Strategic Organizational & Business Ethics Toolkit

Compiled and Edited by:

Jonathan H. Westover, Ph.D.
Utah Valley University

First printed/published in 2014 in the USA
by HCI Press
as part of Leading Innovative Organizations series

Library of Congress Cataloging-in-Publication Data

Strategic Organizational and Business Ethics Toolkit / Jonathan H. Westover, editor.
        p. cm. -- (Leading Innovative Organizations series)
ISBN-13: 978-0692370803; ISBN-10: 0692370803 (HCI Press)
1. Business Ethics. 2. Organizational Strategy. I. Westover, Jonathan H.

Table of Contents

About the Editor

Dr. Jonathan H. Westover is an Associate Professor of Management and Associate Director of the Center for the Study of Ethics at Utah Valley University, specializing in international human resource management, organizational development, and community-engaged experiential learning. He is also a human resource development and performance management consultant. Already a recipient of numerous research, teaching, and service awards and fellowships early in his academic career, Jonathan also recently was named a Fulbright Scholar and was visiting faculty in the MBA program at Belarusian State University (Minsk, Belarus), and he is also a regular visiting faculty member in other graduate business programs in the U.S., UK, France, Poland, and China. Prior to his doctoral studies in the Sociology of Work and Organizations, Comparative International Sociology, and International Political Economy (University of Utah), he received his B.S. in Sociology (Research and Analysis emphasis, Business Management minor, Korean minor) and MPA (emphasis in Human Resource Management) from the Marriott School of Management at Brigham Young University. He also received graduate certificates in demography and higher education teaching during his time at the University of Utah. His ongoing research examines issues of globalization, labor transformation, work quality characteristics, and the determinants of job satisfaction cross-nationally.

Acknowledgements

This text was compiled, edited, and adapted from open source texts at http://www.saylor.org/books and created under a Creative Commons Attribution-NonCommercial ShareAlike 3.0 License without attribution as requested by the work's original creator or licensee. Please contact me for a free copy of the e-text. I would like to thank the many anonymous individuals who contributed their own wisdom and writing to this edited work, particularly those who contributed to the text *The Business Ethics Workshop*. Of course, this text would not be possible without each of their important contributions. Most of all, I would like to publically thank my wife (Jacque) and my six wonderful children (Sara, Amber, Lia, Kaylie, David, and Brayden) for all of their love and support!

Preface

Ethics is about determining value; it's deciding what's worth doing and what doesn't matter so much. Business ethics is the way we decide what kind of career to pursue, what choices we make on the job, which companies we want to work with, and what kind of economic world we want to live in and then leave behind for those coming after. There are no perfect answers to these questions, but there's a difference between thinking them through and winging it. *Strategic Organizational and Business Ethics Toolkit* provides a framework for identifying, analyzing, and resolving ethical dilemmas encountered through working life.

This text's principles:

- **It's your call.** Some of the book's case studies ask for defenses of ethical positions that few agree with (for example, the claim that a drug dealer's job is better than a police officer's). Exercises like this align with the textbook's aim: provoking reasoning freed from customary divisions between right and wrong. In the end, no one completely resists their own habits of thinking or society's broad pressures, but testing the limits sharpens the tools of ethical analysis. These tools can be relied on later on when you face decisions that you alone have to make. The aim of this book is to help make those decisions with coherent, defensible reasoning.

- **Keep it mostly real.** Ethics is an everyday activity. It's not mysterious, head-in-the-clouds ruminating but determining the worth of things around us: Working at an advertising agency is exciting—actors, lights, cameras, and TV commercials—but do I really want to hock sugary breakfast cereals to children? Should I risk my reputation by hiring my college roommate, the one who's habits of showing up late and erratically to class have carried over to working life? These are the immediate questions of business ethics, and while any textbook on the subject must address broad, impersonal questions including the responsibilities of massive corporations in modern societies, this book's focus stays as often as possible on ordinary people in normal but difficult circumstances.

- **Be current.** The rules of ethical thinking don't change much, but the world is a constant revolution. The textbook and its cases follow along as closely as possible, citing from blog posts and recent news stories. As a note here, to facilitate reading some of these citations have been slightly and silently modified.

- **Let's talk about our problem.** Case studies are the most important components of this text because it was written for a discussion-intensive class. Ethics isn't something we know; it's something we do, and trying out our reasoning is the best way to confirm that it's actually working.

Overview of *Strategic Organizational and Business Ethics*

This textbook is organized into three clusters of chapters. The first group develops and explains the main theories guiding thought in business ethics. The goals are to clarify the theoretical tools that may be used to make decisions and to display how arguments can be built in favor of one stance and against others. The questions driving the chapters include the following:

- Are there fundamental rules for action that directly tell us what we ought to do? If so, are the imperatives very specific, including dictates like "don't lie"? Or are they more flexible, more like rules broadly requiring fairness and beneficence to others?

- Are fundamental rights—especially the conviction that we're all free to pursue the destinies we choose—the key to thinking about ethics? If we have these rights, what happens when my free pursuit of happiness conflicts with yours?

- Could it be that what we do doesn't matter so much as the effects of what's done? How can a framework for decisions be constructed around the idea that we ought to undertake whatever action is necessary (even lying or stealing) in order to bring about a positive end, something like the greater happiness of society overall?

- To what extent are perspectives on right and wrong only expressions of the particular culture we live in? Does it makes sense to say that certain acts—say bribery—are OK in some countries but wrong in others?

The second cluster of chapters investigates business ethics on the level of the individual. The goal is to show how the tools of ethical reasoning may be applied to personal decisions made in connection with our nine-to-five lives. The questions driving the chapters include the following:

- What values come into play when a career path is selected?

- Can I justify lying on my résumé? How far am I willing to go to get a raise or promotion?

- Besides a paycheck, what benefits will I seek at work? Money from a kickback? An office romance?
- What do I owe my employer? Is there loyalty in business, or is there nothing more than the money I'm paid and the duties I'm assigned according to my work contract?
- Do I have an obligation to report on someone else doing something I think is wrong?
- If people work for me, what responsibilities do I have toward them inside and outside the office?
- What values govern the way I hire, promote, and fire workers?

The third cluster of chapters considers institutional business ethics. These are general and sweeping issues typically involving corporations, the work environments they promote, and the actions they take in the economic world. Guiding questions include the following:

- What counts as condemnable discrimination in the workplace, and what remedies ought to be tried?
- Which attitudes, requirements, and restrictions should attach to sex and drugs in the workplace?
- Should there be limits to marketing techniques and strategies? Is there anything wrong with creating consumer needs? What relationships should corporations form with their consumers?
- Do corporations hold ethical responsibilities to the larger community in which they operate, to the people who aren't employees or consumers but live nearby?
- Is there a corporate responsibility to defend the planet's environmental health?
- Should the economic world be structured to produce individually successful stars or to protect the welfare of laboring collectives?

Chapter 1:
What is Organizational and Business Ethics?

Chapter Overview

This chapter defines organizational and business ethics and sketches how debates within the field happen. The history of the discipline is also considered, along with the overlap between business and personal ethics.

1.1 What Is Organizational and Business Ethics?
LEARNING OBJECTIVES

1. Define the components of business ethics.
2. Outline how business ethics works.

Captive Customers

Ann Marie Wagoner studies at the University of Alabama (UA). She pays $1,200 a year for books, which is exasperating, but what really ticks her off is the text for her composition class. Called *A Writer's Reference (Custom Publication for the University of Alabama)*, it's the same *Writer's Reference* sold everywhere else, with slight modifications: there are thirty-two extra pages describing the school's particular writing program, the Alabama *A* is emblazoned on the front cover, there's an extra $6 on the price tag (compared with the price of the standard version when purchased new), and there's an added sentence on the back: "This book may not be bought or sold used." The modifications are a collective budget wrecker. Because she's forced to buy a new copy of the customized Alabama text, she ends up paying about twice what she'd pay for a used copy of the standard, not-customized book that's available at Chegg.com and similar used-book dealers.

For the extra money, Wagoner doesn't get much—a few additional text pages and a school spirit cover. Worse, those extra pages are posted free on the English department's website, so the cover's the only unambiguous benefit. Even there, though, it'd be cheaper to just buy a UA bumper sticker and paste it across the front. It's hard to see, finally, any good reason for the University of Alabama English Department to snare its own students with a textbook costing so much.

Things clear up when you look closely at the six-dollar difference between the standard new book cost and the customized UA version. Only half that money stays with the publisher to cover specialized printing costs. The other part kicks back to the university's writing program, the one requiring the book in the first place. It turns out there's a quiet moneymaking scheme at work here: the English

department gets some straight revenue, and most students, busy with their lives, don't notice the royalty details. They get their books, roll their eyes at the cash register, and get on with things.

Wagoner noticed, though. According to an extensive article in the *Wall Street Journal*, she calls the cost of new custom books "ridiculous." She's also more than a little suspicious about why students aren't more openly informed about the royalty arrangement: "They're hiding it so there isn't a huge uproar." [1]

While it may be true that the Tuscaloosa University is hiding what's going on, they're definitely not doing a very good job since the story ended up splattered across the *Wall Street Journal*. One reason the story reached one of the United States' largest circulation dailies is that a lot of universities are starting to get in on the cash. Printing textbooks within the kickback model is, according to the article, the fastest growing slice of the $3.5 billion college textbook market.

The money's there, but not everyone is eager to grab it. James Koch, an economist and former president of Old Dominion University and the University of Montana, advises schools to think carefully before tapping into customized-textbook dollars because, he says, the whole idea "treads right on the edge of what I would call unethical behavior. I'm not sure it passes the smell test." [2]

What Is Organizational and Business Ethics?

What does it mean to say a business practice doesn't "pass the smell test"? And what would happen if someone read the article and said, "Well, to me it smells all right"? If no substance fills out the idea, if there's no elaboration, then there probably wouldn't be much more to say. The two would agree to disagree and move on. Normally, that's OK; no one has time to debate everything. But if you want to get involved—if you're like Wagoner who sounds angry about what's going on and maybe wants to change it—you'll need to do more than make comments about how things hit the nose.

Doing business ethics means providing reasons for how things ought to be in the economic world. This requires the following:

- **Arranging values to guide decisions.** There needs to be a clearly defined and well-justified set of priorities about what's worth seeking and protecting and what other things we're willing to compromise or give up. For example, what's more important and valuable: consumers (in this case students paying for an education) getting their books cheaply or protecting the right of the university to run the business side of its operation as it sees fit?

- **Understanding the facts**. To effectively apply a set of values to any situation, the situation itself must be carefully defined. Who, for example, is involved in the textbook conflict? Students, clearly, as well as university administrators. What about parents who frequently subsidize their college children? Are they participants or just spectators? What about those childless men and women in Alabama whose taxes go to the university? Are *they* involved? And how much money are we talking about? Where does it go? Why? How and when did all this get started?

- **Constructing arguments**. This shows how, given the facts, one action serves our values better than other actions. While the complexities of real life frequently disallow absolute proofs, there remains an absolute requirement of comprehensible reasoning. Arguments need to make sense to outside observers. In simple, practical terms, the test of an ethical argument resembles the test of a recipe for a cook: others need to be able to follow it and come to the same result. There may remain disagreements about facts and values at the end of an argument in ethics, but others need to understand the reasoning marking each step taken on the way to your conclusion.

Finally, the last word in ethics is a determination about right and wrong. This actual result, however, is secondary to the process: the verdict is only the remainder of forming and debating arguments. That's why doing ethics isn't brainwashing. Conclusions are only taken seriously if composed from clear values, recognized facts, and solid arguments.

Bringing Ethics to Kickback Textbooks
The *Wall Street Journal* article on textbooks and kickbacks to the university is a mix of facts, values, and arguments. They can be sorted out; an opportunity to do the sorting is provided by one of the article's more direct assertions:

> *Royalty arrangements involving specially made books may violate colleges' conflict-of-interest rules because they appear to benefit universities more than students.*

A conflict of interest occurs when a university pledges to serve the interest of students but finds that *its own* interest is served by not doing that. It doesn't sound like this is a good thing (in the language of the article, it smells bad). But to reach that conclusion in ethical terms, the specific values, facts, and arguments surrounding this conflict need to be defined.

Start with the values. The priorities and convictions underneath the conflict-of-interest accusation are clear. When university takes tuition money from a student and promises to do the best job possible in providing an education to the student, then it better *do* that. The truth matters. When you make a promise, you've got to fulfill it. Now, this fundamental value is what makes a conflict of interest worrisome. If we didn't care about the truth at all, then a university promising one thing and doing something else wouldn't seem objectionable. In the world of poker, for example, when a player makes a grand show of holding a strong hand by betting a pile of chips, no one calls him a liar when it's later revealed that the hand was weak. The truth isn't expected in poker, and bluffing is perfectly acceptable. Universities aren't poker tables, though. Many students come to school expecting honesty from their institution and fidelity to agreements. To the extent these values are applied, a conflict of interest becomes both possible and objectionable. With the core value of honesty established, what are the facts? The "who's involved?" question brings in the students buying the textbooks, the company making the textbooks (Bedford/St. Martin's in Boston), and the University of Alabama. As drawn from the UA web page, here's the school's purpose, the reason it exists in the first place: "The University of Alabama is a student-centered research university and an academic community united in its commitment to enhancing the quality of life for all Alabamians."

Moving to the financial side, specific dollar amounts should be listed (the textbook's cost, the cost for the non-customized version). Also, it may be important to note the financial context of those involved: in the case of the students, some are comfortably wealthy or have parents paying for everything, while others live closer to their bank accounts edge and are working their way through school.

Finally, the actual book-selling operation should be clearly described. In essence, what's going on is that the UA English Department is making a deal with the Bedford/St. Martin's textbook company. The university proposes, "If you give us a cut of the money you make selling textbooks, we'll let you make more money off our students." Because the textbooks are customized, the price goes up while the supply of cheap used copies (that usually can be purchased through the Internet from stores across the nation) goes way down. It's much harder for UA students to find used copies, forcing many to buy a new version. This is a huge windfall for Bedford/St. Martin's because, for them, every time a textbook is resold used, they lose a sale. On the other side, students end up shelling out the maximum money for each book because they have to buy new instead of just recycling someone else's from the previous year. Finally, at the end of the line there is the enabler of this operation, the English department that both requires the book for a class and has the book customized to reduce used-copy sales. They get a small percentage of Bedford/St. Martin's extra revenue.

With values and facts established, an argument against kickback textbooks at Alabama can be drawn up. By customizing texts and making them mandatory, UA is forcing students to pay extra money to take a class: they have to spend about thirty dollars extra, which is the difference between the cost of a new, customized textbook and the standard version purchased, used. Students generally don't have a lot of money, and while some pass through school on the parental scholarship, others scrape by and have to work a McJob to make ends meet. So for at least some students, that thirty dollars directly equals time that could be spent studying, but that instead goes to flipping burgers. The customized textbooks, consequently, hurt these students' academic learning in a measurable way. Against that reality there's the university's own claim to be a "student-centered" institution. Those words appear untrue, however, if the university is dragging its own students out of the library and forcing them to work extra hours. To comply with its own stated ideals—to serve the *students'* interests—UA should suspend the kickback textbook practice. It's important to do that, finally, because fulfilling promises is valuable; it's something worth doing.

Argument and Counterargument
The conclusion that kickback textbooks turn universities into liars doesn't end debate on the question. In fact, because well-developed ethical positions expose their reasoning so openly (as opposed to "it doesn't smell right"), they tend to invite responses. One characteristic, in other words, of good ethical arguments is that, paradoxically but not contradictorily, they tend to provoke counterarguments.

Broadly, there are three ways to dispute an argument in ethics. You can attack the
1. facts,
2. values,
3. reasoning,

In the textbook case, disputing the facts might involve showing that students who need to work a few extra hours to afford their books *don't* subtract that time from their studying; actually, they subtract it from late-night hours pounding beers in dank campus bars. The academic damage done, therefore, by kickback textbooks is zero. Pressing this further, if it's true that increased textbook prices translate into less student partying, the case could probably be made that the university actually serves students' interests—at least those who drink too much beer—by jacking up the prices.

The values supporting an argument about kickback textbooks may, like the facts, be disputed. Virginia Tech, for example, runs a text-customization program like Alabama's. According to Tech's English Department chair Carolyn Rude, the customized books published by Pearson net the department about $20,000 a year. Some of that cash goes to pay for instructors' travel stipends. These aren't luxury retreats to Las Vegas or Miami; they're gatherings of earnest professors in dull places for discussions that reliably put a few listeners to sleep. When instructors—who are frequently graduate students—attend, they're looking to burnish their curriculum vitae and get some public responses to their work. Possibly, the trip will help them get a better academic job later on. Regardless, it won't do much for the undergraduates at Virginia Tech. In essence, the undergrads are being asked to pay a bit extra for books to help graduate students hone their ideas and advance professionally.

Can that tradeoff be justified? With the right values, yes. It must be conceded that Virginia Tech is probably rupturing a commitment to serve the undergrads' interest. Therefore, it's true that a certain amount of dishonesty shadows the process of inflating textbook costs. If, however, there's a higher value than truth, that won't matter so much. Take this possibility: what's right and wrong isn't determined by honesty and fidelity to commitments, but the general welfare. The argument here is that while it's true that undergrads suffer a bit because they pay extra, the instructors receiving the travel stipends benefit a lot. Their knowledge grows, their career prospects improve, and in sum, they benefit so much that it entirely outweighs the harm done to the undergrads. As long as this value—the greatest total good—frames the assessment of kickback textbooks, the way is clear for Tech or Alabama to continue the practice. It's even recommendable.

The final ground on which an ethical argument can be refuted is the reasoning. Here, the facts are accepted, as well as the value that universities are duty bound to serve the interests of the tuition-paying undergraduate students since that's the commitment they make on their web pages. What can still be debated, however, is the extent to which those students may actually *be* benefitted by customizing textbooks. Looking at the *Wall Street Journal* article, several partially developed arguments are presented on this front. For example, at Alabama, part of the money collected from the customized texts underwrites teaching awards, and that, presumably, motivates instructors to perform better in the classroom, which ends up serving the students' educational interests. Similarly, at Virginia Tech, part of the revenue is apportioned to bring in guest speakers, which should advance the undergraduate educational cause. The broader argument is that while it's true that the students are paying more for their books than peers at other universities, the sequence of reasoning doesn't necessarily lead from that fact to the conclusion that there's a reproachable conflict of interest. It can also reach the verdict that students' educational experience is improved; instead of a conflict of interest, there's an elevated commitment to student welfare inherent in the kickback practice.

Conclusion. There's no irrefutable answer to the question about whether universities ought to get involved in kickback textbooks. What is clear, however, is that there's a difference between responding to them by asserting that something doesn't smell right, and responding by uniting facts, values, and reasoning to produce a substantial ethical argument.

KEY TAKEAWAYS

- Business ethics deals with values, facts, and arguments.
- Well-reasoned arguments, by reason of their clarity, invite counterarguments.

REVIEW QUESTIONS

1. What is the difference between brainwashing and an argument?
2. What does it mean to dispute an argument on the basis of the facts?
3. What does it mean to dispute an argument on the basis of the values?
4. What does it mean to dispute an argument on the basis of the reasoning?

[1] John Hechinger, "As Textbooks Go 'Custom,' Students Pay: Colleges Receive Royalties for School-Specific Editions; Barrier to Secondhand Sales," *Wall Street Journal*, July 10, 2008, accessed May 11, 2011, http://online.wsj.com/article/SB121565135185141235.html.
[2] John Hechinger, "As Textbooks Go 'Custom,' Students Pay: Colleges Receive Royalties for School-Specific Editions; Barrier to Secondhand Sales," *Wall Street Journal*, July 10, 2008, accessed May 11, 2011, http://online.wsj.com/article/SB121565135185141235.html.

1.2 The Place of Business Ethics
LEARNING OBJECTIVES

1. Distinguish the place of business ethics within the larger field of decision making.
2. Sketch the historical development of business ethics as a coherent discipline.

The Boundaries and History of Business Ethics

Though both economic life and ethics are as old as history, business ethics as a formal area of study is relatively new. Delineating the specific place of today's business ethics involves

- distinguishing morality, ethics, and meta-ethics;
- dividing normative from descriptive ethics;
- comparing ethics against other forms of decision making;
- sketching some inflection points in the histories of ethics and business ethics.

Morality, Ethics, and Meta-ethics: What's the Difference?

The back and forth of debates about kickback textbooks occurs on one of the three distinct levels of consideration about right and wrong. Morals occupy the lowest level; they're the direct rules we ought to follow. Two of the most common moral dictates are *don't lie* and *don't steal*. Generally, the question to ask about a moral directive is whether it was obeyed. Specifically in the case of university textbooks, the debate about *whether* customized textbooks are a good idea isn't morality. It's not because morality doesn't involve debates. Morality only involves specific guidelines that should be followed; it only begins when someone walks into a school bookstore, locates a book needed for a class, strips out the little magnetic tag hidden in the spine, and heads for the exit. Above all morality there's the broader question about exactly what specific rules should be instituted and followed. Answering this question is ethics. Ethics is the morality factory, the production of guidelines that later may be obeyed or violated. It's not clear today, for example, whether there should be moral rule prohibiting kickback textbooks. There are good arguments for the prohibition (universities are betraying their duty to serve students' interests) and good arguments against (schools are finding innovative sources of revenue that can be put to good use). For that reason, it's perfectly legitimate for someone like Ann Marie Wagoner to stand up at the University of Alabama and decry the practice as wrong. But she'd be going too far if she accused university administrators of being thieves or immoral. They're not; they're on the other side of an ethical conflict, not a moral one.

Above both morality and ethics there are debates about meta-ethics. These are the most abstract and theoretical discussions surrounding right and wrong. The questions asked on this level include the following: Where do ethics come from? Why do we have ethical and moral categories in the first place? To whom do the rules apply? Babies, for example, steal from each other all the time and no one accuses them of being immoral or insufficiently ethical. Why is that? Or putting the same question in the longer terms of human history, at some point somewhere in the past someone must have had a light bulb turn on in their mind and asked, "Wait, is stealing wrong?" How and why, those interested in meta-ethics ask, did that happen? Some believe that morality is transcendent in nature—that the rules of right and wrong come from beyond you and me and that our only job is to receive, learn, and obey them. Divine command theory, for example, understands earthly morality as a reflection of God. Others postulate that ethics is very human and social in nature—that it's something we invented to help us live together in communities. Others believe there's something deeply personal in it. When I look at another individual I see in the depth of their difference from myself a requirement to respect that other person and his or her uniqueness, and from there, ethics and morality unwind. These kinds of meta-ethical questions, finally, are customarily studied in philosophy departments.

Conclusion. Morality is the rules, ethics is the making of rules, and meta-ethics concerns the origin of the entire discussion. In common conversation, the words *morality* and *ethics* often overlap. It's hard to change the way people talk and, in a practical field like business ethics, fostering the skill of debating arguments is more important than being a stickler for words, but it's always possible to keep in mind that, strictly speaking, morality and ethics hold distinct meanings.

What's the Difference between Normative Ethics and Descriptive Ethics?

Business ethics is normative, which means it concerns how people *ought* to act. Descriptive ethics depicts how people actually *are* acting.

At the University of Alabama, Virginia Tech, and anywhere kickback textbooks are being sold, there are probably a few students who check their bank accounts, find that the number is low, and decide to mount their own kickback scheme: refund the entire textbook cost to themselves by sneaking a copy out of the store. Trying to make a decision about whether that's justified—*does economic necessity license theft in some cases?*—is normative ethics. By contrast, investigating to determine the exact number of students walking out with free books is descriptive. So too is tallying the reasons for the theft: How many steal because they don't have the money to pay? How many accuse the University of acting dishonestly in the first place and say that licenses theft? How many question the entire idea of private property?

The fields of descriptive ethics are many and varied. Historians trace the way penalties imposed for theft have changed over time. Anthropologists look at the way different cultures respond to thievery. Sociologists study the way publications, including Abbie Hoffman's incendiary book titled *Steal This Book*, have changed public attitudes about the ethics of theft. Psychologists are curious about the subconscious forces motivating criminals. Economists ask whether there's a correlation between individual wealth and the kind of moral rules subscribed to. None of this depends on the question about whether stealing may actually *be* justifiable, but all of it depends on stealing actually happening.

Ethics versus Other Forms of Decision

When students stand in the bookstore flipping through the pages of a budget buster, it's going to cross a few minds to stick it in the backpack and do a runner. Should they? Clear-headed ethical reflection may provide an answer to the question, but that's not the only way we make decisions in the world. Even in the face of screaming ethical issues, it's perfectly possible and frequently reasonable to make choices based on other factors. They include:

- The law
- Prudence (practicality)
- Religion
- Authority figures
- Peer pressure
- Custom
- Conscience

When the temptation is there, one way to decide whether to steal a book is legal: if the law says I can't, I won't. Frequently, legal prohibitions overlap with commonly accepted moral rules: few legislators want to sponsor laws that most believe to be unjust. Still, there *are* unjust laws. Think of downloading a text (or music, or a video) from the web. One day the downloading may be perfectly legal and the next, after a bill is passed by a legislature, it's illegal. So the law reverses, but there's no reason to think the ethics—the values and arguments guiding decisions about downloading—changed in that short time. If the ethics didn't change, at least one of the two laws *must* be ethically wrong. That means any necessary connection between ethics and the law is broken.

Even so, there are clear advantages to making decisions based on the law. Besides the obvious one that it'll keep you out of jail, legal rules are frequently cleaner and more direct than ethical determinations, and that clarity may provide justification for approving (or disapproving) actions with legal dictates instead of ethical ones. The reality remains, however, that the two ways of deciding are as distinct as their mechanisms of determination. The law results from the votes of legislators, the interpretations of judges, and the understanding of a policeman on the scene. Ethical conclusions result from applied values and arguments.

Religion may also provide a solution to the question about textbook theft. The Ten Commandments, for example, provide clear guidance. Like the law, most mainstream religious dictates overlap with generally accepted ethical views, but that doesn't change the fact that the rules of religion trace back to beliefs and faith, while ethics goes back to arguments.

Prudence, in the sense of practical concern for your own well-being, may also weigh in and finally guide a decision. With respect to stealing, regardless of what you may believe about ethics or law or religion, the possibility of going to jail strongly motivates most people to pay for what they carry out of stores. If that's the motivation determining what's done, then personal comfort and welfare are guiding the decision more than sweeping ethical arguments.

Authority figures may be relied on to make decisions: instead of asking whether it's right to steal a book, someone may ask themselves, "What would my parents say I should do? Or the soccer coach? Or a movie star? Or the president?" While it's not clear how great the overlap is between decisions based on authority and those coming from ethics, it is certain that following authority implies respecting the experience and judgment of others, while depending on ethics means relying on your own careful thinking and determinations.

Urges to conformity and peer pressure also guide decisions. As depicted by the startling and funny Asch experiments (see Video Clip 1.1), most of us palpably fear being labeled a deviant or just differing from those around us. So powerful is the attraction of conformity that we'll deny things clearly seen with our own eyes before being forced to stand out as distinct from everyone else.

Custom, tradition, and habit all also guide decisions. If you're standing in the bookstore and you've never stolen a thing in your life, the possibility of appropriating the text may not even occur to you or, if it does, may seem prohibitively strange. The great advantage of custom or tradition or just doing what we've always done is that it lets us take action without thinking. Without that ability for thoughtlessness, we'd be paralyzed. No one would make it out of the house in the morning: the entire day would be spent wondering about the meaning of life and so on. Habits—and the decisions flowing from them—allow us to get on with things. Ethical decisions, by contrast, tend to slow us down. In exchange, we receive the assurance that we actually believe in what we're doing, but in practical terms, no one's decisions can be ethically justified all the time.

Finally, the conscience may tilt decisions in one direction or another. This is the gut feeling we have about whether swiping the textbook is the way to go, coupled with the expectation that the wrong decision will leave us remorseful, suffering palpable regret about choosing to do what we did. Conscience, fundamentally, is a feeling; it starts as an intuition and ends as a tugging, almost sickening sensation in the stomach. As opposed to those private sensations, ethics starts from facts and ends with a reasoned argument that can be publicly displayed and compared with the arguments others present. It's not clear, even to experts who study the subject, exactly where the conscience comes from, how we develop it, and what, if any, limits it should place on our actions. Could, for example, a society come into existence where people stole all the time and the decision to *not* shoplift a textbook carries with it the pang of remorse? It's hard to know for sure. It's clear, however, that ethics is fundamentally social: it's about right and wrong as those words emerge from real debates, not inner feelings.

History and Ethics

Conflicts, along with everything necessary to approach them ethically (mainly the ability to generate and articulate reasoned thoughts), are as old as the first time someone was tempted to take something from another. For that reason, there's no strict historical advance to the study: there's no reason to confidently assert that the way we do ethics today is superior to the way we did it in the past. In that way, ethics isn't like the physical sciences where we can at least suspect that knowledge of the world yields technology allowing more understanding, which would've been impossible to attain earlier on. There appears to be, in other words, marching progress in science. Ethics doesn't have that. Still, a number of critical historical moments in ethics' history can be spotted.

In ancient Greece, Plato presented the theory that we could attain a general knowledge of justice that would allow a clear resolution to every specific ethical dilemma. He meant something like this: Most of us know what a chair is, but it's hard to pin down. Is something a chair if it has four legs? No, beds have four legs and some chairs (barstools) have only three. Is it a chair if you sit on it? No, that would make the porch steps in front of a house a chair. Nonetheless, because we have the general idea of a chair in our mind, we can enter just about any room in any home and know immediately where we should sit. What Plato proposed is that justice works like that. We have—or at least we can work toward getting—a general idea of right and wrong, and when we have the idea, we can walk into a concrete situation and correctly judge what the right course of action is.

Moving this over to the case of Ann Marie Wagoner, the University of Alabama student who's outraged by her university's kickback textbooks, she may feel tempted, standing there in the bookstore, to make off with a copy. The answer to the question of whether she *ought* to do that will be answered by the general sense of justice she's been able to develop and clarify in her mind.

In the seventeenth and eighteenth centuries, a distinct idea of fundamental ethics took hold: natural rights. The proposal here is that individuals are naturally and undeniably endowed with rights to their own lives, their freedom, and to pursue happiness as they see fit. As opposed to the notion that certain acts are firmly right or wrong, proponents of this theory—including John Locke and framers of the new American nation—proposed that individuals may sort things out as they please *as long as* their decisions and actions don't interfere with the right of others to do the same. Frequently understood as a theory of freedom maximization, the proposition is that your freedom is only limited by the freedoms others possess.

For Wagoner, this way of understanding right and wrong provides little immediate hope for changing textbook practices at the University of Alabama. It's difficult to see how the university's decision to assign a certain book at a certain price interferes with Wagoner's freedom. She can always choose to not purchase the book, to buy one of the standard versions at Amazon, or to drop the class. What she probably *can't* justify choosing, within this theory, is responding to the kickback textbooks by stealing a copy. Were she to do that, it would violate *another's* freedom, in this case, the right of the university (in agreement with a publisher) to offer a product for sale at a price they determine.

A third important historical direction in the history of ethics originated with the proposal that what you do doesn't matter so much as the *effects* of what you do. Right and wrong are found in the consequences following an action, not in the action itself. In the 1800s John Stuart Mill and others advocated the idea that *any* act benefitting the general welfare was recommendable and ethically respectable. Correspondingly, any act harming a community's general happiness should be avoided. Decisions about *good* or *bad*, that means, don't focus on what happens now but what comes later, and they're not about the one person making the decision but the consequences as they envelop a larger community.

For someone like Wagoner who's angry about the kickback money hidden in her book costs, this consequence-centered theory opens the door to a dramatic action. She may decide to steal a book from the bookstore and, after alerting a reporter from the student newspaper of her plan, promptly turn herself into the authorities as a form of protest. "I stole this book," she could say, "but that's nothing compared with the theft happening every day on this campus by our university." This plan of action may work out—or maybe not. But in terms of ethics, the focus should be on the theft's results, not the fact that she sneaked a book past security. The ethical verdict here is not about whether robbery is right or wrong but whether the protest stunt will ultimately improve university life. If it does, we can say that the original theft was good.

Finally, ethics is like most fields of study in that it has been accompanied from the beginning by skeptics, by people suspecting that either there is no real right and wrong or, even if there is, we'll never have much luck figuring out the difference. The twentieth century has been influenced by Friedrich Nietzsche's affirmation that moral codes (and everything else, actually) are just interpretations of reality that may be accepted now, but there's no guarantee things will remain that way tomorrow. Is stealing a textbook right or wrong? According to this view, the answer always is, "It depends." It depends on the circumstances, on the people involved and how well they can convince others to accept one or another verdict. In practical terms, this view translates into a theory of cultural or contextual relativism. What's right and wrong only reflects what a particular person or community decides to believe at a certain moment, and little more.

The Historical Development of Business Ethics
The long philosophical tradition of ethical thought contains the subfield of business ethics. Business ethics, in turn, divides between ethics practiced by people who happen to be

in business and business ethics as a coherent and well-defined academic pursuit.

People in business, like everyone else, have ethical dimensions to their lives. For example, the company W. R. Grace was portrayed in the John Travolta movie *A Civil Action* as a model of bad corporate behavior. [1] What not so many people know, however, is that the corporation's founder, the man named W. R. Grace, came to America in the nineteenth century, found success, and dedicated a significant percentage of his profits to a free school for immigrants that still operates today.

Even though questions stretch deep into the past about what responsibilities companies and their leaders may have besides generating profits, the academic world began seriously concentrating on the subject only very recently. The first full-scale professional conference on academic business ethics occurred in 1974 at the University of Kansas. A textbook was derived from the meeting, and courses began appearing soon after at some schools.

By 1980 some form of a unified business ethics course was offered at many of the nation's colleges and universities. Academic discussion of ethical issues in business was fostered by the appearance of several specialized journals, and by the mid-1990s, the field had reached maturity. University classes were widespread, allowing new people to enter the study easily. A core set of ideas, approaches, and debates had been established as central to the subject, and professional societies and publications allowed for advanced research in and intellectual growth of the field.

The development of business ethics inside universities corresponded with increasing public awareness of problems associated with modern economic activity, especially on environmental and financial fronts. In the late 1970s, the calamity in the Love Canal neighborhood of Niagara Falls, New York, focused international attention on questions about a company's responsibility to those living in the surrounding community and to the health of the natural world. The Love Canal's infamy began when a chemical company dumped tons of toxic waste into the ground before moving away. Despite the company's warnings about the land's toxicity, residential development spread over the area. Birth defects and similar maladies eventually devastated the families. Not long afterward and on the financial front, an insider trading scandal involving the Wall Street titan Ivan Boesky made front pages, which led John Shad, former head of the Securities and Exchange Commission, to donate $20 million to his business school alma mater for the purpose of

ethics education. Parallel (though usually more modest) money infusions went to university philosophy departments. As a discipline, business ethics naturally bridges the two divisions of study since the theory and tools for resolving ethical problems come from philosophy, but the problems for solving belong to the real economic world.

Today, the most glamorous issues of business ethics involve massively powerful corporations and swashbuckling financiers. Power and celebrity get people's attention. Other, more tangible issues don't appear in so many headlines, but they're just as important to study since they directly reach so many of us: What kind of career is worth pursuing? Should I lie on my résumé? How important is money?

The Personal History of Ethics
Moving from academics to individual people, almost every adult does business ethics. Every time people shake their exhausted heads in the morning, eye the clock, and decide whether they'll go to work or just pull up the covers, they're making a decision about what values guide their economic reality. The *way ethics* is done, however, changes from person to person and for all of us through our lives. There's no single history of ethics as individuals live it, but there's a broad consensus that for many people, the development of their ethical side progresses in a way not too far off from a general scheme proposed by the psychologist Lawrence Kohlberg.

Pre-conventional behavior—displayed by children, but not only by them—is about people calculating to get what they want efficiently: decisions are made in accordance with raw self-interest. That's why many children really do behave better near the end of December. It's not that they've suddenly been struck by respect for others and the importance of social rules; they just figure they'll get more and better presents.

Moving up through the conventional stages, the idea of what you'll do separates from what you want. First, there are immediate conventions that may pull against personal desires; they include standards and pressures applied by family and friends. Next, more abstract conventions—the law and mass social customs—assert influence.

Continuing upward, the critical stages of moral development go from recognizing abstract conventions to actively and effectively comparing them. The study of business ethics belongs on this high level of individual maturity. Value systems are held up side by side, and reasons are erected for selecting one over another. This is the ethics of full adulthood; it requires good reasoning and experience in the real world.

Coextensive with the development of ideas about what we ought to do are notions about responsibility—about justifiably blaming people for what they've done. Responsibility at the lowest level is physical. The person who stole the book is responsible because they took it. More abstractly, responsibility attaches to notions of causing others to do a wrong (enticing someone else to steal a book) and not doing something that could have prevented a wrong (not acting to dissuade another who's considering theft is, ultimately, a way of acting). A mature assignment of responsibility is normally taken to require that the following considerations hold:

- The person is able to understand right and wrong.
- The person acts to cause—or fails to act to prevent—a wrong.
- The person acts knowing what they're doing.
- The person acts from their own free will.

KEY TAKEAWAYS

- Morality is the set of rules defining what ought to be done; ethics is the debate about what the rules should be; meta-ethics investigates the origin of the entire field.
- Normative ethics concerns what should be done, not what is done.
- Ethics is only one of a number of ways of making decisions.
- Business ethics as an academic study is a recent development in the long history of ethical reflection.
- With respect to individuals, the development of ethical thought may be studied, as well as notions of responsibility.

REVIEW QUESTIONS

1. List two basic questions belonging to the field of morality.
2. List two basic questions belonging to the field of ethics.
3. What is one basic question belonging to the field of meta-ethics?
4. What is an example of normative ethics? And descriptive ethics?
5. Explain the difference between a decision based on ethics and one based on the law.
6. Explain the difference between a decision based on ethics and one based on religion.
7. List two factors explaining the recent development and growth of business ethics as a coherent discipline.

[1] Steven Zaillian (director), *A Civil Action* (New York: Scott Rudin, 1998), film.

1.3 Is Business Ethics Necessary?
LEARNING OBJECTIVES

1. Articulate two extreme views of business ethics.
2. Describe the sense in which business ethics is inevitable.

Two Extreme Views of the Business World

At the boundaries of the question about whether business ethics is necessary, there are conflicting and extreme perceptions of the business world. In graphic terms, these are the views:

- Business needs policing because it's a dirty enterprise featuring people who get ahead by being selfish liars.
- Successful businesses work well to enrich society, and business ethicists are interfering and annoying scolds threatening to ruin our economic welfare.

A 1987 *New York Times* article titled "Suddenly, Business Schools Tackle Ethics" begins this way: "Insider-trading scandals in the last year have badly tarnished the reputations of some of the nation's most prominent financial institutions. Nor has Wall Street been the only area engulfed in scandal; manufacturers of products from contraceptives to military weapons have all come under public scrutiny recently for questionable—if not actionable—behavior." [1]

Slimy dealing verging on the illegal, the message is, stains the economic world from one end to the other. A little further into the article, the author possibly gives away her deepest feelings about business when she cracks that business ethics is "an oxymoron."

What will business leaders—and anyone else for that matter—do when confronted with the accusation of sliminess? Possibly embrace it—an attitude facilitated by an infamous article originally published in the *Harvard Business Review*. In "Is Business Bluffing Ethical?" the author suggests businessmen and women should double down on the strategy of getting ahead through deceit because if you're in business, then everyone already knows you're a liar anyway. And since that's common knowledge, taking liberties with the truth doesn't even count as lying: there's no moral problem because that's just the way the business game is played. In the author's words, "Falsehood ceases to be falsehood when it is understood on all sides that the truth is not expected to be spoken—an exact description of bluffing in poker, diplomacy, and business." [2]

The basic argument is strong. Ethically, dishonesty stops being reproachable—it stops being an attempt to mislead—when everyone knows that you're not telling the truth. If it weren't for that loophole, it'd be difficult to enjoy movies. Spiderman swinging through New York City skyscrapers isn't a lie, it's just fun because everyone agrees from the beginning that the truth doesn't matter on the screen.

The problem with applying this logic to the world of commerce, however, is that the original agreement isn't there. It's not true that in business everyone knows there's lying and accepts it. In poker, presumably, the players choosing to sit down at the table have familiarized themselves with the rules and techniques of the game and, yes, do expect others to fake a good hand from time to time. It's easy to show, however, that the expectation doesn't generally hold in office buildings, stores, showrooms, and sales pitches. Take, for example, a car advertisement claiming a certain model has a higher resale value, has a lower sticker price, or can go from zero to sixty faster than its competition. People in the market for a new car take those claims seriously. If they're prudent, they'll check just to make sure (an economic form of "trust but verify"), but it's pretty rare that someone sitting in front of the TV at home chuckles and calls the claim absurd. In poker, on the other hand, if another player makes a comparable claim ("I have the highest hand at the table!"), people just laugh and tell the guy to keep drinking. Poker isn't like business.

The argument that bluffing—lying—in business is acceptable because everyone does it and everyone knows everyone's doing it doesn't hold up. However, the fact that someone could seriously *make* the argument (and get it published in the *Harvard Business Review* no less) certainly provides heavy ammunition for those who believe that most high-level businesspeople—like those who read the *Harvard Business Review*—should have a hard time looking at themselves in the mirror in the morning.

Opposing the view that business life is corrupt and needs serious ethical policing, there's the view that economic enterprises provide wealth for our society while correcting their own excesses and problems internally. How does the correction work? Through the marketplace. The pressures of demanding consumers force companies into reputable behavior. If a car manufacturer lies about its product, there may be a brief uptick in sales, but eventually people will figure out what's going on, spread the word at the water cooler and on Facebook, and in the end the company's sales will collapse. Similarly, bosses that abuse and mistreat subordinates will soon find that no one wants to work for

them. Workers who cheat on expense reports or pocket money from the till will eventually get caught and fired. Of course it must be admitted that some people sometimes do get away with something, but over the long run, the forces of the economic world inexorably correct abuses.

If this vision of business reality is correct, then adding another layer of academic ethics onto what's already going on in the real world isn't necessary. More, those who insist on standing outside corporate offices and factory buildings preaching the need for oversight and remedial classes in morality become annoying nags. That's especially true if the critics aren't directly doing business themselves. If they're ensconced in university towers and gloomy libraries, there may even be a suspicion that what really drives the call to ethics is a burning resentment of all the money Wall Street stars and captains of industry seem to make, along with their flashy cars, palatial homes, and luxurious vacations.

An issue of the Cato Institute's *Policy Report* from 2000 carries an article titled "Business Ethics Gone Wrong." It asserts that some proponents of business ethics aren't only bothersome envious—their resentment-fueled scolding actually threatens our collective economic welfare. Business ethics, according to the author, "is fundamentally antagonistic to capitalist enterprise, viewing both firm and manager as social parasites in need of a strong reformative hand."[3]

These reforms—burdensome regulations, prying investigations, and similar ethical interventions—threaten to gum up the capitalist engine: "If the market economy and its cornerstone, the shareholder-oriented firm, are in no danger of being dealt a decisive blow, they at least risk death by a thousand cuts." [4]

There's a problem with this perspective on the business world. Even if, for the sake of argument, it's acknowledged that economic forces effectively police commerce, that doesn't mean business ethics is unnecessary or a threat to the market economy. The opposite is the case: the view that the marketplace solves most problems *is* an ethics. It's a form of egoism, a theory to be developed in later chapters but with values and rules that can be rapidly sketched here. What are most valued from this perspective is our individual welfare and the freedom to pursue it without guilt or remorse. With that freedom, however, comes a responsibility to acknowledge that others may be guided by the same rules and therefore we're all bound by the responsibility to look out for ourselves and actively protect our own interests since no one will be doing it for us. This isn't to confirm that all businesspeople are despicable liars, but it does mean asserting that the collective force of self-interest produces an ethically respectable reality. Right and wrong comes to be defined by the combined force of cautious, self-interested producers and consumers.

In the face of this argument defending a free-for-all economic reality where everyone is doing the best they can for themselves while protecting against others doing the same, objections may be constructed. It could be argued, for example, that the modern world is too complex for consumers to adequately protect their own interests all the time. No matter how that issue gets resolved, however, the larger fact remains that trusting in the marketplace is a reasonable and defensible ethical posture; it's a commitment to a set of values and facts and their combination in an argument affirming that the free market works to effectively resolve its own problems.

Conclusion. It's not true that doing business equals being deceitful, so it's false to assert that business ethics is necessary to cure the ills of commerce. It is true that the business world may be left to control its own excesses through marketplace pressure, but that doesn't mean business escapes ethics.

Business Ethics Is Inevitable

Business ethics is not about scolding, moralizing, or telling people to be nice. Ethics doesn't have to be annoying or intrusive. On the other hand, it can't just be dismissed altogether because ethics in business is unavoidable. The values guiding our desires and aspirations are there whether they're revealed or not. They must be because no one can do anything without first wanting something. If you don't have a goal, something you're trying to achieve or get, then you won't have anything to do when you get out of bed in the morning. Getting up in the morning and going, consequently, mean that you've already selected something as desirable, valuable, and worth pursuing. And that's *doing* ethics; it's establishing values. The only real and durable difference, therefore, between those who understand ethics and those who don't is that the former achieve a level of self-understanding about what they want: they've compared their values with other possibilities and molded their actions to their decisions. The latter are doing the same thing, just without fully realizing it. The question about whether ethics is necessary, finally, becomes a false one. You can choose to not understand the ethics you're doing (you can always drop this class), but you can't choose to not do ethics.

REVIEW QUESTIONS

1. Why might someone believe the business world needs exterior ethical monitoring and correction?
2. What is the argument that the business world can regulate itself, and why is that an ethics?
3. In your own words, why is business ethics unavoidable?

[1] Sandra Salmans, "Suddenly, Business Schools Tackle Ethics," *New York Times*, August 2, 1987, accessed May 11, 2011, http://www.nytimes.com/1987/08/02/education/suddenly-business-schools-tackle-ethics.html.
[2] Albert Carr, "Is Business Bluffing Ethical?" *Harvard Business Review* 46 (January–February, 1968), 143–53.
[3] Alexei M. Marcoux, "Business Ethics Gone Wrong," *Cato Policy Report* 22, no. 3 (May/June 2000), accessed May 11, 2011, http://www.cato.org/pubs/policy_report/v22n3/cpr-22n3.html.
[4] Alexei M. Marcoux, "Business Ethics Gone Wrong," *Cato Policy Report* 22, no. 3 (May/June 2000), accessed May 11, 2011, http://www.cato.org/pubs/policy_report/v22n3/cpr-22n3.html.

1.4 Facebook and the Unavoidability of Business Ethics

LEARNING OBJECTIVE

1. Show how business ethics stretches beyond working life.

The Facebook Firing

Business ethics in some form is inescapable inside factories, office buildings, and other places where work gets done. The application of business ethics principles and guidance doesn't stop, though, when the workday ends or outside the company door. Because our economic lives mingle so intimately with our private existences, the decisions and reasoning shaping our laboring eventually shape our lives generally. Business ethics, as the problems bedeviling Dawnmarie Souza show, provides a way to examine and make sense of a large segment of our time, both on and off the job.

Souza's problems started when the ambulance she worked on picked up a "17." That's code for a psychiatric case. This particular 17, as it happened, wasn't too crazy to form and submit a complaint about the treatment received from Souza. Since this was the second grievance the ambulance service had received on Souza in only ten days, she sensed that she'd be getting a suspension. "Looks like," she wrote on her Facebook page later that day, "I'm getting some time off.

Love how the company allows a 17 to be a supervisor." She also referred to her real supervisor with some choice four-letter words.

A number of coworkers responded to her post with their own supportive and agreeing comments. Management responded by firing her.

The termination decision came easily to the ambulance service, American Medical Response of Connecticut, since their policy explicitly prohibited employees from identifying or discussing the company or other employees in the uncontrolled public forum that is the Internet. Around the water cooler, at home, or during weekend parties, people can say what they like. Given the semi-permanent record that is the web, however, and the ambulance service's natural inclination to protect its public image, posting there was out of bounds.

But, Souza responded, there's no difference. If people can talk at the water cooler and parties, why can't they post on Facebook? She's not claiming to speak for the company, she's just venting with a keypad instead of vocal chords.

The celebrity blogger and Facebook addict Perez Hilton came down on the company's side: "We think Dawnmarie should be fired, and we support the company's decision to let her go. When you post things online, it's out there for the public to see, and it's a sign of disloyalty and disrespect to deal with a work-related grievance in such a manner." [1]

The Reach of Business Ethics
When someone like Perez Hilton—a blogger most comfortable deriding celebrities' bad hair days—finds himself wrapped in a business ethics debate, you've got to figure the discipline is pretty much unavoidable. Regardless, the Souza episode displays many of the ways business ethics connects with our nonworking existence, whether we like it or not:

- It doesn't sound like Souza displayed any great passion about her job. Maybe she really doesn't care that she got fired. Or maybe she cares but only because it means a lost paycheck. On the other hand, it may just have been a bad day; it's possible that she usually gets up in the morning eager to mount the ambulance. It's hard to know, but it's certain that this—the decision about what we want to do with our professional lives—is business ethics. When choosing a job, what has value? The money it provides? Satisfaction from helping others? Status? Or do you just want something that gives you the most free time possible? There are no rights or wrong answers, but

these are all ethical decisions tangling your personal and professional lives together.

- The mix between the personal and professional on the question of one's job tends to link tighter as people get older. Many of us define who we and others *are* through work. When finding out about someone new, the question—embraced by some and dreaded by others—inevitably comes up. When meeting a woman at a party, when being sent on a blind date, or when discussing old high school friends or the guy who just moved into the next-door apartment, the question hums just below the surface, and it's never long until someone comes out and asks. Of course, for collegians and young people working part-time jobs, it doesn't matter so much because everyone knows that where you work isn't where you'll end up working. Once someone hits the mid-twenties, though, the question "what do you do?" starts to press and it won't let up.

- Perez Hilton wrote that Souza displayed disloyalty to her company when she trashed the management on Facebook. The following questions are raised: What *is* loyalty? What is it worth? When should you feel it? When do you have a right to demand it from others? Is there any difference among loyalty to the company, to family, and to friends?

- One of Hilton's readers posted a pithy response to Hilton in the web page's comments section: "I bet if she were gay, and did the same exact thing, you would be singing a different tune!" Perez Hilton, it's widely known, is about as exuberantly gay as they come. As it happens, in his line of work that orientation isn't professionally harmful. For others, however, the revelation may be career damaging. Hilton, in fact, is despised by some in Hollywood for his habit of outing gay celebrities, people who hide part of themselves in the name of furthering their career. The business ethics question here is also a life one. Would you hide who you are to facilitate things at work? Should you? Doesn't everyone do that to some extent and in some ways?

- Another reader posted this comment: "In the US, your employer owns you. I mean they can make you piss in a cup to check and see what you did over the weekend." Should employers be able to change what you do over the weekend?

- A number of readers defended Souza by upholding the right to free speech—she should be able to say whatever she wants wherever she wants without fear of retribution. In response to those assertions, this was posted, "Of course we have freedom of speech. Employers also have the freedom to employ whoever they wish. Your decision is whether whatever is on your mind is more important than your job." Does freedom of speech—or any other basic liberty—end or get conditioned when the workday begins?

- One commenter wrote, "I'm going to have to agree with the company on this one. An employer expects proper business demeanor even while off the clock." What is "proper demeanor"? Who decides? On the basis of what?

- Many people spend eight (or more) hours a day on the job. There's no shortage of women who see their boss more than their husband, of men who remember the birthday of the guy in the next cubicle before their own child's. Parties tend to include workmates; companies invite clients to ball games. The sheer hours spent at work, along with the large overlaps between professional and social relationships, make separating the ethics of the office and the home nearly impossible.

- This comment is aimed right at Perez Hilton and his Internet gossip column, which wins few points for checking and confirming claims but definitely gets the juicy and embarrassing rumors out about the private lives of celebrities: "Are you insane? All you did for God knows how long is put nasty stuff up about people for the public to see as a sign of disloyalty and disrespect." Assuming that's a reasonable depiction of Hilton's work, the question his career raises is: what are you willing to do to the lives of others to get yourself ahead at work?

Underlining all these questions is a distinction that's easy to make in theory but difficult to maintain in real life. It's one between institutional business ethics and personal business ethics. Institutional ethics in business deals with large questions in generic and anonymous terms. The rules and discussions apply to most organizations and to individuals who could be anyone. Should companies be allowed to pollute the air? What counts as a firing offense? The personal level, by contrast, fills with questions for specific people enmeshed in the details of their particular lives. If Perez Hilton has gotten rich dishing dirt on others, is he allowed to assert that others must treat their employers respectfully?

KEY TAKEAWAY

- The questions pursued by business ethics cross back and forth between professional and personal lives.

REVIEW QUESTIONS

1. What are two reasons business ethics decisions tend to affect lives outside work?
2. What are two ways business ethics decisions may affect lives outside work?

[1] "Facebook-Related Firing Sparks Legal Drama!" *PerezHilton.com* (blog), accessed May 11, 2011, http://perezhilton.com/2010-11-09-woman-fired-over-comments- she-made-about-her-boss-on-facebook-brings-about-court-case#respond.

1.5 Case Studies

Gray Matters

To foster ethical discussion and understanding in the workplace, the Lockheed Martin Company developed a quiz for employees called "Gray Matters." The quiz is multiple choices, with a range of points awarded (or subtracted) depending on the response. Subsequently, the approach has been adopted by a wide range of corporations. Here's a typical question matched with its possible answers and the corresponding points:

Six months after you hired an assistant accountant who has been working competently and responsibly, you learn that she departed from the truth on her employment application: she claimed she had a college degree when she didn't. You're her manager; what should you do?

1. *Nothing because she's doing her job just fine. (–10 points)*
2. *Bring the issue to the human resources department to determine exactly how company policy determines the situation should be handled. (10 points)*
3. *Fire her for lying. (5 points)*
4. *Carefully weigh her work performance, her length of service, and her potential benefit to the company before informing anyone of what happened or making any recommendations. (0 points)*

QUESTIONS

1. The three principle components of business ethics are facts, values, and arguments. What are the facts pertinent to an ethical evaluation of this case? Is there any information not contained in the question that you'd like to have before making a decision about what should be done?
2. From the facts and information provided, can you sketch a set of values and chain of reasoning justifying the answer that the quiz's original authors sanctioned as the right one? (Leave the decision in the hands of the HR department and existing company policy.)
3. You get some points for C (firing her). What values and reasoning may lead to that determination?
4. According to the quiz authors, the worst answer is A. Maybe they're wrong, though. What values and reasoning may lead to the conclusion that doing "nothing because she's doing her job just fine" is an excellent response?
5. One of the most important questions about a situation's facts is "who's involved?"

o Would it be reasonable to say that, ethically, this is an issue just between you and the woman who you hired after she lied on her résumé?

o If you expand the answer about who's involved to include other workmates at the company, as well as the company's clients and shareholders, does that change the ethical perspective you have on what should be done with the lying (but capable) coworker?

6. What's the difference between morality and ethics?

o Would you categorize response B (bring the issue to HR to determine exactly how company policy determines the situation should be handled) as leading to a decision more based on morality or more based on ethics? Explain.

o Would you categorize response D (carefully weigh her work performance, her length of service, and her potential benefit to the company before informing anyone of what happened or making any recommendations) as leading to a decision more based on morality or ethics? Explain.

Who made your iPhone?

Connie Guglielmo, a reporter for Bloomberg news services, begins an article on Apple this way: "Apple Inc. said three of its suppliers hired 11 underage workers to help build the iPhone, iPod and Macintosh computer last year, a violation it uncovered as part of its onsite audit of 102 factories." [1]

Her story adds details. The underage workers were fifteen in places where the minimum legal age for employment is sixteen. She wasn't able to discover the specific countries, but learned the infractions occurred in one or more of the following: China, Taiwan, Thailand, Malaysia, Singapore, South Korea, the Czech Republic, and the Philippines.

Following the discovery, the employees were released, and disciplinary action was taken against a number of the foreign suppliers. In one case, Apple stopped contracting with the company entirely.

The story closes with this: "Apple raised $2.62 to $204.62 yesterday in Nasdaq Stock Market trading. The shares more than doubled last year."

QUESTIONS

1. The ethical question is whether Apple ought to contract (through suppliers) fifteen-year-olds to work on factory floors. Is the fact that the stock price has been zooming up a pertinent fact, or does it not affect the ethics? Explain.

2. From the information given and reasonable assumptions about these factories and the living conditions of people working inside them, sketch an ethical argument *against* Apple enforcing the age workplace rule. What fundamental values underwrite the argument?

3. From the information given and reasonable assumptions about these factories and the living conditions of people working inside them, sketch an argument *in favor of* Apple enforcing the age workplace rule. What fundamental values underwrite the argument?

4. Within the context of the Apple situation, what's the difference between making a decision in terms of the law and in terms of ethics?

5. Assume that in the countries where fifteen-year-olds were working, it's customary for children even younger to earn an adult-type living.

o What is an advantage of following the local customs when making economic decisions like the one confronting Apple?

o Does the custom of employing young workers in some countries change your ethical consideration of the practice in those places? Why or why not?

6. Attributing responsibility—blaming another for doing wrong—requires that the following conditions hold:

o The person is able to understand right and wrong.

o The person acts to cause (or fails to act to prevent) a wrong.

o The person acts knowing what they're doing.

o The person acts from their own free will.

Assuming it's unethical for fifteen-year-olds to work factory shifts making iPhones, who bears responsibility for the wrong?

o Do the fifteen-year-olds bear some responsibility? Explain.

o Does Steve Jobs, the CEO of Apple? Explain.

o Are shareholders guilty? Explain.

o Do people who use iPhones bear responsibility? Explain.

I Swear

Since 2006, students at the Columbia Business School have been required to pledge "I adhere to the principles of truth, integrity, and respect. I will not lie, cheat, steal, or tolerate those who do."

This is a substantial promise, but it doesn't sound like it'll create too many tremendous burdens or require huge sacrifices.

A somewhat more demanding pledge solidified in 2010 when a group of business school students from Columbia, Duke Fuqua, Harvard, MIT Sloan, NYU Stern, Rensselaer Lally, Thunderbird, UNC Kenan-Flagler, and Yale met to formalize the following MBA Oath:

As a business leader I recognize my role in society.

- *My purpose is to lead people and manage resources to create value that no single individual can create alone.*
- *My decisions affect the well-being of individuals inside and outside my enterprise, today and tomorrow.*

Therefore, I promise that:

- *I will manage my enterprise with loyalty and care, and will not advance my personal interests at the expense of my enterprise or society.*
- *I will understand and uphold, in letter and spirit, the laws and contracts governing my conduct and that of my enterprise.*
- *I will refrain from corruption, unfair competition, or business practices harmful to society.*
- *I will protect the human rights and dignity of all people affected by my enterprise, and I will oppose discrimination and exploitation.*
- *I will protect the right of future generations to advance their standard of living and enjoy a healthy planet.*
- *I will report the performance and risks of my enterprise accurately and honestly.*
- *I will invest in developing myself and others, helping the management profession continue to advance and create sustainable and inclusive prosperity.*

In exercising my professional duties according to these principles, I recognize that my behavior must set an example of integrity, eliciting trust and esteem from those I serve. I will remain accountable to my peers and to society for my actions and for upholding these standards. [2]

QUESTIONS

1. The second introductory clause of the MBA Oath is "My decisions affect the well-being of individuals inside and outside my enterprise, today and tomorrow." [3] What's the difference between seeing this as a positive ethical stand in favor of a broad social responsibility held by those in business, and seeing it as arrogance?

2. Looking at the MBA Oath, can you list a set of values that are probably shared by those responsible for its creation?

3. All this pledging and oathing suddenly popping up at business schools drew the attention of the *New York Times*, and soon after, an article appeared: "A Promise to Be Ethical in an Era of Immorality."[4] Many of the readers' comments at the end are interesting. The commenter paulnyc writes that "most students go to MBA programs to advance their careers and to earn more

money, pure and simple, and there is nothing wrong with it." [5]

- o   What values underlie paulnyc's perspective?
- o   How is paulnyc's vision different from the one espoused in the oath?

4. The commenter JerryNY wrote, "Greed IS good as long as it is paired with the spirit of fairness. Virtually all of the major advances in science and technology were made with greed as one of the motivating factors. Gugliemo [sic] Marconi, Alexander Graham Bell, Bill Gates, Henry Ford and Steve Jobs would not have given us the life changing technological advances of our time were it not for personal greed. Remove that element, and your class is destined for mediocrity." [6]

Is it plausible to assert that JerryNY shares most of the values of those who wrote the MBA Oath, it's just that he sees a different business attitude as the best way to serve those values? If so, explain. If not, why not?

5. Eric writes,

I would refuse to take that oath…on principle. The idea that an individual's proper motive should be to serve "the greater good" is highly questionable. This altruistic ethic is what supported the collectivist of communism and National Socialism. If my life belongs first and foremost to "the greater good," it follows that the greatest virtue is to live as a slave. A slave's existence, after all, is devoted primarily for the benefit of his master. The master can be a plantation owner or a King or an oligarchy or a society that demands your servitude.
The only oath I'd be willing to take is, "I swear, by my life and my love of it, that I will never live for the sake of another man, nor ask another man to live for mine." [7]

In your own words, contrast the values the MBA Oath supporters espouse with the values the commenter Eric espouses.

6. The commenter Clyde Wynant is skeptical. He writes this about those who take the MBA Oath: "Call me hyper-cynical, but I can't help wondering if a lot of these kids aren't hoping that having this 'pledge' on their résumé might help them look good." [8]

Is it unethical to take the pledge without expecting to adhere to it simply because you think it will help in your job search, or is that strategy just a different kind of ethics? Explain.

7. The commenter Mikhail is skeptical. He writes, "Give me a break…With the next upswing of the economy, these leeches will be sucking the lifeblood out of our collective economies like the champions they truly are!!! Yes, perhaps opportunistic parasites every last one of them—

but really, it's not their fault—they're just programmed that way." [9]

When he says business school students are programmed, what does he mean? If someone is programmed to be an opportunistic parasite in business, can we blame them for what they do? If so, how? If not, who should be blamed?

8. The commenter *as* is skeptical. He writes, "Don't make me laugh. If they are so concerned about the 'greater good,' go into teaching and nursing." [10]

Assume the MBA Oath does stress the importance of the greater good, and you too are going into the economic world with that as a privileged value. How could you respond to the argument that you really should be doing nursing or something more obviously serving the general good?

9. According to the *Times*, B-schoolers aren't lining up for the MBA Oath: only about 20 percent take the pledge. How could you convince the other 80 percent to sign on?

I.M.P. (It's My Party)

"Look at them!" he said, his eyes dancing. "That's what it's all about, the way the people feel. It's not about the sellout performances and the caliber of the bands that appear here. It's about the people who buy tickets, having a good time." [11]

That's Seth Hurwitz quoted in the *Washington Post*, talking about his 9:30 Club, a small venue playing over-the-hill bands on the way down, and fresh acts scratching their way up.

The story's curious detail is that even though Hurwitz calls his company I.M.P. (It's My Party), he doesn't spend much time at his club. In fact, he's almost never there. Part of the reason is that his workday begins at 6 a.m., so he's actually back in bed preparing for the next day before his enterprise gets going in earnest each night. His job is straightforward: sitting in the second floor office of his suburban DC home, he scrutinizes the music publications and statistics, probing for bands that people want to see and that won't charge too much to appear. He told the *Post* that he won't book an act as a favor, and he won't flatter a group into playing his club to keep them away from the competition by overpaying them. "I don't subscribe," he says, "to doing shows that will lose money."

Hurwitz has been connected with music in one way or another for almost as long as he can remember. The *Post* relates some of his early memories:

He rigged a system to broadcast radio from his basement to his parents and brothers in the living room. "I used to bring my singles into class and play them," Hurwitz said. When he was 16, he decided he wanted to be a deejay and got his chance when

alternative rock station WHFS gave him a spot. "It was from 7:45 to 8—fifteen minutes," he said, laughing. "But that was okay because I wanted to be on the radio, and I had my own show, as a high school student." He said he was fired "for being too progressive." [12]

It's a long way from getting fired for playing music too obscure for alternative radio to where Hurwitz is now: putting on concerts by bands selected because they'll make money.

QUESTIONS

1. Hurwitz is brutally honest about the fact that he'll only contract bands capable of turning a profit. When he was younger and a deejay, he insisted on playing the music he judged best no matter how many people turned off the radio when his show came on (an attitude that cost him the job).
   o What, if anything, is Hurwitz the older concert promoter compromising to get ahead? Is there an ethical objection that could be raised here? If so, what? If not, why not?
   o When Hurwitz was a deejay, he played records that led people to change the station. Then the station changed him. Is this an example of business regulating itself? Is there an ethical side to this, or is it just the way money works? Explain.
   o From the information given, would you judge that Hurwitz is successful in business? Why or why not?
   o Are all these questions part of institutional business ethics or personal business ethics? Explain.

2. Hurwitz says that he doesn't book bands as favors. Presumably at least some of the favors he's talking about would be to friends.
   o Do people who run their own company have an ethical responsibility to separate friends from business?

3. One nice thing about Hurwitz working upstairs in his own house is that he can show up for work in the morning in his pajamas. Should all places of business be like that—with people free to wear whatever they want for work? Explain your answer from an ethical perspective.

4. Most of Hurwitz's shows are on weeknights. Some concertgoers may have such a good time that they can't make it in to work the next day.
   o If you go to a concert on a Wednesday and are too hung over to make it to work on Thursday, what should you tell your boss on Friday? That you were hung over? That your car broke down? Something else? Justify.

o Should Hurwitz accept some responsibility and blame for absent employees? Explain.

[1] Connie Guglielmo, "Apple Says Children Were Used to Build iPhone, iPod (Update1)," Bloomberg, February 27, 2010, accessed May 11, 2011, http://www.bloomberg.com/apps/news?pid=newsarchive&sid=aiEeeQN HkrOY.

[2] "The MBA Oath," MBA Oath, accessed May 11, 2011, http://mbaoath.org/about/the-mba-oath.

[3] "The MBA Oath," MBA Oath, accessed May 11, 2011, http://mbaoath.org/about/the-mba-oath.

[4] Leslie Wayne, "A Promise to Be Ethical in an Era of Immorality," New York Times, May 29, 2009, accessed May 11, 2011, http://www.nytimes.com/2009/05/30/business/30oath.html.

[5] paulnyc, May 30, 2009 (10:58 a.m.), comment on Leslie Wayne, "A Promise to Be Ethical in an Era of Immorality," New York Times, May 29, 2009, accessed May 11, 2011, http://community.nytimes.com/comments/www.nytimes.com/2009/05/30/business/30oath.html?sort=oldest.

[6] JerryNY, May 30, 2009 (10:51 a.m.), comment on Leslie Wayne, "A Promise to Be Ethical in an Era of Immorality," New York Times, May 29, 2009, accessed May 11, 2011, http://community.nytimes.com/comments/www.nytimes.com/2009/05/30/business/30oath.html?sort=oldest.

[7] Eric, May 30, 2009 (10:35 a.m.), comment on Leslie Wayne, "A Promise to Be Ethical in an Era of Immorality," New York Times, May 29, 2009, accessed May 11, 2011, http://community.nytimes.com/comments/www.nytimes.com/2009/05/30/business/30oath.html?sort=oldest.

[8] Clyde Wynant, May 30, 2009 (10:55 a.m.), comment on Leslie Wayne, "A Promise to Be Ethical in an Era of Immorality," New York Times, May 29, 2009, accessed May 11, 2011, http://community.nytimes.com/comments/www.nytimes.com/2009/05/30/business/30oath.html?sort=oldest.

[9] Mikhail, May 30, 2009 (10:35 a.m.), comment on Leslie Wayne, "A Promise to Be Ethical in an Era of Immorality," New York Times, May 29, 2009, accessed May 11, 2011, http://community.nytimes.com/comments/www.nytimes.com/2009/05/30/business/30oath.html?sort=oldest.

[10] as, May 30, 2009 (10:35 a.m.), comment on Leslie Wayne, "A Promise to Be Ethical in an Era of Immorality," New York Times, May 29, 2009, accessed May 11, 2011, http://community.nytimes.com/comments/www.nytimes.com/2009/05/30/business/30oath.html?sort=oldest.

[11] Avis Thomas-Lester, "A Club Owner's Mojo," Washington Post, December 28, 2009, accessed May 11, 2011, http://views.washingtonpost.com/on-success/what-it-takes/2009/12/seth_hurwitz.html.

[12] Avis Thomas-Lester, "A Club Owner's Mojo," Washington Post, December 28, 2009, accessed May 11, 2011, http://views.washingtonpost.com/on-success/what-it-takes/2009/12/seth_hurwitz.html.

NOTES:

NOTES:

Chapter 2:
Theories of Duties and Rights

Chapter Overview

This chapter examines some theories guiding ethical decisions in business. It considers ethics defined by duties and rights.

2.1 The Means Justify the Ends versus the Ends Justify the Means
LEARNING OBJECTIVE

1. Distinguish ethical theory centered on means from theory centered on ends.

A Foundational Question

In business ethics, do the means justify the ends, or do the ends justify the means? Is it better to have a set of rules telling you what you ought to do in any particular situation and then let the chips fall where they may, or should you worry more about how things are going to end up and do whatever's necessary to reach that goal?

Until recently, Eddy Lepp ran an organic medicine business in Northern California. His herbal product soothed nausea and remedied vomiting, especially as suffered by chemo patients. He had a problem, though. While his business had been OK'd by California regulators, federal agencies hadn't approved: on the national level, selling his drug was breaking the law. On the other hand, *not* selling his remedy had a significant downside: it was consigning his clients to debilitating suffering. So when federal agents came knocking on his door, he had to make a decision.

If the means justify the ends—if you should follow the rules no matter the consequences—then when the agents ask Lepp point blank whether he's selling the medicine, the ethical action is to admit it. He should tell the truth even though that will mean the end of his business. On the other hand, if the ends justify the means—if your ethical interest focuses on the consequences of an act instead of what you actually do—then the ethics change. If there are a law forcing people to suffer unnecessarily, it should be broken. And when the agents ask him whether he's selling, he's going to have an ethical reason to lie.

Across the entire field of traditional ethics, this is a foundational distinction. Is it what you do that matters, or the consequences? It's hard to get oriented in ethics without

making a preliminary decision between these two. No one can make the decision for you, but before anyone can make it, an understanding of how each works should be reached. This chapter will consider ethics as focusing on the specific act and not the consequences. Theories of duties and rights center discussion.

KEY TAKEAWAYS

- When the means justify the ends, ethical consideration focuses on what you do, not the consequences of what you've done.
- Traditionally, focusing on means instead of ends leads to an ethics based on duties or rights.

REVIEW QUESTIONS

1. Your mother is ill with diabetes, and you can't afford her medicine. In the pharmacy one day, you notice the previous customer forgot that same prescription on the counter when she left. Why might the premise that the ends justify the means lead you to steal the pills?
2. Why might the premise that the means justify the ends lead you to return the pills?

2.2 Perennial Duties
LEARNING OBJECTIVES

1. Define an ethical duty.
2. Distinguish specific duties.
3. Show how ethical duties work in business.
4. Consider advantages and drawbacks of an ethics based on duties.

Duties

"Should I steal that?"
"No, stealing's wrong."

Basic ethics. There are things that are right and others that are wrong, and the discussion ends. This level of clarity and solidity is the main strength of an ethics based on duties. We all have a duty not to steal, so we shouldn't do it. More broadly, when we're making moral decisions, the key to deciding well is understanding what our duties are and obeying them. An ethics based on duties is one where certain rules tell us what we ought to do, and it's our responsibility to know and follow those rules.

The Madoff Family

If we're supposed to obey our duties, then what exactly *are* they? That's a question Andrew Madoff faced in December 2008 when he learned that some—maybe most, maybe all—of the money he and his family had been donating to the charitable Lymphoma Research Foundation and similar medical investigation enterprises was, in fact, stolen.

It was big money—in the millions—channeled to dedicated researchers hot on the trail of a remedy for lymphoma, a deadly cancer. Andrew, it should be noted, wasn't only a cancer altruist; he was also a victim, and the charitable money started flowing to the researchers soon after he was diagnosed.

It's unclear whether Andrew knew the money was stolen, but there's no doubt that his dad did. Dad—Bernard "Bernie" Madoff—was the one who took it. The largest Ponzi scheme in history, they call it.

A Ponzi scheme—named after the famous perpetrator Charles Ponzi—makes suckers of investors by briefly delivering artificially high returns on their money. The idea is simple: You take $100 from client A, promising to invest the money cleverly and get a massive profit. You spend $50 on yourself, and at the end of the year, you send the other $50 back to the client along with a note saying that the original $100 investment is getting *excellent* results and another $50 should come in next year and every year from then on. Happy client A recommends friends, who become clients B, C, and D. They bring in a total of $300, so it's easy to make good on the original promise to send a $50 return the next year to client A. And you've now got $250 remaining from these three new clients, $150 of which you will soon return to them ($50 for each of the three new clients), leaving you with $100 to spend on yourself. The process repeats, and it's not long before people are lining up to hand over their money. Everyone makes off like bandits.

Bandit is the right term for Madoff, who ran his Ponzi empire for around fifteen years. So many people handed over so much cash, and the paper trail of fake stock-purchase receipts and the rest grew so complicated that it's impossible to determine exact numbers of victims and losses. Federal authorities have estimated the victims were around five thousand and the losses around $65 billion, which works out to about $13 million squeezed from each client.

Madoff had, obviously, rich clients. He met them at his home in New York City; at his mansion in hyper-wealthy Palm Beach, Florida; or on his fifty-five-foot yacht cleverly named *Bull*. He impressed them with a calm demeanor and serious knowledge. While it's true that he was mostly taking clients' money and sticking it in his wallet, the investments he *claimed* to engineer were actually quite sophisticated; they had to do with buying stock in tandem with options to buy and sell that same stock on the futures market. He threw in technical words like "put" and "call" and left everyone thinking he was either crazy or a genius. Since he was apparently making money, "genius" seemed the more likely reality. People also found him trustworthy. He sat on the boards of several Wall Street professional organizations and was known on the charity circuit as a generous benefactor. Health research was a favorite, especially after Andrew's cancer was diagnosed.

Exactly how much money Madoff channeled to Andrew and other family members isn't clear. By late 2008, however, Andrew knew that his father's investment company had hit a rough patch. The stock market was crashing, investors wanted their money back, and Madoff was having trouble rounding up the cash, which explains why Andrew was surprised when his father called him in and said he'd decided to distribute about $200 million in bonuses to family members and employees.

It didn't make sense. How could there be a cash-flow crisis but still enough cash to pay out giant bonuses? The blunt question—according to the Madoff family—broke Madoff down. He spilled the truth: there was little money left; it was all a giant lie.

The next day, Andrew reported the situation to the authorities.

Madoff sits in jail now. He'll be there for the rest of his life. He claims his scheme was his project alone and his children had no knowledge or participation in it, despite the fact that they were high executives in his fraudulent company. Stubbornly, he has refused to cooperate with prosecutors interested in determining the extent to which the children may have been involved. His estate has been seized. His wife, though, was left with a small sum—$2.5 million—to meet her day-to-day living expenses. Bilked investors got nearly nothing.

One of those investors, according to ABC News, was Sheryl Weinstein. She and her family are now looking for a place to live because after investing everything with Madoff and losing it, they were unable to make their house payments. At Madoff's sentencing hearing, and with her husband seated beside her, she spoke passionately about their plight and called Madoff a "beast." The hearing concluded with the judge calling Madoff "evil." [1]

Weinstein was well remembered by Madoff's longtime secretary, Eleanor Squillari. Squillari reported that Weinstein would often call Madoff and that "he would roll his eyes and then they'd go meet at a hotel." Their affair lasted twenty years, right up until the finance empire collapsed.

What Do I Owe Myself? Historically Accumulated Duties to the Self

Over centuries of thought and investigation by philosophers, clergy, politicians, entrepreneurs, parents, students—by just about everyone who cares about how we live together in a shared world—a limited number of duties have recurred persistently. Called perennial duties, these are basic obligations we have as human beings; they're the fundamental rules telling us how we should act. If we embrace them, we can be confident that in difficult situations we'll make morally respectable decisions.

Broadly, this group of perennial duties falls into two sorts:
1. Duties to ourselves
2. Duties to others

Duties to the self-begin with our responsibility to develop our abilities and talents. The abilities we find within us, the idea is, aren't just gifts; it's not only a strike of luck that some of us are born with a knack for math, or an ear for music, or the ability to shepherd conflicts between people into agreements. All these skills are also responsibilities. When we receive them, *they come with the duty to develop them*, to not let them go to waste in front of the TV or on a pointless job.

Most of us have a feeling for this. It's one thing if a vaguely clumsy girl in a ballet class decides to not sign up the next semester and instead use the time trying to boost her GPA, but if someone who's really good—who's strong, and elegant, and a natural—decides to just walk away, of course the coach and friends are going to encourage her to think about it again. She has something that so few have, it's a shame to waste it; it's a kind of betrayal of her own uniqueness. This is the spot where the ethics come in: the idea is that she really *should* continue her development; it's a responsibility she has to herself because she really can develop.

What about Andrew Madoff, the cancer sufferer? He not only donated money to cancer research charities but also

dedicated his time, serving as chairman of the Lymphoma Research Foundation (until his dad was arrested). This dedication *does* seem like a duty because of his unique situation: as a sufferer, he perfectly understood the misery caused by the disease, and as a wealthy person, he could muster a serious force against the suffering. When he did, he fulfilled the duty to exploit his particular abilities.

The other significant duty to oneself is nearly a corollary of the first: the duty to do ourselves no harm. At root, this means we have a responsibility to maintain ourselves healthily in the world. It doesn't do any good to dedicate hours training the body to dance beautifully if the *rest* of the hours are dedicated to alcoholism and Xanax. Similarly, Andrew should not only fight cancer publicly by advocating for medical research but also fight privately by adhering to his treatment regime.

At the extreme, this duty also prohibits suicide, a possibility that no doubt crosses Bernie Madoff's mind from time to time as he contemplates spending the rest of his life in a jail cell.

What Do I Owe Others? Historically Accumulated Duties to Others

The duties we have to ourselves be the most immediate, but the most commonly referenced duties are those we have to others.

Avoid wronging others are the guiding duty to those around us. It's difficult, however, to know exactly what it means to wrong another in every particular case. It does seem clear that Madoff wronged his clients when he pocketed their money. The case of his wife is blurrier, though. She was allowed to keep more than $2 million after her husband's sentencing. She claims she has a right to it because she never knew what her husband was doing, and anyway, at least that much money came to her from other perfectly legal investment initiatives her husband undertook. So she can make a case that the money is hers to keep and she's not wronging anyone by holding onto it. Still, it's hard not to wonder about investors here, especially ones like Sheryl Weinstein, who lost everything, including their homes.

Honesty is the duty to tell the truth and not leave anything important out. On this front, obviously, Madoff wronged his investors by misleading them about what was happening with their money.

Respect others are the duty to treat others as equals in human terms. This doesn't mean treating everyone the same way.

When a four-year-old asks where babies come from, the stork is a fine answer. When adult investors asked Madoff where the profits came from, what they got was more or less a fairy tale. Now, the first case is an example of respect: it demonstrates an understanding of another's capacity to comprehend the world and an attempt to provide an explanation matching that ability. The second is a lie; but more than that, it's a sting of disrespect. When Madoff invented stories about where the money came from, he disdained his investors as beneath him, treating them as unworthy of the truth.

Beneficence is the duty to promote the welfare of others; it's the Good Samaritan side of ethical duties. With respect to his own family members, Madoff certainly fulfilled this obligation: every one of them received constant and lavish amounts of cash. There's also beneficence in Andrew's work for charitable causes, even if there's a self-serving element, too. By contrast, Madoff displayed little beneficence for his clients.

Gratitude is the duty to thank and remember those who help us. One of the curious parts of Madoff's last chapter is that in the end, at the sentencing hearing, a parade of witnesses stood up to berate him. But even though Madoff had donated millions of dollars to charities over the years, not a single person or representative of a charitable organization stood up to say something on his behalf. That's ingratitude, no doubt.

But there's more here than ingratitude; there's also an important point about all ethics guided by basic duties: *the duties don't exist alone.* They're all part of a single fabric, and sometimes they pull against each other. In this case, the duty Madoff's beneficiaries probably felt to a man who'd given them so much was overwhelmed by the demand of another duty: the duty to respect others, specifically those who lost everything to Madoff. It's difficult to imagine a way to treat people more disdainfully than to thank the criminal who stole their money for being so generous. Those who received charitable contributions from Madoff were tugged in one direction by gratitude to him and in another by respect for his many victims. All the receivers opted, finally, to respect the victims.

Fidelity is the duty to keep our promises and hold up our end of agreements. The Madoff case is littered with abuses on this front. On the professional side, there's the financier who didn't invest his clients' money as he'd promised; on the personal side, there's Madoff and Weinstein staining their wedding vows. From one end to the other in terms of fidelity, this is an ugly case.

Reparation is the duty to compensate others when we harm them. Madoff's wife, Ruth, obviously didn't feel much of this. She walked away with $2.5 million.

The judge overseeing the case, on the other hand, filled in some of what Ruth lacked. To pay back bilked investors, the court seized her jewelry, her art, and her mink and sable coats. Those things, along with the couple's three multimillion-dollar homes, the limousines, and the yacht, were all sold at public auction.

The Concept of Fairness

The final duty to be considered—fairness—requires more development than those already listed because of its complexity.

According to Aristotle, fairness is treating equals equally and un-equals unequally. The *treat equals equally* part means, for a professional investor like Madoff, that all his clients get the same deal: those who invest equal amounts of money at about the same time should get an equal return. So even though Madoff was sleeping with one of his investors, this shouldn't allow him to treat her account distinctly from the ones belonging to the rest. Impartiality must govern the operation.

The other side of fairness is the requirement to *treat un-equals unequally.* Where there's a meaningful difference between investors—which means a difference pertaining to the investment and not something extraneous like a romantic involvement—there should correspond a proportional difference in what investors receive. Under this clause, Madoff could find justification for allowing two distinct rates of return for his clients. Those that put up money at the beginning when everything seemed riskier could justifiably receive a higher payout than the one yielded to more recent participants. Similarly, in any company, if layoffs are necessary, it might make sense to say that those who've been working in the organization longest should be the last ones to lose their jobs. In either case, the important point is that *fairness doesn't mean everyone gets the same treatment; it means that rules for treating people must be applied equally.* If a corporate executive decides on layoffs according to a last-in-first-out process, that's fine, but it would be unfair to make exceptions.

One of the unique aspects of the idea of fairness as a duty is its hybrid status between duties to the self and duties to others. While it would seem strange to say that we have a duty of gratitude or fidelity to ourselves, it clearly makes sense to assert that we should be fair to ourselves. Impartiality—the rule of no exceptions—means no exceptions. So a stock investor who puts his own money into a general fund he runs should receive the same return as everyone else. A poor investment that loses 10 percent should cost him no more than 10 percent (he has to be fair to himself), and one that gains 10 percent shouldn't net him any more than what the others receive (he has to be fair to others).

Modern Fairness: Rawls

The recent American philosopher John Rawls proposes a veil of ignorance as a way of testing for fairness, especially with respect to the distribution of wealth in general terms. For example, in society as Madoff knew it, vast inequalities of wealth weren't only allowed, they were honored: being richer than anyone else was something to be proud of, and Madoff lived that reality full tilt. Now, if you asked Madoff whether we *should* allow some members of society to be much wealthier than others, he might say that's fair: everyone is allowed to get rich in America, and that's just what he did. However, the guy coming into Madoff's office at 3 a.m. to mop up and empty the trash might see things differently. He may claim to work just as hard as Madoff, but without getting fancy cars or Palm Springs mansions. People making the big bucks, the suggestion could follow, should get hit with bigger taxes and the money used to provide educational programs allowing guys from the cleaning crew to get a better chance at climbing the income ladder. Now, given these two perspectives, is there a way to decide what's really fair when it comes to wealth and taxes?

Rawls proposes that we try to re-imagine society *without* knowing what our place in it would be. In the case of Madoff, he may like things as they are, but would he stick with the idea that everything's fair if he were told that a rearrangement was coming and he was going to get stuck back into the business world at random? He might hesitate there, seeing that he could get dealt a bad hand and, yes, end up being the guy who cleans offices. And that guy who cleans offices might figure that if he got a break, then *he'd* be the rich one, and so he's no longer so sure about raising taxes. The veil of ignorance is the idea that when you set up the rules, you don't get to know beforehand where you'll fall inside them, which is going to force you to construct things in a way that is really balanced and fair.

As a note here, nearly all children know the veil of ignorance perfectly. When two friends together buy a candy bar to split, they'll frequently have one person break it, and the other choose a half. If you're the breaker, you're under the veil of ignorance since you don't know which half you're going to get. The result is you break it fairly, as close to the middle as you can.

Balancing the Duties

Duties include those to:

- develop abilities and talents,
- do ourselves no harm,
- avoid wronging others,
- honesty,
- respect others,
- beneficence,
- gratitude,
- fidelity,
- reparation,
- fairness,

Taken on their own, each of these plugs into normal experience without significant problems. Real troubles come, though, when more than one duty seems applicable and they're pulling in different directions.

Take Andrew Madoff, for example. Lying in bed at night and taking his ethical duties seriously, what should he do in the wake of the revelation that his family business was in essence a giant theft? On one side, there's an argument that he should just keep on keeping on by maintaining his life as a New York financier. The route to *justifying* that decision starts with a duty to him:

- **Develop abilities and talents.** As an expert in finance, someone with both knowledge of and experience in the field, Andrew should continue cultivating and perfecting his talents, at least those he had acquired on the legitimate side of the family's dealings.

  Beyond the duty to himself, Andrew can further buttress his decision to keep his current life going by referencing a duty to others:

- **Beneficence.** This may demand that Andrew continue along the lines he'd already established because they enabled his involvement with cancer research. He's got money to donate to the cause and his very personal experience with the disease allows rare insight into what can be done to help sufferers. To the extent that's true, beneficence supports Andrew's decision to go on living as he had been.

  On the other side, what's the duty-based argument in favor of Andrew taking a different path by breaking away from his old lifestyle and dedicating all his energy and time to doing what he can for the jilted investors the family business left behind?

- **Respect.** The duty to treat others as equals demands that Andrew take seriously the abilities and lives of all those who lost everything. Why should *they* be reduced to powerlessness and poverty while he continues maximizing his potential as a stock buyer and nonprofit leader? Respecting others and their losses may mean leaving his profession and helping them get back on their feet.
- **Reparation.** This duty advances as the proposal for Andrew to liquidate his assets and divide the money as fairly as possible among the ruined investors. It may be that Andrew didn't orchestrate the family Ponzi scheme, but wittingly or not, he participated and that opens the way to the duty to repayment.

So which path should Andrew follow? There's no certain answer. What duties *do* allow Andrew—or anyone considering his situation—to achieve is a solid footing for making a reasonable and defendable decision. From there, the ethical task is to weigh the various duties and choose which ones pull harder and make the stronger demand.

Where Do Duties Come From?

The question about the origin of duties belongs to meta-ethics, to purified discussions about the theory of ethics as opposed to its application, so it falls outside this book's focus. Still, two commonly cited sources of duties can be quickly noted.

One standard explanation is that duties are written into the nature of the universe; they're part of the way things *are*. In a sense, they're a moral complement to the laws of physics. We know that scientists form mathematical formulas to explain how far arrows will travel when shot at a certain speed; these formulas describe the way the natural world is. So too in the realm of ethics: duties are the rules describing how the world is in moral terms. On this account, ethics isn't so different from science; it's just that scientists explore physical reality and ethicists explore moral reality. In both cases, however, the reality is already there; we're just trying to understand it.

Another possible source for the duties is humanity in the sense that part of what it means *to be* human is to have this particular sense of right and wrong. Under this logic, a computer-guided robot may beat humans in chess, but no machine will ever understand what a child does when mom asks, "Did you break the vase? Tell me the truth." Maybe this moral spark children are taken to feel is written into their genetic code, or maybe it's something ineffable, like a soul.

Whichever, the reason it comes naturally is because it's part of our nature.

What Are the Advantages and Drawbacks of an Ethics Based on Duties?

One of the principal advantages of working with an ethics of duties is simplicity: duties are fairly easy to understand and work with. We all use them every day. For many of us these duties are the first thing coming to mind when we hear the word *ethics*. Straightforward rules about honesty, gratitude, and keeping up our ends of agreements—these are the components of a common education in ethics, and most of us are well experienced in their use.

The problem, though, comes when the duties pull against each other: when one says yes and the other says no. Unfortunately, there's no hard-and-fast rule for deciding *which* duties should take precedence over the others.

KEY TAKEAWAYS

- Duties include responsibilities to one self and to others.
- Duties do not exist in isolation but in a network, and they sometimes pull against each other.

REVIEW QUESTIONS

1. Bernie Madoff was a very good—though obviously not a perfect—fraudster. He got away with a lot for a long time. How could the duty to develop one's own abilities be mustered to support his decision to become a criminal?
2. In the Madoff case, what duties could be mustered to refute the conclusion that he did the right thing by engaging in fraud?
3. Madoff gave up most of his money and possessions and went to jail for his crimes. Is there anything else he should have done to satisfy the ethical duty of reparation?
4. In your own words, what does it mean to *treat equals equally* and *un-equals unequally*?

[1] Brian Ross, Anna Schecter, and Kate McCarthy, "Bernie Madoff's Other Secret: His Hadassah CFO Mistress," *ABCNews.com*, April 16, 2011, accessed May 11, 2011, http://abcnews.go.com/Blotter/Madoff/story?id=8319695&page=1.

2.3 Immanuel Kant: The Duties of the Categorical Imperative

LEARNING OBJECTIVES

1. Define Immanuel Kant's categorical imperative.

2. Show how the categorical imperative functions in business.
3. Consider advantages and drawbacks of an ethics based on the categorical imperative.

Kant

German philosopher Immanuel Kant (1724–1804) accepted the basic proposition that a theory of duties—a set of rules telling us what we're obligated to do in any particular situation—was the right approach to ethical problems. What he set out to add, though, was a stricter mechanism for the use of duties in our everyday experience. He wanted a way to get all these duties we've been talking about to work together, to produce a unified recommendation, instead of leaving us confused between loyalty to one principle and another. At least on some basic issues, Kant set out to produce ethical *certainty*.

Lying is about as primary as issues get in ethics, and the Madoff case is shot through with it:

- Bernie Madoff always claimed that the Ponzi scheme wasn't the original idea. He sought money from investors planning to score big with complicated financial maneuvers. He took a few losses early on, though, and faced the possibility of everyone just taking their cash and going home. That's when he started channeling money from new investors to older ones, claiming the funds were the fruit of his excellent stock dealing. He always intended, Madoff says, to get the money back, score some huge successes, and they'd let him get on the straight and narrow again. It never happened. But that doesn't change the fact that Madoff *thought* it would. He was lying *temporarily*, and for the good of everyone in the long run.

- Sheryl Weinstein had a twenty-year affair with Madoff. She also invested her family's life savings with him. When the Ponzi scheme came undone, she lost everything. To get some money back, she considered writing a tell-all, and that led to a heart-wrenching decision between money and her personal life. Her twenty-year dalliance was not widely known, and things could have remained that way: her husband and son could've gone on without the whole world knowing that the husband was a cuckold and the son the product of a poisoned family. But they needed money because they'd lost everything, including their home, in Madoff's scam. So does she keep up the false story or does she turn the truth into a profit opportunity?

What does Kant say about all this? The answer is his categorical imperative. An imperative is something you

need to do. A *hypothetical* imperative is something you need to do, but only in certain circumstances; for example, I have to eat, but only in those circumstances where I'm hungry. A *categorical* imperative, by contrast, is something you need to do all the time: there are ethical rules that don't depend on the circumstances, and it's the job of the categorical imperative to tell us what they are. Here, we will consider two distinct expressions of Kant's categorical imperative, two ways that guidance is provided.

First Version of the Categorical Imperative

The first version or expression of the categorical imperative: Act in a way that the rule for your action could be universalized. When you're thinking about doing something, this means you should imagine that *everyone did it all the time*. Now, can this make sense? Can it happen? *Is there a world you can imagine where everyone does this thing that you're considering at every opportunity?* Take the case of Madoff asking himself, "Should I lie to keep investor money flowing in?" What we need to do is imagine this act as universalized: everyone lies all the time. Just imagine that. You ask someone whether it's sunny outside. It is sunny, but they say, "No, it's raining." The next day you ask someone else. Again, it's sunny, but they say, "No, it's snowing." This goes on day after day. Pretty soon, wouldn't you just give up listening to what people say? Here's the larger point: if everyone lies all the time, pretty soon people are going to stop listening to anyone. And if no one's listening, is it possible to lie to them?

What Kant's categorical imperative shows is that lying *cannot* be universalized. The act of lying can't survive in a world where everyone's just making stuff up all the time. Since no one will be taking anyone else seriously, you may try to sell a false story but no one will be buying.

Something similar happens in comic books. No one accuses authors and illustrators of lying when Batman kicks some bad guys into the next universe and then strips off his mask and his hair is perfect. That's not a lie; it's fiction. And fictional stories *can't* lie because no one expects they'll tell the truth. No one asks whether it's real or fake, only whether it's entertaining. The same would go in the real world if everyone lied all the time. Reality would be like a comic: it might be fun, or maybe not, but accusing someone of lying would definitely be absurd.

Bringing this back to Madoff, as Kant sees it he has to make a basic decision: should I lie to investors to keep my operation afloat? The answer is no. According to the categorical imperative, it *must* be no, not because lying is directly immoral, but because lying cannot be universalized and therefore it's immoral.

The same goes for Sheryl Weinstein as she wonders whether she should keep the lid on her family-wrecking affair. The answer is no because the answer is *always* no when the question is whether I should lie. You might want to respond by insisting, "She's already done the deed and Bernie's in jail so it's not going to happen again. The best thing at this point would be for her to just keep her mouth shut and hold her family together as best she can." That's a fair argument. But for Kant it's also a loser because the categorical imperative gives the last word. There's no appeal. There's no lying, no matter what.

One more point about the universalization of acts: even if you insist that a world could exist where everyone lied all the time, would you really want to live there? Most of us don't mind lying so much as long as *we're* the ones getting away with it. But if *everyone's* doing it, that's different. Most of us might agree that if we had a choice between living in a place where everyone told the truth and one where everyone lied, we'd go for the honest reality. It just makes sense: lying will help you only if you're the sole liar, but if everyone's busy taking advantage of everyone else, then there's nothing in it for you, and you might just as well join everyone in telling the truth. Conclusion. The first expression of the categorical imperative—*act in such a way that the rule for your action could be universalized*—is a consistency principle. Like the golden rule (treat others as you'd like to be treated), it forces you to ask how things would work if everyone else did what you're considering doing.

Objections to the First Version of the Categorical Imperative
One of the objections to this ethical guidance is that a reality without lying can be awfully uncomfortable. If your boss shows up for work on a Friday wearing one of those designer dresses that looks great on a supermodel and ridiculous everywhere else, and she asks what you think, what are you going to say? "Hideous"? Telling the truth no matter what, whether we're at work or anywhere else, is one of those things that sounds good in the abstract but is almost impossible to actually live by.

Then the problem gets worse. A deranged addict storms into your office announcing that he's just received a message from the heavens. While chewing manically on dirty fingernails, he relates that he's supposed to attack someone named Jones— *anyone* named Jones. "*What*," he suddenly demands, "is *your* name?" Unfortunately, you happen to be named Sam Jones. Now what?

Second Version of the Categorical Imperative
The second expression of the categorical imperative is: Treat people as an end, and never as a means to an end. To treat people as ends, not means is to never use anyone to get something else. People can't be tools or instruments; they can't be things you employ to get to what you *really* want. A simple example of using another as a means would be striking up a friendship with Chris because you really want to meet his wife who happens to be a manager at the advertising company you desperately want to work for.

It'd be hard to imagine a clearer case of this principle being broken than that of Madoff's Ponzi scheme. He used the money from each new investor to pay off the last one. That means every investor was nothing but a means to an end: everyone was nothing more than a way to keep the old investors happy and attract new ones.

Madoff's case of direct theft is clear cut, but others aren't quite so easy. If Weinstein goes ahead and writes her tell-all about life in bed with Madoff, is she using him as a means to her end (which is making money)? Is she using book buyers? What about her husband and the suffering he would endure? It can be difficult to be sure in every case exactly what it means to "use" another person.

Another example comes from Madoff's son, Andrew, who donated time and money to the cause of treating cancer. On one hand, this seems like a generous and beneficial treatment of others. It looks like he's valuing them as worthwhile and good people who deserve to be saved from a disease. On the other hand, though, when you keep in mind that Andrew too had cancer, you wonder whether he's just using other peoples' suffering to promote research so that *he* can be saved.

Summarizing, where the first of the categorical imperative's expressions was a consistency principle (treat others the way you want to be treated), this is a dignity principle: treat others with respect and as holding value in themselves. You will act ethically, according to Kant, as long as you never accept the temptation to treat others as a way to get something else.

Objections to the Second Version of the Categorical Imperative
The principal objection to this aspect of Kant's theory is that, like the previous, it sounds good in the abstract, but when you think about how it would actually work, things become difficult. Almost *all* businesses require treating people as means and not as ends. In the grocery store, the cashier isn't waiting there to receive your respectful attention. She's there

to run your items through the scanner and that's it. The same goes for the guy in the produce section setting up the banana display. Really, just *paying* someone to do a job—no matter what the job might be—is treating them as a means to an end, as little more than a way to get the work done.

If that's right, then you're not going too far by wondering whether the entire modern world of jobs and money would unravel if we all suddenly became Kantians. Paying a janitor to clean up after hours, a paralegal to proofread a lawyer's briefs, a day-care worker to keep peace among children at recess, all these treatments of others seem to fail Kant's test. Defenders of Kant understand all this perfectly and can respond. One argument is that providing someone with a job is *not* treating them as a means to your ends; instead, by allowing them the opportunity to earn a living, you're actually supporting their projects and happiness. Seen this way, hiring people is not denigrating them, it's enabling. And far from being immoral in the Kantian sense, it's ethically recommendable.

KEY TAKEAWAYS

- The first expression of Kant's categorical imperative requires that ethical decisions be universalizable.
- The second expression of Kant's categorical imperative requires that ethical decisions treat others as ends and not means.
- Kant's conception of ethical duties can provide clear guidance but at the cost of inflexibility: it can be hard to make the categorical imperative work in everyday life.

REVIEW QUESTIONS

1. Imagine Madoff lied to attain his clients' money as he did, but instead of living the high life, he donated everything to charity. For Kant, does this remove the ethical stain from his name? Why not?
2. Think back to your first job, whatever it was. Did you feel like you were used by the organization, or did you feel like they were doing you a favor, giving you the job? How does the experience relate to the imperative to treat others as an end and not a means?

2.4 Rights
LEARNING OBJECTIVES

1. Define an ethical right.
2. Distinguish specific rights.
3. Show how ethical rights work in business.

4. Consider advantages and drawbacks of an ethics based on rights.

Rights

An ethics based on rights is similar to an ethics based on duties. In both cases specific principles provide ethical guidance for your acts, and those principles are to be obeyed regardless of the consequences further down the line. Unlike duties, however, rights-based ethics concentrate their force in delineating your possibilities. The question isn't so much *What are you morally required to do*; it's more about defining exactly where and when you're free to do whatever you want and then deciding where you need to stop and make room for other people to be free too. Stated slightly differently, duties tend to be ethics as what you can't do, and rights tend to be about what you can do.

My Property, My Religion, My Nonprofit Organization, My Health Care, My

Grass

Charles Edward "Eddy" Lepp is in jail now, in a prison not too far away from the site of the business that got him in trouble: Eddy's Medicinal Gardens and Ministry. What was Eddy Lepp the gardener and minister up to on his twenty-acre property near a lake in California, about a hundred miles north from San Francisco? Here are the highlights:

- **Ministry.** Lepp claims—and there doesn't seem to be anyone who disputes him—that he's an authentic Rastafarian reverend.
- **Rastafarianism.** Developed over the last century in Africa and the Caribbean, the religion works within the basic structure of Christianity but contains important innovations. Haile Selassie I was the emperor of Ethiopia from 1930 to 1974 and, according to the faith, was also the reincarnation of Jesus Christ. Further, marijuana—called *ganja* by believers—accompanies religious meetings and ceremonies; it brings adherents closer to God.
- **Lepp's Medicinal Gardens.** In fact, this wasn't a garden so much as a collective farm. Lepp oversaw the work of volunteers—their numbers totaling about two hundred—and did some harvesting and planting himself. Many of the farm's marijuana leaves were smoked by the 2,500 members of his zonked-out church as part of Rastafarian celebrations and meetings, and the rest was, according to Lepp, distributed to individuals with serious health problems.
- **Marijuana and health care.** Studies indicate that in some patients marijuana may alleviate nausea and vomiting, especially as connected with chemotherapy.

There's also a list of further symptoms and maladies the drug could relieve, according to some evidence. It should be noted here that many suspect the persons conducting these studies (not to mention the patients receiving the testing) are favorably predisposed toward marijuana in the first place, and the prejudice may contaminate conclusions. What's certain is that from a strictly medical perspective, the question about marijuana's utility remains controversial. Among those who are convinced, however, smoking is a good remedy. That's why in California patients have been granted a legal right to possess and use marijuana medicinally, as long as they've got a doctor's approval. Unfortunately for Lepp, California law can't bar federal prosecutions, and it was the US Drug Enforcement Administration from all the way out in Washington, DC, that eventually came after him. [1]

About retirement age now, Eddy Lepp is one of those guys who never really left Woodstock. Before being incarcerated, he slumped around in tie-dyes and jeans. He liked wearing a hat emblazoned with the marijuana leaf. Out on his semirural farm, he passed the days smoking joints and listening to Bob Marley music.

Everyone seems to like the guy. A longtime activist for the legalization of marijuana, he's even something of a folk hero in Northern California. At his sentencing, the crowd (chanting "free Eddy!") spilled out into the courthouse hallways. The judge didn't seem to mind the spectacle, and she went out of her way to say she didn't want to hit him with ten years of jail time, but federal guidelines gave her no choice. Now there's talk of a pardon.

Like Bernie Madoff, Lepp was touched by cancer. Madoff's son Andrew was stricken and so was Lepp's wife. She died. Also, like Madoff, Lepp was a businessman. Madoff made millions and lived in luxury while robbing investors; Lepp made enough to scrape by from his ministry and farming enterprises.

What's a Right?
One definition of a right in ethics is *a justified claim against others*. I have the right to launch a gardening business or a church enterprise or both on my property, and you're not allowed to simply storm in and ruin things. You do have the right, however, to produce *your own* garden company and church on your property. On my side, I have the right to free speech, to say whatever I want no matter how outrageous and you can't stop me. You can, however, say whatever you want, too; you can respond to my words with whatever comes into

your head or just ignore me completely. A right, in sum, is something you may do if you wish, and others are morally obligated to permit your action.

Duties tend to be *protective* in nature; they're about assuring that people aren't mistreated. Rights are the flip side; they're *liberating* in nature, they're about assuring that you're as free as possible.

Because rights theory maximizes choices in the name of ethics, it's not surprising that Lepp built his court defense on that ground. Lepp fought the law by maintaining that his medical gardens business and church operations involved *his* land and *his* religion. It wasn't that he had a right to grow pot or pray to a specific God; that had nothing to do with it. The point is he had a right *to do whatever* he wanted on that land, and *believe in whatever* he wanted in his mind. That's what rights are about. As opposed to duties that fix on specific acts, rights ethics declares that there are places (like my land) where the acts don't matter. As long as no one else's rights are being infringed on, I'm free.

Finally, duties tend to be community oriented: they're about how we get along with others. Rights tend to center on the individual and what he or she can do regardless of whether anyone else is around or not. That explains why a duty-based ethics coheres more easily with a scene like the one Madoff provoked, a situation that involves winners and losers, criminals and victims. On the other side, an ethics based on rights is more convenient for Lepp and his gardening and religious enterprises. Though he ended up in jail, there were no obvious victims of his crimes; at least no one complained that they'd been mistreated or victimized as individuals.

What Are the Characteristics of Rights?
English philosopher John Locke (1632–1704) maintained that rights are

- **Universal.** The fundamental rights don't transform as you move from place to place or change with the years.
- **Equal.** They're the same for all, men and women, young and old.
- **Inalienable.** They can't be taken, they can't be sold, and they can't be given away. We can't *not* have them. This leads to a curious paradox at the heart of rights theory. Freedom is a bedrock right, but we're *not* free to sell ourselves into slavery. We can't because freedom is the *way* we are; since freedom is part of my essence, it can't go away without me disappearing too.

What Rights Do I Have?

The right to life is just what it sounds like: Lepp, you, and I should be able to go through our days without worrying about someone terminating our existence. This right is so deeply embedded in our culture that it almost seems unnecessary to state, but we don't need to stretch too far away from our time and place to find scenes of the right's trampling. Between the world wars, Ukraine struggled for independence from Joseph Stalin's neighboring Russia. Stalin sealed the borders and sent troops to destroy all food in the country. Millions died from starvation. Less dramatically but more contemporaneously, the right to life has been cited as an argument against capital punishment.

The right to freedom guarantees individuals that they may do as they please, assuming their actions don't encroach on the freedom of others. In a business environment, this assures entrepreneurs like Lepp and Madoff that they may mount whatever business operation they choose. Lepp's garden and ministry were surely unorthodox, but that can't be a reason for its prohibition.

Similarly, *within* a company, the right to freedom protects individuals against abuse. No boss can demand more from an employee than what that employee has freely agreed—frequently through a signed contract—to provide.

On the other side, however, there are questions about how deeply this basic right extends through day-to-day working life. For example, the freewheeling Lepp probably wasn't too concerned about the clothes his volunteer workers chose to wear out in the garden, but what about clothes in Madoff's investment house? He was serving wealthy, urban clients in suits and ties. What would *their* reaction be to a junior investment advisor just out of college who shows up for a meeting in a tie-dye and jeans? Some clients, it's safe to say, would head for the exit. Now, what recourse does boss Madoff have when the casual employee says, "Look, it's a free country; I can wear whatever I want"? Within a rights theory of ethics, it must be conceded that the employee is correct. *It's also true*, however, that Madoff has rights too—specifically, the freedom to fire the guy. What can be taken from this is that, as a general rule, the *enabling side* of a right ethics is that you can do whatever you want, but the *limiting and controlling side* is that the same goes for everyone else.

From the right to freedom, other rights seem to derive naturally. The right to free speech is tremendously important in the commercial world. Lepp's messages to his Rasta flock may have provoked skepticism in some listeners, but no one doubts that he had a right to voice his ideas. The same goes

for Madoff's exuberant claims concerning his investing strategy. Crucially, the same also goes for those on the other side of Madoff's claims; the same freedom Madoff enjoyed also allowed whistle-blowers to answer back that it's *impossible* to legitimately realize such constant and high profits. In fact, in the case of Madoff's investment company, whistle-blowers *did* say that, repeatedly. No one listened, though. The right of free speech doesn't guarantee a hearing.

The right to religious expression also follows from basic freedom. It guaranteed Lepp the space he needed to pioneer his particular brand of gardening Rastafarianism in Northern California. His is, obviously, a weird case, but the right works in more traditional workplaces, too. *USA Today* [2] reported a case where Muslim workers were fired from their jobs in several meatpacking plants in the Midwest because they left the production line in the middle of the day without authorization to go outside and pray. The workers' response? They filed a lawsuit claiming their right to religious expression had been violated.

No doubt it had been.

But the company's response is also weighty. According to the article, "The problem with the Muslim prayer request is that it's not one day or annual, it's every day and multiple times. Further, those times shift over the course of the year based on the sun's position."

The result, according to the company, is that scheduling becomes very difficult, and those who aren't Muslim find it nearly impossible to keep working when they're getting abandoned so frequently during the day. Here we're confronted with a very basic conflict of rights. While no one doubts that freedom exists to practice a religion, isn't it also true that the company—or the company owners if we want to cast this in personal terms—have a right to set up a business in whatever manner they choose, with breaks scheduled for certain times and worker responsibilities strictly defined? In the end, the question about Muslim workers leaving the work floor to pray isn't about one *kind* of religion or another; it's not Christians against Muslims or something similar. The question is about which right takes precedence: the owners' right to set up and run a company as they wish or the employees' right to express their beliefs how and when they choose.

From an ethical perspective—which doesn't necessarily correlate with a legal one—the resolution to this dilemma and any clash about conflicting rights runs through the question of whether there's a way to protect the basic rights of *both* groups. It runs that way because rights are fundamentally about that, about maximizing freedom. In this case, it seems that firing the workers *does* achieve that goal. The owners' initiative inside their company is protected, and the workers are now able to pray when they desire.

To be sure, other ethical approaches will yield different outcomes, but in the midst of rights theory where individual liberty is the guiding rule and the maximization of freedom is the overriding goal, it's difficult for other concerns to get traction. So it may be that the *community as a whole* is better served by looking for a solution that allows Muslims to maintain their prayer schedule *while also* allowing the plant to continue functioning in a normal way. Even if that's true, however, it's not going to affect a rights-theory resolution very much because this kind of ethics privileges what *you* and *I* can do over what *we* can do together. It's an ethics of individualism.

The right to pursue happiness sits beside the right to life and the right to freedom at the foundation of rights ethics. The pursuit gives final direction and meaning to the broad theory. Here's how: it doesn't do much good to be alive if you're not free, so freedom orients the right to life. It also doesn't do much good to be free if you can't pursue happiness, so the right to pursue happiness orients freedom. That's the organizing reasoning of ethical rights; it's how the theory holds together. This reasoning leaves behind, however, the difficult question as to exactly where the pursuit of happiness leads.

In an economic context, one way of concretizing the pursuit of happiness is quite important: it's our right to possessions and the fruits of our work. What's ours, along with what we make or earn, we have a right to keep and use as we wish. Among rights theorists, this particular right attracts a staunch group of advocates. Called libertarians, they understand liberty as *especially* reflected in the right to dominion over what's ours.

Libertarianism is arguably the most muscular area of rights theory, and it's the one where most conflicts—and most stands in the name of personal rights and the pursuit of happiness—take place. This is definitely where Lepp made his stand. A frequently viewed YouTube video reveals exactly what standing up for libertarian rights looks like. In the clip, police have been called to Lepp's Medicinal Gardens. The squad car pulls up the long dirt road, and Lepp goes out to stop it. This is their conversation:

Lepp:	I am demanding that if you do not have a warrant that you leave. You are illegally on my property and I am *demanding that you leave!*
Police officer:	(Into his radio) Can I get some help up here?
Lepp:	This is private property. This is a church function. Again, I am asking, if you do not—
Police officer:	You can ask all you want, Mr. Lepp, but I'm not leaving.
Lepp:	Please leave my property! Under what authority are you standing here? *Sir, I am demanding that you tell me under what authority are you violating my rights!*
Police officer:	Under no authority, Mr. Lepp. As soon as my sergeant gets here, he'll advise you of whatever he wants to advise you of.
Lepp:	Fine, then I suggests you go down and wait for him at the bottom of my property!
The officer stands there silently.	

This is the kind of scene that makes libertarians' blood boil. Lepp, decked out in a t-shirt emblazoned with a marijuana leaf, actually stays fairly mellow, but he makes his point. He makes two points actually, and they need to be distinguished. The first is a *legal* point; it's the question about whether the officer has a warrant. The officer doesn't, but the second point—"under what authority are you violating my rights"—goes beyond the legal and into the ethical. Lepp believes the land is his and he's not infringing on anyone else's freedoms, and therefore, he can do what he wants and the police should leave him alone.

The officer isn't quite sure how to reply to this, which is understandable. It is because this case displays a clear separation between the law on one side and an ethical reality on the other. Moreover, the two appear not only separate but also incompatible; it's difficult to see any way to bring them together. With respect to the law, the case is clear: Lepp was growing massive amounts of marijuana on his farm and growing it for distribution. Federal law explicitly prohibits both the growing and the distributing. It's unambiguous. It's also clear that Lepp was doing it since you could see the crop from the public highway passing by his fields. Everyone saw that marijuana was growing, that people were harvesting it, and that they were planting more. As far as the law goes, Lepp really had no leg to stand on. Once the DEA found out about him, they didn't have any choice but to bring him in. But *ethically*—and in terms of rights theory—there seems to be equal clarity going in the *other* direction. There were few complaints about Lepp's activities. No one was hurt, and it was his land. It's hard to see within a libertarian perspective any way to justify the police harassment, the legal proceedings, or the jail term Lepp ended up getting. This doesn't mean Lepp was treated unjustly; it only means that whatever justice was served on him, it wasn't libertarian.

Libertarianism in the Economic World

Lepp wasn't a big-time businessman. His medicinal garden enterprise produced enough income to get him through the day and little more. When he went to court, he needed a public assistance attorney (not that it would've made any difference). But the issues he brings forward reverberate through the business world. Here are a few hypothetical scenarios where libertarian ethics comes into play:

- A massive brewery is constructed upstream from farmland and soaks up most of the water to make beer, leaving the downstream farms with almost nothing for irrigation. It's the brewery's land, so can't the owners do what they want with the water running through it?
  A strong libertarian argument offers a reason to say yes. Even though it's true that others will be severely harmed by the act, an ethics that *begins* with the freedom to have what's mine doesn't buckle before the demands of others. Now, compare this outcome with the guidance offered by Kant's categorical imperative, the idea that any act must be universalized. Within this framework the opposite conclusion is reached because if *everyone* just dammed up the water channeling through his or her land, then the brewer wouldn't even have the choice: no water would be flowing across the land in the first place. So a duty-oriented ethics leads toward a solution that is more favorable for the larger community, where a rights-based perspective leaves more room for individuality but at the cost of the interests of others.

- Bernie Madoff didn't start off rich. His father was a plumber in Queens. Even before launching his Ponzi scheme, he became wealthy by working hard, being smart, and investing wisely. He grew an investment house from scratch to being among the most prominent in New York. His annual income hit the millions even without the Ponzi stuff. Possibly, there was an administrative assistant of some kind there with him from the beginning. She was hired at, say, $32,000 annually. Years later, Madoff is rich, and she's at $36,000. She still arrives at work in her beater car while Madoff gets the limousine treatment. Is this fair?

A strong libertarian position gives Madoff a reason to say yes. The wealth *did* accumulate from his efforts, not hers. If Madoff hadn't been there the money wouldn't have come in, but, if she'd quit on the first day, he would've hired someone else and the end result probably wouldn't have been much different. The money, in other words, grew because of Madoff's efforts, therefore it's his, and therefore there's no ethical obligation to spread it around.

On the other hand, a duty-based orientation would generate concerns about *gratitude* and *respect*. These perennial duties leave room for wealth redistribution. The argument is that Madoff owes the assistant a higher wage not because of her work performance but as a show of gratitude for her contribution over the years. Similarly, the duty of respect for others doesn't demand that everyone be treated equally. It doesn't mean everyone should get the same wage, but it does demand that people be *respected* as equals. This implies taking into account that the assistant's *efforts* were prolonged and significant, just like Madoff's, and therefore she should receive a salary more commensurate with his.

Negative and Positive Rights

The ethics of rights can be categorized as negative rights and positive rights. Negative rights are fundamental. They require others to not interfere with me and whatever I'm doing. The right to life is the requirement that others not harm me, the right to freedom is the requirement that others not interfere with me, the right to speech requires that others not silence me, the right to my possessions and the fruits of my labors require that others let me keep and use what's mine.

Positive rights, by contrast, are closer to traditional duties. They're obligations others have to help protect and preserve my basic, negative rights. For example, the right to life doesn't only require (negatively) that people not harm me, but it also requires (positively) that they come to my aid in life-threatening situations. If I'm in a car wreck, my right to life requires bystanders to call an ambulance. So if an individual with a rights-based philosophy and an individual with a duty-based philosophy both arrive on a crash scene, they'll do the same thing—just for different reasons. The rights person calls for help to protect the victim's right to life; the duties person calls to fulfill the duty to beneficence, the duty to look out for the welfare of others.

Positive rights can be drawn out to great lengths. For example, the argument is sometimes made that my basic right to freedom is worthless if I don't have my health and basic abilities to operate in the world. This may lead a rights theorist to claim that society owes its member's health care, education, housing, and even money in the case of unemployment. Typically, these positive rights are called welfare rights. Welfare, in this context, doesn't mean government handouts but minimal social conditions that allow the members to fully use their intrinsic liberty and pursue happiness with some reasonable hope for success.

The hard question accompanying positive rights is: *where's the line?* At what point does my responsibility to promote the rights of others impinge on *my own* freedom, my own pursuit of happiness, and my own life projects?

Rights in Conflict

The deepest internal problems with rights ethics arise when rights conflict. Abortion is a quick, hot-button example. On one side (pro-life), support comes from the initial principle: a human being, born or not, has a right to life, which may not be breached. On the other side (pro-choice), every person's original freedom over themselves and their bodies ends all discussion. Now, one of the reasons this debate is so intractable is that both sides find equally strong support *within the same basic ethical framework*. There's no way to decide without infringing on one right or the other.

A complementary case arose around Lepp's Rasta religious gatherings. Though many of his neighbors didn't care, there were a few who objected to having what was essentially mini-Woodstock on the land next door. It was impossible, of course, for Lepp to entirely contain the noise, the smoke from fires, the traffic congestion, and the rest entirely on his property. The question is when does my right to do what I want on my land need to be curtailed so that your right to dominion over yours isn't soiled?

Broadening further, there's the question about Lepp growing marijuana for medicinal purposes. On one side, a rights theory supports his inclination to grow what he wants on his land and sell the fruits of his labors to other adults for their consenting use. His is a farming business like any other. But on the other side, a theory of rights can extend into the realm of positive requirements. The right to the pursuit of happiness implies a right to health, and this may require government oversight of medical products so that society as a whole may be protected from fraudulent claims or harmful substances. The question of marijuana shoots up right here. What happens when socially sanctioned entities like the US Food and Drug Administration decide that marijuana is harmful and should therefore be prohibited? Which rights trump the others, the negative right to freedom or the positive right to oversee medical substances?

A similar question comes up between Madoff and his investors. A pure libertarian may say that individuals have the unfettered right to do as they choose, so if Bernie Madoff lies about investing strategies and his clients go along with it, well, that's their problem. As long as they weren't *forced*, they're free to do whatever they wish with their money, even if that means turning it over to a charlatan. Again here, however, a broader view of rights theory answers that in the complex world of finance and investment, the right to the pursuit of happiness is also a right to some governmental oversight designed to make sure that everyone involved in the financial industry is playing by a single set of rules, ones prohibiting Ponzi schemes and similar frauds.

Examples multiply easily. I have the right to free speech, but if I falsely yell "fire!" in a crowded theater and set off a life-threatening stampede, what's happening to everyone else's negative right to life and positive right to health? Leaving the specifics aside, the conclusion is that, in general, problems with rights theory occur in one of two places:

1. I have negative rights to life, freedom, and my possessions but they infringe on *your* rights to the same.
2. I have a right to freedom and to do what I want but that right clashes with larger, society-level protections put into place to assure everyone a reasonable shot at pursuing their happiness.

What Justifies a Right?

One justification for an ethics of rights is comparable with the earlier-noted idea about duties being part of the logic of the universe. Both duties and rights exist because that's the way things *are* in the moral world. Just like the laws of physics tell us how far a ball will fly when thrown at a certain speed, so too the rules of rights tell us what ought to happen and not happen in ethical reality. The English philosopher John Locke subscribed to this view when he called our rights "natural." He meant that they're part of who we are and what we do and just by living we incarnate them.

Another justification for an ethics of rights is to derive them from the idea of duties. Kant reappears here, especially his imperative to treat others as ends and not as means to ends. If we *are* ends in ourselves, if we possess basic dignity, then that dignity must be reflected somehow: it must have some content, some meaning, and the case can be made that the content is our possession of certain autonomous rights.

Advantages and Drawbacks of an Ethics Based on Rights

Because of its emphasis on individual liberties, rights theory is very attractive to open-roaders and individualists. One of the central advantages of a rights ethics is that it clears a broad space for you and me and everyone else to be ourselves or make ourselves in any way we choose. On the other side of that strength, however, there's a disadvantage: centering ethics on the individual leaves little space of agreement about how we can live together. An ethics of rights doesn't do a lot to help us resolve our differences, it does little to promote tolerance, and it offers few guarantees that if I do something beneficial for you now, you'll do something beneficial for me later on.

Another strong advantage associated with an ethics of rights is simplicity in the sense that basic rights are fairly easy to understand and apply. The problem, however, with these blunt and comprehensible rights comes when two or more of them conflict. In those circumstances it's hard to know which rights trump the others. In the case of Lepp's business—the Medicinal Gardens—it's hard to be sure when his use of his land infringed on the rights of neighbors to enjoy their land, and it's difficult to know when the health product he offered—marijuana—should be prohibited in the name of the larger right to health for all individuals in a society. Most generally, it's difficult to adjudicate between claims of freedom: where does mine stop and yours begin?

KEY TAKEAWAYS

- Rights are universal and inalienable.
- Basic rights include those to life, freedom, and the pursuit of happiness.
- Rights theory divides negative from positive rights.
- Ethical rights provide for individual freedom but allow few guidelines for individuals living and working together in a business or in society

REVIEW QUESTIONS

1. How does the right to pursue happiness license Lepp's Medicinal Gardens?
2. What is a libertarian argument against imprisoning Lepp?
3. One justification Lepp cited for his farm was the health benefits marijuana could provide. Assuming Lepp was right about those benefits, how could they be combined with a rights-based ethics to justify his activities?
4. How could the rights to freedom and the pursuit of happiness be set against Lepp's business?
5. What are positive rights and how could they be mustered against Lepp's farm?
6. If someone drives away from Lepp's farm high as a kite and soon after drives off the road and into a tree, does

Lepp bear any ethical responsibility for this within a rights ethics?

[1] Elizabeth Larson, "Lepp Sentenced to 10 Years in Federal Prison for Marijuana Case, "*Lake County News*, May 18, 2009, accessed May 11, 2011,http://lakeconews.com/content/view/8703/764/; Bob Egelko, "Medical Pot Grower Eddy Lepp Gets 10 Years," *Cannabis Culture Magazine*, May 18, 2009, accessed May 11, 2011,http://www.cannabisculture.com/v2/content/medical-pot-grower-eddy-lepp-gets-10-years.
[2] Emily Bazar, "Prayer Leads to Work Disputes," *USA Today*, October 16, 2008, accessed May 11, 2011, http://www.usatoday.com/news/nation/2008-10-15-Muslim_N.htm.

2.5 Case Studies

Skin and Money

In the mid-1980s in Los Angeles, Somen "Steve" Banerjee and his friend Nick DeNoia pooled money to start a new kind of strip club: men baring it for women. Since they had no idea what they were doing, it didn't go well. What finally helped were a couple of showmen from Las Vegas. Steve Merrit and his partner (professional and romantic) Mark Donnelly came aboard and hatched the idea of a Vegas-type song-and-dance show wrapped around the disrobing.

To find performers, they cruised the muscle beaches outside LA. They brought the guys back to a studio, applied some Village People–style outfits (policeman, fireman, construction worker, and so on), and ran the group through a line-dancing routine.

Their idea was simple but innovative: sex sells; but instead of making the show lustful, they made it entertaining. Drawing on their Las Vegas experience, Merrit and Donnelly understood how to do it, how to produce a fun theatrical fantasy instead of a crude flesh show. The general concept made sense and the execution was professional, but on opening night, no one knew what would happen.

Chippendales exploded. Women went crazy for the performances, first in the United States, then Europe, and then everywhere as Banerjee and DeNoia rushed to form multiple traveling versions of their production. The time they didn't spend together mounting the shows they spent in court fighting over who was entitled to how much of the profits and who really owned the suddenly very valuable Chippendales name and concept. The dispute ended in 1987 after DeNoia was shot dead in his office.

One major problem Chippendales faced is that it wasn't a hard show to copy. Get some muscled guys, some uniform-store costumes, a pop music soundtrack, and pound it all together into a dance routine with a little teasing; you don't need a genius to do it. So others started.

Michael Fullington was a junior choreographer for Chippendales. He struck up a friendship with some of the show guys, and they split away into a group called Club Adonis. The original choreographers—Merrit and Donnelly—also got in on the act, forming their own traveling revue called Night Dreams.

Unhappy with these copycat acts, Banerjee hired a hit man to go around killing the whole bunch. The hit man, it turned out, was an FBI informant. Banerjee ended up in jail. The ensuing investigation led to more charges. There was arson (he'd burned down one of his own clubs for the insurance money some time back) and also another count of conspiracy to murder since it was Banerjee who'd arranged to have his original partner shot.

The case never got to trial. Banerjee agreed to plead guilty, absorb a twenty-six-year sentence, and give up his rights to Chippendales along with nearly all his money and real estate holdings.

While the lawyers worked out the details, Banerjee's wife Irene worked feverishly to organize a group of character witnesses. By bringing a parade of people to testify about her husband's good side at the sentencing hearing, she was hoping to get the jail time reduced a little bit. Or maybe she was hoping to hold on to more of the money and real estate they'd accumulated.

No one got the chance to testify. On the morning of the hearing, Banerjee hung himself in his cell.

Because the trial was never completed, the plea deal never went into effect. And because the guilty man was dead, there was no one left to charge with any crime. Chippendales and all the money and property associated with it went to Banerjee's wife Irene.

QUESTIONS

1. Is being a Chippendale's dancer honorable work?
   - How could the perennial ethical duties to the self—*develop our abilities and talents* and *do ourselves no harm*—be mustered to support the idea that these men should be proud of what they do?
   - Ethically, how does this job compare with working for the Metropolitan Opera in New York, an outfit that calls itself "a vibrant home for the world's most creative and talented artists working in opera"?
2. Is *hiring and training* a Chippendale's dancer honorable? Imagine you were one of the original choreographers cruising California beaches in search of beefcake and dance talent. You bring the guys in, choreograph their routine, and send them up on stage.
   - Thinking just of the perennial duties to the self is hiring and training them honorable? Under what conditions?
     - Thinking just of the perennial duties to others—avoiding wrongful actions toward others, honesty, respect, beneficence (promoting the welfare of others), gratitude, fidelity (keeping promises, honor agreements), and reparation (compensating others when we harm them)—is hiring and training them honorable? Why or why not?
3. With respect to the ethics of duties, is Chippendales a respectable company in terms of how it treats its clients? How does this company compare with the Metropolitan Opera's treatment of its clients (note that the Met occasionally replaces the word *clients* with the more flattering *patrons*)?
4. Leaving aside the legal issues and using only the perennial duties, what ethical case could be made in favor of Banerjee getting a hit man to eliminate the people who were copying his show?
   - Should he have hired someone or done the job himself? Explain.
   - What's the difference between hiring a hit man and hiring a beefcake dancer?
   - How would Kant respond to these questions?
5. The Club Adonis group worked for Chippendales before splitting to do the same thing elsewhere. Use Kant's categorical imperative to show that their action was wrong.
6. According to the perennial duties, did Banerjee do the right thing hanging him in the end?
7. According to Kant, did Banerjee do the right thing hanging him?
8. When Banerjee hung himself, he lost his life, but he did manage to preserves his life's property and wealth for his wife. Can a libertarian ethics be used to show that Banerjee did the right thing?

Two at the Same Time

On a real estate discussion board, [1] someone with the sign-in name BriGuy23 asks, "Does anyone on here find any issue with submitting two offers to buy two different apartments at the same time? My friend thinks that it's unfair due to the fact that one of the offers is definitely going to not go through which means they're tying up the seller's time (and money in a way). From a seller's standpoint I think I would be annoyed but I really don't see anything wrong with it from a buyer's perspective. Thoughts?"

A response comes from middle-aged mom: "Sellers can negotiate multiple offers so there is no reason why a buyer could not make multiple offers on different places. Assuming you are represented by a buyer's agent, I would use the same agent to make both offers. Make certain that your contract gives you an out in the unlikely event both are accepted."

QUESTIONS

1. What does BriGuy23 suspect might be unethical about submitting two offers to buy two different apartments at the same time? Can you wrap this suspicion in the language of the duties?
2. Is middle-aged mom appealing to the concept of fairness to justify making multiple offers at the same time? If she is, then how? If she isn't, what is her reasoning?
3. If Kant decided to make a contribution to this discussion board, what do you think he would write?
4. Middle-aged mom writes, "Make certain that your contract gives you an out in the unlikely event both are accepted." She means that when you make an offer to buy, you actually offer a signed contract to buy the apartment; *but* there's a catch, an escape clause that lets you pull out if you choose. Is that ethical, offering a signed contract offering to buy a property that includes an "out"?
5. You need a date for Saturday night.
   o Would you have any problem with inviting two different people at the same time (by, say, leaving a message on both their phones)? Why or why not?
   o Would you leave yourself an out in case both answers were yes? If not, why not? If so, what would it be and how could it be justified ethically?

Working at American Apparel

Dov Charney is an American immigrant success story, but he's not exactly a "Give me your tired, your poor" kind of immigrant. He's a Canadian who came to America to attend an expensive private university.

He ended up founding American Apparel (AA), a clothing manufacturer producing trendy t-shirts and basics selling mainly to a young, edgy crowd.

Based in Los Angeles, their factory is among the biggest clothes-making operations in the nation. It employs almost five thousand workers. Those workers are well known for a number of reasons:

- Just *having* workers sets AA apart. Nearly all US clothing manufacturers outsource their cutting and sewing to poor countries. From Mexico to China, you can find factories paying locals fifty cents an hour to do the same kind of work they do at AA. The difference is the sewers working in Los Angeles typically get around fifteen dollars an hour. That's not a lot in Southern California, but it's enough to make them—according to AA—the best paid garment workers in the world.
- The workers don't report to bosses so much as each other. They organize as independent teams paid a base wage of eight dollars an hour. On top of that they receive a bonus depending on how much they produce. So they get together, set their own targets, and go for them. This liberating of the workforce led to nearly a tripling of output and was matched by about a doubling of wages.
- The company features a generous stock options program to help workers buy shares in the enterprise.
- On its own initiative, the company provides basic health-care services through a clinic tucked into a factory corner. It provides bikes to employees, helping them zip through the downtown traffic morass without adding pollution to the infamous city smog. There are free telephones in the factory for employees to use to call family members at home.
- Many of those employees' family members are in other countries; AA has a very large immigrant workforce.
- Many of those immigrants are in the country illegally, which partially explains why the company has been on the forefront of amnesty campaigns, organizing public rallies and media events of all kinds for the undocumented. Called *Legalize LA*, the campaign's title references the fact that a tremendous number of Southern Californians outside AA are also illegal immigrants.
- In 2009, the federal government indicated to AA that 1,800 of its workers were using Social Security numbers and other identifying documents that had been purchased, stolen, or just plain invented. In any case, they didn't match up. The company was forced to fire the employees.

QUESTIONS

1. Workers at Charney's America Apparel are the highest-paid mass-production sewers in the world.
   o In terms of Charney's duties to the self, what ethical case can be made in favor of this high pay?
   o In terms of Charney's duties to others, what ethical case can be made in favor of this high pay?
   o Are these wages fair? Why or why not?

2. In terms of duties—either the perennial duties or Kant's categorical imperative—which is more recommendable: keeping the AA plant where and how it is, or moving it to Mexico and cutting the workers' wages in half? Why is the decision you've made the better of the two?

A few factors to consider:
o In Mexico, the workers' *real* pay in terms of local buying power would be much higher, even though the actual amount is less than what they receive here.
o Many of the workers are illegal immigrants from Mexico; their legal situation would obviously be remedied and proximity to family would increase.
o The national Mexican economy would benefit more from AA's presence than does the US economy.

3. Kant's categorical imperative requires that others be treated as ends and never as means.
o In what way could the argument be made that the employees at AA are being treated as *means*, and therefore Charney's plant is unethical no matter how high his salaries may be?
o Besides high pay, the company provides workers with considerable freedom to set their own work pace and schedule. The company also provides a stock purchase program. Do either or both of these factors alleviate the charge that the workers are treated as means and not end? Why or why not?

4. Eighteen hundreds of AA's five thousand workers were using false papers and Social Security numbers to get their job. Charney knew all about that but chose to overlook it.
o Leaving the law aside, how can that overlooking be justified ethically?
o Leaving the law aside, how can Kant are used to cast that action as ethically wrong in terms of lying? In terms of stealing? In terms of using people as means instead of ends?
o Charney and AA support illegal immigrants in two ways: by giving them jobs and by organizing popular protests in favor of their legalization. Ethically, are these two activities recommendable or not? Or is one recommendable and the other not?

5. Assuming it's wrong for illegal immigrants to be working in America, who deserves the sterner ethical reprobation, Charney or the illegal workers? Explain in ethical terms.

6. The basic and natural rights of mainstream rights theory include the following:
o Life
o Freedom
o Free speech
o Religious expression
o The pursuit of happiness
o Possessions and the fruits of our work
o How can these rights be mustered to support Charney's hiring and keeping workers he knows are in the country illegally?
o How can these rights be mustered to ethically denounce Charney for hiring and keeping workers he knows are in the country illegally?
o Thinking about those workers, do these rights give them an ethical license to use false Social Security numbers and identifying documents? Why or why not?

7. Eddy Lepp ended up in jail for his medicinal marijuana garden, yet Charney sleeps in a million-dollar beach house. Is this fair?

Pirates
The following is from an online discussion: [2]

overstand:	I've been having problems with copying cds and trying to burn them…when the copy process gets to 4% the used read buffer will go down to zero and continue fluctuating…will someone let me know the procedures on fixing this.
Retarded chicken:	May I ask what CDs are you copying? Usually big companies put copy protection on their CDs so people don't ILLEGALLY copy their CDs.
-=iNsAnE=-:	why do people post worthless crap like this? its none of your business what cd's he's copying…don't accuse him of making illegal copies of cd's…maybe try posting something useful next time
Flipside:	It's not worthless crap mongloid…Copyright protection does prevent the copying of some disks especially in main-stream programs such as Nero. Try using Clone CD—you may have better luck with a pure duplication program (No fuss).

QUESTIONS

1. The unanswered question here is whether the CD being copied is copyright protected, in other words, whether

this is a piracy case. Assume it is. If retarded chicken had to fill out an ethical argument against CD piracy that relied on either the perennial duties or Kant, what could he say?

2. While overstand may be pirating, no one doubts that the original disc is legitimately his. Maybe he bought it or maybe someone gave it to him; either way, what's the libertarian argument against retarded chicken? How could a libertarian justify overstand's copying?

3. Would a libertarian believe that the company producing the disc has a right to lace it with code that makes duplication impossible? Explain.

4. It sounds like Clone CD is specifically made to help pirates get around the copyright protections manufacturers put on their discs.
   o What's the Kantian case for condemning Clone CD for their project?
   o What's the libertarian case for congratulating them?

Which of the two cases is stronger? Why?

5. Retarded chicken implies that overstand is a thief and -=iNsAnE=- calls retarded chicken's post "worthless crap." Flipside calls -=iNsAnE=- a "mongloid."
   o Is there an ethical case that can be made against the tone of this discussion?
   o Does online interaction foster this tone? If so, can an ethical case be made against the existence of Internet discussion boards?

Gun Shop under Attack

The headline from a local Oakland newspaper reported that a gun shop is closing due to unfair taxes. [3] The gun shop's name was Siegle's Guns. Closing was inevitable, according to owner Mara Siegle, after Oakland residents passed Measure D, which levied a huge tax on gun dealers. They had to pay $24 for every $1,000 earned, in comparison to the $1.20 per $1,000 that all the other retailers in Oakland fork over. "No one can stay in business paying that kind of tax," Siegle said while preparing her going-out-of-business sale. "And that's exactly what Oakland wanted."

No one disputes the point.

The disputes are about whether Oakland should want that and whether it's fair for the city to use taxes as a weapon.

- Tracy Salkowitz says yes to both. "Except for hunting rifles, the sole purpose of weapons is to kill people." Getting rid of gun shops, the logic follows, is a public welfare concern. And about the taxes that brought the store down? She's "delighted" by them.

- Mara Siegle's opinion is that people who don't hunt and shoot for recreation don't understand that guns are a legitimate pastime. "They don't see this side," she says, "because they don't try to." Further, she asserts, over the years gun owners have told her that they own guns to defend themselves.

- Outside the store, mingling customers agreed with Siegle. They said closing gun stores was the wrong way to fight crime and then cursed the city for the unjust taxes.

Amid the winners and losers, Mara Siegle certainly got the rottenest part of the deal. She has two sons, fifteen and seventeen, and she doesn't know what she'll do for income. "I need a job," she said.

A hand-lettered sign posted in the store's backroom for the benefit of Siegle's five full-time employees displayed the phone number of the unemployment office. The sign said, "You paid for it, use it."

QUESTIONS

1. With an eye on the concept of fairness, form an argument in favor of the drastically higher taxes imposed on gun shops.

2. Kant's categorical imperative prohibits killing. Can it be transformed into an argument against a gun shop in Oakland?

3. Would an ethics of duties or an ethics of rights work better for Siegle as she defends her business? Why? What might her argument look like?

4. Unemployment benefits are the result of unemployment insurance, which is not optional. Workers are forced to pay a bit out of each paycheck to the federal government, and if they lose their job, they get a biweekly check partially covering lost wages.
   o Would a libertarian approve of the unemployment insurance program?
   o Would it be right for a libertarian gun shop owner—someone defending her business on libertarian grounds—to accept unemployment benefits after her shop is forced out of business by extreme taxes? Explain.

[1] "Ethical dilemma with submitting two offers at once? (contingency, clause, agent)," City-Data, accessed May 11, 2011, http://www.city-data.com/forum/real-estate/710433-ethical-dilemma-submitting-two-offers-once.html.
[2] "My cd-burner won't let me copy the cd...why...," Hard forum, accessed May 11, 2011, http://www.hardforum.com/archive/index.php/t-711331.html.

[3] Alexandra J. Wall, "Jewish Gun shop Owner Closing Store; Cites Unfair Taxes," *Jweekly*, July 21, 2000, accessed May 11, 2011, http://www.jweekly.com/article/full/13657/jewish-gunshop-owner-closing-store-cites-unfair-taxes.

NOTES:

Chapter 3:
Theories of Consequence Ethics

Chapter Overview

This chapters examines some theories guiding ethical decisions in business. It considers ethics that focuses on the consequences of what is done instead of prohibiting or allowing specific acts.

3.1 What Is Consequentialism?
LEARNING OBJECTIVE

1. Define consequentialism in ethics.

Consequentialism Defined

What's more important in ethics—what you do or what happens afterward *because* of what you did? People who believe ethics should be about what happens afterward are labeled consequentialists. They don't care so much about your act; they want to know about the consequences.

If someone asks, "Should I lie?," one answer is, "No, lying's wrong. We all have a duty not to lie and therefore you shouldn't do it, no matter what." That's not the consequentialist answer, though. Consequentialists will want to know about the effects. If the lie is about Bernie Madoff assuring everyone that he's investing clients' money in stocks when really he plans to steal it, that's wrong. But if a defrauded, livid, and pistol-waving client tracks Madoff down on a crowded street and demands to know whether he's Bernie Madoff, the ethically recommendable response might be, "People say I look like him, but really I'm Bill Martin." The question, finally, for a consequentialist isn't whether or not I should lie, it's *what happens if I do and if I don't?*

Since consequentialists are more worried about the outcome than the action, the central ethical concern is *what kind of outcome should I want?* Traditionally, there are three kinds of answers: the **utilitarian**, the **altruist**, and the **egoist**. Each one will be considered in this chapter.

KEY TAKEAWAY

- Consequentialist ethicists focus on the results of what you do, not what you do.

REVIEW QUESTIONS

1. Under what scenario could a consequentialist defend the act of stealing?

2. Could a consequentialist recommend that a toy company lie about the age level a toy is designed for? What would be an example?

3.2 Utilitarianism: The Greater Good
LEARNING OBJECTIVES

1. Define utilitarian ethics.
2. Show how utilitarianism works in business.
3. Distinguish forms of utilitarianism.
4. Consider advantages and drawbacks of utilitarianism.

The College Board and Karen Dillard

"Have you seen," the blog post reads, "their parking lot on a Saturday?" [1] Its packed. The lot belongs to Karen Dillard College Prep (KDCP), a test-preparation company in Dallas. Like the Princeton Review, they offer high schoolers courses designed to boost performance on the SAT. Very little real learning goes on in these classrooms; they're more about techniques and tricks for maximizing scores. Test takers should know, for example, whether a test penalizes incorrect answers. If it doesn't, you should take a few minutes at each section's end to go through and just fill in a random bubble for all the questions you couldn't reach so you'll get some cheap points. If there *is* a penalty, though, then you should use your time to patiently work forward as far as you can go. Knowing the right strategy here can significantly boost your score. It's a waste of brain space, though, for anything else in your life.

Some participants in KDCP—who paid as much as $2,300 for the lessons—definitely got some score boosting for their money. It was unfair boosting, however; at least that's the charge of the College Board, the company that produces and administers the SAT.

Here's what happened. A KDCP employee's brother was a high school principal, and he was there when the SATs were administered. At the end of those tests, everyone knows what test takers are instructed to do: stack the bubble sheets in one pile and the test booklets in the other and leave. The administrators then wrap everything up and send both the answer sheets and the booklets back to the College Board for scoring. The principal, though, was pulling a few test booklets out of the stack and sending them over to his brother's company, KDCP. As it turns out, some of these pilfered tests were "live"—that is, sections of them were going to be used again in future tests. Now, you can see how getting a look at those booklets would be helpful for someone taking those future tests.

Other stolen booklets had been "retired," meaning the specific questions inside were on their final application the day the principal grabbed them. So at least in these cases, students taking the test-prep course couldn't count on seeing the very same questions come exam day. Even so, the College Board didn't like this theft much better because they sell those retired tests to prep companies for good money.

When the College Board discovered the light-fingered principal and the KDCP advantage, they launched a lawsuit for infringement of copyright. Probably figuring they had nothing to lose, KDCP sued back. [2]

College Board also threatened—and this is what produced headlines in the local newspaper—to cancel the scores of the students who they determined had received an unfair advantage from the KDCP course. As *Denton Record-Chronicle* reported (and as you can imagine), the students and their families freaked out. [3] The scores and full application packages had already been delivered to colleges across the country, and score cancellation would have amounted to application cancellation. And since many of the students applied only to schools requiring the SAT, the threat amounted to at least temporary college cancellation. "I hope the College Board thinks this through," said David Miller, a Plano attorney whose son was apparently on the blacklist. "If they have a problem with Karen Dillard, that's one thing. But I hope they don't punish kids who wanted to work hard."

Predictably, the episode crescendo with everyone lawyered up and suits threatened in all directions. In the end, the scores weren't canceled. KDCP accepted a settlement calling for them to pay $600,000 directly to the College Board and provide $400,000 in free classes for high schoolers who'd otherwise be unable to afford the service. As for the principal who'd been lifting the test booklets, he got to keep his job, which pays about $87,000 a year. The CEO of College Board, by the way, gets around $830,000. [4] KDCP is a private company, so we don't know how much Karen Dillard or her employees make. We do know they could absorb a million-dollar lawsuit without going into bankruptcy. Finally, the Plano school district in Texas—a well-to-do suburb north of Dallas—continues to produce some of the nation's highest SAT score averages.

One Thief, Three Verdicts

Utilitarianism is a consequentialist ethics—the outcome matters, not the act. Among those who focus on outcomes, the utilitarian's distinguishing belief is that we should pursue *the greatest good for the greatest number*. So we can act in whatever way we choose—we can be generous or miserly, honest or dishonest—but whatever we do, to get the utilitarian's approval, the result should be more people happier. If that *is* the result, then the utilitarian needs to know nothing more to label the act ethically recommendable. (Note: Utility is a general term for usefulness and benefit, thus the theory's name. In everyday language, however, we don't talk about creating a greater utility but instead a greater good or happiness.)

In rudimentary terms, utilitarianism is a happiness calculation. When you're considering doing something, you take each person who'll be affected and ask whether they'll end up happier, sadder, or it won't make any difference. Now, those who won't change don't need to be counted. Next, for each person who's happier, ask, how much happier? Put that amount on one side. For each who's sadder, ask, how much sadder? That amount goes on the other side. Finally, add up each column and the greater sum indicates the ethically recommendable decision.

Utilitarian ethics function especially well in cases like this: You're on the way to take the SAT, which will determine how the college application process goes (and, it feels like, more or less your entire life). Your car breaks down and you get there very late and the monitor is closing the door and you remember that…you forgot your required number 2 pencils. On a desk in the hall you notice a pencil. It's gnawed and abandoned but not yours. Do you steal it? Someone who believes it's an ethical duty to not steal will hesitate. But if you're a utilitarian you'll ask: Does taking it serve the greater good? It definitely helps you a lot, so there's positive happiness accumulated on that side. What about the victim? Probably whoever owns it doesn't care too much. Might not even notice it's gone. Regardless, if you put your increased happiness on one side and weigh it against the victim's hurt on the other, the end result is almost certainly a net happiness gain. So with a clean conscience you grab it and dash into the testing room. According to utilitarian reasoning, you've done the right thing ethically (assuming the pencil's true owner isn't coming up behind you in the same predicament).

Pushing this theory into the KDCP case, one tense ethical location is the principal lifting test booklets and sending them over to his brother at the test-prep center. Everything begins with a theft. The booklets do in fact belong to the College

Board; they're sent around for schools to use during testing and are meant to be returned afterward. So here there's already the possibility of stopping and concluding that the principal's act is wrong simply because stealing is wrong. Utilitarian's, however, don't want to move so quickly. They want to see the *outcome* before making an ethical judgment. On that front, there are two distinct outcomes: one covering the live tests, and the other the retired ones.

Live tests were those with sections that may appear again. When students at KDCP received them for practice, they were essentially receiving cheat sheets. Now for a utilitarian, the question is, does the situation serve the general good? When the testing's done, the scores are reported, and the college admissions decisions made, will there be more overall happiness then there would've been had the tests not been stolen? It seems like the answer has to be no. Obviously those with great scores will be smiling, but many, many others will see their scores drop (since SATs are graded on a curve or as a percentile). So there's some major happiness for a few on one side balanced by unhappiness for many on the other. Then things get worse. When the cheating gets revealed, the vast majority of test takers who didn't get the edge are going to be irritated, mad, or furious. Their parents too. Remember, it's not only admission that's at stake here but also financial aid, so the students who didn't get the KDCP edge worry not only that maybe they should've gotten into a better school but also that they end up paying more too. Finally, the colleges will register a net loss: all their work in trying to admit students on the basis of fair, equal evaluations gets thrown into question.

Conclusion. The theft of live tests fails the utilitarian test. While a few students may come out better off and happier, the vast majority more than balances the effect with disappointment and anger. The greater good isn't served.

In the case of the theft of "retired" tests where the principal forwarded to KDCP test questions that won't reappear on future exams, it remains true that the tests were lifted from the College Board and it remains true that students who took the KDCP prep course will receive an advantage because they're practicing the SAT. But the advantage doesn't seem any greater than the one enjoyed by students all around the nation who purchased prep materials directly from the College Board and practiced for the exam by taking old tests. More—and this was a point KDCP made in their countersuit against the College Board—stealing the exams was the ethically *right* thing to do because it assured that students taking the KDCP prep course got the same level of practice and expertise as those using official College Board materials. If the tests hadn't been stolen, then wouldn't KDCP kids be at an unfair disadvantage when compared with others because their test practices hadn't been as close to the real thing as others got? In the end, the argument goes, stealing the tests assured that as many people as possible who took prep courses got to practice on real exams.

Conclusion. The theft of the exams by the high school principal may conceivably be congratulated by a utilitarian because it increases general happiness. The students who practiced on old exams purchased from the College Board can't complain. And as for those students at KDCP, their happiness increases since they can be confident that they've prepared as well as possible for the SAT.

The fact that a utilitarian argument can be used to justify the theft of test booklets, at least retired ones, doesn't end the debate, however. Since the focus is on outcomes, *all* of them have to be considered. And one outcome that might occur if the theft is allowed is, obviously, that maybe other people will start thinking stealing exam books isn't such a bad idea. If they do—if everyone decides to start stealing—it's hard to see how anything could follow but chaos, anger, and definitely not happiness.

This discussion could continue as more people and consequences are factored in, but what won't change is the basic utilitarian rule. What ought to be done is determined by looking at the big picture and deciding which acts increase total happiness at the end of the day when everyone is taken into account.

Should the Scores Be Canceled?
After it was discovered that KDCP students got to practice for the SATs with live exams, the hardest question facing the College Board was, should their scores be canceled? The utilitarian argument for *not* canceling is straightforward. Those with no scores may not go to college at all next year. This is real suffering, and if your aim is to increase happiness, then counting the exams is one step in that direction. It's not the last step, though, because utilitarian's at the College Board need to ask about *everyone else's happiness* too: what's the situation for all the others who took the exam but has never heard of KDCP? Unfortunately, letting the scores be counted is going to subtract from their happiness because the SAT is graded comparatively: one person doing well means everyone getting fewer correct answers sees their score drop, along with college choices and financial aid possibilities. Certainly it's true that each of these decreases will be small since there were only a handful of suspect tests. Still, a descent, no matter how tiny, is a descent, and all the little bits add up.

What's most notable, finally, about this decision is the imbalance. Including the scores of KDCP students will weigh a tremendous increase in happiness for a very few against a slight decrease for very many. Conversely, a few will be left very sad, and many slightly happier. So for a utilitarian, which is it? It's hard to say. It is clear, however, that this uncertainty represents a serious practical problem with the ethical theory. In some situations you can imagine yourself in the shoes of the different people involved and, using your own experience and knowledge, estimate which decision will yield the most total happiness. In this situation, though, it seems almost impossible because there are so many people mixed up in the question.

Then things get still more difficult. For the utilitarian, it's not enough to just decide what brings the most happiness to the most individuals right now; the future needs to be accounted for too. Utilitarianism is a true global ethics; you're required to weigh everyone's happiness and weigh it as best as you can as far into the future as possible. So if the deciders at the College Board follow a utilitarian route in opting to include (or cancel) the scores, they need to ask themselves—if we do, how will things be in ten years? In fifty? Again, these are hard questions but they don't change anything fundamental. For the utilitarian, making the right decision continues to be about attempting to predict which choice will maximize happiness.

Utilitarianism and the Ethics of Salaries

When he wasn't stealing test booklets and passing them on to KDCP, the principal in the elite Plano school district was dedicated to his main job: making sure students in his building receive an education qualifying them to do college-level work. Over at the College Board, the company's CEO leads a complementary effort: producing tests to measure the quality of that preparation and consequently determine students' scholastic aptitude. The principal, in other words, is paid to make sure high schoolers get an excellent education, and the CEO is paid to measure how excellent (or not) the education is.

Just from the job descriptions, who should get the higher salary? It's tempting to say the principal. Doesn't educating children have to be more important than measuring how well they're educated? Wouldn't we all rather be well educated and not know it than poorly educated and painfully aware of the fact?

Regardless, what's striking about the salary that each of these two actually receives isn't who gets more; it's how much. The difference is almost ten times: $87,000 for the principal versus the CEO's $830,000. Within the doctrine of utilitarianism, can such a divergence be justified?

Yes, but only if we can show that this particular salary structure brings about the greatest good, the highest level of happiness for everyone considered as a collective. It may be, for example, that objectively measuring student ability, even though it's less important than instilling ability, is also much harder. In that case, a dramatically higher salary may be necessary in order to lure high-quality measuring talent. From there, it's not difficult to fill out a utilitarian justification for the pay divergence. It could be that inaccurate testing would cause large amounts of unhappiness: students who worked hard for years would be frustrated when they were bettered by slackers who really didn't know much but managed to score well on a test.

To broaden the point, if tremendous disparities in salary end up making people happier, then the disparities are ethical. Period. If they don't, however, then they can no longer be defended. This differs from what a libertarian rights theorist might say here. For a libertarian—someone who believes individuals have an undeniable right to make and keep whatever they can in the world, regardless of how rich or poor anyone else may be—the response to the CEO's mammoth salary is that he found a way to earn it fair and square, and everyone should quit complaining about it. Generalized happiness doesn't matter, only the individual's right to try to earn and keep as much as he or she can.

Can Money Buy Utilitarian Happiness? The Ford Pinto Case Basic questions in business tend to be quantitative, and money is frequently the bottom line: *How many dollars is it worth? What's my salary? What's the company's profit?* The basic question of utilitarianism is qualitative: *how much happiness and sadness is there?* Inevitably, it's going to be difficult when businesses accustomed to bottom-line number decisions are forced to cross over and decide about general happiness. One of the most famous attempts to make the transition easier occurred back in the 1970s.

With gas prices on the rise, American car buyers were looking for smaller, more efficient models than Detroit was manufacturing. Japanese automakers were experts in just those kinds of vehicles and they were seizing market share at an alarming rate. Lee Iacocca, Ford's president, wanted to rush a car into production to compete. His model was the Pinto. [5]

A gas sipper slated to cost $2,000 (about $12,000 today); Ford rushed the machine through early production and testing.

Along the way, unfortunately, they noticed a design problem: the gas tank's positioning in the car's rump left it vulnerable to rear-end collisions. In fact, when the rear-end hit came faster than twenty miles per hour, not only might the tank break, but gasoline could be splattered all the way up to the driver's compartment. Fire, that meant, ignited by sparks or anything else could engulf those inside.

No car is perfectly safe, but this very scary vulnerability raised eyebrows. At Ford, a debate erupted about going ahead with the vehicle. On the legal end, the company stood on solid ground: government regulation at the time only required gas tanks to remain intact at collisions under twenty miles per hour. What about the ethics, though? The question about whether it was *right* to charge forward was unavoidable because rear-end accidents at speeds greater than twenty miles per hour happen—every day.

The decision was finally made in utilitarian terms. On one side, the company totaled up the dollar cost of redesigning the car's gas tank. They calculated

- 12.5 million automobiles would eventually be sold,
- eleven dollars would be the final cost per car to implement the redesign.

Added up, that's $137 million total, with the money coming out of Pinto buyers' pockets since the added production costs would get tacked onto the price tag. It's a big number but it's not that much per person: $11 is about $70 today. In this way, the Pinto situation faced by Ford executives is similar to the test cancellation question for the College Board: one option means only a little bit of suffering for specific individuals, but there are a lot of them.

On the other side of the Pinto question—and, again, this resembles the College Board predicament—if the decision is made to go ahead without the fix, there's going to be a *lot* of suffering but only for a very few people. Ford predicted the damage done to those few people in the following ways:

- Death by burning for 180 buyers
- Serious burn injuries for another 180 buyers
- Twenty-one hundred vehicles burned beyond all repair

That's a lot of damage, but how do you *measure* it? How do you compare it with the hike in the price tag? More generally, from a utilitarian perspective, is it better for a lot of people to suffer a little or for a few people to suffer a lot?

Ford answered both questions by directly attaching monetary values to each of the injuries and damages suffered:

- At the time, 1970, US Government regulatory agencies officially valued a human life at $200,000. (That would be about $1.2 million today if the government still kept this problematic measure.)
- Insurance companies valued a serious burn at $67,000.
- The average resale value on subcompacts like the Pinto was $700, which set that as the amount lost after a complete burnout.

The math coming out from this is (180 deaths × $200,000) + (180 injuries × $67,000) + (2,100 burned-out cars × $700) = $49 million. The result here is $137 million worth of suffering for Pinto drivers if the car is redesigned and only $49 million if it goes to the streets as is.

Ford sent the Pinto out. Over the next decade, according to Ford estimates, at least 60 people died in fiery accidents and at least 120 got seriously burned (skin-graft-level burns). No attempt was made to calculate the total number of burned vehicles. Shortly thereafter, the Pinto was phased out. No one has final numbers, but if the first decade is any indication, then the total cost came in under the original $49 million estimate. According to a utilitarian argument, and assuming the premises concerning dollar values are accepted, Ford made the right decision back in 1970.

If every Pinto purchaser had been approached the day after buying the car, told the whole Ford story, and been offered to change their car along with eleven dollars for another one without the gas tank problem, how many would've handed the money over to avoid the long-shot risk? The number might've been very high, but that doesn't sway a utilitarian conclusion. The theory demands that decision makers stubbornly keep their eye on overall happiness no matter how much pain a decision might cause certain individuals.

Versions of Utilitarian Happiness

Monetized utilitarianism attempts to measure happiness, to the extent possible, in terms of money. As the Ford Pinto case demonstrated, the advantage here is that it allows decisions about the greater good to be made in clear, objective terms. You add up the money on one side and the money on the other and the decision follows automatically. This is a very attractive benefit, especially when you're dealing with large numbers of individuals or complex situations. Monetized utilitarianism allows you to keep your happiness calculations straight.

Two further varieties of utilitarianism are hedonistic and idealistic. Both seek to maximize human happiness, but their definitions of happiness differ.

Hedonistic utilitarian's trace back to Jeremy Bentham (England, around 1800). Bentham was a wealthy and odd man who left his fortune to the University College of London along with the stipulation that his mummified body be dressed and present at the institution. It remains there today. He sits in a wooden cabinet in the main building, though his head has been replaced by a wax model after pranking students repeatedly stole the real one. Bentham believed that pleasure and happiness are ultimately synonymous. Ethics, this means, seeks to maximize the pleasures—just about any sensation of pleasure—felt by individuals. But before dropping everything and heading out to the bars, it should be remembered that even the most hedonistic of the utilitarian's believe that getting pleasure right now is good but not as good as maximizing the feeling *over the long term*. (Going out for drinks, in others words, instead of going to the library isn't recommendable on the evening before midterms.)

A contemporary of Bentham, John Stuart Mill, basically agreed that ethics is about maximizing pleasure, but his more idealistic utilitarianism distinguished low and highbrow sensations. The kinds of raw, good feelings that both we and animals can find, according to Mill, are second-rate pleasures. Pleasures with higher and more real value include learning and learnedness. These aren't physical joys so much as the delights of the mind and the imagination. For Mill, consequently, libraries and museums are scenes of abundant pleasure, much more than any bar.

This idealistic notion of utilitarianism fits quite well with the College Board's response to the KDCP episode. First, deciding against canceling student scores seems like a way of keeping people on track to college and headed toward the kind of learning that rewards our cerebral inclinations. Further, awarding free prep classes to those unable to pay seems like another step in that direction, at least if it helps get them into college.

Versions of Utilitarian Regulation

A narrow distinction with far-reaching effects divides soft from hard utilitarianism. Soft utilitarianism is the standard version; when people talk about a utilitarian ethics, that's generally what they mean. As a theory, soft utilitarianism is pretty laid back: an act is good if the outcome is more happiness in the world than we had before. Hard utilitarianism, on the other hand, demands more: an act is ethically recommendable *only if* the total benefits for everyone are greater than those produced *by any other act*.

According to the hard version, it's not enough to do well; you must do the most good possible. As an example, think about the test-prep company KDCP under the microscope of utilitarian examination.

- When a soft utilitarian looks at KDCP, the company comes out just fine. High schoolers are learning test-taking skills and tricks that they'll only use once but will help in achieving a better score and leave behind a sense that they've done all they can to reach their college goals. That means the general happiness level probably goes up—or at worst holds steady—because places like KDCP are out there.

- When a hard utilitarian looks at KDCP, however, the company doesn't come off so well. Can we really say that this enterprise's educational subject—test taking—is the *very best* use of teaching resources in terms of general welfare and happiness? And what about the money? Is SAT prep *really* the best way for society to spend its dollars? Wouldn't a hard utilitarian have to recommend that the tuition money collected by the test-prep company get siphoned off to pay for, say, *college* tuition for students who otherwise wouldn't be able to continue their studies at all?

If decisions about businesses are *totally* governed by the need to create the most happiness possible, then companies like KDCP that don't contribute much to social well-being will quickly become endangered.

The demands of hard utilitarianism can be layered onto the ethical decision faced by the College Board in their courtroom battle with KDCP. Ultimately, the College Board opted to penalize the test-prep company by forcing it to offer some free classes for underprivileged students. Probably, the result was a bit more happiness in the world. The result *wasn't*, however, the most happiness possible. If hard utilitarianism had driven the decision, then the College Board would've been forced to go for the jugular against KDCP, strip away all the money they could, and then use it to do the most good possible, which might have meant setting up a scholarship fund or something similar. That's just a start, though. Next, *to be true to hard utilitarianism*, the College Board would need to focus *on itself* with hard questions. The costs of creating and applying tests including the SAT are tremendous, which makes it difficult to avoid this question: wouldn't society as a whole be better off if the College Board were to be canceled and all their resources dedicated to, for example, creating a new university for students with learning disabilities?

Going beyond KDCP and the College Board, wouldn't almost *any* private company fall under the threat of appropriation if hard utilitarian's ran the world? While it's true, for example, that the money spent on steak and wine at expensive Las Vegas restaurants probably increases happiness a bit, couldn't that same cash do a lot more for the general welfare of people whose income makes Las Vegas an impossibly expensive dream? If it could, then the hard utilitarian will propose zipping up Las Vegas and rededicating the money.

Finally, since utilitarianism is about *everyone's* total happiness, don't hard questions start coming up about *world* conditions? Is it possible to defend the existence of McDonald's in the United States while people are starving in other countries? Conclusion. In theory, there's not much divergence between soft and hard utilitarianism. But in terms of what actually happens out in the world when the theory gets applied, that's a big difference. For private companies, it's also a dangerous one.

Two further versions of utilitarian regulation are act and rule. Act utilitarianism affirms that a specific action is recommended if it increases happiness. This is the default form of utilitarianism, and what people usually mean when they talk about the theory. The separate rule-based version asserts that an action is morally right if it follows a *rule* that, when applied to everyone, increases general happiness.

The rule utilitarian asks whether we'd all be benefitted if everyone obeyed a rule such as "don't steal." If we would— if the general happiness level increases because the rule is there—then the rule utilitarian proposes that we all adhere to it. It's important to note that rule utilitarian's aren't against stealing because it's intrinsically wrong, as duty theorists may propose. The rule utilitarian is only against stealing if it makes the world less happy. If tomorrow it turns out that mass stealing serves the general good, then theft becomes the ethically right thing to do.

The sticky point for rule utilitarian's involves special cases. If we make the rule that theft is wrong, consider what happens in the case from the chapter's beginning: You forgot your pencil on SAT test day, and you spot one lying on an abandoned desk. If you don't take it, no one's going to be any happier, but you'll be a lot sadder. So it seems like rule utilitarianism verges on defeating its own purpose, which is maximizing happiness no matter what.

On the other hand, there are also sticky points for act utilitarian's. For example, if I go to Wal-Mart tonight and steal a six-pack of beer, I'll be pretty happy. And assuming I don't get caught, no one will be any sadder. The loss to the company—a few dollars—will disappear in a balance sheet so huge that it's hard to count the zeros. Of course if everyone starts stealing beers, that will cause a problem, but in practical terms, if one person does it once and gets away with it, it seems like an act utilitarian would have to approve. The world would be a happier place.

Advantages and Disadvantages of Utilitarian Ethics in Business

Basic utilitarianism is the soft, act version. These are the theory's central advantages:

- **Clarity and simplicity.** In general terms, it's easy to understand the idea that we should all act to increase the general welfare.
- **Acceptability.** The idea of bringing the greatest good to the greatest number coheres with common and popular ideas about what ethical guidance is supposed to provide.
- **Flexibility.** The weighing of individual actions in terms of their consequences allows for meaningful and firm ethical rules without requiring that everyone be treated identically no matter how different the particular situation. So the students whose scores were suspended by the College Board could see them reinstated, but that doesn't mean the College Board will take the same action in the future (if, say, large numbers of people start stealing test booklets).
- **Breadth.** The focus on outcomes as registered by society overall makes the theory attractive for those interested in public policy. Utilitarianism provides a foundation and guidance for business regulation by government.

The central difficulties and disadvantages of utilitarianism include the following:

- **Subjectivity.** It can be hard to make the theory work because it's difficult to know what makes happiness and unhappiness for specific individuals. When the College Board demanded that KDCP give free classes to underprivileged high schoolers, some paying students were probably happy to hear the news, but others probably fretted about paying for what others received free. And among those who received the classes, probably the amount of resulting happiness varied between them.
- **Quantification.** Happiness can't be measured with a ruler or weighed on a scale; it's hard to know exactly how much happiness and unhappiness any particular act produces. This translates into confusion at decision time. (Monetized utilitarianism, like that exhibited in the case of the Ford Pinto, responds to this confusion.)

- **Apparent injustices.** Utilitarian principles can produce specific decisions that seem wrong. A quick example is the dying grandmother who informs her son that she's got $200,000 stuffed into her mattress. She asks the son to divide the money with his brother. This brother, however, is a gambling alcoholic who'll quickly fritter away his share. In that case, the utilitarian would recommend that the other brother—the responsible one with children to put through college—just keep all the money. That would produce the most happiness, but do we really want to deny grandma her last wish?

- The utilitarian monster is a hypothetical individual who *really* knows how to feel good. Imagine that someone or a certain group of people were found to have a much greater capacity to experience happiness than others. In that case, the strict utilitarian would have no choice but to put everyone else to work producing luxuries and other pleasures for these select individuals. In this hypothetical situation, there could even be an argument for forced labor as long as it could be shown that the servants' suffering was minor compared to the great joy celebrated by those few who were served. Shifting this into economic and business terms, there's a potential utilitarian argument here for vast wage disparities in the workplace.

- The utilitarian sacrifice is the selection of one person to suffer terribly so that others may be pleasured. Think of gladiatorial games in which a few contestants suffer miserably, but a tremendous number of spectators enjoy the thrill of the contest. Moving the same point from entertainment into the business of medical research, there's a utilitarian argument here for drafting individuals—even against their will—to endure horrifying medical experiments if it could be shown that the experiments would, say, cure cancer, and so create tremendous happiness in the future.

KEY TAKEAWAYS

- Utilitarianism judges specific decisions by examining the decision's consequences.
- Utilitarianism defines right and wrong in terms of the happiness of a society's members.
- Utilitarian ethics defines an act as good when its consequences bring the greatest good or happiness to the greatest number of people.
- There are a variety of specific forms of utilitarianism.
- Theoretically, utilitarianism is straightforward, but in practical terms it can be difficult to measure the happiness of individuals.

REVIEW QUESTIONS

1. What is a utilitarian argument in favor of a college education? How does it differ from other reasons you might want to go to college or graduate school?
2. How could a utilitarian justify cheating on an exam?
3. What is a "global ethics"?
4. What practical problem with utilitarianism is (to some degree) resolved by monetized utilitarianism?
5. What are two advantages of a utilitarian ethics when compared with an ethics of duties?
6. What are two disadvantages of a utilitarian ethics when compared with an ethics of duties?
7. What's an example from today's world of a utilitarian monster?
8. What's an example from today's world of a utilitarian sacrifice?

[1] "CB-Karen Dillard Case Settled-No Cancelled Scores," College Confidential, accessed May 15, 2011, http://talk.collegeconfidential.com/parents-forum/501843-cb-karen-dillard-case-settled-no-cancelled-scores.html.
[2] Paulina Mis, "College Board Sues Test-Prep Company, Countersuit Filed," Scholarships.com, February 26, 2008, accessed May 15, 2011,http://www.scholarships.com/blog/high-school/college-board-sues-test-prep-company-countersuit-filed/161.
[3] Staci Hupp, "SAT Scores for Students Who Used Test Prep Firm May Be Thrown Out, *Denton Record Chronicle*, February 22, 2008, accessed May 15, 2011.
[4] "AETR Report Card," Americans for Educational Testing Reform, accessed May 15, 2011, http://www.aetr.org/college-board.php.
[5] Case facts taken from Manuel Velasquez, *Business Ethics, Concepts and Cases*, 6th ed. (Upper Saddle River, NJ: Pearson Prentice Hall, 2006), 60–61.

3.3 Altruism: Everyone Else
LEARNING OBJECTIVES

1. Define altruistic ethics.
2. Show how altruism works in and with business.
3. Consider advantages and drawbacks of altruism.

TOMS Shoes

There is no Tom at TOMS Shoes. The company's name actually came from the title for its social cause: Shoes for Tomorrow. Tomorrow shoes—*TOMS Shoes*. The shoes are given away to needy children in Argentina at a one-to-one rate: for every pair bought in the United States, TOMS delivers a pair down there.

They're needed in Argentina's poverty-stricken regions to prevent the spread of an infectious disease, one that flourishes in the local soil and rises up through the feet. A pair of shoes is all that's needed to block the problem.

The project started when young Texan entrepreneur Blake Mycoskie vacationed in Argentina. Not the type to luxuriate in the hotel pool, he got out and learned about the country, good and bad, the food, the sweeping geography, the poverty and diseases. The foot infection, he discovered, was so devastating yet so easy to block that, according to his company's website, he decided he had to do something about it. [1] Initially, he contemplated a charitable fund to buy shoes for the needy children, but that left his project subject to the ebb and flow of others' generosity. It'd be better and more reliable, he determined, to link the community-service project with private enterprise and use revenues from a company to fund the charity. Quickly, Mycoskie determined that he could make the whole machine work most efficiently by starting a shoe company. Simultaneously, he could produce shoes for donation and shoes for sale to finance the effort. So we have TOMS Shoes.

Next, a kind of shoe to produce and sell was required. Mycoskie found inspiration in Argentina's traditional *alpargata*. This is a cheap, workingman's shoe, a slip-on made from canvas with rope soles. [2] For the American adaptation, Mycoskie strengthened the sole, styled and colored the canvas, and added a brand label. The price also got jacked up. The originals cost a few dollars in Argentina; the adaptations cost about forty dollars here.

They're a splashy hit. You find TOMS Shoes at trendy footwear shops, at Whole Foods grocery stores, and all over the Internet. At last check, about half a million pairs have been sold and an equal number donated. Total sales in seven figures aren't far off, and the company was recently featured on a CNBC segment as an American business success story. Notably, TOMS achieved recognition on national TV sooner after its inception than almost any other enterprise in the program's history. It all happened in fewer than four years. Question: how did it get so big so fast? How did some guy transform from a wandering tourist to a captain of the shoe industry in less time than it takes to get a college degree? Answer: celebrities.

Blake Mycoskie's got a warm, round face and a perfect smile. He's got money from his pre-shoe projects and he's smart too. He's also got that contemporary bohemian look down with his bead necklace and wavy, shoulder-length hair. There's no letdown beneath the chin line either; he's fit (he was a tennis pro until nineteen). You get the idea. He commands attention from even Hollywood women, and he ended up coupled with the midrange star Maggie Grace. He introduced her to his TOMS Shoes concept, gave her a few pairs to wear around and show friends, and the ball started rolling. [3]

A few parties later, Scarlett Johansson, Jessica Biel, Benicio Del Toro, Tobey Maguire, Sienna Miller, and Karl Lagerfeld were parading around in TOMS Shoes. There was no stopping it. [4]

Today, when Blake Mycoskie introduces himself, it's not as the CEO of his company; he says he's the *Chief Shoe Giver* at TOMS Shoes, reflecting the idea that charity drives the thriving business, not the other way around.

Is TOMS Shoes Altruistic?

An action is morally right according to the altruist, and to the ethical theory of altruism, if the action's consequences are more beneficial than unfavorable for everyone except the person who acts. That means the actor's interests aren't considered: the altruist does whatever can be done so that *others* will be happier.

It's common to imagine the altruist as poverty stricken and self-sacrificing. When you live for everyone else as the altruist does, it's no surprise that you can end up in pretty bad shape. You might get lucky and run into another altruist like yourself, but if you don't, there's not going to be anyone particularly dedicated to your well-being. On the positive side there's nobility to the idea of dedicating everything to everyone else, but the plain truth is not many of us would choose to live like Gandhi or Mother Teresa.

It doesn't *have* to be that way, though. A suffering life may be an effect of altruism, but it's not a requirement. Living for others doesn't mean you live poorly, only that there's no guarantee you'll live well. You might, however, live well. Blake Mycoskie demonstrates this critical element at the heart of altruism: it's not about suffering or sacrificing; it's about making clear-eyed decisions about the best way to make as many others as happy as possible. If you happen to live the good life along the way—partying with Maggie Grace, Sienna Miller, and friends because that's the fastest route to publicize the TOMS Shoes enterprise—that doesn't count against the project. It doesn't count in favor either. All that matters, all that gets tallied up when the question gets asked about whether the altruist did good, is how things ended up for everyone else.

In the case of TOMS Shoes, the tallying is easy. The relatively wealthy shoe buyers in the United States come off well; they get cool, politically correct footwear to show friends along with a psychological lift from knowing they're helping the less fortunate. On the other side, the rural Argentines obviously benefit also.

Some Rules of Altruism

Altruism is a consequentialist ethics. Like utilitarianism, no specific acts are prohibited or required; only outcomes matter. That explains why there aren't lifestyle requirements for the altruist. Some live stoically like Gandhi while others like Mycoskie get the high life, but they're both altruists as long as the goal of their lives and the reason for their actions is bringing happiness to others. Similarly, the altruist might be a criminal (Robin Hood) or a liar (see Socrates' noble lie). Like the utilitarian, most of the hard questions altruists face concern happiness. They include:

- The happiness definition. Exactly what counts as happiness? In the case of TOMS donating shoes to rural Argentines, the critical benefit is alleviation of disease and the suffering coming with it. Happiness, in other words, is defined here as a release from real, physical pain. On the other hand, with respect to the shoes sold in the States, the happiness is completely different; it's a vague, good feeling that purchasers receive knowing their shopping is serving a social cause. How do we define happiness in a way that ropes in both these distinct experiences?

- Once happiness has been at least loosely defined, another question altruist's face is the happiness measure: how do we know which is worth more, the alleviation of suffering from a disease or the warm happiness of serving a good cause? And even if the answer to that question is clear, *how great* is the difference, how can it be measured?

- Another altruism difficulty is happiness foresight. Even if donating shoes helps in the short term, are the recipients' lives really going to be happier overall? Conditions are hard in the abandoned regions of the third world, and alleviation of one problem may just clear the way for another. So TOMS Shoes saves poverty-stricken Argentines from suffering a debilitating foot disease, but how much good are you really doing if you save people only so that they're free to suffer aching hunger, miserable sickness in places lacking antibiotics, and hard manual labor because there's no other work?

Altruism is a variety of selflessness, but it's not the same thing; people may deny themselves or they may sacrifice themselves for all kinds of other reasons. For example, a soldier may die in combat, but that's not altruism; that's loyalty: it's not sacrificing for everyone else but for a particular nation. The same may go for the political protestor who ends up jailed and forgotten forever. That's self-sacrifice, but she did it for the cause and not for all the others. The fireman may lose his life rescuing a victim, but this is because he's doing his job, not because he's decided to live for the sake of others. All altruists, finally, are selfless, but not all those who sacrifice themselves are altruists.

Personal versus impersonal altruism distinguishes two kinds of altruists: those who practice altruism on their own and leave everyone else alone and those who believe that *everyone* should act only to benefit others and without regard to their own well-being.

The Altruist in Business and the Business That Is Altruistic TOMS Shoes shows that a business can be mounted to serve the welfare of others. A company aiming to serve an altruistic purpose doesn't have to be organized altruistically, however. An individual truly dedicated to everyone else could start a more traditional company (a real estate firm, for example), work like a dog, turn massive profits, and in the end, donate everything to charity. It may even be that during the profit-making phase the altruist CEO is ruthless, exploiting workers and consumers to the maximum. All that's fine as long as the general welfare is served in the end when all the suffering is toted up on one side and the happiness on the other. A business operation that isn't at all altruistic, in other words, can be bent in that direction by an altruistic owner.

Going the other way, the business operation itself may be altruistic. For example, this comes from the College Board's website, the *About Us* page: The College Board is a not-for-profit membership association whose mission is to connect students to college success and opportunity. [5]

That sounds like a good cause. The company doesn't exist to make money but to implement testing that matches students with their best-fit colleges. It is, in other words, an altruistic enterprise, and the world, the argument could be made, is a better place because the College Board exists. But—and this is the important distinction—that doesn't mean everyone who *works* at the College Board is selfless. Far from it, the CEO takes home $830,000 a year. That money would buy a lot of shoes for the poverty-stricken in Argentina. So, there can be altruistic business organizations driven by workers who aren't altruists.

A church is also a business organization with cash flows, budgets, and red and black ink. The same goes for Goodwill. Here's their mission statement: "Goodwill Industries International enhances the dignity and quality of life of individuals, families and communities by eliminating barriers to opportunity and helping people in need reach their fullest potential through the power of work." [6] So, the Salvation Army fits into the group of altruistic enterprises, of organizations that exist, like the College Board, to do public good. It's distinct from the College Board, however, in that a very healthy percentage of those working inside the organization are *themselves* altruists—they're working for the cause, not their own welfare. Think of the Salvation Army red kettle bell ringers around Christmas time.

Conclusion. Altruism connects with business in three basic ways. There are altruists who use normal, profit-driven business operations to do well. There are altruistic companies that do good by employing no altruistic workers. And there are altruistic organizations composed of altruistic individuals.

Advocating and Challenging Ethical Altruism
The arguments for and against an altruistic ethics overlap to a considerable extent with those listed under utilitarianism. The advantages include:

- **Clarity and simplicity.** People may disagree about exactly how much good a company like TOMS Shoes is really doing, but the overall idea that the founder is working so that others can be happier is easy to grasp.
- **Acceptability.** The idea of working for others grants an ethical sheen. No matter what you might think of someone as a person, it's very difficult to criticize them in ethical terms if they really are dedicating themselves to the well-being of everyone else.
- **Flexibility.** Altruists have many ways of executing their beliefs.
  The disadvantages of altruism include:
- **Uncertainty about the happiness of others.** Even if individuals decide to sacrifice their own welfare for the good of others, how do they know for sure what makes others happy?
- **Shortchanging yourself.** Even though altruism doesn't require that the altruist live a miserable life, there doesn't seem to be any clear reason why the altruist shouldn't get an at least equal claim to happiness as everyone else (as in a utilitarian approach). Also, some critics suspect that altruism can be a way of *escaping* your own life: if you spend all your time volunteering, could it be that deep down you're not a good soul so much as just afraid of going out into the competitive world and trying to win a good place for yourself?

KEY TAKEAWAYS

- Altruism defines ethically good as any act that ends up increasing net happiness (or decreasing net unhappiness)

when everything is taken into account except the actor's increased or diminished happiness.
- Altruism doesn't require living a miserable life.
- Altruism intersects with the business world in various ways.

REVIEW QUESTIONS

1. Theoretically, could the most devoted altruist in a society also be its richest and happiest member? How?
2. Does Blake Mycoskie have to be an altruist for TOMS Shoes to be considered an altruistic enterprise?
3. Does TOMS Shoes have to be an altruistic enterprise for Mycoskie to be considered an altruist?
4. What are some other motives that may lead someone to live the life of an altruist?

[1] TOMS Shoes, "One for One Movement," accessed May 15, 2011, http://www.toms.com/our-movement.
[2] TOMS Shoes, accessed May 15, 2011, http://cdn2.tomsshoes.com/images/uploads/2006-oct-vogue.jpg.
[3] Sharon_b, December 14, 2008 (5:24 p.m.), "Blake Mycoskie—he's handsome, rich and helps children in the Third World," Gossip Rocks, accessed May 15, 2011, http://www.gossiprocks.com/forum/news/90958-blake-mycoskie-hes-handsome-rich-helps-children-third-world.html.
[4] Lesley M. M. Blume, "You Are What You Wear," *Huffington Post*, July 30, 2008, accessed May 15, 2011, http://www.huffingtonpost.com/lesley-m-m-blume/you-are-what-you-wear_b_65967.html.
[5] "About Us," College Board accessed May 15, 2011, http://about.collegeboard.org.
[6] "Our Mission," Goodwill Industries International, Inc., accessed May 15, 2011, http://www.goodwill.org/about-us/our-mission.

3.4   Egoism: Just Me
LEARNING OBJECTIVES

1. Define ethical egoism.
2. Show how egoism works in and with business.
3. Consider advantages and drawbacks of egoism.

Ethical Egoism
Ethical egoism: whatever action serves my self-interest is also the morally right action. What's good for me in the sense that it gives me pleasure and happiness is also good in the sense that it's the morally right thing to do.

Ethical egoism mirrors altruism: If I'm an altruist, I believe that actions ought to heighten the happiness of others in the world, and what happens to me is irrelevant. If I'm an egoist, I believe that actions ought to heighten my happiness, and what happens to others is irrelevant.

Could someone like Blake Mycoskie—someone widely recognized as an altruistic, social-cause hero—actually is an egoist? Yes. Consider things this way. Here's a young guy and he's out looking for money, celebrity, good parties, and a jaw-dropping girlfriend. It wouldn't be the first time there was a guy like that.

Put yourself in his shoes and imagine you're an ethical egoist: whatever's good for you is good. Your situation is pretty clear, your moral responsibility lists what you should be trying to get, and the only question is *how* can I get it all?

That's a tall order. Becoming a rock star would probably work, but there are a lot of people already out there going for it that way. The same goes for becoming a famous actor. Sports are another possibility; Mycoskie, in fact, made a run at pro tennis as a younger man, but like most who try, he couldn't break into the upper echelon. So there are paths that may work, but they're hard ones, it's a real fight for every step forward.

If you're smart—and Mycoskie obviously is—then you might look for a way to get what you want that doesn't force you to compete so brutally with so many others. Even better, maybe you'll look for a way that doesn't present any competition at all, a brand new path to the wish list. The idea of a celebrity-driven shoe company that makes a profit but that also makes its founder a star in the eyes of the Hollywood stars is a pretty good strategy.

Obviously, no one can look deep into Mycoskie's mind and determine exactly what drove him to found his enterprise. He may be an altruist or an egoist or something else, but what's important is to outline how egoism can actually work in the world. It can work—though of course it doesn't work this way every time—just like TOMS Shoes.

Egoism and Selfishness

When we hear the word *egoist*, an ugly profile typically comes to mind: self-centered, untrustworthy, pitiless, and callous with respect to others. Some egoists really are like that, but they don't *have* to be that way. If you're out to maximize your own happiness in the world, you might find that helping others is the shortest and fastest path to what you want. This is a very important point. Egoists aren't against other people, they're for themselves, and if helping others work for them, that's what they'll do. The case of TOMS Shoes fits right here. The company improves the lives of many; it raises the level of happiness in the world. And *because* it does that, the organization has had tremendous success, and because of that success, the Blake Mycoskie we're imagining as an egoist is getting what he wants: money, great parties, and everyone loving him. In short, sometimes the best way to one's own happiness is by helping others be happier.

That's not always the way it works. Bernie Madoff destroyed families, stole people's last dimes, and lived the high life all the way through. For an ethical egoist, the only blemish on his record is that he got caught.

Madoff *did* get caught, though, and this too needs to be factored into any consideration of egoists and how they relate to others. Just as egoists may help others because that serves their own interests, so too they may obey social customs and laws. It's only important to note that they obey not out of deference to others or because it's the morally right thing to do; they play by the rules because it's the *smart* thing to do. They don't want to end up rotting in jail.

A useful contrast can be drawn in this context between egoism and selfishness. Where egoism means putting your welfare above others', selfishness is the refusal to see beyond yourself. Selfishness is the inability (or unwillingness) to recognize that there are others sharing the world, so it's the selfish person, finally, who's callous and insensitive to the wants and needs of others. For egoists, on the other hand, because working with others cooperatively can be an excellent way to satisfy their own desires, they may not be at all selfish; they may be just the opposite.

Enlightened Egoism, Cause Egoism, and the Invisible Hand

Enlightened egoism is the conviction that benefitting others—acting to increase their happiness—can serve the egoist's self-interest just as much as the egoist's acts directly in favor of him or herself. As opposed to altruism, which claims that it's our ethical responsibility to serve others, the enlightened egoist's generosity is a rational strategy, not a moral imperative. We don't help others because we ought to: we help them because it can make sense when, ultimately, we only want to help ourselves.

One simple and generic manifestation of enlightened egoism is a social contract. For example, I agree not to steal from you as long as you agree not to steal from me. It's not that I don't take your things because I believe stealing is morally wrong; I leave you alone because it's a good way to get you to leave me alone. On a less dramatic level, all of us form mini social contracts all the time. Just think of leading a group of people through one of those building exits that makes you cross two distinct banks of doors. If you're first out, you'll hold the door for those coming after, but then expect someone to hold the next door for you. Sure, some people hold the door because it's good manners or something like that, but for most of us, if no one else ever held a door open for us, pretty soon we'd stop doing them the favor. It's a trivial thing, of course, but in the real world people generally hold doors open for others because they've agreed to a social contract: everyone else does it for me; I'll do it for them. That's enlightened egoism, and it frequently works pretty well.

TOMS Shoes can be understood as a more sophisticated version of the same mentality. It's hard to discern exactly what the contract would look like if someone tried to write it down, but it's not hard to see the larger notion of enlightened egoism. Shoes are donated to others not because of a moral obligation but because serving the interests of others helps Blake Mycoskie serve his own. As long as shoe buyers keep holding up their end of the bargain by buying his product, Mycoskie will continue to help them be generous and feel good about themselves by donating pairs to people who need them.

Cause egoism is similar to, but also distinct from, enlightened egoism. Enlightened egoism works from the idea that helping others is a good way of helping me. Cause egoism works from the idea that giving the *appearance* of helping others is a promising way to advance my own interests in business. As opposed to the enlightened egoist who will admit that he is out for himself but happy to benefit others along the way, the cause egoist claims to be mainly or only interested in benefiting others and then leverages that good publicity to help him. Stated slightly differently, enlightened egoists *respect* others while pursuing their own interests, while cause egoists just fake it.

Adam Smith (1723–90) is known for making a connected point on the level of broad economic trade and capitalism. In the end, it usually doesn't matter whether people actually care about the well-being of others, Smith maintains, because there exists an invisible hand at work in the marketplace. It leads individuals who are trying to get rich to enrich their society as well, and that enrichment happens regardless of whether serving the general welfare was part of the original plan. According to Smith, the person in business generally

> Intends only his own gain, but is led by an invisible hand to promote an end which was no part of the original intention. By pursuing his own interest he frequently promotes that of the society and does so more effectively than when he directly intends to promote it. [1]

What's the invisible hand? It's the force of marketplace competition, which encourages or even requires individuals who want to make money to make the lives of others better in the process.

The invisible hand is a central point defenders of egoism in business often make when talking about the virtues of a me-first ethics. Egoism is good for me, but it frequently ends up being good for everyone else, too. If that's right, then even those who believe the utilitarian ideal of the general welfare should guide business decisions may be forced to concede that we should all just become egoists.

Here's a quick example. If you open a little takeout pizza shack near campus and your idea is to clear the maximum amount of money possible to pay your tuition, what kind of business are you going to run? Does it make sense to take a customer's twelve dollars and then hand over an oily pie with cheap plastic cheese and only three pepperonis? No, in the name of pursuing your own happiness, you're going to try to charge a bit less than Domino's and give your customers something slightly better—maybe you'll spread richer cheese, or toss on a few extra pepperonis. Regardless, you're not doing this for the reason an altruist would; you're not doing it because you sense an ethical obligation to make others' lives better. As an egoist, you don't care whether your customers are happier or not. But if you want your business to grow, you better care. And because you're ethically required to help your business grow in order to make tuition money and so make yourself happier, you're going to end up improving the pizza-eating experience at your school. Better food, less money. Everyone wins. We're not talking Mother Teresa here, but if ethical goodness is defined as more happiness for more people, then the pizza place is ethically good. Further, *anybody* who wants to start up a successful pizza restaurant is, very likely, going to end up doing good. If you don't, if you can't offer some advantage, then no one's going to buy your slices.

Going beyond the quality-of-life benefits of businesses in society, Smith leaned toward a second claim that's far more controversial. He wrote that the entrepreneur trying to do well actually *promotes society's well-being more effectively than when directly intending to promote it.* This is startling. In essence, it's the claim that for the most dedicated altruist the most effective strategy for life in business is…to act like an egoist. Within the economic world at least, the best way for someone who cares only about the well-being of others to implement that conviction is to go out and run a successful profit-making enterprise.

Clearly, this is a very powerful argument for defenders of ethical egoism. If it's true that egoists beat altruists at their own game (increasing the happiness of everyone else), then egoism wins the debate by default; we should all become egoists. Unfortunately, it's impossible to prove this claim one way or the other. One thing *is* clear, however: Smith's implicit criticism of do-gooders can be illustrated. Sometimes individuals who decide to act for the good of others (instead of seeking profit for themselves) really do end up making the world a worse place. Dr. Loretta Napoleoni has shown how attempts by Bono of U2 to help the destitute in Africa have actually brought them more misery. [2] Bono threw a benefit concert and dedicated the proceeds to Africa are most needy. The intention was good, but the plan wasn't thought all the way through and the money ended up getting diverted to warlords who used it to buy guns and bullets.

Still, the fact that some altruistic endeavors actually make things worse doesn't mean they're all doomed. Just as surely as some fail, others succeed.

The same mixed success can be attributed to businesses acting only for their own welfare, only for profit. If it's true that the pizza sellers help improve campus life, what about the entrepreneurial honor student who volunteers to write your term paper for a price? It's hard to see how a pay-for-grades scheme benefits students in general, even though the writer may make a tidy profit, and that one student who paid for the work may come out pretty well.

The invisible hand is the belief that businesses out in the world trying to do well for themselves tend to do good for others too. It may even be that they do more good than generous altruists. It's hard to know for sure, but it can be concluded that there's a distance between ethical egoism in reality and the image of the egoist as a ruthless destroyer of broad social happiness.

Some Rules of Egoism
Egoism, like altruism, is a consequentialist ethics: the ends justify the means. If an egoist were at the helm of TOMS Shoes and he cared only about meeting beautiful people and making huge money, he'd have no scruples about lying all day long. There'd be no problem with smiling and insisting that the reason TOMS Shoes exists is to generate charitable shoe donations to the poor. All that matters for the egoist is that the lie works, that it serves the goal of making TOMS as attractive and profitable as possible. If it does, then deviating from the truth becomes the ethically recommendable route to follow.

Personal egoism versus impersonal egoism distinguishes these two views: the personal egoist in the business world does whatever's necessary to maximize his or her own happiness. What others do, however, is considered their business. The impersonal egoist believes *everyone* should get up in the morning and do what's best for themselves and without concern for the welfare of others.

An impersonal egoist may find comfort in the invisible hand argument that the best way for me to do right with respect to society in general is to get rich. Of course it's true that there's something crude in shameless money grubbing, but when you look at things with rational eyes, it is hard to avoid noticing that the kinds of advances that make lives better—cars affordably produced on assembly lines; drugs from Lipitor to Chap Stick; cell phones; spill-proof pens; whatever—often trace back to someone saying, "I want to make some money for myself."

Rational egoism versus psychological egoism distinguishes two reasons for being an ethical egoist. The rational version stands on the idea that egoism makes sense. In the world as it is, and given a choice between the many ethical orientations available, egoism is the most reasonable. The psychological egoist believes that, for each of us, putting our own interests in front of everyone else isn't a choice; it's a reality. We're made that way. Maybe it's something written into our genes or it's part of the way our minds are wired, but regardless, according to the psychological egoist, we all care about ourselves before anyone else and at their expense if necessary.

Why would I rationally choose to be an egoist? Maybe because I figure that if I don't look out for myself, no one will. Or maybe I think almost everyone else is that way, too, so I better play along or I'm going to get played. (The Mexicans have a pithy phrase of common wisdom for this, "O te chingas, o te chingan," which means "either you screw everyone else, or they'll screw you.") Maybe I believe that doing well for myself helps me do well for others too. The list could be drawn out, but the point is that there are numerous reasons why an intelligent person may accept ethical egoism as the way to go.

As for those who subscribe to the theory of psychological egoism, obviously there's no end of examples in business and history to support the idea that no matter how much we may want things to be otherwise, the plain truth is we're made to look out for number one. On the other hand, one problem for psychological egoists is that there *do* seem to be examples of people doing things that are irreconcilable with the idea that we're all only trying to make ourselves happier:

- Parents sacrificing for children. Any mom or dad who works overtime at some grinding job for cash to pay their children's college tuition seems to be breaking the me-first rule. Here, the psychological egoist responds that, when you really think about it, there may be something there for the parents after all: it could be the pride in telling friends that their children are getting their degrees.

- Mother Teresa or similar religious-based advocates for the needy. Anyone spending their time and energy making things better for others, while living painfully modestly, seems like a good candidate to break the rule of psychological egoism. Here, the psychological egoist responds that perhaps they see a different reward for themselves than earthly pleasures. They may believe, for example, that their suffering on this earth will be more than compensated by paradise in heaven.

The Four Relations between Egoism and Business

Structurally, there are four possible relations between ethical egoism and business life:

1. You can have egoists in egoist organizations. This is mercenary capitalism. Individuals do whatever work is required so long as it benefits them to the maximum. Naturally, this kind of person might find a good home at a company entirely dedicated to maximizing its own health and success, which can mean one looking to maximize profits without other considerations. A good example is executives at the Countrywide mortgage firm. They OK'ed thousands of mortgages to clients who had no way to repay the money. Then they bundled and sold these mortgages to banks and other financial institutions, making a quick profit. When the loans later collapsed, those institutions fell into bankruptcy. The Countrywide executives quickly formed a new company to buy those same loans back at pennies on the dollar, thus once again turning millions in profits. [3]

2. You can have egoists in nonegoist organizations. Possibly, the CEO of the College Board fits into this category. His salary of just under a million dollars annually sounds pretty good, especially when you consider that he gets it working for a nonprofit company that exists to help high school students find the college best fitted to them. It's also possible that Blake Mycoskie of TOMS Shoes fits this profile: he lives an extremely enviable life in the middle of a company set up to help people who almost no one envies.

3. You can have nonegoists in egoist organizations. Somewhere in the Countrywide mortgage company we could surely find someone who purchased shoes from TOMS because they wanted to participate in the project of helping the rural poor in Argentina.

4. You can have nonegoists in nonegoist organizations. Think of the red kettle bell ringers popping up outside malls around the holiday season.

Advocating and Challenging Ethical Egoism

The arguments for an egoistic ethics include the following:

- **Clarity and simplicity.** Everybody understands what it means to look out for them first.

- **Practicality.** Many ethical theories claim to protect our individual interests, but each of us knows ourselves and our own interest's best. So doesn't it make sense that we as individuals take the lead? Further, with respect to creating happiness for ourselves, there's no one closer to the action than us. So, again, doesn't it make sense that each of us should be assigned that responsibility?

- **Sincerity.** For those subscribing to psychological egoism, there's a certain amount of honesty in this ethics not found in others. If our real motive beneath everything else is to provide for our own happiness first, then shouldn't we just recognize and say that? It's better to be sincere and admit that the reason we don't steal is so that others don't steal from us instead of inventing some other explanations which sound nice but are ultimately bogus.

- **Unintended consequences.** In the business world, the concept of the invisible hand allows egoists to claim that their actions end up actually helping others and may help them more than direct charity or similar altruistic actions.

- Finally, there's a broad argument in favor of egoism that concerns **dignity**. If you're out in the world being altruistic, it's natural to assume that those benefiting from your generosity will be grateful. Sometimes they're not, though. Sometimes the people we try to help repay us with spite and resentment. They do because there's something *condescending* about helping others; there's a message wrapped up in the aid that those who receive it are incapable of taking care of them and need someone superior to look out for them. This is especially palpable in the case of panhandlers. If you drop a dollar into their hat, it's hard to not also send along the accusation that their existence is base and shameful (you refuse to look them in the eye; you drop the money and hurry away). To the extent that's right, an egoism that expects people to look out for themselves and spurns charity may actually be the best way to demonstrate respect for others and to acknowledge their dignity.

Arguments against ethical egoism include the following:

- **Egoism isn't ethics.** The reason we *have* ethics is because there are so many people in the world and in business who care only about themselves. The entire idea of ethics, the reasoning goes, is to set up some rules for acting that rescue us from a cruel reality where everyone's just looking out for number one.

- **Egoism ignores blatant wrongs.** Stealing candy from a baby—or running a company selling crappy baby food—strikes most of us as unacceptable, but the rules of egoism dictate that those are recommendable actions as long as you can be assured that they'll serve your interests.
- **Psychological egoism is not true.** The idea that we have no choice but to pursue our own welfare before anything else is demonstrated to be false millions of times every day; it's wrong every time someone makes an anonymous contribution to a cause or goes out of their way to help another without expecting anything in return.

KEY TAKEAWAYS

- Egoism defines ethically good as any act that raises the actor's overall happiness (or decreases unhappiness) without counting anyone else's increased or diminished happiness.
- Egoism does not mean ignoring the existence and welfare of others, though they are not necessarily advocated either.
- Though egoists act in the name of their own happiness, others may benefit.
- Egoism intersects with the business world in various ways.

REVIEW QUESTIONS

1. What's the difference between egoism and selfishness?
2. In what situation would an egoist decide that a lie is morally wrong?
3. In the real world, is there any way to distinguish an enlightened egoist from a cause egoist?
4. What are some reasons someone may become a rational egoist?
5. What is the *invisible hand*?
6. If you were starting a small business, would you prefer that your partner is a utilitarian, an altruist, or an egoist? Why?

[1] Adam Smith, *An Inquiry into the Nature and Causes of the Wealth of Nations* (London: Strahan and Cadell, 1776), bk. 4, chap. 2.

[2] Can Tran, "Celebrities Raising Funds for Africa End Up Making Things 'Worse,'" *Ground Report*, May 14, 2008, accessed May 15, 2011, http://www.groundreport.com/World/Celebrities-Raising-Funds-For-Africa-End-Up-Making/2861070.

[3] Eric Lipton, "Ex-Leaders of Countrywide Profit from Bad Loans," *New York Times*, March 3, 2009, accessed May 15, 2011, http://www.nytimes.com/2009/03/04/business/04penny.html.

3.5 Case Studies

Cheaters

KDCP is Karen Dillard's company specialized in preparing students to ace the Scholastic Aptitude Test. At least some of the paying students received a solid testing-day advantage: besides teaching the typical tips and pointers, KDCP acquired stolen SAT tests and used them in their training sessions. It's unclear how many of the questions that students practiced on subsequently turned up on the SATs they took, but some certainly did. The company that produces the SAT, the College Board, cried foul and took KDCP to court. The lawsuit fell into the category of copyright infringement, but the real meat of the claim was that KDCP helped kids cheat, they got caught, and now they should pay.

The College Board's case was very strong. After KDCP accepted the cold reality that they were going to get hammered, they agreed to a settlement offer from the College Board that included this provision: KDCP would provide $400,000 worth of free SAT prep classes to high schoolers who couldn't afford to pay the bill themselves. [1]

QUESTIONS

1. Can you form a quick list of people who'd benefit because of this decision and others who'd end up on the losing side? Then, considering the situation globally and from a utilitarian perspective, what would need to be true for the settlement offer to be ethically recommendable?
2. As for those receiving the course for free—it's probably safe to assume that their happiness increases. Something for nothing is good. But what about the students who still have to pay for the course? Some may be gladdened to hear that more students get the opportunity, but others will see things differently; they'll focus on the fact that their parents are working and saving money to pay for the course, while others get it for nothing. Some of those who paid probably actually earned the money *themselves* at some disagreeable, minimum wage McJob. Maybe they served popcorn in the movie theater to one of those others who later on applied and got a hardship exemption.
   - Starting from this frustration and unhappiness on the part of those who pay full price, can you form a utilitarian case against the settlement's free classes?
   - From a utilitarian perspective, could the College Board have improved the settlement by adding the stipulation that the settlement's terms (and therefore the free classes) not be publicly disclosed?

o   Once word got out, could a utilitarian recommend that the College Board lie or that it release a statement saying, "No free classes were part of the settlement"?

3. There was talk about canceling the scores of those students who took the SAT after benefitting from the KDCP classes that offered access to the stolen exam booklets. The students and their parents protested vigorously, pointing out that they'd simply signed up for test prep, just like students all across the nation. They knew nothing about the theft and they presumably didn't know they were practicing on questions that might actually appear on their exam day. From the perspective of *rule utilitarianism*, what's the case for canceling their scores? From the perspective of *act utilitarianism*, what's the case for reinstating the scores?

4. The College Board CEO makes around $830,000 a year.
    o   What is a utilitarian case for radically lowering his salary?
    o   If you were a utilitarian and you had the chance—and you were sure you wouldn't get caught—would you steal the money from the guy's bank account? Why or why not?

5. It could be that part of what the College Board hoped to gain through this settlement requiring free classes for the underprivileged was some positive publicity, some burnishing of their image as the good guys, the socially responsible company, the ones who do the right thing.
    o   Outline the case for this being an act of an altruistic company.
    o   Outline the case for this being an act of an egoistic company.

UFC

Ultimate Fighting Championship (UFC) got off to a crushing start. In one of the earliest matches, Tank Abbott, a six-footer weighing 280 pounds, faced John Matua, who was two inches taller and weighed a whopping four hundred pounds. Their combat styles were as different as their sizes. Abbott called himself a pit fighter. Matua was an expert in more refined techniques: he'd honed the skills of wrestling and applying pressure holds. His skill—which was also a noble and ancient Hawaiian tradition—was the martial art called Kuialua.

The evening went poorly for the artist. Abbott nailed him with two roundhouses before applying a skull-cracking head butt. The match was only seconds old and Matua was down and so knocked out that his eyes weren't even closed, just glazed and staring absently at the ceiling. The rest of his body was convulsing. The referee charged toward the defenseless

fighter, but Abbott was closer and slammed an elbow down on Matua's pale face. Abbott tried to stand up and ram another, but the referee was now close enough to pull him away. As blood spurted everywhere and medics rushed to save the loser, Abbott stood above Matua and ridiculed him for being fat. [2]

The tape of Abbott's brutal skills and pitiless attitude shot through the Internet. He became—briefly—famous and omnipresent, even getting a guest appearance on the goofy, family-friendly sitcom *Friends*.

A US senator also saw the tape but reacted differently. Calling it barbaric and a human form of cockfighting, he initiated a crusade to get the UFC banned. Media executives were pressured to not beam the matches onto public TVs, and doctors were drafted to report that UFC fighters (like professional boxers) would likely suffer long-term brain damage. In the heat of the offensive, even diehard advocates agreed the sport might be a bit raw, and the UFC's original motto—"There are no rules!"—got slightly modified. Head butting, eye-gouging, and fish-hooking (sticking your finger into an opponent's orifice and ripping it open) were banned. No matter what anyone thinks of UFC, it convincingly demonstrates that blood resembles sex. Both sell and people like to watch. The proof is that today UFC events are among the most viewed in the world, among the most profitable, and—this is the one part that hasn't changed since the gritty beginning—among the most brutal.

QUESTIONS

1. Two of the common arguments against ultimate fighting—and the two main reasons the US senator argued to get the events banned—are the following:
    o   They're brutal; UFC celebrates violence and hatred and injury, and therefore, it's immoral.
    o   Besides the bumps, bruises, and broken bones—which usually heal up—the fighters also suffer long-term and incurable brain damage. Therefore, the sport is immoral even though it might be true that in their prime, the fighters make enough money to compensate the physical suffering endured in the octagon.

    How could a utilitarian defend the UFC against these two criticisms?

2. How could the concept of the *utilitarian sacrifice* apply to John Matua?

3. How would a hedonistic utilitarian's reaction to UFC differ from an idealistic utilitarian's reaction? Is there

anything at all in UFC that might convince an idealistic utilitarian to promote the sport as ethically positive?

4. How could a proponent of monetized utilitarianism begin portioning up the experiences of Abbott, Matua, the UFC sponsors, and the spectators in order to construct a mathematical formula (like Ford did with the Pinto) to decide whether UFC should be banned?

5. Think of UFC as a business, one compared to a biotech company that pioneers cutting-edge, life-saving drugs. Now, how would a utilitarian decide which one of these two companies was the more ethically respectable?

6. Why might an altruist sign up to be a UFC fighter? Why might an egoist sign up to be a UFC fighter?

Lottery

In her blog *Majikthise*, Lindsay Beyerstein writes, "State lotteries are often justified on the grounds that they raise money for social programs, especially those that target the neediest members of society. However, the poorest members of society tend to spend (and, by design lose) the most on lottery tickets. Some state lottery proceeds fund programs that benefit everyone, not just the poor. Often state lottery money is being systematically redistributed upward—from lotto players to suburban schools, for example." [3]

QUESTIONS

1. How is the lottery an example of the utilitarian monster?

2. How can you set yourself up to argue in favor of or against the ethical existence of the lottery in terms of monetized utilitarianism?

3. Lotteries are about money and about fun—that is, even for the losers, there's a benefit in the thrill of watching the numbers turn up. Could the case be made that, from a hedonistic utilitarian standpoint, the lottery is ethically recommendable because it serves the welfare not only of the winner but also of the millions of losers?

4. One of Lindsay Beyerstein's concerns is that the lottery tends to redistribute money from the poor toward the rich.

   o Does a utilitarian necessarily consider this redistribution unethical?

   o What kinds of things would a utilitarian have to look into to decide whether the inverse Robin Hooding is necessarily a bad thing?

5. The lotteries under discussion here are run by states, and Lindsay Beyerstein is not a big fan. She calls these lotteries "a tax on idiocy" meaning, presumably, that people are just throwing their money away every time they buy a ticket. Now, one of the arguments in favor of egoism as an ethical stance is that no one knows what

makes each of us happy better than each of us. So, it follows, we should all just try to get what we want and leave other people alone. How can this view of egoism be fashioned to respond to the idea that the lottery is a tax on idiocy?

Honest Tea

Seth Goldman founded Honest Tea in 1998. He calls himself the Tea EO (as opposed to CEO) and his original product was a bottled tea drink with no additives beyond a bit of sugar. Crisp and natural—that was the product's main selling point. It wasn't the only selling point, though. The others aren't in the bottle; they're in the company making it. Honest Tea is a small enterprise composed of good people. As the company website relates, "A commitment to social responsibility is central to Honest Tea's identity and purpose. The company strives for authenticity, integrity and purity, in our products and in the way we do business…Honest Tea seeks to create honest relationships with our employees, suppliers, customers and with the communities in which we do business." [4]

Buy Honest Tea, the message is, because the people behind it are trustworthy; they are the kind of entrepreneurs you want to support.

The mission statement also relates that when Honest Tea gives business to suppliers, "we will attempt to choose the option that better addresses the needs of economically disadvantaged communities." [5] They'll give the business, for example, to the company in a poverty-stricken area because, they figure, those people really need the jobs. Also, and to round out this socially concerned image, the company promotes ecological ("sustainability") concerns and fair trade practices: "Honest Tea is committed to the well-being of the folks along the value chain who help bring our products to market. We seek out suppliers that practice sustainable farming and demonstrate respect for individual workers and their families." [6]

Summing up, Honest Tea provides a natural product, helps the poor, treats people with respect, and saves the planet. It's a pretty striking corporate profile.

It's also a profile that sells. It does because when you hand over your money for one of their bottles, you're confident that you're not fattening the coffers of some money grubbing executive in a New York penthouse who'd lace drinks with chemicals or anything else that served to raise profits. For many consumers, that's good to know.

Honest Tea started selling in Whole Foods and then spread all over, even to the White House fridges because it's a presidential favorite. Revenues are zooming up through the dozens of millions. In 2008, the Coca-Cola Company bought a 40 percent share of Honest Tea for $43 million. It's a rampantly successful company.

Featured as part of a series in the *Washington Post* in 2009, the company's founder, Seth Goldman, was asked about his enterprise and his perspective on corporate philanthropy, meaning cash donations to good causes. Goldman said, "Of course there's nothing wrong with charity, but the best way for companies to become good citizens is through the way they operate their business." Here are two of his examples: [7]

- Switching from Styrofoam to postconsumer waste might help a packaging company make a more meaningful contribution to sustainability than a token donation to an environmental nonprofit.
- Investing in a local production facility or even a community bank could help support a local economy more effectively than a donation to a nearby jobs program.

Organizations in the economic world, Goldman believes, can do the most good by doing good themselves as opposed to doing well (making money) and then outsourcing their generosity and social responsibility by donating part of their profits to charities. That may be true, or it may not be, but it's certain that Goldman is quite good at making the case. He's had a lot of practice since he's outlined his ideas not just in the *Post* but in as many papers and magazines as he can find. Honest Tea's drinks are always featured prominently in these flattering articles, which are especially complimentary when you consider that Honest Tea doesn't have to pay a penny for them.

QUESTIONS

1. Make the case that Seth Goldman founded Honest Tea as an expression of his utilitarian ethics.
   - What kinds of people are affected by the Honest Tea organization? Which groups might benefit from Honest Tea and how? Which groups might not benefit?
   - Would this be a hedonistic or idealistic utilitarianism? Why?
   - Would it be possible to construe Honest Tea within a framework of monetized utilitarianism?
   - Would this be a soft or hard utilitarianism?

2. Make the case that Seth Goldman founded Honest Tea as an expression of his ethical altruism.

   - Altruists serve the welfare of others. How does Honest Tea serve people's welfare?
   - What would have to be true about Goldman in terms of his particular abilities and skills for this enterprise to fall under the heading of altruism?
   - Does Goldman sound more like a personal or an impersonal altruist?

3. Make the case that Seth Goldman founded Honest Tea as an expression of his ethical egoism.
   - What are some of the benefits Goldman could derive from Honest Tea?
   - Before running Honest Tea, Goldman was a big-time mutual fund manager. What kind of benefits could Honest Tea have offered that he couldn't find in the world of finance?
   - Does Goldman sound more like a personal or an impersonal egoist?
   - In the real world, does it make any difference whether Goldman does enlightened egoism or cause egoism?

4. In this case study, two kinds of drink manufacturers are contrasted: Honest Tea and the hypothetical drink company run by some mercenary businessman lacing drinks with bad chemicals to maximize profits. Looking at this contrast, how could a defender of egoism claim that the *best* way for healthy drinks to make their way into the general public's hands (in the medium and long term, anyway) is for Goldman *and* the mercenary businessman *and* everyone else to all be egoists?

5. Assume that Seth Goldman is a cause egoist, someone faking concern for the general welfare in order to provide for his own happiness and pleasure. How could the concept of the invisible hand be introduced to make the claim that Goldman is actually doing more good for the general welfare than he would if he were a utilitarian or even an altruist?

Your Business

Think about something you do with passion or expertise—a dish you like to cook and eat, a sport you play, any unique skill or ability you've developed—and figure out a way to turn it into a small business. For example, you like baking cookies, so you open a bake shop, or you like hockey and could imagine an improved stick to invent and market.

QUESTIONS

1. If your business is like most others, you're going to need some money to get it up and going, more money than you've got right now. That means you'll need to find a partner for your venture, someone to help you get the

cash together and then run things afterward. Would you prefer a utilitarian, an altruist, or an egoist for your partner? Why?

2. Do you think the invisible hand would be in effect for your business? Just by trying to make money, do you imagine you'd end up improving people's lives? If this business works, is it even possible that you'd help others *more* than you would by volunteering time for a charity organization? Elaborate.

3. Assume that doing well in society and not just doing well (making money) is important to you. Within the business you have in mind, with which of these three options do you suspect you'd accomplish more general good?

   o Just making money and trusting the invisible hand to take care of the rest

   o Making money and donating part of it to charity— that is, to people specialized in serving the general welfare

   o Attempting to do good *within* your business by, for example, buying recycled materials or by paying wages slightly above what people could get for the same work at other companies

4. Is there a potential cause egoism angle to your business? Could you set it up to make it seem like the *reason* you're running your enterprise is to help others when really you're just trying to make money? For a consequentialist, is there anything wrong with that?

[1] missypie, April 29, 2008 (2:22 p.m.), "CB-Karen Dillard case settled-no cancelled scores," College Confidential, accessed May 15, 2011, http://talk.collegeconfidential.com/parents-forum/501843-cb-karen-dillard-case-settled-no-cancelled-scores.html.

[2] David Plotz, "Fight Clubbed," *Slate*, November 17, 1999, accessed May 15, 2011, http://www.slate.com/id/46344.

[3] Lindsay Beyerstein, "Lotteries as Regressive Taxes," *Majikthise* (blog), January 23, 2006, accessed May 15, 2011, http://majikthise.typepad.com/majikthise_/2006/01/lotteries_as_re.html.

[4] "Our Mission," Honest, accessed May 15, 2011, http://www.honesttea.com/mission/about/overview.

[5] "Our Mission," Honest, accessed May 15, 2011, http://www.honesttea.com/mission/about/overview.

[6] "Our Mission," Honest, accessed May 15, 2011, http://www.honesttea.com/mission/about/overview.

[7] "On Leadership: Seth Goldman," *Washington Post*, accessed May 15, 2011, http://views.washingtonpost.com/leadership/panelists/2009/11/the-biggest-dollars.html.

NOTES:

Chapter 4:
Theories Responding to the Challenge of Cultural Relativism

Chapter Overview

This chapter examines some theories guiding ethical decisions in business. It considers reactions to the possibility that there are no universal definitions of right and wrong, only different customs that change from one society to another.

4.1 What Is Cultural Relativism?
LEARNING OBJECTIVES

1. Define cultural relativism.
2. Show how cultural relativism defies traditional ethics.

Nietzsche and the End of Traditional Ethics

"God is dead," the declaration attributed to Friedrich Nietzsche, stands along with "I think, therefore I am" (René Descartes, 1641) as philosophy's most popularized—and parodied—phrases. The t-shirt proclaiming "Nietzsche is dead, signed, God" is funny, but it doesn't quite answer what Nietzsche was saying in the late 1800s. What Nietzsche meant to launch was not only an assault on a certain religion but also a suspicion of the idea that there's one source of final justice for all reality. Nietzsche proposed that different cultures and people each produce their own moral recommendations and prohibitions, and there's no way to indisputably prove that one set is simply and universally preferable to another. The suspicion that there's no final appeal—and therefore the values and morality practiced by a community can't be dismissed as wrong or inferior to those practiced elsewhere—is called cultural relativism.

Example: For most of us, the killing of a newborn would be among the most heinous of immoral acts; a perpetrator would need to be purely evil or completely mad. The Inuit Eskimos, however, regularly practiced female infanticide during their prehistory, and it was neither evil nor insane. Their brutal living conditions required a population imbalance tipped toward hunters (males). Without that gender selecting, the plain fact was the entire group faced starvation. At another place and time, Bernal Diaz's *The Conquest of New Spain* recounts the Spanish invasion of the Americas and includes multiple reports of newborns sacrificed in bloody ceremonies that made perfect sense to the locals, but left Spaniards astonished and appalled. The ethics of infanticide, the point is, differ from one culture and

time to another. Further, these differences seem irreconcilable: it's extremely difficult to see how we could convince the Inuit of the past to adopt our morality or how they could convince us to adopt theirs. And if that's right, then maybe it no longer makes sense to talk about right and wrong in general terms as though there's a set of rules applying to everyone; instead, there are only rights and wrongs as defined within a specific society.

Finally, if you accept the cultural relativist premise, then you're rejecting the foundation of traditional ethics. You're rejecting the idea that if we think carefully and expertly enough, we'll be able to formulate rules for action that everyone—people in all times, places, and communities—must obey if they want to consider themselves ethically responsible.

Cultural Relativism in Business Ethics

In the world of international business, *Entrepreneur* magazine introduces the pitfalls of ethical variation across cultures with this statement from Steve Veltkamp, president of Biz$hop, an American import-export business: "Bribery is a common way of doing business in a lot of foreign places." [1]

If that's true, then US businesses trying to expand into markets abroad—and competing with local businesses already established there—are probably going to consider doing what everyone else is doing, which means getting in on the bribery action. As the *Entrepreneur* article points out, however, this leads to a problem: "While bribes are expected in many countries, the United States' 1977 Foreign Corrupt Practices Act prohibits payments made with the aim of gaining or maintaining business."

So American hands are tied. If a construction company is bidding on the contract to build an airport in a foreign nation, one where the local politicians will be expecting to get their palms greased, they're at a distinct disadvantage since they're not allowed to play by the local rules. Still there is (as there almost always is) a loophole: "Not all payments are prohibited by the act. Some payments are acceptable if they don't violate local laws. Gifts, for instance, to officers working for foreign corporations are legal."

There's no bribing, but gifting, apparently, gets a green light. There's a problem here, too, however: "It can be difficult to determine the difference between a gift and a bribe in a given situation. 'If you give a gift to someone and it leads to a business deal, is that a bribe or a gift?' asks Veltkamp. 'In some cultures, gift-giving is an entrenched part of doing business. If you look at it in a certain sense, maybe it's a bribe, since they won't talk to you until you've made that gesture.'" Now what? Over there, cash changes hands and it's called an acceptable gift, while those watching from back here see an illegal bribe.

There are two ways of looking at this dilemma. One is to say, well, this has to be one or the other, either a gift or a bribe; *it has to be either moral or immoral.* Given that, we need to take out our traditional tools—our basic duties, the utilitarian doctrine that we should act to serve the greater good, and so on—and figure out which it is. Nietzsche went the other way, though. He said that situations like this don't show that we need to use ethics to figure out which side is right; instead, the situation shows what moral rules *really are*: just a set of opinions that a group of people share and nothing more. In the United States we believe it's wrong to grease palms, and so it is. In some other places they believe it's honorable to hand money under the table, and so it is.

If that's true, then specific convictions of right and wrong in business ethics will never be anything but cultural fashions, beliefs some community somewhere decides to hold up for a while until they decide to believe something else. *Anything,* the reasoning goes, may be morally good or bad in the economic world; it just depends on where you happen to be, at what time, and who else is around.

KEY TAKEAWAYS

- Cultural relativism is the suspicion that values and morality are culture specific—they're just what the community believes and not the result of universal reason.
- For cultural relativists, because all moral guidelines originate within specific cultures, there's no way to dismiss one set of rules as wrong or inferior to those developed in another culture.

REVIEW QUESTIONS

1. Why do you imagine the term *cultural relativism* was chosen to mean what it does?
2. Do you believe cultures are irreconcilably different? Or is it that deep down people are people and we're really all the same? How does this distinction relate to the difference between cultural relativism and traditional theories of ethics?

[1] Moira Allen, "Here Comes the Bribe," *Entrepreneur*, October 2000, accessed May 11, 2011: http://www.entrepreneur.com/magazine/entrepreneur/2000/october/32 636.html.

4.2 Nietzsche's Eternal Return of the Same
LEARNING OBJECTIVES

1. Define Nietzsche's eternal return of the same.
2. Show how the idea of the eternal return provides guidance for professional life.
3. Consider the advantages and a drawback of the eternal return.

Responding to Cultural Relativism by Leaving Common Morality Behind

If, along with cultural relativists, you accept that rules distinguishing right from wrong shift around from place to place and time to time, it becomes difficult to keep faith in morality. It's difficult because verdicts seem flimsy and impermanent, and because this hard question seems inescapable: Why should I go out of my way to do the right thing today if what counts as the right thing might change tomorrow?

One response to the question is to give up on morality, disrespect the whole idea by labeling all the customary regulations—*don't lie, don't steal, strive for the greatest good for the greatest number*—a giant sham. Then you can live without the inhibiting limits of moral codes. You can go beyond any idea of good and evil and lead an unconstrained life exuberantly celebrating everything *you* want to do and be.

Wallace Souza: TV Reporter, Politician, and Dealer

Some careers are more vivid and alive than others. TV crime reporting is intense work, especially the action-type shows where the reporter races to the scene, interviews witnesses, and tracks down shady characters. Politics is another throbbing life; the adrenalin of crime chasing isn't there, but you get the brimming confidence and energy that comes with power, with deciding what others can and can't do. Drug dealing excites too, in its way, with thrilling danger and the pleasures of fast money. People, finally, who want to live exuberantly, who prefer risk to caution and find it easy to say things like "you only go around once" are probably going to find something attractive in these lines of work and may opt for one or another.

Then there's Wallace Souza. He opted for all three. At the same time. The most visible of his roles—TV reporter—also yielded the most visible success. His program aired from the Brazilian state of Amazonas, a jungley place far from cosmopolitan São Paulo and touristy Rio de Janeiro. Known as a haven for cocaine cartels, and as a training ground for revolutionary militants charging into neighboring Columbia and Venezuela, it's a natural spot to bring cameras and look for dramatic action. A number of reporters were stationed in the region, but none seemed so uncannily skilled at reaching scenes first and getting video over the airwaves than Mr. Souza. In fact, on occasion, he even reached scenes before the police.

The dogged TV reporting, along with Souza's editorializing complaints about the region's jaded criminals, made him a popular hero and sealed his bid for a seat in the local congress. He didn't allow his state capital work to interfere with his TV role, however. Actually, the two jobs fit together well: one day he was reporting on the deplorable free-for-all in the jungle and the next he was in the capital meeting with high-ranking police officers, reviewing their strategies and proposing laws to fix things.

The perfect image began to crack, though, when it was revealed that the reason Souza so frequently reached the best crime scenes first is that he was paying hit men to assassinate local drug dealers. He wasn't, it turned out, just the first to know about the crimes, he knew even before they happened. In an especially brazen move, during one of his last TV programs, he put up pictures of several notorious criminals and asked his viewers to phone in and votes on which one they'd like to see killed.

At this point, Souza seemed like an overzealous crusader: he was drawing vivid attention to the crime plague and doing something about it with his hit men. You could doubt his methods, but his dedication to his community's welfare seemed noble—until it was revealed that he was actually also a major drug dealer. And the criminals getting killed and shown on his program weren't just random outlaws; they were Souza's drug-trade competitors. [1]

What Is the Eternal Return of the Same?
One report on Souza's exploits included the suggestion that his willingness to cross every moral line—to lie, traffic drugs, order killings, whatever—fit him for the title of the Antichrist. [2]

That title, as it turns out, was one Nietzsche enjoyed assigning to himself. It's definitely also a fit for Souza in the sense that he seemed to live without shame, fear, or regard for good and evil. What's notable about Souza's business ventures is that they *pay no heed to the very idea of morals*. It's not that they skirt some rules or follow some guidelines while disobeying

others; it's not like he's trying to get away with something—it's much more like morality doesn't exist. Now, bringing this back to Nietzsche, who shared the sentiments, the question Nietzsche asked himself was, if morality really is canceled, then what? How should we live? The answer was a thought experiment called the eternal return of the same.

Imagine, Nietzsche proposed, that every decision you make and everything you feel, say, and do will have to be repeated forever—that is, at the end of your life, you die and are immediately reborn right back in the same year and place where everything started the time before, and you do it all again in exactly the same way. Existence becomes an infinite loop. With that disturbing idea established, Nietzsche converted it into a proposal for life: we should always act as though the eternal return were real. Do, Nietzsche says, what you would if you had to live with the choice over and over again forever. The eternal return, finally, gives us a reason to do one thing and not another: it guides us in a world without morals.

How Does the Eternal Return Work?
Start with the eternal return as it could be applied to an altruist, to someone dedicating life to helping others. One way to do altruism would be by working for a nonprofit international organization that goes to poverty-wrecked places like Amazonas and helps coca farmers (the coca leaf is the base for cocaine) shift their farms to less socially damaging crops. This would be difficult work. You might figure on doing it though, getting through it, and feeling like you've done some good in the world. *But* would you do it infinitely? Would you be willing to suffer through that existence once and again *forever*? Remember, the world would never get better; every time you'd just go back to being born on earth just the way it was before. Obviously, people can make their own decisions, but it seems fairly likely that under the condition of the eternal return there'd be fewer people dedicating themselves—and sacrificing their own comfort and interests—to social well-being.

What about some other lines of work? Would there be fewer snowplow operators, long-haul pilots, teachers willing to work in troubled schools? What kind of professional lives, Nietzsche forces us to ask, would be too hellish, bothersome, or exhausting to be repeated forever? Those lives, whatever they are, get filtered by the eternal return; they get removed from consideration.

If certain careers and aspirations are out, then what's in? What kind of existence in the economic world does the eternal return recommend? One possibility is Wallace Souza.

The question is, why would *his* career trajectory fit the eternal return?

The job of a reporter is fast and dramatic, the kind of thing many imagine themselves doing if they weren't tied down by other commitments. People with children frequently feel an obligation to get into a safe and conservative line of work, one producing a steady paycheck. Others feel a responsibility toward their aged parents and a corresponding obligation to not stray too far just in case something goes wrong. So trekking off into the Brazilian jungle in search of drug operations may well be exciting—most of us would probably concede that—but it'd be irreconcilable with many family responsibilities. One thing the eternal return does, however, is *seriously* increase the burden of those responsibilities. When you sacrifice something you want to do because of a sense of obligation, you may be able to swallow the loss once, but Nietzsche is demanding that you take it down over and over again. Family responsibilities may count, but at what point do you say "enough"? Can anyone oblige you to sacrifice doing what you really want forever?

Taking the next step into Souza's amoral but dramatic career, assuming you do decide to become a crime reporter, and you're inside the eternal return where everything will recur infinitely, then aren't you going to go about making your reporting work as exciting and successful as possible? Probably, yes. So why not hire some hit men to fire things up a bit? Normally, of course, our moral compass tells us that killing others to get ahead isn't really an option. But with all morality canceled, it becomes an option, one just like any other. Be a banker, be a reporter, be a killer, there's no real difference. Just choose the one you'd most like to do repeatedly without end.

Souza also chose to be a drug dealer. Again, this is one of those jobs many would find exciting and satisfying. Thrills and easy money are attractive; that's part of the reason Hollywood produces so many films about traffickers and their lives. Most of us wouldn't actually *do* something like that, though, at least partially because dealing drugs feels morally wrong. But inside the eternal return, that shame factor falls away; when it does, the number of people entering this field of work might well increase.

It's critical to note that Nietzsche's eternal return is *not* the idea that you should go off and be a crime-reporting, hit man–hiring drug dealer. Instead, Souza's life just exemplifies one thing that *could* happen in the world of your career if you accept Nietzsche's proposal of living beyond any traditional moral limit. Regardless, what the eternal return definitely

does do is force you to make decisions about your professional life in very different terms than those presented by traditional ethical theories. There's no consideration of sweeping duties; there's just you and a simple decision: the life you choose now will be repeated forever, so which will yours be?

What's the Reward of Morality?
One of the strengths of Nietzsche's idea is that it forces a very important question: *Why* should I want to be morally responsible? Why should a salesman be honest when lying could win her a healthy commission? Why should a factory owner worry about pollution spewing from his plant when he lives in a city five hundred miles away? Now, a full elaboration of this question would be handled in an airy philosophy class, not an applied course in business ethics. Nietzsche, however, allows a taste of the discussion by puncturing one of the basic motivations many feel for being virtuous: the conviction that *there'll be a reward later for doing the right thing today.*

The certainty of this reward is a critical element of many religious beliefs: when you die, there'll be a final judgment and you'll enjoy heaven or suffer punishment at the other extreme, depending on how you behaved on earth. A similar logic underwrites Hinduism's concept of reincarnation: the life you are born into next will be determined by the way you live now. This discussion could be drawn out in more directions, but no matter what, Nietzsche spoils the idea that you take the moral high road because you'll be repaid for it later. Within the eternal return, there is no later; all that ever happens is exactly the same thing again.

Advantages and a Drawback of the Eternal Return
One advantage of the eternal return is that it adds gravity to life. Forcing you to accept every decision you make as one you'll repeat forever is compelling you to take those decisions seriously, to think them through. Another connected advantage of the eternal return is that it forces *you* to make your own decisions. By getting rid of all guidelines proposed by ethics, and by making your reality the one that will repeat forever, Nietzsche forces you to be whom you are.
The disadvantage of the eternal return is Wallace Souza. If everyone is just out there being themselves, how are we going to live together? How can we make peaceful and harmonious societies when all anyone ever thinks about is what's best for themselves forever?

KEY TAKEAWAYS

- The eternal return is a thought experiment in which you imagine that the life you choose will repeat forever.

- According to the eternal return, when faced with a dilemma in the business world—what career should I choose, should I kill (or maybe just lie or cheat) to get ahead?—you should imagine living the decision over and over again forever.

- The eternal return maximizes individuality but does little to help individuals live together in a community.

REVIEW QUESTIONS

1. In your own words, what is the eternal return?
2. Why might the eternal return be considered a reasonable response to cultural relativism?
3. Write down some factors leading to a significant decision you've made. It could be about choosing a field of study or a career path. Now, can you walk through each of the factors within the eternal return? Are there any decisions you made that you'd take back and change?
4. If you knew the eternal return was true, could you still make the reasonable decision to choose an altruistic profession? Why or why not?

[1] Dom Phillips, "Brazil Crime Show Host 'Used Murder to Boost Ratings,'" *Times*, August 13, 2009, accessed May 12, 2011, http://www.timesonline.co.uk/tol/news/world/us_and_americas/article6 793072.ece.
[2] Danny Gallagher, "Brazilian Crime Show Host Kills for Ratings?" *TV Squad*, August 14, 2009, accessed May 12, 2011, http://www.tvsquad.com/2009/08/14/brazilian-crime-show-host-kills-for-ratings.

4.3 Cultural Ethics
LEARNING OBJECTIVES

1. Define cultural ethics.
2. Consider how cultural ethics works in the business world.
3. Examine the truth of cultural ethics.
4. Consider advantages and drawbacks of a culturist's ethics.

What Is Cultural Ethics?

Culturists embrace the idea that moral doctrines are just the rules a community believes, and they accept that there's no way to *prove* one society's values better than another. Culturists don't, however, follow Nietzsche in taking that as a reason to turn away from all traditional moral regulation; instead, it's a reason to accept and endorse whichever guidelines are currently in effect wherever you happen to be. The old adage, "when in Rome, do as the Romans do," isn't too far from where we're at here.

Gift or Bribe or Both?

The *Entrepreneur* magazine article posed a problem for Americans going overseas to do business. In some places, passing money under the table is necessary to spark negotiations and win contracts. However, bribery is illegal in the United States, and US law makes it illegal for Americans to do that kind of thing abroad. Gifts, on the other hand, are allowed. But, according to the *Entrepreneur* article, it can be difficult to determine the difference between a gift and a bribe. In some cultures, a gesture may be seen as a gift, and in others it looks like a bribe.

Looking at this uncertainty, what a culturist sees is *not* ambiguity about whether handing the money over to a potential client is a legal gift or an illegal bribe. That's not it at all. A culturist sees it as *both* a gift and a bribe. In one culture—a nation overseas where the payment is occurring and where similar payments always occur when business is getting done—there are no moral qualms. It's right to give a cash gift because that's the rule of the country; it's the way things are commonly and properly done there. By contrast, from the perspective of American business culture, the conclusion that's drawn with equal force is that it's an immoral bribe because that's what US customs and normal practices tell us.

Cultural Ethics and International Bribery

Culturists see moral rules as fixed onto specific societies, but that doesn't help anyone know what to do when confronted with an unfamiliar set of beliefs. How, the really important question is, does a culturist *act* when forced to make decisions in a place and among people whose beliefs are different and unfamiliar? The *Entrepreneur* interview with Steve Veltkamp provides one answer.

> *What can you do if your overseas associate demands a bribe? Veltkamp doesn't recommend asking embassies or consulates for assistance, as "they have to stick to the official line." Instead, he believes "the best resource in almost every country of the world is the U.S. Chamber of Commerce, where you can find Americans who live in the country and understand how things are done."* [1]

Immediately you can see how different the culturist approach is to moral dilemmas. The message is: get in touch with the locals and try to do as they would in the same situation.

Most traditional ethical theories go in exactly the opposite direction. They say that it doesn't necessarily matter what people are actually doing. Stronger, the entire point of studying ethics has normally been to *escape* conventional wisdom and ingrained habits; the idea of doing what we ought to do requires a step away from those things and a cold, rational look at the situation. So, a morality based on duties sets up guidelines including *don't lie, don't steal* and appeals to men and women in business to follow them. Acting in an ethically responsible way in the world means obeying the dictates and refusing to be swayed by what the guy in the next cubicle is up to. Handing someone money under the table, consequently, while publicly insisting that everything's on the up and up can't be condoned no matter what anyone else does; it can't be right because it entails at least implicit lying. More specifically for the culturist, *Entrepreneur* advises overseas business people to *avoid* seeking guidance from embassies or consulates because those people have to stick to "the official line." What's the official line? Presumably, it's the set of practices delineated and approved by the State Department back in Washington, DC. The strength of these practices is that they're formed to be universal, to work at every embassy everywhere in the world. A culturist, however, looks at that and says it's silly. There are no practices that work everywhere in the world. The advice government bureaucrats give is worthless; it's less than worthless because it departs from the error of conceiving ethics as a set of rules fitting a transnational reality. What people in business should actually do is get in contact with people who really know something about ethics, and that requires turning to the locals, including the chamber of commerce, because they're on the scene.

Conclusion. The culturist deals with the question about whether a bribe is ethically respectable by ignoring all dictates received from other places and obeying the customs and standard practices of those who live and work where the decision is being made.

Cultural Ethics and the News Reporting of Wallace Souza

Another example of how culturist ethics works comes from the flamboyant TV reporter Wallace Souza. Like many action crime reporters the world over, he raced to violent scenes hoping to get the first and best video. What counts, however, as good video in Brazil is different from what typically gets shown in the United States. Here's a description of what Souza sent over the airwaves: "In one of Mr. Souza's shows on his Canal Livre programme, a reporter approached a still-smoldering body in a forest. 'It smells like a barbecue,' he says. 'It is a man. It has the smell of burning meat. The impression is that it was in the early hours…it was an execution.'" [2]

This is not the kind of report we see in the US media, and one of the differences is the ethics. Typically in the United States, a certain respect is accorded to the deceased, even if they're criminals. It's considered an exploitation to directly *show* dead bodies, especially smoldering ones. There's quite a bit of cultural analysis that would go into this prohibition, but simplifying, it's not just that reporters hold an ethical responsibility to others to not exploit their deaths graphically; they also have a responsibility to viewers to not show images that may be (or probably would be) disturbing. By contrast, and as the Souza report shows, in Brazil the rules are different and this kind of visual makes it over the airwaves without raising eyebrows or triggering moral objections.

More generally, the question about what you're allowed to show on TV to boost the ratings and so make more money is an extremely rich area of examples for cultural ethics. How graphic is the violence allowed to be on *CSI Miami*? How far is the wardrobe malfunction allowed to go on the *Real Housewives of Orange County*? These kinds of basic questions about decency and ratings (which means advertising revenue) seem tailor made for those who believe the answers don't depend on anything more than what people in a certain culture will accept. They seem cut out for those believing that the value we call decency is nothing more (or less) than the line drawn between the number of people who will watch and the number who turn the TV off in disgust.

Is Culturalist Ethics True?

If it's true that there's no ethics but the kind a culturalist proposes, then this book loses a good deal of its usefulness. It's lost because the main object is to help readers form and justify rules to guide their professional lives. Conceding that the culturalists are right, however, is also admitting that there's no reason to carefully analyze problems: you're far better served just checking around to see what most other people are doing in similar situations. Ethics isn't a test of your ability to think reasonably and independently; it's more a responsibility to follow the crowd.

Culturalism isn't true, however, at least not necessarily. You can see that in the reasoning underneath the cultural approach. The reasoning starts with an observation:

In certain societies, handing money under the table is commonly considered an appropriate, ethically respectable part of business activity, and in others it's considered both illegal and unethical.

And moves quickly to a conclusion:

Right and wrong in the business world is nothing more than what's commonly considered right and wrong in a specific community.

On the surface, this argument looks all right, but thinking it through carefully leads to the conclusion that it's not valid. A valid argument is one where the conclusion *necessarily* follows from the premises. For example, if you start from the definition that *all unmarried men are bachelors*, and then you observe that your friend John is an unmarried man, you can, in fact, conclude that he's a bachelor. You must conclude that. But that's not the situation with the culturalist argument because the conclusion *doesn't* necessarily follow from the premise. Just because no broad international agreement has been reached about what counts as bribery doesn't mean no agreement will ever be reached. Or making the same point more generally, just because no trans-cultural theory based on universal reason *has yet* to conquer all local beliefs and habits everywhere on the globe doesn't mean no such theory *will ever* accomplish that goal.

Taking the same situation in the less ambiguous world of the physical sciences, there was a time when some believed the earth centered the sun and planets, while others believed the sun was at the center, but that didn't mean the dispute would linger forever. Eventually, tools were found to convince everyone that one side was right. So too in business ethics: one day an enterprising ethicist may find a way to indisputably *prove* on the grounds of a universal and reasonable argument that greasing palms is a bribe and not a gift, and it's immoral, not moral. We don't know if that will happen, but it might. Consequently, the fact that we're unsure now as to whether any single ethics can deal with the whole world doesn't require shooting to the other extreme and saying there'll *never* be anything but what people in specific nations believe and that's it. The culturalist argument, in other words, isn't necessarily persuasive.

It is worrisome, though. And until someone can find a way to do for ethics what scientists did for the question about the earth's relation to the planets, there will always be individuals who suspect that no such proof will ever come. Count Nietzsche among them. In the field of contemporary philosophy and ethics, those who share the suspicion—those who doubt that no matter how hard we try we'll never be able to get beyond our basic cultural perspectives and disagreements—belong to a movement named postmodernism.

What Are Some Advantages and Drawbacks of Culturalist Ethics?

One general advantage of a culturalist ethics is that it allows people to be respectful of others and their culture. A deep component of any society's existence, uniqueness, and dignity in the world is its signature moral beliefs, what the people find right and wrong. A culturalist takes that identity seriously and makes no attempt to change or interfere. More, a culturalist explicitly acknowledges that there's no way to compare one culture against another as better and worse. Though you can *describe* differences, you can't say one set of moral truths is better than another because all moral truths are nothing more than what a society chooses to believe.

A more specific advantage of a culturalist ethics in the economic and business world is that it adapts well to contemporary reality. Over the last decades we've seen an explosion of international commerce, of large corporations tearing loose from specific nations and functioning globally. This economic surge has outpaced the corresponding understanding surge: we have no trouble switching dollars for euros or for yen, and we can buy Heineken beer from Germany and ride in a Honda made in Japan, but few of us speak English, German, and Japanese. In that kind of situation, one where some dilemmas in business ethics end up involving people we can't really talk to, culturalism provides a reasonable way to manage uncertainties. When we're in the United States, we follow American customs. If we're sent on an overseas trade venture to Germany or Japan, we pretty much do as they normally do there. Just in practical terms, that may well be the easiest way to work and succeed in the world, and a culturalist ethics allows a coherent justification for the strategy.

The Disadvantages

The major disadvantage of a culturalist ethics is that it doesn't leave any clear path to making things better. If a community's recommended ethical compass is just their customs and normal practices, then it's difficult to see how certain ingrained habits—say business bribery—can be picked up, examined, and then rejected as unethical. In fact, there's no reason why bribery should be examined at all. Since moral right and wrong is just what the locals do, it makes no sense to try to change anything.

This view stands in stark contrast with what we usually believe—or at least would like to believe—about ethics: there can be progress; we can become *better*. In science, we know progress occurs all the time. Our collective knowledge about the sun's position relative to the planets went from wrong to right with time and effort, and we'd like the same to happen for moral uncertainties. That's why it's so easy to imagine that bribery is a dirty, third-world practice, and part of our responsibility as a wealthy and developed nation is to lead the way in cleaning it up. We clean the moral world of bad business ethics just like our scientists rid the physical world of misperceptions. More, that's a central aim of America's anti-bribery legislation as it applies to overseas acts: it's to cure other cultures of their bad habits. If you're a culturalist, however, then the bad habit isn't bribery; it's one nation trying to impose a morality on another.

However you may come down on the question about whether nations should be trying to improve ethical customs in other places, what's inescapable is that if you're a culturalist, you don't have any ground to stand on when it comes to criticizing the moral practices of businessmen and women in foreign countries. You don't because what's going on elsewhere is an independent and legitimate ethical system and can't be judged inferior to our own.

Another problem with a culturalist ethics is that it provides few routes to resolving conflicts *within* a society. For example, should I be allowed to go into business for myself on the land I bought in the middle of a residential neighborhood by opening a motorcycle bar? In Houston, the answer's yes. There's a community consensus there that owning a piece of land allows you to do (almost) whatever you want with it. In legal terms, that translates into Houston being the only major American city without zoning regulations. Up the road in Dallas, however, there's a similar community consensus that the rights of landownership are curtailed by the rights of nearby landowners. The result is strict zoning laws likely prohibiting Harley conventions in the middle of family neighborhoods. At this point, a culturalist has no problem; people in Houston have their codes of right and wrong and people in Dallas have theirs. What happens, though, in Austin, Texas, which is about midway between Houston and Dallas? What if about half the population believes in landowner rights at all costs and the other half goes for a more community-oriented approach? A cultural ethics provides few tools for resolving the dispute beyond sitting and waiting for one side or the other to take control of the town. This means ethics isn't helping us solve disagreements; it only arrives when, really, it's no longer needed.

KEY TAKEAWAYS

- Proponents of cultural ethics embrace the idea that moral doctrines are just the rules, beliefs, and customs of specific communities.

- Doing the right thing within a culturalist framework relies less on traditional ethical reasoning and more on detecting local habits.
- The culturalist view of ethics is neither true nor false. It's a reaction to the world as it is: a place with vastly divergent sets of moral codes.
- A culturalist ethics respects other societies and their practices but loses solid hope for ethical progress.

REVIEW QUESTIONS

1. If you're doing business overseas as a cultural ethicist, why would it make sense to consult the local chamber of commerce? Who else might you consult for moral guidance? Why?
2. You go abroad to win a contract and discover that a cash gift is necessary, so you hand it over and win the business. On returning to the United States, you put the $200 gift on your expense report. The boss is infuriated, calls your act an "unethical, wrongheaded bribe" and says she won't reimburse you the $200. What arguments could you use to convince her that you did the right thing and should be reimbursed?
3. Souza's bloody TV program is popular in Brazil, especially the parts where he shows video of horridly dead bodies. How could a culturalist argue that the episodes should *not* be shown on American TV?
4. A cultural ethics is neither true nor false. Explain.

[1] Moira Allen, "Here Comes the Bribe," *Entrepreneur*, October 2000, accessed May 12, 2011, http://www.entrepreneur.com/magazine/entrepreneur/2000/october/32636.html.
[2] Dom Phillips, "Brazil Crime Show Host 'Used Murder to Boost Ratings,'" *Times*, August 13, 2009, accessed May 12, 2011, http://www.timesonline.co.uk/tol/news/world/us_and_americas/article6793072.ece.

4.4 Virtue Theory
LEARNING OBJECTIVES

1. Define virtue ethics.
2. Elaborate basic virtues and show how they work in business.
3. Indicate how virtue is acquired.
4. Note an advantage and drawback of the theory.

What Is Virtue Ethics?
Contemporary virtue ethics is an updated version of a theory first proposed in ancient Greece. Today's proponents acknowledge that it's very difficult to set up a list of moral rules that are going to solve ethical dilemmas across cultural lines. Typically, they don't go quite so far as the culturalists;

they don't believe that basic regulations of right and wrong are *completely* independent from one community to another. In practical terms, however, there's agreement that the world is too diverse and changing to be controlled by lists of recommendations and prohibitions. So proponents of virtue suggest that we change the focus of our moral investigations. Instead of trying to form specific rules for everyone to follow—*don't bribe, don't exploit the deceased on TV*—they propose that we build virtuous character. The idea is that people who *are* good will do the good and right thing, regardless of the circumstances: whether they're at home or abroad, whether they're trying to win new clients or making a decision about what kind of images are appropriate for public TV.

In a vague sense, we all know what it means to have a virtuous character; we all know people who can be counted upon to do the right thing. Think of a business situation where true character shines through. A local TV station has seen advertising revenue plummet and layoffs have to be made. Who should go? Should Jim get to stay because his wife just had their first child? Should Jane get to stay because she's fifty-seven and probably won't be able to find another job? Should John—who's a tireless worker and the station's best film editor—be laid off because he was hired only two months ago? It's a hard choice and there's no way to know for sure what's right. It is certain, however, that there are better and worse ways of handling the situation.

One strategy is to not think too much about it, to just know that two employees have to go, so you take the names that happen to come to mind, you send them an e-mail, and you instruct security to make sure they're escorted from the building. Then you go hide in the bathroom until they're gone. In other words, you weasel out. In the same situation, another person will draw up criteria for making the decision and will stand up and inform those who are being let go why the decision was made. The thoughts (complaints, regrets, excuses) of those being released will be honored and heard attentively, but the decision will stand. From the person in charge of deciding, there'll be honesty, respect, and firmness. This is virtue. You can't read it in a book, you can't memorize principles, and you can't just follow some precooked decision-making process. You have to have certain qualities as a person to do the right thing in a hard situation.

Virtue ethics is the idea that we can and should instill those qualities in people and then let them go out into the complex business world confident that they'll face dilemmas well. What decisions will they make? What will they do when faced with questions about who should be laid off or, in another

case, whether to hand over a bribe in a place where everyone is bribing? We don't know. But we rely on their good character to be confident they'll do right.

Under this conception, these are the primary tasks of ethics:
* Delineate what the virtues are.
* Provide experience using the virtues.

The experience is especially important because virtue isn't so much a natural characteristic like height or hair color; it's more of an acquired skill: something you need to work at, practice, and hone. Also, like many acquired skills, doing it—once a certain level of mastery has been reached—is rewarding or satisfying. Typically, a person driven by virtue has nurtured a moral instinct for acting in consonance with the virtues. Doing right feels right. Conversely, *not* acting in consonance with the virtues is discomforting; it leaves a bad taste in the mouth. At the risk of trivializing the subject, there's a very limited comparison that can be made between learning virtue and learning more rudimentary activities like golf or dancing. When someone has acquired the skill, hitting a good shot or taking the right steps in perfect time feels good. Conversely, missing a putt or stepping on your partner's foot leaves you consternated.

What Are the Virtues and Vices?
Every advocate of virtue ethics will present a constellation of virtues that they believe captures the essence of what needs to be acquired to *be* virtuous. Typically, there'll also be a set of anti-virtues or vices to be avoided to fill out the picture. Here's a set of virtues overlapping with what most proponents will offer:
* Wisdom (both theoretical and practical)
* Fairness
* Courage
* Temperance
* Prudence
* Sincerity
* Civility

On the outer edges, here's a common pair of vices to be avoided. Notice that what counts as a vice here isn't synonymous with the common use of the word, which implies a weakness of the physical body manifested as the inability to resist drunkenness, drugs, and similar:
* Cowardice
* Insensibility

How Do the Virtues and Vices Work in a Business Environment?

Wisdom as a virtue is frequently divided into theoretical and practical variations. Theoretical wisdom is what you get reading books and hearing college lectures. It's the acquired ability to concentrate and understand sentences like the one you're reading now, even though it's not very exciting and allows almost no cheap thrills—words like *sex* and *drugs* don't come up much. Those possessing theoretical wisdom know the scholarly rules of the world in the abstract but not necessarily in practice. In the world of business, for example, someone may be able to explain the fine points of Immanuel Kant's complicated and dense ethical ideas, but that doesn't mean they'll be able to apply the lessons when sitting in someone's office in a foreign country.

Practical wisdom (sometimes called prudence) is the learned ability to take a deep breath and respond to situations thoughtfully. For example, everyone feels like exploding sometimes, especially at work after you've had too much coffee and you didn't get the raise you wanted. After that, some guy in a meeting takes a cheap shot and jokes about how you didn't win an overseas account because you didn't bribe the right person. What do you do? Scream the guy's head off? Talk about it quietly after the meeting? Let it pass like nothing happened? Practical wisdom doesn't give an answer, but in the heat of the moment, it's the virtue of making the decision coolly, of doing something you won't regret later. Frequently, an association is set between practical wisdom and finding a spot between extremes. In this case, perhaps it would be excessive to go off right there in the meeting room (because the outburst would tend to confirm that you're not real smart), but it might also be excessive to let the jab go as though nothing had happened (because the same guy may feel emboldened to keep poking at you). So practical wisdom would be the ability to navigate a middle, prudent, route—perhaps one leading to the decision to discuss the matter quietly but sternly after the meeting.

Fairness is the virtue of judging people's acts dispassionately, evenhandedly, and from all points of view. When forming judgments about a potential client who seems to be asking for a bribe, the verdict is going to partially depend on where the client is. If he's in the United States, that's one thing; if he's in a country where clients customarily get cash under the table, that's another. No one is saying the first is wrong and the second right, but the different contexts need to be considered, and fairness is the ability to consider them, to make evenhanded judgments even in very different situations.

Courage is the virtue of moderate boldness. If you're an action crime reporter, you won't hide in a bush while pushing your cameraman out into the open to try to get some exciting footage. You won't, in other words, be a coward. At the same time, you won't be rash either, you'll know that sometimes you need to take a risk to get a good story, but it doesn't make a lot of sense to stand up and film from the middle of a gunfight.

Temperance is the virtue of self-control with respect to pleasure, especially the pleasures of the body and the senses. Curiously, Wallace Souza stands as an embodiment of this skill. As a major league drug dealer, he no doubt had constant access to good, cheap, feel-good substances. Even so, he managed to control his intake, not letting it interfere with his day job as a TV reporter, and his other day job as a legislator. More generally in the workplace, temperance mixes well with the learned ability to delay gratification. For example, doing good work is frequently rewarded with a better job, but it's hard to find someone who feels as though they get everything they deserve every time. Temperance enters here as the ability to bear down and keep trying. It's also, on the other side, the ability to know when a larger change (perhaps looking for work at another company) may be necessary to get ahead.

Sincerity is the ability to reveal yourself to others with confidence that you'll be respected. It fits between the extremes of frigidity and emoting. Souza or any TV reporter has to do more than just give cold facts; some human, emotional component must be added to the mix. On the other hand, no one's going to watch a reporter who arrives at a crime scene, reports that he feels sad, and breaks down in tears. Similarly in international business negotiations, to establish good contact across cultures, there has to be some sharing of humanity. You need to reveal what kind of food you like or something similar to the people on the other side. You don't want to go too far, though, and talk about how Japanese food reminds you of a childhood vomiting episode (especially when doing business in Tokyo).

Civility is the virtue of showing consideration for others without humiliating yourself. As a virtue it doesn't mean eating with the right fork or remembering to say "thank you" to clients. Instead, it's the disposition to show others that you take them seriously while also respecting yourself. This means establishing ground rules for behavior that are independent and neutral. In essence, the idea is, when having lunch with your boss, you don't eat like you're sitting in front of the TV in your family room; you respect her, and you expect the same from her. Civility is the virtue of habitually being and expressing yourself in a way that establishes your presence solidly without threatening or impinging on others.

Vices

On the outside of the virtues, there are vices. Just as the accomplishment of a virtue—acting in harmony with it—yields a sense of satisfaction and confidence that you're living well, living a good life, so too the vices produce a sensation of unease. It's not exactly a sting of conscience (like a child feels when caught stealing); it's more a sense of weakness, deflation, and failure. *Cowardice*, for example, is a vice. It may save your job if you mess up and don't confess to the problem being your fault; but for the person trained in virtue, the job will have lost its dignity. *Insensibility* is another vice. Had Souza understood that, he may have thought twice about those people's dead bodies he rolled out for television. He may have thought of their living parents, their children. And even if he hadn't, after he'd presented the images he would've felt that he'd lapsed, that he hadn't done as well as he could.

How Do I Become Virtuous?

Virtues aren't a list of actions you can write on the back of your hand and refer to; they're ways of living, and the only route to becoming virtuous is to actually live those ways. Every society will have its own institutions for instilling virtue, and within societies different institutions will seem more apt for some than for others. In the United States, the kinds of groups that are sought out as instillers of virtue include the family, churches, schools, sports teams, Boy and Girl Scouts, volunteer and community organizations, the armed forces, AmeriCorps, and similar.

Companies play a role, too. The virtuous organization will be led by individuals who *are* virtuous, and it will reward workers—at least partially—based on their progress toward being good people. This kind of organization won't rely on employee handbooks and compliance rules to dictate behavior; instead, it will devise strategies for nurturing the skills of a good life. They may include mentor programs, carefully calibrated increases in responsibility and independence for employees, and job performance assessments that not only measure numerical results but also try to gauge an individual's moral contributions to the organization's undertaking.

Finally, when confronted with moral questions—"What kind of images should I broadcast on my TV report?" or "Should I hand money under the table?"—the answer won't be *yes* or *no*. It's never a yes or no; it's always to do what my good character dictates.

An Advantage and Drawback of Virtue Ethics

The principal advantage of virtue ethics is its flexibility, the confidence that those who *are* virtuous will be equipped to manage unforeseeable moral dilemmas in unfamiliar circumstances. The principal drawback is the lack of specificity: the theory doesn't allow clear, yes-or-no responses to specific problems like whether I should offer a bribe.

KEY TAKEAWAYS

- Virtue ethics concentrates on forming good character and then trusting people to do the right thing. At the heart of ethics, the formation of good character replaces the defining of specific guidelines for action.
- A society's institutions play a key role in instilling virtue.
- The basic virtues tend to stress moderation, the ability to avoid taking extreme action in the face of dilemmas.
- Virtue ethics grants flexibility insofar as those who are virtuous should manage any situation well.

REVIEW QUESTIONS

1. Would you call Souza's colorful professional life a profile of the virtue of courage? Why or why not?
2. How might the virtue of civility come forward in the case of international bribery, in the case that you've gone abroad in pursuit of a contract and the prospective client demands some cash under the table?
3. What are some societal institutions you've come in contact with that could be understood as teaching virtue? What virtue(s) do they instill, and how?

4.5 Discourse Ethics

LEARNING OBJECTIVES

1. Define discourse ethics.
2. Show how discourse ethics can function in a business context.
3. Note an advantage and drawbacks to the theory.

What Is Discourse Ethics?

Proponents of discourse ethics reverse the order in which we normally address ethical uncertainties. Instead of starting with one theory or another and then taking it out into the world to solve problems, they start with a problem and try to create a moral structure to solve it. Ethical solutions become ad hoc, custom generated to resolve specific conflicts. It doesn't matter so much, therefore, that people come to an issue like bribery from divergent moral terrains because that difference is erased by the key element of discourse ethics: a foundational decision to cut away from old ideas and make new ones.

How Does Discourse Ethics Work?

When a dilemma is faced, those involved gather and try to talk it out. The discussion is constrained by two basic limits: conversation must be reasonable and civil, and the goal is a peaceful and consensual resolution. As long as these ideals control what we say, we can call the result ethically respectable.

Take the dilemma of international bribery: you've left your home office in New Jersey and gone to Somalia seeking to win construction business on a new airport. As the recent Transparency International *Corruption Perception Index* shows, [1] you're going to discover that its customary to pass some cash to a prospective client before he'll be willing to do serious business. Company policy, however, prohibits bribes. What do you do? If you're playing by hometown, American rules, your responsibility to company policy and to broad honesty and fairness requires you to walk away. But if you're playing Somali rules where greasing a palm seems fair and acceptable, your obligation to win contracts for the company that's paying your salary requires you to pass some cash. Discourse ethics comes in here with this: instead of trying to impose one side's convictions on the other, the effort will be to overcome the divide by constructing a new and encompassing moral framework through common agreement. American rules and Somali rules are both thrown out, and new ones get sought. Here are steps on the way:

1. **Define the immediate stakeholders**—that is, those who're most affected by the dilemma and may be gathered to resolve it. In this case, they include you and your client. Since your responsibilities to the company are reported through your supervisor, she too could be included.

2. **Establish a language for discussion.** In the international world this is actually a real problem. Sensibilities must be respected, and if you're in Somalia, just assuming that everyone will speak English might be a step backward. On the other hand, you probably don't speak Somali. This step then becomes a rehearsal for the larger problem—just as you're separated by moral codes, so too you're separated by languages—and you're going to have to find a solution. You may choose a third language, you may hire an interpreter, or maybe your client will be able to speak English. In any case, an agreement must be reached.

3. **Establish the goal**, which in discourse ethics is always the peaceful and consensual resolution to the dilemma.

4. **Define the problem.** Here, it's that when cash passes from you to the client, you feel like you're handing over an illegitimate bribe, but he feels like he's receiving a typical and acceptable gift. This stage of the process would require fairly lengthy elaborations by all those involved of exactly what they understand their obligations and interests to be. Your supervisor would need to explain the company policy, why it exists and how she's responsible for upholding it. Your client might point out that his salary is quite low, and the reason for that is simple: *everyone* accepts that his income will be supplemented by gifts. (Here, he might sound something like a waitress in New York City explaining to a foreign diner that her salary is absurdly small, but everyone expects there'll be some tipping, and it'll be more than two shiny quarters.) You, finally, explain how you're being stretched between two obligations: the one to respect company policy and the other to do the job of winning contracts.

5. **Propose solutions.** Discourse ethics is open, a kind of ethical brainstorming: those involved offer solutions, modify each other's' proposals, and try to discern whether a common ground can be mapped. In this case, someone may propose that the prospective client offer substantial evidence that money is expected and customary for someone in his position in Somalia. If the evidence can be produced, if it shows that payments are nearly universal, and it shows about how much they normally are, then perhaps all parties can be satisfied. Your supervisor, seeing that the amount actually forms part of a normal salary and isn't some extraordinary payment, may be able to reason that the money isn't a bribe because it's not doing what bribes typically do, which is afford an unfair advantage. In this case, if everyone's paying, then no advantage will be had. It's important to note here that the logic isn't *if everyone does it then it's all right*, because discourse ethics doesn't generalize like that. All conversations and solutions are about getting agreement on this one case. So your supervisor feels like handing cash over isn't a bribe any more than tipping a waitress is. Your client, having received the money, will obviously be satisfied. You, finally, will be free to fulfill your professional obligation to win the client without sacrificing your obligation to respect company policy and your obligation to yourself to work in a way that's honest.

If this—or any—solution is reached, then discourse ethics will have done what it promised: open a way for concerned parties to reach agreements alleviating conflicts. Whatever the agreement is, it's an ethically recommendable solution because the definition of what's ethically recommendable is just agreements reached through discussion.

An Advantage and Drawbacks to Discourse Ethics

The main advantage of discourse ethics is that the search for solutions opens the door all the way. Everything's on the table. That gives those involved just about the best hope possible for a resolution benefitting everyone joined in the discussion.

There are two main drawbacks to discourse ethics. The first is that everything's on the table. If what's morally acceptable can be as broad as anything a group agrees to, there's the potential for ugly solutions. On the face of it, the international bribery resolution—*hand some money over because it's not really a bribe and it's more like tipping a waiter*—seems pretty harmless. But it doesn't take much to see a slippery slope developing. If this kind of gifting is OK in Somalia where salaries are low, then why not in the United States too if it happens that a particular client has a low salary relative to others in that line of work? Or why not *every* client because, really, pay in that line of work is substandard? This can go on and on, and before you know it, the entire economy is corrupted. Obviously, that won't *necessarily* happen, but it could, and this is one of the reasons so many insist that any serious attempt to do ethics must begin with some basic defining of inbounds and out-of-bounds, some dividing of right from wrong. Discourse ethics doesn't do that.

The second drawback to discourse ethics is that for every ethical dilemma faced, you have to start over. Since the entire idea is to clear the deck and make a new solution, anyone facing a significant number of ethical dilemmas in their line of work is going to be constantly clearing the deck and beginning anew. Of course there may be some components of past discussions that could be carried forward—what you learned on the trip to Somalia may be helpful in Uzbekistan—but that doesn't change the fact that the ethical recommendation to start from zero and talk problems out is going to lead to a lot of talking.

KEY TAKEAWAYS

- Discourse ethics solves dilemmas by asking those involved to discuss the matter reasonably until they can find a consensual and peaceful solution.
- Discourse ethics allows tremendous latitude in the search for solutions to conflicts, but it risks allowing solutions that many would consider unethical.

REVIEW QUESTIONS

1. A five-step process was discussed to chart the advance of discourse ethics. Summarize each of these steps in your own words.
2. Describe a business situation where discourse ethics might work well. Why might it succeed?
3. Describe a business situation where discourse ethics might not work well. Why might it fail?

[1] "Corruption Perceptions Index 2009," Transparency International, accessed May 12, 2011, http://www.transparency.org/policy_research/surveys_indices/cpi/2009/cpi_2009_table.

4.6 Ethics of Care

LEARNING OBJECTIVES

1. Define the ethics of care.
2. Show how an ethics of care functions in a business context.
3. Note advantages and drawbacks to the theory.

The Rules of an Ethics of Care

Sometimes advocated under the titles of community ethics or feminist ethics, an ethics of care switches the focus of moral regulation from the individual to networks of social relationships. The basic question isn't about yourself; it's not "What should I do?" Instead, it's always about a larger us: "What should be done to nurture the connections among those of us closest to each other?"

A quick example dilemma: There's a flaming car wreck involving your sister and a Nobel Prize–winning medical scientist, and you have the strength to rescue only one of the two. Which should you save? A strict utilitarian—someone believing we should always act to bring the greatest good to the greatest number—will go for the scientist. Saving him will likely produce future medical breakthroughs in turn saving many others, which means the greater good will be served by dragging him out. But how many of us would actually do that? Wouldn't you go for your own sister before some scientist you've never met? And wouldn't most of the rest of us agree that we'd do the same thing? If the answer is yes, an ethics of care provides a way of understanding and justifying the impulse, which is, before anything else, to protect those bound to us.

There are three critical steps on the way to formalizing care as a coherent ethical orientation. Each is a shift away from traditional ethics.

1. At the center of attention, independent actors are replaced by a web of interrelated individuals. (Ethics is not about me and you; it's about us.)
2. The impartial application of abstract principles is replaced by the maintenance and harmonizing of human relationships. (Ethics is less about the fair imposition of rules and more about crafting social integration.)
3. Tensions between the rights of individuals get replaced by conflicts of responsibility to others in established relationships. (Ethical tensions aren't my rights versus yours; it's me being torn between those I care for.)

In the international bribery example up to now, we've treated all those involved as anonymous individuals: it hasn't mattered whether or how long they've known each other. It's only important to know that there's a supervisor X back at the US company headquarters, and there's the person Y who's gone abroad to win a contract, and there's the prospective client Z expecting a bribe. That's it. Maybe the three have never exchanged more than fifty words in a single conversation, or maybe they're all cousins who meet for family blowouts every two months. We haven't asked because it hasn't mattered what their personal relationships may be. That will have to change, however, within an ethics of care because there are no anonymous, single individuals: everyone has a place—near or far, integral or accidental—within a social network. For that reason, all morality resembles the car wreck. It's charged with human attachment, and because the ethics of care makes those attachments the center of deliberation, you have to know how people are related to each other before beginning to know how they should treat each other.

Turning this perspective toward the bribery example, the overseas client, let's say, is an old and loyal client of the company, and also one who's always gotten a little extra from one or another employee. About the company, it's not an anonymous multinational but a medium-sized, extended-family concern. Brothers, uncles, nieces and nephews, and a hodgepodge of others all work there. For years, it can be added, this overseas contract has been vital to the company's success. Now all this counts for something within an ethics of care. As opposed to the traditional idea that the best moral lessons show us how to coldly, impersonally, and impartially apply abstract rules, here we're checking to see who's involved, because the reason we have morality is to vitalize our human relationships.

An ethics geared to strengthen bonds isn't necessarily easy to enact. Take a company like Oil-Dri, about which *Forbes* recounts,

Oil-Dri now makes about $240 million a year in revenues. At the company's 50th anniversary party, the CEO asked anyone related to anyone else at the organization to stand up. Of the company's 700 or so employees, almost 500 rose. [1]

This is obviously an organization where relationships matter and where management is accounting for human concerns and networks when hiring people. No doubt there's a lot of camaraderie in this workplace, but imagines how difficult it must be to dole out promotions when everyone knows everyone else in that personal, almost familial way. Within a more traditional ethics, one of the first steps to making a promotion decision is to clear away all the personal stuff before evaluating each employee directly and simply assess his or her professional merits. Within an ethics of care, however, any promotion decision—more or less any decision at all, for that matter—is going to require the subtle, complex, and difficult balancing of many individual and highly emotional situations and circumstances.

Something similar happens within typical families. Most parents trot out the idea of treating all their children identically—they all get their first car at the same age and so on—but if a sibling has special problems at one stage of their development, they'll normally get special treatment in the name of preserving the family unit. The other brothers and sisters probably complain, but if they're old enough they understand that protecting those who are vulnerable is one of the first imperatives of caring for each other as a group. An ethics of care in essence takes that model from the family and extends it out into the world of business. Applying it to the promotion question, if there's a member of Oil-Dri saddled by, let's say, a difficulty with alcohol, then that might actually be a *positive* consideration within care-based thought. Promoting someone who has had problems and reinforcing their attempt to get past them may serve the general harmony of the entire group. As a result, someone who's less qualified in purely professional terms may get the promotion in the name of caring for the social web.

How Might the Case of International Bribery Be Managed within an Ethics of Care?

Traditionally, ethics features questions about the competing rights of individuals. For example, when I offer a bribe, am I impinging on the right of another to compete on a level playing field for the same business? Starting from an ethics of care poses a different question: does giving a bribe reinforce or weaken the bonds of human relationships defining my place in the world? The answer, obviously, depends. If the company is Oil-Dri where everyone's deeply connected, and it's an old client, and a little gift of cash has always been slid under the table, then the maintenance of that network's vitality and human health becomes a powerful argument in favor of continuing the practice.

Keeping the wheels turning isn't the only solution, however. Discomfort with doing something that seems underhanded may lead the overseas representative to try a different way of keeping the contract going, one that's based less on money under the table and more on aboveboard selling points. Quality of service as proven by work performed in previous years may offer a way to keep the business and personal link intact. There may be, in other words, a less controversial route to the same end of maintaining and enforcing existing relationships.

Alternatively, a different client, one not demanding a bribe, may be sought to purchase the company's goods and services. Nothing in an ethics of care requires those participating to preserve *every* bond. Sometimes it happens in families that a member becomes so toxic and damaging to the rest that the connection needs to be severed in the name of maintaining the larger whole. The overseas bribery relationship may be one of those cases. It's hard, of course, to break away, but there are other potential clients out in the world and going after them may, in the final analysis, do more for the social health of the core group than clinging to a problem at all costs.

Finally, enrolling in an ethics of care doesn't mean going blind to what's going on outside the circle of care. One fact from the larger world that should be taken account of comes from a recent article in the *Washington Post* about foreign business bribes: prosecutions of international bribery by the US government are picking up. [2] Ethical concerns should normally be distinguished from legal considerations, but there's no doubt that few events interrupt human relationships like a jail term. Cutting the bribery relationship, therefore, may be necessary regardless of how important the particular client and business are for the larger whole.

Conclusion. The activation of an ethics of care may justify continuing to pay money under the table. Or it may lead toward a less controversial way of maintaining the business relationship. Or it may cause a break between the company offering services and the overseas client demanding a bribe. There's no way to know for sure which path will be the right one, but in every case the choice will be made in the name of preserving and nurturing the human relationships surrounding the decision.

Advantages and Drawbacks of an Ethics of Care

The advantages of a care-based ethics include the following:

- It can cohere with what we actually do and think we ought to do, at least in cases like the car accident cited at this section's beginning. In a certain sense, it corresponds with our natural instincts to act in favor of and protect those under our care and those involved in our lives.

- It humanizes ethics by centering thought on real people instead of cold rules. Presumably, everyone agrees that ethics is ultimately about people: unlike the hard sciences, the end results of morality are tallied in human lives. To the extent that's right, an emphasis on care seems well suited to the general practice of ethics.

- It allows us to focus our energy and concern on those who are closest to us. Everyone knows that there's injustice in the world, just as we all know we can't solve every problem. The ethics of care allows us to focus our energy naturally on the most immediate human needs.

The main disadvantage of an ethics of care is that it threatens to devolve into tribalism: There's my group, and I take care of them. As for all the rest of you, you're in your groups and in charge of yourselves. This isn't *every man for himself*, but it comes close to *every social group for itself*.

KEY TAKEAWAYS

- An ethics of care makes the nurturing of our immediate communities and the protecting of those closest to us the highest moral obligation.
- In business, an ethics of care asks us to review decisions not in terms of hard rules but in terms of how they will affect the people with whom we share our lives.
- An ethics of care humanizes moral decisions, but it threatens tribalism.

REVIEW QUESTIONS

1. What are the three major steps an ethics of care takes away from most traditional theories? Can you put each one in your own words?
2. An ethics of care is frequently compared to the morality guiding a family. Can you think of another comparison that encapsulates how this ethics works?
3. Imagine that you had two parents and a sister working for Oil-Dri in the United States. The overseas client you've been sent to do business with is a half-brother from your father's first marriage. He demands a bribe. How could the ethics of care be used to justify accepting or refusing?

[1] Klaus Kneale, "Is Nepotism So Bad?" *Forbes*, June 20, 2009, accessed May 12, 2011, http://www.forbes.com/2009/06/19/ceo-executive-hiring-ceonewtork-leadership-nepotism.html.

[2] Carrie Johnson, "U.S. Sends a Message by Stepping Up Crackdown on Foreign Business Bribes," *Washington Post*, February 8, 2010, accessed May 12, 2011, http://www.washingtonpost.com/wp-dyn/content/article/2010/02/07/AR2010020702506.html.

4.7 The Cheat Sheet: Rules of Thumb in Applied Ethics

The following tables summarize the theories considered in this textbook. The first includes the traditional theories and the second encapsulates the contemporary theories built to respond to cultural relativism.

Table 4.1 The Traditional Theories

Name	Guidance for ethical action	Focus of our efforts	Typical questions asked in the effort to fulfill obligations	Conception of the person implied by the theory	Strengths and weaknesses	Type of theory
Duty	Learn the basic duties to ourselves and others, and obey them.	The duties.	To whom do I have obligations? What are the obligations? How do the obligations weigh against each other?	We are rational actors.	Gives clear guidance in many situations but is inflexible in the face of special cases.	Non-consequentialist
Fairness	Treat people identically unless they differ in ways relevant to the situation. (Treat equals equally and un-equals unequally.)	Resist prejudice and personal feelings.	Does everyone get an equal chance? (If they don't, how are the differences justified?)	We are rational actors.	Promises egalitarianism, but can be difficult to implement in complex reality.	Non-consequentialist
Kant	Learn the basic duties to ourselves and others, and obey them.	The categorical imperative in two articulations: actions must be universalizable *and* treat others as ends and never as means.	Is the act I'm considering universalizable? Am I being careful not to treat others as means to an end?	We are rational actors.	Gives clear guidance in many situations but is inflexible, especially in the face of special cases.	Non-consequentialist
Rights theory	Maximize freedom.	Learn the individual's basic rights, live them, and respect others' right to live them.	Does doing what I want impinge on the basic freedoms of others?	We are distinguished by the possession of dignity.	Allows individuality, but does little to resolve conflicts between individuals.	Non-consequentialist
Egoism	Increase my well-being and happiness.	Learn about my desires and welfare, and serve them	What makes me happy over the long term? How can I get that?	We are driven toward pleasure and away from pain.	Good for me in the short term, but might not help us live together as a society.	Consequentialist
Altruism	Increase the well-being and happiness of others.	Learn about others' desires and welfare, and serve them.	What makes others happy over the long term? How can I help them get that?	We are driven toward pleasure and	Others benefit, but it may be difficult to justify devaluing yourself.	Consequentialist

Name	Guidance for ethical action	Focus of our efforts	Typical questions asked in the effort to fulfill obligations	Conception of the person implied by the theory	Strengths and weaknesses	Type of theory
				away from pain.		
Utilitarianism	Increase the well-being and happiness of everyone collectively.	Learn about the desires and welfare of everyone, understood as an aggregate, and serve them.	What brings the greatest happiness and good to the greatest number over the long term? How can I help us get that?	We are driven toward pleasure and away from pain.	The general welfare is served, but injustices at the individual level may persist.	Consequentialist

Table 4.2 The Contemporary Theories Responding to Cultural Relativism

	Guidance for ethical action	Focus of our efforts	Typical questions asked in the effort to fulfill obligations	Strengths and weaknesses	Reaction to cultural relativism
Eternal return of the same	Be myself.	Think through the eternal return.	Would I do this if it had to be repeated in the same life, which recurred forever?	Maximizes individual authenticity but provides no specific recommendations for action.	Abandons morality altogether.
Cultural ethics	Follow local customs and practices.	Learn local customs and practices.	What do the locals do?	Helps you fit in but allows little hope for ethical improvement.	Accepts the proposal that moral rules are just a particular community's beliefs.
Virtue ethics	Develop good moral character.	Learn and practice the virtues.	Am I acting with integrity and in accordance with values learned?	Allows flexibility but provides little specific guidance.	Tries to protect against cultural relativism by developing an adoptable but consistently moral character.
Discourse ethics	Produce solutions to moral dilemmas.	Talk it out: use rational conversation to reach a peaceful, consensual agreement.	What do you think? How about this possibility?	Provides a broad range of possible solutions but every conflict must be addressed from scratch.	Replaces a culture's moral rules with the attempt to fabricate new rules to function in specific situations.
Ethics of care	Nurture and protect immediate relationships.	Respond to the needs of those nearest us.	Which solution preserves healthy and harmonious relationships among those involved?	Humanizes morality but risks tribalism.	Replaces a culture's moral rules with loyalty to those whose lives touch our own.

4.8 Case Studies

I Wouldn't Change a Thing

Tamica Tanksley graduated from Temple University in Philadelphia in 2000. About a decade later she worked her way into an important role in the office of Pennsylvania State Senator Vincent Hughes: she's co-director of his community affairs outreach and efforts. Though not a celebrity or mightily important in politics, what she's done with her life up to now earned her a brief write-up and a chance to answer a few interview questions in Temple's Internet Alumni magazine. [1]

She describes her job responsibilities as linking the senator with "community leaders, educators, religious organizations, constituents and various institutions within the public and private sector." It all comes naturally to her. As she puts it, "I didn't choose politics, politics chose me. And if I had to do it all over again, I wouldn't change a thing…Working in the government sector where my daily responsibilities afford me the opportunity to empower and inspire everyday people is a career that ignites my passion for people."

It's not just heavy, public service trudging, though; Tanksley also finds the job "fun" because it allows her "creative juices to flow into a sea of possibilities," and in a different part of the interview she calls the work, in a sense, victorious: "As a citizen and voter, I've learned that this game of life is not won by standing on the sidelines. In order to provoke change and improve the quality of life for everyone, we must get into the game because victories are won on the field."

How'd she get the job? The way a lot of people start off in politics, by serving in that same office as a volunteer worker. Finally, since it's a Temple University website, the interviewer tries to get in a plug for the school and succeeds with this memory Tanksley produces of Dr. Jean Brody's public relations course and the prof's infamous (at least on the Temple campus) red pen: "While I was often saddened by my white paper being flooded by red pen marks, I quickly learned that Dr. Brody and her red pen refined the best in me. With each passing assignment, the red marks lessened and my knowledge and experience increased. Moreover, it was the red that encouraged me to do my best work, which has ultimately contributed to the dedicated worker I am today."

QUESTIONS

1. Tanksley reports about her young life up to this point that "if I had to do it all over again, I wouldn't change a thing." Can you use this as a point of departure for

   o defining Nietzsche's eternal return and showing how it works?
   o characterizing Tanksley's professional life as one fit for approval by Nietzsche's eternal return?

2. The values guiding Wallace Souza's work as a news reporter in remote Brazil—especially the kinds of images judged appropriate for TV there—are quite different from those guiding TV reporting in the United States. Why does Nietzsche believe this kind of cultural clash is a reason to subscribe to the eternal return and simultaneously abandon traditional ethical theories, which attempt to pertain universally?

3. Tanksley reports about her young life up to this point that "working in the government sector where my daily responsibilities afford me the opportunity to empower and inspire everyday people is a career that ignites my passion for people." How might an advocate of the eternal return respond to this sentiment? Explain.

4. Whose life seems more in tune with how you imagine yourself living the eternal return, Souza's or Tanksley's? Why?

5. For virtue ethics, knowing what to do with your life—responding to its problems, choosing goals to reach for—isn't something you can just figure out no matter how intelligent you may be or how many ethics classes you've taken. To succeed, you also need a good society, one that does two things:
   o Teaches the virtues through its institutions
   o Provides a way to practice using the virtues

   How could Dr. Jean Brody be considered a teacher of virtue? What particular virtues did she teach Tanksley, and how did she provide a way to practice using them?

Mordidas

In Mexico City, police salaries are extremely low. They live decently enough, though, by adding bribes (*mordidas* in Spanish) to their wages. During a typical week they pull in bribe money that more or less equals their monthly salary. All the locals know how it works, especially when it comes to the most avid collectors, the traffic cops. In the standard procedure, the officer pulls a car over, takes out his codebook, walks up, and hands it to the driver. Ostensibly, he's allowing confirmation that the law actually prohibits whatever was done. This is what actually happens: the driver slips about fifty pesos (a little under five dollars) into the book, closes it, hands it back, and is free to go. [2] The practice is so routine that frequently the procedure is abbreviated and participants don't even bother trying to hide the payoff or going through the codebook pantomime. They may approach the officer's patrol car and directly drop the money onto the guy's lap. [3] Or they may stay in their own car and just hand cash out to be directly pocketed. [4] Regardless, the transaction is smooth and efficient.

Despite the bribery's efficiency and its penetration to society's core, not everyone in Mexico City is happy with the constant mordidas. According to a story in the city's largest circulation daily, a mayor in one of the suburbs decided to take a lonely stand against the informal police action. Since *all* the police are in on it, he couldn't resort to an *Untouchables*-styled internal affairs operation. And since all the citizens considered the payoffs perfectly normal, he couldn't appeal to them for help either. Really, he was left with only one choice. To interrupt the habit, he made traffic tickets illegal. His suburb became a free driving zone where anybody could do whatever they wanted in their car and the police couldn't respond. A lot happened after that, but there's no doubt that the payoffs stopped. [5]

QUESTIONS

1. About the bribery in Mexico City, not only is it the way things have been done as long as anyone can remember, but the process actually makes a lot of sense; it's even very economically efficient because the middlemen are being cut out. Instead of having to pay an administrative staff to process traffic tickets, then accept deposits into the city's account, and then redistribute the money back out as part of police salaries, here the money goes straight into the officer's pocket.
    o   What is cultural relativism, and how does the vision of ethics associated with it diverge from the traditional ethical theories?
    o   The Mexico City process of getting and paying off a traffic ticket is different from the US process. What values and advantages can be associated with the process in Mexico City? How can it be justified in ethical terms?
    o   The Mexico City process of getting and paying off a traffic ticket is different from the US process. What values and advantages can be associated with the process in the United States? How can it be justified in ethical terms?
    o   The Mexico City process of getting and paying off a traffic ticket is different from the US process. How can that difference be converted into an argument in favor of the idea that cultural relativism is the right way to look at things? Does the argument convince you? Why or why not?
    o   Your company, FedEx, has sent you to Mexico to open a branch in Mexico City. You'll be there for

three months, with all expenses paid. Can you make the case with a culturalist ethics that FedEx should reimburse not only your car rental and gas but also the two mordidas you had to pay even though you obviously don't have any receipts?
    o   After you return from your successful overseas experience, FedEx assigns you to train a set of recruits to go to Mexico and open more branch offices. When you to talk about the police and mordidas, would you counsel a culturalist approach, or would you advise them to go by the book (as that phrase is understood in the United States)? How would you justify your decision?
    o   For owners of office buildings in Mexico City, FedEx is a great client. They pay their rent every month and they're probably willing to negotiate an amount in dollars, which is extremely attractive because the Mexican peso is prone to the occasional and steep devaluation. As a result, if you're opening up a new FedEx office, you're going to have building owners lining up, trying to rent you space. Does a decision to play by local rules and pay mordidas to cops also allow you to play by local real estate rules, which allow you to take a generous cash gift in exchange for renting in one building instead of the place across the street? Why or why not?
    o   You are sent to Mexico City to rent office space. You find two equally good spaces only distinguished by the fact that one owner offers a larger bribe than the other. No one's watching, no one will ever know, you can do whatever you want. What do you do? Why?

2. Think of yourself as a virtue ethicist.
    o   Very quickly, what are some of the virtues you personally attempt to live by, and what social institutions played a role in shaping your character?
    o   If you were sent to Mexico on a work assignment and found yourself in the situation typically faced by local drivers after being caught driving a bit fast, how would you handle the situation? Which virtues might come into play?
    o   Most advocates of virtue ethics believe companies—like other organizations including schools, churches, and community associations—play a role in instilling virtue. If you were training FedEx recruits destined to open branch offices in Mexico City and you wanted to prepare them for the ethical challenges of bribery, what virtues would you seek to instill in them? Can you think of any life experiences that some recruits may have had that

may have formed their character to respond well to the situation on the Mexican streets?

o   The mayor in suburban Mexico City who decided to cancel traffic tickets was, in fact, fighting against what he saw as corruption. Most advocates of virtue ethics believe government organizations play a role in instilling virtue in its citizens. Could this action be considered part of that effort? What virtues might it instill? How would it help people become better practitioners of those virtues?

3.   The video *Mordida in the Booklet* (http://businessethicsworkshop.com/Chapter_4/C4.html) shows a motorcycle officer getting paid off. One curious aspect is how long and intense the discussion stretches between the officer and the pulled-over driver. What they're doing is negotiating the amount. The fifty peso price tag is a good average, but the number can drop or climb depending on the give and take. [6]

o   What is the five-step process of discourse ethics? How could this bribery negotiation be understood within it?

o   According to Transparency International's *Corruption Perception Index*, Mexico is a place where people doing business make many informal agreements involving bribery, kickbacks, insider dealing, and all sorts of similar practices. Except for the fact that those involved are wearing suits, most of these scenes resemble the one between the motorcycle police officer and the driver: people talk for a while, come to a mutually satisfying, peaceful conclusion, and some money changes hands. Do you see this as an indictment of discourse ethics, a justification of the approach, or something else? Justify.

4.   In the newspaper article about the Mexico City suburb where the Mayor decided to ban traffic tickets, the reporter interviewed a police officer described as "an old transit cop whose juicy bribes had helped buy his gold necklaces and bracelets." This was the old cop's reaction to the situation (translated from Spanish): "I got my buddies together and I told them, 'This sucks, now what're we going to do for money?'"

An ethics of care shifts the focus of moral thought away from the fair imposition of rules and toward the maintenance of immediate personal relationships. Ethics isn't about treating everyone equally so much as it is about keeping companions together.

o   Listening to this officer, who do you suppose exists within his web of social responsibility?

o   Assuming this officer practiced the ethics of care, would he treat these two drivers differently after pulling them over: his nephew and some out-of-towner he's never seen before? Why might he (not) treat them differently? Are there circumstances under which he'd actually demand more money from the nephew? What could those be?

o   According to the newspaper article, in the first two months of ticketless existence in the suburb, about two hundred people were struck by moving vehicles, and twenty were killed. From the perspective of the ethics of care, can these numbers be used to form an argument against this policy and in favor of a return to the previous, corrupted reality?

Money for Nothing

In his blog *the z spot*, author Z raises two questions about people receiving unemployment paychecks. Both are laced with suspicion of fraud. First, people who are collecting unemployment checks are required to show they're at least trying to get a job, but Z writes that some are "showing up for interviews in jeans and t-shirts." Then he asks, "Do these people really want the job, or are they just showing up to say that they are actively seeking work?" [7]

He goes from there to a second critical point. "Some people," Z says, "are collecting unemployment checks even though they're actually working." What they do is turn in their unemployment form listing the days they worked, and those are deducted from the check they receive. That sounds OK in the abstract, but, he adds, "The problem is that these people who are 'on call' are not taking shifts that are offered to them. Those shifts don't get deducted from their unemployment. So, while there are people who are actually unemployed, struggling and looking to find work, there are Union employees sitting at home deciding when they do and don't want to come in. And collecting unemployment."

From the posting's response section, here are two contributions:

1.   It's not easy for me to swallow that my taxes are supporting people who could be working.

2.   I have a question. I live in Wisconsin and I know of somebody who is collecting unemployment but is not actually going to any job interviews or is even applying for jobs. Is this illegal? If so, how can I report this without them knowing?

QUESTIONS

1.   If you were using the eternal return to chart your way through life, would you have any problem "sitting at

home deciding when you do and don't want to come in while collecting unemployment"? If you're all right with that, how would you respond to the complaint from the response section that someone is paying taxes to support your lifestyle?

2. Thinking about the people showing up for job interviews in jeans and t-shirts, what might be lacking in their character according to a virtue ethicist? If the government is one of those institutions proponents of virtue look to for the instillation of good character, what might the government do in this situation in the name of encouraging virtue?

3. The second cited response to Z is a question about how an unemployment cheat can be reported "without them knowing."
   o About this silent reporting, why is this *not* what a proponent of discourse ethics would recommend?
   o How could the five-step process of discourse ethics be applied to the situation? Would the guy complaining about paying taxes be included in the discussion? What kind of proposals might be voiced to rectify the situation?

4. Starting from the ethics of care, is there a situation you could imagine that would justify the actions of workers who take some shifts but decline others, and collect unemployment for those declined hours?

A Single Parent in the Army

The post of cook in the mess hall is probably one of the Army's least dangerous assignments, the closest you get to actual battle is a food fight, but it's still a military job where you go and do what your orders command. For Specialist Alexis Hutchinson, a twenty-one-year-old Army cook, that meant catching a flight to Afghanistan. She missed hers, though, intentionally. She regretted abandoning her unit, but felt she had no choice. The single mother of a ten-month-old, she says she couldn't find anyone to care for her child during the absence; the only potential help, her mother, was already overwhelmed by caring for three other relatives with health problems. Hutchinson's fear, according to her lawyer, was that if she showed up at the airport, the Army "would send her to Afghanistan and put her son with child protective services."

For its part, a military spokesman says, "the Army would not deploy a single parent who had nobody to care for a child." The situation is under review, but for the present, just like anyone else who refuses deployment, she's under military arrest on her base in Georgia. [8]

QUESTIONS

1. Virtue ethics
   o The military is cited by virtue ethicists as a potential character-building institution, one of the places a society molds a good citizenry. What are some of the virtues the military could be expected to instill? How are those reflected in this situation?
   o Families are a cited source of virtue. What values should we expect family life to instill? How are those virtues reflected in this situation?
   o Is there any way to bring the military virtues and the family virtues together for Hutchinson? If so, what might it be? If not, why not and what should she do?

2. Proponents of discourse ethics walk through a five-step process on the way to reaching a negotiated settlement to moral conflicts. What might the five steps look like here?

3. One of the objections to discourse ethics is that it can set up a slippery slope—that is, the people involved can form a solution that bends the rules a little bit, and next someone else wants a little flexibility too, and then someone wants a little more, and before long, the rules have completely disappeared and everyone's doing whatever they want. Could you sketch out how this process could happen here, with the end result being the Army more or less losing the values at the core of its existence?

4. Ethics of care
   o One of the key elements composing an ethics of care and distinguishing it from traditional ethical theories is this: At the center of attention, independent actors are replaced by a web of interrelated individuals. Ethics, in other words, isn't about me and you, it's about us. In Hutchinson's case, she finds herself in the midst of at least two networks of "us," two communities of people to whom she owes an allegiance and care. Describe these communities and the links binding them.
   o Another of the key elements composing an ethics of care and distinguishing it from traditional ethical theories is this: The impartial application of abstract principles is replaced by the maintenance and harmonizing of human relationships. Ethics, in other words, is less about the fair imposition of rules and more about crafting social integration. Can you find an example of this conflict between an ethics of rules on one side, and an ethics of relationships on the other, in Hutchinson's situation?

- o Another of the key elements composing an ethics of care and distinguishing it from traditional ethical theories is this: Tensions between the rights of individuals get replaced by conflicts of responsibility to others in established relationships. Ethical tensions, in other words, aren't my rights versus yours, it's me torn between those I care for. In the case of Hutchinson, how is she torn?
- o In general, do you believe there's a place for an ethics of care in the military? If so, where? If not, why not?

[1] "Tamica Tanksley, SCT '00," Temple University, accessed May 12, 2011,
http://www.myowlspace.com/s/705/index.aspx?sid=705&gid=1&pgid=1021&cid=1612&ecid= 1612&ciid=3725&crid=0.

[2] Business Ethics Workshop video, accessed May 12, 2011,
http://businessethicsworkshop.com/Chapter_4/Mordida%20in%20the%20booklet.html.

[3] Business Ethics Workshop video, accessed May 12, 2011,
http://businessethicsworkshop.com/Chapter_4/How_to_purchase_a_police_ officer.html.

[4] Business Ethics Workshop video, accessed May 12, 2011,
http://businessethicsworkshop.com/Chapter_4/Quick_mordida.html.

[5] Alejandro Almazán, "Fin de la mordida," *El Universal*, November 16, 2003, accessed May 12,
2011, http://www2.eluniversal.com.mx/pls/impreso/noticia.html?id_nota = 54910&tabla=ciudad.

[6] Business Ethics Workshop video, accessed May 12, 2011,
http://businessethicsworkshop.com/Chapter_4/Mordida%20in%20the%20booklet.html.

[7] Business Ethics Workshop, accessed May 12, 2011,
http://businessethicsworkshop.com/Chapter_4/Unemployment_fraud.html.

[8] "Mother Refuses Deployment," *New York Times*, November 16, 2009, accessed May 12,
2011, http://www.nytimes.com/2009/11/17/us/17soldier.html.

NOTES:

Chapter 5
Employee's Ethics: What's the Right Job for Me?

Chapter Overview

This chapter examines some ethical decisions facing employees. It considers the values that underlie and guide choices about the kind of work you choose to pursue.

5.1 Finding Jobs to Want
LEARNING OBJECTIVES

1. Delineate ethical dilemmas and considerations in job seeking.
2. Discuss how values guide the search for a job.
3. Define job sequencing.

What Kind of Work Is Out There?
A question posed on a web discussion board: *What Is Your Nightmare Job?* Here are some answers:

*   Lung gunner (in a poultry processing plant: ram a nozzle down the chopped neck of a chicken and suck out the lungs)
*   Roofer (Miami, summertime)
*   Urinalysis monitor (watch guys pee for eight hours, making sure no one's switching their own for some friends who hasn't been using drugs)
*   Toll booth operator (apparently evil drivers heat quarters with cigarette lighters and drop them into the hands of unsuspecting operators) [1]

That last part about hot coins may be urban legend, but no matter what, there are jobs on the list that are going to make you cringe.

The *Wall Street Journal* has a similar list, but theirs includes both a top and bottom twenty—the best and worst jobs you can try to get or struggle to avoid.[2] Here are a few from one group:

*   Child-care worker
*   Lumberjack
*   Butcher
*   Seaman
*   Nuclear decontamination tech
*   Nurse
*   Firefighter

And a few from the other group:

*   Actuary
*   Parole officer
*   Accountant
*   Medical laboratory technician
*   Paralegal assistant
*   Meteorologist
*   Historian

Can you tell which jobs belong in the twenty best and which are among the twenty worst? You might have a fix on the answer, but probably there's one or two on each list that don't seem to fit. That's because once you get away from the extremes—the horribly bad and enviously good jobs—it's difficult to define exactly what counts as good work.

Let's take a look at two jobs: child-care worker and actuary. It's probably true that no one really likes changing diapers at the day care center, and certainly it's smellier and dirtier than being an actuary, which is a statistical job. Actuaries take a calculator and reams of data and try to figure out how old people are likely to be when they die. This is important information for companies selling life insurance since they've got to make sure their clients live long enough—and *pay* long enough—to more than cover the lump sum that gets doled out at the end. Now there's a fair amount of money at stake here, and that's why good actuaries get paid big money. The money is one reason being an actuary gets ranked as one of the best jobs by the *Wall Street Journal*. So the actuary advantages are the money, it's not stinky work, and also it's worth noting that there's not much stress since no one will know for sure whether your calculations are right or wrong for decades. Add it all up and you've got a potentially desirable job and career path, the kind you may want to put at the center of your working life.

Still, is it *really* better than a bottom-twenty job as a day care worker? If you do go the day care route, it's true that you've got to wash your hands constantly, but the rest of the day, being with excited children, helping them take their first steps, recite the alphabet, and learn how to play with one another, that must be worth *something*; there must be a human, emotional reward in it. Undeniably, when you punch out from the day care center on Friday night you won't have as much money to spend as your friend whose charting future death rates, but it's also true that when you come back on

Monday you'll be engaged with young lives instead of death. You'll be human for the day instead of a calculator.

On the other hand, no one likes poop under the fingernails. It's hard to get away from that.

Finally, what's really curious about that first list taken from the Internet discussion board is that for almost all of them, there's some lone voice speaking up in favor in the comments part of the web page. A toll booth operator, for example, wrote in to say that he likes his job because there's no boss staring over his shoulder. And roads don't go out of business, so he doesn't have to worry too much about corporate downsizing or economic recessions. Nearly every job, it seems, looks OK to *someone*. Even in the worlds of lung gunners and urinalysis monitors, there are people who are decently happy with what they're doing.

Why Is a Career Decision Ethical Instead of Just a Personal Decision about Jobs?

Normally we think of ethics as providing guidelines for how to treat other people—don't steal, don't lie. But ethics is also about how we treat ourselves and the responsibilities we have to ourselves. One of the deepest of the responsibilities is making thoughtful and independent decisions about what's worth doing and what isn't. Narrowing this to economic reality, the most tangible choice you're going to have to make is *where am I going to go to work when I wake up in the morning?* This decision—choosing a job and a career path—is about *value*. Every time the alarm goes off, you affirm what definitely matters in your life and what's really not so important.

These value judgments are rehearsed in comparing the so-called bottom-twenty job in the day care center with the so-called top-twenty job of an actuary. There are big advantages to being an actuary: money and relatively fixed hours (no parents get stuck in traffic and leave you with a screeching three-year-old until 8:00 p.m.). But day care also has advantages: you work in a life-affirming profession while reaping the human reward of helping children learn.

It's true that on paper being an actuary probably looks better. But life doesn't happen on paper. That's why, every day, people make the decision to go work at the day care center, despite everything. Or to be a teacher at an inner-city junior high school. Or to be a lumberjack because the opportunity to work outdoors outweighs the sore muscles. The possibilities are nearly endless.

In the end, you're the only one who can decide what to do when the alarm goes off, and you have an ethical responsibility to yourself to make the best decision you can.

Seven Values for Ranking Jobs

To start thinking about jobs in terms of the values they respond to, these questions are pivotal. For me, how important is it that my work

1. is meaningful,
2. allows leisure time,
3. accumulates money,
4. bestows power,
5. radiates prestige,
6. is comfortable,
7. provides security?

The question about meaningful work is the hardest to cleanly answer. Even defining exactly what counts as "meaningful" isn't easy. Definitely, its work that holds significance for you or the larger community apart from how much you're paid, how big your office is, how long your vacations stretch. Still, it's difficult to pin down exactly what counts as a meaningful job. Unlike money, which you can just add up, meaning is more like a color: hard to describe, changes a bit depending on the light and people tend to have their own palettes of good and bad.

On her blog, Kendra Kinnison writes that she "believes her purpose in life is to use her ability to discover connections and present them in an innovative way to support the creation and building of healthy businesses and to inspire others to accept Jesus Christ and to discover and utilize their gifts." [3]

She's got it down. There's nothing about salary or how many employees she has working underneath her. She *does* want to be in business; it's not like her religion has led her off to be a missionary. But at the same time she wants to work on her terms and within her priorities. Probably, there are career slots where she wouldn't fit too well (imagine her trying to help others and spread her faith while working at a used car dealership), but maybe starting up a local day care center would suit her ideals. True, the *Wall Street Journal* tells us that are a bad job, but it doesn't sound like it would be a bad one for her.

Look at the Greenpeace recruitment page: http://greenpeace.org/international/about/jobs. Their job openings read like anti-ads, like they're trying to *discourage* your application. There are some uplifting parts about "challenging work," but nothing about the potential for huge, year-end bonuses, or rapid advancement, or generous health insurance, or comfortable working conditions. In all those terms, working for Greenpeace sounds pretty bleak. Which is part of the reason it's so clear that this is a job for people who want meaning in their professional lives, a purpose separate from their own comfort, and one involving the environment?

Not all meaningful work has to be based on faith or tied to internationally known advocacy organizations. Chances are there's a woman not too far from where you live who's in the music business at the grassroots level: she offers piano lessons. Knock on her door and ask why she does it year after year; she may say she believes in music, its beauty, and its contribution to what she considers a full life. Your college athletic director might say something similar about sports. Or go to the nearest farmer's market—you won't find a lot of money changing hands; it's definitely not big business, but you'll probably run into someone eager to discuss the virtues of organic food in terms that sound more like a crusade than a menu choice.

Actually, organic food *is* big business. Beyond seeds in the fields and the scattered crates of the farmers' market, there's a growing, and growingly profitable business in the massification of the organic. Anyone walking through the local Whole Foods will see a lot of the color green. What won't be seen—but what's definitely up above—is an impressive corporate structure with big-salary managers making million-dollar stocking decisions every day. As far as money goes, they're doing well for themselves—like any multibillion-dollar corporation, Whole Foods pays its leading executives big money. [4] But hunched over a desk and tapping on a keypad, hasn't their work been bleached of the meaning and devotion that abides with the vegan wearing dirty overalls and trying to sell strawberries in an empty parking lot Saturday mornings? Maybe. Or maybe not. Meaningful work doesn't *require* that the only jobs you'll accept are low paying.

More jobs and kinds of work could be added here, but whatever you believe in, you should be able to find some employment that lets you approach it. As for how close you can get to truly meaningful work that will probably depend to some extent on trade-offs, on how much you're willing to give up in terms of leisure time, job security, and other comforts. Regardless, the real key is that meaningful work sets a specific purpose *before* everything else. With respect to lining up a career path, you don't start with a list of jobs and then find one that suits your interests; it's the opposite: you start with your deep interest and then find a job that lets you pursue it.

Finally, two cautionary points: While it's true that people devoted to meaningful work frequently sacrifice money, leisure time, and job security, the logic doesn't work the other way. Most of the time, low pay, short vacations, and a constant threat of unemployment don't mean you've chosen a noble career; they just mean you've got a crappy job.

And on the other side, there *are* the holy grails out there. Probably, some higher-ups at Whole Foods got into the line of work because they find the promotion of organic food meaningful, and they ended up with enviable salaries as well (in other words, they're in it for the organic cause more than the money, but they're happy to get the money). In a different direction, Michael Jordan loved basketball and also ended up getting paid handsomely to play. The photographer Annie Leibovitz loves and is dedicated to photography, but she's not making many sacrifices to do it: traveling to exotic places, living well, and meeting interesting people. Former vice president Al Gore believes in saving the planet as much as any sweating deckhand on the Greenpeace boat; the difference is he wrote a book about it that sold millions of copies and made him millions of dollars.

Conclusion about meaningful work: dedicating your professional life to a cause or activity that you believe in doesn't mean low wages and long hours. A lot of times it does, but that's not the point.

Another question shaping job seeking is leisure time. How important is it? In a sense, this is the mirror image of meaningful work. If you believe in something like promoting organic food, playing basketball, taking pictures, saving the planet, or even watching game shows on TV, it's perfectly reasonable to find a job in some other field that provides the income you need in the fewest hours possible and then lets you get out and do what you really want with the rest of your time. More or less, what you say here is I'm just going to X out that part of my life where I'm working. In the extreme case, the attitude is, "I don't care how bad it is, I just want to get through it."

The Discovery Channel series *The Deadliest Catch* about crab fishing in the Arctic shows how cold, smelly, and ugly work can be; but a few months of it and you get a year's worth of wages and the free time to spend it. One important concept here is instrumentalism, which means that work becomes an instrument—a tool allowing you to get or do something else.

The third question about jobs and values involves money. Like sacrificing hours of work to get leisure, punching the clock to accumulate cash makes your job an instrument. Money is also the easiest way to organize your professional life. You can count it; if one job pays more than another, its better.

But this easiness can also be a trap. For anyone just out of college and facing a hazy and unclear world where all the decisions seem so difficult, it's easy to get tempted by the smoothest route: just check the possibilities out there and go for whatever pays the most. At least that way you know you're not messing things up completely. So there's something to be said for going that safe route, but this also needs to get underlined. From the perspective of your responsibilities to yourself, the better-paying job is only the better job *if you've already made the decision* to value career options in terms of how much they pay.

There's nothing necessarily wrong with that decision. Of course the Hollywood movies and the Habitat for Humanity volunteers hanging around campus looking for recruits are all going to tell you that you've got to follow your heart, do meaningful work, and contribute to society. And if you face them up and flat out say you're just in it for the money, there are always going to be whispers about greed and accusations like being a sellout.

In defense of money, though, dedicating your career to getting it makes a lot of sense, and it can do a lot of good, too:

- If you've got student loans, it's good to be able to pay them back, as it's the fulfillment of a duty to fidelity.
- If you do feel a need to support causes like protecting the planet, most advocacy organizations will be happy to receive a cash donation. The truth is, they'd probably rather have the money than a few volunteer hours.
- Making money means participating in an economy that's getting richer, and doesn't that end up making life better for everyone? Faced with Habitat for Humanity volunteers who ask you to join them in building shelter for the needy, couldn't you even make the case that contributing to an economy that functions well actually helps people more—at least in the long run—by producing jobs so they can purchase their own home instead of relying on volunteers to build one?
- You may have children. Clothes are expensive. Summer camp is expensive. The holidays are expensive. True, little ones might still be a long way off, but when they come, a new set of responsibilities arrive, too, and just about the only way you can begin preparing for them

now is by making sure that, on the money side at least, the house is in order.

There's more to this list, but when it comes to choosing a job with an eye on the salary factor, it's important to spend some time with this question: *Why is it, exactly, that money has value for me?*

If you're looking for power, you could do a lot worse than being a judge. True, you spend your days listening to lame excuses for shoplifting and the bogus assurances of repentance from drug dealers, but with the pound of a (little wooden) hammer, you get a police officer to rumble over and haul people off to jail. In court, even someone mouthing off is enough to slap them with contempt and assign them to a few hours of lockup.

The military, politics, policing: all these fields will appeal to anyone who sets the possession of power as one of the most valuable aspects of a job. Less directly, people in the news media can decide which issues center popular attention by mentioning them on the radio broadcast, the TV news show, or the current affairs blog. That's serious influence, shaping what people are thinking and talking about in our shared world.

Obviously, bosses in most fields of work have power. Usually they like to say that they have "responsibilities," but frequently part of holding the responsibility to carry out a project is having the ability to hire and fire the people participating. Advertising is also about power. It's not as explicit as the ability to get someone hauled off to jail or sent to the unemployment line, but masters of the craft can get people to believe that they really *need* some electronic device that they didn't even know existed thirty seconds ago. There's power in schools, too. If you're in this class as a distribution requirement, that means someone has decided for you what you're supposed to know.

The bottom line is that power—and the various jobs that grant it—exist in many places, and some are more transparent holders of force than others. So one of the keys to understanding power as a career option is being sensitive to the different ways it works. Commanding a platoon of soldiers fits the bill, but so does sending out an army of TV commercials.

Even more than money, power is vilified as a career goal. If you tell your friends that all you care about is money, they might think you're greedy, but they'll probably keep in touch over the years, figuring you could invite them to your

Hamptons beach house for a great weekend. If you tell everyone that all you care about is power, though, they'll probably think you're weird and drop you off their Facebook friends list.

The image we get from popular culture of a power-hungry careerist is a drooling madman with clenched fists, too much caffeine, and maybe a copy of Machiavelli's *The Prince* on the nightstand. And it's not just the movies. Deborah Gruenfeld, a professor in the Stanford Graduate School of Business and expert in the psychology of power in the workplace believes: "Those in positions of power can be observed to act in a manner that is peculiar and that often has no connection to reality." [5]

Ouch.

There must be *something* there, though. If power were really so bad, we wouldn't have to worry about it since no one would want it. But people *do* want it; it's just that hardly anyone wants to admit it.

In a sense, prestige is the opposite of power. Almost everyone says they'd love a job granting prestige, but not many are willing to give up much for it. Going all the way back to the *Wall Street Journal* article, "historian" is on the top-twenty list of desirable jobs, and "philosopher" is there, too, on the longer, uncut version of the story. Salary isn't the reason they're included among the twenty best, and there's not much direct power to those jobs either. (Despite what you think, professors don't get any rush out of failing people. Only rarely, anyway.) There *is* job security if you're a tenured university professor, but the main benefit of a prestigious job is the "wow" factor:

> *"What do you do for a living?"*
> *"I'm a historian."*
> *"Wow."*

After a few minutes in which everyone in the conversation acknowledges that this is very interesting, the talk switches back to more normal topics. Later on, people quietly wonder why anyone would choose to spend more or less his or her entire life in school. That doesn't detract from the prestige of the career path, though.

Being a doctor is prestigious, and (even if we hate to admit it) being a lawyer is, too, although it's also true that part of the prestige accrues from the fact that you know people who have these jobs probably have some money too.

The Paul Teutuls (father and son), along with Mikey Teutul, hold prestige jobs at Orange County Choppers, and they were prestigious even before the TV show.

One of the thorny parts of prestige as a career goal is the difficulty in finding jobs that straight-out specialize in that. Frequently, what makes this kind of job attractive isn't *purely* prestige, usually there's something else mixed in. Being a judge is prestigious, but partially because you know there's some real power there. Being a struggling rock musician is pretty good in terms of prestige, but only if there's some sober hope that one day you'll convert into a legitimate star and not just end up with no money and damaged eardrums. On the other end of the musical spectrum, a jazz musician who tells people that's what he does for a living can usually count on getting a few people to say "that's cool" or "that's so interesting," but again, part of the reason is the mixing of the music with the sense that this person has found *meaningful* work, something they'd probably be doing for free if no one was paying.

Finally, the signature difference between prestige and meaningful work is that prestigious jobs by definition demand an audience. People dedicated to a meaningful cause like protecting the welfare of animals can labor in obscurity all their lives doing simple things that virtually no one notices, like running a kennel for out-of-town dog owners where the pets get treated with extraordinary levels of respect. But for this work to cross from meaningful into prestige, someone at some point has to look and say, "Wow."

Comfort on the job comes in all forms, spanning from the size of your desk, to how often you need to travel in cramped airplanes, to the clothes you need to wear while on the clock. The *Wall Street Journal* article grades jobs to some extent on comfort, though they call the category "Environment." Here are some components of an (un)comfortable workday:
- Physical demands (crawling, stooping, bending, etc.)
- Work conditions (toxic fumes, noise, etc.)
- Physical environment extremes
- Stamina required
- Degree of confinement

This is a good list of factors that move the needle on the comfort scale, but there's something very important missing from it. On the comfort scale, Arctic fishermen aren't going to score highly in terms of physical working conditions; they're cold and wet and living in a cramped space. The food's bad. On the other hand, it takes a certain type of person to sign up for a job like that—a very, very specific kind of person. And if you're seriously thinking about it, there's a decent chance you're going to hit it off with—you're going to feel comfortable with—the *other* people who are doing it. The boat, consequently, will be uncomfortable, but the company of people you're with may be comforting.

Looking not just at the physical characteristics of the job but the other characters that'll be there doing it with you is important for the obvious reason: you spend a lot of time at work. ("I spend more time with you guys than with my husband/wife" is a constant refrain in some offices.) So if your sense of humor works well with a bunch of people you happen to know, and it turns out that many of them are nurses, which tell you something about how you're going to feel about seeing them bright and early every morning, Monday through Friday.

In his book *Vital Friends: the People You Can't Afford to Live Without*, Tom Rath organizes data from Gallup polls and studies to show that employees who have good friends in the office tend to stay longer in a job. It's difficult to *prove* things about happiness, of course. It's even hard to know exactly what happiness is, but it seems fair to suspect that there might be a connection between duration in a job and happiness with the job. And if there is, then feeling comfortable with the people you work with—laughing when they laugh, watching the same TV shows, whatever—should be a job consideration.

Pushing the importance of workmates in a different direction, in a blog post, a woman calling herself Penelope (she doesn't give a last name) makes a point about flourishing at work: "You'll learn the most on a job by having a great mentor looking after you." [6] If that's true, then if you choose to work in a profession that's full of the kind of people you respect, admire, understand, and get along with, you're likely to do better for yourself than working with the kind of people you don't take seriously (or who don't take you seriously). Fitting in, the point is, with the people at work isn't just a fringe benefit; it's a critical value to factor into the selection of one or another career line.

For the young, job security seems like a distant virtue, a fuddy-duddy aspiration for the over-the-hill crowd. In fact, even for the not-so-young it's fuddy-duddy. It's also one of the most volatile of the values you can assign to your job search, one of the most prone to surges and retreats. When you wake up at 3 a.m. and then can't get back to sleep because there's a recession and you know cutbacks are coming, all of a sudden holding a position that maybe isn't too glamorous but is certainly necessary—like being a day care worker—doesn't seem so bad.

The day you learn your family will be growing by one is another of those moments when security's importance blows up. And the day your husband loses his job, that'll be another security surge.

Then there's age. It's a delicate subject—for legal reasons no employer wants to go on record saying they won't hire people older than fifty—but there comes a point when years become a disadvantage for job seekers, which explains why an entire subfield of the résumé-writing business has now sprung up to manage the problem. Jeanne Knight, a certified career coach and résumé expert, says, "What candidates can do to make themselves look younger in a résumé is only list ten to fifteen years of work experience. Also, drop graduation dates and make sure you list any seminars or workshops that focus on new technology."[7]

So you can figure that if older people are going that far to camouflage their overabundant experience, it must be hard to get hired after fifty. And if that's true, you better have good job security at forty-nine.

Finally, the easiest way to define job security is just the confidence that you won't be fired next week, but the discussion broadens very naturally. For example, demographic trends tell us that the American population is aging, so if you're deciding between studying to be an athletic trainer or a nurse, you may well figure that over the next twenty years it's probably going to be easier to find work in the nursing home than the gymnasium, and that holds regardless of how secure any single job may appear right now. Or again, computer technologies keep entering our lives faster and from more directions, and that's a good clue about future job prospects.

In any case, if you're reading this, it's possible that you're what marketers are calling a millennial, meaning someone born between 1980 and 1995, more or less. If you fit the category, the TV show *60 Minutes* believes you think this: "We have options. We can keep hopping jobs. No longer is it bad to have four jobs on your résumé in a year. Whereas for our parents or even generation X, that was terrible. But that's the new reality for us. And we're going to keep adapting and switching and trying new things until we figure out what it is." [8]

Probably, the value of job security arrives along with the realization that companies can say the same thing about employees. A lot of them do.

Balancing the Values

One factor can be chosen to weigh more heavily than everything else combined when sorting out the values for initiating a job search. The imbalance would go a long way toward efficiently filtering career possibilities. For many, however, the priorities won't sort out so easily: it'll be necessary to balance competing values, to trade one against another when considering specific jobs and career paths. Someone may, for example, value both money and comfort, but that doesn't help answer the question about whether a job on an Alaskan crabbing ship is more or less attractive than a summer on the beach in the lifeguard stand. In the longer term, holding the two values won't help to decide between the career of an undersea welder or an office worker. How can individuals get a grip on what their own priorities are, and how much each weighs? In his essay "Strategic Planning—For the Good Life," Robert Solomon offers a provocative question: "Looking back over your life from a rocking chair, what would you like to remember—and how would you like to be remembered?" [9]

Of course, the idea isn't to lock you into a life plan based on how things might look in the distant future. You have no way of knowing how things will be, and if you're a millennial, we know you don't like life plans anyway. Instead, the idea is to try to get a revealing angle on the question of what values in work really matter for you. The aim is to step away from everything and get a different perspective, a fresh look at the problem.

That's important because real life, moving along fast as it does, can narrow your perspective, get you caught seeing things more or less the way everyone around you does. Faced with a career center job board filled with interview schedules of visiting corporate recruiters, isn't it easiest just to sign up for the ones your friends are signing up for? If everyone in your sorority is talking about going to work at one agency or another, or if half the people you know are getting teaching degrees, the temptation's there to just follow along.

When looking at things from extreme or unusual angles, those herding forces recede. At least for a bit you can make yourself turn away from what everyone else is doing, leaving you no choice but to arrange your own priorities for determining the kind of work you want to get involved with. Importantly, the idea isn't to eliminate other people from consideration but to eliminate consideration that just imitates what other people are thinking. Here's the beginning of a list of questions aiming to do that, aiming to shake up thinking about the career choice and force some sorting of the basic values determining which way the choice is going to go:

- Of the seven discussed values—meaning, leisure time, money, power, prestige, comfort, security—can you rank them, or at least group them, from the most to least important for you? Can you take some of the jobs or careers you've been considering and loosely rank them in terms of how well they fit with your list of values?

- To make the list of values more manageable, can you cut it down by just eliminating some concerns that you really don't share?

- Are there any values you think should be added to the list?

- Can you make a short list of *other people* whose opinions are important to you, and then loosely imagine how they would rank the seven values for evaluating jobs? If you can, is their ranking similar to yours or different? If it's similar, are you sure you're thinking for yourself? If it's different, are you sure your values for work align with the kind of life that you respect?

- What would you like to tell your parents you've decided to do for a living?

- Career day at the elementary school. You're standing in front of your own child's class talking about your work. What kinds of things would you like to report and be proud to say? Looking back at your original list of values for jobs, does it correspond with the classroom scene?

- You've got six months to live: what do you do? Is it something that might be related to work or is it a pure leisure activity? (Can you imagine any job that would allow you to do that activity, whatever it is, throughout your career?)

- You'll live 600 years—and have to work during 550 of them—does that change your work priorities? Should it?

- You'll live 600 years—and have to work during 55 of them—does that change your work priorities? Should it?

- For you, is the term *couch potato* a slur or just the name of a comfortable lifestyle? Are there anti–couch potato and pro–couch potato career tracks?

- Your rich uncle dies and leaves you a sum of money and private instructions to use it to put poor children through school in Mexico. It's also enough to pay your college and leave a good amount left over for whatever. No one's watching—no one will ever know. What do you do? What does this tell you about the place money have in your life?

- Madonna and Mick Jagger are among the world's two richest rock stars. Imagine you could have all their money, but be a complete unknown and have no sense of rhythm. Would you prefer that or would you trade all the money to have their success, voice, and rhythm for one year on a world tour? Does the decision correspond with your original ranking of the seven values?

- For you, which would be better: spending big money or having people know you've got big money to spend? If it's the second, is there a way to command respect from others that's easier to achieve than wealth?

- Friday night, you're with a new group of people who know little about you. Would you rather tell them you've been invited to a dinner at the White House for notable citizens or you'll be having dinner tomorrow at your own expansive beach house?

- You sign up for a blind dating service, hoping to meet someone to marry. The only thing you get to choose about the man or woman you'll be paired with is his or her job. What job would you choose to match you? Next, imagine that you're not ready for marriage, still exploring, and you go to the same service. What's the job this time? If the two jobs are really different, does that reflect anything about where you're at with respect to the kind of work you want for yourself?

- Do you like being in charge, no one is telling you what to do, even telling other people what to do? Be honest, no one's listening. By the way, would your answer change if people *were* listening?

- A brutally long Friday at work comes to an end at 9 p.m. On the elevator ride down with some people in the office, there's a power outage. No one's around to fix the machinery or let you out. What kind of people would you like to have in the elevator with you? Is it possible to match these people up with the kind of people frequently involved in one or another profession? (Alternatively, what kind of people would lead you to investigate how your keys or the pen in your pocket could be used as a suicide implement?)

- If you could wear anything you wanted to work every day, nose rings included, what would it be? Is there really an office anywhere where people do dress that way? What would you be willing to give up to work there, and what does that tell you about the importance of environment (or comfort in the broad sense) for your work?

- At the end of every month, your boss gives you a choice. You can have your $4,000 check or you can spin a lottery wheel with a range of numbers from $1 to $8,000. Would you take the $4,000 check or spin? Does this tell you anything about the importance of job security?

- If you've had time to read through this entire list of questions, do the answers you gave more or less correspond with the ranking of the seven values—

meaning, leisure time, money, power, prestige, comfort, security—that you set up at the beginning?

Whose Job Is It, Anyway?

No one can decide for you what line of work to start down; it's a decision only you can make and that you have to make for yourself. This doesn't mean, however, that your life is the only one involved in the decision. Here's a blog post: "I think people need to find the right job for them, the one that will make them happy. My parents are always telling me to get a successful and well-paying job, however the job that I really want to do probably isn't the best paying job, but it would make me happy if I fulfill my dream. I think people need to go out and do what they want and they will be successful in different ways."[10]

Sounds good, but is it right? If you've adopted egoism (morality = self-interest) as your ethical compass, then it is. Egoism makes the job search *relatively* easy; just find the one that will make you most happy.

On the other hand, if you think of yourself as more of a utilitarian—someone guided by the conviction that the morally recommendable act is the one bringing the greatest good to the greatest number—then it's not clear whether this is the right way to go or not. On one side, it's true that pursuing your dream of professional satisfaction is good, but your parents' satisfaction—*everyone's* satisfaction—has to be factored in too. It could be that your parents' wishes—and the happiness they enjoy if you follow their advice—outweigh the happiness and welfare *you* take from a career they recommend against.

Staying with the parents, and taking their side, what kind of ethical arguments can they launch against your career choice? One of the strongest is going to be *obligation* in the sense of *gratitude*, in the sense that we have a duty to repay those who've given to us. Most of us sense this as the courtesy of returning favors. Sometimes we feel it in an inverted form as the desire to decline a gift that seems so great we won't be able to pay it back. The case could be made that this sense of obligation and gratitude is a virtue, the result of a proper upbringing. Or it may be more like a duty, a sense of fairness inherent in the idea of ethics in the first place. Regardless, it's too late to go back now for you and your parents. All you can do is add up everything they've done for you and everything you've done for them. It's doubtful that there's any kind of balance.

In Portuguese, the word commonly used to say "thank you" is *obligado*, meaning I'm obligated, and there aren't many instances where the word is more apt than the parental relation with children. Faced with the obligation, these are possible responses:

- I accept my obligation and will follow the career path my parents' desire.
- I accept my obligation, but I'll pay it off by bringing up my own children and letting them off the hook when they hit adulthood (or through some other mechanism of repayment).
- I accept my obligation, but I won't respect it.

Of course people are always free to pursue that last course, to say the obligation is there and I don't care. But if you want to continue acting ethically, that shifts the burden onto you to build a structure for *justifying* walking away.

Moving from parents to others, what kind of ethical responsibilities do you hold to your spouse if you're married and to children if they arrive? There's nothing wrong with being, say, a starving actor working for that one break on the way to fame. But it's a different thing entirely when you're asking *someone else* to starve too so that you can go on trying to be the next Johnny Depp.

Do you owe anything to that math teacher who saw that you had exceptional ability with numbers and used her own time after class to patiently tutor you on the subject? She probably wouldn't have bothered if she knew you were going to end up working at something that doesn't involve math-related skills. She did bother, though, so does that create a responsibility—even if it's only a small one—to *use* that ability in your professional life, to find a job that exploits your skill with numbers that she helped you acquire?

Finally, at the broadest level, what obligations do you have to the impersonal community around you, to all those people you barely know or have never met—the woman behind the counter at the gas station, the plant worker in Germany who helped assemble your car, some taxi driver in Thailand whose life will never touch yours in any way? Do you owe anything to *them* when thinking about your long, eight-hour days?

This Is the *Perfect* Job for Me…Right Now

One way of dividing up the responsibility felt to yourself and to the others who share your world is career sequencing—that is, defining zones of life and evaluating each separately in terms of work priorities and aspirations. Meaningful labor—signing up for a rugged, low-paying trip on the Greenpeace ship—may fit with your values right out of school. The trip allows a broad ethical vision of work, one seeking to incorporate the welfare of others at a good time for you, while your own needs are limited. Later on, lucrative

work—signing up for a desk job administering a tourist cruise ship where the hours are fewer and the pay higher—might prove the better fit.

Making the move from meaningful work to a more salary-centered vision of the workplace may simply correspond to the realization that walking around in ripped jeans and a t-shirt doesn't work with a receding hairline. Or it may be that the others you hope to benefit with your time have come closer to home: it's not that you want to make the world a better place anymore so much as make the world better for your family.

The Tuck School of Business has published a report on sequencing in today's world. [11] Among the findings: employees, led by women especially, are *professionalizing* the movement in and out of the workplace. Exiting the daily grind to have a child is no longer understood so universally as *leaving* work so much as a planned interruption to pursue personal goals. The difference between leaving and interrupting is that many women now step off the career track fully intending to return in the not-so-distant future and to resume the professional trajectory already established. It's not putting on the brakes so much as taking a detour.

Men, the study finds, are following suit. Some are taking paternity leaves, more or less along the lines pioneered by women, but the study also finds workers interested in professional detouring for the following reasons:

- An avocation outside of work
- Stress and burnout
- Entrepreneurship

In all three cases, space along the career's way is being pried open for different values to enter and at least temporarily redefine the relation with work.

Why *don't* people sequence? What keeps them in jobs they'd like to get away from, at least temporarily? Fear that they won't be able to get their jobs back leads the list. The study also shows, though, that many employees in essence think that sequencing is wimpy, and it'll mark them as unreliable and, therefore, un-promotable. That perception may not be right, though. The study is a snapshot of a changing situation, so it's difficult to draw too many conclusions, but the authors do sense that that the direction of evolution is *toward* sequencing, not away. More and more higher-level managers are willing to accommodate employees who want to take detours; they're willing to make space for them to come and go (as long as the coming and going isn't constant).

To the extent that's right, the ethical relation with job selection transforms. It's no longer the formation of values for choosing a career track leading into the indefinite future; instead it's a *process*. The ethical question about your work, "What's the right kind of job for me?," is now a lingering concern, and answering is a constant responsibility.

Do I Have to Decide?

Some millennial are big on job hopping, on experimenting with work first and *then* deciding on a path instead of doing all the ethical considering up front. This is an attractive option.

There's a risk here, though: it's the trivialization of professional life. If you're just going to take whatever job comes along and see how it works out, then why bother even thinking about it at all? In fact, why bother switching? If you're not going to do the work beforehand to get a grip on the kind of employment, on the general direction of professional interest that supports the values you've decided to live by, then how are you going to know the right job when you find it? Why switch jobs, in other words, when you don't know what you're looking for?

This was one of Saint Augustine's (AD 400) durable pieces of wisdom. It's very simple: if you don't know what you're seeking before you start looking, then how are you going to know when you've found it? Trial and error, in other words, when you're looking for the right kind of job (or the right romantic partner, or the right beer, or whatever) *only* works if you already know what's going to count as an error and what counts as success.

Of course no one's going to get everything down perfectly at the beginning. Ethically, there's a kind of bind here paralleling the first job and experience catch (you can't get your first job without experience, and you can't get experience without your first job). Similarly, you can't know exactly what kind of work fits your values and outlook until you've learned how things really are out there in the nine-to-five world, but that's not a convincing reason to fall off the other extreme and just spin the wheel, take whatever comes your way, and switch jobs without thinking.

KEY TAKEAWAYS

- Pursuing a specific job is an economic and also an ethical decision.
- Specific values shape the ethics of the job search.
- Job seekers hold ethical responsibilities both to themselves and to others.

- Job sequencing allows workers to manage shifting ethical responsibilities as their lives evolve.

REVIEW QUESTIONS

1. What are some of the differences between a job that provides meaningful work, and one that provides prestige?
2. Can leisure time—maximizing it—be pursued on its own as a value in the job search, or does it need to be combined with other values? If it needs to be combined, which values might work best?
3. If money is selected as the prime value a job seeker decides to pursue, what other values may become easier to reach because of the money, and which values may be pushed further away?
4. What's the difference between power and prestige? Can you think of a job that grants power but little prestige and one that grants prestige but little power?
5. For you, what are the components of comfort—do they include flexible hours, working in an office instead of outside, something else? Can you rank the components as more and less important?
6. What responsibilities to others may a job seeker consider when looking for a job?
7. What is career sequencing? What are some reasons a person may choose to sequence, and what are some reasons a person may choose not to be a sequencer?

[1] Michael Froomkin, "What Is Your Nightmare Job?" Discourse.net, July 19, 2007, accessed May 16, 2011,http://www.discourse.net/archives/2007/07/what_is_your_nightma re_job.html.
[2] Sarah E. Needleman, "Doing the Math to Find the Good Jobs," *Wall Street Journal*, January 6, 2009, accessed May 16, 2011, http://online.wsj.com/article/SB123119236117055127.html.
[3] About Kendra, accessed May 16, 2011, http://businessethicsworkshop.com/Chapter_5/Kinnison_bio.html.
[4] Hannah Clark, "Whole Foods: Spinning CEO Pay," accessed May 16, 2011, http://www.forbes.com/2006/04/20/john-mackey-pay_cx_hc_06ceo_0420wholefoods.html.
[5] Psychology of Power, accessed May 16, 2011, http://businessethicsworkshop.com/Chapter_5/Power_in_business.html.
[6] "How to Pick the People You Work With," *Penelope Trunk* (blog), May 6, 2009, accessed May 16, 2011, http://blog.penelopetrunk.com/2009/05/06/how-to-pick-the-people-you-work-with.
[7] Ric Romero, "'Get the Job' Pt. 4: De-Aging Resumes," *ABC7*, September 3, 2008, accessed May 16, 2011, http://abclocal.go.com/kabc/story?section=news/7_on_your_side &id=6369394.
[8] "The Millennial Are Coming," *60 Minutes*, CBS News.com, May 23, 2008, accessed May 16, 2011, http://www.cbsnews.com/stories/2007/11/08/60minutes/main347 5200.shtml.

[9] Joanne B. Ciulla, Clancy Martin, and Robert Solomon, eds., "Strategic Planning—for the Good Life," in *Honest Work: A Business Ethics Reader* (Oxford: Oxford University Press, 2007), 106–7.

[10] Karen Sternheimer, "How Great Is Being a Sociologist?" *Everyday Sociology* (blog), January 24, 2009, accessed May 16, 2011, http://nortonbooks.typepad.com/everydaysociology/2009/01/how-great-is-being-a-sociologist.html.

[11] Tuck Executive Education, *Changing the Career Ladder: Paving Flexible Pathways for Today's Talent* (Hanover, NH: Dartmouth, 2011), accessed May 16, 2011, http://worklifefit.com/pdf/TuckSurveysummary.pdf.

5.2 Working for Ethically Complicated Organizations

LEARNING OBJECTIVES

1. Define reasons why an organization's work may be viewed as unethical.
2. Consider how working for ethically troubling organizations can be managed.

The Psilocybin Project

The Harvard Psilocybin Project began in 1960 and included some of the university's leading and most innovative professors, especially from the psychology and related departments. One of their projects—the Concord Prison Experiment—used the newly developed drug psilocybin on inmates. Professors wanted to discover whether the medication could reduce antisocial behavior and recidivism. Another project, this one carried out in tandem with the Harvard Divinity School, used the same drug to experiment with the bond felt between young theology students and their chosen profession. In both cases, significant, even mind-blowing success was initially reported.

The experiments didn't last. Other Harvard professors raised questions about the ethics of using this drug on humans. An intense conflict erupted in the university. The ethical propriety of the entire Psilocybin Project, the decision came down, was, in fact doubtful. That quickly led to the project's shuttering and then to the dismissal of several well-known professors who protested too loudly in favor of their work and its value, both scientific and moral.

Not all of those fired professors just went away. Outside the university some continued defending their work with principled stands and meticulous arguments. One of those defenders, Dr. Leary, achieved such broad public recognition that he ended up being mentioned in a song by The Who.

Not only did Timothy Leary defend the Psilocybin Project from outside university walls, he also continued with his avid experimentation. Pretty soon the experiments weren't only outside the university; they were also outside the law because psilocybin, like its close relative LSD (lysergic acid diethylamide), was categorized as an illegal substance.

Is it immoral to experiment on people—especially on prisoners who may feel pressured to participate—with psychedelic drugs, concretely with magic mushrooms (the organic source of psilocybin)? Assume just for the sake of argument that it is wrong and the experiments were immoral. Now *who* should feel guilty? The leaders of the Psilocybin Project seem like good candidates since they knew exactly what was going on, and they were the ones handing the doses over. What about the graduate students who followed their professor's lead and joined in the distribution and application of the drugs? Or the administrators at the university who financed the project but maybe didn't know exactly what the experiments involved? What about the undergrads whose tuition money paid for all this? What about the chemists who derived the substance from mushrooms? Or the lab techs who actually made the stuff? What about the secretary who happened to be assigned to work in the psych department and processed some of the paperwork? Where do we draw the line?

One of the most difficult constellations of questions facing conscientious job seekers is: what kind of organization is it OK to work for? Specifically, to what extent am *I* personally responsible for the things my company does? There are the two questions here:

1. What makes a company's work—or universities, or a nonprofit organization's—unethical?
2. I've got an attractive job offer from an unethical organization: can I work there anyway?

What Makes an Organization's Work Unethical?

In a world spattered with poverty and desperation, exploitation of workers is one of the most frequently cited areas of corporate abuse. Advocacy organizations peopled by volunteers who enjoy traveling have proven very effective at locating and drawing attention to overseas sweatshops. The Nike company pays athletes millions to break a sweat for a few hours so they can get some good action video for commercials selling athletic shoes, but they pay sewers in Asia only a few dollars to sweat all day long making those shoes. And what about the cameraman hired to shoot the commercial? He's earning a lot more than the sewer, but his wages are still closer to the sweatshop level than the NBA star level.

In *An Economic Analysis of a Drug-Selling Gang's Finances*, authors Steve Levitt and Sudhir Alladi Venkatesh report on a drug gang studied over the course of several years. It turned out that the street dealers weren't even getting minimum wage for their dangerous efforts: about $200 a month for dealing. Above them, however, the gang leader made between $4,000 and $11,000 a month. It's unclear whether he paid taxes. [1]

Questions about wages and sweatshops will be pursued more fully in later chapters, but here it's enough to note that vast discrepancies in wages throughout a company raise concerns that the organization is exploiting employees. That may lead job seekers to think twice before signing on, even if they're not the ones being exploited.

Exploitation of consumers is another murky direction. It's true that many immigrants from Asia, Latin America, and elsewhere received interest-only home loans in the early 2000s with repayment schedules beginning low but later ballooning to monstrous levels. It's also true that no one forced them to sign the contract; they hold responsibility for their acts, no doubt. However, considering their imperfect English and little knowledge of the American world, is it fair for the mortgage company to even offer these kinds of loans, which seem more predatory than cooperative?

Tobacco companies selling addiction sticks, which sometimes become cancer sticks, aren't clearly removed from charges of exploiting their own buyers.

Breakfast cereals aimed at children frequently boast on the box that the nuggets or the puffs contain 100 percent of the recommended daily allowance of various vitamins and minerals. They don't say anything about sugar highs and crashes. In all these cases, questions about whether consumers are being respected may lead potential employees to question whether they want to get involved in the operation.

Environmental exploitation is frequently invisible in the sense that few people suffer direct consequences of pollution, deforestation, and poisoned water and soil. There are orange alert days in many cities now when children are told not to play outside. But for the most part, companies that pollute may carry on without being held directly responsible for harmful consequences. Of course there are extreme cases like the Love Canal, the neighborhood constructed on a landfill covering thousands of rusting steel barrels of industrial waste. Families living there reported acid slicks running down the street during rains, puddles of rancid chemicals forming in their yards, and birth defects at astronomical levels. Whether, finally, an organization exploits the environment in obvious or not-so-obvious ways, workers may ask if ethical obstacles stand between them and continued employment.

Ethically dubious missions and connections is another category of corporate irresponsibility. The case of Harvard experimenting with acid fits here. So too the drug gang studied by Levitt and Venkatesh. Questions could also be directed toward organizations specializing in reuniting families across borders (people smuggling).

Almost any social hot-button issue is going to double as a source of ethically challenged industries; there'll be people for it and others against it, but either way the questions are there. Circles of controversy surround

- abortion doctors,
- judges sending inmates to death row,
- advocates of assisted suicide.

One thing all these people, professions, and institutions have in common (besides inciting ethical debates) is that they need to hire workers—telephone operators, assistants and administrators, marketers and finance people—just like any other business. You can work for them.

You could also work for a specific kind of lawyering outfit, the one specializing in clients who are very wealthy and very guilty: there'll always be law firms—especially in the field of tax law—specializing in raising a reasonable doubt where there really isn't any.

Massage parlors need receptionists and janitors just like every other business. The horse racetrack hires a small army of diverse workers to keep taking bets. The state lottery contracts actors, directors, film editors, and media experts to make and run ads showing jubilant winners tossing money in the air; on the other hand, they don't spend much time hiring statisticians to explain to the public what the small print on the back of their ticket means: "Really, the chances you'll haul in the Super Magnum Jackpot are about zero."

Conclusion. Ethically conscientious individuals don't have to look too hard to find jobs that make them ask, am I participating in something that's wrong?

I've Got a Job Offer at an Unethical Company; Can I Work There Anyway?

Yes. The question is how.

Ignore it all is one option, pretend like the ethical stain isn't there or at least that you don't see it. Here's an example of what that strategy can look like. Most cities have at least one free and local alternative culture publication, usually published on newspaper-grade paper; it comes out on Thursdays and is called The *Observer* or something like that. Their reporters hit the street to get the latest on the alternative music scene and idealistic political grassroots operations and government abuses and, above all, altruistic, principled causes. The *Dallas Observer* is the Dallas version. In the November 5, 2008, publication there's an article called "Pole Dancing—Good for the Body, But What About a Woman's Soul?" It comes with an honest and thoughtful objection to the caricature of femininity that was developed and mass produced with the express goal of turning on a male audience. [2]

A few pages after the author finishes making a strong moral case against the exploitation of this caricature, the full-page spread devoted to Debbie comes. She's looking tight in her white bikini. She wants to talk to you, and her phone number's right there on the page. In little print it says it costs $1.49 per minute. On the next page there's Robert. He's wearing even less. The phone call costs the same.

It's not anybody's fault that Debbie and Robert (or whatever their real names are) figure so prominently on the advertising pages of a newspaper that's so set against stereotypes like Debbie and Robert. It's only a fact that *that's* where the money comes from to keep the otherwise idealistic and ethically elevated paper in business. So what can the reporters do? They can object to the ads; but without them and their revenue, there won't be any publication left to print their articles decrying these kinds of ads. It's a tough spot. There's no clear way out, which is why it's understandable to go forward pretending you don't see the contradiction.

There are pacifists working for Boeing, the same company that makes warplanes. Somewhere there must be a volunteer at the Society for the Prevention of Cruelty to Animals who holds down a day job at L'Oreal, a company vilified on Internet petitions for its animal testing. [3] There are parents working at General Mills who'd die before giving their kids Cocoa Puffs. There are strict Catholics working for the pharmaceutical company that manufactures birth control pills. The list will never end because it's always possible to pretend you don't see the conflict between your own moral convictions on one side and the actions of the company you work for on the other.

But the decision to remain blind is difficult because pretending you don't see essentially means you're lying—lying to yourself. The question raised here is this: can that lying be justified ethically?

If you're a strict believer in the standard duties, which normally include the duty to honesty, you're going to have problems. You can, however, argue that you have a still *more*

compelling duty to provide for your family and loved ones. So if the job you have is the best one you can get, and then you can make the case that your responsibility to them is greater than your responsibility to be honest with yourself. Making a similar argument but from a slightly different direction, a utilitarian can point out the benefits a paycheck brings—not just for the worker but also for the family and the economy generally—and from there say that lying to yourself is good because it produces a greater general good.

Of course there are arguments that could be raised against these justifications and so the debate rolls on. What's important is that pretending an ethical conflict between your convictions and your company simply isn't there may be justifiable.

Explicitly Accepting Employment at an Ethically Difficult Workplace

Another option for accepting a job offer in an organization you consider to be morally stained is to explicitly accept that I work at an ethically difficult company and go on to justify the decision. There are two directions for consideration here:
1. How seriously wrong do I believe the company's actions are?
2. How close is my work to those actions I believe wrong?

There's a difference between working for a firm that experiments on animals (L'Oreal) and working for one that experiments on humans (the Harvard psychedelic drug project). Most ethically challenged jobs are more like the former than the latter. That's not a license to simply discount the reality that the work may participate in a larger and objectionable process, but it does open the way to a move from *an absolute to a balanced ethical stance*: it's not that "something's going on there that's wrong and therefore I can't be involved at all"; instead "something's going on there that's wrong, but things could be a lot worse, plus, the right and good things I can achieve by taking this job are pretty significant." So start with the idea that even if you think experimenting on animals is wrong, it's not as bad as experimenting on humans. Then add the good things that could come from working for an animal-abusing company.

Here are two possibilities:
1. The post allows me to maximize the use of my personal strengths. Ethics isn't only about duties to others; there are also duties to you. Maximizing your own potential is one of them.
2. The post allows me to better equip myself to get an improved job further down the line. If you *really* want to avoid touching unethical work, then your best option

may be to do whatever's necessary to build the strongest résumé possible. Once you've done that, your options for working will increase and correspondingly the possibilities for ethically satisfying employment.

Moving to the next question—*how close is my work to those actions I believe are wrong?*—there's a difference between experimenting on animals and preparing the tax return for a company that experiments on animals. Making this point sharper, if you adamantly refused to participate in *any* company that has *anything* to do with animal testing, then you're not going to be able to participate in anything. You're not going to be able to buy paper from the company that sells paper to the animal testers. You're not going to be able to use Google because people at the animal testing company buy advertisements on Google search pages. The list is endless in an economy that's totally interlinked, and our economy is pretty close to totally interlinked.

Now, if that's right, then the relationship between you and the immorality that indisputably exists in the economic world—and probably in the company you work for in one way or another—isn't an issue of right and wrong so much as a question of *distance*. In other words, when you're contemplating a job, the question isn't whether something bad is happening there; it's "how close does the stink get to my office?"

More, it may even be that accepting a job at a company can be a route to changing that company's policy. Of course that's going to be more than difficult at a giant concern like L'Oreal, but if you're interested in the environment, you may end up at a small local firm that sells plastic (not biodegradable) bottles of water, and you can advocate the forming of a company recycling program. It's a small thing. Almost absurd. But it's no closer to absurd than the other choice, which is the big thing: simply refusing to work for any company that acts objectionably in the world in one way or another.

KEY TAKEAWAYS

- There is a wide range of reasons why an organization's work may be viewed as unethical.
- There are multiple strategies for managing concerns about working for ethically troubling organizations.

REVIEW QUESTIONS

1. What are four reasons an organization's actions may be viewed as ethically troubling?

2. Ethically, how could you justify ignoring the fact that there's a conflict between your convictions and the actions of the company you work for?

3. Why might a potential employee of an ethically troubling organization ask how seriously wrong the organization's actions are?

4. Explain why working for almost any organization may be ethically troubling.

5. If someone were working for an organization involved in ethically troubling activities, what questions may they ask themselves as they consider whether they should continue working there?

[1] Steven D. Levitt and Sudhir Alladi Venkatesh, "An Economic Analysis of a Drug-Selling Gang's Finances," *Quarterly Journal of Economics* 115 (August 3, 2000): 755–89.
[2] Megan Feldman, "Pole Dancing—Good for the Body, but What about a Woman's Soul?" *Dallas Observer*, November 6, 2008, accessed May 16, 2011,http://www.dallasobserver.com/2008-11-06/news/pole-dancing-classes-mdash-good-for-the-body-but-what-about-a-woman-s-soul.
[3] Cherry Marrone, "Stop L'Oreal's Animal Testing," Care 2 Petition Site, accessed May 16, 2011, http://www.thepetitionsite.com/1/stop-loreals-animal-testing.

5.3 Case Studies

The Ethics of Grunge Work

In February 1989, Jason Everman joined a new act called Nirvana as a backup guitarist. A few months later the group's first record, a raw and noisy effort titled *Bleach*, was recorded and released by an obscure local distributor.

Everman played in the 1989 summer tour supporting *Bleach*, then was kicked out of the band: the rest of the guys found him too show bizzy on stage and too introverted off it. *Bleach* scored a minor success on the college radio circuit. Nirvana's 1991 follow-up, *Never mind*, is one of the more important and financially lucrative pieces of recorded music in history.

In 1990, Everman joined Sound garden to play bass on their promotional tour for the EP *Loudest Love*. Not meshing with the other band members, he was sent packing after the tour's end.

Sound garden's 1991 release *Bad motor finger* scored a moderate success with the indie crowd. The 1994 follow-up, *Super unknown*, debuted at number one on the *Billboard 200* album chart. It stayed there.

In 1994, Everman joined the US Army Rangers and then a Special Forces unit. He toured in Afghanistan and Iraq. He was honorably discharged in 2006.

Fifteen minutes of fame came to Everman on November 10, 2008, when he was featured in a *New Yorker* piece titled "Theatre of War." While being interviewed to provide a veteran's perspective on war, a friend of Everman's breaks in to add that besides being a warrior, Everman had once been a musician. The article's author was skeptical. But, she writes, later investigation revealed that Everman had, in fact, been a small-time rock star.

During the interview Everman related that he's a devotee of the Renaissance intellectual Benvenuto Cellini, who believed that in order to live a full life, you must develop each of the soul's three parts: the artist, the warrior, and the philosopher. At the time of the interview, Everman—bearded and heavily tattooed—was studying philosophy at Columbia University in New York City.

Kurt Cobain (b. 1967), Aberdeen, Washington
Cobain was born into a broken home and eventually lived with a born-again Christian family. He adopted the religion. The faith didn't last; soon he was spray painting "God is Gay" onto random pickup trucks in the neighborhood.

In 1981, his uncle gave him a choice between a bike and a guitar for his birthday. He went for the guitar.

By March 1988, Cobain had formed a noisy outfit called Nirvana. They were playing dives around Seattle, doing bad covers, and making up some of their own songs. They decided to make a record. No one wanted to sponsor them. They decided to go ahead anyway and pay for it themselves. None of them had any money.

In 1989, another local musician, Jason Everman, agreed to pay the $606.17 it cost to make the record if they'd let him join the group. They did. They recorded *Bleach*. Though he's named on the credits and pictured (hazily) on the cover, Everman didn't actually play on any of the tracks. Cobain said the credit was a symbolic thanks to Everman for paying the $600 it cost to record the album. Everman never got his money back.

The group took the music on the road, and when they returned home, they kicked Everman out.

The group's next record, *Never mind*, knocked Michael Jackson's disco sensation *Dangerous* off the top of the charts in January 1992.

In 1991, Cobain met Courtney Love. They did massive drugs, got married, and she got pregnant.

While revolving through detox programs and heroin binges, Cobain wrote music for the next album. *In Utero* debuted at number one in 1993.

In 1994, Cobain committed suicide with a shotgun. These are fragments of his note:

> *I haven't felt the excitement of creating music for too many years now. For example when we're backstage and the lights go out and the roar of the crowds begins, it doesn't affect me the way it used to. The fact is, I can't fool you, any one of you. It simply isn't fair to you or me. The worst crime I can think of would be to rip people off by faking it and pretending as if I'm having 100% fun. Sometimes I feel as if I should have a punch-in time clock before I walk out on stage.*
>
> *I can't stand the thought of the self-destructive death rocker I've become. I don't have the passion anymore, and so remember, it's better to burn out than to fade away.* [1]

QUESTIONS

1. Consider the seven values used for ethically defining jobs: meaningful work, leisure time, money, power, prestige, comfort, and security.
   o Just from what you've read about Everman and Cobain, which values do, they share? Where do they diverge?
   o Are there any values not on the list that could be added to apply to the careers of either Everman or Cobain?

2. *Everman worked to live; Cobain lived to work.*
   o What does that mean?
   o Do you think it's true? Explain.
   o Does this split also divide up the seven values used for ethically defining jobs? If not, why not? If so, what's the split?

3. Everman is a sequencer; he wholeheartedly followed one career path, then a second, and a third. He's a different *kind* of sequencer than the more standard version: a man or woman following a single main career path interrupts it to do something else (have a child, start a small company, travel around the world) and then returns to the old job.
   o What's the difference between these two kinds of sequencing in terms of the value of work and what it can give you?
   o Would it be useful to have different names for these two types of sequencers, or would that be splitting hairs?

4. According to Everman, Cellini believed that in order to live a full life, you must develop each of the soul's three

parts: the artist, the warrior, and the philosopher. Assuming this is true; must it *necessarily* involve one's work life? Is it possible to define a full life that doesn't include any reference to your gainful employment (in other words, is it possible to live fully without worrying about what your job is)? What values for work are implied by your response?

5. Cobain comes to believe that he's unethically exploiting consumers.
   o In what sense is he unethically exploiting consumers?
   o What does Cobain's feeling reveal about the values he associates with his work life?
   o Was Cobain's response to his perceived failure justifiable? Explain.
6. Whose career would you rather have: Everman's or Cobain's? Why? What does that tell you about *your* values?
7. In the career you've chosen for yourself (just pick one, if you haven't), what would it mean to burn out? What would it mean to fade away?
8. Is it better to burn out or fade away? Justify in terms of the values that can be attached to working life.

Cop or Drug Dealer?

Roberto Pulido, a ten-year veteran of the Boston Police Department, was arrested by the FBI and charged with protecting drug dealers, cocaine dealing, identity theft, obstruction of justice, robbery, assault and battery, and money laundering. [2]

QUESTIONS

1. What are some of the advantages to being a policeman? What are some of the advantages to being a drug dealer? Presumably, Pulido started out being an honest cop, and over the course of ten years fell (or climbed) into the illegal drug business. Can you imagine how the seven values of his work might have shifted as this transformation developed?
   o Which values grew in importance?
   o Which might have fallen away?
   o Could any of the values have been maintained through the shift in professions?
2. Officer Pulido is a career sequencer, but it's a unique kind of sequencing because his two careers actually contradict each other. It's not that he took time off to follow some outside interest, and it's not that he pursued various jobs that all fit into a larger plan. He did one thing and then the opposite. Is there a sense in which he has canceled out his professional life? Explain.

3. Imagine that you are considering two career directions: joining the police academy or growing some pot in the basement and getting a start in the drug-dealing business.
   o Regardless of whether you'd ever actually do it, what ethical theory (duties, rights, utilitarianism, some other) could be employed to justify the decision to go the drug route?
   o What ethical theory (duties, rights, and utilitarianism, some other) could you employ to justify the decision to go the police route?
4. Apply Nietzsche's theory of eternal recurrence to the cop/drug-dealer choice. You would have to choose one life and live it over and over forever. Which would you choose? Why? Does that tell you anything about what you should do with the one and only life you have?
5. Doctors and pharmacists deliver powerful, addictive drugs that send waves of tremendous pleasure through the users' bodies (and sometimes those meds result in abuse and death). So that makes three career directions that have something in common: doctor, pharmacist, and street drug dealer. Now, in terms of the seven values of work, what do the jobs have in common, and where do they diverge?
6. From the newspaper report on the Pulido case, "Pulido bought a Hyde Park building where his wife began teaching dance to children—and where once a month for the next several years Pulido hosted and provided protection for drug-and-sex parties. Admittance ran from twenty to forty dollars, and narcotics were often in open use. Lap dances in the "boom-boom room" cost an additional twenty dollars. As many as one hundred people attended on a given night, including well-known felons, drug dealers, and law-enforcement officers— some in uniform." Compare and contrast Pulido's wife's job and Pulido's. Which post is most desirable for the person valuing prestige?
7. How could Pulido's drug operation be characterized as unethical in terms of the exploitation of consumers?
8. In a sense, Pulido's wife worked for her husband. By running a dance school out of the building where Pulido operated, she provided cover for his operation.
   o How could the argument be made that she has an ethical responsibility to resign from her job by shutting down the dance classes so that her husband could no longer use the space to sell drugs?
   o In ethical terms, how could she justify pretending not to know what was going on in her building once a month?
   o In ethical terms, and assuming she explicitly recognizes and accepts that she's providing space

and cover for her husband's activities, how could she justify continuing to work for his operation?

9. Assuming you were a drug dealer, who would you sell to, and *not* sell to? Why? Does this tell you anything about how willing you might be in the future to work for an ethically challenged corporation?

Investigative Fashion Journalism

The blogger Dahlia (she doesn't provide her last name) wants to invent a new career. She calls it investigative fashion journalism. In condensed and slightly altered form, here's what she writes:

Investigative Fashion Journalism is a different kind of job. When people talk investigative journalism they think Watergate, Area 51, etc. Also, due to watching too many movies, there's the fear that the consequences of investigative journalism include losing your job, your family, your money, and on the very rare occasion—your life. (Though last I've heard, the fashion journalists that I've admired are still very much alive.) Part of the fun is being your own detective by trying to dig up evidence, to see what the big cover up is about. I mean, how many of you were actually aware that illegal immigrants working long hours in manufacturing jobs were happy being paid minimum wage in Europe?

We love scandals. And what better scandals can you uncover than the fashion industry? I mean I know celebrity gossip is hot right now, but exposing a multi-billion dollar industry gives me a bigger high, but that's just me. Also, by exposing the corruption like those working illegal immigrants, you can change how the industry works and perhaps enforce better practices for all current and new companies coming into the mix. If you lead by good example others will follow, right?

If local universities would offer such a program in journalism, I'd sign up for it in a heartbeat. Unfortunately, for now, I'm resolved to my fashion blog. [3]

QUESTIONS

1. "Part of the fun," she writes, "is being your own detective by trying to dig up evidence, to see what the big cover up is about." Is there a connection between "fun" and meaningful work? Where does fun fit in the consideration of values to be weighed when considering a career track?

2. What career-related values do you suspect light up Dahlia and, more generally, the kinds of people who try to make up jobs for themselves?

3. Ethically troubling exploitation in the fashion industry.

○ Do you think *she* thinks there's exploitation in the fashion industry? Where?

○ If there is exploitation—if something ethically reproachable is going on—what's *her* relation to that blemish? Is she guilty too? Explain.

Octomom

In January 2009, the woman known as Octomom gave birth to octuplets. Her real name is Nadia Suleman; she's a single mother who'd split from her husband because they were unable to have children together. She was on welfare when she conceived the children via in-vitro fertilization. She already had six young ones at home.

All her children were implanted by Dr. Michael Kamrava. The delivery required forty-six doctors, nurses, and attendants.

In 2009, she was offered $1 million to star in a pornographic movie. She refused, but later that year she signed a contract for each of her children to earn $250 a day to star in a reality show.

QUESTIONS

1. Make the ethical case that a nurse should not seek employment in the office of Dr. Michael Kamrava, even though he pays well.

2. Justify a nurse's decision to work in the office of Dr. Michael Kamrava, because he pays well.

3. What alignment of work-related values may have led Nadia Suleman to reject work as a porn star but accept the role of reality TV actress (along with her many children)?

Paralegal or Lawyer?

Sally Kane, an attorney and writer, drew up a list comparing the practical realities of two careers, paralegal and lawyer.

Here's a summary:

Paralegal: A few months training.
Lawyer: A few years of school after college.
Paralegal: Low-cost education.
Lawyer: Law school is EXPENSIVE.
Paralegal: Earning limit under $100,000 in most markets.
Lawyer: The sky.
Paralegal: A paralegal now is pretty much a paralegal forever.
Lawyer: Working as a lawyer opens doors to other careers.
Paralegal: One of the fastest-growing careers in United States.
Lawyer: Job outlook above average.
Paralegal: Limited responsibility and stress.

Lawyer: High responsibility and stress.

Paralegal: Overtime pay.

Lawyer: If there's work until 11 pm, you work to 11 pm.

Paralegal: Once you've got the job, no more school.

Lawyer: You need to keep updating your knowledge (every year, if you're a tax attorney).

Paralegal: Shorter learning curve and your work is routine and mundane.

Lawyer: Long learning curve and your work is intellectually challenging and varied.

Paralegal: Cubicle.

Lawyer: Private office. [4]

QUESTIONS

1. This comparison is a list of facts. Can you go through the list and attach ethical *value* to the facts? In terms of what value(s) does each fact make a job more or less desirable?
   o Make the ethical case that it's better to go the paralegal route.
   o Make the ethical case that it's better to go the lawyer route.
2. If you've developed a short list of career options, can you go through and make up a sort of career decision spreadsheet that resembles the one just constructed for lawyers and paralegals? It would list the two or three jobs you're considering. Then one column would list the *factual* advantages and disadvantages of each one, things about vacation time, salary, working conditions, and so on. Finally, there'd be your unique part: the notation of which of those facts held value and importance in your life and with respect to the role you imagine work to have for you in the coming years.

[1] Wikipedia, "Death of Kurt Cobain," accessed May 16, 2011, http://en.wikipedia.org/wiki/Death_of_Kurt_Cobain#Suicide_note.

[2] David S. Bernstein, "Cop or Drug Dealer?" *Phoenix Boston*, November 9, 2006, accessed May 16,

2011, http://thephoenix.com/Boston/News/26961-Cop-or-drug-dealer/?rel=inf.

[3] Dahlia, "Investigative Fashion Journalism," *Dualité*, July 7, 2008, accessed May 16, 2011.

[4] Sally Kane, "Should You Become a Paralegal or Lawyer?" *About.com*, accessed May 16,

2011, http://legalcareers.about.com/od/legalcareerbasics/a/paralegallawyer.htm.

NOTES:

Chapter 6
Employee's Ethics: Getting a Job, Getting a Promotion, Leaving

Chapter Overview

This chapter examines some ethical decisions facing employees. It considers the values that underlie and guide choices about how you go about getting a job, how you maneuver for a better one, and what the right moment is for leaving.

6.1 The Résumé Introduction
LEARNING OBJECTIVES

1. Define ways job seekers may misrepresent themselves on a résumé.
2. Construct an ethical framework for managing the dilemmas of crafting a résumé.

Robert Irvine's Stretched Résumé

For many job seekers the first—and maybe the only—chance they get to impress a potential employer is a résumé. What are the ethics of presenting your qualifications on a sheet of paper?

Robert Irvine is a muscled chef from England who you may have seen hosting the Food Network's popular *Dinner: Impossible*. It's a good job. The TV show generates free publicity for his cookbook *Mission: Cook!* and affords him the kitchen credibility to open his own restaurants. That was the idea he brought to St. Petersburg, Florida, in 2008. His concept for south Florida, actually, was two restaurants: Ooze and Schmooze. Ooze was going to be the accessible, entry-level place and Schmooze the highbrow complement. His biography—the summary of his professional life and experiences that he presented to potential investors—was impressive. According to the *St. Petersburg Times*, he advertised his résumé as including:

- A bachelor's of science degree in food and nutrition from the University of Leeds.
- Royal experience working on the wedding cake for Prince Charles and Princess Diana.
- He was a knight, as in *Sir* Robert Irvine, Knight Commander of the Royal Victorian Order, handpicked by the Queen.
- For several consecutive years, he'd received the Five Star Diamond Award from the American Academy of Hospitality Sciences.
- He'd served as a White House chef. [1]

Everything came to an end, though, at least temporarily, when Food Network fired him for résumé lies. Here's the truth about the listed items:

- The claimed BS degree? According to a press officer at the University of Leeds, "We cannot find any connection in our records between Robert and the university."
- The royal wedding cake? Well, he did help pick some of the fruit that went into it.
- The knighthood? No.
- The Five Star Diamond Award? True, but it's not the AAA's prestigious Five Diamond Award or Mobil's five stars. The American Academy of Hospitality Sciences is actually a guy's apartment in New York, and the award is granted to anyone who pays a fee.
- White House chef? Kind of. But he didn't prepare sophisticated dishes for the president or anything like that; he cooked food for the cafeteria line, serving military workers at the White House.

Certainly, Robert Irvine isn't the first guy to stretch his résumé, but he does an excellent job of exploring the many ways people *can* misrepresent themselves when trying to get a job. Generally, there are two kinds of résumé abuses. Positive résumé misrepresentations are those items on a résumé that simply aren't true. Examples include:

- **False credentials.** These are certificates of accomplishment that don't exist. Irvine said he had a BS degree. He didn't. This kind of misrepresentation is especially tempting for job seekers who didn't quite finish their degree. One of the obvious practical problems is that claims like this can be verified or disproven by human resource departments. (Or, as in Irvine's case, by enquiring newspaper reporters.)
- **False experience.** Untruthfully claiming to have participated in projects. Irvine asserted that he'd been a White House chef, meaning he'd planned sophisticated menus and prepared dishes for dignitaries. He didn't. He cooked assembly-line food in the cafeteria for White House staff workers.
- **Embellished experience.** This is the easiest kind of résumé misrepresentation. Irvine really did work on the royal wedding cake, but only picking fruit, not actually making it. His claim, therefore, isn't directly false, but incredibly misleading. The same could be said about the

Five Star Diamond Award. While technically true, it's not the meaningful award that people imagine it to be.

- **False chronology.** Anyone who's suffered long periods of unemployment—or just been fired from a job and taken a while to find another one—has surely been tempted to adjust the dates on their résumé to make it seem as though they went smoothly from one post to another.
- **False references.** Listing someone to vouch for your experience who really won't or can't. Irvine said he'd been selected by the Queen of England for a knighthood. It never got to the point where someone actually called her to ask, but if they would've, she would've drawn a blank. Of course people don't normally list royalty as a reference, but in everyday life, it's easy to commit the same misrepresentation. One fraternity brother could list another as a former boss. A woman could list a brother-in-law.

Negative résumé misrepresentations are those items that would appear on a *complete* résumé, one listing all your working experience, but that conveniently get left out of the one you submit to a potential employer. If you were fired from your first job at McDonald's years ago because you kept forgetting to take the fries out of the oil pit, no one's going to object when you drop those months off your work history. On the other hand, if, up until two months ago, you were in charge of the vehicle fleet for a hotel, and you were fired for taking your girlfriend out in the company limo after hours, leaving that off your résumé is misleading new prospective employers.

In the case of Irvine, things worked out for him in the end. After he publicly recognized the truth and cleaned up the most outrageous resume claims, he got his TV show back.

The Ethics of Stretching the Résumé

It's hard to define all the ethical lines dividing what should and shouldn't be included in a job applicant's résumé, but steps can be taken to control the situation. If you're sitting at your desk trying to figure out whether there should be any deleting, fudging, or exaggerating, two questions can help get a hold of the situation:

1. Who will be affected by my decision?
2. Does it matter what everyone else is doing?

The first person affected by your decision is you, and everyone's closest ethical responsibility is the one they hold to themselves, the responsibility to respect their own dignity and abilities. One way of taking that responsibility seriously is to look back at the jobs you've held and ask what kinds of tasks they entailed and how those experiences and the skills taken from them might be stated in a broad and appealing way. Probably, Irvine went overboard when he translated the fact that he'd chosen fruit included in a royal wedding cake into the claim that he participated in assembling and cooking it. But it also seems like it'd be a mistake to say that he'd been a simple "fruit picker" on a wedding cake job. In the culinary world, his was important fruit picking. Irvine's mistake, in other words, wasn't that he tried to make himself look good, it's that he couldn't find a way to do it without essentially lying about his experience.

The duty to present yourself positively to potential employers may also justify the decision to leave certain, let's say, unfortunate aspects of your professional life off the résumé. Irvine doesn't talk much about how his endeavor to create restaurants in St. Petersburg fell apart in a sorry mess. If tomorrow he goes out and tries to stir up investors for a new pair of restaurants somewhere else, he has an obligation to be honest with them about what happened last time. But if he's looking for a job as a TV cook, or just as a cook in a restaurant, then he may be able to justify leaving that bad episode unmentioned. The reasoning? The fact that he's bad at mounting restaurants doesn't mean he's a bad TV personality or an error-prone cook. The one job has little in common with the others. So if he's applying to be a cook, he could possibly leave the negative information about his other business ventures out based on the idea that it's simply not applicable to the employment being sought.

The duty to you, finally, points toward a résumé presentation that sets your accomplishments and skills in boldface while not dwelling on extraneous shortcomings.

Another person affected by your résumé decisions—the choice about how much truth to tell and hide—is the person doing the hiring. If you claim experience you don't really have and skills you don't possess, the supervisor who oversaw your contracting won't just be disappointed and angry as he watches you stumble and trip over tasks that should be easy. The botched hiring will also reflect negatively on him when superiors evaluate *his* performance and make decisions about pay raises and promotions. He's going to suffer because you lied. There is, in other words, a loser when you scam to get a job that you're not really qualified for. More, that harm accrues to the company as a whole. Maybe costs will increase because more training than expected will be necessary. Maybe an account will be lost when you fumble an assignment that should be automatic.

Your potential future workmates also have a stake in your application for a job. If you claim, as Irvine did, to have worked on the Charles and Diana wedding cake, it seems fair for your boss to assume you'll be able to manage producing first-rate cakes for ordinary people. If you can't, if you have no idea how to serve up even a simple layer cake, someone else on the team is going to have to step in and do your work for you. They probably won't get your paycheck at the end of the month, however.

Other applicants for a job also have a stake in your own application. It's a competitive world, and while you're the one who can best make the case for your ability, making false claims doesn't just give you an opportunity you may not otherwise receive: it takes an opportunity away from someone else.

What's Everyone Else Doing?

The first step in getting control of your résumé's relation with the hard truth is working through how any particular decision affects those involved. The second step is *determining whether it matters what everyone else is doing.* The question is important because applying for jobs doesn't happen in a vacuum. If *everyone* stretches their qualifications to the extent Irvine demonstrated, then obviously you may want to consider whether you need to do the same just to get a fair shake.

A web page with a very truthful URL, Fakeresume.com, and takes up the question about how much fibbing is going on out there. Under the heading "The UGLY Truth About How People Are Outsmarting You!" they assert,

> *Over 53% of job seekers lie on their résumés. Over 70% of college graduates admit to lying on their résumés to get hired. Can you afford not to know the techniques, tricks and methods they use?* [2]

Fair question. Of course no one knows exactly how much cheating goes on, but as Irvine attests, there's definitely some out there. So should you get in on it? The argument in favor roughly corresponds with the web page's pitch. If *everyone's* doing it—if exaggeration is expected—then employing the same misrepresentations that guide everyone else isn't really lying. Like driving sixty down a fifty-five-miles-per-hour highway when all the other cars are going that fast too, your exaggerations are following the rules as everyone seems to understand them. From this point of view, you may even have a duty to exaggerate because *not* doing so, as the web page claims, isn't being an ethical hero, it's just being outsmarted. And in a competitive environment, you at least have the moral obligation to not let yourself be snookered.

On the other side, where do these percentages—53 percent, over 70 percent—come from? The web page doesn't say, and if they're not true, then doesn't the whole argument—do it because everyone else is doing it—reduce to an excuse to lie? In the case of Fakeresume.com, it couldn't be more obvious what's going on. The site is offering you a way to not tell the truth and not feel bad about it. Instead of offering moral guidance, it's inventing a way for you to justify taking the easy path, to justify padding the résumé without having to consider whether that's the right thing to do.

Conclusion. In the midst of résumé-stretching dilemmas, what other people are doing matters. Hiring is relative; there's hardly anyone who's perfect for any job, recruiters take the applicant who's best suited. Your obligation—to yourself and to the recruiter—is to show why you may be the best suited of the applicants. That may mean (using the language of Fakeresume.com) use the résumé-enhancing techniques commonly employed. It doesn't mean, however, just imagining that everyone else is laying their pants off and then using that as an excuse to lie yourself.

Résumé Verification and the Law

One problem Robert Irvine faced was his very public personality. To stir up interest in the restaurants he planned for St. Petersburg, he had to stir up interest in himself. All the commotion drew the attention of a local newspaper reporter who ended up blowing the whistle on the résumé exaggerations and concoctions.

More ordinarily, job applicants don't need to worry about reporters prying into their claims. Most medium and larger companies do, however, pass résumés through human resources departments and they typically confirm the significant, objective claims of job seekers. Items like degrees obtained can typically be verified. So too dates of previous employment and job titles. Every company will follow its own internal guidelines, of course, so it's impossible to make a table listing the misrepresentations that will and won't slip through, but it's certain that objectively false information may come to light sooner or later.

If false information does come to light, are there *legal* complications? Probably not. Because résumés aren't binding, signed agreements between the applicant and employer, they're generally protected by free-speech guidelines. In the case of Irvine, if he claimed he was Superman, there's nothing the police could do about it. That said, efforts have been made to take some action against the most extreme cases of résumé misrepresentations. A number of legislative measures have been proposed to punish those who lie about a military record and honors received. Also, in Washington State in 2006, legislation was advanced to fine and briefly imprison applicants found guilty of claiming advanced degrees they didn't actually earn. The measure ultimately failed. [3]

Conclusion. Most résumé misrepresentations don't cross into illegality. This is one of those areas in the business world where legal right and wrong diverges clearly from ethical right and wrong.

Ethical Egoism and Résumé Misrepresentations

Ethical egoism means your moral responsibility is to act in your own interest no matter what that may require. This provides a license for outright résumé invention (a false BS degree and imaginary knighthood for Irvine). But, as is always the case with egoism, the question must be asked whether job seekers *really* serve their own interests when they claim things that may later be revealed to be false or when they land jobs they later won't be able to perform because their qualifications were fake.

One specific warning for the egoist comes from the admissions department at the Massachusetts Institute of Technology. One of the world's elite universities, the task of selecting each year's freshman class is as daunting as it is important for a school dedicated to preserving its reputation. The head of that office in 2007 was Marilee Jones. One of her central skills was the ability to distinguish high schoolers who'd truly excelled from those who got great grades by taking easy classes. Her widely admired skill, in other words, was filtering out grade sheets (which are students' résumés) that misleadingly stretched the students' classroom accomplishments. She went on using that skill until it was discovered that twenty-eight years earlier, when she'd first applied to work at the school, she'd invented a few degrees for herself. She was fired on the spot. [4]

KEY TAKEAWAYS

- There are multiple kinds of positive résumé misrepresentations and negative résumé misrepresentations.
- Managing the dilemmas of crafting a résumé requires accounting for obligations to all those who will be affected by the résumé.
- Circumstances involving the specific post being sought, along with commonly accepted practice, may determine

the extent to which misrepresentations are ethically objectionable.

REVIEW QUESTIONS

1. Who are the people affected by résumé truth decisions?
2. What are five distinct ways you may choose to misrepresent yourself on your résumé?
3. What's the difference between legal and ethical approaches to the question about padding the résumé?
4. Why might a job seeker have a duty to blur parts of his or her work history?
5. Why might an egoist lie on the résumé, and why not?

[1] Ben Montgomery, "TV Chef Spiced Up His Past Exploits," *St. Petersburg Times*, February 17, 2008, accessed May 17, 2011, http://www.sptimes.com/2008/02/17/Southpinellas/TV_chef_spiced_up _his.shtml.

[2] Fakeresume.com accessed May 17, 2011, http://fakeresume.com.

[3] Candace Heckman, "Lying on Résumé Could Land You in Jail," *SeattlePI*, March 3, 2006, accessed May 17, 2011, http://www.seattlepi.com/local/261747_diplomamill04.html.

[4] Marcella Bombardieri and Andrew Ryan, "MIT Dean of Admissions Resigns for Falsifying Resume," *Boston Globe*, April 26, 2007, accessed May 17, 2011: http://www.boston.com/news/globe/city_region/breaking_news/2007/0 4/mit_dean_of_adm.html.

6.2 What Am I Worth?

LEARNING OBJECTIVES

1. Distinguish the free market from other methods for determining a just salary.
2. Consider the justification of wage demands.

Bogus Job Offer Converted into a Real Raise?

In her blog *Female Science Professor*, the author considers a problem. She's got a lab research assistant whom she calls *post doc*, which presumably means he got his PhD, but he's still hanging around the university and working for low pay. She wants to give him a raise. The higher-ups, however, won't approve it. So she writes,

> *I'm pretty sure I could get a colleague at another institution to send my post doc an e-mail expressing an interest in hiring him away from my institution (but without any real intention of doing so). With such a letter in hand, there's a good chance I could get the raise approved. Ethical? No. Should I do it anyway?* [1]

Actually, the ploy may be considered ethical within a purely market-driven framework for setting salaries. Cutting the details and reducing to the situation's essence, the worker is in effect threatening to not show up for work anymore unless there's a larger paycheck. That means the employer is being forced to determine if the employee is worth the extra money. The answer will follow from a survey of available workers in the market, and an answer to the question as to whether another can be found to perform the same duties equally well without demanding more pay. If not, then the increase will probably be granted. If a replacement *can* be found, then things will get awkward as the lab assistant tries to walk back his threat. The walking back is an etiquette problem, though, not an ethical one. From this perspective, in terms of ethics, all that happened is the worker tried to get a raise and didn't. Obviously there's a loose end here; there's the question about whether the *lying* is ethical. It depends. Placing the question in the context of organized labor, is it ethical for a union organization to bluff, to say they'll go on strike while knowing they really won't? What about less direct lies? An employee that's actually satisfied with her salary may feign unhappiness in order to squeeze out a little extra. Further, almost all hard-nosed business negotiation entails a bit of posturing. Not many cars have been sold without the seller at least initially insisting, "Well, I can't *possibly* go below *x* price for this fine automobile." And then, after a visit with the manager or some other contrived breakthrough, the seller decides, "Well, in this *special* case, maybe I can do a *little* better."

In one form or another, a pure market economy occasionally (or maybe frequently) reduces to both sides insisting that they can't pay more or give less, and in the end, both sides meet somewhere in the middle. As for the previous claims about other jobs or threats to go on strike or insisting that the price can't possibly come down or whatever, all that washes away when hands finally shake.

The ethical foundation undergirding and justifying participating in business this way is libertarian in nature. It starts with the premise that we're all independent actors out in the business world trying to accrue the most for ourselves, and others are out to do the same thing. We all know the rules, we're all adults. When we negotiate a pay raise, we may exaggerate circumstances or say some things that aren't true. But at the end of the day, no one forces the employer to pay more; it's the employer's choice. As for the employee, the empty threat to leave may be presented at the bargaining table, but it's not so much a lie as a commonly used negotiating technique, just a way of upping the pressure. It is, therefore, ethically acceptable to invent another job offer but only within the confines of business negotiating and only because everyone knows the give-and-take happens that way. There is another side to this, however. If you don't accept that negotiating in business is a kind of special-rules game where posturing and exaggerating are customary, then you may want to argue that talking about salaries isn't any different from any other kind of conversation. If it's not, then the ethical argument against leveraging an imaginary job offer to force a pay raise finds a solid foundation on the bedrock duty not to lie regardless of the circumstances. For anyone who begins from the ethical foundation that any morally acceptable act must not breach certain ironclad principles—*don't lie, don't steal,* and similar—it becomes impossible to justify making up a nonexistent job offer, even if that's the way the game of business is being played by others.

The Role of the Larger Community in Determining Wages

There are two broad ways to get a fix on your own economic worth. One operates within the open market: economic free agents meet and sessions of no-holds-barred negotiations result in an answer. The other broad approach to setting wages places the issue within the context of a larger community. Here, it's not so much that we're bargaining individuals dealing to get the best possible result; instead, we're part of a business organization and a larger society, and wages get distributed across it in accordance with guidelines and norms. There are multiple kinds of guidelines. They include:

- my value to the organization,
- the ability of the organization to pay,
- the community wage level,
- the wages paid to other employees in the organization,
- my experience and seniority relative to others in the organization,
- the future jobs a post may prepare me for.

Trying to determine what a fair salary would be for post doc in terms of his value to the organization requires determining how much of the organization's profit he actually produces. A researcher in a science lab may, under this system, labor for years without any pay at all if his investigative work fails to produce a marketable product. On the other hand, if after years of labor his research finally yields a breakthrough, his wages conceivably shoot to astronomical levels.

Needless to say, this wage-determining structure won't work very well for lab researchers or for any kind of job that requires years of labor before any return may be anticipated. It does function, however, for businesses like American Apparel. They pay their clothing sewers a small base wage, and then a large secondary amount that rises or falls depending on their output, on the number of garments they add to the inventory. In essence, each week workers bring home a paycheck corresponding with the value they've added to the company. That means the relation between the sewers and American Apparel is fundamentally *cooperative*; it's not a worker negotiating against the organization but the two laboring together and splitting the fruits of the efforts. [2]

Another broad context into which the wage question may be fitted is the **organization's ability to pay**. A lab assistant may choose, for example, to accept a pay cut to help the firm weather a period when no one seems able to invent anything that can be sold. The hope would be that, later on, when someone finally gets that breakthrough and profits zoom, everyone's wages will shoot up too.

A third context for setting wages is the community wage level. Going back to American Apparel, their Los Angeles factory pays workers more than twice the US minimum wage, plus benefits. That's not a lot of money for California, but it's ten times more than what sewers in countries including China make for similar work, which doesn't mean, within this context, that those overseas workers are being abused, only that salaries should be comparable with what others in the immediate area make. Two employees may receive, therefore, radically different paychecks for the same work, but that's ethically appropriate if the wage levels are initially set to correspond with local costs of living and standard practices.

Organizational wage level is another way of standardizing employee pay. In this case, a lab researcher would base demands for a raise on the argument that others working in the same lab are being paid more than he is. It doesn't matter, it follows, and how much researchers are being paid at other, competing locations. They may receive more, or possibly less. Regardless, the standard is set within that single organization, and people with comparable experience doing comparable work should receive similar checks.

Seniority **relative to others in the organization** also provides a salary framework. Here, the emphasis doesn't rest so much on abilities or contribution to the organization, it's the amount of time an employee has been doing it that counts most. In a research lab like the one *Female Science Professor* is blogging about, her assistant's demand for a raise would be based on the idea that he should be getting more than those hired after him, and less than those who've been employed longer. There's a comforting sense of fairness here as the wages get aligned with factors that aren't subjective; it's much easier to tally an employee's time working than to determine how much he might get paid elsewhere or measure his exact contribution to the organization. One drawback to this approach is that it allows little room for rewarding exceptional ability or effort. Potentially, the only reward an

employee receives for working more efficiently than others is that he gets more work to do.

This particular drawback to a seniority system for determining wages is called a perverse incentive; it's a system of rewards that actually encourages workers to perform poorly or inefficiently. Take the case of American Apparel's sewers and imagine that wages were determined *solely* based on the length of their employment. Sewers would have little reason to produce more garments than their workmates. They may even feel like their main task at work each day is to find as many ways as possible to rest and not do anything. Why not? Their wages won't be affected. Obviously, in most private enterprises, slackers like these find themselves out of a job. But in sectors where firing individuals is extremely difficult—government jobs being a prime example—a seniority system for setting wage levels threatens to incentivize glum, nonresponsive employees.

Finally, pay may be calibrated by the **future prospects the post creates**. Here, the lab assistant may complain about low pay, but the response may be that the particular lab where he's working is quite prestigious, and gaining experience there will allow an advantage against other candidates when he goes out to find employment elsewhere later on. The wages lost now, the reasoning goes, will be more than recouped in the future.

An extreme form of this future-prospects salary structure is an internship. This is a short-term job with little pay and few benefits. Sometimes, there's no pay at all. The upside is the experience. When it's added to the résumé, it should make a job seeker more attractive to employers. If everything works, the time may be a good investment, a good way to get into a line of work, or get in at a higher level. The ethical problem, however, lies in the possibility of abuse that's unavoidable when someone is working essentially for nothing. Here's a snippet from an entry on Craigslist:

> I agree that calling work for no pay an 'internship' is just a fancy spin for disrespecting the talents and the person being 'used'. Unfortunately, in this society…many people think it's ok to offer no pay for legitimate work. [3]

He might be right. This complaint is definitely right if the organization offering the internship knows beforehand that the worker's prospects in the market won't really be improved by the experience acquired. In that case, it seems like an internship really is just a "fancy spin for disrespecting the talents and the person being used."

There are two kinds of questions to ask about a worker who's laboring for low (or no) wages with the idea that the experience will pay off in the long run. The first involves employers implying there'll be improved job prospects while knowing there probably won't be. The other is more prudential: assuming the employer is acting in good faith, the worker still needs to ask, "Is it worth it?" It's impossible to know the answer beforehand, but by making the best judgment possible you can get a grip on the question about whether a higher wage ought to be demanded.

Conclusion. For employees trying to measure their worth in business—how much they ought to be paid for their work—the guiding question is, "What are the criteria used to measure whether a paycheck is too fat or too lean?" Are wages set by the market, or is it my value to the organization or something else that determines the pay scale?

KEY TAKEAWAY

- An appropriate salary level may simply be the result of the hardest negotiating possible, or it may be determined by broader guidelines.

REVIEW QUESTIONS

1. How can an employee ethically justify inventing a job offer in order to pressure the boss into granting a raise?
2. From the employee's perspective, in what line of work might *value to the organization* function not very well as a gauge for setting salary levels?
3. How could a company justify paying accountants in its St. Louis office less than accountants in the New York City office?
4. From the employee's perspective, in what line of work might *experience and seniority* function well as a gauge for setting salary levels?
5. Does an employer have an ethical responsibility to offer an intern a job at full pay once the internship is successfully completed? Why or why not?

[1] "Proposed Ethical Lapse," *Female Science Professor* (blog), July 1, 2009, accessed May 17, 2011, http://science-professor.blogspot.com/2009/07/proposed-ethical- lapse.html.
[2] Nick Schou, "The Low Cost of High Wages," American Apparel, *OC Weekly*, December 28, 2005, accessed May 17, 2011, http://www.americanapparel.net/presscenter/articles/20051228ocweekly.html.
[3] Craigslist San Diego, "Comments RE: internship posts& low pay," January 5, 2010.

6.3 Plotting a Promotion
LEARNING OBJECTIVES

1. Distinguish two job promotion tracks.
2. Define ethical responsibilities of those seeking a job promotion.

Two Kinds of Job Promotions

Two major promotion tracks run through many organizations: one based on accomplishment, the other on competition. Accomplishment promotions are those scheduled for workers attaining specific, predetermined goals. For example, in an office of stockbrokers those who achieve a certain number of clients or reach a level of total investment money under their direction may automatically be elevated. An *account executive* could become a *vice president of accounts* after she's gathered more than ninety-nine clients or has garnered accounts valued at more than a million dollars. Along with the new title, there may come a pay raise and additional benefits.

The ethical questions rising around this system are fairly straightforward and tend to involve transparency—that is, a clear explanation of the rules and rewards from the beginning. Does it count, for instance, if a broker games the system by signing up one hundred clients who each invest only piddling amounts? That could lead to a system where a vice president oversees one hundred clients but only $500 of assets, while a lowly account executive labors with ninety clients and $900,000 in assets.

Every industry and organization will have its quirks and ways of twisting the numbers to make things appear better (or worse) than they really are. Keeping those angles under control is a manager's concern, however. Establishing a level playing field, that's the kind of thing managers are paid to take care of, and the dilemmas surrounding this subject, will be considered from their perspective in later chapters. From the employee's perspective, there aren't many problems: if the goals are set, then you have every right to try to meet them as best as you can to get the step up.

The stickier ethical territory comes with competitive promotions. These are situations where workers within a group aren't only teammates laboring to reach the organization's goals but also competitors vying for that one slot that comes open on the hierarchy's next level up. In this situation, what are the ethics of trying to get the promotion?

Dirty Tricks

Colin Gautrey has written a book with a captivating title: *21 Dirty Tricks at Work*. In a short article, he summarizes two of the most commonly used by stealthy promotion seekers to either inflate them or sabotage their coworker competitors.

- **The creative magpie.** This time-honored strategy of self-service is exaggerating involvement in successful ideas—or flat out stealing credit for them—while steadfastly forgetting to mention others' contributions.

- **E-mail to the gods.** A contemporary and clever scheme for ruining your colleagues' advancement chances, it entails writing an e-mail incidentally detailing a colleague's work-related failure and "accidentally" copying the message to supervisors and clients. [1]

The business of getting a promotion, if Gautrey's tricks are any indication, can get pretty rough. One way to determine what you're willing to do is by separating and looking at each one of the ambitious worker's ethical responsibilities with respect to self-advancement. In broad strokes, those seeking promotion at the cost of others in their work group are located at the center of four responsibilities: those to

- themselves,
- their coworkers,
- their managers,
- the organization in general.

The Four Responsibilities

What do ambitious employees owe themselves? Most ethical theories encourage those who desire to advance at work to go after the success. Duty-based ethical structures, for example, include the responsibility all of us should have to respect our own skills and dignity, and if professional excellence is among them, then there's a responsibility to excel, to do well at work. So if getting the promotion requires acting to be sure superiors know when you've done a good job—and in competitive environments it does—then there's a moral imperative there to act, to ensure that credit is received. There's no shame, in others words, in at least discreetly blowing your own horn. Of course there'll always be people in the workplace; perhaps this is even the majority, whose ambitions for their lives aren't about professional success so much as having a fulfilling family life or pursuing an after-five interest. For these individuals, just avoiding the whole career advancement race—even if it means getting less money at the end of the month than others—makes perfect sense.

What do ambitious employees owe their workmates? To begin, the same ethical framework of duties requiring individuals to respect their own ability and dignity also demands that much for others. So while it may be that singing your own praises and advertising your accomplishments as the creative magpie does is respectable, it's harder to justify obscuring the accomplishments of others. Further, if the respect for yourself is balanced by the same respect for others, it seems like there's an obligation to actively ensure that superiors are aware of not only your own contributions but also those made by another. There is, in essence, a good sportsmanship rule in effect. (And certainly, any ethics functioning from a base of respect for ourselves and others will prohibit the outright stealing of others' ideas and accomplishments.) On the other hand, an ethical egoist—someone insisting that individuals are free agents and the world will work out for the best if everyone steadfastly pursues their own interests—will see things somewhat differently. From this point of view, the responsibility to trumpet the accomplishments of others falls to those others. If they want to claim credit for a job well done, they may, but if they don't, it's no one else's responsibility to do it for them. Finally, what's important to see is that there are different intermediate points between trumpeting your own accomplishments and claiming the accomplishments of others as your own. Acting ethically requires determining which point you're at and justifying the stance.

The responsibilities workers hold to their superiors start with honesty. The basic problem with the creative magpie strategy on this ethical front is that it means passing on to managers misleading or false information about who contributed how much to a project. This affects managers negatively—potentially *very* negatively—because next time something needs to get done urgently and at the highest possible level, they may not aim the assignment at those employees most apt to produce the best results. Their performance as a manager, it follows, will be adversely affected when the work performed under their direction comes in at a quality level below expectations. The career prospects of a manager, finally, will be hindered when a subordinate sacrifices honesty in the attempt to advance his or her own career.

The last responsibility that employees looking to be promoted ought to consider is their obligation to the organization in general. Here, both the magpie strategy and the e-mail to the gods trick raise serious questions. The worker's central obligation to the organization is to help it flourish: they're being paid to help the enterprise reach its goals. The problem with the magpie strategy on this front is the same as the problem experienced by managers. When workers who do the best work see the credit stolen by others, the organization loses some of its ability to produce at the highest possible level. Moving on to the e-mail to the gods strategy (the appending of harmful information about other workers to e-mails and then seeing that clients receive the information), this is especially damaging. Even if the information is true, and should perhaps be shared with managers *inside* the organization, it's nearly impossible to see how any organization can benefit when clients find out the work being done is substandard.

Conclusion. For ambitious employees looking to advance quickly in a situation where they're competing against their own coworkers, the recipe for success is obvious: get credit for doing better work than the others. One way to accomplish that is to actually *do* better work and make sure superiors know about it. There are other ways too. Navigating the ethics of those ways requires workers to carefully evaluate their obligations to themselves, their coworkers, their managers, and their organization.

KEY TAKEAWAYS

- Accomplishment promotions and competitive promotions are distinct and occur on different ethical terrains.
- Those pursuing competitive promotions ought to consider their responsibilities to themselves, their coworkers, their managers, and their organization.

REVIEW QUESTIONS

1. Who is hurt by the creative magpie strategy and in what specific ways?
2. You're working on a project with another worker and he's not doing well. His contributions need constant correction. Does your obligation to the organization's well-being provide ethical justification for informing superiors about the shortcomings? Does the ethical situation change if you're also competing with that workmate for a promotion? If it changes, how and why? If not, why not?

[1] Colin Gautrey, "Dirty Tricks at Work—Five Ways to Protect Yourself," *EzineArticles.com*, accessed May 17, 2011, http://ezinearticles.com/?Dirty-Tricks-at- Work---Five-Ways-to-Protect-Yourself&id=2703788.

6.4 Looking for a Better Job Outside the Company
LEARNING OBJECTIVE

1. Consider ethical dilemmas confronting employees as they move from one organization to a competitor.

Ethical Issues along the Way to a New Job

Most people who leave one job for another make the transition smoothly; they learn of a new position, apply, interview, and win the post. Notice is provided to the current employer. The split is amicable. Everyone goes forward. On some occasions, however, ethical turbulence occurs because obligations to the *current* employer are broken along the way out. These are some of the most commonly encountered flashpoints:

- **Time abuse.** The use of company time to seek another job.
- **Equipment-use abuse.** Using the firm's equipment as part of the effort to find a job elsewhere.
- **Skill theft.** Taking specific, job-related abilities acquired at one company to another.
- **Client adoption.** Moving to a new company and helping it appropriate part of the former company's client base.
- **Market adoption.** Moving to a new company and helping it appropriate part of the former company's market.
- **Idea appropriation.** Taking ideas belonging to the old company to the new one.

Musical Chair Stockbrokers

Successful stockbrokers share some basic skills. One is the ability to manage reams of information about diverse investments. The options they need to organize run from humdrum treasury bills, which are safe investments but don't earn very much, to stock in companies like Google, which first went on sale in 2004 at a price of $85. By 2007, that same share cost more than $600. Other start-up companies also began selling shares in 2004, but it's harder to remember their names since they went broke. Now it's not the stockbrokers' job to determine which investments are reliable and which more explosive; that's handled by specialized analysts. What stockbrokers do is arrange the possibilities into clear groups of more and less speculative investments, then they provide options to their clients.

Talking and helping clients choose good options is another key stock broking skill. To do that, brokers need to understand clients' situations and aspirations. If you're a young client with some extra cash, you may want to take a risk. But if you're nearing retirement, you may figure it's best to play it safe. Regardless, the stockbroker-client relationship tends to be fairly sticky once it's fully established because they've spent real time talking seriously: to help their broker work, clients need to open up about themselves, their current reality, and their hopes for the future. After that, it's difficult to just switch out of the relationship.

How do stockbrokers make money? They get a small percentage of every investment they oversee, and the larger brokerage firm, say, Smith Barney, gets a cut too. At least that's the way it works on a day-to-day basis. There is, however, another option for brokers, at least for ones who've accumulated a good, trusting client list. They can switch firms for money. For *a lot* of money because brokerage houses fall over themselves rushing to offer large signing bonuses to those employees who can bring a long client list with them.

After a deal to jump to another brokerage house has been struck, the stealth begins. One way or another, the broker needs to get his or her client files. It's a delicate operation; computers in most brokerages don't have USB drives, so you can't just pull the information off the hard drive. You've got to print it all out or find some way to access the mainframe with a thumb drive. Regardless, brokers need to get those files because they hold each client's investment history and notes brokers use to remember their clients' stories, their family members, and all the little things that make the personal relationship work.

With the client information in hand, the broker prepares for the nail-biting day of the actual switch. A letter is written to clients (though not yet sent) reporting the broker's move to the new firm, and explaining why it's a good change—or just not bad—for the clients' interests. Instructions and the necessary forms are included for clients to transfer their accounts easily and fast. The day before the change, the letters are delivered to the central post office. The next morning, the broker resigns and hurries out of the office. With the first step outside, she hits the call button on her cell phone. A long and frantic day has begun: starting with the largest investor and running down the list, she telephones to explain what's happening, and to ask each client to stick with her through the switch.

Back at the old office, intense damage control begins. The manager rushes to divide up the ex-worker's client list among the remaining brokers, and they start phoning, pleading with the clients to stay with the old, reliable firm.

Usually, most clients go.

For the moment, that's the end of it. But the switching will fire up again because a brokerage house that's lost a rainmaker may go after one of the major brokers at another house. More, a broker who's jumped ship once for money might be tempted to do it again. Eventually, the wheel may get going so fast that no one can keep straight who's working where.

Facing the possibility that the whole thing could spin out of control, the poaching brokerage houses mutually disarmed in 2004 by drawing up a protocol for broker recruiting. The legally binding agreement—which all employees were asked to sign—allowed brokers to take their clients' names and contact information when changing jobs, but nothing else, none of the investment history. That made the switch *much* more difficult since office-jumping brokers would need to rebuild their client relationships almost from scratch.

Neither Bernadette Holland nor Amy Villani wanted to do the rebuilding when they jumped from the Smith Barney brokerage house in Bethlehem, Pennsylvania, to Janney Montgomery Scott LLC of Philadelphia in late 2008, so they took their client files with them. At least that's what Smith Barney maintained when they filed a lawsuit against the two women. Their complaint alleged, "The brokers took with them customer files and information, despite their written assurances that they had complied with the protocol for broker recruiting, which expressly prohibits them from taking such files." [1]

Time Abuse
Time abuse is the use of company time to seek another job. On the surface, it's unethical. We need to be careful here, however, to distinguish exactly what "company time" means. Many jobs and work contracts are task related instead of time defined. That is, workers are hired to accomplish certain goals. In the construction business, a roofer may be signed up to get shingling done on a building before a certain deadline. In a case like that, there is no such thing as company time. The roofer's free to work whenever and consequently to *not* work whenever. As long as the job gets done by the deadline, the obligation is fulfilled. So if he wants to sit up on the roof and field calls for new jobs, it's hard to see ethical problems.

Problems do rise when workers are paid for their time. Most stockbrokers receive a base salary, a benefits package, or both as part of their work agreement. In exchange, they're supposed to use the working day to pursue the brokerage's interests, which means finding new clients and serving those already held. If Holland and Villani sat in the office talking with competing brokerage houses, they were breaking their obligation of fidelity—that is, their duty to honor their professional agreements. Of course they could respond that *all* workers take breaks. They eat a snack, sneak out for a cigarette, extend lunch. All those things are true. It's also true, however, that the case can be made that those departures actually *help* employees do their job by providing the refreshment that comes with the occasional break from work. In the cases of Holland and Villani, it seems almost impossible for them to find a way to fold conversations with competing brokerages into the obligation to their current one.

Could those conversations be justified even while recognizing that they breach the duty to fidelity? Yes. The brokers could argue that another obligation simply outweighs their responsibility to maintain their working agreement with Smith Barney. Scratching the surface a bit on the Smith Barney situation provides an example. According to a story detailing the case in the *Investment News*,

> *Recruiters and executives from rival firms said the Smith Barney reps and advisers are continuing to leave the firm this year as it prepares to take the minority stake in a joint venture with Morgan Stanley, also of New York. Citigroup will exchange Smith Barney for a 49% stake in the new firm, dubbed Morgan Stanley Smith Barney, and a $2.7 billion cash payment.* [2]

Smith Barney, this means, was being taken over by Morgan Stanley, and Smith Barney brokers were fleeing in droves.

Of course every ship-jumping broker will have unique reasons for leaving, but it does seem plausible that at least some brokers believed this new management wouldn't serve their interests well, and, by extension, their clients' interests. On this foundation, Holland and Villani could build an argument. Once it became clear that the kind of service they'd been offering their clients would be impossible under the new management, they could conclude that their service responsibility to clients outweighed their responsibility to honor a commitment to Smith Barney. From there, the case may be made for the two to use company time to pursue the possibility of working for another brokerage.

Finally, it's easier from an ethical perspective if the two could just isolate any discussions with potential future brokerage houses to non-business hours, to lunch breaks, and after 5:00 p.m. If that's not possible, however, then the decision to impose on the working day will have to find an ethical justification.

Equipment-use abuse is occupying an employer's computers, telephones, and similar as part of the effort to find a job elsewhere. In the case of the two Smith Barney brokers, just as they may have used hours, so too they may have used Smith Barney's equipment to negotiate their moving to another firm. This isn't a strong form of theft (assuming Holland and Villani didn't carry the machines out the door), but it's a betrayal of the obligation they received when they accepted the equipment—the obligation to use it to serve Smith Barney's interests. Or to at least to not subvert Smith Barney. Visiting Facebook once in a while, in other words, is OK, but sending e-mails to competitors, not so much.

Skill Theft

Skill theft is taking specific, job-related abilities acquired at one company to another. Stock broking—like many posts—requires extensive, job-specific training, and it can't be picked up along the way: legally, you can't work in the field until you've completed the required courses and passed subsequent exams. Typically, the company pays for the learning. The larger houses organize their own stock broking universities: new recruits are gathered and privately hired teachers lead them through the materials. What's learned? Beyond the Wall Street knowledge about stocks and bonds, there are guidelines to master about providing recommendations and specific rules to follow that ensure clients understand the risks involved in creating a portfolio, especially on the more speculative side of the investment spectrum. Stock broking is also a job in sales: brokers need to learn the delicate art of touting their own services without making promises about returns that can't necessarily be kept. Finally, there's quite a bit of technical knowledge that needs to be acquired so brokers can adeptly manage job-related and sometimes complicated software programs. All of this is expensive. When a company hires, they're making a major commitment and incurring a real cost.

What obligations does the cost create? The answer divides onto a legal side and an ethical one. With respect to the law, many hiring organizations incurring significant training costs write clauses into job contracts protecting against the loss if a fresh employee comes aboard for the training and then tries to leave and work elsewhere. Called a repayment clause, it stipulates that departing workers may be billed for their training. In a typical clause, the cost must be repaid completely if the employee leaves immediately, and then a declining percentage are repaid if the departure occurs after three, six, nine months, and so on.

Frequently, ethics and the law fail to overlap. In this case, however, an ethical solution to the problem of leaving an organization and taking your training with you may correspond with the strictly legal one. To the extent it's possible to monetize the investment an employer makes in an employee, returning the money could satisfy several fundamental moral duties. The *duty to not harm others* is satisfied because the recouped funds may be applied by the organization to hire and train another employee. The *duty of fidelity*—keeping obligations—is satisfied insofar as the contract's clauses are honored. Finally, the *duty to reparation*—to repay others when we harm them—is explicitly satisfied. The conclusion is that a stockbroker who takes a firm's training and leaves may justifiably claim that the action was ethically acceptable because the contractual obligation was honored.

What if the contractual obligation *isn't* honored? Is there any way for an employee to build an ethical case against repaying the company for training received? On the discussion board just mentioned, two routes are indicated. The first works from a utilitarian ethics, from the idea that the right action is the one bringing the greatest good to the greatest number. A contributor called there_are_many_questions writes,

> *I recently took a promotion at my current job and part of this was to study a level 4 course they had chosen. I had also applied to university, and due to the competitiveness of the course I wasn't sure that I would get in. Hence the reason I agreed to go for the promotion. As it happens I have been accepted into university and I begin my course shortly. I knew that I would be required to pay back the cost of the course fees but it turns out, that they were more then I was originally told. To add, because I am becoming a full time student I am unlikely to have a permanent income.* [4]

So this person applied to a competitive university and wasn't sure about getting in. Faced with the uncertainty, he or she took a promotion at the current company, which required company-provided training. In the end, as it turned out, there_are_many_questions got into the university and so left the company. Now the company wants the course fees back. As the writer notes, it's probable that he or she won't be able to pay them while enrolled as a student.

Looking at this situation, there's no doubt here that the abandoned company has a strong ethical case. "Why is there_are_many_questions paying a university for classes when he or she already owes us for classes taken?" Good question. Here's a utilitarian response: when *everyone's* interests are fully taken into account, the decision to go to university and shaft the company does, in fact, serve the greater good. The abandoned company is damaged, no doubt, but really, unless it's a small company on the brink of bankruptcy, it seems likely that they'll absorb the loss and move on. Further, there_are_many_questions had just been *promoted* by the company, so, obviously, he or she had been doing good work for them; it's not as though the entire professional relationship will be a pure loss. The jilted

company, finally, will suffer the employee's abandonment, but probably get over it without suffering lasting damage. There_are_many_questions, on the other hand, has a singular opportunity. The university is competitive—so much so that there was real uncertainty about gaining admission. To leave that opportunity behind simply to honor the clause of a contract seems like a choice causing real unhappiness, one that will continue over the long term. There'll always be that feeling of "what if?," as in "What if I'd just walked and gone to the university to learn to do what I really wanted?" In sum, when you weigh on one side the damage caused to the company by a departing employee who doesn't refund training costs, and on the other side you weigh the damage done to there_are_many_questions if the university course is abandoned to repay the company's training, it feels like there's an imbalance. When viewed dispassionately from outside the situation, the greater good really is served by walking away from the debt and going to the university. No one is saying that walking away from debts is ethical, but it would be more *unethical* to let the university opportunity pass. Another justification for walking away from the debt to the company could emerge along the lines of ethical egoism indicated by a contribution coming from Suze. She says the employee should hand over a bit of money and then "tell them to whistle for the rest, or else you will see them in court. I doubt they will pursue it." [5]

Solid ethical egoism. The right thing to do is the right thing for you, and that's it. If you can get away with not paying, Suze says, and then go for it. The reasoning is the company "probably won't pursue it." If they do, well then you might have to come up with the money. Until that happens, though, her advice is to protect your own interests, let the company take care of theirs, and see where things end up.

Client Adoption

Client adoption is moving to a new company and helping it appropriate part of the former company's client base. Holland and Villani are perpetrators. In fact, this is the central idea behind their move: to transfer clients along with them.

With respect to the law, Holland and Villani are completely free to take their clients. It's a black-and-white legal situation. All that's in dispute is how much client information they can carry to their new office. And the ethics? The situation here seems fairly clear also, at least with respect to the brokers and the brokerage. There's no doubt that both Holland and Villani on one side, and the Smith Barney brokerage house on the other, have a certain claim on the clients. While it's true that the brokers did most of the work, the brokerage provided the infrastructure and opportunity. One way to adjudicate these competing claims when the broker and brokerage split is to check whether any prior agreements regulate the separation. In this case, an agreement does exist: the protocol for broker recruiting. The fact that the agreement is there indicates that all parties involved accept that brokers transferring and taking clients is part of the way things normally work: it's fair. What needs to be settled, and what the protocol does presumably settle, are the rules for the process.

One difference, however, between ethics and the law in this situation is that ethical considerations open a broader scope onto the situation: the stakeholders increase. Where the law is concerned only with the brokerage house and the brokers, an ethical evaluation incorporates the clients as important since they're tangibly affected by any decision. So what are the clients' rights? How are they exposed by shifting brokers? Their first clear right is to say "no." They're under no obligation to follow when a broker changes firms, and there's good reason to stay put. The paperwork involved in moving is significant. More, not all houses offer the same investments instruments, so there may actually be a cost involved as items in the portfolio are sold on one side so that a comparable product may be purchased from the new brokerage. This means the client really loses when they move along with a broker.

The clients are in a tough spot, though. Typically, they've invested a good bit of their own energy and time in fostering a broker-client trust and mutual understanding. There's no guarantee—and this is especially true for longtime clients—that another broker would easily understand how the current portfolio fits together with the client's life. If that's right, then any client choosing to remain with the old firm will more or less have to start over by rebuilding their investments in consultation with whichever new stockbroker gets assigned to their case. More complications could be added, but the point is, the clients aren't just bystanders. The brokers' decision to change houses is going to affect them, and they may end up losing either way.

How do the clients' interests—and the ethical responsibility to consider them—fit into the stockbrokers' job switching? One way to begin reasoning toward an answer comes from Immanuel Kant's categorical imperative, specifically the idea that we are to treat others as ends and never as means. Kant's proposal is that we're obligated, regardless of circumstances, to not treat others as tools or instruments; treating another as a "means" is just using them to get something else. So the question here for brokers when considering whether they hold an ethical license to do all they can to carry clients to a

new firm becomes relatively simple. It would *not* be ethically recommendable if the change failed to serve the *clients'* interests. If it doesn't, if it turns out that the only people who come out ahead in all this are the brokers because they get a nice bonus from the new brokerage house for bringing over a busload of new investors, then what's happening is the clients are reducing to mere means. They're the tools the brokers use to get a payoff for them.

On the other hand, if the change *does* serve the clients' interests, then Holland and Villani can say that they aren't reducing the clients to nothing more than a payday, they're actually treating the clients the way they themselves would want to be treated in that situation. In Kant's language, the clients become "ends," they're no longer tools, and their interests can be considered a *reason* for Holland and Villani to make the switch. Now, we know from the case that Smith Barney was in the process of being engulfed by Morgan Stanley when Holland and Villani were making their move. If the brokers really believed that the services they could provide would be harmed by the change in corporate structure as Smith Barney became Morgan Stanley, and if they really believed their client services could be bettered by shifting over to the new brokerage house, then there's space for claiming that bringing the clients along is morally right.

Market Adoption

Market adoption occurs when an employee moves from one company to another and helps the new employer appropriate part of the former company's market. On the surface, this resembles client adoption. A firm's market—the people to whom they deliver goods or services—is a collection of clients, a set of people who pay for the company's efforts. Even so, there are important differences between a market and a client, and they result in radical changes to the ethical atmosphere.

The fundamental difference between a client and a market is that clients have names and markets have definitions. Clients are individuals with whom a company has cultivated a relationship; markets are aggregates of people at whom companies aim their products. When Holland and Villani changed brokerage houses, they tried to take clients with them because they were people they'd really talked to; they knew their phone numbers and life stories. A market, on the other hand, is composed of people you don't know; it's just anyone who shares a set of characteristics. For example, a brokerage house may want more business from middle-aged adults starting to think about retirement. So what do they do? They put up TV ads showing a fiftyish husband and wife at the dinner table talking about something they'd like to do together, say, visit China for a month. They can't go now. They're both working full time scraping money to pay for the kids' college and making mortgage payments. When they *retire*, though, they'll have the time; the kids will be done with school, the house will be paid for. What they need to do now is plan the financial landscape. They have a question: what kind of investments guarantees their trip? The commercial ends with a tagline: "Smith Barney: For the Journey of Your Life." That's a bad commercial, but it shows what a market is. Smith Barney doesn't care who shows up at their branch offices the next day. They don't care if it's Sam Smith or Jane Jones; they just want fifty-year-olds with some money to invest.

Many companies are constantly trying to convert markets into clients, trying to replace purely economic relationships with personal ones because people tend to stick with their brands. Markets, by contrast, shift easily; whichever company has the best TV commercial or the lowest prices, that's the one that gets the largest chunk.

Our economy is built on the idea of competition for markets: the premise that they're open and may be pursued by any organization is the basis for business activity. Obviously, there are islands of exception, things like trash collection performed by the city government. But for the most part, it's nearly impossible to form an ethical argument against employees leaving one company and going to another and then chasing the same market. To be against it isn't to be against one action or another on the part of an employee; it's to be against the entire economic structure in which we live. (It's possible to be against that structure, but that's a different debate.)

Idea Appropriation

Idea appropriation occurs when an idea belonging to the old company is given over to the new one. If a chemist at Coca-Cola accepts a job at Pepsi and promptly reveals Coke's secret formula, that's idea theft. In the brokerage business at the level Holland and Villani worked, there probably weren't too many secrets to steal. Clients yes, but no shadowy formulas for stock picking or anything like that.

Higher up in Smith Barney, however, it's perfectly possible that analysts responsible for selecting stock winners (and weeding out losers) had developed an algorithm, a kind of recipe of numbers to produce answers. In the finance industry, those who rely on numbers—share price, a company's annual earnings, and so on—to make stock predictions are called *quants*, which is short for quantitative data analyst. They take these numbers, stick them into a

secret mathematical formula, and out pops another number presumably showing whether the stock is a good buy or not. These formulas are a brokerage's concealed idea and, presumably at least, a key to their success: clients are going to flock to those brokerages consistently providing good stock-buying tips. Now if you happen to be a quant at Smith Barney, and you're offered a similar position at a competing firm, can you take the formula with you?

This is a knotted question, both legally and ethically. Starting with the law, a company's ideas are broadly divided into two categories: trade secrets and patented or copyrighted information. Trade secrets consist of nonpublic information that

- concerns a company's own activities and that if known by competitors would negatively affect the company's ability to compete against them;
- is owned by the company (though it may not be copyrighted or patented) because it was developed by the company or purchased from another company;
- is meant to remain secret as is made clear by explicit directives, security measures, or contractual agreements with employees. [6]

Trade secrets (which are sometimes called proprietary data) are ideas a company develops and uses, and that they don't want anyone to know about. In the case of the quants at Smith Barney, a formula for picking stock winners kept under lock and key would be a trade secret.

The other broad category of ideas belonging to companies is patented or copyrighted information. This is more or less a trade secret but without the secret. It's an idea a company develops that helps it compete, but the strategy for protecting the idea from competitors is different. Instead of pretending like the idea doesn't exist, or doing everything possible to make sure the details don't leak, what the company does is make the idea public by registering it with the government, claiming thereafter the sole right to use the idea. After registration, the idea's no longer a secret, but that doesn't matter since anyone else who tries to use it is vulnerable to being sued.

So the recipe for Coke is a trade secret but not patented. If you can figure out what it is, you're free to use it. The word *Coke*, on the other hand, is copyrighted. Everyone knows what it is, but you're not allowed to use it, or at least not use it to label your own soft drink. The result of all this for an employee switching companies is that the legal questions involving stolen ideas tend to involve trade secrets. You can't steal an idea that's copyrighted because everyone knows that idea already. But a trade secret—the recipe for Coke, the formula an investment house like Smith Barney uses to pick stocks—that definitely *can* be stolen; it can be revealed to the new company.

The Economic Espionage Act of 1996 makes the theft of trade secrets a federal crime. The law is clear on the issue. The problem is it's hard to *prove* that a trade secret is stolen. If you steal the recipe for Coke, you might disguise the theft by adding a tad more sugar to the version you make. Or, if you steal one of Smith Barney's quantitative stock-picking formulas, maybe you adjust the numbers slightly: not so much that it effects the predictions, but enough to make the formula different. In these cases it's going to be hard to absolutely prove the formula is stolen. In broad strokes, finally, the law of intellectual property is clear. When you get down into specific cases, however, things rapidly get twisted. What are the ethics? If you're a quant at Smith Barney and you get a call from your broker friends—Holland and Villani—saying that they're taking their clients to a new firm and they'd like you to come along, bringing Smith Barney's secret formula for stock picking as well, what kind of ethical responses are possible?

The "no" response is easily justified on moral grounds. The trade secret is company property, really no different from a computer or a desk, and taking it—even if you're taking it by memorizing it and carrying it out in your mind—is theft just like stealing objects. Further support for the no answer comes from the responsibility to fidelity, the responsibility to maintain agreements. Almost all companies that work with trade secrets write a clause into employment contracts stipulating confidentiality on sensitive matters. So the ethical obligations not to steal, and to keep our word, make a good case for declining the request to steal an idea.

Going the other way, some situations allow a reasonable argument to be mounted in favor of leaving with the trade secret or proprietary data. One justification is authorship. Someone who provides a company with an invention can fairly expect to be rewarded by the company. Inventing an idea is labor like any other, and in any field people who do exemplary work can expect promotions and rewards from the larger organization. If, unfortunately, an inventor feels as though the company isn't providing a reward—a promotion, a healthy bonus, or similar—then he or she may feel justified in leaving with his or her work, just as a good accountant may feel the need to look for employment elsewhere after being repeatedly passed over for promotion. The basic argument here is one of fairness. If a quant at Smith Barney invents an algorithm for stock picking that produces excellent results

and then sits by and watches others who've contributed less receive larger year-end bonuses, the conclusion may be reached that for balance to be restored, it's necessary to take the algorithm to another firm where a reward will be guaranteed.

Another ethical argument could be located in the difficulty that may exist in separating the *skills* an employee gains on the job from an idea or a certain kind of knowledge developed on the job. A quant who figures out a good algorithm may be able to claim that, as a skilled manipulator of numbers as they relate to economic markets, his ability as an analyst allows him to take the strategy with him. Stated differently, because of the unique skills possessed, when the quant is hired for a new brokerage, he would be able to just reinvent the algorithm. That's possible because of the rare analytic talents the quant possesses, not because the old algorithm is being stolen. In general, it can be very difficult to separate skills as they relate to ideas from the ideas themselves. And in this case, it may be that the quant's skills provide a license to regenerate the stock-picking algorithm for whatever firm is paying the salary.

Finally, an ethical case for the revelation of a trade secret may be made on humanitarian grounds. It's difficult to envision a good example of this is in the world of stock picking, but in the no-less-lucrative field of medical research, a humanitarian context for taking an idea easily comes into focus. If a cure for cancer were invented by a private company, the stock value would blow through the roof, but only if they kept the drug formula secret and sold the serum at a fairly high price. In this case, a worker in the company may feel justified in taking a job with an international health nonprofit, and then revealing the serum's formula and the technique for its production so that it could be made and distributed at a low cost to all those in need throughout the world. A theft would be committed and a wrong done, but an obligation to the greater good, to the health benefits the theft would allow, may justify a departing worker's carrying a company's secret out the door.

KEY TAKEAWAYS

- Using time and equipment paid for by a current employer to look for a new job is ethically problematic.
- Job skills provided by employers may create employee obligations.
- Employees transferring from one company to another—and asking established clients to follow—face a broad range of ethical concerns.

- Ideas belonging to an organization may not be taken to another without raising ethical concerns.

REVIEW QUESTIONS

1. Ethically, is there a difference between a worker sitting at her desk during office hours and working on her Facebook page and one who's trolling Monster, looking to find a new job somewhere else? If not, why not? If so, what's the difference?
2. If a company pays for your job training, is there a way to calculate how long you need to work there to satisfy the obligation to use the training for the company's benefit?
3. In business terms, what's the difference between trying to steal clients from your old employer and trying to steal market share? In ethical terms, what's the difference?
4. What's the difference between a trade secret and a patented idea?

[1] Bruce Kelly, "Smith Barney Seeks Restraining Orders against Four Ex-Reps," investmentnews.com, accessed May 17, 2011.http://www.investmentnews.com/article/20090224/REG/90224997 1.

[2] Bruce Kelly, "Smith Barney Seeks Restraining Orders against Four Ex-Reps," investmentnews.com, accessed May 17, 2011.http://www.investmentnews.com/article/20090224/REG/90224997 1.

[3] "Repayment of Course Fees," I-resign.com, accessed May 17, 2011, http://www.i-resign.com/uk/discussion/new_topic.asp?t=648.

[4] There_are_many_questions, April 4, 2009 (4:26 p.m.), "Repayment of Course Fees," I-resign.com, accessed May 17, 2011, http://www.i-resign.com/uk/discussion/new_topic.asp?t=648.

[5] Suze, January 6, 2005 (5:42 p.m.), comment to bradley, "Repayment of Course Fees," I-resign.com, accessed May 17, 2011, http://www.i-resign.com/uk/discussion/new_topic.asp?t=648.

[6] Manuel Velasquez, *Business Ethics: Concepts and Cases 6th Edition* (Upper Saddle River, NJ: Pearson, 2006), 357. List adapted for this text.

6.5 Take This Job and…
LEARNING OBJECTIVE

1. Define and consider ethical issues surrounding the decision to quit.

The Ethics of Quitting

There's a difference between giving a few weeks' notice that you've decided to leave your job in cold Minneapolis to try your luck in Florida, and suddenly walking out three days before the year's most important presentation, the one your team was responsible for creating. The first scenario won't cause many objections, but the second raises this question: what do departing workers owe employers?

If the answer is sought through a prism of fairness—through the idea that justice in the workplace requires equal treatment all around—the answer might be "not very much." Since most work contracts offer employment only at will, employers are typically positioned to let workers go at any time for any reason that's convenient. And they do.

> *When Ameritech was letting people go they would call them into a conference room and say their services were no longer needed. They would then show them to the door. Any coats or personal effects left at their desk would be shipped to them.* [1]

Especially in larger organizations where layoffs can come massively, the employee's pleading, "You shouldn't fire me because we just bought a house and had our first child," isn't going to persuade too many CEOs. If it doesn't, it's going to be difficult to justify the demand that employees, no matter how vital they may be to the company, come in to work when they plainly don't want to.

It's also true, however, that many employers extend benefits going beyond contractual obligations, and yes, some bend over backward to keep their workers on, even when it doesn't make strict business sense. When Malden Mills burned to the ground, owner Aaron Feuerstein spent millions keeping all three thousand employees on the payroll with full benefits for months. Some asked whether he was a fool. [2] Maybe he was, but he proves that every situation is different: some employers are cutthroats, others doggedly loyal when it comes to the people doing the work.

This is the important point for anyone thinking about leaving their organization in a lurch. If the ethical justification for splitting is built on the idea of fairness—which in this case reduces to the principle that the employee owes the organization the same loyalty that the organization displays for the employee—then it's the worker's responsibility to ask how the organization responds to employees' needs.

It should be underlined that this ethical attitude isn't quite a form of *turnabout is fair play*: the argument isn't so much that if a company has screwed (or not) people in the past, then they should get screwed (or not) now. The argument from fairness is simply that the weight of self-interest when set against the interests on the other side should be more or less balanced.

A different framework for considering the question of walking out on a job virtually without warning comes from the utilitarian perspective, from the idea that in any situation the morally right act is the one increasing happiness for all those involved. Looking at the question this way, workers considering leaving need to weigh their benefit from walking out against the suffering incurred by everyone else.

The "everyone else" includes the worker's fellow employees. If a presentation really does need to be done and given in three days and you disappear, there's just not going to be time to hire someone else and get them up to speed; those who are already there and on the project are going to have to do your share. It's worth noting here that the concern about whether the company has previously demonstrated loyalty to its workers doesn't arise within this perspective. What matters is a calculation of what serves everyone's best interest now and going forward. So even if you feel no loyalty to the company—and even if the company demonstrates no loyalty to its employees—you may still decide to stay on until a more convenient separation time can be found just so that you don't wrong those who work with you.

%$&^*#!

Everyone who's ever worked anywhere has felt the temptation at one point or another to not just quit but to go out in flames: march into the boss's office, let loose an avalanche of %$&^*#!, and storm out. It would feel good. But should it leave you feeling guilty afterward? Within a utilitarian scheme, the answer is "maybe not." If ethical justification is based on the idea that the right path is the one bringing the greatest good to the greatest number, then it might just be that the release and clean break the outburst allows is worth the scene and the discomfort (or maybe the private joy) others feel about the whole thing. Of course, by the same reasoning, anyone standing outside that door and taking one last breath before storming through better consider their own long-term happiness. Probably, bawling out the boss isn't going to help your future job-seeking prospects.

KEY TAKEAWAYS

- Most ethical issues surrounding the quitting of a job gather around those cases where the leaving is abrupt.
- The ethics of leaving a job involves a range of people and their interests.

REVIEW QUESTIONS

1. If you feel as though you've been mistreated at work, can an ethical justification be formed for walking away at a moment of maximum pain for the company? Explain.
2. Can you think of a kind of job or line of work where any employee could walk off at any time without ethical qualms? What characteristics of the job allow that freedom?

[1] James Carlini, "Ready to Leave? Why You Shouldn't Give Two Weeks' Notice," *WTN News*, April 27, 2005, accessed May 17, 2011, http://wistechnology.com/articles/1757.
[2] "Malden Mills: A Study in Leadership," Organizational Productivity Institute, Inc. *Quality Monitor Newsletter*, October 1996, accessed May 17, 2011, http://www.opi-inc.com/malden.htm.

6.6 Case Studies

Cooking a Résumé

Chef Robert Irvine's résumé was impressive. According to the *St. Petersburg Times*, he advertised his experience as including:

- A bachelor's of science degree in food and nutrition from the University of Leeds.
- Royal experience working on the wedding cake for Prince Charles and Princess Diana.
- He was a knight, as in *Sir* Robert Irvine, Knight Commander of the Royal Victorian Order, handpicked by the Queen.
- For several consecutive years, he'd received the Five Star Diamond Award from the American Academy of Hospitality Sciences.
- He'd served as a White House chef.

The truth—when the newspaper revealed it on a splashy front-page article—wasn't quite so overpowering:

- The claimed BS degree? According to a press officer at the University of Leeds, "We cannot find any connection in our records between Robert and the university."
- The royal wedding cake? Well, he did help pick some of the fruit that went into it.
- The knighthood? No.
- The Five Star Diamond Award? True, but it's not the AAA's prestigious Five Diamond Award or Mobil's five stars. The American Academy of Hospitality Sciences is actually a guy's apartment in New York, and the award is granted to anyone who pays a fee.
- White House chef? Kind of. But he didn't prepare sophisticated dishes for the president or anything like that; he cooked food for the cafeteria line, serving military workers at the White House. [1]

After the truth came out, Chef Irvine was fired from his popular TV show on the Food Network, *Dinner: Impossible*. A few months later, however, after the scandal blew over and he'd corrected his résumé, he reapplied for his old job, was rehired, and he's on TV today.

QUESTIONS

1. When Irvine first applied for the job as TV show chef, he had to consider whether he should "embellish" his résumé, and if so, how far he should go. What ethical responsibilities should he have considered? To whom?

2. The five types of positive résumé misrepresentations are
   - false credentials,
   - false experience,
   - false chronology,
   - embellished experience,
   - false references.

   Negative résumé misrepresentations have also been discussed. Looking back at Irvine's résumé adventure, can you label each of his transgressions?

3. Are some of the lies worse than others in the sense that they relate directly to his ability to be a successful TV chef? Are others less objectionable because they don't relate to the job he was applying for? Why or why not?

4. *It's better to seek forgiveness than ask permission.* In a sense, that's what Irvine did. He lied on his résumé, got the job, did well, got caught having lied on the résumé, got fired, sought forgiveness, got it, and got back a TV show job he might never have received had he not lied in the first place. Ethically, how could you go about justifying his course of action?

5. The Internet site Fakeresume.com includes the following advice for job seekers: "Hiring Managers Think You're Lying Anyway!! Yep that's right, the majority of human resources managers assume that EVERYONE embellishes, exaggerates, puffs up and basically lies to some extent on your résumé. So if you're being totally honest you're being penalized because they're going to assume that you embellished your résumé to a certain extent!" [2] Assume you believe this is true; can you make the ethical case for being honest on your résumé regardless of what hiring managers think?

6. Assume Fakeresume.com is right. *Everyone* "embellishes, exaggerates, puffs up and basically lies to some extent on their résumé." On the basis of the obligations you hold to others (hiring managers, coworkers, and other applicants) and to yourself, could you form the argument that you have an ethical responsibility to lie?

7. You have a friend you like and respect. You've spent a lot of time with him over the years in school and you know he's very responsible, a hard worker, and smart. He'd be good at almost any entry-level type job; you're sure of it. He comes to you and asks you to fake having been his boss for a pizza delivery business. "I just want," he says, "someone out there who I can count on to say I'm the good, responsible type. You know someone who's always on time for work, that kind of thing." Would you do it? Justify your answer.

Inmate Wages

An Internet posting carries a simple Q&A thread: someone's searching for a good upholstery shop in Maryland. An unexpected answer comes back from Fenny L: criminals. A local jail has a job-training program for their inmates and they contract the men at $1.50 per hour. [3]

The responses to the suggestion are intense and all over the place, but many circle around the ethics of the numbingly low wage, leading Fenny L to introduce a new thread. Here are the three main points she makes.

- While I object to slave labor…at the same time, I don't see this as slave labor. If I wished to become a professional uhhh…upholsterer (what do they call themselves?!?) I would need to spend money on the classes and etc. The Dept. of Corrections doesn't charge the inmates for these classes—thusly; I don't see a problem with only paying the inmates $1.50 for their work.

- Also, we use free/cheap labor ALL the time…in the form of Interns. Interns are often paid nothing, or extremely little—because they want the job experience…that is their compensation. In turn, I feel that the inmates are getting job experience so that they can earn an honest living once they get out.

- Finally, I think that the Dept. of Corrections has to make the wages obscenely low—because let's be honest…how many people would feel comfortable with having a convict in their home to do work? The only way they can be competitive and offer the inmates this opportunity, is to make it worth the consumer to utilize them—by having obscenely low wages. [4]

QUESTIONS

1. Suppose you made a mistake and ended up in jail for a few months. While there, you participated in this program. Now you're out and seeking an upholstering job.
   - You're considering leaving the jail part of this episode off your résumé. Whose interests should you consider before going ahead? What ethical case could you make for leaving it off your résumé?
   - Given the kind of work you'd be doing—going into peoples' homes and upholstering—does the nature of your "mistake" (drunk driving versus shoplifting, for example) influence the ethical consideration of

whether you ought to acknowledge this part of your life on your résumé? How?

o   Maybe for the first several years you should leave your prison training on your résumé, but is there a kind of statute of limitations, a certain amount of time that, once passed, gives you an ethical license to leave something negative off your résumé? How would you calculate the amount of time and based on what factors?

2. Sometimes a split opens between a community-wage level (what people in general in a certain place are paid for certain labor) and an organizational-wage level (what people at a specific organization are paid for the same labor). The split clearly opens here; the prisoners are paid much less than other upholsterers in the larger community.

o   Fenny L believes this split is justified by the ethics of a market economy. She makes the point that most people really don't want crooks wandering around their house, so in order to get business; the prison needs to make its offer attractive by cutting labor prices. She's probably right in terms of economics, but in terms of ethics, do you find this reasoning convincing? Why or why not?

o   Can you form an ethical argument in favor of the prisoners demanding a pay raise to make their salary comparable with other upholsterers?

3. If you were an upholsterer and your company had a practice of hiring ex-convicts because they'd work for lower wages, could you make the ethical argument that you deserve a higher wage than those other workers with similar experience and skills because you'd never had trouble with the law? What would your argument look like?

4. If you were an upholsterer looking to wiggle a pay hike, would you ask a friend to pose as the boss from a competing outfit and offer you the same job at a higher salary? In considering the question, what are the specific ethical obligations tugging one way or the other, and to whom do you have the obligations?

5. Fenny L. believes the workers are receiving a fair wage because they're getting valuable training and experience that will improve their future job prospects. That's probably true, but the fact remains that the workers are being paid much less money, for the same work, than others.

o   Is an internship—or any post where you receive less than the community-wage level for a certain kind of work—a humiliation? Why or why not?

o   Is there an ethical objection to allowing you to be humiliated? Explain.

6. Many jobs require company-sponsored training, and frequently employees enrolling in corporate training programs sign repayment clauses, promising to repay the training's cost if they leave before a certain amount of time has passed, say, one year. Is there an ethical argument here for the idea that repayment clauses are a form of prison and therefore unethical? Why or why not?

7. Upholstering is not a job where experience counts very much. Yes you need some initial training and practice, but once you've got that, ten years more experience isn't going to make you a significantly better upholsterer of common items. Accepting that reality, if you were the upholsterer who'd been with the company the longest, could you still translate your seniority into an ethical argument that you deserve a higher wage than others who've been around less time? Explain.

Dirty Tricks

In his book *21 Dirty Tricks at Work*, author Colin Gautrey gives his readers a taste of how intense life at the office can get. Here are two of his favorite tricks. [5]

QUESTIONS

1. **The exposure trick.** Coercing a coworker by threatening to make public a professional or personal problem. If you're angling for a raise, and you know something damaging about your supervisor, you may be tempted by the tactic of exposure. Imagine you know that your supervisor has a prescription drug habit and it's getting worse. Her performance at the office has been imbalanced but not so erratic as to raise suspicions. You plan to confront her and say you'll spill the beans unless she gets you a raise. Whose interests are involved here? What responsibilities do you have to each of them? What ethical justification could you draw up to justify your threat?

2. **The bystander trick.** Knowing that someone is in trouble but standing on the sidelines and doing nothing even when intervention is clearly appropriate and would be helpful to the business. At an upholstering company you're in competition for a promotion with a guy who learned the craft in jail, through the Department of Corrections' job-training course. He hadn't revealed that fact to anyone, but now the truth has come to light. You've worked with him on a lot of assignments and seen that he's had a chance to make off with some decent jewelry but hasn't taken anything. You could

speak up to defend him, but you're tempted to use the bystander trick to increase the odds that you'll win the duel. What ethical argument could you draw up to convince yourself that you shouldn't stand there and watch, but instead you should help your adversary out of the jam?

The End of Destiny's Child

The R&B group Destiny's Child was composed of Beyoncé Knowles, Kelly Rowland, and Michelle Williams. They started slow in 1990 (Beyoncé was nine), giving mini-concerts in crumbling dance halls around Houston, and then kept at it through small-time talent shows, promised record deals that never materialized, and the disintegration of Rowland's family (Beyoncé's parents took her into their home). They finally got a crummy but real record deal in 1998 and made the most of it.

By 2002 they'd become a successful singing and dance act. But soon after, they broke up under the pressure of Beyoncé's solo career, which seemed to be speeding even faster than the group effort.

In 2004 they reunited for a new album, *Destiny Fulfilled*, which went triple platinum. On the European leg of the subsequent world tour, Beyoncé quit more definitively. She took the fan base with her and began evolving into the hugely successful Beyoncé we know now: pop music juggernaut, movie celebrity, clothing design star…The other two members of the original group? Today they appear on B-list talk shows (when they can get booked) and are presented to viewers as Kelly Rowland, formerly of Destiny's Child, and Michelle Williams, formerly of Destiny's Child.

According to the *New York Times* it shouldn't be surprising that things ended up this way: "It's been a long-held belief in the music industry that Destiny's Child was little more than a launching pad for Beyoncé Knowles's inevitable solo career." [6]

Which leads to this question: Why did she go back in 2004 and do the *Destiny Fulfilled* album with her old partners? Here's what the *New York Times* reported: "Margeaux Watson, arts and entertainment editor at *Suede*, a fashion magazine, suggests that the star does not want to appear disloyal to her former partners, and called Beyoncé's decision to return to the group a charitable one." But "from Day 1, it's always been about Beyoncé," Ms. Watson said. "She's the one you can't take your eyes off of; no one really cares about the other girls. I think Beyoncé will eventually realize that these girls are throwing dust on her shine." [7]

1. Destiny's Child rolled money in, and it needed to be divided up. Assume the three singers always split money equally, going way back to 1990 when it wasn't the profits they were dividing but the *costs* of gasoline and hotel rooms, which added up to more than they got paid for performing. About the money that finally started coming in faster than it was going out, here are two common theories for justifying the payment of salaries within an organization: *Money is apportioned according to the worker's value to the organization*, and *money is apportioned according to the experience and seniority relative to others in the organization*.
   o How would these two distinct ways of divvying up the revenue change the salary assigned to the three singers?
   o When success came, how could Beyoncé ethically justify demanding a greater share of the pie?
   o How could you justify experience and seniority as the ethically preferable route to follow when paying the three singers making up Destiny's Child?
2. There are a lot of rhythm and blues groups out there, singing as hard as they can most nights on grimy stages for almost no audience, which means the organizational-wage level of Destiny's Child was way, *way* above the wage level of other organizations in the same line of work.
   o When the members of Destiny's Child cash their paychecks, should they feel guilty about getting so much more than others in their profession who work just as hard as they do, but in different organizations where the pay is less? Why or why not?
   o Cashiers at Whole Foods Market get paid more than cashiers at Wal-Mart. Should the Whole Foods cashiers feel guilty? Why or why not?
3. Beyoncé didn't break clean from Destiny's Child. She rejoined the organization because, according to Watson, "she didn't want to appear disloyal to her former partners." Beyoncé felt an ethical responsibility to mind the interests of Kelly Rowland and Michelle Williams. As she thought about leaving the group more definitively, what other people (if any) do you suppose she should have considered in order feeling ethically justified in finally and permanently taking off on her own? What are the obligations she holds to Rowland, Williams, and any others you have added to the list?
4. Destiny's Child was a pop group; their hits included "Say My Name," which isn't too different from Beyoncé's smash "Single Ladies (Put a Ring on It)." The videos are pretty close, too: nearly identical mixes of rhythm,

dancing, fun, and sexy provocation. After comparing the video of "Say My Name" [8] with "Single Ladies," [9] it's hard to deny that Beyoncé benefited from her time in Destiny's Child. Very possibly, she feels as though she owes Rowland and Williams part of her success, and that's why she did the reunion record and tour. Now, if you were Rowland or Williams, could you form an ethical argument that Beyoncé owes you more than that based on the following:

o **Client appropriation.** When Beyoncé left, she benefited from a group of devoted listeners constructed by Destiny's Child. Do you suppose these would be clients, a market, or some mix? How do you imagine Beyoncé benefited from them and what should she do to repay the obligation?

o **Skill theft.** When Beyoncé left, Destiny's Child still had gas in its engine: the group was selling CDs and touring successfully. It could do that because of the skills the three members learned years earlier through tireless rehearsals and small-time concerts. During all those years they were training for musical success, but when they got it, Beyoncé quickly left the organization. She went out on her own and kept doing what she'd learned to do with Rowland and Williams. Given that, use an ethical theory to make the case that Beyoncé is significantly obligated to the other two. What is her obligation? Is there some point—either after a certain amount of time has passed or an amount of money has been paid or something else—where the obligation will have been satisfied? Explain.

Stolen Intel

Biswamohan Pani, a low-level engineer at Intel, apparently stole trade secrets worth a billion dollars from the company. His plot was simple. According to a *Business week* article, he scheduled his resignation from Intel for June 11, 2008. He'd accumulated vacation time, however, so he wasn't actually in the office during June, even though he officially remained an employee. That employee status allowed him access to Intel's computer network and sensitive information about next-generation microprocessor prototypes. He downloaded the files, and he did it from his new desk at Advanced Micro Devices (AMD), which is Intel's chief rival. Pani had simply arranged to begin his new AMD job while officially on vacation from Intel.

Why did he do it? The article speculates that "Pani obtained Intel's trade secrets to benefit himself in his work at AMD without AMD's knowledge that he was doing so, which is a fairly frequent impulse among employees changing jobs: to take a bit of work product from their old job with them."[10] According to Nick Akerman, a New York lawyer who specializes in trade secret cases, "It's amazing how poorly most companies [protect their trade secrets]." [11]

After being caught, Pani faced charges in federal court for trade secret theft, with a possible prison term of ten years. He pleaded innocent, maintaining that he downloaded the material for his wife to use. She was an Intel employee at the time and had no plans to leave.

QUESTIONS

1. Can the fact that Pani got the information so easily be used to build an ethical case that what he did wasn't wrong? If not, why not? If so, what does the case look like?

2. Ethically, does it matter whether Pani was a key author of the taken documents? Why or why not?

3. According to the article, a lot of people do what Pani did. Is that a justification for his action? Explain.

4. Did Pani have a responsibility to formally end his employment status with Intel before joining AMD, or is it OK for him to be vacationing from Intel while working at AMD? Whose interests need to be considered to answer this question thoroughly?

5. As James Carlini, a professor at Northwestern University, points out in an essay, [12] it is accepted wisdom in the world of business ethics that employees leaving a company ought to provide two-week' notice to employers. Use the Pani case to make the argument that employees should notify employers that they're leaving only at the last moment.

6. Pani left Intel after receiving a poor job review. Probably he was mad about that. From a utilitarian perspective—one that defines the ethical good as the greatest good for the greatest number over the long haul—would Pani have acted more ethically had he stormed into his boss's office and screamed at the guy and quit instead of biting his tongue, getting a job elsewhere, and doing what he did? Explain.

[1] Ben Montgomery, "TV Chef Spiced Up His Past Exploits," *St. Petersburg Times*, February 17, 2008, accessed May 17, 2011, http://www.sptimes.com/2008/02/17/Southpinellas/TV_chef_spiced_up_his.shtml.
[2] Fakeresume.com accessed May 17, 2011, http://fakeresume.com.

[3] Fenny L., April 7, 2009, "Searching for good upholstery shop in MD," accessed May 17, 2011, http://www.yelp.com/topic/gaithersburg-searching-for-good-upholstery- shop-in-md.

[4] Fenny L., April 17, 2009, "Ethics of Inmate Wages," accessed May 17, 2011, http://www.yelp.com/topic/washington-ethics-of-inmate-wages.

[5] "21 Dirty Tricks," The Gautrey Group, accessed May 17, 2011, http://www.siccg.com/fre/DirtyTricks.php.

[6] Lola Ogunnaike, "Beyoncé's Second Date with Destiny's Child," *New York Times*, November 14, 2004, accessed May 17, 2011, http://www.nytimes.com/2004/11/14/arts/music/14ogun.html?_r=1.

[7] Lola Ogunnaike, "Beyoncé's Second Date with Destiny's Child," *New York Times*, November 14, 2004, accessed May 17, 2011, http://www.nytimes.com/2004/11/14/arts/music/14ogun.html?_r=1.

[8] "Destiny's Child—Say My Name," YouTube video, 4:00, posted by "DestinysChildVEVO," October 25, 2009, http://www.youtube.com/watch?v=sQgd6MccwZc.

[9] "Beyoncé—Single Ladies (Put a Ring on It)," YouTube video, 3:19, posted by "beyonceVEVO," October 2, 2009, http://www.youtube.com/watch?v=4m1EFMoRFvY.

[10] Michael Orey, "Lessons from Intel's Trade-Secret Case," *Bloomberg Businessweek*, November 18, 2008, accessed May 17, 2011, http://www.businessweek.com/print/technology/content/nov2008/tc200 81118_067329.htm.

[11] Michael Orey, "Lessons from Intel's Trade-Secret Case," *Bloomberg Businessweek*, November 18, 2008, accessed May 17, 2011, http://www.businessweek.com/print/technology/content/nov2008/tc200 81118_067329.htm.

[12] James Carlini, "Ready to Leave? Why You Shouldn't Give Two Weeks' Notice," *WTN News*, April 27, 2005, accessed May 17, 2011, http://wistechnology.com/articles/1757.

NOTES:

Chapter 7:
Making the Best of the Job You Have as You Get from 9 to 5

Chapter Overview

This chapter examines some ethical decisions facing employees. It considers the values guiding choices made over the course of a workday.

7.1 Taking Advantage of the Advantages: Gifts, Bribes, and Kickbacks

LEARNING OBJECTIVES

1. Define a conflict of interest.
2. Show how gifts in the business world may create conflicts of interest.
3. Delineate standard practices for dealing with gifts.
4. Consider how receiving gifts connected with work may be managed ethically.
5. Define bribes and kickbacks in relation to gifts.
6. Show how the ethics of bribes and kickbacks can be managed inside the ethics of gifts.

Living the High Life

If you're young, looking for work, and headed toward a big city (especially New York), then you could do a lot worse than landing a job as a media buyer for an advertising agency. According to an article in *New York* magazine, it's working out well for twenty-four-year-old Chris Foreman, and it's working out despite a salary so measly that he can't afford his own place, a ticket to a movie, or even to add meat to his homemade spaghetti. [1]

This is what makes the job click for Foreman: as a media buyer, he oversees where big companies like AT&T place their advertisements. And because those ads mean serious money—a full page in a glossy, top-flight magazine costs about five times what Foreman earns in a year—the magazines line up to throw the good life at him. Thanks to the generosity of *Forbes* magazine, for example, Foreman spends the occasional evening on the company's vast Highlander yacht; he drinks alcohol almost as old as he is, munches exquisite hors d'oeuvres, and issues orders to white-suited waiters. While guests arrive and depart by helicopter, Foreman hobnobs with people the rest of us see only on movie screens. A scan of the Highlander guest book turns up not just celebrities but serious power too: Margaret Thatcher was a guest once.

A night on the Highlander is a good one, but it's far from the only event lighting up Foreman's glitzy life. A few of his other recent outings are listed in the article, with some estimated cash values attached: An all-expenses-paid ski weekend (worth almost $1,000, in Foreman's estimation); tickets to see Serena Williams at the US Open ($75 each); invites to the *Sports Illustrated* Swimsuit Issue party, where he chatted with Heidi Klum and Rebecca Romijn-Stamos; prime seats for sold-out Bruce Springsteen concerts ($500 each); dinners at Cité, Sparks, Il Mulino, Maloney & Porcelli, and Monkey Bar, to name a few of his favorites ($100 a pop).

Foreman observes the irony of his life: "It's kind of crazy, I had dinner at Nobu on Monday [the kind of restaurant few can afford, even if they're able to get a reservation], but I don't have enough money to buy socks." [2]

The Highlander's spectacularly wealthy owner is Steve Forbes. If he invites former British Prime Minister Margaret Thatcher aboard for a holiday weekend, you can understand why: she's not just an interesting person; she's living history. Serena Williams would be an interesting guest, too, in her way. The same goes for Heidi Klum and Ms. Romijn-Stamos, in a different way. What they all have in common, though, is that you know exactly what they've got, and why a guy with a big bank account would treat them to an evening. But what, exactly, does Mr. Forbes expect to get in return for inviting media buyer Chris Foreman? The answer: "We media buyers are the gatekeepers—no one at AT&T actually purchases the ads. If at the end of a buying cycle, your budget has an extra $200,000, you'll throw it back to the person who treated you best." [3]

The answer, in a word, is money.

What's Wrong with Gifts and Entertainment?

The fundamental problem with the gifts Foreman received and the free entertainment he enjoyed is that they create a conflict of interest, a conflict between professional obligations and personal welfare. As a paid media buyer, it's Foreman's job and obligation to buy ads in the magazines that will do his clients the most good, that'll deliver the biggest bang for the buck. But against that, as a single twenty-four-year-old guy in New York City, it's in his personal interest to purchase ads in *Forbes* magazine since that probably gets him invited back to the Highlander with its free drinks, exquisite dinners, and, if he's lucky, some face time with women he's already seen quite a bit of in *Sports Illustrated*. This is a tough spot, and there are two broad ways it can play out:

1. Foreman can do the parties at night, go home, sleep, wake up with a clear head, and buy the best ads for his client. Let's say the advertising money he's spending belongs to AT&T and they're trying to attract new clients in the forty-five to fifty-five demographic of heavy cell phone users. He takes that target, checks to see what magazine those people like to read more than any other, and buys a full pager there. If the magazine happens to be *Forbes*, great, if not, then *Forbes* doesn't get anything back for its party. In this case, Foreman knows he's done right by AT&T and his employer. To the best of his ability, he guided advertising money to the spot where it'll do the most good. There remains a potential problem here, however, which is the *appearance* of a conflict of interest. Even though Foreman didn't let the parties affect his judgment, someone looking at the whole thing from outside might well *suspect* he did if it happens that *Forbes* gets the ad buy. This will be returned to later on in this chapter.

2. The darker possibility is that *Forbes* isn't the best media buy, but they get the ad anyway because Foreman wants to keep boarding the Highlander. In this case, Foreman is serving his own interest but failing his obligations to his employer and to his client.

In pure ethical terms, the problem with the second possibility, with selling out the client, can be reduced to an accusation of lying. When Foreman or any employee signs up for a job, shows up for work, and then accepts a paycheck, they're promising to be an agent for the organization, which is formally defined in commercial law as someone acting on *behalf* of the organization and its interests. In some situations it can be difficult to define exactly what those interests are, but in Foreman's it's not. He does well for his employer when he gives the clients the best advice possible about spending their advertising dollars. That's his promise and he's not fulfilling it.

Redoubling the argument, in the case of the typical media buyer, there's probably also an explicit clause in the employment contract *demanding* that all media advice be objective and uncorrupted by personal interest. Even without that formal step, however, the shortest route to an ethical condemnation of buying ads because a night on the Highlander (or some other gift) has been received is to underline that the act turns the media purchaser into a liar. It makes him or her dishonest every time they come into work because they're not providing the objective and impartial advice they promise.

In discussing conflicts of interests, it's important to keep in mind that those who find themselves caught up in one haven't necessarily been corrupted. Just because Foreman finds himself torn between giving impartial advice to his client and giving the advice that gets him good parties *doesn't* mean his judgment is poisoned. That said, it's *extremely* difficult to walk away from a conflict of interest unstained: any time serious gifts or rich entertainment gets injected into a business relationship, suspicious questions about professionalism are going to seep in too.

Finally, there are two broad ways of dealing with gifts, especially those creating conflicts of interest. They can be flatly refused, or rules can be formulated for accepting them responsibly.

Refusing Gifts and Entertainment

One way to avoid the gift and conflict of interest problem altogether for Chris Foreman or anyone in a similar situation is to simply refuse any gifts from business partners. Far more frequently than private businesses, government organizations take this route. The approach's advantage, obviously, is that it wipes out the entire question of wrongdoing. The disadvantage, however, is that it dehumanizes work; it seems to forbid many simple and perfectly appropriate gestures of human interaction.

Here's an example of what can happen when efforts to eradicate conflicting interests go to the extreme: it's from a *New York Times* front-pager about the state governor:

> *Governor David A. Paterson violated state ethics laws when he secured free tickets to the opening game of the World Series from the Yankees last fall for himself and others, the New York State Commission on Public Integrity charged on Wednesday.* [4]

So, the governor is in trouble because he got some tickets to watch his home team play in the baseball championship? That's going to make Chris Foreman's head swim. Without getting into the details of the Paterson case, accepting these tickets doesn't seem like a huge transgression, especially for someone whose job pays well and is already packed with gala events of all kinds. It's not as though, in other words, Peterson's going to be blown away by the generosity or become dependent on it. In the case of Foreman who could barely afford to eat, it's reasonable to suspect that he may come to rely on his occasional trip to the Highlander, but it just doesn't seem likely that the governor's judgment and ability to fulfill professional obligations are going to be distorted by the gift provided by the New York Yankees baseball club. More, as the state's elected leader, a case could probably be made that the governor actually had a professional responsibility to show up and root for the home team (as long as the visitors aren't the Mets). As a final note, since the now former governor is legally blind, the value of the gift seems limited since he couldn't actually see the game he attended.

Despite this case's apparent frivolity, the general practice of eliminating conflict of interest concerns by simply banning gifts can be justified. It can be because so many gifts, just by existing, create the appearance of a conflict of interest. An appearance of conflict exists when a reasonable person looking at the situation from outside (and without personal knowledge of anyone involved) will conclude from the circumstances that the employee's ability to perform his or her duties may be compromised by personal interest. This is different from an *actual* conflict because when there's really conflict, the individual *feels* torn between professional obligations and personal welfare. Almost certainly, Foreman was tempted to help out *Forbes* because he really liked the parties. But the case of Governor Paterson presents only the appearance of a conflict of interest because we don't know whether he even wanted the tickets to the Yankees game. Given the fact that he's blind, he may well have preferred staying home that night. Still, for those of us who can't know his true feelings, it does seem as though there might, potentially, be some incentive for Paterson to return the Yankee favor and provide them some special advantage. It's almost certain that at some time in the future, the baseball club will have an issue up for debate by the state government (perhaps involving the construction of a stadium or maybe just a license to sell beer inside the one they currently have), and as soon as that happens, the appearance of conflict is there because maybe Paterson's response will be colored by the tickets he got.

Conclusion. Refusing to accept any gifts from business associates is a reasonable way of dealing with the ethical dilemma of conflicting interests. By cutting the problem off at the roots—by eliminating not only conflicts but the appearance of them—we can go forward with confidence that a worker's promise to represent the organization faithfully is uncorrupted by the strategic generosity of others.

What Other Remedies Are Available for Conflict of Interest Problems Stemming from Gifts?

Categorically refusing gifts may be recommendable in some cases, but in most economic situations a total ban isn't realistic. People make business arrangements the same way they make friendships and romance and most other social things—that mean invitations to the Highlander if you're lucky, or just to a few Budweiser's in the hotel bar. And if you turn everyone down every time, it's probably going to dampen your professional relationships; you may even lose the chance to get things done because someone else will win the contract between drinks.

So where does the line get drawn for accepting gifts with ethical justification? Whether you happen to be a renowned politician in a large state or someone just out of school trying to make a go of it in the world, there are a number of midpoints between Governor Paterson's obligation to refuse tickets to a game he couldn't see anyway and Chris Foreman's raucous partying on the Highlander. Three of the most common midpoints are:
1. transparency,
2. recusal,
3. organizational codes.

Transparency, as the word indicates, manages the acceptance of gifts by publicly recognizing their existence. The idea is that if Foreman is willing to openly acknowledge exactly what he's getting from *Forbes* magazine, then we can trust that there's nothing underhanded going on, no secret agreements or deals. Of course the gifts may still influence his judgment, but the fact that they're public knowledge at least removes the sense that he's trying to get away with something.

Recusal is abstaining from taking part in decisions contaminated by the appearance of a conflict of interest. Foreman could, for example, keep going to Highlander parties but not manage any media buying for the demographic that reads *Forbes*. It's fairly easy to imagine a team of media buyers working together on this. Every time something comes up that might be right for *Forbes*, Foreman passes the decision on to Sam Smith or whoever and so removes himself from the conflict.

In the public sphere, especially politics and law, it's common for judges and legislators to remove themselves from considering issues bearing directly on their welfare. A judge who owns stock in the Omnicom communications group may recuse herself from hearing a civil case brought against the company. Legislators deciding what the salary should be for legislators may ask for recommendations from an independent panel.

Organizational codes are one of the theoretically easiest but also one of the more practically difficult ways to handle gifts. The advantage of a code is that it can provide direct responses for employees trying to decide whether they can accept a gift. In Oregon, for example, legislators are prohibited from accepting gifts valued at more than fifty dollars. Assuming the code is reasonable—and in this case it was judged so by the state's supreme court—legislators may assert that by implication accepting a gift valued under that amount is, in fact, ethical.[5]

However, the problem with codes is that, like laws, they frequently leave gray areas. That's especially true in a media buyer's world where so much is spent on entertaining. In that kind of reality, it's very difficult to put a specific price on everything. A night on the Highlander, obviously, is worth a lot to Foreman, but how does it appear in the accounting books of dollars and cents? Because it's hard to know, monetary limits provide only vague ethical guidance for those in Foreman's line of work.

The broader lesson is that gifts come in so many forms—and with values that can be so difficult to accurately measure—that it's virtually impossible to write something encompassing all the specific possibilities. Many codes of conduct, therefore, end up sounding noble but are really just saying, "Figure it out for yourself." Take a look at the last lines from the Code of Conduct from Omnicom, a massive group of companies including many leading advertising firms that purchase ads in *Forbes*:

> *We expect each employee to exercise good judgment and discretion in giving or accepting any gift. No set of specific rules can anticipate or capture every possible instance in which an ethical issue may arise. Instead, all of us must be guided by the overarching principle that we are committed to fair and honest conduct and use our judgment and common sense whenever confronted with an ethical issue.* [6]

Questions to Ask before Accepting a Gift

In their book *Moral Issues in Business*, authors William Shaw and Vincent Barry formulate a list of questions that, when answered, can provide support and clarity for making decisions about whether a gift may be accepted. They're not going to tell you what to do—there's no magic guide—but they can help you see things more clearly. In modified form and with some additions and subtractions, here's the list. [7]

- **Is there a conflict of interest, or the appearance of a conflict, that arises because of the gift?** Not every gift raises conflict of interest concerns. Maybe a marketer at *Forbes* gets a late cancellation for a Highlander night and can't find any targeted media buyer to fill the spot, so the invite gets handed off to a buyer specializing in purchasing ads for young teenagers. Why not? It'd just go to waste otherwise. And should that lucky media buyer say yes? It's difficult to find an ethical reason not to since no conflict of interest concerns seem to arise.

- **What's the gift's value?** This can be an easy one. When Foreman was invited to a Springsteen concert he could just look at the tickets and see that he'd been offered something worth $500. On the other hand, getting the chance to chat up a *Sports Illustrated* swimsuit model on the Highlander is going to be harder to quantify. In those cases where a value can be set, the number allows a clean dividing line: anything above the a specified amount gets categorized as potentially influencing a decision and so causing a conflict of interest, while any gift worth less may be considered nominal, too small to threaten professionalism. What's the magic number? That depends on who's involved and the general context, but many organizations are currently setting it at $25, which is, not incidentally, the limit the IRS sets for business deductions for gifts to any single person during one year.

- **Is the gift provided out of generosity or for a purpose?** No one can peer into the soul of another, but something offered during the holiday season may be more acceptable than the same thing offered just before a major advertising buy is being made.

- **What's the gift's purpose?** Just because a gift isn't an outpouring of generosity so much as an expression of self-interest *doesn't* mean there's a corrupting intent. For example, if *Forbes* magazine sends Foreman a free copy of each issue, that's more like advertising for themselves than an attempt to buy the guy off. Almost all of us have had the same experience: we've received calendars or notepads in the mail from a local real estate agent or insurance seller. These aren't attempts to buy us, just ways to present their services. On the other hand, it's hard to see how tickets to a Springsteen concert given by a magazine can be anything but an attempt to induce the receiver to give a gift back by throwing some ad money the publication's way.

- **Is it a gift or entertainment?** Traditionally, a distinction has been drawn between giving gifts and paying for entertainment. As a rule of thumb, the former is something you can take home and the latter is enjoyed on the spot. Presumably, entertainment raises fewer ethical concerns because it isn't a payoff so much as a courtesy extended to a media buyer in exchange for hearing a pitch. If someone from *Forbes* wants to convince Foreman that her magazine is the best place for advertising dollars, then it doesn't seem so bad, buying him a lunch or a few beers while he hears (endures) the pitch. After all, it's her job to sell the magazine and it's his to know the advantages all the magazines offer. This is just normal business. Gifts, on the other hand, seem much more like bribes because they don't exist in the context of normal business conversations. Take the tickets to a Springsteen concert; they have nothing to do with business and can't be justified as a courtesy extended within the boundaries of normal exchanges between magazines and ad buyers. Finally, with respect to the parties on the Highlander, those are technically entertainment since Foreman can't take the yacht home afterward. It doesn't sound, though, like a lot of business talk was going on.

- **What are the circumstances?** There's a difference between *Forbes* magazine handing concert tickets to media buyers to mark the launching of a new column in the magazine and their constant, ongoing provisioning. As part of the launch campaign, it's much easier for Foreman to accept the gift without feeling trapped by an obligation to throw business *Forbes'* way since he can respond to the gesture simply by being aware that the new column is there and taking it into account when he makes future buying decisions.

- **What power do I have to bestow favors in return for gifts?** Foreman's job title is *assistant* media buyer, meaning he probably doesn't actually decide which magazine gets the business. He just gathers research data and makes a recommendation to the boss. Does this free him to enjoy the Highlander night's guilt free? Hard to be sure, but it definitely helps him fulfill his professional obligations: it's just much easier to do the data mining and recommendation writing in the back office than it is to be the guy sitting out front telling *Forbes* magazine the answer's "no," even though the parties were great. If that's the way things go, Foreman may be a coward for letting his boss deliver the bad news to *Forbes*, but that's a personal ethical failure, not a business one.

- **What's the industry accepted practice?** In New York state government, as the Paterson case shows, the accepted practice is no gifts, period. In the looser world of Manhattan media business, *New York* magazine sums things up: "Everybody in our industry is guilty of it. Many of those who travel for work take their boyfriends and call it a vacation." [8]Care should be taken here to avoid the conclusion that whatever everyone else is doing is OK. That's not it at all. But it is true that if

everyone's guilty—if *all* the magazines are lavishing gifts on media buyers, and all the buyers are accepting—it's going to be much easier for Foreman to satisfy his professional obligations. It's going to be easier for him to tell *Forbes* "no" (assuming the demographic facts recommend that) when all the magazines are gifting about equally and everyone's accepting than it would be if *Forbes* were the only magazine giving the gifts and he was the only one accepting.

- **What's the organization's policy?** As the Omnicom Code of Conduct illustrates, sometimes policy provides words but no guidance. As the New York government policy (which prohibits all gifts) shows, however, sometimes there is guidance. When true guidance *is* provided, an employee may fairly reason that following it is fulfilling professional obligations to the employer.

- **What's the law?** Generally, laws on gift giving and receiving apply to public officials and those working with them (politicians, judges, lawyers, businesses doing work for the government). As is always the case, the legal right doesn't in itself make ethical right. It can, however, provide the foundation for making an ethically recommendable decision, assuming other factors—many of which will come up through the set of questions just listed—have not been ignored.

Conclusion: gifts cause a conflict of interest when they threaten to corrupt an employee's judgment on business matters related to the interests of the person or organization providing the gift. Sometimes gifts are given with that intention, sometimes not. Regardless, and no matter what the law or corporate philosophy may be, it's frequently the employee who ends up deciding whether a gift will be accepted. If it is, a responsibility follows to justify accepting it.

What's the Difference among Gifts, Bribes, and Kickbacks?

One advantage of the developed framework for thinking ethically about gifts in the midst of advertising business relationships is that it provides a compact way to manage the ethics of bribes and kickbacks.

Bribes are gifts—everything from straight cash to entertainment—given to media buyers with the direct purpose of corrupting their professional judgment by appealing to their personal welfare. When a representative from *Forbes* magazine gives Chris Forman tickets to the Springsteen show with the intention of spurring Foreman to *consider* buying ad space in *Forbes*, that's a gift; it's left to

Foreman to decide whether he can accept it without betraying his obligation to serve his employer's interests. When, on the other hand, the rep gives the same tickets with the intention of getting Forman to *directly buy* the space, that's a bribe. A bribe, in other words, is an extreme conflict of interests where the individual's personal interest completely overwhelms the professional responsibilities implied by his job. If Foreman accepts this kind of gift—one where he knows the intention and accepts that the objectivity of his judgment will be blinded—then he's crossed into the zone of bribery. Receiving bribes, finally, seems unethical for the same reason that accepting gifts can be unethical: it's betraying the promise to act as an agent for the organization. Kickbacks resemble bribes except that instead of the gift or entertainment being given over first and then the ad space getting purchased, the ad space is purchased and then a portion of that revenue is sent back to the media buyer as cash or Springsteen tickets or whatever. Regardless of whether the media buyer gets his reward first and then buys the ad space, or buys the space and then gets rewarded, what's happening on the ethical level doesn't change. Personal interest is being exploited to corrupt professional judgment. That means accepting the reward becomes a form of lying since it's a betrayal of the implicit promise made to do the job right when you sign the contract.

In the Real World, What's the Difference among Gifts, Bribes, and Kickbacks?

In actual day-to-day business it can be extremely difficult to distinguish among gifts, bribes, and kickbacks because at bottom all of them spark conflicts of interest. All of them, consequently, are also going to incite at least remote suspicions of corruption. Of course it's always easy to find examples at one extreme or the other. On the safe side, if a woman seeking your business pays for one cup of coffee for you once, it's unlikely that you'll give her proposal any special consideration, and it's doubtful that she'd expect it. If she offers to make your car payments on the other hand, it's pretty clear something's going on. Usually, however, the lines are blurry and the reality more like the one Foreman lived through. The exact monetary value of what he received wasn't certain. Did he get the invitations with the intention of having his judgment tainted or were they extended as a courtesy and in accordance with the industry's common practice? Would he get more and better invitations if he sent *Forbes* magazine some extra dollars? While these questions don't have certain answers, the ethics can be rendered in straightforward form. Agents of an organization have a duty to act in favor of the organization's interests regardless of what happens after hours.

REVIEW QUESTIONS

1. Why do gifts create conflicts of interest?
2. What is the main advantage and disadvantage of dealing with gifts and conflicts of interest by prohibiting the acceptance of gifts?
3. What questions could you ask yourself to help frame the question as to whether you can ethically accept a business-related gift?
4. What's the difference between a conflict of interest and the appearance of a conflict?
5. What's the difference between a gift and a bribe?
6. What's the difference between a bribe and a kickback?

[1] Sarah Bernard, "Let Them Eat Crab Cakes," *New York*, accessed May 19, 2011,http://nymag.com/nymetro/news/media/features/2472.
[2] Sarah Bernard, "Let Them Eat Crab Cakes," *New York*, accessed May 19, 2011,http://nymag.com/nymetro/news/media/features/2472.
[3] Sarah Bernard, "Let Them Eat Crab Cakes," *New York*, accessed May 19, 2011,http://nymag.com/nymetro/news/media/features/2472.
[4] Nicholas Confessor and Jeremy "Paterson's Ethics Breach Is Turned Over to Prosecutors," *New York Times*, March 3, 2010, accessed May 19, 2011,http://www.nytimes.com/2010/03/04/nyregion/04paterson.html?hp?hp.
[5] Bill Graves, "Oregon Supreme Court Upholds $50 Gift Limit for Legislators, Public Officials," *OregonLive.com*, December 31, 2009, accessed May 19, 2011,http://www.oregonlive.com/news/index.ssf/2009/12/oregon_supreme_court_upholds_5.html.
[6] "Code of Conduct," Omnicom Group, last updated October 16, 2008, accessed May 19, 2011, http://www.omnicomgroup.com/corporategovernance/codeofconduct.

[7] William Shaw and Vincent Barry, *Moral Issues in Business* (Belmont, CA: Thomson Wadsworth, 2007), 398–99.

[8] Sarah Bernard, "Let Them Eat Crab Cakes," *New York*, accessed May 19, 2011, http://nymag.com/nymetro/news/media/features/2472.

7.2 Third-Party Obligations: Tattling, Reporting, and Whistle-Blowing

LEARNING OBJECTIVES

1. Define third-party obligations.
2. Elaborate three standard responses to third-party obligations.
3. Define whistle-blowing.
4. Consider justifications and requirements for whistle-blowing.

Caught in the Crossfire

A hypothetical situation. You work at Omnicom, at the desk next to Chris Foreman. Like him, you're an assistant media buyer. Though your area of concentration is distinct (you're in charge of placing ads on radio stations) you team up with him from time to time to run numbers, and you know enough about how it all works to recognize when something's going wrong. In your opinion, it is. Chris is sending ads to *Forbes* that would deliver more for the client if they'd been placed in *Business Week*. Further, you believe he's doing it in exchange for the gifts. You can't prove that but you do know this: he's occasionally supplementing his lousy income by selling some of what he's receiving—concert tickets, vouchers for limo service, things like that—on eBay. You've tried talking about it, bringing the subject up one way or another, but he doesn't want to talk back. And when you say it directly, when you ask whether it's right to accept gifts from *Forbes* and convert them to money, he laughs. "*Everyone* does it," he says.

This situation is different from most of those discussed so far for an important reason: you're not directly faced with an ethical dilemma; you're not the one placing the ads or accepting the gifts. Still, you do work with Chris, sometimes even sending over marketing data that he uses for his accounts. You're a third party, which in this situation means you're not directly responsible for what's going on but you're caught in the cross fire between Foreman and *Forbes* magazine.

There are infinite variations on this kind of predicament. The financier-fraudster Bernie Madoff asked his secretary to cover up his affairs by answering his wife's phone calls and saying he was in a meeting and couldn't be interrupted. In the student union of your campus, maybe the breakfast menu offers omelets cooked with fresh eggs, but you work there and know the manager occasionally messes up the stocking order and so ends up selling omelets made from a preordered mix of egg-like chemicals. What do you do? It can be a hard call and at least two questions arise on the way to making it:

1. You need to decide if something truly unacceptable is happening.
2. You've got to determine whether it's any of your business.

   If, finally, something unacceptable *is* happening and you *should* do something about it, you're facing a third-party obligation. This is an ethical responsibility to correct something you're not actually doing.

Why Should I Get Involved? Ethics and Self-Interest

When confronted with a third-party obligation, employees may get involved for a number of reasons. One is as a response to an ethical responsibility. Another: as an opportunity to benefit themselves.

Tattling, as any child knows, is revealing an ethical transgression involving others, and revealing it *for your own benefit*. Take the case of assistant media buyer Chris Foreman and another assistant media buyer who learns that Foreman is shortchanging the ad agency's client for personal benefit. If you're that other assistant media buyer and you're crafty, you may see not only an ethical lapse here but also your own personal chance. Every senior media buyer has several assistants underneath, and when the time comes for promotion, there'll be space, presumably, for only one assistant to advance. Getting Foreman out of the way may not be a bad career move.

It's an extremely ambiguous ethical move, however. On one hand, there's solid justification for getting the truth known about Foreman. He's clearly not fulfilling his professional obligations to the company. However, if you turn him in *because* that'll give you a leg up on the promotion ladder, you can hardly say that ethical righteousness has driven your action. On the other side, this should also be noted: the fact that you may benefit from revealing unethical behavior probably can't justify keeping everyone in the dark.

Typically, we think of ethical restrictions as painful, as obstacles you put between yourself and what you really want. That's not always the case, though; they don't necessarily make you suffer, they may make others suffer and serve your interests. When they do, you have weaponries ethics—that is, perfectly reasonable moral dictates used to attack others and benefit yourself. Tattling, finally, is the use of weaponries ethics; it's doing the right thing for selfish reasons.

Responding to a Third-Party Obligation: Reporting

Regardless of the motivation for responding to a third-party obligation, there are two broad paths the response can take: reporting and whistle-blowing.

Reporting ethical transgressions means bringing them to light, but only *within* the organization. In most situations, this route is the most direct way for third parties to balance their basic and immediate obligations. Staying with the advertising scenario where you believe Foreman is essentially accepting bribes from *Forbes*, you have an obligation not only to halt the bribery but also to protect the agency's interests. Obviously, a noisy public blowup about Foreman misspending a client's money is going to damage the advertising company's business. Reporting—because it stays inside agency walls—promises to rectify the bribery without causing larger publicity problems.

Bringing this into the real world, because reporting ethical problems does allow them to be addressed without harming the agency, the Omnicom Code of Conduct includes this:

> *All reports of possible violations about which management becomes aware will be promptly considered. We will not punish any employee or representative for making any report in good faith.* [1]

It's in Omnicom's interest to get ethical dirty laundry washed in-house.

Up to here, the situation's resolution has come easily. But there's another, potentially complicating, obligation to consider: the human link to Chris Foreman. Almost all organizations rely on and seek to nurture bonds of shared responsibility and dependence between employees: in working life, when someone's sick or just having a bad day, the others have to pick up the slack. That nurturing explains why anyone who's entered a fast-food restaurant knows the workers aren't "coworkers" but "teammates." In most organizations, some form of the camaraderie holds, and you can't just break those bonds from one moment to the next. That means if you're working with Foreman and you know he's doing wrong, you may well feel an obligation to *not* report anything because you don't want to cause him problems. Reporting, the conclusion is, a coworker for ethical lapses is easy. But in the real world there are no coworkers; there are only flesh and blood people.

Next, even if those human connections to others don't move you, you also have obligations to *yourself* and your own welfare to consider, and turning others in to company authorities can ultimately come back against you. By giving rise to distrust and possibly resentment among other colleagues who fear they may be the next ones to get reported, you may be in essence isolating yourself in your own cubicle.

In the end, seeing what Foreman is doing and stretching ethical obligations through the situation, you may find yourself torn between reporting him and not. There's no automatic resolution to this dilemma, only the attempt to weigh the obligations and get a sense of which outweigh the others.

Responding to a Third-Party Obligation: Whistle-Blowing

Whistle-blowing is bringing ethical transgressions to light publicly outside the organization. A recent case involved one of the many advertising agencies gathered under the Omnicom umbrella, Leo Burnett. Two employees—Vice President Greg Hamilton and Comptroller Michelle Casey—alleged, and a subsequent federal investigation backed them up, that Leo Burnett was overbilling the government for their work on the US Army's "Army of One" recruiting campaign. The agency was supposed to calculate its hourly rate with a formula dividing charges between the more expensive work done directly in Leo Burnett's offices and the less costly hourly labor performed by subcontractors. What Leo Burnett did was simple: they billed subcontractor work at the higher in-house rate. The accounting in these massive campaigns—TV, radio, and prints ads as well as sponsorships and events—is so knotted that a virtual army of accountants is required to keep track of where all the money is going. In that kind of numerical chaos, the agency could expect that switching a few hours from one column to another deep inside the mountain of paperwork would go unnoticed by outside auditors. It did go unnoticed—until Hamilton and Casey told the government what was going on.

Almost inevitably a lot of dust gets kicked up when employees turn on their employers noisily and publicly. In this case, the US Justice Department lawyers rode in, and they probably wanted a scalp on their wall: they have limited resources, limited time and money, and when they take something on they want to win, and they want people to know about it. Back on the agency's side, they're going to defend themselves, and that typically entails attacking their accusers, maybe labeling them disgruntled, incompetent, or worse. In this case, there was also a tug-of-war over money. The agency obviously wanted to keep as much as it could, the government wanted money back, and thanks to the False Claims Act, Hamilton and Casey also demanded their share, which came to almost $3 million.

The False Claims Act is a federal law designed to encourage whistle-blowing on private contractors who are attempting to defraud the government. Whistle-blowers are entitled, under the law, to 30 percent of the damages the government obtains. The incentive doesn't apply to situations involving only private companies, but even there whistle-blowers may encounter suspicions that ulterior motives—not a dedication to doing the right thing—finally spurred their loud assertions about misdeeds.

Finally, with respect to the Leo Burnett fraud, the full details will never be known. Because the case never went to trial, there was little public exhibition of evidence and testimony. To head the whole mess off, Leo Burnett agreed to settle. In the words of a published report, "Leo Burnett denied any wrongdoing and said in a statement that it agreed to the settlement 'to avoid the distraction, burden and expense of litigation.'" [2]

Every case of whistle-blowing is different, but a few questions get to the heart of most instances:

- What, exactly, is whistle-blowing?
- What justifies whistle-blowing?
- What weighs against whistle-blowing?
- Can the whistle-blower expect protection?
- Is whistle-blowing morally required?

What Is Whistle-Blowing?

Whistle-blowing is bringing an organization's ethical transgressions to public light. Spilling the beans to the family over dinner, however, doesn't count; the truth must be exposed to an authority or institution capable of taking action. In the case of the advertising agency, Hamilton and Casey took their information to the federal government. They also could have selected one of the important industry publications—say, *Advertising Age* magazine. Any information published there would draw attention from those involved and give the client (in this case the US Army) the opportunity to act on behalf of its own interests. The news media—a newspaper, a TV station—may have been a possibility in this case, given the large scope of the fraud and the national interest underneath it. Other possibilities could be listed, but what's important is that the report of misdeeds goes to someone who can *do* something about it (or at least provoke others to do something). Finally, whistle-blowing may be anonymous. However, in practical terms, that's frequently not a real option because government authorities, like private ones (editors of industry publications and so on), are far less likely to spend time tracking down the truth about accusations when even the accuser is unwilling to stand behind them.

What Justifies Whistle-Blowing?

Whistle-blowing needs careful justification because it requires violating the obligation any employee has to protect the interests of the employer. Here are five items that could be checked before publicly lighting up an organization's misdeeds from the inside. Importantly, the fact that the items may all be checked *doesn't oblige* action, but it does raise the possibility as ethically justifiable.

1. There is clear evidence of *continuing wrongdoing* by the organization or *continuing effects* of past wrongdoing. In the business world, actions that are entirely locked in the past are the subject of history, not ethics.

2. The *wrongdoing must be serious*. In the case of Leo Burnett, the case wouldn't cross this threshold if only one hour of labor had been attributed to the higher-cost office. But the threshold would be crossed if the agency significantly overcharged many hours for years, bleeding the account of its resources and ultimately damaging the army's ability to recruit new, top-flight soldiers.

3. *The organization's established, internal channels for reporting and correcting problems have been exhausted.* Most organizations provide clear ways for employees to voice concerns internally. A conversation with a supervisor is an obvious example. At larger organizations, sometimes an entire internal department has been mounted to receive and act on the concerns of employees. Here's the web page of a typical example; it links to Wal-Mart's internal department for ethics:http://ethics.walmartstores.com/Statementofethics/RaiseAConcern.aspx. Whether, finally, there's a clear, formal route for internal reporting or not, employees have a responsibility to try to resolve problems in ways that benefit—or do the least possible damage to—the organization, and therefore the possibility of raising concerns internally needs to be explored fully. (As always, there are special cases. If, for example, the CEO of a small advertising company is robbing its client's money, there may be no internal route to resolution, leaving external whistle-blowing as the only moral corrective. Also, though whistle-blowing is defined as taking action *outside* the organization, the definition could be stretched to include the act of bringing wrongdoing to light directly before high officials within an organization by skipping over the normal chain of authority.)

4. *There's unmistakable and convincing evidence of misconduct.* The evidence must be unmistakable in the sense that it clearly indicates wrongdoing; it can't be that an innocent explanation seems as likely as a guilty one. In the Leo Burnett accounting books, if it turns out that on one page all the internal hours are in the external hour's

column and vice versa, that may be an attempt to defraud the government, or it may just be that the data-entry guy came to work one morning hung over and ended up confusing the numbers. Further, the evidence must also be compelling in the sense that there's enough of it for a reasonable person to conclude the misdeeds are actually occurring. So even if you're certain numbers are being entered incorrectly intentionally, but it turns out that the difference—the amount of extra money Leo Burnett is making—is trivial, then it's going to be hard to justify creating a stink. It may be, for example, that someone in the accounting department is making small adjustments in order to balance errors found elsewhere in the giant balance sheet.

5. *There's reason to believe that whistle-blowing will resolve the problem.* In the case of Leo Burnett—or any business that's overcharging a client—you can be pretty sure that bringing the fraud to light will spark action, at least by the defrauded client. On the other hand, if you're in the production department of the advertising agency (in other words, you're actually filming commercials) and you regularly get shipped down to Mexico to shoot campaigns because everything's cheaper down there and you learn that some of the extras in the commercial's background are working longer hours than local regulations allow, you might reasonably figure that you can talk all you want in public, but it's not going to make any difference.

What Weighs against Whistle-Blowing?
The three heaviest arguments against whistle-blowing are:
1. legal requirements for confidentiality,
2. prudential concern for one's career and personal welfare,
3. an employee's sense of loyalty to the organization.

A legal requirement for confidentiality may weigh against whistle-blowing by binding employees to not share a company's internal information. The requirement traces back to a section contained in many work contracts. Called a confidentiality clause, here's a basic version:

> *Employees may have access to records and other information about customers and other employees, including proprietary information, trade secrets, and intellectual property to which the Company holds rights. Employee agrees to keep all such information strictly confidential and to refrain from discussing this information with anyone else without proper authority.*

While this is most directly aimed at protecting consumer information (say, credit card numbers) and company trade secrets (Coke's secret formula), it may also be read as

safeguarding the kind of information a whistle-blower wants to make public. In the case of the Leo Burnett agency, what Vice President Hamilton and Comptroller Casey told the government did, in fact, involve "records and other information about customers."

The second major argument against whistle-blowing, self-interest operates in both the professional and personal sense. Turning against the company may be the right thing to do, but it's almost inevitably a painful thing to do, at least according to a survey published in the *New York Times*. What condition, the study sought to determine, do whistle-blowers find themselves in a few years afterward?

- One hundred percent who worked for private business were fired.
- Twenty percent could still not find work at the time this survey was taken.
- Seventeen percent lost their homes.
- Fifty-four percent had been harassed by peers at work.
- Fifteen percent viewed their subsequent divorce as a result of whistle-blowing.
- Eighty percent suffered physical deterioration.
- Eighty-six percent reported significant emotional stress (depression, anxiety).
- Ten percent reported having attempted suicide. [3]

It doesn't sound good. Of course every case is different, and if you look on the other side of these numbers, they leave room for the possibility that at least some people do the right thing and get on with their lives just fine. Still, there are no guarantees and ethics isn't only about duties to others and the world outside, all of us have equal duties to ourselves: duties to maximize our potential, protect those nearest to us, and defend our own welfare.

Finally, the values and reasons supporting loyalty as a reason for not blowing the whistle will be considered in their own section further on.

Protecting the Whistle-Blower
As the survey data about whistle-blowers reveal, there's not a lot of protection for them. That isn't for a lack of trying, however. At both the state and federal levels, reams of laws have been enacted to protect those who expose wrongdoing organizations. Perhaps the most notable is the Sarbanes-Oxley Act. Passed in 2002 by the federal government as a response to a series of disastrous accounting frauds at large companies, Sarbanes-Oxley is a massive piece of legislation intervening in many parts of the business world, and

especially in aspects connecting to an organization's finances and transparency.

Specifically with respect to whistle-blowers, the law attempts to encourage it by protecting whistle-blowers at publicly traded companies that report activities to government agencies. (The act doesn't apply to privately held firms dealing exclusively with other private firms.) Employers are prohibited from taking retaliatory action (firing, demoting, harassing), and whistle-blowers are provided clear avenues for lawsuits should such retaliation occur. Here's the legislative language: "In order to establish a case under Sarbanes-Oxley, an employee must prove that she (1) reasonably believed that her employer was breaking the law; (2) engaged in whistle blowing activity as defined by the statute; (3) suffered an adverse employment action; and (4) that *there was a causal connection between the whistle blowing activity and the adverse employment action.*" [4]

The problem is that last clause. Everyone who's ever had a job knows that mistakes happen every day. Deadlines are missed, projects contain errors, and goals aren't met. Bosses who have it in for you aren't going to have many difficulties converting those mishaps into reasons for denying wage hikes and even outright firing. In your heart you may know—everyone may know—that you're suffering retaliation for reporting the company, but *proving* it can be difficult.

The bottom line is—and as the previous survey shows—if you publicly divulge information seriously damaging your employer, you're probably going to be gone. And even if you find some protection in one or another law, it's difficult to imagine that your career is going anywhere inside the company. Worse still, prospective new employers are, very likely, going to hesitate before extending a job to someone who has already caused serious problems for a former employer. Taken all together, the bleak reality is that in most cases whistle-blowers can't count on getting back the life they had before they publicly disclosed their organization's misdeeds.

Is Whistle-Blowing Morally *Required*?

Given the abundant reasons—financial, professional, emotional, and ethical—against whistle-blowing, are there any cases where a moral argument can be formed to *require* publicizing an organization's unethical actions? Probably, but they're few. Here's a possible rule of thumb: whistle-blowing is required when the act can prevent harm to others in ways that are serious and go *beyond the bottom line*. If someone is getting ripped off, the reasoning goes—if an advertising company is overcharging its clients—whistle-

blowing may be justified, but not required. All that's at stake is money. On the other hand, if a nuclear power plant is being constructed near a residential area and you learn the contracting company you work for is using cheap cement to boost the profit margin, it seems as though you have little choice—the weight of elementary personal integrity in the face of potentially lethal wrongdoing probably requires personal sacrifice.

What about the hypothetical Chris Foreman situation? You're working with him and have acquired sufficient evidence to know that he's selling out his client by sending their ad dollars to *Forbes* magazine in exchange for Highlander nights. You've reported the matter internally and received no response. Do you go public? You'd certainly be justified in taking the story to *Ad Age* magazine. Just running down the list of conditions justifying whistle-blowing, they all get checked:

1. There's clear evidence of continuing wrongdoing by the organization.
2. The wrongdoing is serious (at least in the world of advertising).
3. The organization's established, internal channels for reporting and correcting problems have been exhausted.
4. There's unmistakable and convincing evidence of misconduct.
5. There's reason to believe that whistle-blowing will resolve the problem.

The question remains, however, whether the issue affects life beyond business and the bottom line. It doesn't appear to. At bottom, this is the case of a client—AT&T mobile phone services—getting poor service from an Omnicom company. That should be corrected, and presumably market forces will correct it sooner or later, but whether they do or don't, there's no requirement here to seriously jeopardize your own financial, professional, and emotional welfare.

What about the case of Leo Burnett? Again here a client is getting a raw deal, but there's an important difference: this is the army, not a telephone company. If it's true that the recruiting budget is being seriously hindered, the situation may be crossing the line from justified whistle-blowing to justified and required. If it does cross that line, the reason will be that protecting your own financial and emotional welfare is trumped by the responsibility to help soldiers in war resist mortal danger as totally as possible. The fact that the army isn't getting the best recruits possible doesn't just affect people in the pocketbook, it threatens those on a live battlefield. Faced with that reality, it will be hard for individuals including Burnett employees Hamilton and Casey to keep quiet just because they don't want to lose their jobs.

KEY TAKEAWAYS

- Third-party obligations arise when you know of wrongdoing by an organization or by individuals within it, and though you aren't directly at fault, you're in a position to correct the problem.

- In some cases, third-party obligations can be opportunities to sabotage a fellow worker for personal gain.

- Responses to third-party obligations include reporting the problem inside the organization for correction and publicizing the problem, also known as whistle-blowing.

- Because whistle-blowing harms the organization, employees must take into account their responsibility to defend the organization's interests before publicly decrying the wrongdoing.

- In some cases whistle-blowing is not justified, in some it is, and in some extreme cases, whistle-blowing may be ethically required.

- In practical terms, whistle-blowing can be devastating for the employee.

REVIEW QUESTIONS

1. Create a hypothetical third-party obligation involving an employee of a major company.
2. What does it mean to deploy weaponries ethics?
3. What questions can be asked to help determine whether whistle-blowing is justified?
4. What questions can be asked to help determine whether whistle-blowing is ethically required?
5. Why might an employee hesitate before whistle-blowing?
6. The Sarbanes-Oxley Act tries to protect whistle-blowers. Why is it not very effective?

[1] "Code of Conduct," Omnicom Group, last updated October 16, 2008, accessed May 19,
2011, http://www.omnicomgroup.com/corporategovernance/codeofcond uct.
[2] Mehhen Streit, "Leo Burnett Settles Suit for $15.5 Million," *Chicago Business*, January 6, 2009, accessed May 19,
2011, http://www.chicagobusiness.com/cgi-bin/news.pl?id=32498.
[3] Survey cited in Manuel Velasquez, *Business Ethics: Concepts and Cases*, 6th ed. (Upper Saddle River, NJ: Pearson, 2006), 378.
[4] Welch v. Cardinal Bankshares Corp., 2003-SOX-15 at 35 (ALJ 2004).

7.3 Company Loyalty
LEARNING OBJECTIVES

1. Define company loyalty.
2. Elaborate three degrees of company loyalty.

Two Kinds of Loyalty

There is narrow company loyalty and broad company loyalty. The narrow definition pertains to employment: the loyal employee sticks with the company instead of looking for work elsewhere, especially during economic booms when jobs are plentiful and moving on is easy.

This kind of loyalty, however, is in trouble according to an article from the Harvard Business School: "The very nature of the relationship between employers and employees has undergone a fundamental shift: Today, workers not only don't expect to work for decades on end for the same company, but they don't want to. They are largely disillusioned with the very idea of loyalty to organizations." [1] Part of the reason for the shift—and part of the reason employees don't stay at companies for decades—is that many employers don't hesitate to fire their workers at the drop of the hat when it serves the company's interest. On the other side, according to the article, it's also true that today's workers don't hesitate to move on to a new job when a better one, or maybe just a different one, comes along. Regardless of who went first, the fact is company loyalty—whether it's going from the company to the worker or the worker to the company—isn't what (we are told) it once was.

The broad definition of company loyalty goes beyond employment questions and measures an employee's willingness to sacrifice income, leisure time, personal relationships, family responsibilities, and general life aspirations in the name of the organization. To create this dynamic of sacrifice, two distinct kinds of relationships with the organization are required:

1. Attachment to the organization that is non-instrumental. This means the attachment isn't maintained only because it serves the employee's concrete interests, such as the need for a salary to pay the rent and grocery bills.
2. A deposited value in the organization that goes beyond any individual and their attachment; the organization's value continues even without those who currently feel it.

Probably, there's not a lot of this kind of deep loyalty in the advertising field. Agencies are constantly stalking new clients, even trying to steal them from others. For their part, most clients are constantly looking for better deals and ways to refresh their image, and they are usually open to proposals from new firms interested in handling their communication.

More, companies that employ advertising agencies constantly "put their account up for review," which means the current account holder has to compete with new entrants just to maintain the business. There are exceptions, of course, but for the most part advertising agencies are constantly clinging to the business they have, seeking new opportunities, and always on the lookout for fast money. In that kind of cutthroat environment—one where it's your job to sing the praises of Burger King one day and McDonald's the next—it's going to be difficult for workers to feel as though they should (or even can) be true to their current employer.

Other kinds of organizations seem more likely to instill feelings of loyalty. A religious hub—a church, a synagogue, a mosque—is one obvious example. Most priests are attached to, and deeply concerned by, the welfare of their church; they *serve* their institution and aren't working there for the money (which probably isn't great). Further, most also believe their institution has value beyond them: the importance was there before they arrived (or were even born) and will continue after they leave. Taken together, these elements create space for true employee loyalty to the organization. Something similar—the existence of a space for labor that's not about money and similar rewards—could be found surrounding many who work for Greenpeace, Doctors Without Borders, political parties, the CIA, the United Nations.

Other professions open on both sides of the line—that is, there's ample space for an instrumental relationship (I keep this job because it makes *me* happy) and one based on broad loyalty. Some medical doctors are in it for the money but others for the care, for the principle that bringing health to others is a good cause. Law is another example. Ambulance-chasing lawyers just want payoffs, but some judges believe in the law as something larger than themselves and a basic force for civilization that's worth serving. Moving down to street level, there are police officers who just like a steady paycheck and others in the field to serve and protect: they see their work as improving the lives of others and the general community.

Three Degrees of Loyalty

Within a dynamic of employee loyalty, there are three levels of dedication: obedience loyalty, balanced loyalty, and free agency.

Obedience loyalty, which is an extreme case, works from the idea that the organization is worthy and the employee is comparatively worthless or only worthwhile to the extent he or she serves the organization. This extreme will be reached

only rarely, but there are glimmers of it in some professional activities. One quick way to identify these kinds of labors is to check whether the truly dedicated are willing to sacrifice even their lives for the cause their organization embodies. The armed forces come to mind here. Some political organizations command this devotion, especially in revolutionary times. Some workers' devotion to their labor union has been sufficient to put their lives in danger. The exploring scientist Charles Darwin believed in accumulating knowledge and put his life at risk in the field as he tracked rare species and ecosystems.

Not so dramatic or extreme, some professions and organizations can suck the *emotional* life out of employees. Or they may take vast chunks of the employee's time. Undercover police work exemplifies by requiring a loyalty reflected as self-sacrifice to an extent few of us would contemplate. April Leatherwood, for instance, went undercover in Memphis for an entire year. Almost entirely separated from family and friends, she lived on the street, wore the same clothes every day, went without brushing her teeth, and rarely bathed. That was an ugly year of her life, one sacrificed for the job. [2]

Balanced loyalty is a situation where both the employee and the organization recognize in each other an independent value. In this case, the employee can be expected to make sacrifices—possibly even do things he or she would normally consider unethical—in the name of serving the larger organization. One example would be a lawyer working in a public defender's office, one who believes that the system of law and the rules of its enforcement are noble and should be respected to some important extent that is independent of the particular lawyer's welfare and beliefs. The loyalty can be reflected in a number of ways. First, it's simply the case that most public defender positions don't pay as well as similar posts in private firms. Pushing further, the public defender may be asked to represent and defend a client she knows (or *strongly* suspects) is guilty. In this case, presumably, she's being asked to do something she wouldn't do in her day-to-day life—that is, serve the interests of a guilty man. More, presenting a full-blown legal case for the defendant's innocence would essentially be lying and, again, something the lawyer might not typically do.

At the same time, this lawyer probably won't be sacrificing *everything*; she'll recognize that her life and aspirations have value also, and there may come a point where she decides the sacrifices demanded by the job are too great to bear. Perhaps she's just had a child and needs to up her income, or, maybe a man she helped set free has committed a gruesome crime. However the situation might be, when the lawyer leaves the office of the public defender for a higher paying job at a large private firm, she has demonstrated a balanced sense of loyalty. She's willing to sacrifice in the name of a larger organization she respects. But only up to a point.

Other demonstrations of balanced loyalty to the organization could include

- buying the company's products (though they aren't the personal preference),
- evangelizing in public life (telling your friends how great the company or its products are),
- voting for the political candidate the company affirms will best serve its interests,
- moving for the company.

Free agency is the extreme on the bottom end: the absence of loyalty. Some theorists propose that this should be the default state for most employees for this reason: it's ultimately *impossible* to be loyal to a typical company because profit-making institutions just aren't the kinds of things that can properly demand or receive any loyalty. The entire idea of loyalty, the argument goes, only exists in a reality where individuals stand by others to some extent without conditions (example: parents who love each other and their children unconditionally). Money-making businesses, on the other hand, are incapable of that kind of unconditional fidelity. On the contrary, the only desire most private enterprises know is the one to serve its own interests by making more profits. If that's right—if companies have no loyalty to give—then its employees *can't* enter into that kind of relationship. Instead, in the business world at least, you and I are forced to pursue our own interests—a higher salary or whatever—just as the larger company pursues its own.

Translating this into the working world, the absence of company loyalty is the idea that workers find value in their organization *only* because it serves their own interests. Of course it's impossible to know the souls of others, or exactly what their deepest values are, but there might be a hint of this free-agent loyalty in the Leo Burnett case. Two high-level and highly paid workers served the company well—and were compensated well—until they turned whistle-blower against the firm. When vice president Hamilton and comptroller Casey alleged that Leo Burnett was overbilling the government for their work for the US Army, they weren't just doing the right thing, they were doing a lucrative thing for themselves since the False Claims Act promised 30 percent of damages the government obtained. If the money is the *reason* they turned on the agency, they exemplify free-

agent loyalty. They worked hard for the organization because the pay was good, but the moment they saw the chance to get even more money by turning against it, they jumped. At bottom, that means, their loyalty is only to themselves.

KEY TAKEAWAYS

- Company loyalty defined narrowly concerns employees sticking with the organization instead of looking for work elsewhere.
- Company loyalty defined broadly emerges from the idea that the organization possesses nobility that's worth serving, even if employees don't benefit personally from the contribution.
- The three degrees of company loyalty are obedience loyalty (the worker exists to serve the organization's interests), balanced loyalty (workers and organizations share interests), and free agency (the organization exists to serve the worker's interests).

REVIEW QUESTIONS

1. Name an organization that might inspire obedience loyalty. Why is obedience inspired? What does the loyalty look like?
2. Name an organization that might inspire balanced loyalty. Why is it inspired? What does the loyalty look like?
3. Name an organization that might inspire an attitude of free agency. Why is it inspired? What does the free agency look like?
4. Take a career you're (considering) pursuing. On the scale from obedience loyalty to free agency, where do you imagine most employees in that line of work are located? Why?

[1] Lauren Keller Johnson, "Rethinking Company Loyalty," Harvard Business School Working Knowledge, September 19, 2005, accessed May 19, 2011,http://hbswk.hbs.edu/item/5000.html.
[2] Kristina Goetz, "A Year of Living Dangerously Takes a Toll on Undercover Memphis Officer," *Commercial Appeal*, August 30, 2009, accessed May 19, 2011,http://www.commercialappeal.com/news/2009/aug/30/year-of-living-dangerously-takes-its-toll.

7.4 Stress, Sex, Status, and Slacking: What Are the Ethics of Making It through the Typical Workday?
LEARNING OBJECTIVE

1. Consider ethical questions attached to several issues commonly arising during the workday.

Bringing the Office Home: High-Stress Work

No book can cover the ethics of everything happening on every job, but four issues arising in most workplaces sooner or later are stress, sex, status, and slacking off. Starting with stress, what happens if the workday doesn't end when the workday ends? For those enduring—or choosing—high-stress jobs, there's no five o'clock whistle; even if they're shopping or watching a baseball game, the job's effects hum in the background. One simple example—and also one all of us see on the street every day—come from an article in the *USA Today*. It recounts an academic journal's finding that overweight people pack on still more pounds when their work continually produces serious anxiety. If you're overweight, the study shows, and you're stressed in the office, there's a high likelihood your stomach or your thighs are going to keep growing. [1]

One of the central arguments Aristotle made in ancient Greece was that doing right isn't the highest goal of ethics. The careful understanding of our values and purposes centers on, ultimately, living a good life. Doing the right thing is part of that goodness, but happiness is there too, so one of the issues stress at work brings forward is this: how is my decision to accept stressful employment affecting my happiness and the happiness of those around me? Here are some more specific questions that could be asked on the way to pinning down the ethics of stress:

- What positive returns, exactly, am I getting from my stressful job?
- Are there prospects for reduced stress in the future?
- What are the costs of the stress? Is it affecting my weight, my leisure time, my friends, my marriage and family?
- Who is affected? Is anyone else suffering stress because I'm stressed out? Are people suffering from my stress in other ways?

Stress at work isn't only a psychological problem or a medical one—it's also laced with questions about value. It's the most fundamental ethics: what's worth doing and what isn't? It's impossible to know, of course, exactly where the line should be drawn and when stress is worth accepting. Any answer that will be justifiable, however, will have to begin with a clear understanding of exactly what the costs and benefits are.

Office Romance

Hooking up at work is one eternal way of making the time fly, but what's going on in today's offices is somewhat different from the past. An article from the *Wall Street Journal* indicates how the meaning of sex in the office is shifting: "Marriage is a priority for most Americans—more than 90 percent of American adults eventually marry—but

these days it may not happen, as it so often did before, in the immediate post-high-school or post-college years. The truth is that we're marrying later." [2]

When marriages were typically celebrated at the end of the schooling years, work-related romances went hand in hand with infidelities. In that environment, questions arose about the organization's role in any affair that may be occurring during company time.

The entire context of discussion changes, however, when a large number of people flowing into the workforce are unmarried and are looking to wed. Inevitably, the office is going to become a mating ground—people pass eight hours a day there—and one of the questions young workers are going to start asking when they think about jobs and careers is, will I be able to meet someone if I get into one or another line of work?

The aspiration to connect introduces a thorny dimension to employment decisions made by young people (and some older ones too). If you're a guy working on a heavy construction job, the pay may be good, but there's probably not going to be a woman in sight. On the other hand, doing the coursework to earn paralegal certification may be a headache, but getting into the field isn't a bad way to meet successful and interesting women.

What's going on here is that as society changes—as marriage and family life get pushed back into time that used to be reserved for work—the factors shaping the way we think about which jobs are more desirable than others simply on a day-to-day basis are changing, and part of your responsibility to yourself is to keep track of what you *really* want from your 9 to 5 time. One of the standard moral obligations we share is the responsibility to be sincere not only with others but also with ourselves about important decisions touching the business part of life. And if romance is part of what you want from work, then the possibilities have to be taken into account just like salary and other benefits.

Status

Chris Foreman, the media buyer who enjoyed yacht evenings on the Highlander and tickets to all kinds of major events, received a piddling salary. He thought about changing jobs but decided not to. One reason was that all the entertainment added a lot of indirect money to his income. There was another reason too—the special, VIP privileges he constantly received from his benefactors: "There's a feeling of superiority. When you pass by a line at a screening because you're on the list you do get that ego boost. You're thinking, *Ha, ha! I'm not a chump.*" [3]

Status on the job makes a difference in quotidian working life, but it's hard to quantify; it's not like a salary, which is an objective number and can be directly compared with others on a pay scale. How much is it worth, the question is, to wing by others forced to stand in line?

Knotting matters further, defining exactly what counts as status isn't easy, and any answer is going to move and slide depending on who you talk to. For some, being a lawyer is impressive and lucrative, for others it's dirty and, well, lucrative. For some, being a test pilot is exciting and respectable, for others it's scary and weird. Many people seated in first class on an airplane rush to get on early so that all the economy travelers get to see them as they file past. Some of those people headed toward the back of the plane see the first-class passengers as legitimate power elites, but others get the feeling that most of them are really chumps: the reason they're in first class is because they used frequent-flyer miles to bump up, and the reason they have a lot of those is because their bosses always make them take the trip to see clients instead of bothering to do it themselves.

More generally, in the world of New York City media buyers, status seems linked with superiority, with being visibly more privileged than those forced to stand in lines. For others, however, status will be quieter. The teacher, the nurse—they find status not as superiority but as social importance.

Conclusion. Status means different things to different people, but anyone looking to get it from a job should ask how much is really there, and how much is it going to help me get out of bed in the morning and want to go to work?

Slacker's Paradise
Typical ways of getting through the day include throwing yourself into your work (frequently with the hope of a promotion or pay raise), firing up an office romance, and enjoying the status a post allows. Another way of making it from 9 to 5 is by trying to *avoid* doing work, by working to do as little as possible. This is the slacker reality, and there are two routes into it: Personal slackers adopt the attitude for their own private reasons. The context slacker is dedicated to not working because the incentive system of the labor contract—or some other external factor—encourages slacking off.

Beginning with the personal slacker, the attitude starts with a decision: You take a typical job and make it your project to expend as little effort as possible. The reasons for adopting this stance depend on the person. Maybe there's a passive-aggressive element, some personal frustration with life or perhaps a somewhat idealistic attempt to make a statement. In any case, the motives behind this kind of behavior should be pursued in a psychology course. Here all that matters is that for one reason or another the private decision gets made to get through the day by working to not work.

The second slacker pathway starts with a context. Here's an example from an online discussion board: "Haha I worked in a union job and they were there to punch in…take a lunch…take 2 15min breaks…and punch out. They had n0 incentive to work hard because they would get a 0 dollar raise." [4]

The key here is the incentive, the idea that working hard doesn't benefit the worker because labor agreements are so protective and constricting that, on one side, it's almost impossible to fire a worker, and on the other, it's nearly impossible to reward one for superior performance. That means there are islands in the general economy where the traditional rule regarding performance and reward—the rule that doing well gets you ahead—doesn't apply very well.

One of the curiosities of these islands is that it's not right to conclude that there's no incentive to do anything. Actually, there *is* an incentive system in place even when, as the discussion board poster writes it, "hard work gets a 0 dollar raise." In this case, the incentive is negative. If union rules (or whatever rules happen to be in effect) mean workers can't compete against each other with the best performer winning a better post, the workers can still compete. It's just that since wages are fixed, the competition turns negative: the most successful worker is the one who manages to do the least work. It makes perfect sense: if you do less work than anyone else, and you're paid the same amount as everyone else, you have, in fact, found a way to win. You get the highest salary; you're the one paid most for the least work.

Is slacking ethically acceptable? Whether someone is a contextual or personal slacker, when success is defined not as how well you do but how little you do, two basic questions arise:
1. Is someone or some organization being cheated?
2. Is there something fundamentally unethical about *being* a slacker?

The first question applied to those trapped—willingly or not—in contextual slackerism leads quickly to the conclusion that the organization bears at least as great a burden of responsibility as the employee for deficient work motivation. Applied to the personal slacker, the question about whether an employer was cheated becomes more difficult. There does seem to be an element of reneging on implicit or explicit pledges to fulfill responsibilities here, but it's also true that most employment contracts in the United States (though not so much in Europe where this question would require more prolonged consideration) leave the organization broad latitude for dismissing workers whose performance is inadequate.

Next, is there something fundamentally unethical about slacking off? Most basic ethical theories are going to return some form of a yes verdict. From a utilitarian perspective—one trying to maximize the common good and happiness—it seems like problems are going to arise in most workplaces when coworkers are forced to pick up assignments the slacker was supposed to complete or could have completed easily with just a bit more effort. Similarly, basic ethics of duties include the one we all have to maximize our own potential and abilities, and rigorously avoiding work seems, in most cases, to run against that aspiration. Probably, a satisfying ethical defense of the slacker lifestyle would need to be founded on a personal project going well beyond the limited economic world. Slacking off, in other words, would need to be part of someone's life ambition, and therefore its questions belong to general ethics, not the more limited field of economic values treated here.

KEY TAKEAWAYS

- Stress at work invites ethical considerations of workers' obligations to their own happiness.
- Office romance may broaden the range of values applying to career choices.
- Status deriving from one's work can be an important compensation, but it is difficult to quantify.
- Slacking off—working to not work—may result from an employee's work environment or it may be a personal choice.

REVIEW QUESTIONS

1. What are some of the ways stress at work can cause unhappiness in life?
2. Why the office is an important scene of romance in today's world?
3. What do you imagine the rewards of status to be?
4. What kind of work contract would encourage slackerism?

[1] Nanci Hellmich, "Study: Overweight People Gain More When Stressed by Work," *USA Today*, July 8, 2009, accessed May 19, 2011,http://www.usatoday.com/news/health/weightloss/2009-07-08-obesity-stress_N.htm.

[2] Christine Whelen, "Older but Wiser," *The Wall Street Journal*, November 3, 2006.

[3] Sarah Bernard, "Let Them Eat Crab Cakes," *New York*, accessed May 19, 2011,http://nymag.com/nymetro/news/media/features/2472.

[4] Eazy E, "IS it me or are most Union workers lazy?," *Yahoo! Answers*, accessed May 19, 2011, http://answers.yahoo.com/question/index?qid=20081008004353A An1iL7.

7.5 Case Studies

Payola and the iPhone App

The word *payola* traces back to rock and roll's early days, back when the only large-scale way new acts could get their name and music out was on the radio. Deejays in the 1960s controlled their own playlists much more than today, so a band could drive into town, play a few concerts, and pay off a few deejays to get their songs into the rotation. When they rolled out toward the next stop, they left behind the impression that they were the next big thing.

It's not illegal for a deejay, radio station, or anyone at all to accept money in exchange for playing someone's music, but US law does make pay for play illegal if the sponsorship isn't openly divulged, if the song isn't treated, in other words, as a commercial.

Today's media world provides almost infinite ways for musicians, video commentators, moviemakers, and iPhone app developers to get word out about what they're doing. Anyone can post a video on YouTube or give away software on a web page. Payola is still out there, though. *Wired* magazine ran a story about it in the world of iPhone apps. It works like this. You invent an iPhone app but can't get anyone to notice. What do you do? One possibility is offer money to one of the well-known iPhone app review sites in exchange for a review of your creation. That gets the word out pretty well, so developers are starting to pay up. This modern payola scheme is enraging the iPhone community, however. Jason Snell, who works for Apple's own app-review website complains, "Readers need to know that true editorial reviews are fair, and aren't the product of any quid pro quo involving money or any other favors." [1]

Michael Vallez, owner of the app-review site *Crazy Mike's Apps*, disagrees. He charges for reviews without disclosing that to his readers, but he doesn't guarantee a positive report. If he thinks the app isn't worth buying, he sends the money back and cancels the review.

The *Wired* article concludes with an opinion from Kenneth Pybus, a professor of journalism and mass communication: "Undisclosed paid reviews are indisputably unethical because they manipulate the public. That's an easy call to say it's ethically wrong because that is a disservice to readers. It ought to be information that applies to readers and not information that advances you financially."

QUESTIONS

1. Professor Pybus believes there's a conflict of interest operating when Vallez accepts money to write reviews for his website *Crazy Mike's Apps*. What, exactly, is the conflict?

2. Vallez says that his actions do not cause a conflict of interest, only the appearance of a conflict.
   o What's the difference between a conflict of interest and the appearance of a conflict of interest?
   o How could Vallez argue that in his case there's only an appearance, and, on close inspection, there really is no conflict here?

3. Three standard strategies for alleviating ethical concerns surrounding conflicts of interest are
   o transparency,
   o recusal,
   o organizational codes.
   How could each of these strategies be applied to the conflict-of-interest issue at *Crazy Mike's Apps*?

4. You develop an iPhone app and you pay Vallez to review it. He tries the app, likes it, and writes up a positive paragraph.
   o Make the case to defend the payment as an ethically acceptable gift. Are there limits to how much you could give before it would shift from a gift to a bribe? If there is a limit, how was the number chosen?
   o Vallez says that if he doesn't like an app he returns the money and refuses to review it. Does this fact interfere with the possibility of justifying the payments as a standard, business-type gift?

5. Old style payola—paying to get a rock band on the airwaves isn't dead. According to a story from ABC News, the practice is alive and well; the only difference is that it's no longer the deejays who get the cash, it's high-level executives because they're the ones who set today's playlists. Here's a comment from Foo Fighters drummer Taylor Hawkins: "I think back in the '70s they used to pay people with hookers and cocaine, and now they're just doing it with straight-up money. So they can all go out and buy their own hookers and cocaine." [2]

There's a difference in the business world between providing entertainment and giving gifts. What is the distinction?
   o Why might entertainment be considered less ethically objectionable than gifts?
   o Leaving aside moral concerns about hookers and drugs, ethically, is there a difference between a rock group's manager inviting radio executives out on a hooker and cocaine evening on one side and just sending those cash on the other? If there's a difference, what is it? If not, why not?

The Decorator's Kickback
On a message board, Ms. G. C. from Miami writes,

Here's the problem: an interior decorators bid is broken down into two parts-(A) the decorator's services and (B) the cost of labor and supplies. Most customers think (B) is a fixed cost- they forget it's not the decorator's fault if cabinetmakers charge an arm and a leg. So, where do customers look the closest when they're comparing costs? That's right, (A)-the decorator's fee.

Well, decorators are creative people and for years they've been doing some very creative bidding. They've been low balling (A) and padding (B), expecting the laborers to kick back a percentage of their inflated fees to the decorator. Surprised? Everyone's doing it. Everyone, that is, except me. It's deceptive. And as a Christian, I think it's just plain wrong. The customer's final cost is about the same either way you cut it, so most decorators don't feel they're doing anything wrong. Are they right?
Needless to say, "blowing the whistle" on such a widespread and accepted practice would only damage my professional reputation.[3]

QUESTIONS

1. Mrs. G. C. confronts a third-party obligation. What is it?
2. Ethics can be weaponries—that is, used in your personal interest. Show how this could be the case here. Does the fact that she would benefit by getting these kickbacks eliminated somehow make her position less morally respectable? Why or why not?
3. Typically, according to Mrs. G. C, a client contracts an interior decorator. Later that decorator hires a laborer, and the laborer gives the designer a kickback. There's a conflict of interest here, what is it? What is the ethical case against this kickback scheme?
4. *Consequence theories* of ethics represent the point of view that acts themselves are not good or bad; all that matters are the consequences. Therefore, lying isn't bad if it

happens that a fleeing criminal is asking you which way is the best escape route, and you point him down the street leading to the police station. Duty theorists, by contrast, believe that certain acts including lying and stealing are wrong regardless of the context and consequences.

- o Do you suppose Mrs. G. C. adheres to a consequence ethics or a duty ethics? Why?
- o Could you use the idea of consequence ethics to try to convince her to simply join the crowd and do what everyone else is doing? What would that case look like?

5. If you wanted to put an end to this pervasive kickback practice in the interior decorating world and only had time to present one argument, which of the following would you choose?
   - o The practice should be stopped because it involves unethical kickbacks.
   - o It should be stopped because it's dishonest in the sense that consumers are misled.
   - o It should be stopped because the straight shooter is getting the shaft.

Why did you choose that argument and how could it be elaborated more fully?

6. Imagine that Mrs. G. C. from Miami reveals her name and makes a whistle-blowing cause out of her unhappiness with the standard practice in her profession.
   - o What kind of reprisals and negative effects might she expect?
   - o Do you believe whistle-blowing is justified in this situation? Why or why not?
   - o Is it required? Why or why not?

Sex, Money, and Whistle-Blowing

Like all recent NBA All-Star players, Kevin Johnson made a lot of money during his pro basketball career. It drained out fairly quickly too. A few hundred-thousand went to the family of a sixteen-year-old high-school girl in Phoenix after a he-said, she-said sex accusation. A decade later, a similar story emerged, but at a different place: this time it was three girls in Sacramento, California, who attended St. Hope Academy. They took their stories—each told of a similar incident involving Johnson—to the recruitment advisor, Jacqueline Wong-Hernandez. Soon after, Ms. Wong-Hernandez was gone. Her resignation was a protest over the way the complaints were handled internally at the school, which was by dismissing them. Not only did St. Hope Academy take no action, the local police also decided not to

press any charges in a case that essentially came down to one person's word against another's.

St. Hope Academy, as it happens, wasn't a public school but a private business, and Kevin Johnson was the founder and CEO. A lot of the money flowing into the young institution came from the federal government as grants from the AmeriCorps program. After accusations surfaced that the grant money wasn't spent appropriately, the school agreed to pay back $423,836.50 to the government (about half of what the school had received). The first payment, about $73,000, was made by Kevin Johnson himself.

So things probably would have ended, except for an AmeriCorps inspector general named Gerald Walpin. He believed Johnson had gotten way too good a deal: the school should have been forced to pay back much more of the grant money it had received. On May 5, 2009, he took the accusation to a California congressman who in turn brought public attention to the issue. On June 10, Mr. Walpin was fired. In an editorial statement, the *Washington Times* complained, "Mr. Walpin was fired with no explanation and no warning to Congress; even though the act governing inspectors general says IGs can be removed only after the president gives Congress 30 days' notice and a reason for the firing. Rather than investigate the IG's serious complaints, Mr. Obama fired him. In short, he snuffed out the whistleblower rather than heed the whistle." [4]

A local Sacramento TV station doing some follow-up uncovered a report detailing hush money payments at St. Hope and noted that the former NBA All-Star "often described himself as a personal friend" of another avid basketball player, President Obama. [5]

QUESTIONS

1. How were the following two faced with a third-party obligation?
   - o Jacqueline Wong-Hernandez
   - o Gerald Walpin

2. In general, there are three possible responses to third-party obligations, do nothing, report the problem, become a whistle-blower. How would you categorize the response made by
   - o Wong-Hernandez?
   - o Walpin?

3. What questions can be asked to help determine whether whistle-blowing is justified? How might they be answered in the case of
   - o Wong-Hernandez?

- o   Walpin?

4. What questions can be asked to help determine whether whistle-blowing is ethically required? How might they be answered in the case of
    - o   Wong-Hernandez?
    - o   Walpin?

Loyal to the Badge

When police officer April Leatherwood went undercover in Memphis, she changed her name to Summer Smith. She didn't change her socks for a year—no showers or brushing her teeth either.

Her daily routine was to hang out on the street smoking and trying to befriend drug addicts. They'd take her to their dealers, where she'd make a buy and then try to find out who was the next person up the ladder. Her work resulted in about three hundred arrests, everyone from two-bit drug sellers to major movers who organized the street-level crime from luxury apartments.

Why'd she do it? According to the newspaper article relating her story, she loved the camaraderie of the department and its protect-and-serve mission.

When she emerged from the undercover program, she was promoted to detective. Unfortunately, her three-year romantic partner had moved on, and it was difficult to get the bad memories out of her mind. Still, when the reporter asked whether she'd do it again, she said, "Yeah." [6]

QUESTIONS

1. The two ideas on which company loyalty—or organizational loyalty to broaden the title—is built are the following:
    - o   An attachment to the organization that is non-instrumental, meaning the attachment is not maintained only because it serves the employee's concrete interests, such as the need for a salary.
    - o   A deposited value in the organization that goes beyond any individual and their attachment: the organization's value continues even without those who currently feel it.

    How are these ideas manifested in the case of April Leatherwood?

2. Three measures on the scale of loyalty intensity are *obedience loyalty*, *balanced loyalty*, and *free agency*. Given what you've read about Leatherwood, where would you put her on this scale? Why?

3. Think about one of the career lines you're considering, or the one you're currently on, and imagine your company loyalty was similar to Leatherwood's.
    - o   What kinds of sacrifices do you imagine you'd make for the organization?
    - o   Thinking about yourself, really, would you be able to make those sacrifices?

4. Leatherwood's pay is not high, about $50,000 a year. That works out to about $7 an hour for the twelve undercover months. Obviously she enjoyed no status while she was undercover. Now, however, she has appeared in the newspaper and made detective grade in the department. In your opinion from what you've read, do you believe she has acquired a level of status through her work?
    - o   If she has acquired a status, how would you describe it, what is it based on, how is it different from the status enjoyed by, say, a senator or a movie star?
    - o   Does this status—assuming she's acquired it—compensate what she suffered? Explain.

[1] Brian X. Chen, "Fallout from Wired.com's iPhone App Payola Story," *Wired*, Gadget Lab, March 24, 2010, accessed May 19, 2011, http://www.wired.com/gadgetlab/2010/03/app-review-payola-reaction.

[2] Brian Ross, Richard Esposito, and Vic Walter, "Pay to Play: Music Industry's Dirty Little Secret," *ABCNews.com*, February 8, 2006, accessed May 19, 2011,http://abcnews.go.com/Primetime/story?id=1591155&page=1.

[3] Ms. G. C. from Miami, "The Case of the Casual Kickback," Urbana.org.

[4] "Editorial: Stonewalling on Walpin-gate," *The Washington Times*, July 10, 2009, accessed May 19, 2011,http://www.washingtontimes.com/news/2009/jul/10/stonewalling-on-walpin-gate.

[5] "Report: Johnson Offered to Pay Accuser," *KCRA.com*, November 20, 2009, accessed May 19, 2011, http://www.kcra.com/news/21679385/detail.html.

[6] Kristina Goetz, "A Year of Living Dangerously Takes a Toll on Undercover Memphis Officer," *Commercial Appeal*, August 30, 2009, accessed May 19, 2011,http://www.commercialappeal.com/news/2009/aug/30/year-of-living-dangerously-takes-its-toll.

NOTES:

Chapter 8:
Getting, Promoting, and Firing Workers

Chapter Overview

This chapter examines some ethical decisions facing managers. It considers the values that underlie and guide the hiring, promoting, and firing of workers.

8.1 Hiring
LEARNING OBJECTIVES

1. Locate ethical tensions affecting the breadth of a hiring search.
2. Define applicant screening and mark its ethical boundaries.
3. Define applicant testing and consider what makes an appropriate test.
4. Draw the lines of an ethical interview process.

Help Wanted, but from Whom?

The Central Intelligence Agency's hiring practices are widely known and well depicted in the movie *The Recruit*. After discretely scouting the special capabilities of a young bartender played by Colin Ferrell, Al Pacino catches him at work, orders a drink, carries on a one-sided and cryptic conversation, performs a magic trick with a ripped newspaper, announces that "things are never quite as they appear," and finally admits that he's actually a job recruiter. Ferrell seems annoyed by the man's presence.

Pacino returns to the newspaper, pulls out a page covered by an ad announcing "Two Day Specials." He circles the letters *c*, *i*, and *a* in "Specials" and walks out. Colin Ferrell follows. [1]

Actually, that's not true. The CIA doesn't hire that way. They advertise on CareerBuilder just like any other company. You can understand, though, why they wouldn't mind scouting out their applicants even before allowing people to apply; they don't want to end up hiring double agents.

Something like that happened soon after Procter & Gamble grew jealous of a competitor's hair-care products. Salon Selective, Finesse, and Thermasilk were all doing so well for Unilever that P&G contracted people to get hired over at Unilever and bring back secrets of their success. The corporate espionage—which P&G executives characterized as a "rogue operation"—led to a multimillion-dollar settlement between the companies and left behind the lesson that when you're the boss and you're hiring, you've got to make sure that the people you bring in will be loyal to the company. [2]

The problem is you've also got to make sure that they're going to do good work, the best work possible.

Between the two requirements there's a tension stretching through every decision to hire a new worker. On one side, you want to limit the people you even consider to those few who, for one reason or another, you know won't be a total disaster. On the other side, no company can survive playing it safe all the time; generally, the corporations able to hire the best talent will win over the long run. And one way to get the best talent is to cast as large a net as possible, let a maximum number know that a position is available, and work through the applications carefully no matter how many pour in. Conclusion. Hiring employees can be safe or risky depending on how broadly you announce a job opening.

Three Strategies for Announcing a Job Opening: Nepotism, Internal Public Announcement, Mass Public Announcement Start on the safe side of hiring. Nepotism is granting favored status to family members. In the case of hiring, it means circulating information about open jobs only to your relatives. Naturally this happens at many small businesses. A sales representative at a small firm importing auto accessories meets a woman at work. She's also a rep. Marriage follows. A year later he decides to quit his job and strike out on his own with a new website project that reviews and sells the same kind of car products. Things go well, page hits climb, sales increase, and soon he needs help so he hires…his wife. They've worked together before, and they both know the field. Most important, the risk is minimal. Since he's waking up with her in the morning he can figure she's not going to skip out on work just because it's a nice spring day. And is she going to steal office supplies? A little money from the payroll? An important client? Probably not. This is a case where nepotism makes sense.

But what about the other way? What if the husband's solo venture flops, and at the same time, his wife's career flourishes. Now he needs a job, and she's got the power to hire. A job opens up. Probably, she's got junior staff ready for the post, but can she push them aside and bring her husband in?

There *is* some justification: she's worked with him before, and she knows he performs well. Plus, as a boss of his own (failed) business, he's obviously got leadership experience and he has demonstrated initiative. All that counts for something. But if she goes with him she's going to breed resentment in her group. You can hear it:

"Hey, what do you need to get a promotion around here?"
"A last name."

And

Now you might be asking why nepotism bugs me so much. It's the presumption. It's the attitude. It's just one more example of how life isn't fair. Am I jealous? I don't know. I guess I take advantage of the company in other ways…LOL. What can I learn from this? That life is good if you're born into the right family? That I need to control my attitude and stop letting petty crap drive me to drink? [3]

That last paragraph comes from a blog entry titled "Nepotism Sucks." It does for his company too: few firms can be successful with employees musing about how they "take advantage of the company" while they're punctuating comments about their work with LOL. As for the central issue, he's right. Basic fairness isn't being honored: people are getting considered for a job because of who they're related to, and it's not this blogger's fault that his last name is wrong. On the other hand, "Is Nepotism So Bad?" titles an article on Forbes.com that compiles a list of large companies—including *Forbes*—where nepotism has been the norm…and successful. According to the article, experts estimate that executive-level nepotism works out about 40 percent of the time. What are the advantages to bringing in your own? Familiarity with the business and trust are noted. Another advantage is also underlined: frequently, relatives don't want to let their own relatives down. Sons work harder for fathers, cousins for cousins, brothers for sisters. There's a productivity advantage in nepotism. Arguably, that factor weighs more heavily than the bitterness arising when deserving workers already employed don't get a chance to apply for a job because it already went to the boss's sister-in-law. [4]

Finally, at least theoretically, there's a creative solution to the bitterness caused by nepotism: make virtually every post a nepotism-first position. Oil-Dri, a producer of absorbent materials, celebrated its fiftieth anniversary with a party for all employees. "Would everyone," the group was asked at one point, "who is related to someone else in the company please

stand up?" Of the seven hundred employees, about five hundred left their seats.

Internal public job announcements occupy a middle spot on the continuum between playing it safe (only letting selected people you're *certain* will be loyal and at least moderately capable know when a job is available) and going for the best talent (broadcasting the post as broadly as possible and accepting applications from anyone).

An example of an internal public job announcement comes from the *National Review*, a political magazine and website run by the kind of people who wear suits and ties to baseball games. Their blog is called *The Corner*, and the magazine's editors fill it with thoughts and arguments about the day's political debates in Washington, DC. There's also a bit of insider humor, provocation, and satire tossed back and forth between posters. If you keep reading for a few weeks, you'll start to sense an intellectual soap opera developing along with the libertarian-conservative politics; there's an undercurrent of shifting alliances, snarkiness, and thoughtful jabs.

You'll also notice that *National Review* places job announcements on *The Corner* blog. There aren't a lot of openings, but every couple of weeks a little announcement appears between posts.

The National Review Online is seeking an editor with web capabilities. Send applications to _____@nationalreview.com.

It's pretty ingenious. The *only* people who are going to be reading *The Corner* are

- *sincerely* interested in the wonkish subjects these guys publish about;
- not out there just looking for *any* job (at the time they see the announcement, they're not looking for a job at all because it's not a job site);
- compatible on a personal level with the *National Review* crew. The posters let personalities shine through, and if you don't have chemistry with their style of humor and talk, you're simply not going to be reading them.

What an internal public job announcement seeks to do is get the most applications in the hopper as possible, and so the announcement is published on a free Internet page that anyone can see. That's the public part. *But* because the page is only commonly followed by people who are *already inside* the world of public policy defining the employees at *National Review*, the bosses don't need to worry about the wrong kind of people sending in résumés. That's the "internal" part. Recruiters can get a lot of applicants—

increasing their chances of finding really talented people—without worrying too much about a bunch of lefties who really prefer websites like *Daily Kos* trying to fake their way into the organization.

Mass public job announcements are just what they sound like. You need someone and you post the position at Monster, CareerBuilder, and The Ladders. Here you're giving up confidence that applicants will fit into the organization naturally, and you're even risking corporate spying moles like those that infested Unilever. In exchange, however, you're getting the broadest selection possible of people to toss their hat into the ring, which maximizes your chances of finding stellar work performance.

Beyond the advantage of many applicants, there are good ethical arguments for mass public job announcements. The simplest is *fair play*: everyone should get an equal opportunity to take a run at any job. Just past that, there are concerns about discrimination that are eased by mass announcements. While there's no reason to launch charges of inherent racism at nepotistic hiring practices, it might well be true that if a small business is initiated by an Asian family, and they start hiring relatives, the result at the end of the day is a racial imbalance in the company. Again, no one is equating nepotism with racism, but the *appearance* can develop fairly easily whenever job announcements are not publicized as widely as possible. The parallel case can be made with respect to internal public job announcements. If 90 percent of the people who come in contact with the "help wanted" message happen to be women, sooner or later, there's going to be some guy out there who complains. So, one argument in favor of mass announcements is the stand it helps take against illegal and unethical discrimination.

Another argument for mass announcements is *reciprocity*. If a company is trying to sell a product to the general public, to anyone who's willing to pay money for it, then shouldn't they allow everyone a shot at becoming an employee? It doesn't seem quite right to profit from anyone—to try to sell, say, a car to anyone who walks in the door—and then turn around and not give all those consumers a decent chance at earning a living there at the dealership.

Conclusion. Announcing a job opening is not automatic. You can announce the spot more publicly or less so. There are advantages and disadvantages to the various approaches, but there's always an ethical responsibility to clearly account for the reasons why one approach is selected over another.

Ethical Perils of Job Announcements

Ethical perils of job announcements include:

1. describing a position in ways that don't correspond with the reality,
2. announcing a post to people who really have no chance for the job.

Once you've identified the demographic pool you'd like to recruit from, it's easy to oversell the job in the announcement you post. The most blatant cases—*You can earn $300 per hour working from home!*—are obvious frauds, but even sincere attempts can cause misunderstandings. Say a job requires "occasional travel." Fine, but does that mean occasionally during the year or occasionally during the month?

The much more severe case of insincerity in job announcements is posting one before an audience that has no reasonable chance of getting the job. When Hooters posts a "server wanted" sign, we all know what they're looking for just like when the rough bar next door advertises for a bouncer. But what if it's a formal restaurant advertising for a waiter? If the place is across town, you can't just drop in to check out the kind of people they hire. So maybe you go through the application process and make the telephone calls and finally go in for the interview. As you walk through the door, the first thing they check out is your weight profile. Then your jaw line, haircut, eyes, and the rest. They want to see how you compare with the other waiters who all look like they model on the side.

If you're lucky, you see yourself fitting right in, but if you're like most of us, you know the interview's over before it started; the whole thing has been a huge waste of time.

Now put yourself on the other side. As the restaurant manager trying to fill the position, you know you *should* put the requirement that applicants be devastatingly handsome into the ad. The duty to be honest requires it. The duty to treat others as an end and not a means requires it. The idea that our acts should be guided by the imperative to bring the greatest good to the greatest number requires it. Almost every mainstream ethical theory recommends that you tell the truth about what you're looking for when you announce a job. That way you don't waste peoples' time, and you spare them the humiliation of being treated as irrelevant. So you should want to put in the ad something about how only potential movie stars need apply.

But the law virtually requires that you *don't* put the line in. If you explicitly say you'll *only* consider exceptionally attractive men for your job, you open yourself to a slew of lawsuits for unfair and discriminatory hiring practices. In fact, even Hooters aren't safe. In 2009 the chain was sued by a Texas man named Nikolai Grushevski because they refused to hire servers who looked, well, like him. When it gets to that point—when hairy guys can get away with calling lawyers because they aren't hired to serve food in short shorts and halter tops—you can understand why restaurants don't want to publicly admit exactly what they're looking for. [5]

Bottom line: if Hooters just comes out and states what it is that makes their kind of employee, they can get sued. So they're much better off just making the announcement ambiguous. That way, when it turns out that no hairy guys ever seem to get hired, they can always say it's because they didn't seem so adept at dodging tables while shooting around with trays of beers and sandwiches. Or whatever. One lie is as good as another so long as it keeps the restaurant out of the courtroom.

For managers, this is a tight spot. They're caught between what's right and the law. In ethical terms, they're stretched between two conflicting duties: to tell the truth and to get the famous Hooters Girls into the restaurant.

Screening

Reducing a large pool of applicants to a manageable selection of people for serious consideration is applicant screening, sometimes referred to as filtering. Screening begins with the job announcement. Requirements like "three or more years of experience" and "willingness to work the night shift" go a long way toward eliminating applicants.

It's impossible, though, to completely define the perfect applicant beforehand, and even if you could, there's almost always going to be someone like Nikolai Grushevski who shows up. So screening continues as the preliminary review of applications and applicants to see who can be quickly crossed off the list without any serious consideration.

Legally, who can be crossed out? The default response is no one. In its broadest form, civil rights employment law guarantees equal opportunity. *All* applicants deserve to be considered and evaluated *solely* on their ability to do the job, and the federal government's Equal Employment Opportunity Commission is stocked with lawyers who are out there doing their best to make sure the rules are upheld. For managers, that means they've got to take all applicants seriously; they've got to pursue interview questions about ability, training, experience, and similar. Now, this is where a guy like Grushevski can come in the door and say, "Look, I can deliver a round of burgers and beer as well as any

woman." He's probably right. Still, he's not the right person for the job; there's no reason for a manager to lose valuable time dealing with him.

Similarly, a wheelchair-bound man shouldn't be a beach lifeguard; an eighty-year-old shouldn't be flying commercial jetliners; the seven foot one and 330-pound Shaquille O'Neil isn't going to be a horse jockey. There is a legal way for companies to summarily screen out inappropriate applicants: by appealing to bona fide occupational qualifications (BFOQs). BFOQs are exceptions granted to equal opportunity requirements. A form of legalized discrimination, they let managers cross off job applicants for reasons that are normally considered unfair: gender, physical size, religious belief, and similar. (As a note, race isn't allowed to be considered a BFOQ.)

When do bosses get this easy way out? When they can show that the otherwise discriminatory practices are required because of a *business' nature*. So while it's clear that Shaquille O'Neil's intimidating size doesn't mean he'll be a bad accountant, the nature and rules of horse racing require that riders be diminutive, and that means Shaq would be a disaster. A horse owner can show that the job *requires* a physically little person to be successful. Thus size becomes a BFOQ and a legitimate way of screening applicants for that particular job.

A maker of men's clothes can reasonably screen out women from the applicant pool for models—but they can't eliminate female applicants from consideration for a *sales* position. Or they could, but *only* if they could show that maintaining a masculine public image was integral to the success of the company. For example, you could imagine a company called Manly Incorporated, which sold products based on the premise that every employee was a quality control officer.

Along similar lines, a Catholic school may screen atheists from the search for a teacher, but it's harder to justify that filter for janitors. At the airport security line women can be assigned to pat down women and men to men, but either may apply for the job to hand check the carry-on bags.

Another common screen is education. Imagine you have just opened a local franchise of Jan-Pro, which offers commercial cleaning services to car dealerships, gyms, banks, churches, and schools. [6] What level of education will you be looking for in potential employees? Since the job involves mixing chemicals, it seems like requiring some basic education is a fair demand, but is a college degree necessary for the work? You may have one as a manager, but that doesn't mean you should necessarily demand that much from employees. And on the other side, is it fair to screen out someone who's got *too much* education, say a master's degree in chemistry? It does seems reasonable to suspect that this kind of person will soon become bored pushing a vacuum over carpets.

Then again, do you *know* that will happen? Is it fair to screen based on what you *suspect* might occur?

Another type of screening catches high-risk lifestyles. Smoking is one of the most often cited, and the Humana company in Ohio is one of a growing number that's directly banning smoking—on or *off* work—by new employees. [7]

These healthy lifestyle policies set off firestorms of ethical debates. With respect to smoking and in broad strokes, the company has an interest in prohibiting smoking because that should mean healthier workers, fewer sick days, lower health insurance premiums, and higher productivity. In short: better working workers. On the other side, job applicants (at least the smokers) don't believe that they're less productive than everyone else, and anyway, they resent being excluded for a recreational habit pursued on their own time. In long discussion boards—there are hundreds online—the debate plays out. Here's one exchange from a typical board:

bonos_rama:	I wouldn't hire anyone that has a habit of leaving their desk every hour to stand outside for 10 minutes. Doesn't matter if it's to smoke, drink coke, or pass gas that they're leaving, it's bad for productivity.
Mother of a Dr.:	But it's OK to stand by the coffee pot and discuss sports and politics? Productivity actually improves when you get away from the computer every hour.
matt12341:	Even discounting the productivity argument, smokers tend to have more long-term health problems, leading to higher insurance premiums so companies end up paying more.
jamiewb:	What if we apply this logic to people who are overweight? What about people who have a family history of cancer? Or a higher incidence of diabetes? As long as it doesn't impact job performance, I don't think it's fair to refuse to hire smokers.
happily-retired:	I think it is a great idea to not hire smokers. Up next should be obesity, as it leads to diabetes, heart problems, joint problems, etc. Companies following that path would be demonstrating
	good corporate citizenship by fostering a healthier America.
Zom Zom:	Yes, the good citizenship of fascism. Now my employer has the right to dictate what I do with my body? "Land of the free," unless your boss doesn't like the choices you make. [8]

You can see that underneath the back-and-forth, this is ultimately a debate about ethical perspectives. One side tends toward a utilitarian position: the greater good in terms of health and related issues justifies the filtering of smokers in hiring decisions. The other side tends toward a fundamental rights position: what *I* do with *my* time and body is my decision only. Both sides have strong arguments.

Criminal record screening is another common filter for job applicants. Most states won't allow employers to deny someone fair consideration for a job *only* because of a prior criminal conviction. There's wiggle room, though. In New York, Article 23-A of the correction law certifies that employment *may* be denied if:

- there's a direct relationship between the criminal offense committed and the employment sought,
- the applicant would pose an unreasonable risk to property or the safety or welfare of others.

Those are big loopholes. The first one means the Brinks armored car company can legally refuse to consider ex-bank robbers for a position. It may also apply to the shoplifter who wants to be a cashier or the drug dealer who wants a job in the pharmacy.

The second exception is still broader and applied in *Grafter v. New York City Civil Service Commission.* [9] In that case, the Fire Department of New York refused to hire Grafter because he'd been caught drunk driving on his last job. A potentially drunken fireman *does* seem like a risk to the welfare of others. Pushing that further out, the same would probably go if he applied to be a taxi driver. In fact, the list of jobs that may seem dangerous for others if the worker is drunk extends a long way, probably everything in construction, transportation, or anything with heavy equipment. So the law *does* allow employers to resist hiring convicts across a significant range of wrongdoing.

Finally, the basic ethical tension pulls in three competing directions for any manager facing a criminal hiring decision:

1. **The ethical responsibility to recovering criminals.** Rehabilitation (via honest work) is good for ex-convicts.
2. **The manager's responsibility to the company.** Managers need to avoid problems whenever possible and keep the machine running smoothly so profits flow smoothly too.
3. **The company's responsibility to the general public.** If a taxi syndicate is hiring ex-drunk drivers, you've got to figure something's going to go wrong sooner or later, and when it does, the person who put the driver behind the wheel will be partially responsible.

Social media is another potential filter. Fifty-six percent of millennial believe that the words and pictures they put on Facebook and Twitter shouldn't be allowed to factor into hiring decisions. [10] Recruitment officers, they're saying, shouldn't be going through online photo albums to check out the kinds of things you and your buddies do on Friday nights. From the employers' side, however, the argument in favor of checking the pages is simple. If an applicant is sufficiently incautious to leave pictures of massive beer funnel inhalations available for just anyone to see—and if they do that while they're trying to put their best face forward as job seekers—then God knows what kind of stuff will be circulating once they've got a job. As a manager, it's part of *your* job to protect the company's public image, which means you've got to account for clients and others maybe running the same Google and Facebook searches that you are.

It's an easy scenario to imagine: you hire someone with a flamboyant online life. Soon after, a client working with her gets nosey does a Google image search, and what comes in at the top of the list is a picture of your new employee slamming beers, chain-smoking cigarettes, or maybe inhaling something that's not legal. This isn't good and the person who looks really bad is the supposedly mature manager who allowed the whole thing to happen by hiring her.

Of course there's always the standard but still powerful argument that what employees do after hours is their own business, but one of the realities inherent in the Internet is that there is no such thing as "after hours" anymore. Once something goes online, it's there all the time, forever. Managers need to take account of that reality, which might mean rethinking old rules about privacy.

Testing

Once an ad has been placed, and applicants have been pooled, and the pool has been screened, the real hard work of hiring begins: choosing from among apparently qualified people. One tool used in the selection process is applicant testing. There are various sorts of tests, but no matter the kind, for it to be legitimate; it should itself pass three tests. It ought to be:

- **Valid.** The test must measure abilities connected to the specific job being filled. A prospective roadie for Metallica shouldn't be asked to demonstrate mastery of Microsoft Excel, just as there's no reason to ask an accountant to wire up his cubicle with speakers blasting 115 decibels.
- **Normalized.** The test must be fair in the sense that results are adjusted for the circumstances of the testing session. If you're checking to see how frequently applicants for the post of TV weatherman have predicted sunshine and it turned out to rain, and one woman gets tested in Phoenix while another takes Seattle, it's pretty easy to see who's going to win in terms of raw numbers. Those numbers need to be adjusted for the divergent levels of difficulty.
- **Constant.** The results any test taker achieves over time should be similar. Just like a broken clock is right twice a day, an applicant for an interior design job who happens to be color-blind might once in a while throw together a carpet-sofa combination that doesn't clash. A good test eliminates the lucky hits, and also the unlucky ones.

Of the many kinds of hiring tests now in use, the most direct try to measure the exact skills of the job. Skill tests can be simple. They're also relatively easy to control for validity, normalization, and constancy. For example, applicants for a junior-level position in copyediting at a public relations firm may be given a poorly written paragraph about a fictional executive and asked to fix up the spelling and grammar.

Psychological and personality tests are murkier; it's more difficult to show a direct link between the results and job performance. On one side, you've got a test that probes your inspirations and fears, your tastes and personal demons. On the other side, the test's goal is to reveal how well you can handle plain work assignments. Here's an example of the disconnect. The following is a true-or-false question that Rent-A-Center placed on one of its employee application tests: I have no difficulty starting or holding my bowel movement. [11]

Well, it's hard to see the link between bathroom performance and the ability to rent washer and drier sets. Rent-A-Center wouldn't be asking, though, if they didn't think the link was there. And they could be right; there may be some connection. One of the firmest sources of belief in the link between personality profile and job performance is the very interesting Minnesota Multiphasic Personality Inventory (MMPI). That specific test is the origin of the bathroom question. Other true-or-false choices on the long test include the following:

- I am very attracted to members of my own sex.
- Evil spirits possess me sometimes.

Now, the MMPI is a real test with a long and noble history. One of the things it tries to do is establish *correspondences*. That is, if we take a group of successful executives at Rent-A-Center and we discover that they nearly universally have trouble in the bathroom, then it may make sense to look for people who suffer this discomfort when looking to recruit future company leaders. As for the *why* question—as in *why is there a link between bathroom habits and success?*—that doesn't matter for a correspondence test; all that matters is that some link is there. And if it is, then you know where to look when you're hiring.

Theoretically, correspondence testing makes sense. Still, it's hard to know how *applicants* are going to react to questions about sexual attraction and evil spirits. Obviously, some are going to find the whole thing too weird and not turn in responses that actually match their profile. As for applicants and employees of Rent-A-Center, they filed a lawsuit. [12]

Inescapably, correspondence-type personality tests are vulnerable to lawsuits because they're explicitly based on the premise that no one knows *why* the results indicate who is more and less suitable for a post. The administrators only know—or at least they think they know—that the correspondence is there. It's not obvious, however, like it is with a simple skill test, so it makes sense to imagine that some are going to doubt that the test is valid; they're going to doubt that it really shows who's more and less qualified for a job.

So the problems with psychological tests include validity failure and lawsuits. Problems with constancy and normalization could also be developed. Added to that, there are invasion of privacy questions that are going to get raised whenever you start asking perspective employees about their bathroom habits and bedroom wishes.

On the other hand, it needs to keep being emphasized that the tests do happen, and that's not a coincidence. At the Universal Studios Hollywood theme park, recruiter Nathan Giles reports that the tests he administers—with true-or-false questions including "It's maddening when the court lets guilty criminals go free"—actually do produce valuable

results. They correlate highly, he says, with personal interviews: if you do well on the test, you're going to do well face to face. And though the application and interpretation of these tests are expensive, in the long run they're cheaper than interviewing everyone. Finally, if that's true, then don't managers have a responsibility to use the tests no matter how heated the protests? [13]

Lie detectors in the Hollywood sense of wires hooked up to the fingers for yes-or-no interrogations are illegal except in highly sensitive and limited cases, usually having to do with money (bank guards) and drugs (pharmaceutical distribution). Written honesty tests are legal. Generally, the questions populating these exams resemble those found on psychological tests, and deciphering the results again works through correlation. Obviously, the test can't work directly since both honest and dishonest people will answer "yes" to the question "are you honest?" Here are some typical questions that do get asked:

- I could help friends steal from my company.
- I'm not an honest person and might steal.
- I return quarters I find on the street to the police station.

Medical tests are generally only considered appropriate when the specific job is labor intensive. As always, there's a difference between testing and prying, and it's your responsibility as a manager to limit the questioning to specifically work-related information. Questions about *past* physical problems are generally considered off limits as are *future* problems that may be indicated by family health history. A simple example of an appropriate medical test would be a vision examination for a truck driver.

When Michael Phelps—the thick-grinned Olympic swimming hero—got photographed pulling on a bong, he immediately failed the drug test with one of his employers: Kellogg's breakfast cereal. He wouldn't be hired again, the company explained, because smoking pot "is not consistent" with the company's image.

The National Organization for Reform of Marijuana Laws rushed to disagree, insisting that the problem's not that the drugs are bad; it's the *law* that's outdated and wrongheaded. They were supported, NORML claims, by the *Washington Post* and *Wall Street Journal*. [14]

However that might be, it's seems difficult to object to Kellogg's argument. The *reason* they'd hire Michael Phelps in the first place is to brand their product with the image of beaming, young health, not zoning out in front of the TV eating Doritos. Whether it's legal or not, pot smoking is going to clash with the job description.

But what if he hadn't been caught by someone with a camera? Would Kellogg's have the right to demand a drug test before signing Phelps up as a representative? It depends where you are. Because there's no broad federal law on the subject, the rules change depending on your state, even your city. If you're looking for a job and you share a pastime with Michael Phelps, you may be in trouble in Alaska where any employer can test any applicant at any moment. In Arizona, on the other hand, you have to get written warning beforehand, which might allow for some cleanup. And if you're applying for a government job in Berkeley, California, you can party on because a local ordinance prohibits testing. [15]

Looking at the Berkeley law allows a sense of the central ethical conflict. On one side, the employers', the obvious and strong argument is that drug use negatively affects work performance, so evaluating job prospects in terms of their future productivity implies, it almost *requires*, making sure they're not distracted or disoriented by drug habits. In contrast, the Berkeley ordinance persuasively states that mandatory drug testing fails two distinct tests:

1. It assumes guilt instead of innocence.
2. It invades the individual's privacy.

Deciding about drug tests seems to come down to deciding whose legitimate rights deserve higher billing: the employer's or the employee's.

In 1971 the US Supreme Court banned intelligence quotient (IQ) testing except in very limited circumstances after finding that the tests disparately affected racial minorities. Further, serious IQ tests (as opposed to seven-question Internet quizzes) are extremely expensive to apply, so even if it were legal, few employers would use the test with any frequency.

Conclusion. Tests applied by employers to job applicants include those probing skills, psychological profile, honesty, medical condition, and drug use.

Interviewing

In 1998 the Indianapolis Colts had a very good problem. Holders of the top pick in the National Football League draft, they had to choose between two exceptional players: two that everyone agreed radiated Super Bowl talent. Both were quarterbacks. Peyton Manning had a better sense of the field and smoother control of the ball; Ryan Leaf had a larger frame and more arm strength. Which would make the better

employee? The call was so close that the team with the *second* choice, the San Diego Chargers, didn't care much who the Colts selected; they'd be happy with either one. The Colts didn't have the luxury of letting the choice be made for them, and as draft day approached they studied film of the players' college games, poured over statistics, measured their size, speed, and how sharply and accurately they threw the ball. Everything. But they couldn't make a decision.

So they decided to interview both candidates. The key question came from Colts coach Jim Mora. He asked the young men, "What's the *first thing you'll do if drafted by the Colts?*" Leaf said he'd cash his signing bonus and hit Vegas with a bunch of buddies. Manning responded that he'd meet with the rest of the Colts' offense and start going over the playbook. Mora saw in Manning a mature football player ready for the challenges of the sport at its highest level. In Leaf he saw an unpredictable kid.

More than a decade later, Peyton Manning heads into another season as starting quarterback. Having won the Super Bowl, set countless team and NFL passing records, and assured himself a spot in the NFL Hall of Fame, you can understand that the Colts are happy with their selection.

Ryan Leaf has recently been indicted on burglary and drug charges in Texas. He got the news while in Canada at a rehab clinic. As for football, after a rocky first few seasons, his performance collapsed entirely. He hasn't been on a field in years.

Interviews matter. Grades, recommendation letters, past successes, and failures on the job—all those numbers and facts carry weight. But for most hiring decisions, nothing replaces the sense you get of a candidate face to face; it's the most human part of the process.

Because it's so human, it's also one of the most ethically treacherous. Two factors usually weigh heavily in deciding which questions should and shouldn't be asked:

1. Fairness
2. Pertinence

Fair questioning means asking similar questions to all applicants for a post. If the position is entry level, many candidates will be young, inexperienced, and probably easily flustered. That's normal. So too there's nothing necessarily wrong with trying to knock applicants off rhythm with a surprise or trick question. The problem comes when one candidate gets pressed while another gets softballs.

What do tough questions look like? One answer comes from Google. There are always blog entries circulating the Internet from applicants talking about the latest weird questions asked by that successful and unpredictable company:

- How many golf balls can fit in a school bus?
- You are shrunk to the height of a nickel and your mass is proportionally reduced so as to maintain your original density. You are then thrown into an empty glass blender. The blades will start moving in 60 seconds. What do you do?
- How much should you charge to wash all the windows in Seattle?
- Every man in a village of 100 married couples has cheated on his wife. Every wife in the village instantly knows when a man other than her husband has cheated, but does not know when her own husband has. The village has a law that does not allow for adultery. Any wife who can prove that her husband is unfaithful must kill him that very day. The women of the village would never disobey this law. One day, the queen of the village visits and announces that at least one husband has been unfaithful. What happens?
- Explain a database in three sentences to your eight-year-old nephew. [16]

We're a long way from "why do you want to work at Google?" and even further from "what was your biggest accomplishment or failure in your last job?" Those are softballs; anyone going into Google for an interview is going to have prepared answers to those. It's like reading from a script. But looking at the hard questions Google actually poses, there is no script, and you can see how things could go south quickly. You can't figure out about golf balls and school buses, and you start to get nervous. Next, the blender question seems odd and threatening, and it's all downhill from there. Some interviews just don't go well and that's it. As an applicant, you probably don't have too much to complain about as long as the next guy gets the same treatment. But if the next guy gets the softballs, the fairness test is getting failed. As a manager, you can go hard or soft, but you can't change up.

On the question of pertinent interview questions, the Google queries seem, on the face, to be troublesome. Is there any job that requires employees to escape from a blender? No. But there are many jobs that require employees to solve unfamiliar problems calmly, reasonably, and creatively. On that ground, the Google questions seem perfectly justifiable as long as it's assumed that the posts being filled require those skills. By confronting prospective employees with unexpected problems demanding creative solutions, they are, very possibly, rehearsing future job performance.

When the Colts were interviewing Peyton Manning and Ryan Leaf, something similar happened at the key moment. At first glance, it seems like the question about the first thing each player would do after draft day wouldn't reveal much about all the other days to come. But the guys probably weren't prepared for the question, and so they had to reveal how they'd face a rapidly shifting reality that they had no experience in dealing with, a reality just like the one they'd face the day after the draft when they'd go from being college students on campus to wealthy adults in the big world. *That* makes the question pertinent. And that explains why the answers that came back were telling. They distinguished a great hire from one of the sports world's monumental bungles.

On the other side, what kinds of questions reveal employees' personalities' but *not* their job skills? Interview consultants typically warn managers to avoid asking about these subjects:

- Sex life
- Opinions about homosexuality
- Beliefs about contraception
- Personal finances
- Religious faith
- Political affiliations

Except in special circumstances (a job is with a church, a political party, or similar), these kinds of questions fall under the category of privacy invasion.

Finally, there are legal red lines to respect. While managers should ensure that applicants are old enough to work and so can confirm that people are, say, eighteen or older, it's discriminatory in the legal sense to hire one person instead of another because of an age difference. This means asking "how old are you?" is an off-limits question. It's also illegal to ask about citizenship, though you can ask whether applicants are legally authorized to work in the United States. It's illegal to ask about disabilities, except as they relate directly to the job. It's illegal to ask about *past* drug and alcohol use, though you may ask applicants whether they are *now* alcoholics or drug addicts.

The interviewer's fundamental responsibility is to choose the best applicant for the job while giving everyone a fair shot. Being fair isn't difficult; all you need to do is just ask everyone the standard questions: Why do you want to work for our company? What are your strengths? How do you work with others? Do you stay cool under pressure? The problem here, though, is that it's easy to get gamed. It's too easy for applicants to say, "I love your company, I'm a team player, and I never get mad." Since everyone knows the questions and answers, there's a risk that everything will be fake. And that makes identifying the *best* applicant nearly impossible.

One response to this is to junk the standard questions and come up with surprising and (seemingly) crazy questions like they do at Google. Another strategy is a different *kind* of interview. A situational or behavioral interview asks candidates to *show* how they work instead of talking about it. Here's how it goes. Instead of asking an applicant, "Do you stay cool under pressure?" (the correct response is "yes"), the question gets sharpened this way:

> *You know how jobs are when you need to deal with the general public: you're always going to get the lady who had too much coffee, the guy who didn't sleep last night and he comes in angry and ends up getting madder and madder…at you. Tell me about a time when something like this actually happened to you. What happened? How did you deal with it?*

It's harder to fake this. Try it yourself, try inventing a story. Unless you're a real good liar, you're going to hear the slipperiness in your own voice, the uncertainty and stammering that goes with making things up. Probably, most people who get hit with situational questions are going to opt for the easiest route, which is tell the truth and see how it goes. So the advantage to this kind of interview is that it helps sort out qualified candidates by giving an unvarnished look at how they confront problems. On the other side, however, there's also a disadvantage here, one coming from the fairness side. If candidate A has spent years at the counter of Hertz and candidates B through G have all been working in the Hertz back office, of course the counter person is going to do better.

KEY TAKEAWAYS

- In publicizing a job opening, a tension exists between limiting the job announcement to ensure that applicants are appropriate, and widely publicizing the announcement to ensure that applicants include highly qualified individuals.
- Decisions about how broadly to publicize a job opening can be implemented through nepotism, internal public job announcements, and mass public job announcements.
- Screening job applicants makes the hiring process more efficient but raises ethical concerns.
- Common screening techniques involve BFOQs, educational requirements, high-risk lifestyles, criminal record, and an applicant's social media history.

- Testing allows applicants' suitability for a post to be measured but raises ethical concerns.
- Common tests include skill tests, psychological and personality tests, honesty tests, medical tests, and drug tests.
- Applicant interviewing provides valuable information for evaluating job candidates, but questions ought to be fair and pertinent to job-related concerns.

REVIEW QUESTIONS

1. Why might an employer opt for nepotism when hiring?
2. What is an advantage of a mass public job announcement?
3. Invent a job description that would allow applicants to be screened by a BFOQ.
4. Why might an applicant pool be screened for use of social media?
5. List the three requirements for a fair and legitimate job-applicant test.
6. How do psychological and personality tests work through correspondence?
7. Imagine a job and then an interview question for applicants that would *not* be pertinent and one that would be pertinent.
8. Why might a behavioral interview be used?

[1] R. Donaldson (director), *The Recruit* (Burbank, CA: Touchstone Pictures, 2003), film.

[2] "Fortune: P&G Admits Spying on Hair Competitors," *Business Courier*, August 30, 2001, accessed May 24, 2011,http://cincinnati.bizjournals.com/cincinnati/stories/2001/08/27/daily43.html.

[3] Marti's Musings, "Nepotism Sucks," August 30, 2004, accessed May 24, 2011,http://businessethicsworkshop.com/Chapter_8/Nepotism_sucks.html.

[4] Klaus Kneale, "Is Nepotism So Bad?," *Forbes*, June 20, 2009, accessed May 24, 2011,http://www.forbes.com/2009/06/19/ceo-executive-hiring-ceonewtork-leadership-nepotism.html.

[5] "Texas Man Settles Discrimination Lawsuit Against Hooters for Not Hiring Male Waiters," *Fox News*, April 21, 2009, accessed May 24, 2011,http://www.foxnews.com/story/0,2933,517334,00.html.

[6] "2011 Fastest-Growing Franchise," *Entrepreneur*, accessed May 24, 2011,http://www.entrepreneur.com/franchises/fastestgrowing/index.html.

[7] Megan Wasmund, "Humana Enforces Mandatory Stop Smoking Program," wcpo.com, June 16, 2009, accessed June 7, 2011,http://www2.wcpo.com/dpp/news/local_news/Humana-Enforces-Mandatory-Stop-Smoking-Program.

[8] "Humana: We Won't Hire Smokers," *Newsvine.com*, June 16, 2009,http://sorrelen.newsvine.com/_news/2009/06/16/2935298-humana-we-wont-hire-smokers.

[9] Grafter v. New York City Civil Service Commission, 1992.

[10] Wei Du, "Job Candidates Getting Tripped Up By Facebook," *MSNBC.com*, August 14, 2007, accessed May 24, 2011, http://www.msnbc.msn.com/id/20202935/page/2.

[11] Martin Carrigan, "Pre-Employment Testing—Prediction of Employee Success and Legal Issues," *Journal of Business & Economics Research* 5, no. 8 (August 2007): 35–44.

[12] Karraker v. Rent-A-Center, 2005.

[13] Ariana Eunjung Cha, "Employers Relying on Personality Tests to Screen Applicants, *"Washington Post*, March 27, 2005, accessed May 24, 2011,http://www.washingtonpost.com/wp-dyn/articles/A4010-2005Mar26.html.

[14] Paul Armentano, "The Kellogg Company Drops Michael Phelps, The Cannabis Community Drops Kellogg's," *NORML* (blog), February 6, 2009, accessed May 24, 2011,http://blog.norml.org/2009/02/06/the-kellogg-company-drops-michael-phelps-the-cannabis-community-drops-kelloggs.

[15] American Civil Liberties Union, "Testing Chart," aclu.org, accessed May 24, 2011,http://www.aclu.org/FilesPDFs/testing_chart.pdf.

[16] Michael Kaplan, "Want a Job at Google? Try These Brainteasers First,"*CNNMoney.com*, August 30, 2007,http://money.cnn.com/2007/08/29/technology/brain_teasers.biz2/index.htm.

8.2 Wages

LEARNING OBJECTIVES

1. Explore the limits of wage confidentiality.
2. Delineate the uses and ethics of wages as a work incentive.

Two Salary Issues Facing Managers

Two salary issues facing managers are wage confidentiality and the use of wages as a work incentive. Starting with wage confidentiality, in the private sector it's frequently difficult to discover what an organization's workers are paid. Because of freedom of information laws, many salaries in government operations and contracting are available for public viewing, but in the private sector, there are no laws requiring disclosure except in very specific circumstances.

The main ethical reason for keeping wage information concealed is the right to privacy: agreements struck between specific workers and their companies are personal matters and will likely stay that way. Still, ethical arguments can be mounted in favor of general disclosure. One reason is to defend against managerial abuse. In a law firm, two paralegals may have similar experience, responsibilities, and abilities. But Jane is single and living in a downtown apartment while John has just purchased a home where his wife is living and caring for their newborn. Any boss worth his salt is going to see that Jane's got no local commitments and, who knows, she may just up and decide to spend a few months traveling, and then make a run at living in some different city. Maybe she likes skiing and a few years in Denver don't sound bad. John, on the other hand, is tied down; he can't just walk away from his job. He can always get a new one, of course, but if money's tight and a recession is on, there's an incentive to raise Jane's salary to keep her and not worry so much about John who probably won't be going anywhere anyway. That seems to be taking unfair advantage of John's personal situation, and it also seems like paying someone for something beyond the quality of the work they actually do. But if no one knows what anyone else is making, the boss may well get away with it.

Stronger, the boss may actually have an *obligation* to try to get away with it given his responsibility to help the company maximize its success.

Another argument against confidentiality is the general stand in favor of transparency, and in this case, it's transparency as a way of guaranteeing that ethical standards of equality are being met. Since the signing of the Equal Pay Act in 1963, the ideal of "equal pay for equal work" has become a central business ethics imperative in the United States. But it's hard to know whether the equality is really happening when no one knows how much anyone else is making.

Of course, workers *do* frequently know how much other people are getting. In an extreme case, if you're laboring in a union shop, it's probable that your wage scale will be set identically to those of your companions. Even if you're not unionized, though, people still talk at the water cooler. The result is, in practice, that some wage transparency is achieved in most places. From there, arguments can be mounted for the expansion of that transparency, but in most cases, the weight of privacy concerns will carry the day.

Another wage issue concerns its use to provide a work incentive. Many sales positions have the incentive explicitly built in as the employees receive a percentage of the revenue they generate. (That's why salespeople at some department stores stick so close after helping you choose a pair of pants; they want to be sure *they* get credit for the sale at checkout.) In other jobs, generating a motivation to work well isn't tremendously important. The late-night checkout guy at 7-Eleven isn't going to get you out of the store with cigarettes and a liter of Coke any faster just because his salary has been hiked a dollar an hour. Between the two extremes, however, there are significant questions.

Probably, the main issue involving the use of wages as a carrot in the workplace involves clarity. It's quite common, of course, for managers to promise an employee or a team of workers a pay hike if they win a certain account or meet productivity goals. Inevitably, the moment of the promise is warm and fuzzy—everyone's looking forward to getting something they want, and no one wants to sour things by overbearingly demanding specifics. The problems come afterward, though, if the terms of the agreement have been misunderstood and it begins to look like there's an attempt to worm out of a promised salary increase. It is management's responsibility as the proposers of the accord to be sure the terms are clearly stated and grasped all around:

- What, exactly, needs to be accomplished?
- How much, exactly, is the wage hike?

The mirror image of promised wage hikes to encourage improved worker performance is the bonus paid at year's end to employees marking a job well done. In a letter to the editor of the Greensboro *News-Record* in North Carolina, a teacher cuts to the central ethical problem of the bonus: on the basis of what do some employees receive one while others don't? Some teachers, the writer states, "at schools with high 'at-risk' populations and students coming from homes where education is just not valued, work themselves into a tizzy every year, but because of the clientele they serve, will never see that bonus money. Inversely, schools with middle-class clienteles have teachers who work hard, but also others who merely go through the motions but usually can count on that bonus because their students come from homes that think education matters. Where is the justice in this?" [1]

It's not clear where the justice is, but there's no doubt that bonuses aren't serving their purpose. The problem here isn't a lack of clarity. No one disputes that the rules for assigning a bonus are clear. The problem is that the rules don't seem to account for divergent working conditions and challenges. The important point, finally, is that even though a bonus is extra money outside the basic salary structure, that doesn't mean it escapes the question, "Where's the justice in this?," coming with every decision about who gets how much.

KEY TAKEAWAYS

- Wage confidentiality pits the right to privacy against the desire for, and benefits of, transparency.
- Wages and bonuses are used to provide a work incentive, but problems arise when the pay increments don't obviously align well with promises or with job performance.

REVIEW QUESTIONS

1. Why might a company want to maintain wage confidentiality?
2. What is an example of a payment bonus becoming disconnected from work performance?

[1] Bill Toth, "Entire State ABC Bonus System Unfair," *News-Record.com*, Letters to the Editor, August 19, 2008, accessed May 24, 2011, http://blog.news-record.com/opinion/letters/archives/2008/08/.

8.3 Promoting Employees

LEARNING OBJECTIVES

1. Distinguish criteria for promoting employees.
2. Locate and define ethical issues relating to promotion.

The Drinking Strategy

If you want a promotion, does going out for drinks with the crew from work help the cause? Here's a blog post; it's about two uncles—one who goes drinking with the crew and one who doesn't—and you'll see why the answer might be yes:

> *Look at my uncles, they both work for Ford and one has been in his position for 10-plus years and still doesn't have a company car, while my other uncle has a company car, increase salary, paid training. Even though he comes home to my auntie blinded drunk in the end it's all worth it if you want to be noticed.* [1]

Get hammered to get promoted! Too good to be true? Probably.

But not entirely, the Reason Foundation commissioned a report on the question of whether drinkers earn more money than nondrinkers. [2] The title "No Booze? You May Lose" pretty much tells what the study concluded about the link between social drinking with workmates and promotions. A few things should be noted, though. Drinking doesn't mean coming home blind drunk every night; it just means taking down alcohol in some amount. And the payoff isn't huge, but it *is* respectable: about 10 percent pay advantage goes to the wet bunch compared to those workers who stay dry. The really interesting result, though, is that guys who *drink in bars* at least once a month get another 7 percent pay advantage on top of the 10 percent. The bad news for drinking women is that for them, going to the bars doesn't seem to help.

So there are two findings. First, just drinking is better than not drinking for your wallet. Second, at least for men, drinking socially at bars is even better. One of the study's authors, Edward Stringham, an economics professor at San José State University, comments on the second result: "Social drinking builds social capital. Social drinkers are networking, building relationships, and adding contacts to their Blackberries that result in bigger paychecks." [3]

Now, going back to the blog comment about the drunken uncle, isn't this more or less what the blogger sees too? Here are the next lines from the entry:

No senior management wants to promote a boring old fart. They want outgoing people, in and outside of work. They want social people. If you can display your social abilities to them, it means that you want more than the 9am to 5pm, thank God, time to go home. They want people who enjoy working with the company and the people who they work for. [4]

That sounds reasonable, and it may explain why there's some serious scientific evidence that partying with the workmates does, in fact, lead to promotions in the company.

The link between lifting a glass and moving up may be solid, but is it *right*? From the worker's side, there's not a lot you can do about the situation so you may want to leave some Thursday and Friday evenings available for happy hour regardless of whether you think that's the way promotions ought to be arranged. From management side, however, there *is* a stark issue here. When you sit down to look at two candidates in your company for one promotion, do you have a right to consider how well they mix after hours? Do you have a *duty* or *responsibility* to consider it?

There are two issues:
1. Should you consider a worker's party aptitude?
2. If you do, how should you manage it?

The reasons for *not* considering party ability are many. Two stand out. First, workers are being paid for what they do from nine to five. That's the job. If you're going to start considering other things, then why stop at parties? You could give the promotion to the better player on the company softball team, or the one who's got curlier hair, or whatever. Second, workers may not have an equal opportunity to party. The guy who lives closer to work and isn't married obviously holds an advantage over the guy who has diabetes when gin and tonics become job qualifications.

On the other hand, when workmates gather after work to drink, what do they talk about? Well, work. That's why people say a new advertising campaign or a fresh product idea got scratched onto a napkin. It's not a metaphor. Further, the ability to labor together with others—teamwork—that's a real job qualification, and it's reasonable to suppose that people who get along well drinking will carry the camaraderie over to the next morning's breakfast meeting (where coffee and tea are served). This explains why companies including Deloitte Consulting encourage and even to some extent *pressure* employees to socialize outside the office. [5]

Finally, it's a hard call—there are reasonable arguments to be made on both sides. It's also difficult to be absolutely certain how the party qualification should be managed *if* it's included in the performance evaluation. On one hand, a strong case can be made for transparency and openness, for simply stating that after-hours socializing is, in fact, a part of the job. To *not* inform workers, the argument goes, that hanging out is a job requirement is really a form of lying: it's dishonest because the default understanding typical employees are going to have is that what counts in determining the quality of work *is* the work, period. Whether the assigned task got outlined in a cubicle or on a bar stool is irrelevant. Therefore, any manager who secretly totes up the social aptitude of the workers is not being honest about the way workers are graded. It's the equivalent of a college teacher assigning grades partially based on class participation without listing that in the syllabus.

On the other hand, all teachers know that listing class participation as part of a student's grade can lead to brown nosing, and there's a similar threat in the workplace: if employees are told to party, then at least a few are going to tag along for drinks even when they really don't want to go and end up souring the evening for everyone. If you as a manager believe in honesty above all, then you may accept that cost. On the other hand, if your vision of corporate responsibility dovetails more closely with profit maximization, you may be able to build an ethical case around the idea that in the name of evaluating employees as perfectly as possible some elements of that evaluation may have to remain close to the vest.

Three Considerations for Promotion: Work Performance, Seniority, Projected Work Performance

When managing a promotion, there are three fundamental considerations; work performance is the most obvious. The person most deserving to step up to a higher level of responsibility is the one who's best managed current responsibilities. This may be measured by accounts won, contributions to a larger group, or some other work-related factor, but the key is that the measured performance be related with the job.

The problem comes in determining exactly what that word *related* means. When read narrowly, it means that the employee who looks best on paper—the one who's written the best reports, achieved the highest sales, won the most cases—will be the most deserving. When read broadly, however, the range of considerations can expand dramatically to include contributions having to do with personality, chemistry, and other characteristics tangential to nine-to-five tasks. This is where questions about going out for drinks after work start to gain traction and importance. Finally, it's not clear that after-hours socializing should be considered part of work performance, but the fact that it *can* be included shows how broad this category is.

The second consideration when weighing a promotion is seniority. Seniority is preference for promotion granted to the person who's been with the company the longest. A *strong* or *pure* seniority system simply reduces the choice to comparisons of time with the firm: the promotion goes to the longest-serving employee. There's a taste of fairness here since no one will be overlooked for a job because of a personal conflict with the boss, or because he doesn't smile enough at work, or because her skirt is too short or his necktie too absurd or whatever. More, there's an inherent tranquility in the fact that all employees know exactly where they stand. The connected problem, obviously, is that good work is not directly rewarded. This explains why the seniority system seems especially suited to production line jobs or any kind of labor where experience is more important than analytic skills, high-level training, or creativity. If it's true that experience is what matters on a job, then a seniority system should produce promotions that more or less dovetail with expertise and the ability to do a good job.

A weak seniority system considers time with the company as a positive element, but only as one component in evaluating candidates for a promotion. The advantage of this kind of system is the encouraging of worker loyalty. The retention of good workers is nearly the highest human resources priority of any company, and rewarding seniority plus performance gives good workers a reason to stick around. Equally important, it helps retain good, loyal workers without forcing the company to promote old-timers who've never really learned to get the job done well.

The third promotion consideration is projected performance, which evaluates candidates in terms of what they'll be able to do in the future. A tool used by companies to groom young people for future leadership roles, the escalation normally goes to highly qualified individuals currently working at a level beneath their ability. For example, a health insurance company may hire a college graduate with a strong premed profile and hope to keep that person out of medical school by pulling her up the career ladder at a crisp rate. She simply doesn't have the experience, however (no one does), to just *start* near the top. In order for her to play a leadership role in the future, she does need to be familiar with how the company works at every level, including the lowest. That means spending some time on the front lines, say, manning telephones, answering questions from (frequently frustrated or angry) customers. Of course it's difficult to really stand out

in this kind of work, so if she's going to move up, it's going to have to be because she's expected to stand out at something more demanding later on.

Other employees are going to be tempted to resent the rapid ascension since many of them have done just as well at the same job for a longer time. Within the narrow view of performance evaluation (your job performance equals how well you do the work) their resentment is justified. The rule of equal treatment is being severely broken. But if you're in management, you have a responsibility to the company (and to shareholders if the company is public) to be successful. And you need to face the problem that highly educated and qualified young people have options. Arguably, retaining them is a higher priority—not just financially but also ethically—than keeping more replaceable talent content.

KEY TAKEAWAYS

- Work performance is defined in diverse ways, and managers may have a right to consider after-hours activities as part of that definition.
- Three common criteria for awarding promotions are seniority, work performance, and projected performance. Each contains specific ethical tensions.

REVIEW QUESTIONS

1. Why might someone's social skills be considered a factor in receiving a promotion?
2. What are some advantages and disadvantages of seniority promotion?
3. Why might a promotion be based on projected performance?

[1] Maya, "Alcohol: Income Booster?," *Monster* (blog), September 20, 2006, accessed May 24,
2011, http://monster.typepad.com/monsterblog/2006/09/alcohol_income_.html.
[2] Bethany L. Peters and Edward Stringham, "No Booze? You May Lose," Reason Foundation, September 1, 2006, accessed May 24,
2011,http://reason.org/news/show/127594.html.
[3] Bethany L. Peters and Edward Stringham, "No Booze? You May Lose," Reason Foundation, September 1, 2006, accessed May 24,
2011,http://reason.org/news/show/127594.html.
[4] Maya, "Alcohol: Income Booster?," *Monster* (blog), September 20, 2006, accessed May 24,
2011, http://monster.typepad.com/monsterblog/2006/09/alcohol_income_.html.
[5] *Deloitte Consulting: WetFeet Insider Guide* (San Francisco: WetFeet), accessed May 24,
2011, http://www.wellesley.edu/Activities/homepage/consultingclub/wetfeet%20-%20deloitte_consulting.pdf.

8.4 Firing

LEARNING OBJECTIVES

1. Define legal guidelines on firing employees.
2. Elaborate justifiable reasons for deciding to fire.
3. Set standards for the actual firing process.
4. Consider ways of limiting the need to terminate employees.

Optimal Level Firing

A study funded by the CATO Institute and titled "The Federal Government Should Increase Firing Rate" concludes this way: "The rate of 'involuntary separations' is only about one-fourth as high in the federal government as in the private sector. No doubt private-sector firing *is below optimal* as well since firms are under threat of expensive wrongful discharge lawsuits." [1]

There is, in other words, an *optimal level* for firing, and in both the public and private sectors it's not being met. People aren't being fired enough.

The strictly economic question here is, "What *is* the optimal firing level?" No matter the answer, there's an ethical implication for the workplace: firing workers is a positive skill. For managers to perform well—for them to serve the interest of their enterprise by maximizing workplace performance—the skills of discharging employees must be honed and applied just like those of hiring and promoting. On the ethical front, these are the basic questions:

- When *can* an employee be fired?
- When *should* an employee be fired?
- *How* should an employee be fired once the decision's been made?
- What steps can management take to support workers in a world where firing is inevitable?

When *Can* an Employee Be Fired?

In the world of for-profit companies, most work contracts offer at-will employment. Within this scheme, a clause is written into the contract offering employment only as long as the employer desires. Stated more aggressively, managers may discharge an employee whenever they wish and for whatever reason. Here's a standard version of the contractual language:

> *This is an "At Will" employment agreement. Nothing in Employer's policies, actions, or this document shall be construed to alter the "At Will" nature of Employee's status with Employer, and Employee understands that Employer may*

terminate his/her employment at any time for any reason or for no reason, provided it is not terminated in violation of state or federal law.

The legal parameters for firing seem clear.

Things blur, however, once reality hits. As the Cato study authors note, simply the fear of a possible lawsuit does impinge to some extent on the freedom to fire, especially when the discharged worker fits into a protected group. This means older workers, foreigners, or disabled workers may protest that no matter what reasons are *given* for termination—assuming some are given—the *real* reason is their age, nationality, or disability. Further, gender protection may be claimed by women fired from largely male companies and vice versa.

Another round of blurring occurs on the state level where legislation sometimes adds specific employee protections, and so curtails employers' rights. In Minnesota, for example, firing may not be based on a worker's participation in union activities or the performance of jury duty.

These varied and frequently changing legal protections are the reason managers are typically instructed to keep detailed records of employee performance. If those can be produced to show a pattern of incompetence or simply inadequate results, they can justify a dismissal before a judge, if it ever comes to that.

Even though legal complexities mean managers are well advised to be careful about firing workers, and it's prudent to be sure that there are directly work-related reasons for the dismissal, none of that changes the fact that at-will hiring gives wide latitude to the company, and fired workers are typically left with few good avenues of protest. One way to see how tilted the table is toward the employer and away from the employee is to compare the American at-will firing system with the European model, where a reasonable cause for termination must be demonstrated. In the United States, employers may more or less fire anyone for any reason, and the burden of showing the termination was illegal or unfair falls entirely on the worker. In Europe, by contrast, the legal burden falls largely on the *employer*. Instead of the worker having to show the firing was wrong, now the company has to show the firing was right. This is a big deal. It's like the difference between innocent until proven guilty and guilty until proven innocent. Just because firing means the company holds the burden of proof: it must demonstrate that the worker wasn't holding up his or her end of the employment contract. That's a lot harder to do than just producing some work evaluations to buttress the claim that she wasn't fired because she's Jewish or he wasn't let go because he's Asian. As opposed to the European reality, the conclusion is, employees in the United States hired at will have little recourse against a company that wants them out. Finally, it's worth noting that elements of just cause law have been working their way into the American legal system in recent years.

When *Should* an Employee Be Fired?

Because the legal footing is usually more or less solid for American managers, the real hard questions about terminating employees aren't legal ones about what can't be done but ethical ones about what should be done.

Sometimes firing is unavoidable. Economic slowdowns frequently bring furloughs and terminations. When the company's books turn red, and after the entire easy cost cutting has been done, people need to be cut. Who? There are three broad philosophies:

1. Inverted seniority
2. Workload
3. Recovery preparation

Inverted Seniority occurs when the last worker hired is the first released. This works especially well for assembly-line-type labor where one worker can replace another easily. As long as replacement *is* possible, dismissing the most recently hired allows clear and impersonal rules to make downsizing orderly.

Workload firings focus the pain of job cuts on that part of the company suffering most directly from a falloff in business. An office furniture supply company may find its line of hospital products unaffected by an economic downturn (people keep getting sick even if they don't have a job) so layoffs are taken from other divisions. This may mean losing workers with higher seniority or better job performance, but it minimizes cash-flow disruption.

Recovery preparation takes the long view on an economic slowdown: firings and layoffs are executed not so much to compensate for the present downturn but to sharpen the company for success when the economy bounces back. Staying with the office furniture supply company, the owner may see better long-term opportunities for profits in the nonhospital units, so the downsizing may occur across the board. The idea is to keep those slow-moving units at least minimally prepared to meet new demand when it eventually comes.

Sometimes economic slowdowns don't reflect a problem with the larger economy, they're the result of fundamental changes in the market, frequently brought on by technological advance. For example, the popularization of digital photography has shrunk the market for old fashioned film. Seeing this coming, what can a company like Kodak do? They're probably going to let workers from the old film side go to create room for new hires in the digital division. This is potentially unfair to terminated workers because they may be doing exemplary work. Still, it would be unfair—and financially disastrous—to the company as a whole to not change with the times.

Rank and yank is a management philosophy promoted by former General Electric Company CEO Jack Welch. Every year, he counsels, the entire workforce should be ranked and the bottom 10 percent ("There's no way to sugarcoat this," he says) should be fired to make room for new employees who may be able to perform at a higher level. Here, the responsibility to the company is being weighed far heavier than the one to the employee because, theoretically at least, those in the bottom 10 percent may be doing fine on the job—fulfilling their responsibilities adequately—it's just that others out there who could be hired to replace them *may* do it better. In the hope they will, workers who've done nothing wrong are sacrificed. [2]

There are two main criticisms of this practice. First, it's a betrayal of employees who are fulfilling their contractual obligations (they're just not over performing as well as others). Second, it's counterproductive because it lowers morale by drowning workers in the fear that even though they're doing what's being asked, they may end up in that dreaded bottom 10 percent.

Employee misbehavior is the least controversial reason to fire a worker. Here, the ethics are relatively clear. Employees aren't being mistreated when they're dismissed because it's their own actions that lead to their end. Standard definitions of misbehavior include:

- rudeness toward clients or customers,
- drinking or drugs on the job,
- theft of company property or using company property for personal business,
- frequent and unexplained absences from work,
- entering false information on records,
- gross insubordination,
- fighting or other physical aggression,
- harassment of others (sexual, sexual orientation, religious, racial, and similar).

How Should an Employee Be Fired Once the Decision's Been Made?

At the Friday all-staff meeting the office manager stands up to announce, "The good news is the following people have *not* been fired!" He reads a list of seventeen names. There are nineteen people at the meeting.

That's from a (perhaps unemployed) comic's stand-up routine. Unfortunately, people have written into the *CNNMoney.com* with real stories that aren't so far removed:

- An employee received news of her firing in a curt letter delivered to her home by FedEx.
- A man tells of being halted at the building door by security and being humiliatingly sent away.
- People report that they arrived at their office to find the lock changed and their stuff thrown in a box sitting on the floor. [3]
  All these are inhumane firings in the sense that no flesh and blood person took the trouble to present the bad news.

It's easy to understand why inhumane firings occur: not many people enjoy sitting down with someone and telling them they're out. So it's tempting to yield to cowardice. Instead of facing the worker you've fired, just drop a note, change the lock, and talk to security. On the ethical level, however, firing an employee is no different from working with an employee: as a manager, you must balance your duties to the company and the worker.

How can the manager's duty to the organization be satisfied when terminating a worker? First, to the extent possible, the fired person should leave with a positive impression of the organization. That means treating the employee with respect. No mailed notices of termination, no embarrassing lockouts, just a direct, eye-to-eye explanation are probably the most reliable rule of thumb.

Second, the terminated employee should not be allowed to disrupt the continued work of those who remain. If deemed necessary, security personnel should be present to ensure the ex-worker leaves the premises promptly. Also, if the worker is involved in larger projects, a time for severance should be found when their contribution is minimal so that other members of the team will be able to carry on near normally. (It may be recommendable to arrange the termination to coincide with the finishing of a larger project so that everyone may start fresh with the new, substitute employee.)

Third, the financial costs of the termination should be minimized. This means having clear reasons for the termination and documents (pertaining to worker performance or behavior) supporting the reasons to guard against lawsuits. Also, there should be clear understandings and prompt payment of wages for work done, as well as reimbursements for travel expenses and the full satisfaction of all monetary obligations to the employee. This will allow the human resources department to close the file.

With duties to the company covered, how can the manager's duty to the employee be satisfied? Consultants—both legal and ethical—typically share some bullet-point answers. First, the employee should be addressed honestly and directly with a clear explanation for termination. Speak firmly, the advice is; don't waver or provide any kind of false hope. Further, the termination should not come as a total surprise. Previous and clear indications should have been given concerning employee performance along with specific directions as to what areas require improvement. Many companies institute a structure of written warnings that clearly explain what the employee's job is and why their work is not meeting expectations.

Second, getting fired is embarrassing, and steps should be taken to minimize the humiliation. The employee should be the first to know about the discharge. Also, the severance should occur in a private meeting, not in view of other workers. To the extent possible, the employee should have an opportunity to say good-bye to workmates or, if this is the preference, to leave discreetly. For this reason, a meeting late in the day may be chosen as the appropriate time for notice to be given.

Third, to the extent possible and within the boundaries of the truth, an offer should be extended to provide a recommendation for another job.

Fourth, make sure the employee gets all the money coming for work done, without having to jump through hoops.

What Steps Can Management Take to Support Workers in a World Where Firing Is Inevitable?

One response to the inescapable reality that firing happens is preemptive; it's to reduce the moral uncertainty and hardship *before* they arise. Two strategies serve this purpose: actions can be implemented to minimize the occasions when firing will be necessary, and steps can be taken to reduce the severity of the firing experience for employees when it happens.

In her book *Men and Women of the Corporation*, Rosabeth Moss Kanter generates a list of measures that corporations use to diminish firings, and reduce the professional impact for those who are let go. Here's an abbreviated selection of her recommendations, along with a few additions:

- Recruit for the potential to increase competence, not simply for narrow skills to fill today's slots.

- Rotate assignments: allow workers to expand their competence.

- Retrain employees instead of firing them.

- Offer learning opportunities and seminars in work-related fields.

- Subsidize employee trips to work-related conferences and meetings.

- Provide educational sabbaticals for employees who want to return to school.

- Encourage independence and entrepreneurship: turn every employee into a self-guided professional.

- Keep employees informed of management decisions concerning the direction of the company: What units are more and less profitable? Which ones will grow? Which may shrink?

- Ensure that pensions and benefits are portable. [4]

KEY TAKEAWAYS

- At-will firing grants employers broad legal latitude to discharge employees, but it does not erase ethical concerns.

- Justifiable worker firings include cases where workers bear none, some, or all of the blame for the discharge.

- The act of firing a worker requires managers to weigh responsibilities to the organization and to the ex-employee.

- Steps can be taken to limit the need for, and effects of, employee discharge.

REVIEW QUESTIONS

1. What's the difference between at-will and just cause firing?
2. How might fundamental changes in the marketplace require a company to fire workers?
3. What is *rank and yank*?
4. When managers fire employees, what duties do they hold to the organization, and what are the duties to the dismissed worker?
5. What are some steps organizations can take to protect their workers from the effects of discharge if firing becomes necessary?

[1] Chris Edwards and Tad DeHaven, "Federal Government Should Increase Firing Rate," Cato Institute, *Tax and Budget*, no. 10 (November 2002), accessed May 24, 2011, http://www.cato.org/pubs/tbb/tbb-0211-10.pdf.

[2] Allan Murray, "Should I Rank My Employees?," *Wall Street Journal*, accessed May 24, 2011, http://guides.wsj.com/management/recruiting-hiring-and-firing/should-i- rank-my-employees.

[3] "Worst Ways to Get Fired," *CNNMoney.com*, September 6, 2006, accessed May 24, 2011, http://money.cnn.com/blogs/yourturn/2006/09/worst-ways-to-get-fired.html.

[4] List adapted from Rosabeth Moss Kanter, *Men and Women of the Corporation* (New York: Basic Books, 1993),

8.5 Case Studies

Fashionable

In her blog *Love This*, MJ (full name not provided) relates that she's been an aspiring clothes designer since she started sewing tops for her Barbie dolls. Things weren't going well, though, as she tries to break into the industry. One thing she notices is that there aren't a lot of female fashion designers out there—Vera Wang, Betsey Johnson, and a few more. Not many. So she starts trying to figure it out with questions like these:

- Do women want straight guy designers to dress them because they dress to please the men? It could make sense: what that designer likes, the man in her life is going to love too.

- Do women prefer gay men to dress them because gay men are their new girlfriends? Gay men are usually more receptive to trends and physical appearances too.

- Do women prefer women designers because she knows a woman's body better?

- Do men have the same issue? Do some men prefer a lesbian designer? Would they balk at being dressed by a gay designer? [1]

QUESTIONS

1. Assume MJ is right when she hypothesizes that most women like straight male designers because straight guys are the ones they're trying to impress, so they want clothes straight guys like. Now imagine you've been put in charge of a new line of women's clothes. Your number one task: sales success. You've got five applicants for the job of designing the line. Of course you could just ask them all about their sexual orientation(s), but that might leave you open to a discrimination lawsuit. So could you devise a test for new applicants that's fair—that gives everyone an equal chance—but still meets your requirement of finding

someone who produces clothes that straight guys get excited about?

2. Four standard filters for job applicants are
   o education level,
   o high-risk lifestyle,
   o criminal record,
   o flamboyant presence in social media.

   Which of these might be used to winnow out applications for a job as a clothes designer? Explain in ethical terms.

3. MJ wonders whether women might prefer women designers because she knows a woman's body better. Is there a bona fide occupational qualification for a women's fashion company to hire only women designers? Is there a difference between a BFOQ based on sex and one based on sexual orientation?

4. MJ asks, "Do women prefer gay men to dress them because gay men are their new girlfriends?" Assume you think there's something to this. Could you design a few behavioral interview questions that test the applicants' ability to become girlfriends (in the sense that MJ means it) with their clients? Would these be ethically acceptable interviews, or do you believe there's something wrong and unfair about them?

God at Work

The University of Charleston is a private, nonreligious institution with a very particular job opening: the Herchiel and Elizabeth Sims "In God We Trust" Chair in Ethics. According to the job description, the successful candidate for this job as a professor "must embrace a belief in God and present moral and ethical values from a God-centered perspective." [2]

QUESTIONS

1. You're in charge of getting applicants for this post and you've got a small advertising budget. What ethical responsibilities should you consider when determining where to place the ad? How broadly should you advertise the position?

2. According to Erwin Chemerinsky, a law professor at Duke University, "The description that 'candidates must embrace a belief in God and present moral and ethical values from a God-centered perspective,' violates the Civil Rights Act as religious discrimination in employment." [3] Imagine you're in charge of every step of the process of filling this job. How could you respond in terms of
   o bona fide occupational qualifications (BFOQs),
   o testing,
   o interviewing?

3. You're the university president. The person who currently holds the In God We Trust Professorship has, by all accounts, been doing a mediocre to poor (but not directly unacceptable) job. One day you happen to trip across the person's blog page and notice that your professor claims to be a sadist and practices a mild form of devil worship (also, the prof's favorite movie is *The Omen*). Right now the In God We Trust Professor of ethics is down the hall lecturing to seventy-five undergrads. You sneak to the door and listen from outside. The professor sounds just like always: dull and passionless, but the talk is about the Bible, and nothing's being said that seems out of line with the job description. Still, you decide to terminate the relationship.
   o In a pure at-will working environment, you can just fire the professor. But imagine you want to demonstrate just cause. How does this change the way you approach the situation? What would your just causes be?
   o The professor's classes are passionless because he doesn't believe in what he's teaching. Still, his teachings are not directly *wrong*. Does this case show why a manager may be ethically required in certain situations to implement a strategy of *rank and yank*? Explain.

Testing Baseball Players' DNA

The *New York Times* reports that there's a "huge difference between sixteen and nineteen years old," when you're talking about prospects for professional baseball. A kid whose skills knock your socks off for a sixteen-year-old just looks modestly good when he practices with nineteen-year-olds. [4] This is a significant problem in the Dominican Republic, which produces excellent baseball players but little in the way of reliable paperwork proving who people really are and when they were born. The Cleveland Indians learned all about that when they gave a $575,000 bonus to a seventeen-year-old Dominican named Jose Ozoria, only to later find out he was actually a twenty-year-old named Wally Bryan.

This and similar cases of misidentification explain why baseball teams are starting to apply genetic tests to the prospects they're scouting. Typically, the player is invited to provide a DNA sample from himself and his parents to confirm that he's no older than he claims. The player pays for the test and is reimbursed if the results show he was telling the truth.

QUESTIONS

1. Many experts in genetics consider testing an unethical violation of personal privacy.
   o What does it mean to "violate personal privacy"?
   o Can a utilitarian argument (the greatest good for the greatest number should be sought) in favor of DNA testing in the Dominican Republic be mounted? What could it look like?

2. In the baseball world, other tests that clearly *are* allowed as part of the hiring process include testing a player's strength and speed. Is there anything in the fair application of these tests that may ethically allow—even require—that baseball teams extract DNA to confirm the age?

3. Assume you accept that testing a prospect's age is a bona fide occupational qualification (after all, the job is to be a *prospect*: a developing player, not an adult one). Once you accept that, how do you draw the line? Couldn't teams be tempted to use DNA facts for other purposes? The *Times* article interviews a coach who puts it this way: *I know [the baseball teams taking the DNA samples] are looking into trying to figure out susceptibility to injuries, things like that. If they come up with a test that shows someone's connective tissue is at a high risk of not holding up, can that be used? I don't know.* [5] Can you formulate an ethical argument in favor of teams secretly using DNA tests to do just that, check for as many yellow and red flags as possible in the young prospect's genetic code?

4. Baseball scouting—the job of hiring excellent future players and screening out mediocre ones—is very competitive. Those who do it well are paid well; those who don't are cycled out quickly to make room for someone else. You have the job, you have the DNA sample. What do you do? Why?

5. You decide to do the test in question four. The problem is people aren't trees; you can't age them just by counting genetic rings—you also need to do some cross-testing with the parents' DNA. You do that and run into a surprise: it turns out that the young prospect's father who's so proud of his athletic son isn't the biological dad. Now what?
   o Is there an argument here against DNA testing, period? What is it?
   o Remember, the family paid for the test. Do you have a responsibility to give them these results? Explain.

6. Lou Gehrig was the first athlete ever to appear on a box of Wheaties. From 1925 to 1939 he played for the Yankees in every game: 2,130 straight appearances, a record that lasted more than fifty years. He was voted into the baseball Hall of Fame in 1939. He died in 1941 from a genetic disorder—yes, Lou Gehrig's disease—that today's DNA tests would identify. Is there an ethical argument here against DNA testing of prospects or one in favor? Or is the argument about this more theoretical—should the rules be decided regardless of what has actually happened at some time or place? Explain.

7. In a different sport, the sprinter Caster Semenya won the world eight-hundred-meter challenge in 2009 with a time that few men could equal. She looked, in fact, vaguely like a man, which led the International Athletics Federation to run a genetic gender test. She is, it turns out, neither a woman nor a man; she's a hermaphrodite: a little bit of both. Does the fact that genetic tests don't always return clean, black-and-white results make their use less advisable from an ethical perspective? Why or why not?

Windfall at Goldman

Goldman Sachs is an expansive financial services company. Many clients are institutional: private companies and government organizations wanting to raise cash seek Goldman's help in packaging and then selling stock or bonds. On the other side, private investors—wealthy individuals wanting to multiply their riches—receive a hearty welcome at Goldman because they have the cash to purchase those stocks and bonds. Ultimately, Goldman Sachs is a hub where large companies, governmental powers, and wealthy people come and do business together.

Executives at Goldman Sachs are among the world's highest paid. According to a *New York Times* article, "At the center of Goldman's lucrative compensation program is the partnership. Goldman's partners are its highest executives and its biggest stars. Yet while Goldman is required to report compensation for its top officers, it releases very little information about this broader group, remaining tightlipped about even basic information like who is currently a partner." [6]

The rest of the article investigates this shadowy partnership. The conclusions: "Goldman has almost 860 current and former partners. In the last 12 years, they have cashed out more than $20 billion in Goldman shares and currently hold more than $10 billion in Goldman stock."

This tally of accumulated wealth in Goldman stock doesn't even include the standard salary and cash bonuses the partners receive, but leaving that aside, here's the math: $30 billion divided by 860 divided by 12 should give some sense of the wealth each of these corporate stars is accumulating over the course of a year. To give a provisional idea of how large the number of dollars is here, when you try plugging $30 billion into an iPhone calculator, you find the screen can't even hold a number that long. Using a different calculator yields this result: $2.9 million per partner every year.

The 2.9 million can be compared with the salary earned by the average American: $50,000 a year. The Goldman partner gets that in less than a week. This huge money explains the clawing fight that goes on inside Goldman to become a partner. The odds are long. Each time the books are opened to admit a new class, only 1 of 330 Goldman employees makes the cut. It is, in the words of one former partner, "a very Darwinian, survival-of-the-fittest firm."

In the public comments section of the *New York Times* story about Goldman, a person identified as GHP picks up on the firm's characterization as a "Darwinian, survival-of-the-fittest" place. He wrote, "The French revolution was also very Darwinian, let's give that a try." During the French Revolution, the wealthy and powerful were rewarded with a trip to the guillotine.

Probably, GHP isn't just annoyed about how much money executives at Goldman make, he, like a lot of people, is peeved by the fact that the company was bailed out by the federal government during the 2008–9 financial crisis. Had the taxpayers (people making $50,000) not kicked in, Goldman might've gone bankrupt, and all that money its partners accumulated in stock would've vanished. As it happens, the US government's bailout was masterminded by US Treasury Secretary Henry Paulson. His previous job was CEO (and partner) at Goldman.

QUESTIONS

1. Goldman is dominated by a "Darwinian, survival-of-the-fittest" mentality. What does that mean?
   o In ethical terms, how can this mentality be justified?
   o Would a company dominated by this mentality, whether it's Goldman or not, be more likely to announce job openings to a limited public, or as a massive public announcement? Why?
2. Describe the advantages of a "behavioral interview." If you were in charge of hiring for a company seeking employees who flourish in a survival-of-the-fittest environment, what kind of question might you ask in a behavioral interview? Why?
3. One contributor to the *New York Times* comments section writes, "There are sure to be lots of pointed,

angry posts about how unfair it is that these guys make so much money etc. But if we are honest, there is a fair amount of envy and pure remorse that we weren't bright enough to go down that path! And these guys are very bright." How could these comments be construed to explain why high wages and big bonuses are used by Goldman to motivate its workers? What is it that makes big money (or the possibility of big money) function as a powerful motivator to encourage employees to work hard and well? Ethically, how can this use of big money be justified?

4. One difference between offering an employee a wage increase and offering a bonus is that the latter doesn't come automatically the next year. The employee has to earn it from scratch all over again.
   o Why might managers at Goldman award their best workers with a bonus instead of a wage increase?
   o By appeal to an ethical theory, could you make the case that, in general, employees should be paid mainly through a bonus system? How would the theory work at two extremes: wealthy Goldman executives and waitresses at a corner diner?
5. Given the kind of work that's done at Goldman—bringing wealthy people and powerful organizations together to make deals—why might party aptitude (the ability to mix socially after hours) be considered when deciding who does and who doesn't make partner at Goldman? How could that decision be justified ethically? How could it be criticized ethically?
6. Make the case that in theoretical terms, managers at Goldman have an ethical responsibility to institute the process of rank and yank.

The Five O'Clock Club

A *Washington Post* story about firing employees relates that some companies use "the surgical method: terminations that last about 15 seconds, after which former employees are ushered off company property."[7]

It doesn't have to be that way, though. For about $2,000 per fired employee, the outplacement company Five O'Clock Club will help employers manage the actual termination moment more compassionately. Later on, the fired worker receives a year of career coaching to help get back on track. What do the Five O'Clock Club recommend managers do at the critical moment when giving the bad news? To answer, according to the *Post*, they offer a booklet titled *How to Terminate Employees While Respecting Human Dignity*, which "asks managers to approach layoffs with the understanding that, 'unlike facilities and equipment, humans have an intrinsic worth beyond their contribution to the organization.'" [8]

Then some catchphrases are provided for managers to use:

- George, you've been a trooper. I'm sorry that this organization has moved in a different direction.
- George, you have made many good friends here. We hope those friendships will continue.
- George, you have made considerable and long-lasting contributions and they are acknowledged and appreciated. [9]

Five O'Clock Club vice president Kim Hall—who downs a lot of Tylenol and coffee on the job—relates several other phrases that may be helpful:

- I know this is hard, but you'll get back on your feet.
- The timing could actually work in your favor. A lot of people take vacation in the summer. There's no competition for job hunters.
- Maybe this is a chance to begin your dream career. Follow your heart.[10]

In sum, the Five O'Clock Club helps workers feel better when they're fired, and helps them get on with their lives. Meanwhile, employers get a hedge against lawsuits. The outplacement service, according to the Five O'Clock Club literature, "can redirect anger or anxiety away from the organization and…encourage the newly-fired to sign their severance agreements so they can get on with their lives." [11]

QUESTIONS

1. The Five O'Clock Club charges $2,000 per firing. If you were fired, would you prefer to receive the compassionate end the Five O'Clock Club provides, or just get shown the door but also get to keep that $2,000 for yourself?
   o If you're the boss, do you have the right to decide this for the fired employee? Why or why not?
   o If you're the boss, do you have the *responsibility* to decide this for the fired employee? Why or why not?

2. According to the Five O'Clock Club, "Unlike facilities and equipment, humans have an intrinsic worth beyond their contribution to the organization."
   o Does this sound like utilitarian ethical thinking to you, or is it more in line with the notion of an ethics guided by basic duties and rights? Why?
   o Probably, everyone agrees that humans aren't just machines that can be installed and replaced. But can an ethical argument be made to *treat people in the*

workplace as machines—that is, to abruptly hire them when they're useful and fire them when they're not? What ethical theory (or theories) could help you make the case?

3. In general terms, here are three firing situations:
   o an economic downturn (good workers are sacked because the company can't afford to keep them)
   o rank and yank (workers are fulfilling their duties but not as well as most of the others)
   o misbehavior (a worker is fired directly because of something done or not done)
   Looking at these three contexts and the Five O'Clock Club, do you think their services should be hired in all three situations? Do the ethics of firing change depending on *why* the person is being fired? Explain.

4. Recall some of the Five O'Clock Club's pre-packed firing sentences:
   o George, you've been a trooper. I'm sorry that this organization has moved in a different direction.
   o George, you have made many good friends here. We hope….
   o George, you…are acknowledged and appreciated.
   o Maybe this is a chance to begin your dream career. Follow your heart.

   The contrasting method of firing employees—the surgical method—is to look the person in the eye, say you're fired, and have security march the ex-employee out the door, all in less than a minute.
   o Is it possible to make the case that the surgical method is actually more compassionate and respectful?
   o Is there a place for compassion in business? From a manager's perspective, how should compassion be defined within a business context?

5. Maybe the Five O'Clock Club gets hired because a company really wants to help and support fired employees. *Or* maybe the company doesn't really care about them; all they want is to avoid wrongful termination lawsuits. Ethically, does it matter *why* the company contracts the Five O'Clock Club? Explain.

[1] "Sexual Orientation in the Fashion Industry," *Love This!* (blog), accessed May 24, 2011,http://lovethis.wordpress.com/2007/07/28/sexual-orientation-in-the-fashion-industry.

[2] Rob Capriccioso, "Divinely Inspired Bias?," *Higher Ed*, March 1, 2006, accessed May 24,
2011, http://www.insidehighered.com/news/2006/03/01/charleston.

[3] Rob Capriccioso, "Divinely Inspired Bias?," *Higher Ed*, March 1, 2006, accessed May 24,
2011, http://www.insidehighered.com/news/2006/03/01/charleston.

[4] Michael S. Schmidt and Alan Schwarz, "Baseball's Use of DNA Raises Questions," *New York Times*, July 21, 2009, accessed May 24, 2011,http://www.nytimes.com/2009/07/22/sports/baseball/22dna.html?hp.

[5] Michael S. Schmidt and Alan Schwarz, "Baseball's Use of DNA Raises Questions," *New York Times*, July 21, 2009, accessed May 24, 2011,http://www.nytimes.com/2009/07/22/sports/baseball/22dna.html?hp.

[6] Susanne Craig and Eric Dash, "Study Points to Windfall for Goldman Partners," *New York Times*, January 18, 2011, accessed May 24, 2011,http://dealbook.nytimes.com/2011/01/18/study-points-to-windfall-for-goldman-partners/?hp.

[7] Eli Saslow, "The Art of Letting Employees Go," *Washington Post*, August 9, 2009, accessed May 24, 2011, http://www.washingtonpost.com/wp-dyn/content/article/2009/08/08/AR2009080802659.html?hpid=topnews.

[8] Eli Saslow, "The Art of Letting Employees Go," *Washington Post*, August 9, 2009, accessed May 24, 2011, http://www.washingtonpost.com/wp-dyn/content/article/2009/08/08/AR2009080802659.html?hpid=topnews.

[9] Eli Saslow, "The Art of Letting Employees Go," *Washington Post*, August 9, 2009, accessed May 24, 2011, http://www.washingtonpost.com/wp-dyn/content/article/2009/08/08/AR2009080802659.html?hpid=topnews.

[10] Eli Saslow, "The Art of Letting Employees Go," *Washington Post*, August 9, 2009, accessed May 24, 2011, http://www.washingtonpost.com/wp-dyn/content/article/2009/08/08/AR2009080802659.html?hpid=topnews.

[11] Eli Saslow, "The Art of Letting Employees Go," *Washington Post*, August 9, 2009, accessed May 24, 2011, http://www.washingtonpost.com/wp-dyn/content/article/2009/08/08/AR2009080802659.html?hpid=topnews.

NOTES:

NOTES:

Chapter 9:
Deciding on a Corporate Culture and Making It Work

Chapter Overview

This chapter examines some ethical decisions facing managers. It considers how leaders guide organizations by selecting and then instilling the specific values and culture that define a workplace.

9.1 What Is Corporate Culture?
LEARNING OBJECTIVES

1. Define the concept of corporate culture or, more broadly, organizational culture.
2. Learn to recognize and distinguish specific organizational cultures.
3. Consider ways that a culture may be instilled in an organization.

I'm a Mac, and I'm a PC

"I'm a Mac, and I'm a PC" is the first line from a set of advertisements produced for Apple. [1] Two guys stand in front of a white screen, a step or two apart. The one pretending to be an Apple Macintosh computer looks a lot like you'd expect the typical Apple computer user to look: casual, young, and cool; he's not stressed but certainly alert and thoughtful. He hasn't had a haircut in a while, but the situation isn't out of control. He speaks up for himself without being aggressive. His t-shirt is clean, his jeans reliable, and his tennis shoes stylish. The PC, on the other hand, can't relax in a polyester suit that's a half size too small, especially for his inflated waistline. Bulky glasses slide down his greasy nose. Short, parted hair glues to his head. He's clean, shaven, and very earnest. In one of the commercials, the PC man talks about the things he does well: calculation, spreadsheets, and pie charts. The Mac responds that he feels more comfortable helping users make their own movies and organize their music collections.

Underneath these ads there are two very different corporate cultures, two very different *kinds* of companies making two very different products even though both sell their machines in the store's computer section. Now, because this is advertising and it's paid for by Apple, we should take the claims being made with a grain of salt. And, obviously, Apple didn't air these spots because they wanted to exhibit their corporate culture. They wanted to sell computers (and hammer the competition in the process). None of that,

however, changes the fact that the commercials do a good job of displaying what a difference between corporate cultures looks like. It looks like these two guys. They're both capable and dedicated, but everything about each of them makes the other one squirm; it's hard to imagine they could work well together because their habits and comportments—everything from how they dress to the way the talk—is so completely different.

The same can be said about workplaces. It's easy to imagine a kind of office where PC fits nicely. People there would wear ties and skirts. They'd be punctual. Their days and working styles would be regimented and predictable. Employees would have their own cubicle offices, and anyone proposing an "informal Friday" break from the dress code would be looked on with suspicion. By contrast, Mac would function well in an open, warehouse-like space with a bike rack out front. Flextime would be common—that is, people arriving earlier or later in the morning depending on their preference and on the circumstances of their lives (whether they have children, when they can avoid rush-hour traffic). Regardless of when they show up, they take responsibility for making sure they log a full workday. The attire would be casual and diverse. Maybe the boss wears jeans. Some people would probably be annoying others with their loud music, but everyone would force smiles and be tolerant.

One of the reasons the Apple ad works well is that it resists the temptation to simply say Apple is superior. Yes, PC is dorky and Apple is cool, but Apple does admit that PC really is better at analytic-type activities like producing clean spreadsheets. The same mixed findings apply to corporate culture. At the PC office, the clothes aren't nearly as comfortable as the ones you find at the Mac place, but at least there aren't any guys wearing jeans that fall a little too low over their back end. And the flextime scheduling at Apple may make for a happier workforce, but only until it happens that a project suddenly arises and needs to be executed immediately, and one of the key participants has flex-timed and already left for the day. The other team members are left, that means, to do his share of the work. What about the bike racks outside? Everyone agrees that it's great that the Mac people are peddling to work, but only until a morning thunderstorm pops up and no one can make it to the office. The point is there are advantages and drawbacks to every corporate culture. It's hard to say that one is better than another (just like Macs work for some people while others prefer PCs), but it's certainly true that there are different value systems beneath the distinct cultures.

Anyone who has a management role in any organization will be expected to have a grip on what values guide the enterprise and how they reflect in the day-to-day life of people on the job. Further, some managers—and all entrepreneurs—will not only need to apply guiding values; they'll have to select and create them.

Definitions of Corporate Culture

Corporate culture is easier to get intuitively than put into words. Because you can't touch it, measure it, or take its picture (even though you can show two people in an advertisement who obviously *belong* to different corporate cultures), it's not surprising that there's no consensus definition attached to the term. Here are three attempts to put the idea in words. A corporate culture is:

- "the shared beliefs top managers have in a company about how they should manage themselves and other employees, and how they should conduct their business"; [2]
- "the pattern of shared values and beliefs that gives members of an institution meaning and provides them with rules for behavior in their organization"; [3]
- "a general constellation of beliefs, mores, customs, value systems and behavioral norms, and ways of doing business that are unique to each corporation, that set a pattern for corporate activities and actions, and that describe the implicit and emergent patterns of behavior and emotions characterizing life in the organization." [4]

There are common threads to these cited definitions and some points that may be added:

- Corporate culture is *shared*; it's not like a regulation or a code that's imposed from some specific place outside the organization. The culture may begin that way, but once installed, it belongs to all those participating in the workplace.
- Corporate culture provides *guidance*. It's not a potted plant to be looked at; corporate culture *tells* an employee that the Daffy Duck necktie is too far out there and should be left in the closet. The pumpkin necktie, however, is OK as long as we're coming up on Halloween. Analogously, though more significantly, it tells a salesman whether it's OK to flagrantly lie to a customer, to stretch the truth a little, or only to play it straight.
- Corporate culture provides *meaning* in the organization; it tells members why they are there. At Goldman Sachs, the bottom line really is the bottom line: people are there

to make money. At Greenpeace, by contrast, people arrive in the morning to protect the planet, and while it's true that many receive a paycheck for their efforts, that's not the reason they show up for work.

- Corporate culture is top heavy; management carries the heaviest burden. Unlike simple office codes—such as turning in your expense reports within a week of terminating travel—that apply to people more or less uniformly, the burden of understanding and promulgating the organization's culture falls heavily, though not exclusively, on the leaders.
- A corporate culture is a *constellation* of values, a set of ways of seeing the business world.
- The constellation of cultural values is *dynamic*; everyone involved every day stretches and pushes the organization's culture.
- An organization's culture is *organic*; it's born and grows with the organization. It dies there too.
- The organization's culture includes *life values*, ones that cross beyond purely business concerns to touch questions including, "Is it OK to date someone from work?" "Can I cry at my desk?" "Will anyone object if I have a shouting match with my wife from the telephone in my cubicle?"

This list isn't exhaustive. It does, however, show how thoroughly corporate culture penetrates the workday.

What's My Organization's Culture?

Managers' job responsibilities include protecting and promoting their organization's culture. Fulfilling the responsibility requires determining exactly what culture lives in the workplace. There's no secret decoding mechanism, but there are a number of indicating questions that may be asked. One of the most natural is to brainstorm associated words. For example, imagine visiting two offices, one filled with people who look like the Apple Mac from the commercial, and the other with those who'd fit naturally into the office where PCs are bought and used. Just looking at the commercial and jotting words as they flow might lead to lists beginning this way:

- On the Apple side: sloppy, fun, warm, loose, careless, resigned, informal, smart, creative, soft-spoken, controlled, cool, and haughty.
- On the PC side: uptight, formal, reliable, demanding, uncomfortable, determined, perfectionist, detail oriented, disciplined, unconcerned with appearances, and geeky.

These are short, rapidly composed lists, but they're developed enough to observe two profiles of work-life peeking out. You can see that that the Apple office is going to fit closely with values including comfort, innovation, and independence, while the PC office will be more compatible with values including reliability and responsibility. You can count on the PC office to get things done, but if you're looking for something outside the box, you may be better off going the Apple route.

Other questions getting at the heart of an organization's culture and basic values include these dealing with the workplace time: How many hours are expected at work each week? Is there flextime? Is there telecommuting? Is there a punch clock or some other kind of employee time-in-the-office monitoring? Is it more important that the employee be present or that the work gets done? In some offices it's the former; in others, the latter.

Then there are questions about employee interaction. Is each worker situated in a private room or a more open, common space? Do people tend to compete with each other or is teamwork a higher value? To the extent there's individual competition, how far does it go? Is it a good-natured jousting, or closer to hostile blood sport? Of course different kinds of organizations are going to recommend themselves to one side or the other of the spectrum. For example, a doctor's office, an archeological dig, a construction company are relatively good places to value teamwork. A stockbroking office, a pro basketball team, and an actors' studio are spots where you may want to encourage individuals to outdo those around them.

What's the workplace mood? Fun? Somber? Energetic? Modern? Traditional? Many Volkswagen dealerships are remarkable for their huge windows and sunlight; it's a kind of work environment for the sales staff meant to encourage an open, airy feel conducive to car buying. Elevated heating and cooling costs go along with all that glass, however, and different workplaces where money is valued more than ambience may choose to cut operating costs with a drabber space. Going beyond the architecture, different offices have different moods. It's pretty rare that you see practical jokes or trash-basket basketball games going on at the dentist's office. On the other hand, anyone who's ever operated a call center telephone knows there's a solid chunk of each workday dedicated to high jinks.

Is the workplace personalized? Some office cubicles burst with family snapshots and personal memorabilia. Most assembly lines, on the other hand, are practically devoid of individual touches.

Are employee's workers or people doing work? If the former—if the value the organization attributes to those receiving paychecks is limited to what they do to earn the check—then few resources will be dedicated to supplemental and benefits. On the other side, a corporate culture valuing its employees as people may provide extra vacation time, health insurance, and retirement plans. Branching out further, you can get an idea of a workplace culture by checking to see if a gym or exercise room is provided. Day care for those with young children is another sign of the corporate culture that values workers as integral people.

Dress codes reflect the organization's values. Is uniformity or individuality more highly prized? If uniformity is the rule, what kind is it? In some advertising agencies, for example, the people who work in the creative department conceiving the commercials at first appear to be a diverse collection of independent-minded dressers, but get a few together and you'll immediately perceive a uniform that's as binding as the most traditional office—it's just that ratty jeans replace slacks and clever t-shirts replace neckties.

Another cultural indicator runs through the employees' leisure time. Where do people hang out? Do they go to football games, the opera, and church? Do they spend their weekend mornings on family excursions because they have spouses and children, or are they still in bed, sleeping off the night before? More, is leisure time spent with coworkers? Do employees get together just because they enjoy each other's company? If they do, the social outings are more likely to occur in connection with organizations seeking a harmonious workforce and expending resources to foster camaraderie on the job. They're less likely to occur at organizations where everyone is fiercely competing with everyone else, as sometimes happens, for example, at stockbrokerages.

Healthy community interaction is a value emphasized in some corporate cultures. Everyone has seen the "adopt a highway" signs indicating that a local firm or group has taken responsibility for keeping a stretch of highway litter-free. The professional sports leagues have traditionally asked players to dedicate some season and off-season time to community outreach. Other kinds of organizations, by contrast, may not even have a local community. Telecommuting and cloud computing mean employees can easily form a functioning organization with members living in different states, even different countries.

Social cause activism is another marker of corporate culture. The shoemaker TOMS Shoes fights rural poverty in developing nations by donating shoes. Other companies focus entirely on doing well in the for-profit marketplace.

Political action may (or may not) infuse a corporate culture. Many companies steer clear of overt or even hints of political partisanship for fear of alienating one or the other half of the electorate. This is especially true for larger enterprises spread across the entire country, drawing consumers from liberal corners of San Francisco, conservative bastions of north Dallas, and the libertarian towns of New Hampshire. Local businesses, however, especially those catering to relatively homogenous communities, may find no downside to flipping the switch on political activism and breeding partisanship as a guiding value. The company Manhattan Mini Storage provides (obviously) storage for household items in Manhattan. Their big competition comes from warehouses in New Jersey. The Manhattan Mini Storage billboard ads read, "If You Store Your Things in New Jersey, They May Come Back Republican." This appeal may work pretty well in central New York City, but it won't seem very funny most other places.

Like politics, religious belief and doctrine are rarely set at the center of the largest corporations, but smaller outfits operating in a narrow social context may well embody a particular faith.

Conclusion. Taken together, these categories of values begin shaping the particular culture defining an organization.

How Is Organizational Culture Instilled?

A specific culture may be instilled in an organization through a set of published rules for employees to follow or by the example of leaders and employees already working inside the organization.

Instilling a culture through established rules typically means publishing an organizational code governing behavior, expectations, and attitudes. The multinational firm Henkel—the company that invented laundry detergent and today produces many cleaning and health products sold under different brand names around the world—has published this kind of code. It's quite long, but here's an edited section:

> *Shared values form the foundation of our behavior and our actions throughout Henkel. Every single person plays a key role here. It is the sum of our actions that makes Henkel what it is—a lively corporate culture in which change is embraced as opportunity and everyone is committed to continuous improvement.*
> *Our Values*

1. *We are customer driven.*
2. *We develop superior brands and technologies.*
3. *We aspire to excellence in quality.*
4. *We strive for innovation.*
5. *We embrace change.*
6. *We are successful because of our people.*
7. *We are committed to shareholder value.*
8. *We are dedicated to sustainability and corporate social responsibility.*
9. *We communicate openly and actively.*
10. *We preserve the tradition of an open family company.* [5]

This statement sounds good in general. The stubborn problem, however, with trying to capture a corporate culture with a string of dictates and definitions parallels the ones constantly faced in ethics when trying to make decisions by adhering to pre-established rules and duties: frequently, the specific situation is far more complicated than the written code's clear application. So, in the case of Henkel, we learn that they *embrace change*, but does that mean employees can change the dress code by showing up for work in their pajamas? Does it mean managers should rank and yank: should they constantly fire the lowest-performing workers and replace them with fresh, young talent in order to keep turnover going in the office? There's no way to answer those questions by just looking at the code. And that creates the threat of an at least perceived cultural dissonance within the organization—that is, a sense that what actually happens on the ground doesn't jibe with the lofty principles supposedly controlling things from above.

Social Conditioning

The second form of instilling a culture doesn't work through rules but through social conditioning; it's not about written codes so much as the cues provided by the customs of the workplace, by the way people speak and act in the organization. New employees, in other words, don't read handbooks but look around, listen, and try to fit in.

In his book *Business Ethics*, O. C. Ferrell lists some of the social ways a culture infiltrates the organization. [6] Selecting a few of those and adding others yields this list:

1. **The founder's ethical legacy to the organization may contribute to its living culture.** Wal-Mart's founder Sam Walton was a legend in austerity; he industriously minimized costs so in-store prices could be lowered correspondingly. This is a continuing aspect of Wal-Mart's cultural legacy, though it can be controversial on other fronts. Some complain that Wal-Mart is in

essence encouraging third world sweatshop labor by ruthlessly granting contracts to lowest-cost providers.

2. **Stories and myths embedded in daily conversations may indicate culturally appropriate conduct.** Warren Buffett, leader of the Berkshire Hathaway investment group is a kind of Yogi Berra of the finance world, a highly skilled professional with a knack for encapsulating pieces of wisdom. Here's a paraphrase of one of Buffett's thoughts, "I'm rich because I've always sold too early and bought too late." Conservative investing, the lesson is, yields value for shareholders. It's also a high ethical value within the corporate culture he tries to nurture.

3. **Heroes or stars in the organization may consistently communicate a common message about the organization's guiding values.** There's a difference between lists of values written up in a handbook and a group of leaders who together consistently talk about guiding values and live by them.

4. **The dress, speech, and physical work setting may be arranged to cohere with the organization's values.** The United Nations threw a wrench into its own efforts to reduce global carbon emissions by scheduling its thirteenth annual global warming meeting in Bali. The weather was nice there, but since most participants came from the United States and Europe, it became difficult not to notice that the values of the organization's handbook (control of carbon emissions) didn't jibe with the values of the organization's members (burn tons of jet fuel to work in a place with sunny beaches). On the other hand, the UN Foundation—which advocates reduced greenhouse gas emissions and similar—recently moved into an environmentally friendly building with cubicles formed from a biodegradable product and many similar, environmentally friendly features. [7]

5. **An organizational culture may reinforce itself through self-selective processes.** A self-selective process is one where individuals effectively select themselves into a group as opposed to being chosen by others. Hiring presents a good example. Presumably, when an organization hires new employees, certain filters are constructed to reduce the applicant pool to those most likely to succeed. The process becomes self-selective, however, when job interviews are conducted as they are at Google. There, perspective employees are faced with bizarre questions that have nothing to do with the typical "Why do you want to work at Google?" and "Why would you excel at this job?" Instead, they get the following:

   o You have five pirates, ranked from five to one in descending order. The top pirate has the right to propose how a hundred gold coins should be divided among them. But the others get to vote on his plan, and if fewer than half agree with him, he gets killed. How should he allocate the gold in order to maximize his share but live to enjoy it? (Hint: One pirate ends up with 98 percent of the gold.)

   o A man pushed his car to a hotel and lost his fortune. What happened?

   o Explain the significance of "dead beef."

In response, some applicants will dive into the challenges excitedly, while others will find the whole process really weird and prefer not to be caught within a mile of a place where job interviewers ask such bizarre questions. In the end, those who enjoy and want to continue with the job application process are precisely those who will fit in at Google. Perspectives, that means, select themselves.

Conclusion. Two ways a corporate culture may be instilled and nurtured in a workplace are a list of codes to be followed and a set of social techniques that subtly ensure those sharing a workspace also share values corresponding with the organization.

KEY TAKEAWAYS

- An organizational culture is the set of values defining how and why members live at work.

- Distinguishing an organizational culture requires observing a range of values from the way people dress to the degree of cooperation and competition in the workplace.

- An organization's culture may be instilled through codes and rules.

- An organization's culture may be instilled through social cues and pressures.

REVIEW QUESTIONS

1. List five aspects of a corporate or organizational culture.
2. Describe two workplace decisions that may be determined by a corporate culture.
3. List some questions you could ask about a workplace that would start to give you a sense of its culture.
4. What are five ways that an organization may attempt to instill a culture through social conditioning?
5. In your own experience in a job or any organization, what's an example of social conditioning that enforced the place's culture?

[1] "'Get a Mac' Collection," YouTube video, 9:39, posted by "Aploosh," February 26, 2007,http://www.youtube.com/watch?v=siSHJfPWxs8.

[2] "Can this Man Save Labor?" *BusinessWeek*, September 24, 2004, 84.

[3] Robert Kuttner, "Labor and Management—Will They Ever Wise-Up?" *BusinessWeek*, May 9, 1994, 16.

[4] Simon Head, "Inside the Leviathan," *New York Review of Books*, December 16, 2004, 88.

[5] Henkel North America, *Vision and Values* (Düsseldorf, Germany: Henkel AG & Co., 2008),http://businessethicsworkshop.com/Chapter_9/images/HenkelNorthAmerica_ Vision_and_Values.pdf.

[6] O. C. Ferrell, John Fraedrich, and Linda Ferrell, *Business Ethics*, 7th ed. (Boston: Houghton Mifflin, 2008), 181.

[7] "UN Foundation Green Building," YouTube video, 2:23, posted by "unfoundation," February 14, 2008, accessed May 25, 2011, http://www.youtube.com/watch?v=15_MdcSUlSY.

9.2   The Relation between Organizational Culture and Knowing the Right Thing to Do

LEARNING OBJECTIVES

1. Delineate an ethically questionable organizational culture.
2. Consider responses to an ethically questionable organizational culture.
3. Define compliance in the business world.
4. Discuss a way of measuring compliance.

Dishonesty in the Fish Market

A frequently recurring business ethics question involves dishonesty: when, if ever, is it OK to lie, to stretch the truth, to not tell the whole truth? A simple scene of deceit goes like this: A fish dealer sells both expensive salmon caught in the wild and relatively cheap farmed salmon. Occasionally, he switches the farmed for the wild—a change that's very difficult to detect through appearance or taste, even by expert chefs—and pockets the difference. Randy Hartnell is a fish dealer in New York who suspected that a lot of that kind of dishonest fish switching was going on among his competitors. He investigated and published an Internet report. As he tells it, he visited the famed Fulton Fish Market in lower Manhattan and found some dealers openly admitting that the fish they were selling as wild had actually come from a farm. [1]

This led the *New York Times* to do a follow-up story. Using sophisticated chemical tests, the *Times* confirmed that, yes, at six of eight places sampled, fish being sold as wild for about thirty dollars per pound was actually farmed salmon, which typically sells for about ten dollars a pound.

In the six bad cases, the person who actually made the switch participated in an organization where one or both of two things were true about the culture:

1. Profit was understood as being more important than honesty.
2. Honesty was presumably important, but recalcitrant workers paid little attention and sacrificed the truth to make a buck.

These are two very different situations, and they lead to distinct discussions: One has to do with choices being made about what specific culture to instill in an organization. The other concerns compliance, which, in the business world, measures the distance between what an organizations *says* it believes and what its members actually do.

An Ethically Questionable Corporate Culture

The first situation—one where a fish seller puts profit above honesty because that's just the way things are done in the company—is one which most outside observers would categorize as fundamentally corrupt. Everyone inside the operation knows what's going on—principal and peripheral members are lying to bring in money—and newcomers are meant to pick up on and continue the practice. The organization itself is dishonest.

What responses are available? First, we need to check whether a serious attempt is being made, or there's a real interest in making a serious attempt, to justify the deceitful actions. If there isn't, if management and leaders of a fish-selling business aren't interested in ethical debates, there's not much ethical arguments can do about it. For those wishing to change a situation like this, the law (criminal and civil) presents good venues for action. Bad publicity in the *New York Times* might do the trick too.

If, on the other hand, there *is* an interest on the organization's part in justifying their actions from an ethical viewpoint, we could ask, "Can institutionalized lying be justified and, if so, how?" Three possible answers run through three distinct ethical theories: duty theory, consequentialist-utilitarian theory, egoism:

1. **Can basic duty theories justify putting profits above honesty?** Probably not. Duty theories affirm that right and wrong is determined by a set of unchanging rules, and they typically include *don't steal, don't lie*, and similar. Because this kind of ethics *starts* from the proposition that dishonesty is wrong, it's hard to see a non-frivolous way of justifying the fish seller's deceit.
2. **Can a consequentialist-utilitarian theory justify putting profits above honesty?** Utilitarian theory is oriented by the common welfare. Acts in business—whether it's lying or doing anything else—are defined as acceptable or reproachable depending on whether they

end up doing the most good for the most people. Any act, the theory affirms, that ultimately makes more people happier is good.

In this case, we can imagine an organization promoting lying as a common operating principal and making the case that the ethical stance is, in fact, good. Every Christmas, department stores deploy heavy men in red suits to proclaim that they live at the North Pole and ride a sleigh pulled by reindeer. The stores promote these fictions—addressed to innocent children, no less—to make money. Almost no one finds that ethically objectionable, however. One reason is that they're implicitly accepting the affirmation that an act making people happier in the end is good, even if it's dishonest. Similarly, the CIA covert operations branch (undercover spying, insofar as it truly exists) fits a utilitarian mold. In this organization, lying is good because it ultimately serves the American national interest and the basic principles of liberal democracies. Again here, the effects of what's done matters more than what's done. Finally, can this reasoning be applied to the lying fish seller? Maybe. As the *New York Times* story notes, the truth is that even the highest-level chefs and experts have a hard time distinguishing farmed from wild salmon. There is, therefore, a kind of placebo effect for food. If the fake stuff tastes just as good as the real thing, and the only real difference between selling one or the other is that the fish dealer makes out like a bandit, then an argument could be formed that the double-dealing does, in fact, increase happiness (the fish dealer's) without hurting anyone else. Therefore, the dishonesty is ethically justifiable. In practical terms, however, it's difficult to see how this strategy could get too far. Sooner or later someone *is* going to notice the difference, and as people begin to feel scammed (and therefore unhappy), the justification for the double-dealing crumbles.

3. **Can an ethical theory of egoism justify putting profits above honesty?** Egoism is a coherent ethical approach to the world that does offer some justification for a deceitful fish trader. On this account, the ethical good for organizations and individuals in the economic world is defined as just whatever serves the organization's or individual's interest. And switching in the farmed stuff in for the wild is good for the fish sellers. (It's hard to find any other explanation for the fact that, as the *New York Times* discovered, fully 75 percent of the places where fish was sold had some switching going on.) By definition, then, the dealing is ethically justifiable under this theory. Of course, most proponents of egoism in the business world don't stop

there. They go on to note that other, honest dealers who are pursuing *their* interests have a good reason to reveal the fraud. And, as it turns out, that's just what honest dealer Randy Hartnell did, presumably helping his own business in the process.

Organizational cultures that incorporate lying as an acceptable part of day-to-day business do exist. Whether or not these cultures are ethically justifiable depends on the deep theoretical stances people adopt when going into business.

The Ethics of Compliance

What happens when an organization's principles are laudable, but they don't get put into practice by the people actually doing the work? What happens, the question is, when an enterprise (say, a fish-selling operation) internally promotes basic values including honesty, but outside in the world where the transactions happen, the lesson is lost and individual sellers are swapping farmed for wild salmon?

In the business world, this is called a breakdown in compliance. Of course there are different reasons for compliance failure, everything from a bad-apple employee to a misunderstanding of directions, but the broadest explanation is simply that key elements of the organization's guiding philosophy aren't getting through to the members. One response to this possibility is a corporate culture ethics audit.

A corporate culture ethics audit attempts to loosely measure how open channels are between the ethical values stationed at the top, and the actual practices down below, and one common way of doing the measuring is with a questionnaire addressed to all an organization's members. Strings of questions can be answered simply yes/no or on a numerical scale from strongly agree (5) down to strongly disagree (0). These questionnaires can be distributed and the responses coming back summed and compared with previous samples in the same workplace or against results drawn from other workplaces. The goal is to get a sense of where people are at in terms of putting company ideals into practice.

It goes without saying that a simple questionnaire can, at best, provide only a crude picture of what's actually going on inside an organization. The process must begin somewhere, however, and two attempts at drawing up auditing questionnaires come from O. C. Ferrell's *Business Ethics* [2] and Dr. Arthur Gross Schaefer. [3] Combined, and with additions, subtractions, and modifications, the following corporate ethics audit emerges. (As a quick note, this test could be nuanced by changing the responses from yes or no, to agree or disagree on a one-through-five scale. Some audits also add a section for comments.)

A Corporate Culture Ethics Audit
Answer *yes* or *no*.

Part 1: Corporate Culture as Defined and Understood throughout the Organization

1. Are codes of ethics and business practices clearly communicated to employees?
2. Are there rules or procedures in company publications that may be consulted?
3. Is there a value system and understanding of what constitutes appropriate behavior within the organization that is shared by members at all levels of the organization?
4. Is there open communication going both ways between superiors and subordinates on questions concerning ethics and organizational practices and goals?
5. Have employees ever received advice on how to bring behavior into closer alignment with the organization's values and norms?
6. Does the organization have methods for detecting ethical and behavioral concerns?
7. Are there penalties that are publicly discussed for transgressions of the organization's rules and values?
8. Are there rewards for decisions corresponding with the organization's culture (even if they don't result in a profit)?
9. Do people at work act in a way that's consistent with what they say are the organization's values?
10. Do employees spend their time working in a cohesive way that is in accord with the organization's values?
11. Does the organization clearly and directly represent its activities and goals in its public communications?

Part 2: Corporate Culture as Organic and Encompassing

1. Does the company recognize the importance of creating a culture that is concerned about people and their self-development as participants in the organization's values?
2. Do employees treat each other with a respect, honesty, and fairness that correspond to the organization's values?
3. Are leadership decisions made with an opportunity for input from all relevant sources?
4. To what extent does leadership, the board of trustees or executive committee, view its responsibility as one to represent the entire organization?
5. Are leadership positions open to all members (insofar as such openness coincides with the organization's values)?

6. Does the professional staff provide services to all members in accordance with organizational policy and regardless of board or leadership status?
7. Are employees satisfied that day-to-day responsibilities correspond with what the organization's culture has led them to expect?
8. Is turnover low?
9. Are emotional outbursts springing from ambiguity about responsibilities within the organization rare? (*I'm in charge here!*)
10. Is there an absence of open hostility and severe conflict that goes beyond the internal competition provided for by the organization's culture?
11. Does the organization address contract negotiations, work expectations, and compensation levels in a way that corresponds with the organization's values?
12. Are there shared and commonly held beliefs about how to succeed in the organization?
13. Are there day-to-day rituals, habits, and practices within the organization that create direction and prevent confusion on ethical and business matters?
14. Do the dress, speech, and physical work setting prevent an environment of fragmentation or inconsistency about what is right and appropriate for the organization?
15. Does the organization's involvement in community activities correspond with the effects of the organization's day-to-day activities?

In its simplest form—with this audit rendered as a string of yes-or-no questions—the yes answers may be summed with a higher number indicating more compliance within the organization.

This audit can be applied to the question initiating this section. If we assume a fish seller is misrepresenting farmed salmon as the more expensive wild variety and if we assume that the larger business for which the fish seller works actually does value honesty within its corporate culture, then we should expect to see an audit like this produce a low score. We should expect to see that employees either aren't getting the message as to what the corporate culture is, or they're seeing it as just words, not real values supported on a day-to-day basis by the company's leaders.

KEY TAKEAWAYS

- A corporate culture may be evaluated in ethical terms: it may be justified as ethically respectable or challenged as ethically reproachable.

- Compliance in the business world means the organization's members are acting in accord with the organization's stated policies and values.
- Compliance may be loosely measured with a corporate culture ethics audit.

REVIEW QUESTIONS

1. In what ways can an ethically questionable organizational culture be challenged by outsiders? In what situations might one way be preferable to another?
2. What is an example of compliance, and an example of failure of compliance, in a fish-selling business that openly values honesty?
3. What does a *corporate ethics audit* do and how does it do it?

[1] Randy Hartnell, "N.Y. Times Calls Wild Salmon a Gamble for Consumers," *VitalChoices*2, no. 25 (April 22, 2005), accessed May 25, 2011,http://www.imakenews.com/vitalchoiceseafood/e_article000389904.cfm.

[2] O. C. Ferrell, John Fraedrich, and Linda Ferrell, *Business Ethics*, 7th ed. (Boston: Houghton Mifflin, 2008), 181.

[3] A. G. Schaefer and Anthony Zaller, "Strategic Modeling: The Ethics Audit for Non-Profit Organizations," accessed May 25, 2011,http://www.austincc.edu/npo/library/documents/Strategic%20Modelng%20The%20Ethics%20Audit%20for%20Nonprofit%20Organizations.pdf.

9.3 Two Ethically Knotted Scenes of Corporate Culture: Clothes and Grooming

LEARNING OBJECTIVE

1. Consider how the organization's values are reflected in dress codes and grooming codes.

Scenes of Corporate Culture: Dress Codes

Corporate culture is visible on the big issues, including whether a fish-selling business is honest about what consumers are receiving. It also exists, however, in the customs and rules making up quotidian life in the workplace. One of these quotidian scenes is a dress code, and a glimpse of how one can work comes from *Apple Insider*, a gossipy online magazine devoted to what's going on—everything from life at work to product development—inside Apple. The site got its hands on a survey Apple ran of its employees, a version of a corporate culture audit. What Apple was trying to do was get a grip on the corporation's values as the employees understood them.

According to the study, one notable aspect of Apple culture is the leisurely dress code. "I never dressed nicer than sweat pants. I often came in wearing whatever I slept in the night before and walked around the office barefoot. Nobody cared," said a customer solutions specialist who works for Apple in Austin, Texas. [1]

The survey presents this as one of the positives of working for Apple. On the other hand, there are people who go to bed at 3 a.m. after a rough party night and still wake up a full hour before leaving for work at 7:45 the next morning because no matter how tired they are, they wouldn't be caught dead on the street without a shower, some makeup, and the rest. Now, what makes Apple's culture appealing for many is that both kinds of people can fit in. If you want to dress nicely, great. If grunge is your style, still great. It sounds like this ethical stance in favor of individualism at the core of Apple Incorporated works well.

Listen, though, to the next lines that the same pajama-clad employee wrote in the survey: "There were a lot of communications problems. Micro management to the extreme. I had six different supervisors that did not communicate together and gave me six different answers." Well, if part of the corporate culture is to let people be independent to the extreme, dressing however they want, then it's going to be hard to stop each individual supervisor from supervising in his or her own unique way. This is one of the profound truths about corporate culture: it's difficult to have part way. If you're going to raise the values of diversity and individuality, then that's probably what you're going to get across the board. If it's in the way people dress, then it's probably also in the management style and in the customer relations and in the way people treat each other at work.

Of course no one is going to make the claim that a corporation allowing people to show up for work in pajamas is a scene of great ethical debate. It is, however, a scene of very broad debate. It shows how the values an organization decides to raise up permeate the company; they color everything.

Grooming Codes

Personal hygiene is less easily controlled by the organization than dress because it's more intimate than clothes and, frequently, more difficult to define. It's easy to require a necktie; it's harder to figure out exactly what "well-groomed hair" is.

Some grooming codes aren't questions of ethics so much as safety or hygiene. For safety reasons, you don't want a guy who hasn't had a haircut since the 1960s running the table saw in a lumberyard because his hair may get caught up in the blade with some Hollywood movie results. Similarly with respect to a woman working as a chef in a restaurant, if she refuses to wash her hands or cut her fingernails, the health safety of patrons eating the food she prepares is sufficiently concerning to allow and probably require that the cook be ordered to clean up or be fired.

While health and hygiene issues can normally be resolved by appeals to common reason, more difficult ethical dilemmas arise around the organization's desire to maintain a uniform and presentable workforce as a way of boosting appeal to consumers. It's safe to say that business would decline at a McDonald's if employees were allowed to show up for work un-bathed, unshaven, and wearing pajamas. On the other side, however, employees do have lives outside the nine to five, and workplace requirements concerning haircuts and beards obviously wash over to those personal hours.

The conflict between a business's desire for grooming uniformity and the individuals' personal freedom to appear in public as they wish centers the case of *Brown v. Roberts and Company* argued before the Massachusetts Supreme Court in 2008. [2] The journey to a lawsuit began when the owner of a Jiffy Lube station hired a consultant to improve the business, and one recommendation was a grooming policy requiring neatly combed and trimmed hair, along with the prohibition of beards and mustaches. Consumers, the consultant reported, found that cleanliness and uniformity provided an implicit assurance of trustworthiness and good work. The problem for Jiffy Lube employee Bobby Brown was that he practiced a version of Rastafarianism. For more than a decade he'd faithfully subscribed to a religion that didn't permit him to shave or cut his hair.

After refusing to abide by the new Jiffy Lube grooming guidelines, Brown was removed from his normal routine, which included working the register and greeting customers, and banished to the lower bay where, out of customer sightlines, he performed the dirty work of servicing cars and trucks. He sued to get his old duties back. The Jiffy Lube owner refused to back down. In court, the owner provided statistics showing that cleaning up the customer service personnel actually improved business, and, the owner added, he had the right to control the public image of his company regardless of whether it improved business or not. Brown countered that his grooming was protected by the fact that it was a religious necessity. The grooming requirement, he maintained, didn't just interfere with his personal life and religion, it completely desecrated both of them. For its part, the high court punted the issue back down to a lower court. The law in these cases may be hazy, but the ethics will come down to the foundational views shaping the organization's

working culture. Here are three different solutions to Brown versus Jiffy Lube as they emerge from three distinct organizational cultures:

1. An authoritarian culture defines right and wrong inside a business as just what the highest-ranking individual orders. In this case, the owner is in charge of his shop, and if he determines that all employees must wear short hair, that's the way the workplace will be. Since there's no higher code, authority or appeal, people who want to be part of the company will need to accept obedience to the boss.

2. A consequentialist, utilitarian outlook will produce a workplace culture that most highly values the collective welfare of all those involved. The issue is no longer boss versus employee; it's what's best for everyone. If this mentality controls the Jiffy Lube franchise, someone may propose that Brown bundle his hair up underneath a cap or agree to work only limited hours up front at times when visits from walk-ins and new clients are minimal. That way the business can prosper (possibly triggering wage increases for all employees), while Brown's inconvenience is minimized.

3. An ethics of care produces an organizational culture distinct from the previous two. Instead of seeing the workplace as controlled by an owner, and instead of seeing it as a scene of compromise in the name of the general welfare, a Jiffy Lube structured by care will conceive of the workforce as something near a family. In this case, the ethical justification for action will always trace back to the question about whether the act will strengthen and nurture the bonds of all those involved in working together. In the case of Jiffy Lube, this guideline will probably lead to a decision to allow Brown to return to his customary role. It may be that some business will be lost, but if that's the cost of maintaining the harmony of the work unit *as* a unit, then the cost will be paid. Of course the owner may still appeal to Brown to cut his hair and shave, but just as members of a family learn to respect (or at least tolerate) the idiosyncrasies and uniqueness of each member, so too a business culture governed by care will ultimately be more interested in preserving Brown's ties to the group than reforming his character, habits, and presentation.

Conclusion. Some businesses have an interest in controlling the way employees look. The degree to which they'll control appearances depends on the ethical stance defining their internal values and culture.

KEY TAKEAWAYS

- An organization's fundamental values show through in codes regulating dress and grooming.
- The implications of these particular codes and the values beneath them stretch broadly through the organization.

REVIEW QUESTIONS

1. What might a dress code tell you about an organization's larger culture?
2. Why might a business install a grooming code?
3. Why might a utilitarian vision of the workplace and its values lead to an only partially enforced grooming code?

[1] Kasper Jade and Katie Marshal, "Employees Offer Mixed Reactions to Corporate Life, *"Apple Insider*, March 30, 2005, accessed May 25, 2011,http://www.appleinsider.com/articles/05/03/30/employees_offer_ mixed_reactions_to_apple_corporate_life.html.
[2] Bobby T. Brown vs. F. L. Roberts & Co., Inc., accessed May 25, 2011,http://www.socialaw.com/slip.htm?cid=18640&sid=120.

9.4 What Culture Should a Leader Choose to Instill?
LEARNING OBJECTIVES

1. Show that different kinds of businesses and organizations lend themselves to distinct cultures and guiding values.
2. List and describe questions that may help leaders choose an appropriate organizational culture.
3. Show how specific aspects of an organizational culture may be founded on ethical theory.

Choosing the Right Organizational Culture for Me

For those starting a business, the first question about the values and culture of the new workplace is the simplest: *What should they be?* There's no right or wrong answer, but there are different ways that any set of values may be justified.

Diverse fields of work will lend themselves more naturally to one or another organizational style and tone. A fish seller delivering to markets, restaurants, and homes, for example, one entrusted with providing food for others to sell and cook, will need to value punctuality and reliability. This kind of firm must honor its contracts by getting orders delivered to clients when promised and by making sure the quality (at least the quality that consumers perceive) is up to standard. Further, the physical workplace—which stretches from the office where orders are received to trucks delivering goods—will probably function best if the values of fairness, respect, and openness are enforced. The various individuals entrusted with any one account must be able to work together well and

produce results individually that the entire group stands behind.

On the other hand, if the small company you're forming happens to be a rock band, then creativity (as they say in the business world, the ability to think outside the box) steps forward as a cardinal value. When trying to get a nightclub or bar to book your group, you may lie about (or "exorbitantly exaggerate") the response your songs have gotten from people who've listened to you in the garage. You may promise that you've got material to present a forty-five-minute show and run out after half an hour. You may not foster mutual respect in the workplace: the lead guitarist may secretly instruct the soundman to reduce the hapless bass player's volume to near zero or the drummer may show up for work blind drunk and flinging expletives. All those failures in reliability and respect will wash away, though, if you've got a new sound and people like hearing it. Fish sellers and rock bands, finally, are different kinds of businesses and the organizational values surrounding them may be similarly divergent.

Even within the same pursuit, even when two corporations are producing comparable products, there's no requirement that their cultures be similar. In fact, that's a central point of the "I'm a Mac, I'm a PC" advertising campaign. The appeal being made in these ads isn't that Apple is better because their processors run a gigahertz faster than a PC's or because the screen images are crisper or the battery life is longer. Fundamentally, Apple is making the case that the values—as displayed by the style of clothes the actors wear and their way of standing and speaking—are ones the purchaser may want to participate in. Apple, in essence, turns corporate culture into a selling point.

Refocusing on the problem of determining a set of values for an organization, there's a two-step process: decide the values, and then justify them. One way to proceed is by posing some questions aimed at the core of workplace culture.

What Counts as Success?

In some organizations (especially nonprofits and political groupings), success gets defined socially. Perhaps it's an effort to eradicate homelessness, or diminish the effects of poverty, or advance a legislative agenda. In this kind of endeavor, one existing to serve the greater good, a utilitarian ethical perspective could be employed to justify the organization's existence and goals. The *reason* for the organization's existence fits well with the theory that acts are ethically good if they bring the greatest good to the greatest number.

By contrast, if success for an organization is economic not social, if it's about me getting rich and not the general welfare, other theoretical foundations may be more recommendable. A culturalist ethics—one that defines moral right and wrong as just what the larger society dictates—might work in this case, at least in the United States where private enterprise and the pursuit of wealth have customarily been regarded as a virtue. Alternatively, a rights-based theory, one that maximizes individuals' liberty to pursue their own happiness (as long as the rights of others aren't infringed upon in the process) may work well for those choosing to establish a corporate culture that raises profit as the main goal of the business.

Am I a Collectivist or an Individualist?

If I believe that people work best when they work together, then I may choose to raise collectivism as a central virtue. Individuals are rated professionally in terms of their workgroup's accomplishments. This kind of organization would recognize a single person's accomplishment only when it served the efforts of others and individual rewards like bonuses and similar would be severely limited. By contrast, benefits received by one member like health insurance or a year-end bonus would likely be received by all. In the business world, finally, assembly-line work would be a good candidate for collectivism because any finished product is only as good as the weakest part.

On the other hand, someone starting their own business may believe that individuals don't work best when teaming up with colleagues but when competing against them. In this case, an individualistic corporate culture might be established with workers granted incentives to outperform their colleagues. Pay and benefits in this kind of organization would likely be closely linked to performance and success; those who do well for the company would receive a healthy percentage of the revenue they generate. Further, on the other side, employees shouldn't make the mistake of thinking that just because the organization is doing well, *they're* doing well. They're not, at least not unless they can show how they contribute personally and significantly to the success. Finally, this orientation of values may be constructed by someone starting up a wholesale fish-selling operation, and hiring a sales force to go out and lure restaurants away from their current providers and give the new company a chance.

What Do I Value More, the Means or the Ends?

One of the curious aspects of the farmed or wild salmon story is that for many (though definitely not all) consumers, there's really no difference. Their palettes aren't sufficiently trained, their cooking expertise insufficiently developed for the distinctions between the two kinds of fish to register inside their mouth. If that's right, if a consumer really can't distinguish farmed from wild salmon, then is there any harm in selling the farmed variety as wild (at a 200 percent markup)? Some people will answer *yes* and others *no*. If you're on the *yes* side, if the kind of organization you want to set up will be ruled by what members do more than the results of what's been done, then an ethics based on duties suggests itself as the right way to go. Within this kind of enterprise, the basic ideas of honesty and respect for others will prevail; they will guide the way people act inside the workplace and also the way the business interacts with customers. You can take people at their word inside this business because telling the truth is a basic element of the organization's culture.

On the other side, if you look at this and say, "well, consumers are just as happy either way, but selling the farmed fish as wild makes *me* a lot happier because my profit margin jumps," then you'll find a more comfortable spot on the consequentialist side of the ethical spectrum. Here, what people do is less important than the outcome. Decisions about whether an act is acceptable or not is answered by looking at the act's consequences and nothing else. In this case—and assuming people really can't tell the difference between the two fish—the way opens to affirming that the general welfare really is improved by the sleight of hand. The fish seller is better off, and no one else has grounds for complaining.

This ethical dilemma—one between valuing the sincerity and the ethical protocol of the actual transaction, and one valuing just the end result and consumer satisfaction—plays out in many and diverse organizational environments. There's the fish seller debating selling cheap product that tastes expensive. In 2004 Ashlee Simpson got caught lip-synching on *Saturday Night Live* when the soundtrack kicked in before she opened her mouth and Tom Petty's 2008 Super Bowl halftime performance looked fishy. Does it really matter, though? In Simpson's case, it obviously does because she got caught and it ruined her show, but if everything had fit together right, do you think it's OK for her to pretend she's live and then go to the tape without anyone noticing? Are people who paid money to see her sing getting cheated?

One organization where this dilemma plays out in quite dramatic terms is police work. It's an old-time policing phrase that more good has been done with the business end of a nightstick than through every courthouse in the land. It's unclear whether that's true, but it gets right to the heart of the question about means or ends. Should a police department be more focused on going by the book, treating all suspects as the written law dictates, or should they be more focused on the ends—that is, punishing criminals and minimizing crime in a community? Take a situation where an officer knows a man is guilty of a violent assault but the evidence isn't there. Is it OK to plant something? As is the case of the fish seller and the stage performer, the basic values—the way the members have learned to live and act within organization—will dictate what ultimately happens.

How Do I See My Employees?

Many small businesses have only one employee: the owner who doubles as the employer. Others, however, require a workforce. If people need to be hired, the question about how they're to be valued can't be avoided. Are they paid mercenaries? Something closer to extended members of a family? Somewhere in between? One type of business where this question can rise quickly is a franchise. In a franchise operation, a parent company sells the rights to a certain name and kind of product to an individual to start their own branch. Domino's Pizza is a good example. Though there are corporate-owned stores, many of the local Dominos are owned by their managers. These entrepreneurs agree to buy basic material from the mother business—the pizza dough and so on, as well as the signage and participation in advertising campaigns—and in exchange they're allowed to command their own small outpost of the pizza empire. The extent of corporate control over particular franchises varies from one business to another, but since the actual owner is the person there from day-to-day and in charge of hiring and firing, the culture surrounding the place is going to be largely determined by the values the owner installs.

With respect to employees, what are the possibilities? A libertarian culture comes close to the mercenary system. Under this ethical umbrella, freedom and the individual pursuit of his or her own happiness become guiding values. Ethical good is defined as that freedom and pursuit, while reprobation is assigned to those acts interfering with others doing the same. In this case, the owner may (though not necessarily) adapt a somewhat disinterested attitude with respect to employees. A certain job is offered at a certain wage and the applicant is free to accept or decline. Acceptance means nothing more than assuming the responsibilities in exchange for a paycheck. Initiating a Domino's Pizza business, of course, requires hiring many drivers to deliver the product. These aren't great jobs, driving around and knocking on doors with pizzas, but they may work for students and others who need a little income. Neither the employer nor employee expects any loyalty from each other nor does the relation continue forward just as long as both benefit nothing more.

Alternatively, a franchise owner may want to welcome employees as integral parts of the business. An ethics of care suits this purpose. Within this theory, good is defined not as freedom or the pursuit of happiness but as the maintenance and fortifying of social networks and relationships. The workplace becomes paternalist (or maternalist) as workers begin seeing themselves participating in an organic unit. In this case, the owner is much less likely to fire workers who foul up (bring pizzas to the wrong address, incorrectly input customer orders into the computer), and probably more likely to share revenue and benefits with workers as much as possible. Drivers are likely to be trained at other tasks (making pizzas and taking orders being the main opportunities) so that they can participate more fully in the enterprise.

The above questions posed and answered are only a beginning, only the first of many steps on the way to defining and implementing a corporate culture. It's also true, however, that in the real world people don't have time to sit down and extensively draw up every detail of their ethical business plan before commencing; every new manager will have to decide for him or herself how far to go on paper before actually beginning to run their operation, whether it's a Domino's Pizza franchise or something else. Many will probably just go ahead with the enterprise and pick up ethical things along the way. This isn't necessarily a bad idea: it's hard for anyone to know what they believe until they've experimented a bit. It is worth noting, however, that these kinds of decisions will have to be made at some point. Staying with the Domino's example, every franchise has a few drivers who mess up more than the rest and every manager has to draw a line somewhere to mark the point where the driver is let go. When that happens, a decision about the values of the organization—the extent to which drivers are more like mercenaries or members of a big business family—will have to be made.

Some further questions that a manager may ask to help sort out the organizational culture of the operation include the following:

- **Who are my consumers?** Are they purely a way for me to make money, or something closer to a social network with a financial element attached?
- **Am I a short or long termer?** Do I see my business as a lifelong project, or is this a quick hit and then I'll move on to something else?
- **Who am I responsible to?** Am I doing this for me, my family, the community, the world?
- **What are the vital ingredients of success?** Does my organization need to value analysis, competence, reliability, creativity, or something else to thrive?

- **What's my organization's relation with the law?** Do I want to obey the letter and spirit of the law, just the letter, just the spirit, or do whatever I can get away with?
- **Am I a delegator or a micromanager?** Will I give employees goals and let them find ways to accomplish them, or will I monitor their performance every step of the way?

If you're starting your own business or joining up with friends to put something together, the first ethical questions you're likely to face are those concerning the organizational culture of your enterprise. It's true that you can put decisions off, but for most businesses at some point, there'll need to be a coherent response.

KEY TAKEAWAYS

- People initiating their own business will need to instill an organizational culture.
- The kind of culture instilled will depend on the style of leadership and the contingencies of the type of business.
- Straight-ahead questions about the most basic elements of the endeavor (what I want from my business, how I will see employees and consumers, and similar) may help define an appropriate corporate culture.

REVIEW QUESTIONS

1. Why might diverse fields of work lend themselves to divergent internal cultures?
2. Picture a business you may want to initiate one day. What are some questions you could ask that might help you get a sense of the kind of culture and values you would erect inside the enterprise?

9.5 Styles and Values of Management
LEARNING OBJECTIVES

1. Define the concept of a leadership style.
2. Consider what values underlie specific leadership styles.
3. Investigate what kinds of enterprises may be suited to one or another leadership style.

Selecting a Leadership Persona

A persona of leadership is the image you adopt, the kind of person you decide to be when you stand in front of others as a director. What values will be most important to your particular leadership role, and how will they be transmitted? Psychologist Daniel Goleman has identified the following leadership styles in his book *Primal Leadership*: [1]

- Visionary. This leader guides an organization's members toward a shared vision. Establishing and communicating that vision become the primary leadership task and subordinates are granted significant leeway to reach the vision.
- Coach. Members of the organization are challenged to meet specific, relatively accessible goals, and they're closely supervised—and encouraged—as they work.
- Affiliative. This leader fosters social harmony within the organization and focuses on the human and emotional dynamic of the workplace over immediate work requirements. Nurturing a well-integrated team that works well together is considered the best way to reach the organization's goals.
- Democratic. These leaders seek active participation from an organization's members and value consensus in decision making.
- Pacesetter. This leader challenges members of the organization to work and meet goals by setting a strong example, possibly one that most members will be unable to match.
- Commander. This leader gives clear directions and expects compliance.

Of course there are other ways of leading, and elements of these six models may be mixed in a single person, but taken together this group of strategies represents common ways of fostering specific values in the workplace. Two examples— John Buford and Carol Smith—illustrate how the strategies and values function together.

John Buford

In a short video from the *Washington Post*'s continuing "On Leadership" series, the story of John Buford at Gettysburg in 1863 is examined. [2] Buford, a general in the Federal army leads a small force of cavalrymen on a mission to locate and engage Robert E. Lee's Confederate forces. He finds them near Gettysburg and hatches a plan to arrange the coming battle on terrain that will favor the North. While his small group aligns itself on the high ground and begins battling the vastly superior Confederate force, Buford sends word to the main Federal army of his location and the advantage he's holding. His group is nearly wiped out, but they resist just long enough for Federal reinforcements to flow in and occupy the adventitious ground. Days later, they'll win the battle. The South never recovered.

Here are the episode's key aspects according to the *Washington Post*'s Ed Ruggero:

- As a cavalryman, Buford was accustomed to operating far from headquarters and direct oversight. He was empowered to and able to make his own decisions.
- No preconceived plan can account for all contingencies, so all overarching strategies must leave room for leaders on the ground to shift strategies as the situation requires and take rapid action.
- Buford asked for and got significant (life) sacrifices on the part of his soldiers in the name of the greater good and larger cause.

Along with Buford's autonomy and decisiveness, the significant ethical trait leaping out of the organization he led was the uniform willingness of those working with him to sacrifice for the larger goal. There is, at the heart of this organization's culture as it was fostered by Buford, a sense of the importance of the collective over the individual. Buford isn't the kind of leader who seeks to maximize the individual initiative of the members of his organization and he doesn't set his team loose into competition with each other. Instead, he fosters firm camaraderie. Within the six types of leadership personas laid out by Goleman, Buford is, not surprisingly, a *commanding leader*.

Coming at this value from a different angle, Buford's can be called transformational leadership. In his book *Business Ethics*, O. C. Ferrell defines this as the ability to transform the members of an organization into devoted and unselfish advocates of its goals. In a word, it means the ability to inspire. [3]

As the *Washington Post* video underlines, business isn't war. Still, lessons in leadership—and the basic values animating one or another model—may be common to the two. So what kind of business might invite this commanding style? One possibility, one place that might do well under this model of leadership is a Domino's Pizza franchise. First, because it's a franchise outfit, because it's an outpost of the central organization granted wide latitude and independence, the local manager and owner must be able to make decisions independently. There must be an ability to see a way forward and act even without approval from superiors. For example, all Domino's locations share in the benefits of the central corporation's advertising budget, but every individual manager is free to supplement those efforts. A franchisee may decide to send drivers to an apartment complex delivering discount coupons to every door or something similar. What's important is that every neighborhood is different and offers unique opportunities. Success will require a leader who can get a sense of what might work at a particular place without constantly calling into corporation headquarters for guidance.

Further, with respect to the employees, the commanding style of leadership may be suitable when you take into account that most drivers have relatively little experience in the pizza business and aren't particularly motivated for the Domino's team. Almost no one signs up to deliver food because they enjoy it or see a bright future in that line of work. Given that reality, a commanding style—leadership that demands employees follow directions carefully and one that values deference to the delivery policy and rules—may work to keep the operation flowing well. More, the values of transformational leadership—devotion to the organization and the unselfish advocacy of its goals—may function to rally the drivers, to inspire a belief in the cause of the business even if, as is obvious, winning the neighborhood pizza delivery war is far less dramatic and important than Gettysburg.

Carol Smith

Here are a few snippets from a newspaper interview of Carol Smith, a senior vice president and chief brand officer for the Elle Group:

Q:	What is the most important lesson you've learned about leadership?
A:	The importance of winning over employees as opposed to bossing employees…I sit in the middle of the table, always. I don't want to sit at the head of the table. I want to be part of the process and part of the decision.
Q:	Let's talk about hiring.
A:	You've got to meet someone three times, and one of them better be over a meal. It's like a little microcosm of life. Throughout a meal, the personality comes out. Are you going to connect with us? Are you going to be part of the team, or are you going to be one of these independent players who want to take all the credit? Are you good with assistants? Those are things you can find out in some subtle ways when you eat with someone. [4]

Referring these thoughts back to the list of six leadership personas, Smith reflects skills and practices of at least two distinct leadership styles: democratic and affiliative. Her custom of sitting in the middle of the table instead of stationing herself at the head isn't an empty gesture, it's part of the way she broadcasts openness to counter suggestions and input. Further, this kind of culture—one that values give-and-take and some sense of equality in the decision-making process—is bolstered by the distinction Smith draws between being a boss and being bossy. Being a boss means ultimately making, and taking responsibility for, decisions; being bossy means cowing people into grumbling obedience. It's presenting herself as the former while resisting the latter that Smith believes makes her style work in her particular organization. Democratic leadership, finally, isn't the same as political democracy; there's no indication that Smith decides by taking a vote. But where the two do overlap is in the process preceding decisions: a high value is assigned to an open airing of differences, and to the insistence that all sides be heard and respected.

Smith also participates in an affiliative strategy for managing. When she invites potential new hires to dinner, she's checking to see if they'll add to the organization's social harmony. Notice that Smith is probing for information about whether the new hire will mix with superiors, equals, *and* subordinates in the workplace. Every direction of social interaction is important. Of course the idea here isn't that no work gets done because so much stress is placed on people getting along, it's the opposite: because emotional integration is highly valued in the office, members of the organization are likely to work well together in pursuit of the organization's goals.

One way of summarizing Smith's management strategy is that she's a *negotiator*, always trying to find ways to get people to come together in agreement. She's not so interested in locking her employees in a march toward her company's goals; instead, she activates their participation and then balances individual efforts to keep everyone on the same page. This quality can be called transactional leadership, which means leadership dedicated to getting the members of an organization onboard through give-and-take and inclusion. [5]

Moving into a general business environment, what kind of business might invite the style of leadership Smith promotes? Starting with what can be excluded, a Domino's franchise probably wouldn't work very well. In that business, driver turnover is very high, so she'd spend inordinate amounts of time balancing the social dynamic of a workplace that changed personalities on a weekly basis. Also, input from drivers who consider their work to be a McJob and have no experience in the pizza business would be of limited value. It's very possible, in other words, that the values Smith privileges would quickly lead a Domino's Pizza restaurant—

or any enterprise depending on a large, high-turnover workforce—into red ink.

Apple Incorporated, on the other hand might be a good fit for Smith. We know from the Apple employee survey that the workplace values tolerance and individualism. Within a social dynamic like that, one where people are free to work (and show up for work) as they wish, the great danger is a collapse of the group effort into individualistic, self-centered projects and agendas. It takes alchemy of personalities to make sure these different types of people are functioning well together despite their explosively individualistic outlook. The value of social harmony as promoted by an affiliative leadership style, consequently, might be crucial for this kind of workplace. Apple also sounds like a place where democratic-type leadership could bear fruit. One of the great advantages of diversity in the office is a wealth of viewpoints. For the right kind of leader—one valuing and encouraging contributions from every direction—that diversity can be translated into a maximum number of options for action. Of course if the leader is weak, those divergences will result in chaos; the trick is to maintain openness to the input of others without sacrificing authority and surrendering to rampant individualism.

Conclusion. No one style of leadership will work in every situation and very few individuals will find that they naturally fall into one category or another. But a sense of the range of possibilities, and an ability to understand the different values holding them up, maximizes a leader's chances for success.

KEY TAKEAWAYS

- A persona of leadership is the role adopted when leading an organization.
- There are a number of basic personas or leadership styles that may be mixed on an individual basis.
- Leadership styles are not good or bad in themselves, but some are more or less suited to certain individual personalities and specific kinds of businesses.

REVIEW QUESTIONS

1. What are Goleman's six leadership prototypes?
2. Are there any other leadership prototypes that could be added to Goleman's list? Explain.
3. What is transformational leadership, and can you think of a kind of organization to which it might be well suited?
4. What is transactional leadership, and can you think of a kind of organization to which it might be well suited?

[1] See Daniel Goleman, *Primal Leadership* (Cambridge: Harvard University, 2002).

[2] "On Leadership at Gettysburg: 'Find Those Confederate Forces,'" *Washington Post* video, 4:40, http://www.washingtonpost.com/wp-dyn/content/video/2010/04/21/VI2010042100960.html.

[3] O. C. Ferrell, John Fraedrich, and Linda Ferrell, *Business Ethics*, 7th ed. (Boston: Houghton Mifflin, 2008), 134.

[4] "No Doubts: Women Are Better Managers," *New York Times*, July 25, 2009, accessed May 25,

2011, http://www.nytimes.com/2009/07/26/business/26corner.html?_r=1&8dpc.

[5] O. C. Ferrell, John Fraedrich, and Linda Ferrell, *Business Ethics*, 7th ed. (Boston: Houghton Mifflin, 2008), 134.

9.6 Case Studies

Culture on the Trading Floor

On Wall Street, S&T means sales and trades of stock, and it's generally carried out by teams working for a bank or investment house. It's their job to sniff out the best buys (and recommend them to their clients), while also picking up on which shares may be in for a fall so they can be unloaded fast. On one of Wall Street Oasis.com's forum pages, welcome2nyc starts a thread this way: I was curious to know the culture of S&T. Can anyone give an honest opinion? [1]

QUESTIONS

1. What is a corporate culture?

2. A contributor named credit derivatives posts this about the culture at Deutsche Bank Equities: "These guys were brilliant and no-nonsense. Very tolerant atmosphere, but very focused. These guys argued over the correct pricing approach for equity swaps as opposed to which March Madness bound team had the best chance of winning it all."

   An "equity swap" is a complex financial bet, but in the end it comes down to this: one side believes a stock will go up (or down) more than another, and they put money on it.
   - There's not a lot of information here, but from what you have, can you brainstorm a short list of words fitting the culture and values Deutsche Bank fosters?
   - One important characteristic of corporate culture is employee interaction: the way workers relate to each other on the job. At Deutsche Bank, does it sound like the culture values teamwork among workers, competition, or some mix? Explain.

3. BigFatPanda writes, "I'd rather work on a desk with the trash talk, like where people are on the verge of cutting each other."

"A desk" is Wall Street talk for a team of analysts working together on investment strategies.
- How would you describe the culture BigFatPanda prefers?
- One of the recurring questions all managers face is "Will more and better work get done if people work together or compete with each other?" It's pretty obvious where BigFatPanda comes down on this. From what he says and the way he says it, what do you suppose are some of the potential disadvantages of this organizational culture of competition?

4. jjc1122 writes, "When I used to work at the Chicago mercantile exchange, there were a lot of crazy stuff. traders routinely doing coke in the bathroom, old Irish guys hurling racial insults, fights, and sleeping with their hot female clerks."

He adds that his experience dates from 2005, but he'd heard that things were actually a lot crazier in the earlier part of the decade.
- Two aspects of corporate culture are workplace mood (the social energy and decorum of an office) and leisure time (what coworkers do and the way they relate to each other when not at work). How has jjc1122's manager tuned those aspects of the organization's culture?
- One aspect of working culture involves *life values*—that is, the extent to which on-the-job experience leaks out to color non-work concerns and life. What kinds of life values are exhibited by this organization? What kind of theoretical ethical argument could be made to criticize the manager's promotion of these values?
- The two basic ways that an organizational culture is instilled are codes (established rules guiding an organization's members) and social conditioning (guidance is provided by following the cues and examples of others in the organization). Do you suspect the values of jjc1122's Chicago Mercantile Exchange workplace were established more by codes or social conditioning? Why?
- The instillation of a workplace culture through social conditioning functions in a variety of ways. Three are listed here. Can you fill in for each how it may have worked in the Chicago Mercantile Exchange in 2005?
  1. Stories and myths embedded in daily conversations may indicate culturally appropriate conduct.

2. Heroes or stars in the organization may consistently communicate a common message about the organization's guiding values.

3. The dress, speech, and physical work setting may be arranged to cohere with the organization's values.

o One social way that an organizational culture may reinforce itself is through a self-selective process. What is a self-selective process? How might that process have worked to reinforce the values guiding work life at the Chicago Mercantile Exchange?

5. Bondarb writes, "When I am out with Goldman people and somebody tells a joke they all look at the most senior GS person there to see if they are allowed to laugh." GS is Goldman Sachs, the global investment bank.

o Make the case that employees constantly looking to superiors for guidance—even whether they should laugh at a joke—shows that a strong, clear corporate culture exists at Goldman.

o Make the case that employees constantly looking to superiors for guidance—even whether they should laugh at a joke—shows that a weak, ill-defined corporate culture exists at Goldman.

Corporate Culture at Herschend Family Entertainment
Joel Manby is CEO of Herschend Family Entertainment, a $300 million corporation employing more than 10,000 people at two dozen theme parks around the country. They put on everything from massive aquariums to Dollywood, the Dolly Parton theme park in Tennessee.

In an interview, Manby discusses the corporate culture infusing the properties. It's composed of eight attributes:
1. Patience
2. Kindness
3. Honesty
4. Humility
5. Respectfulness
6. Selflessness
7. Forgiveness
8. Commitment

Manby exemplifies the corporate values he's trying to instill this way, "You can dislike somebody, but you can still respect them, forgive them, and treat them with humility and honesty. We also have a phrase: 'admonish in private, praise in public.' So you don't embarrass people."

Manby explains that 50 percent of a Herschend executive's year-end bonus is awarded on the basis of how well the organization's culture is exhibited and promoted. As he puts it, "You have to put your money where your mouth is."

He concludes with this: "It's all about hiring the right people. You know, this culture either resonates with people or it doesn't. If it doesn't, they're not going to enjoy working here." [2]

QUESTIONS

1. The characteristics of corporate culture elaborated in this chapter were the following. Corporate culture is
   o shared,
   o a provider of guidance,
   o a provider of meaning in the organization,
   o top heavy,
   o a constellation of values,
   o a dynamic constellation of values,
   o organic,
   o inclusive of life values.

   Choose three of these characteristics and show how the culture Manby promotes at Herschend Family Entertainment relates with each one.

2. What is a corporate culture ethics audit? What does it attempt to measure?

3. If a corporate culture ethics audit were taken of this company, how do you suppose it would fare? Why?

4. Before coming to Herschend, Manby was CEO of Saab, a division of General Motors. His time there was marked by a very different organizational culture. According to him, "I don't want to bash GM, but intimidation was part of the culture there. You would get ridiculed in meetings. The CEOs had big egos and had no problem making you look silly. I once missed one of my numbers. I didn't miss it by that much, but the president of all of Saab calls me and orders me to fly over there [to Europe]. I get there Monday morning, he chews me out for four hours, and then I get on a plane and fly back. It was so humiliating, so uncalled for. I figured, if that's the way I'm going to be treated, I don't need that. That's when I began looking at other opportunities." [3] Manby lists the attributes of the culture at Herschend—patience, kindness, honesty, and so on. What might a similar list look like for Saab?

5. Corporate culture provides an organization's meaning; it defines what counts as success.
   o For Herschend, what counts as success?
   o For Saab, what counts as success?

6. A corporate culture distinguishes workers from people who work. What is the distinction?
   o How does Herschend fit into this distinction?
   o How does Saab fit into this distinction?

7. Manby says, "Apple's culture, for example, would be very different from ours, but Steve Jobs is still an incredibly successful CEO. I'm not pretending we're right and others are wrong; it's just our culture, and it works for us." Explain how Manby can say that a set of ethical values isn't right or wrong, but one set (at Saab) is wrong for him, and another set (at Herschend) is right for him?

Even Better Than the Real Thing

The web store FinerBags.com sells fakes—very good copies of purses originally made by Louis Vuitton and similar high-end brands. The price is right: a $1,800 Prada bag can be purchased as a copy for about $180. At Finer Bags, they're totally open about what they're doing, and their home page lists the advantages of buying their products. According to the leadership at Finer Bags, "Millions of replica handbags can be found on internet these days, they are not a rare thing anymore. Maybe the Louis Vuitton handbag that your friend bought is a perfect replica. Maybe the Louis Vuitton Monogram Speedy 30 that Linda paid $1,200 for is a replica handbag. Maybe those replica bags all were bought from finerbags.com." [4]

QUESTIONS

1. Would you call honesty part of the corporate culture at Finer Bags? Yes, no, or both? Explain.

2. Corporate cultural dissonance occurs when what actually happens on the ground doesn't jibe with the principles supposedly controlling things from above. Do you suspect that dissonance is occurring here? Why or why not?

3. This company is selling counterfeit purses, bags designed to trick people into thinking they're real when they're not. No one denies that.
   o Could you use a utilitarian argument (bring the greatest good and happiness to the greatest number) to justify this corporate culture and business endeavor as ethically respectable?
   o Could you use either a basic duties argument (right and wrong is defined by preexisting principles) or Kant's categorical imperative (to be right an act must be universalizable) to make the ethical case that this company should put itself out of business?

4. This line from the web page is curious: "Maybe the Louis Vuitton Monogram Speedy 30 that Linda paid $1,200 for is a replica handbag." It's important to know that the price of the real thing is about $1,200. The point being made is that people can end up paying full price for a copy. If that's true, it sounds like Finer Bags is inviting

people like you and me to realize that we can buy their fakes and then sell them as real, pocketing the difference.
   o Imagine you buy a few replicas for $120. Then you spread word around campus that your mom is a major department store buyer and handed off a few Louis Vuitton Monogram Speedy 30s that you're now selling at the absurdly low price of…$800. Can you sketch an argument to ethically justify your business model? What kind of ethical theory could it be based on? How would you respond to a consumer who discovered the trick?
   o Imagine you have so much success that you hire some friends to go around selling bags at nearby colleges. Would you tell them the truth about the source of your bags or keep up the mommy lie? Why? What ethical justification could you sketch to support your decision?
   o One reason to lie to the people you hire to sell the bags elsewhere is to help them do their job well. If they believe the bags are the real thing, they may find it much easier to enthusiastically promote their product. Is there any ethical difference between lying to employees to help them improve their work performance as purse salespeople and lying to consumers about what they're getting when they make a purchase? If not, why not? If so, what's the difference?
   o Can you think of examples in the world where managers don't tell their employees the whole truth about a situation and believe they're doing the right thing? What is such a situation? Is it the right thing?
   o Assume you're running the fake purse outfit and hiring sales reps for other schools. You decide to maintain the lie about the purses' origin. How do you think your small business would fare on a corporate culture ethics audit? Why?

5. Assume you're running the fake purse outfit and hiring sales reps for other schools. You decide to reveal the truth about the purses' origin to the reps. What you need to do next is instill a corporate culture that fosters lying. Common ways of instilling a workplace culture include the following:
   o The founder's ethical legacy to the organization may contribute to its living culture.
   o Stories and myths embedded in daily conversations may indicate culturally appropriate conduct.
   o Heroes or stars in the organization may consistently communicate a common message about the organization's guiding values.
   o The dress, speech, and physical work setting may be arranged to cohere with the organization's values.

o   An organizational culture may reinforce itself through self-selective processes.

How might these or other strategies of social conditioning be used to create a working culture that values lying?

6. If you discuss this case in class, there'll be people loudly proclaiming that this fake bag business is despicable and completely wrong. Then they'll go home, hit up finerbags.com on the Internet, and spend the next hour trying to figure out if they can make the scheme work on your campus. It is good money. Now, is there any ethical difference between someone who lies in a social situation like a class and someone who lies as a way of doing business?

[1] welcome2nyc, March 20, 2010 (9:09 p.m.), "Culture on the Trading Floor…Changed?," WallStreetOasis.com, accessed May 25,

2011,http://www.wallstreetoasis.com/forums/culture-on-the-trading-floorchanged.

[2] Steve Tobak, Undercover Boss: Escaping GM's Abusive Corporate Culture," *The Corner Office* (blog), *BNET*, March 30, 2010, accessed May 25, 2011, http://blogs.bnet.com/ceo/?p=4254.

[3] Steve Tobak, Undercover Boss: Escaping GM's Abusive Corporate Culture," *The Corner Office* (blog), *BNET*, March 30, 2010, accessed May 25, 2011, http://blogs.bnet.com/ceo/?p=4254, brackets in the original.

[4] Business Ethics Workshop, accessed May 25, 2011,http://businessethicsworkshop.com/Chapter_9/finer_bags.html.

[5] Jada Yuan, "As the Disco Ball Turns," *New York*, April 30, 2007, accessed May 25, 2011,http://nymag.com/news/features/31277.

[6] Steve Lewis, "Good Night Mr. Lewis: Carmen D'Alessio's Fabulous Life," blackbookmag.com, December 11, 2008, accessed May 25, 2011,http://www.blackbookmag.com/article/good-night-mr-lewis-carmen-dalessios-fabulous-life-part-two/5463.

NOTES:

Chapter 10
Discrimination, Victimization, and Affirmative Action

Chapter Overview

This chapter examines issues and ethics surrounding discrimination in the workplace.

10.1 Racial Discrimination
LEARNING OBJECTIVES

1. Define racial discrimination.
2. Distinguish different ways that racial discrimination occurs in the workplace.
3. Consider legal aspects of racial discrimination in a business environment.
4. Discuss ethical aspects of racial discrimination in a business environment.

The White Running Back

Toby Gerhart is a bruising running back. Coming out of college at six feet and 225 pounds, he was drafted by the Minnesota Vikings football team with their first-round pick in 2010. It was a controversial choice. His playing style is unorthodox: he runs standing almost straight up and doesn't do much faking and cutting. Most NFL runners get low and slip away from tacklers. Gerhart chugs and blows through things.

That's not Gerhart's only distinction. In a league where running backs—almost all of them—are black, he's white. On the days leading to the draft, Gerhart feared his skin color might be expensive. An anonymous quote had been circulating, suggesting that his position in the draft order could fall, bringing his paycheck down along with it: "One longtime NFL scout insisted that Gerhart's skin color will likely prevent him from being drafted in Thursday's first round. 'He'll be a great second-round pick up for somebody, but I guarantee you if he was the exact same guy—but he was black—he'd go in the first round for sure,' the scout said." [1] As it turned out, the scout was wrong. But the question of race in sports had flared, and the media came to it. One story appeared on an MSNBC-affiliated website called *theGrio.com*. Writer John Mitchell pointed out that twenty-seven of the NFL's thirty-two general managers (those ultimately responsible for draft-day selections) were white, and so, he asserted, it was "virtually impossible" that racism could work against Gerhart. [2]

John Mitchell is black. In fact, if you go to *the Grio.com*'s contributor page, you'll find that, as a rough estimate, 90 percent of the website's writers are black, a number that's far, far out of proportion with the global percentage of black writers out there. The disproportion, however, would be less surprising for anyone who'd read the description the site presents of itself: "TheGrio.com is devoted to providing African Americans with stories and perspectives that appeal to them but are underrepresented in existing national news outlets. The Grio features aggregated and original video packages, news articles, and blogs on topics from breaking news, politics, health, business, and entertainment, which concern its niche audience." [3]

On that same page, surfers are directed to a video story about *the Grio.co*-produced by NBC New York, which is a station aimed at the general market, not *the Grio.com*'s niche audience. The story tells of *the Grio.com*'s origin and in an interview with the website's founder, he remarks that his contributors are very diverse: "We have conservatives, liberals, old folks, young folks, rich folks, poor folks, politicians and plain folks." [4]

The NBC story also informs us that the idea for creating a site that aggregated news stories involving the black community was taken to NBC executives who agreed to sponsor the website. We don't learn which specific NBC execs received the proposal, but a quick check of the network's directors and programming directors and so on leads to the strong suspicion that most were white.

Questions about racial discrimination are tangled and difficult. Here are a few of the knotted uncertainties arising from the Gerhart episode and its treatment in the press:

- The story about Toby Gerhart in *theGrio.com* claimed that the white Gerhart couldn't suffer racial discrimination because the people who'd be drafting him (or not) were white. Is that true, is it impossible for whites to be racists against other whites?
- Overwhelmingly, running backs in the NFL are black. These are painful but very high-paying jobs with long vacations and lots of fringe benefits. Most young guys would be happy with the work, but a certain racial group holds a near monopoly. Is there racism operating here?
- *The Grio.com*'s workforce is, according to its founder, very diverse in many ways but completely dominated by a single racial group. Racism?

- MSNBC, which sponsors *theGrio.com*, currently has a prime-time TV lineup (Joe Scarborough and Mika Brzezinski in the morning and Chris Matthews, Ed Schultz, Rachel Maddow, and Lawrence O'Donnell at night) that's all white. Racism?

What Exactly Is Racial Discrimination?

Racial discrimination in the economic world can be defined in three steps:

1. An employment decision—hiring, promoting, demoting, firing, and related actions—affects an employee or applicant adversely or positively.
2. The decision is based on the person's membership in a certain racial group rather than individual ability and accomplishment with respect to work-related tasks.
3. The decision rests on unverified or unreasonable stereotypes or generalizations about members of that racial group.

The first step—someone has to suffer or benefit from the discrimination—is important because without that, without something tangible to point at, you're left making an accusation without evidence.

The second step—discrimination is based on race as opposed to job qualifications—is critical because it separates the kind of racism we typically consider vile from the one we normally accept as reasonable. For example, if actors are being hired to play Toby Gerhart in a biography about his life, and all the finalists for the role are white guys, well, the casting company probably *did* discriminate in terms of race, but this particular discrimination overlaps with qualifications helping the actor play the part. This contrast with the alleged racial discrimination surrounding the Gerhart draft pick: the suspicion that he couldn't be very good at running over other people with an oblong leather ball cradled in his arm because his skin is white. If that's a baseless premise, then it follows that within this definition of racism, *the Grio.com*'s claim that Gerhart has no reason to fear unfair discrimination because so many NFL general managers are white is, in fact, wrong. Whites can exhibit racial discrimination against other whites just as blacks can discriminate against blacks and so on.

The difference between discriminating in favor of white males to play Gerhart in a movie and discriminating against white males as running backs is more or less clear. Between the extremes, however, there are a lot of gray areas. What about the case of hiring at *theGrio.com*? Just looking at the list of contributors, it's hard to avoid wondering whether they're picking people based on skin color as opposed to writing ability. On the other hand, since *theGrio.com* explicitly states that its mission is to tell stories affecting the black community, a case could be made that black writers are more likely to be well qualified since it's more likely that their lives significantly connect with that community. It's not, in other words, that contributors are hired because they're black; it's the fact that they're black that helps them possess the kind of background information that will help them write for *theGrio.com*.

The definition's third step—an employment decision rests on unverified or unreasonable stereotypes or generalizations about members of a racial group—is also important. Staying on *theGrio.com* example, there's a difference between finding that in specific cases contributors well suited to the site also tend to be black, and making the stronger generalization that whites, Asians, Hispanics, and so on are by nature *incapable* of understanding and connecting with the realities covered by the web page. This second and generalizing claim eliminates the *opportunity* for those others to participate.

Finally, questions about racial discrimination center on purely racial divisions but overlap with another distinction that can be similar but remains technically different: ethnicity.

Race concerns descent and heredity. It's usually visible in ways including skin, hair, and eye color. Because it's a biological trait, people can't change their race. Ethnicity is the cluster of racial, linguistic, and cultural traits that define a person as a member of a larger community. The Hispanic ethnic group, for example, contains multiple races, but is unified by common bonds tracing back to Spanish and Portuguese languages and customs. Though it's not common, one's ethnicity may change. A girl born in Dublin to Irish parents but adopted by an Argentine family living in East Los Angeles may ultimately consider herself Hispanic. The US Census Bureau divides individuals in terms of race and, with a separate question, ethnicity. It's not unusual, however, for the two categories to be mixed in a business environment. Many organizations place Hispanic on the list of racial options when measuring their workforce's diversity. In the real world, the line between race and ethnicity is blurry.

Locating Racism in Business

Questions about racism swirl around the Toby Gerhart episode, but it's equally clear that getting a firm grip on which people and institutions involved actually *are* racist is difficult. Nearly all running backs in the NFL are black, and at least one scout presumes that racial discrimination in favor of that color is an active part of the reason. But there could also be social and cultural reasons for the imbalance. Maybe young black men are more likely to devote themselves to football because they see so many successful role models. Or it may be that players—regardless of their race—come from a certain economic class or geographic part of the country where, in fact, blacks happen to be the majority. More explanations could be added. No one knows for sure which is right.

On the other side, just as it's prudent to be careful when using words like racist and pointing fingers, there is real evidence indicating wide and deep currents of racism in US business life. Generally, there are three evidence types:
1. Experimental
2. Statistical
3. Episodic

One experimental indication of racism in hiring comes from economist Marc Bendick. He paired applicants for gender and appearance, loaded them with similar qualifications, and sent them to New York City restaurants in search of waiter jobs. The only notable difference between the two applicants was their race; whites, blacks, Asians, and Hispanics participated. After 181 restaurant visits in which the two applicants appeared within an hour of each other, the results were tabulated. Because four racial groups were investigated there are a lot of cross-tabs, but the basic finding was simple: with everything else as equal as possible, whites were significantly more likely to be given information about job duties, receive second interviews, and be hired. According to Bendick, "The important thing is that we repeated the experiment dozens of times so that we can be pretty sure when a pattern emerges it really is differences in employer behavior and not a random effect." [5]

In terms of statistical evidence of racism, racial disparities are significant in many areas. Income is not atypical. According to the US Census Bureau, in 2006 the median personal income for Asians was $36,000; for whites $33,000; for blacks $27,000; and for Hispanics $24,000. [6] The disparities contract significantly—but not all the way—when you adjust for education levels. Surveying only those who hold bachelor's degrees yields these numbers: white, $44,000; Asian $42,000; black $42,000; Hispanic $37,000. Going back a little more than a decade, the federal Glass Ceiling Commission produced a set of striking statistics. According to its study, 97 percent of the senior managers of *Fortune* 500 companies are white (and 95 percent are male). That compares with a broader economic reality in which 57 percent of the working population is female, or minority, or both. [7]

Episodic evidence of racism in business life is real-world episodes where decisions seem to have been made based on racial distinctions. The venerable clothier Abercrombie & Fitch, which once outfitted JFK and now sells heavily to collegians, garnered considerable (and unwanted) media attention when Jennifer Lu, a former salesperson at the store, took her story to the CBS news program *60 Minutes*. According to Lu, she was fired soon after corporate executives patrolled the store where she worked and informed the store's manager that the staff was supposed to look like the models in the store's display posters. If you've been in Abercrombie, you may remember that they tend to have the blonde, blue-eyed, football team captain look. Like Toby Gerhart. In an interview with *60 Minutes*, Anthony Ocampo says, "The greeters and the people that worked in the in-season clothing, most of them, if not all of them, were white. The people that worked in the stock room, where nobody sees them, were mostly Asian-American, Filipino, Mexican, and Latino." [8]

A lawsuit against the store was settled out of court when Abercrombie agreed to pay almost $50 million to negatively affected employees and beef up their minority hiring. They also stated that their custom of seeking out new sales staff at predominantly white fraternities and sororities should be modified.

Categories of Racial Discrimination

When discrimination exists in a business environment, it can be distinguished into several categories. First, there's a division between institutional and individual discrimination. Institutional discrimination is exemplified in the Abercrombie lawsuit. The preference given to white, football-player types wasn't one person at one store; it was part of the corporate culture. Managers were instructed to include a certain look while excluding others, and presumably their job depended on their ability to meet that demand. The manager, in other words, who fired Jennifer Lu may (or may not) have thought it was a terrible thing to do. Regardless, the manager's personal feelings had nothing to do with the firing. Instructions were provided by higher-ups, and they were followed.

Individual racial discrimination, on the other hand, can occur in any organization no matter how determined leaders may be to create an organizational culture prohibiting it. The NFL, for example, established a requirement (commonly called "the Rooney Rule") in 2003 requiring teams to interview minority candidates for football operations posts. It's part of a broader effort by the league to ensure against racial discrimination. Still, this comes from a 2005 article by *Sports Illustrated* writer Dan Banks: "One Asian stereotype concerns size. A NFL personnel man told me on Thursday the problem with Chang is 'the kid is short.' But when I noted that Chang was 6-1½ and 211 pounds, and taller than San Diego's Drew Brees—the talent scout replied: 'But he plays short. And he's 211, but he looks frail.'" [9]

A second broad distinction within the category of racial discrimination divides isolated from regularized incidents. An isolated case of racial discrimination is a one-time deal. Regularized incidents are repeated occurrences fitting into a pattern.

The final distinction cuts through all those mentioned so far; it divides sun intentional from intentional discrimination. Take as a general example a seventy-year-old who grew up in a time and place where racism was normal and accepted almost without objection. For someone coming from those circumstances, it's hard to imagine that from time to time some of that old way of seeing the world isn't going to slip through. Of course the fact that racism is unintentional doesn't make it less racist, but just like in everything else, there's a difference between doing something without thinking about it and doing something with premeditation and full understanding.

The Legal Side of Discrimination

A complex web of legal precedents and civil rules apply to racial discrimination. At the center, the Civil Rights Act of 1964 covers all employers in both private and public organizations that have fifteen or more workers. The act's crucial language can be found in Title VII, which confronts a host of discriminatory practices:

> *It shall be an unlawful employment practice for an employer (1) to fail or refuse to hire or to discharge any individual, or otherwise discriminate against any individual with respect to his compensation, terms, conditions or privileges of employment, because of such individual's race, color, religion, sex, or national origin; or (2) to limit, segregate or classify his employees or applicants for employment in any way that would deprive or tend to deprive any individual of employment opportunities or otherwise adversely affect his status as an employee, because of such individual's race, color, religion, sex, or national origin.* [10]

You notice that employee is referred to as "his," not "his or hers," and employers are also "his," not "his or hers." That's not a snarky comment; it's just an example of how treacherous the issues of unfair discrimination are. Even those with the best intentions find it difficult to pull completely away from what others may perceive as signs and appearances of unfair practices.

The difficulty partially explains why the Civil Rights Act has been repeatedly modified and supplemented. The Equal Employment Opportunity Act of 1972 set down new rules and created a powerful commission to enforce and report on the status of anti-discriminatory efforts across the nation. These reports have played a role in many civil lawsuits brought by individuals or groups against employers suspected of discriminatory treatment.

Additional requirements—some involving affirmative action (to be discussed further on)—were compiled for companies doing business with the US government. While these measures don't bind organizations operating independently of government contracts, the pure size and spending power of Washington, DC, does send the measures far into the world of business.

So the legal and governmental bulwark set up against racial and other types of discrimination stands on four legs:

1. Racial and similar types of discrimination are directly illegal.
2. Civil lawsuits may be filed by those who feel they've suffered from discriminatory practices.
3. Government oversight (the Equal Employment Opportunity Commission) is continuous.
4. Government regulations insist that companies wanting to do business with deep-pocketed Washington, DC, implement exemplary anti-discriminatory practices.

The Ethics of Discrimination: Arguments against the Practice

It's difficult to locate a mainstream ethical theory for workplace life that can be twisted to support racial discrimination as it's defined in this chapter. The arguments mounted against it generally fall into three groups:

1. Fairness arguments typically operate from the assertion that discrimination divides up society's opportunities in an unacceptable way. (These kinds of arguments are sometimes called "justice arguments.")
2. Rights arguments typically assert that discrimination contradicts the victims' basic human rights.
3. Utilitarianism arguments employed in the economic world frequently assert that discrimination reduces a society's economic productivity and so harms the general welfare, the happiness of the society.

Fairness, as Aristotle defined the term, is to treat equals equally and un-equals unequally. People, that means, are to be treated differently if and only if there are job-pertinent differences between them. Burly men should be favored over thin ones when you're hiring an offensive lineman in the NFL, but not when you're looking to contract a coach.

The philosopher John Rawls advocated an ingenious way to, at least as a thought experiment, promote fairness. He proposed that individuals imagine the reality surrounding them as shaken up, with people pulled from their situation and randomly inserted into another. So if you're a white guy in college looking for a summer job, you probably don't mind too much that Abercrombie & Fitch is looking for your type more than any other. But if you imagine getting shaken up with your black, Asian, and Hispanic classmates and you don't know beforehand what race you're going to get assigned, then maybe you think twice about whether Abercrombie should be allowed to hire whites so pervasively. This is called a veil of ignorance test: you need to imagine how you'd like society to be if you don't know beforehand exactly where you'll be placed in it. The imagined reality, presumably, will be one where everyone gets a chance that's fair.

Rights arguments against discrimination typically depart from the premise that as humans we're all endowed with a certain dignity and freedom that abides regardless of circumstances. These attributes are an essential part of what we are: they're like pregnancy in the sense that you can't have them halfway. You're either pregnant or you're not; you either possess full dignity and freedom just like everyone else or you don't. If all of us do possess dignity and freedom, then it's a short step to see that discrimination is an affront to them. Treating one group differently than another is to wrongly claim that they have different levels of basic dignity. Or, from the viewpoint of freedom, discrimination grants one group more freedom in the world than another. Again, the argument here is that dignity and freedom can't be measured or parceled out; as essential rights, everyone must hold them perfectly, and they must be respected fully.

The utilitarian argument holds that we ought to act in the business world in a way that maximizes our collective happiness and welfare. If that's right, then we all have an interest in ensuring that the most qualified people occupy the various working slots in our economy. Possibly the examples of professional football and Abercrombie don't lend themselves very well to this argument, but if we move to other professions, the inadvisability of discrimination becomes clearer. In the field of medical research, we wouldn't want to lose a breakthrough because the one person who'd have the idea that could cure cancer happens to be Hispanic.

The argument, therefore, is simply that as a society we benefit when each individual member is allowed the maximum opportunity to contribute.

The Ethics of Discrimination: Racism versus Job Qualification

While few argue that discrimination is good or justified, there are equally few who deny that some situations do, in fact, allow for discrimination (the actor hired to play Martin Luther King is black, the person hired to monitor the women's locker room is a woman). Between these extremes there stretches a tense set of debates about where the line gets drawn. When is some limited discrimination acceptable?

The lawsuit against Abercrombie & Fitch alleging that the company hires a disproportionately white sales force and favors white employees for the best positions never went to court. Former employee Jennifer Lu turned up on *60 Minutes*, CBS news started running stories about how Asians and Mexicans were confined to the stockroom, and with the bad publicity storming, Abercrombie opted to settle the matter and move on. That was probably a good business decision.

Others, however, wanted to push the issue out to see the ethical consequences. One of those was lawyer and talk show host Larry Elder. He made this point: "Abercrombie & Fitch ought to have the right to set their own policies. Look, there's a restaurant called Hooters. Hooters require you to have certain kinds of physical accoutrements, and I think people understand that. Should they have a right to hire waitresses because they want to attract a certain kind of clientele who want to ogle at the waitresses? I think so." [11]

Closing off the argument with respect to Abercrombie & Fitch, the point is that Abercrombie isn't selling only clothes but also a look, an image, a kind of social message. And that message is crystallized by the kind of people they hire to walk around their showrooms and smile at consumers: white, attractive, fit, upper-middle-class. Not coincidentally, one of the company's subsidiary lines of clothes is called *Prep School*. And if *that's* what they're selling—not just clothes but a social message—they should be able to hire the best possible messengers, just as Hooters is allowed to hire the kind of waitresses their clientele wants to ogle and just as the movie producer is allowed to hire a black actor to play Martin Luther King. There's no racial discrimination here; it's just business. At bottom, it's no different from *theGrio.com*, which is selling a specific product and image that naturally leads to an almost entirely black organization. In every case, it's not that the business starts out with a certain racial (or gender) type that they'll contract; it's that they start out with something they want to sell, and as it happens a certain racial type lends itself to the business.

There are two types of responses to this argument. The first is to push back against the premise that the one racial type *really does* serve the business's interest better than the others. Rebecca Leung, the CBS reporter for the Abercrombie & Fitch case, shapes her story this way. The idea, Leung asserts, of prep schools and the all-American pursuit of upper-middle-class life that Abercrombie tries to represent belongs equally to all races. There's no justification, Leung leads viewers to believe, for associating that ideal with a skin color. That's why her report ends this way:

> *"All-American does not mean all-white," says Lu.*
> *"An all-American look is every shade," Lueng asks.*
> *"Yes, absolutely."* [12]

The other kind of response to the argument that Abercrombie's business model lends itself to hiring whites is to concede the point but then to insist that it doesn't matter. Because society's general welfare depends on rallying against poisonous discrimination, it should be avoided in every possible case, even those where there might be some rational, business-based reason for engaging in the practice. Abercrombie, the argument goes, may have good reason for seeking out white sales staff. But even so, the larger social goal of developing a color-blind society requires Abercrombie's participation, and the company ought to be required to participate even against its own short-term economic interest.

Conclusion

For historical reasons in the United States, discrimination in the reproachable sense of the word comes into sharpest focus on questions concerning race. *Any* distinguishing characteristic, however, can be levered into a scene of unfair marginalization. Women, for example, have suffered mistreatment in ways analogous to the kind discussed here for racial groups. And it doesn't stop there. Age, national origin, religion, weight, whatever, *all* of us have features that can be singled out by others and then converted into favoritism or negative prejudice in the workplace. Somewhere there's probably a high executive who's convinced that individuals with knobby knees can't do good work. In ethical terms, all these cases may be understood and handled as the question of race has. That is, by thoughtfully determining whether the identifying feature—the skin color, gender, age, religion, weight, the knobbiness of the knees—actually has a bearing on the person's ability to successfully accomplish the tasks fitting the job.

KEY TAKEAWAYS

- Racial discrimination is adverse treatment stemming from unfounded stereotypes about a person's race.
- Favoring or disfavoring members of a racial group may imply racism, or it may reflect a legitimate job requirement.
- Evidence of racial discrimination may be accumulated experimentally, statistically, and episodically.
- Racial discrimination in business can be divided into multiple kinds and intentions.
- The Civil Rights Act of 1964 is a key legal document in the history of discrimination.
- Ethical arguments against discrimination are generally built on theories of fairness, rights, and utilitarian arguments.

REVIEW QUESTIONS

1. In your own words, what are the three steps defining racial discrimination?
2. What's the difference between racial discrimination and a preference for race based on an occupational qualification? Provide an example.
3. List and define the six categories of discrimination in a business environment.
4. What are the main legal and governmental remedies set up against discrimination?
5. Why kind of business may favor Asians when hiring, and draw both reasonable defenses and criticisms of the practice?
6. What is the utilitarian argument against racism in the economic world?

[1] Michael Silver, "Race Factors into Evaluation of Gerhart," *Yahoo! Sports*, April 20, 2011, accessed May 31, 2011, http://sports.yahoo.com/nfl/news?slug=ms-gerhartstereotype042010.

[2] John Mitchell, "White Running Back's Draft Status Won't Be Hamstrung by Race,"*TheGrio.com*, April 22, 2010, accessed May 31, 2011,http://www.thegrio.com/opinion/white-running-backs-draft-status-wont-be-hamstrung-by-race.php.

[3] "About theGrio," *TheGrio.com* accessed May 31, 2011, http://www.thegrio.com/about.

[4] "About theGrio," *TheGrio.com* accessed May 31, 2011, http://www.thegrio.com/about.

[5] "City Room," *New York Times*, NY/Region, March 31, 2009, accessed May 31, 2011,http://cityroom.blogs.nytimes.com/2009/03/31/racial-bias-seen-in-hiring-of-waiters.

[6] U.S. Census, "Table PINC-03. Educational Attainment—People 25 Years Old and Over, by Total Money Earnings in 2005, Work Experience in 2005, Age, Race, Hispanic Origin and Sex," in *Current Population Survey* (2006).

[7] George E. Curry, "Race, Gender and Corporate America," *District Chronicles*, April 24, 2005, accessed May 31,

2011, http://www.georgecurry.com/columns/race-gender-and-corporate-america.

[8] Rebecca Leung, "The Look of Abercrombie & Fitch," *60 Minutes*, November 24, 2004, accessed May 31,

2011,http://www.cbsnews.com/stories/2003/12/05/60minutes/main587099.shtml.

[9] Don Banks, "Hurdles to History: From Size, Stereotypes, System, Chang Fights Skeptics, *"Inside the NFL* (blog), *Sports Illustrated*, April 15, 2005, accessed May 31,

2011,http://sportsillustrated.cnn.com/2005/writers/don_banks/04/15/chang/index.html.

[10] Civil Rights Act of 1964 (Pub. L. 88-352, 78 Stat. 241, enacted July 2, 1964).

[11] Rebecca Leung, "The Look of Abercrombie & Fitch," *60 Minutes*, November 24, 2004, accessed May 31,

2011,http://www.cbsnews.com/stories/2003/12/05/60minutes/main587099.shtml.

[12] Rebecca Leung, "The Look of Abercrombie & Fitch," *60 Minutes*, November 24, 2004, accessed May 31,

2011,http://www.cbsnews.com/stories/2003/12/05/60minutes/main587099.shtml.

10.2 Gender Discrimination and Occupational Segregation

LEARNING OBJECTIVES

1. Define gender discrimination.
2. Consider the ethics of occupational segregation.
3. Discuss the doctrine of comparable worth.
4. Define the glass ceiling.
5. Examine the case of motherhood.

10.3 Discrimination: Inferiority versus Aptness

Discrimination in the workplace moves in two directions. One is hierarchical, one group or another is stereotyped as simply superior or inferior. Historically, many cases of race discrimination fit on this scale. Discrimination can also move horizontally, however. In this case, divisions are drawn between different groups not so much in terms of general capability, but as naturally suited for some and naturally unsuited for other tasks and occupations. Gender discrimination frequently fits into this category.

Here's a list of professions where the workers are more than 90 percent women:

- Dental hygienists
- Preschool and kindergarten teachers
- Secretaries and administrative assistants
- Dental assistants
- Speech-language pathologists
- Nurses
- Child-care workers
- Hairstylists and cosmetologists
- Receptionists and information clerks
- Payroll clerks

And another where the workers are 99 percent (not a typo) male:

- Logging workers
- Automotive body repairers
- Cement masons
- Bus and truck mechanics
- Electrical power-line installers and repairers
- Tool and die makers
- Roofers
- Heavy vehicle equipment service technicians
- Home appliance repairers
- Crane and tower operators

The lists come from a blog called *The Digerati Life*. [1] The author is a software engineer living in Silicon Valley. Because she's a she, 78 percent of her colleagues don't use the same bathroom. [2]

What Exactly Is Gender Discrimination?

Gender discrimination defines analogously with the racial version:

1. An employment decision—hiring, promoting, demoting, firing—adversely or positively affects an employee or applicant
2. The decision is based on the person's gender rather than individual merit.
3. The decision rests on unverified stereotypes or generalizations about members of that gender.

The difference, again, is that the stereotypes and generalizations tending to surround women in the United States during our lifetimes have branded the group as naturally suited to some types of work and not others; and, correspondingly, men also find their natural roles pointing in some directions and not others. This division of labor raises provocative questions. More sparks fly when two other factors add to the mix: concrete and broad statistics showing that women receive lower wages than men when doing distinct but comparable work; and women who *do* pursue career lines dominated by men can find their advance up the promotion ladder halted by a difficult-to-see barrier, a kind of glass ceiling.

So three ethical issues connecting with gender discrimination in the workplace are occupational segregation, comparable worth, and the glass ceiling.

Occupational Segregation: The Causes

What causes occupational segregation? One explanation is biological. Differences, the reasoning goes that are plainly visible physically also exist on the level of desires and aspirations. Women and men are simply divergent; they pursue distinct goals, define happiness in separate ways, and tend to have dissimilar kinds of abilities. For all those reasons, women gravitate to different kinds of professions. Now, if all those things are true, then we should expect to see just what we do see: significant occupational segregation.

The biological explanation also functions less directly when career paths and family paths conflict. Women who physically carry children find themselves removed—willingly or not—from work for significant periods. If you see that coming in your not-distant future, then you may opt into a field where that kind of absence is less damaging to the company and your own long-term prospects.

One clean argument against the biological explanation for gender segregation in the workforce starts with the suspicion that visible physical differences may be leading us to mistakenly believe that there are underlying psychological differences where few actually exist. People, the reasoning goes, are making an invalid argument when they suppose that because women and men look different on the outside, they must be different on the inside too. There's no reason that's necessarily true, just like there's no reason to think that a Cadillac painted blue and one painted pink are going to perform differently on the road.

A second and frequently cited explanation for occupational segregation is social precedent. Young men and women making career decisions normally have very limited experience in the workplace and so depend on what others have done. It's very reasonable, therefore, for a young man trying to decide between, say, going to work as an assistant to a dentist and going to assist a roofer to notice that a lot of other guys are working on roofs, but not many are in dentists' offices. Women see the same thing, and the occupational segregation that already exists in society gets repeated. In this case, it's the individual men and women themselves who are effectively volunteering for professional separation.

A third explanation—and the one drawing the sharpest ethical attention—is discriminatory prejudice. Those in charge of hiring stack the deck to favor one gender over another because of unverified generalizations about differences between men and women. In his book *Business Ethics*, Manual Velasquez relates an experiment done by the ABC news program *Primetime Live*. Two early careerists— Chris and Julie—were outfitted with hidden microphones and tiny cameras and sent out to answer the same help-wanted ads. Their experiences were for TV entertainment,

not a scientific study, but they do illustrate how discriminatory occupational segregation can work. [3] Both she and he were in their mid-twenties, blond, and attractive. They presented virtually identical résumés, and both claimed to have management experience. What they got from their interviewers, however, was very different. When Julie appeared at one company, the recruiter spoke only of a position answering phones. The same day the same recruiter offered Chris a management job. In a gotcha-follow-up interview, the flustered recruiter told the camera that he'd never want a man answering his phone.

Another instance wasn't quite so clear-cut. The two visited a lawn-care company. Julie received a typing test, some casual questions about her fiancé, and was offered a job as a receptionist. Chris's interview included an aptitude test, some casual talk about keeping the waistline trim, and a job offer as a territory manager. When confronted in his gotcha interview, the owner strongly defended his actions by pointing out that being a manager at a lawn-care service means actually doing some of the outdoor work; and Chris— an objectively stronger candidate in the physical sense— seemed more apt for that. The question to ask here—and it's one that comes up time and again in discussions of occupational segregation—is the extent to which the outdoor work requirement is a legitimate reason for hiring Chris or an excuse for excluding Julie (because the owner doesn't believe women should be in that line of work).

The Ethics of Women's—and Men's—Work
What kind of ethical arguments can be mounted for and against the idea that occupational segregation ought to exist? Possibly the strongest argument in favor runs through a utilitarian theory—one that judges as ethically correct any act that raises a society's overall happiness. The theory's cutting edge is the requirement that individual interests be sacrificed if that serves the greater good. For example, occupations requiring hard physical strength (firefighter, logger, construction) may require strength tests. These tests, which more or less measure brute power, are going to weed out most women—so many, in fact, that it may make practical sense to essentially designate the job as a male realm, and to do so even though it may be unfair to a very few physically strong women. That unfairness is erased, in ethical terms, by the requirement that the general welfare be served.

There are a number of responses to this argument. One is to say that the general position of firefighter should be open to everyone, but every firehouse should make sure there are a few big guys in the mix in case smoke-inhalation victims need to be carried down perilous ladders. Another response is to concede that there are some occupations that may be right for one or another gender but draw the line firmly there and demand equal opportunity everywhere else. Another, more polemical argument is to assert that the goal of a gender-neutral society is so important and worthwhile that if it means sacrificing performance in some occupations, then the sacrifice should be made. The greater good is better served by occupational equality than by the certainty that the 250-pound weight-lifting guy will be the one who happens to be in the firehouse when the alarm goes off even if it goes off because it's your apartment that's on fire.

Another way to argue against occupational segregation of *any* kind, no matter the circumstances, starts from rights theory and the premise that the highest ethical value is personal freedom and opportunity: what's always recommendable is maximizing our ability to pursue happiness as each of us sees fit. Within this model, it becomes directly unethical to reserve some jobs for women and others for men because that setup limits both men and women; it impinges on their basic freedom.

Like utilitarian theory, this freedom-based argument can be twisted around to work in the other direction. If individual freedom is the highest ethical good, the reasoning goes, then shouldn't business owners be able to hire whomever they like? There may be an owner out there who simply doesn't want to hire guys. Perhaps there's no rational reason for the exclusion, but if individual freedom is the highest good, there's no strong ethical response to the preference. The only open pathway is to say that if you don't like the fact that this owner isn't hiring men, then you should make your own company and you can hire as many of them as you wish.

Comparable Worth
Going back to the list of gender-concentrated occupations, some on the women's side really aren't so different from those on the men's side in terms of skill and training required, effort exerted, and responsibility held. Take hairstylists and cosmetologists from the woman's list and automotive body repairers from the guy's list. While it's true that a lot of the hairdressers wouldn't be caught dead working in the body shop and vice versa, their jobs really aren't so different: fixing hair and giving cars makeovers. The wages *are* different, though, at least according to statistics that come from the *San Jose Mercury News*. Doing hair will net you about $20,000 a year, and working in the car shop gets you $35,000. [4]

This reality is at odds with the doctrine of comparable worth, which states that when two occupations require comparable levels of skill, training, effort, and responsibility, they should be rewarded with comparable salaries. The gender problem associated with comparable worth is that statistical evidence suggests that so-called women's work has consistently garnered lower wages than men's work. The hairdresser and the body shop example isn't an anomaly but a representative of the larger reality. According to the US government, the median income of American working women is $27,000, while for men it is $39,000. More, the differences hold when adjusting for educational levels. For high school grads, it is $21,000 versus $32,000. For college grads, it's $40,000 versus $60,000. At the PhD level, it's $55,000 versus $78,000. [5] These statistics don't tell the whole story, however; they never do. As it happens, statistician is one of those professions where there's a notable pay gap between genders—$49,000 versus $36,000 as a median salary—and women get the $49,000. [6]

Glass Ceiling
What happens when a woman goes into a field traditionally dominated by men and starts strong, receiving salary and treatment comparable with her male workmates but then hits a promotion wall? Called the glass ceiling, it's the experience of women topping off in their career for, apparently, no reason beyond the womanhood. A good example of the glass ceiling—and also of breaking it—comes from Carly Fiorina, the former CEO of the very masculine Hewlett-Packard. In an interview with the web magazine *Salon*, she discusses the topic candidly. Five of her ideas come through loudly. [7] First, in Silicon Valley Fiorina believes there is a glass ceiling at many companies.

Second, she buys the notion that women and men are fundamentally different, at least in this way: they feel comfortable with different kinds of languages and ways of communicating. Compared with Silicon Valley guys, she says, "Women tend to be more communicative, collaborative, and expressive. The stylistic differences get in the way [of mutual understanding]. That's why diversity in the workplace takes real work." [8]

Third, differences in the *way* women and men communicate ultimately doom many women's professional ascent. As the office culture becomes increasingly male on the way up, women are decreasingly able to communicate with and work well with colleagues.

Fourth, Fiorina believes that given the way things are now in Silicon Valley, if a woman wants to break through to the highest echelons of management, she's probably going to have to learn male rules, and then play by them. For example, she once pulled on cowboy boots and a cowboy hat, stuffed socks down her crotch, and marched into a hall full of (mostly) men to proclaim, "Our balls are as big as anyone's in this room!" In the *Salon* interview, she explains it this way:

Fiorina:	Part of the reason I succeeded in Silicon Valley was that I talked to people in a language they understood. When I negotiated in Italy, I ate a lot of pasta and drank a lot of wine. In bringing a team together to focus on a common goal, you have to find common language.
Interviewer:	And the language of the business world remains male?
Fiorina:	Yes, and particularly that case you cited, it was an incredibly male-dominated, macho culture. They understood balls and boots, they understood what that meant. [9]

Fifth, in the medium to long term, Fiorina believes the way to truly demolish the glass ceiling is for women to work their way up (like she did) and occupy more high-level posts. "When I went to HP," she says, "I hoped I was advancing women in business by putting women in positions of responsibility. But it's clear that we don't yet play by the same rules and it's clear that there aren't enough women in business, and the stereotypes will exist as long as there aren't enough of us." [10]

The Special Case of Motherhood

One advantage Carly Fiorina had on the way up was a husband who cooperated extensively in rearing her children. Still, women alone physically bear children and frequently hold principal responsibility for their care at least through the breast-feeding stage or further. For that reason, a discrete area of business ethics has been carved out for managing the tension between the legitimate interest businesses have in employees continuing their labors without the occasional childbearing and rearing interruption, and the legitimate interest professional women and society generally hold in motherhood and in ensuring that a healthy generation will be arriving to take over for the current one.

One proposal has been the creation of a dual-track career system: one for women who plan to have children at some point in the not-so-distant future and another for those who either do not plan to have children or envision someone else as assuming primary child-care responsibility (a husband, a relative, a paid nanny). Under this scenario, companies would channel women planning for motherhood and child rearing

into positions where work could be interrupted for months or even years and then resumed more or less from the same spot. A potential mother would receive an at least informal guarantee that her spot would be held for her during the absence, and upon resumption of duties, her career would continue and advance as though there had been no interruption. In fact, in many European countries including Spain, France, and Germany, such leave is actually required by law. In those countries, the birth of a child automatically qualifies one of the parents (the laws generally treat fathers and mothers indiscriminately as caregivers) for an extended leave with the guarantee of job resumption at the end of the period. Laws in the United States are not so worker oriented (as opposed to business oriented), though some companies have taken the initiative to offer extended parental absences without adverse career effects. These include Abbott Laboratories, General Mills, IKEA, and others.

Theoretically, granting professional leaves for the fulfillment of parental responsibilities makes sense. The problem is that in the real world and in many industries, it's nearly impossible to go away for a long time and then resume responsibilities seamlessly. In the interim, projects have been completed and new ones have begun, clients have changed, subordinates have been promoted, managers have moved on, and the organization's basic strategies have transformed. Reinsertion is difficult, and that leads to the fear that companies and managers—even those with the best intentions—will end up channeling those they presume will seek parental leaves into less important roles. The potential mother won't be the one chosen to pursue research on the company's most exciting new product—even if she's the best researcher—because the firm won't be able to just put product development on hold at some point in the future while she's away. The end result is that the so-called mommy track for professional life becomes the dead end track.

There are no easy solutions to this problem, though there are ways to limit it. Technology can be a major contributor. Just something as simple as Skype can allow parents at home with young children to "come into" the office regularly. Further, companies can, and increasingly are, providing day care facilities in the building.

Ethically, one way to manage the conflict between professional life and parenting is to locate the interests of those involved, set them on a scale, and attempt to determine how the issue weighs out. So, who are the primary stakeholders along the mommy track: whose interests should be considered and weighed? The mother, to begin with, has a right to pursue success in professional life, and she has the choice to embark on motherhood. A born child has a right to nurturing care, and to the love parents give. A business owner has a right to hire employees (and fire) employees in accord with rational decisions about what will benefit the organization and help it reach its goals. The coworkers and subordinates linked to a prospective parent have the right to not be bounced around by someone else's personal choices. Society as a collective has a responsibility to nurture the growth of a new generation fit to replace those who are getting old.

The next step is to put all that on the scale. In the United States today, the general consensus is that the business owners' rights to pursue economic success outweigh the parents' interest in being successful in both professional and family life and society's concern for providing an upcoming generation. That weighing can be contrasted with the one done in most countries of Western Europe where, not incidentally, populations are shrinking because of low birthrates. In Europe, there's a broad consensus that the workers' interest in combining professional and personal lives, along with society's interest in producing a next generation, outweighs the business's interest in efficiency and profit. For that reason, the already-mentioned laws guaranteeing extended family leave have been implemented.

KEY TAKEAWAYS

- Gender discrimination can take the form of occupational segregation.
- Strong ethical arguments may be formed for and against some forms of occupational segregation.
- The doctrine of comparable worth prescribes comparable pay for distinct occupations that require similar capability levels.
- The glass ceiling blocks women from advancing to the highest professional levels for reasons outside of dedication and capability.
- The fact that women can also be mothers introduces a broad set of ethical questions about the rights of employers and a society's priorities.

REVIEW QUESTIONS

1. What are the three steps defining gender discrimination?
2. What are some of the causes of occupational segregation?
3. What is an argument in favor of some occupational segregation? What is an argument against occupational segregation?
4. What is comparable worth?

5. What are two explanations for the existence of a glass ceiling?
6. How might the existence of a career track dedicated to those who expect to rear children be criticized in ethical terms?

[1] Silicon Valley Blogger, "Traditional Jobs for Men and Women and the Gender Divide," *The Digerati Life* (blog), May 29, 2007, accessed May 27, 2011,http://www.thedigeratilife.com/blog/index.php/2007/05/29/traditional-jobs-for-men-and-women-the-gender-divide.
[2] Claire Cain Miller, "Out of the Loop in Silicon Valley," *New York Times*, April 17, 2010, accessed May 31, 2011,http://www.nytimes.com/2010/04/18/technology/18women.html?pagewanted=1.
[3] Manuel Velasquez, *Manual Business Ethics: Concepts and Cases* (New Jersey: Prentice Hall, 2002), 306.
[4] Silicon Valley Blogger, "Traditional Jobs for Men and Women and the Gender Divide," *The Digerati Life* (blog), May 29, 2007, accessed May 27, 2011,http://www.thedigeratilife.com/blog/index.php/2007/05/29/traditional-jobs-for-men-and-women-the-gender-divide.
[5] "Table PINC-03. Educational Attainment—People 25 Years Old and Over, by Total Money Earnings in 2005, Work Experience in 2005, Age, Race, Hispanic Origin and Sex," Current Population Survey (CPS), accessed May 31, 2011,http://pubdb3.census.gov/macro/032006/perinc/new03_000.htm.
[6] Jeanne Sahadi, "39 Jobs Where Women Make More than Men," *CNNMoney.com*, February 28, 2006, accessed May 31, 2011,http://money.cnn.com/2006/02/28/commentary/everyday/sahadi_paytable/index.htm.
[7] Rebecca Traister, "The Truth about Carly," *Salon*, October 19, 2006, accessed May 31, 2011, http://www.salon.com/life/feature/2006/10/19/carly_fiorina.
[8] Rebecca Traister, "The Truth about Carly," *Salon*, October 19, 2006, accessed May 31, 2011, http://www.salon.com/life/feature/2006/10/19/carly_fiorina.
[9] Rebecca Traister, "The Truth about Carly," *Salon*, October 19, 2006, accessed May 31, 2011, http://www.salon.com/life/feature/2006/10/19/carly_fiorina.
[10] Rebecca Traister, "The Truth about Carly," *Salon*, October 19, 2006, accessed May 31, 2011, http://www.salon.com/life/feature/2006/10/19/carly_fiorina.

10.4 The Diversity of Discrimination and Victimization
LEARNING OBJECTIVES

1. Indicate characteristics beyond race and gender that may be targeted for discrimination.
2. Form a general definition of discrimination in the workplace.
3. Define minority status.
4. Analyze victimization.

The Diversity of Discrimination

There's a difference between history and ethics. Historically, racism and sexism have been the darkest scourges in the realm of discrimination. In straight ethical terms, however, discrimination is discrimination, and any isolatable social group is equally vulnerable to negative prejudice in the workplace. The Civil Rights Act of 1964 extends protection to those stigmatized for their religion or national origin. In subsequent years, amendments and supplements have added more categories, ones for age and disability. Currently, there are no federal laws prohibiting discrimination based on sexual orientation, though measures have been enacted in states and localities. Other measures identifying and protecting further distinct groups exist on local levels.

What holds all these groups together is that they fit into the most general form of the definition of discrimination in the economic realm:

1. A decision affects an individual.
2. The decision is based on personal characteristics clearly removed from job-related merit.
3. The decision rests on unverified generalizations about those characteristics.

Even though discrimination in the realm of business ethics can be wrapped up by one definition, it remains true that distinct groups victimized by discrimination have unique and diverse characteristics affecting the way the issue gets managed. Two types of characteristics will be considered here: discrimination based on traits that are *concealable* and discrimination based on traits that are (eventually) *universal.*

Concealable and In-concealable Status
One of the enabling aspects of race and gender discrimination is that it's normally easy to peg someone. If you don't think Asians do good work, you're probably going to see who not to hire. The same goes for gender, age, and many disabilities.

Other traditionally discriminated-against groups aren't so readily identifiable, though: the characteristics marking them as targets are concealable. For example, it's not so easy to detect (and not so difficult to hide) religious beliefs or sexual orientation. John F. Kennedy, many young people are surprised to learn today, faced considerable resistance to his presidential ambitions because of his religion. In fact, he considered the fact that he was the first Roman Catholic president of the United States as one of the higher virtues of his story. While the Protestant-Catholic divide has faded from discriminatory action in America, other splits have taken its place—Christian and Muslim, for example. No matter the particular religion, however, most individuals going into the work world do have the opportunity to simply reduce that part of their identity to a nonissue by not commenting on or displaying their religious beliefs.

A similar point can be added to considerations of national identity. Only a generation ago Italians were disdained as "wops." Legendary football coach Joe Paterno (no stranger to insults himself: "If I ever need a brain transplant, I want it from a sports reporter because I know it's never been used.") remembers being derided as a wop in his career's early days. If you wander down the street calling people a "wop" today, however, hardly anyone will know what you're talking about, which indicates how quickly discrimination against a group can fade when the source (in this case nationality) isn't readily visible.

Ethical questions raised by the possibility of invisibility include "In the business world, do those who feel they may be discriminated against for a personal characteristic that they can conceal have any responsibility to conceal it?" and "If they choose not to conceal, and they're discriminated against, do they bear any of the blame for the mistreatment?"

Universality versus Individuality
One obvious reason it's easy for white men to discriminate against racial minorities and women is that they don't have to worry about riding in that boat themselves. Age is different, however. All of us have gray years waiting at the end of the line. That hasn't stopped people from denying jobs to older workers, however. Take this report from California:

> *When a then-emerging Google recruited engineer Brian Reid in the summer of 2002, it appeared to have landed a Silicon Valley superstar. Reid had managed the team that built one of the first Internet search engines at AltaVista. He'd helped co-found the precursor company to Adobe Systems. He'd even worked on Apollo 17.*
>
> *But within two years, Google decided that the 54-year-old Reid was not a "cultural fit" for the company and fired him, allegedly after co-workers described him as "an old man," "slow," "sluggish" and "an old fuddy-duddy." Reid responded with an age discrimination lawsuit blasting Google's twenty something culture for shunning his generation in the workplace.* [1]

Reid can take satisfaction in knowing that, eventually, these twenty something are going to get what's coming to them. Is it more than that, though? Is the fact that they too share that fate a *license* for their discrimination? Assuming those who fired Reid aren't hypocrites, assuming they accept that one day they too will be subject to the same rules, can Reid really claim any kind of injustice here? In terms of fairness at least, it seems as though the Google whippersnappers should be able to treat others in terms they would accept for themselves.

On the other side, if his work performance matches his younger peers, if the only difference between Reid and the others is that his hair is gray and he doesn't know who Lady Gaga is, then his case does fit—at least technically—the definition of invidious discrimination. Google might be wrong on this one.

Regardless of which side you take, there's a fundamental ethical question here about whether discrimination can count when it's based on a characteristic that's universal, that everyone shares.

What Is a Minority?

The boundaries marking who can rightfully claim to belong to a group falling victim to systematic discrimination in the workplace are shifting and uncertain—in different times and places the victims share different characteristics. For that reason, it makes sense to try to form a definition of personal vulnerability that doesn't rely only on describing specific personal traits like skin color or gender but that can stretch and contract as society evolves. The term minority, as understood within the context of workplace discrimination, is sometimes summoned to perform this role.

To be part of a minority means to belong to a group of individuals that are the minority *within a specific organizational context*. Whites, for example, are not a minority population in the United States, but white students are a minority at the University of Texas–San Antonio. Similarly, women make up more than 50 percent of the population but count as a minority in corporate boardrooms where they represent only a small percentage of decision makers.

Being part of a minority doesn't just mean suffering a numerical disadvantage; it also means having so few peers in a situation that you're forced to adapt the language, the styles of dress, the sense of humor, the non-work interests, and so on of people very different from yourself. In the case of the minority white population at University of Texas–San Antonio, it's difficult to claim that their numerical minority status also forces them to adapt in any significant way to the Hispanic majority—whites can get by just fine, for example, without speaking any Spanish. By contrast, the case of Carly Fiorina wadding up socks in her crotch and screaming out that she has big balls, this is minority behavior. For minorities in a man's world, if you want to get ahead you have to adapt. To a certain extent, you need to speak and act like a man.

The term minority can be defined by three characteristics:

1. Physical and/or cultural traits set a group of individuals within a community apart from the customs and members that dominate the collective.
2. The physical and/or cultural traits that set the group apart are either disapproved of, or not understood by the dominant group. In Carly Fiorina's case, these traits included her gender and, more importantly, her feminine use of language. As she put it, "The stylistic differences get in the way" [2] of trying to communicate well with male colleagues. She was a minority because she wasn't well understood.
3. A sense of collective identity, mutual understanding, and common burdens are shared by members of the minority group. Fiorina sensed this collective identity and burden very clearly when she said, "I hoped I was advancing women in business by putting women in positions of responsibility. But it's clear that we don't yet play by the same rules as men, and it's clear that stereotypes about women in business will exist as long as there aren't enough of us." [3]

The advantage of using the term *minority* to name a group vulnerable to discrimination in the workplace is connected to the rapidly changing world, one where those subjected to discriminatory treatment come and go. For example, a tremendous influx of Spanish-speaking immigrants from Mexico have recently made that group a target of sharper discrimination, while the marginalization that the Irish once experienced in the United States no longer seems very threatening. There's no reason to believe that this discriminatory evolution will stop, and in the midst of that shifting, the term minority allows the rules of vulnerability to discrimination in the workplace to remain somewhat steady.

What Is a Victim?

As the number of characteristics classified as vulnerable to discriminatory mistreatment has expanded, so too has a suspicion. It's that some of those claiming to suffer from discrimination are actually using the complaints to abuse others, or to make excuses for their own failures. This is called victimization.

To accuse someone of being a victim is to charge that they are exploiting society's rejection of discrimination to create an unfair advantage for themselves. There are a range of victimization strategies running from strong to weak. Strong victimization is individuals in protected groups who aren't suffering any discrimination at all claiming that they are and making the claim for their own immediate benefit. This is what's being alleged in an Internet post where a supervisor writes the following about an employee:

> *This person came out & stated in this meeting that I use a racial slur on a very regular basis in my vocabulary. With my profession, this is something that is EXTREMELY HARMFUL to my status in my job, my respect in my job & community, my reputation, etc. But that word has NEVER been in my vocabulary. I am SO UPSET I do not know what to do!* [4]

Assuming this supervisor's allegations are true, then the employee was never subjected to racist language or offended by slurs. There was no workplace discrimination. Instead, it sounds like the employee may actually be disgruntled and is aiming for revenge by getting the supervisor in trouble. If that's what's going on, then the accusation of racial discrimination has become a workplace weapon: the charge can be invented and hurled at another with potent effect.

Weak victimization occurs when someone works in a context where discrimination is a constant subject of attention, one permeating daily life in the office. In that situation, it can happen that a worker suffering an adverse work evaluation (or worse) comes to the conclusion that it wasn't poor job performance but minority status that actually caused the negative review. (Possibly, one of the few universal human truths is that we all find it easier and more comforting to blame others for our problems than ourselves.) In the interview with Carly Fiorina—which was done not long after she'd been fired from Hewlett-Packard—the interviewer broaches this possibility *very* gingerly. Here's how she puts the question:

> *I'm predisposed to be sympathetic to the notion that you were treated differently because of your gender. But I've also read a lot about actual business mistakes you made.*

Fiorina comes back with an ambiguous answer and the interviewer lets it go. For a while. Suddenly, however, after a few softball questions she tries again, more forcefully:

Interviewer:	I want to press you on the fact that you missed a quarter's projections big-time…
Fiorina:	Wouldn't be the first top company that missed a quarter either. Or the last.
Interviewer:	Right. But that miss was huge. And you wrote in the book that "building a culture of accountability and execution of discipline
	requires real and clear consequences for failure to perform." If you had been told that you were fired because you missed the quarter, would you have understood? [5]

What's being intimated here is that Fiorina got so caught up in being a woman in a man's world that when she got fired, she was so invested in that battle-of-the-sexes way of seeing things that she ended up suspecting sexist discrimination where maybe there wasn't any.

Weak victimization means that someone is twisting discrimination claims into an excuse for their own imperfections, shortcomings, and failures. Everyone faces adversity in their lives. When that happens, the choices are deal with it or collapse. Accusing someone of being a victim in the weak sense is saying they're collapsing; they're using racism or sexism or whatever as an excuse to not confront what most people face every day: an imperfect and sometimes difficult world. So weak victimization is an accusation tinged with exasperation. Here's what the accusation sounds like in longer form, as posted on an Internet forum:

> *I genuinely don't believe that in this country that persecution of minorities exists anymore. This is not to say that these things don't exist, of course they do in isolation, but being black or gay or a woman is not in any way a barrier to achieving anything that you want to achieve.*
>
> *I told her that she was playing the victim against an oppression that doesn't exist, is looking for excuses about things she can't do rather than looking at what she can do (which is anything she wants) and that she's being patronizing towards all those from 'minority' groups who had gone on to be successful. Thatcher didn't whine about latent sexism, Obama didn't complain that being black meant he wasn't able to do the most powerful job in the world.* [6]

In the ensuing discussion, quite a few posters pick up on the claim that "being black or gay or a woman is not in any way a barrier to achieving anything that you want to achieve." Some agree, some not so much. What's certain is that somewhere between Carly Fiorina stuffing socks down her pants and Carly Fiorina leading one of the world's most powerful companies and somewhere between black slavery and a black president, there's a line. No one knows exactly where, but it's there and it divides a reality where sexism and racism are vile scourges from another reality where they're things people whine about.

An ethical argument against victimization—against someone playing the role of a victim of discrimination—can be outlined quickly. It begins with the duty to respect your own dignity, talents, and abilities. Those blaming their failures on others are essentially giving up on their own skills; they are concluding that their abilities are worthless when they may not be. If Carly Fiorina believes that her gender makes success in Silicon Valley impossible, and it really doesn't, then by denying her own talent she's subtracting from her own dignity.

KEY TAKEAWAYS

- Discrimination may be applied in a society to a group defined by any physical or cultural trait.

- A successful general definition of discrimination in the workplace must evolve as society and the face of discrimination change.

- Minority is a general category meant to include those vulnerable to discrimination.

- Victimization occurs when vulnerability to discrimination converts into a weapon to use against others, or an excuse for failure.

REVIEW QUESTIONS

1. In your own words, explain the general definition of discrimination.
2. What's the difference between a concealable and in-concealable characteristic that may leave one vulnerable to discrimination?
3. In your own words, define what it means to be a minority.
4. What's the difference between strong and weak victimization?

[1] "Ex-Google Worker's Case Goes to High Court," *San Jose Mercury News* (CA), May 24, 2010.
[2] Rebecca Traister, "The Truth about Carly," *Salon*, October 19, 2006, accessed May 31,
2011, http://www.salon.com/life/feature/2006/10/19/carly_fiorina.
[3] Rebecca Traister, "The Truth about Carly," *Salon*, October 19, 2006, accessed May 31,
2011, http://www.salon.com/life/feature/2006/10/19/carly_fiorina.
[4] UT alum, August 24, 2005 (9:09 a.m.), "Falsely Accused of Racist Slur," ExpertLaw Forum, accessed May 31,
2011, http://www.expertlaw.com/forums/showthread.php?t=2887.
[5] Rebecca Traister, "The Truth about Carly," *Salon*, October 19, 2006, accessed May 31,
2011, http://www.salon.com/life/feature/2006/10/19/carly_fiorina.
[6] Gerogerigegege, February 26, 2010 (10:27), "Does Racism/Sexism/Homophobia Exist in Any Meaningful Way in Modern Britain?," *DrownedinSound.com*, accessed May 31,
2011,http://drownedinsound.com/community/boards/social/4248929.

10.5 The Prevention and Rectification of Discrimination: Affirmative Action

LEARNING OBJECTIVES

1. Define affirmative action.
2. Elaborate arguments for and against affirmative action.
3. Discuss the ethics of affirmative action.
4. Indicate why some organizations implement affirmative action policies.

Race-Based Scholarships

"The scholarship," according to Carlos Gonzalez, an overseer appointed by a federal court, "was designed essentially as a jump-start effort to get the process of desegregation under way." He was talking about a new race-based scholarship at Alabama State University (ASU). It was triggered by a federal court's finding that "vestiges" of segregation remained within the Alabama university system: the state was ordered to spend about $100 million to racially diversify the student body.

Two years later, 40 percent of ASU's budget for academic grants went to minority students even though they represented only about 10 percent of the student population. That meant minority students got about $6 of aid for every $1 going to everyone else.

One beneficiary of diversification was a grad student who accumulated $30,000 in scholarship money. She said that she would've attended the school anyway, but getting the money because of her skin color was an added bonus. "I think it's wonderful," she exclaimed, according to a CNN report. [1]

Not everyone came off so well. One big loser was another grad student, Jessie Tompkins. The effort to balance the student body racially meant funding he'd been promised got reassigned to others. He remembered the moment vividly. He'd received an assistantship for three years, but when he went to apply the next year, he learned that the scholarships had been reserved for those with a different skin color. "I said, 'Ma'am?' She said, 'You can apply, but you won't get it.'" [2]

As word of the new scholarship policy circulated, temperatures rose. They heightened even more when news got out that the race balancers were more lucrative than the old funding mechanisms that had been available to everyone. The minority set-asides paid for tuition, books, and for room and board, and then added on almost $1,000 for personal use. While the new students got all that just for showing up inside their color-appropriate skin, Tompkins remembered that he hadn't even received enough to fully cover tuition; in exchange for his aid, he'd worked for the school by helping coach the track team and by scheduling tennis court use.

The situation reached a boil with one more detail: the revelation that the minority scholarship recipients weren't as academically qualified as those including Tompkins who were now suddenly being turned down at the funding office. To qualify for financial aid, the new recipients only needed a C average, significantly below what had been required of all applicants in the earlier, color-blind system. That led the editor of the university newspaper, Brandon Tanksley II, to express his frustration and anger this way, "It's not that they're minority students, it's that they're not competitive." [3] As for Jessie Tompkins, with his scholarship no longer available, he was forced to drop out and take a job handling packages at United Parcel Service. The next year he returned on a part-time-student basis and once again applied for his old scholarship. Again he was rejected. In a newspaper interview he said, "We don't need race-based quotas. I don't want anyone telling my children they're the wrong color. If you want something, you work for it; you just work for it." [4] Eventually, Tomkins connected with the Center for Individual Rights, a nonprofit public interest law firm with conservative and libertarian leanings. The firm was experienced with this kind of complaint: it had previously led a charge against the University of Texas's affirmative action program. In an article in the *Wall Street Journal*, Tompkins compares himself to a plaintiff in that important case, Cheryl Hopwood: "We were bumped aside, regardless of our qualifications, because of our race." [5]

Tompkins says he's just like Hopwood, even though she's a woman and he's a man, and even though she's white and he's black.

As for the administration at the traditionally black Alabama State, they chose not to respond to Tompkins directly, but they did stand behind their affirmative action program. William Hamilton Harris, president at ASU, defended the set-asides this way, "Bringing whites and blacks together on campus will broaden the quality of education and the quality of life at Alabama State." [6]

What Is Affirmative Action?

The Civil Rights Act aimed to blind organizations to gender and race and similar distinctions removed from merit. The idea behind the law is an ideal, a theoretically perfect society where discrimination in the invidious sense doesn't exist. Unfortunately, the real world rarely lives up to ideals. Affirmative action enters here, at the realization that things won't be perfect just because we make laws saying they

should be. What affirmative action does—as its name indicates—is *act*. It's not a requirement that organizations stop discriminating; it's a set of preferences and policies that aggressively counter discrimination, usually in ways that themselves hint at discrimination. There is, even ardent defenders admit, a troubling element of fighting fire with fire where affirmative action operates.

In practice, affirmative action comes in various strengths:

- In the strongest form, quotas are employed to guarantee that individuals from disadvantaged groups gain admittance to an organization. A number of slots—whether they are seats in a classroom or posts in an office—are simply reserved for individuals fitting the criterion. Since quotas inescapably mean that certain individuals will be excluded from consideration for certain posts because of their race, gender, or similar trait, they're relied on only infrequently.

- In strong form, significant incentives are deployed to encourage the participation of minority groups. In universities, including the historically black Alabama State University, special scholarships may be assigned to attract whites to campus. In private companies, bonuses may be offered or special accommodations made for targeted individuals. A mentor may be assigned to guide their progress. Statistics may be accumulated and care taken to ensure that salary hikes and promotions are being distributed to members of the aggrieved demographic.

- Moderate affirmative action measures typically mean something akin to *the tie goes to the minority*. Whether a university is admitting students to next year's class or a business is hiring new sales representatives, the philosophy here is that if two candidates are essentially equally qualified, the one representing a disadvantaged group will be selected.

- Weak affirmative action measures refuse to directly benefit one or another identity group. Steps are undertaken, however, to ensure that *opportunity* is spread to include minority candidates. Frequently, this means ensuring that the application pool of candidates for a post or promotion includes individuals from across the spectrum of genders, races, and similar. A commitment to implement his policy was part of the Abercrombie & Fitch discrimination lawsuit settlement. The company in essence said they'd been doing too much recruiting at overwhelmingly white fraternities and sororities, and they promised to branch out.

The history of affirmative action has been brief and turbulent. Since the early 1970s, the courts—including the

US Supreme Court—have visited and revisited the issue, and repeatedly reformed the legally required and allowed strength of affirmative action. The specific physical and cultural traits affirmative action policies address have also stretched and contracted. In the midst of all that, individual states have formed their own rules and guidelines. And for their part, companies have scrambled to bring policies into line with accepted practice and, in some cases, to take the lead in establishing standards. Because there's no sign that the legal and historical developments will settle in the near future, this section will concentrate only on the ethics and the broad arguments surrounding affirmative action.

Arguments for and against Affirmative Action Policies

Arguments in favor of affirmative action include the following:

1. Affirmative action is necessary to create fairness and equal opportunity in organizations because discrimination is so ingrained. When Carly Fiorina went to Hewlett-Packard, she found a culture so thoroughly masculine that it was difficult for her to communicate well with her colleagues. In that kind of environment, one where it's difficult for a woman to really make herself understood, forcing women into the workforce is necessary to open channels of communication so that more may flow without needing the help. Similarly at the historically black Alabama State University, the concern was that few white students would want to be the first to confront the specific traditions and customs of the longtime black school. Consequently, it's necessary to force the doors open with attractive scholarships so that later, with the comfort level raised, more whites will follow.

2. Affirmative action will stimulate interest in advancing at lower levels of the organization. Even if Hewlett-Packard *really is* gender neutral with respect to picking a CEO, it may be necessary to put a woman in the post so that younger women at the company feel that the way is open to the very highest levels. In other words, it's not until people actually *see* that they can become a CEO or enroll at Alabama State that they really make the attempt. In the absence of that seeing, the aspiring may not be there and the result is a company without women leaders, or a historically black university without whites, even though the doorways are wide open to them.

3. Affirmative action benefits third parties. Sometimes we think of affirmative action as being about a tight set of winners and losers. When Carly Fiorina went to HP, it's very possible that a white guy didn't get the job. When a white student got a scholarship at Alabama State, Tompkins lost his. But the stakeholders don't end there.

Society *as a whole* will be more harmonious as discrimination recedes. To the extent that's true, the tangible benefits of affirmative action climb significantly even while it remains true that there are individual losers.

4. Affirmative action can reduce tensions in a university, an office, or any organization by offering assurances that discrimination of minorities will not be tolerated, and also by opening the workplace to a diversity of viewpoints.

5. Affirmative action benefits organizations by helping them reach their goals. The more open an organization is to all candidates for all positions, the better the chance that they'll find someone truly excellent to fill the role. Affirmative action, by expanding the range of people considered for posts, helps the organization excel in the long term.

6. Affirmative action is necessary as compensation for past wrongs. Even if tomorrow all discrimination magically disappears, there'd still be a long legacy of suffering by minorities who didn't get the opportunities available to their children. By giving those children a little advantage, some of the historical unfairness balances out.

Common arguments against affirmative action include the following:

1. Affirmative action is discrimination (just in reversed form), and therefore it's wrong. When you privilege a minority at the expense of, say, a white male, you're treating the white male unfairly because of skin color and gender, and that *must* be unacceptable because the reason we have affirmative action in the first place is that we've all agreed that racial and gender discrimination are unacceptable.

2. Affirmative action is discrimination (just in reversed form), and therefore it reinforces what it combats. When you privilege a minority at the expense of, say, a white male, you're treating the white male unfairly, and so you're sanctioning the way of thinking that caused the problem in the first place. When you start selecting people for scholarships or jobs because of their skin color or gender, the larger point is you're reinforcing the habits of discrimination, not eliminating them.

3. The best way to eliminate discrimination is to let the law, markets, and time do their work. The law, which prohibits discrimination, should be enforced scrupulously, no matter who the in-fractor might be. More, companies that *are* discriminatory will put *themselves* out of business in the long term because competitors that hire the best talent regardless of minority status will eventually win out. With time, the

conclusion is, discrimination will be stamped out, but trying to hurry the process may just create social rancor.

4. Affirmative action can be unfair and damaging to third parties. Surgeons, firefighters—those kinds of jobs are vital to all individuals. Lives are at stake. If a surgeon who otherwise would have failed medical school eventually got her degree because the school needed to graduate a few minority female doctors to fulfill their affirmative action requirements, the people who pay may be patients.

5. Affirmative action is unfair to minorities who are treated as tokens. Minority candidates for positions who would win the post on merit alone see their hard work and accomplishments tarnished by suspicion that they didn't really earn what they've achieved. Minorities, consequently, can *never* be successful because even when they merit respect in the classroom or in the workplace, they won't get it.

6. Affirmative action creates a tense organization. The web of resentments lacing through classrooms and offices touched by affirmative action are multiple and complex. Nonminority workers may resent special privileges given to those favored by affirmative action. Also, because such privileges are handled discretely by HR departments, the tensions might exist even where affirmative action isn't active: suspicion that others are receiving special treatment can be as aggravating as the certainty that they are. The list of potential angers continues, but the larger problem with affirmative action is the social stress it may create.

7. Affirmative action damages organizations. By forcing them to evaluate talent in ways outside of merit, it diminishes their competitiveness, especially against companies from other states or nations where affirmative action implementation is less rigid.

8. Affirmative action doesn't compensate past wrongs. Those who suffer today because their scholarship or their promotion is taken by an otherwise undeserving minority are paying the price for past discrimination even though they may have never discriminated against anyone. Further, those who benefit today aren't the ones who suffered in the past.

Finally, an important point to note about the debate swirling around affirmative action is that there's broad agreement on the goal: diminishing and eliminating discrimination in organizations. The conflicts are about how best to do that.

The Greater Good versus Individual Rights: The Ethical Prism of Affirmative Action

In business ethics, few subjects raise emotions like affirmative action. There are a number of reasons, and one is that the ethics are so clear. In all but its weakest form, affirmative action stands almost straight up on the divide between individualism and collectivism.

- Do you belief ethics are about individual rights and responsibilities, or should ethics revolve around society and what benefits the larger community?
- Where does right and wrong *begin*? Is it with you and me and what we do? Or is it the society as a whole that must be set at the start and before any other concern?

If you believe that individuals center ethics, it's going to be hard (not impossible) to defend favoritism, no matter how noble the goal. An ethics based on fundamental personal duties—especially the requirement for fairness—demands that all men and women get an even shot in the workplace. Any swerve away from that principle, whether it's to favor whites at a historically black university in Alabama, or women in Silicon Valley, or any other minority group anywhere else, is going to be extremely difficult to justify. Further, if you believe that ethics begins with individuals and their rights to freedom and to pursue happiness, then blocking the opportunities allowed for some just because they don't fit into a specific race or gender category becomes automatically objectionable.

On the other side, if you believe in the community first, if you think that society's *overall* welfare must be the highest goal of ethical action, then it's going to be hard (not impossible) to deny that some form of affirmative action balancing, at some places and times, does serve the general welfare and therefore is ethically required. Thinking based on utilitarianism accepts that divvying out opportunities in terms of minority status will harm some individuals, but the perspective demands that we only bear in mind the *total* good (or harm) an action ultimately does. With respect to affirmative action, it may be true that its proponents sometimes push too far, but it's very difficult to look at workplaces and schools through the second half of the twentieth century and not concede that society as a whole does in fact benefit in at least some of the instances where special efforts are made to support the opportunities of some historically disadvantaged groups. Specific individuals may suffer when these social engineering strategies are implemented, but the general benefit outweighs the concern.

Why Do Public Institutions and Private Companies Implement Affirmative Action Policies?

There are a number of reasons organizations implement affirmative action policies, and not all are motivated by social idealism. First, some companies are simply required to do so because they want to work for the US government. According to current law, all businesses holding contracts with Washington, DC, in excess of $10,000 are required to have at least a weak affirmative action program in place. With respect to public institutions including universities, since their funding derives to a significant extent from the government, they typically are subject to governmental policy directives.

Another very practical reason affirmative action policies are implemented is to prevent future lawsuits. The suing of organizations, businesses, and individuals for damages alleging discrimination can be quite lucrative, as the $40 million lawsuit against Abercrombie & Fitch indicates. More, a business may even choose to quickly hand over millions of dollars to settle a lawsuit of dubious merit just to avoid the bad publicity of a nasty, public, and prolonged court fight. Lawyers, of course, have picked up on this and are constantly probing for weak organizations, ones where just the appearance of some kind of discrimination may be enough for a shakedown. Given that reality, prudent companies will take preventative action to insulate themselves from claims that they're discriminatory, and an affirmative action policy may serve that purpose.

A set of more positive reasons for an organization to implement affirmative action policies surrounds the belief that companies benefit from a diverse workforce:

- Diversity may help win business with a new consumer group.
- Diversity may help break minds out of ruts or just shake things up creatively.
- An affirmative action policy may be part of an organizational strategy to benefit from underused human resources in an area. This strategy generally begins with a utilization analysis, which is a spreadsheet representation of all the work positions in an organization, along with the characteristics of those filling the slots and then a comparison between those numbers and the demographic of qualified people in the immediate geographic region. If, to take a simple example, the company's legal team is 90 percent white, and local data shows that 50 percent of the area's lawyers are Asian, that tends to indicate the area's legal resources are being underutilized: there are a lot of good Asian

legal minds out there that for some reason aren't getting into the company workforce.

Finally, regardless of whether an affirmative action policy may help the bottom line by protecting against lawsuits or by improving employee performance, some organizations will implement a program because they believe it's part of their responsibility as good corporate citizens in a community to take steps to serve the general welfare.

KEY TAKEAWAYS

- Affirmative action seeks to end discrimination by giving some amount of preference to minorities.
- There are multiple strong arguments in favor of and against affirmative action.
- The ethics of affirmative action center on the question of whether the individual or the community should receive priority.
- Organizations implement affirmative action policies for reasons of self-interest or for altruistic reasons.

REVIEW QUESTIONS

1. What are the differences between strong and weak affirmative action?
2. Explain two arguments in favor of affirmative action.
3. Explain two arguments against affirmative action.
4. Why does conflict between individualism and collectivism exist at the core of the ethics of affirmative action?
5. Why may a company pursue a strong affirmative action policy?

[1] Brian Cabell, "Whites-only Alabama Scholarship Program Raising Eyebrows," *CNN*, October 30, 1999, accessed May 31, 2011,http://www.cnn.com/US/9910/30/white.scholarships/index.html.
[2] June Kronholz, "Double Reverse: Scholarship Program for whites Becomes a Test of Preferences," The Center for Individual Rights, *Wall Street Journal*, December 23, 1997, accessed May 31, 2011, http://www.cir-usa.org/articles/103.html.
[3] June Kronholz, "Double Reverse: Scholarship Program for whites Becomes a Test of Preferences," The Center for Individual Rights, *Wall Street Journal*, December 23, 1997, accessed May 31, 2011, http://www.cir-usa.org/articles/103.html.
[4] June Kronholz, "Double Reverse: Scholarship Program for whites Becomes a Test of Preferences," The Center for Individual Rights, *Wall Street Journal*, December 23, 1997, accessed May 31, 2011, http://www.cir-usa.org/articles/103.html.
[5] June Kronholz, "Double Reverse: Scholarship Program for whites Becomes a Test of Preferences," The Center for Individual Rights, *Wall Street Journal*, December 23, 1997, accessed May 31, 2011, http://www.cir-usa.org/articles/103.html.
[6] June Kronholz, "Double Reverse: Scholarship Program for whites Becomes a Test of Preferences," The Center for Individual Rights, *Wall*

Street Journal, December 23, 1997, accessed May 31, 2011, http://www.cir-usa.org/articles/103.html.

10.6 Case Studies

The Zinger and the Slur

Football coach Joe Paterno's on-field prowess is only slightly more legendary than his sharp tongue. This is one crowd favorite: "If I ever need a brain transplant, I want one from a sports writer because I'll know it's never been used." [1]

Most people find this to be pretty funny. And though it rubs some sports writers the wrong way, no one is going to file a lawsuit or claim anti-discriminatory protection is needed to protect the offended. On the other hand, JoePa—as he's called around Pennsylvania—he suffered taunting as a younger man. People called him a "wop," a slur attacking someone's Italian heritage (like the more common "guido" or calling a Chinese person a "Chink").

QUESTION

1. From an ethical viewpoint, and within a discussion of discrimination, why does the brain transplant zinger get a green light while the wop slur seems objectionable?

Working at Columbia University

This comes from the Columbia University website: "As an equal opportunity and affirmative action employer, the University does not discriminate against or permit harassment of employees or applicants for employment on the basis of race, color, sex, gender (including gender identity and expression), pregnancy, religion, creed, national origin, age, alienage and citizenship, status as a perceived or actual victim of domestic violence, disability, marital status, sexual orientation, military status, partnership status, genetic predisposition or carrier status, arrest record, or any other legally protected status." [2]

QUESTIONS

1. Looking at this list of characteristics that Columbia doesn't discriminate against, can you quickly put in your own words what each of them means?

2. What's the difference between unintentional and intentional discrimination?
   - Are some of these characteristics more vulnerable than others to unintentional discrimination? Which ones? Why?
   - Are some of these characteristics more vulnerable than others to intentional discrimination? Which ones? Why?

3. Which of the protected characteristics are concealable, meanings that in most cases a job applicant could fairly easily hide or not reveal whether he or she has the trait? Which aren't so concealable?

4. Which characteristics are universal (we're *all* afflicted and therefore vulnerable to discrimination) and which ones are individual (some of us have the trait and some don't)? In your opinion is one group more vulnerable to discrimination? Why?

5. If you wanted to stop discrimination at Columbia University, could you rank the protected characteristics in terms of their importance? Which forms of discrimination would be most important to combat and which wouldn't matter so much? Or are they all equally important? Justify your answer.

6. Are there any characteristics you would add to the list? In terms of doing ethics, is there any problem with a list this long?

7. Are there any characteristics that really shouldn't be on the list? Which ones? Why?

8. Hypothetically, John Smith has applied for a maintenance post at Columbia. The job entails routine and emergency plumbing and fixing of general problems, everything from burned-out light bulbs to graffiti. More or less, the job is to walk around and make sure things are in working order. He'd be working the night shift from 11 p.m. to 7 a.m. His assigned buildings would be a classroom and three coed dorms. He has been arrested three times for attempted rape of young women, but there was never enough evidence to convict.
   - Susan Rieger heads the Columbia University employment office. It's part of her job to defend the school's policies. In ethical terms, how do you suppose she might defend Columbia's refusal to discriminate on the basis of arrest record?

9. Columbia won't discriminate on the basis of religious belief. Historically, some creeds have been singled out more than others for abuse, but one that's not often found on the list of mistreatment is Haitian Voodoo. Houngan Hector of New Jersey identifies himself as an *asogwe* priest of Haitian voodoo. His story is interesting. He claims to have been "mounted" by an ancestor at the age of seven, and so began his spiritual journey. Eventually, it led Houngan Hector to perform spiritual cleansings for money. They haven't always gone well. According to this newspaper story in the *Philadelphia Daily News*: "Lucille Hamilton paid $621 to have her 'spiritual grime' removed by voodoo high priest Houngan Hector in an ordinary townhouse in Camden County. Hamilton, 21, a male living as a woman, flew in on Friday from her home in Little Rock,

Arkansas to take part in the three-day spiritual cleansing. By Saturday night Hamilton was dead, and authorities are awaiting results of an autopsy and toxicology tests to determine exactly what happened."[3] Here's Houngan Hector's advertisement for his services on his MySpace page, as it was reported in *Odd Culture*: "I have over 15 years of experience helping individuals resolve their issues, and well over 9 years of helping people through the means of the Haitian Voodoo tradition. Having gotten individuals out of jail, brought lovers back, and improved people's financial situation, I keep myself humble remembering it is not I who does it. It is God and Ginen who resolves." [4] The three basic ethical arguments against discrimination (and, in this case, discrimination based on personal religious belief) are *fairness*, *rights*, and *utilitarianism*.

o   Choose one and make the case that Houngan Hector—who was never charged with any crime—should be treated like any other applicant for a job at Columbia University.

o   Can any of the three arguments be used to show that discriminating against Haitian voodoo believers is ethically acceptable, even recommendable?

Susan Rieger in Trouble: Randy Raghavendra and Zenobia White-Farrell

Susan Rieger heads Columbia University's Office of Equal Opportunity and Affirmative Action, and she has a tough case with Randy Raghavendra. He's an analyst at Columbia's Office of Institutional Real Estate who got passed over for a promotion. The spot went to a younger white woman. Raghavendra, who's a dark-skinned Indian American, accused that "Columbia practices blatant racial discrimination and various deceptive tactics to keep out blacks and other dark-skinned minorities from higher-paying managerial and executive positions of power." [5]

QUESTIONS

The case's specifics go back and forth:

1.   Raghavendra points out that when he interviewed for the promotion, it had *already* been given to the white woman. His interview, therefore, was a "joke," as he put it, "a fake interview." The university answered that the hiring for that post had been handled by an outside headhunting company, which was a common practice at Columbia. Assume the outside company did engage in discriminatory practices. Does the fact that it's an independent enterprise cleanse Columbia University of responsibility? Or is the university equally responsible?

Or is it actually worse that they're hiding behind an outside firm? Justify your answer.

2.   An administrator at the university once asked Raghavendra, "Do you often get hassled at airport security?" The suggestion, according to Raghavendra, was that he looked like a potential terrorist. The administrator didn't deny the comment but affirmed that the idea that it was racist was "bizarre" and "silly beyond belief."

o   How could you make the case that this is an example, of individual, isolated, unintentional discrimination?

o   Who gets to decide whether a comment is racist? How is the decision made? Does or doesn't this conflict resemble the one you see on MTV videos where blacks openly refer to each other with a specific term that would earn a white person who used the word a lifetime ban from the channel?

3.   Raghavendra argues that he didn't get his own office while several white workers in lower posts did have their own office as well as a separate mailbox. The university responded that office and mailbox space is distributed by seniority: the lower-level white workers who had their own office had worked there longer. Seniority is viewed by most as a generally fair way of distributing offices. It's also fair, according to common opinion, to divide them up in terms of rank. Would it be right or wrong, however, for Columbia to simply say that either of the two systems will be used interchangeably, but the choice will be made in terms of minorities: whichever system allots the best offices to minorities will be implemented? Justify your answer.

4.   Raghavendra originally took his case to Susan Rieger, head of the Office of Equal Opportunity and Affirmative Action. After three months he withdrew it, however, claiming that they played games with him and never really investigated the charges. The university responded that he "failed to utilize internal administrative remedies provided by Columbia." Raghavendra is claiming that Columbia discriminates against him. As an employee of Columbia, does he have any ethical responsibility to try to work out the issue inside that organization? If so, what is the responsibility? As a member of society, does he have an obligation to take his claim outside the university? If so, what is the responsibility?

5.   Raghavendra sued for punitive damages. That's money as punishment for discrimination, and it's an amount beyond that which may have been lost in wages and benefits because of mistreatment. More, as part of any

settlement, Raghavendra wanted to be awarded a job assignment as manager of finance and accounting at Columbia. He says he'd like to stay at the university after the suit is settled. Does this decision affect the way you see his case against Columbia? Why or why not? Should it? Why or why not?

6. Raghavendra notes that there are no African Americans in higher-level positions in his office. There is a Pakistani who has a higher title, but Raghavendra points out "he's not really that dark-skinned." Within the context of the ethics of discrimination, what does it mean to be a victim? What types of victimhood are there? Is there any reason to ask here whether Raghavendra might be one of these kinds of victims? If so, what is it? If not, why not?

7. What makes the case especially difficult for Rieger, the Columbia point person on all this, is that she's trying to balance discrimination claims while fending off a lawsuit herself. Her post had been occupied—on a provisional basis—by Zenobia White-Farrell, a black woman. Columbia offered to make the job permanent with a salary of $80,000. White-Farrell responded that she'd accept but only on the condition that the salary was upped to $100,000. Columbia offered only $83,000. White-Farrell resigned. Soon after, Columbia hired Rieger at a salary of $107,000. White-Farrell sued, alleging discrimination.

   o What factors could possibly have justified offering Rieger so much more than White-Farrell?

   o How could you describe this case as an example of a glass ceiling for minority women?

   o The Columbia nondiscrimination code protects both gender minorities (women) and racial minorities. Is White-Farrell *more* protected than Rieger because she fits two categories and Rieger only one? Does the answer affect the ethical strength of White-Farrell's case? Justify your answer.

   o Assume that, strictly in terms of merit, Rieger deserved a higher salary than White-Farrell for the same job. Rieger had, say, more years of experience and a higher degree. Could you make a utilitarian argument that because the ethically right thing to do is just that which serves the general society's welfare, White-Farrell should have been offered $100,000, even though, again, strictly in terms of merit, she didn't deserve that much?

8. Columbia University is an Affirmative Action institution. They aren't satisfied with gender and racial

neutrality; it's the institution's policy to promote and to some extent favor minority candidates for jobs.

   o Can you make the case that, with respect to the particular job of overseeing all hiring at the university, there's a good practical reason—which is also ethically acceptable—to seek a white male to direct the office? What is the case?

   o Can you make the case that with respect to this particular job, there's a good practical reason—which is also ethically acceptable—to seek a multiple minority (a gender plus racial minority or some similar combination) to direct and oversee hiring? What is the case?

9. The name of the office Susan Rieger leads is the *Office of Equal Opportunity and Affirmative Action*. What is "Equal Opportunity?" What is "Affirmative Action?" Does the title of this office make sense? If so, how? If not, why not?

Google Celebrates Diversity…and Profit

This statement comes from Google CEO Eric Schmidt on the corporate web page titled "Google Celebrates Diversity": "Our products and tools serve an audience that is globally and culturally diverse—so it's a strategic advantage that our teams not only encompass the world's best talent but also reflect the rich diversity of our customers, users, and publishers. It is imperative that we hire people with disparate perspectives and ideas, and from a broad range of cultures and backgrounds. This philosophy won't just ensure our access to the most gifted employees; it will also lead to better products and create more engaged and interesting teams." [6]

This is a very carefully worded paragraph, and beneath its motivational tone there are firm statements about diversity in the Google workplace. They include the following:

- Google carefully avoids mentioning race, gender, and similar requirements for any particular position. The company doesn't get involved in discussions about how many Catholic females over fifty years old and with a disability work there. Like most contemporary organizations, Google avoids strict quota systems.

- Google will seek to hire "the world's best talent."

- Google, *apart from hiring the best raw talent*, will seek employees reflecting "the rich diversity of our customers."

There are also clear justifications for the diversity side of the hiring strategy. Google will take action to contract a rainbow of workers because

- diversity in hiring will help Google connect with its diverse consumer base,

- diversity in hiring will ensure Google has access to all gifted employees,
- diversity in hiring will help Google produce better products,
- diversity in hiring will help Google create more engaged and interesting teams.

Concretely, what is Google doing to diversify the people forming its company? Besides directly hiring a diverse workforce, the company offers a number of scholarships and internships aimed at those historically underrepresented in the technology industry. [7]

QUESTIONS

1. In a nutshell, the commonly cited arguments in favor of affirmative action include the following:
   - It creates fairness and equal opportunity within organizations.
   - It benefits third parties: society *as a whole* will be more harmonious as discrimination recedes.
   - It reduces tensions in an organization.
   - It benefits organizations by helping them reach their goals.
   - It is compensation for past wrongs.

   Which of these arguments appear to stand behind affirmative action at Google? Explain. Are any of the other justifications applicable even though they may not be the *reason* Google seeks diverse talent?

2. In sweeping terms there are two types of arguments in favor of affirmative action. First, it serves a broad social good by integrating society. Second, companies employing affirmative action do better in the marketplace than those that don't. If you had to choose one of these as a better and more persuasive argument for affirmative action, which would you choose? Why?

3. At some publicly funded universities, scholarships are, in essence, set aside for minorities. Google privately funds scholarships that are, in essence, set aside for minorities. Taxpayers, in other words, fund one affirmative action endeavor and private investors the other. Now, is one endeavor ethically superior to the other? Why or why not?

4. In a nutshell, the basic arguments against affirmative action include the following:
   - It is essentially discrimination, and therefore it reinforces what it combats.
   - The best way to eliminate discrimination is to let equal opportunity law, markets, and time do their work.
   - It is unfair to minorities who are treated as tokens.
   - Forcing organizations to evaluate talent in ways outside of merit diminishes their competitiveness.
   - It creates resentment and tensions in an organization.
   - It doesn't compensate past wrongs (because those benefitting and suffering today aren't those who suffered and benefitted in the past).

   Looking at this list, how do you suppose Google CEO Eric Schmidt might argue against each item?

5. With an eye on these arguments against affirmative action, can you make the case that Google's efforts are ethically reproachable?

6. What does the *veil of ignorance* test for discrimination? Put yourself under the veil of ignorance. Now, do you believe Google's hiring policies are ethically good or bad? Why?

Susan Rieger in More Trouble: Madonna Constantine
Madonna Constantine is a professor of psychology and education specializing in race studies and prejudice. Growing up as one of five children in a lower-middle-class family in Lafayette, Louisiana, she'd benefitted from parents who never finished college and vowed she would: they saved and scrimped together enough money to get her started at the upper level. Constantine took it from there. She began her remarkable journey at Xavier in New Orleans. Next, she went to the University of Memphis, and then to the University of Texas, and Temple University, and finally to the Ivy League's prestigious Columbia, where she earned tenure with more than thirty articles authored and published: "Most people may go up for tenure with 15 or 20 articles," she said. "I figured as a black woman, I needed at least double that." [8]

As it turned out, the numbers weren't the whole truth. Constantine had plagiarized significant amounts of her writings from students and another professor. Upon discovering the truth, Columbia fired her. Constantine responded, "I am left to wonder whether a white faculty member would have been treated in such a publicly disrespectful and disparaging manner."[9]

Next, she sued Columbia for racial discrimination.

Columbia University is having a rough time: Randy Raghavendra, Zenobia White-Farrell, and Madonna Constantine are all suing the traditionally very white institution for color discrimination.

QUESTIONS

1. In your own words, and in general terms since there isn't space here to provide every detail of every case, what would it mean to accuse these people of being victims? What's the difference between strong and weak victimhood?

2. With the facts provided, create a picture of Madonna Constantine as a victim. What kind of victim would she be? How could that conclusion be supported?

3. Sketch an argument that society *as a whole* is better off with occasional cases of discrimination than it is with occasional cases of victimhood.

4. Use a utilitarian argument to make the case that *even if* Columbia's affirmative action policies are fostering cases of victimization, they should maintain those policies.

[1] Mike Bianchi, "Panthers Gm Proves Paterno Barb Wrong," *Orlando Sentinel*, January 31, 2004, accessed May 31, 2011, http://articles.orlandosentinel.com/2004-01-31/sports/0401310276_1_sports-writer-silly-stuff-recruiting-visits.

[2] "Office of Equal Opportunity and Affirmative Action," Columbia University, accessed May 31, 2011, http://www.columbia.edu/cu/vpaa/eoaa.

[3] "Transvestite Dies At Voodoo Ceremony," *OddCulture*, accessed May 31, 2011, http://oddculture.com/culture/transvestite-dies-at-voodoo-ceremony.

[4] "Transvestite Dies At Voodoo Ceremony," *OddCulture*, accessed May 31, 2011, http://oddculture.com/culture/transvestite-dies-at-voodoo-ceremony.

[5] "NRI Sues Columbia University for Racism, *Times of India*, November 22, 2003, accessed May 31, 2011, http://businessethicsworkshop.com/Chapter_10/susan_rieger_in_trouble.html.

[6] "Diversity@Google: A place to be you," Google, accessed May 31, 2011, http://www.google.com/corporate/diversity/index.html.

[7] "Diversity and students," Google, accessed May 31, 2011, http://www.google.com/diversity/students.html.

[8] Elissa Gootman, "Noose Case Puts Focus on a Scholar of Race," *New York Times*, October 12, 2007, accessed May 31, 2011, http://www.nytimes.com/2007/10/12/education/12columbia.html?_r=1&pagewanted=all.

[9] Karen W. Arenson and Elissa Gootman, "Columbia Cites Plagiarism by a Professor, *"New York Times*, February 21, 2008, accessed May 31, 2011, http://www.nytimes.com/2008/02/21/education/21prof.html.

NOTES:

Chapter 11:
Sex and Drugs at Work

Chapter Overview

This chapter examines the ethics of sex in the marketing world, and discusses issues raised by romance among workmates. Drug use is considered from the side of prevention and in terms of performance enhancement.

11.1 Is There Anything Special about Sex?
LEARNING OBJECTIVES

1. Consider the ethics of using sex to promote products and services in the marketplace.
2. Investigate the ethics of sleeping with the boss in exchange for professional advancement.

Sex in the Office

That subtitle got your attention. It gets everyone's attention, which explains why there's so much of it in the business world. Marketing efforts lead the way because people tend to pay attention to the TV when scantily clad people appear. More broadly, sex happens—either explicitly or just as a suggestion—almost everywhere business does. It's exploited in the commercials, showing up on the office computer screens, joked about in the bathroom, discussed in the organizational code of conduct, and going on underneath cubicle desks. The economic world is charged with it. Some of the more intense questions about the ethics of sex in the workplace include:

- What's the ethics of using sex to sell products?
- What's the ethics of using sex to sell yourself?
- What's the ethics of looking for sex at work?

Sex Sells

The Russian anchorwoman Svetlana Pesotskaya caused a stir in international media circles when she started doing her reporting topless. Her news program—utterly conventional except for the clothing issue—is called *The Naked Truth*. One of the broadcast's more entertaining aspects is watching male guests as they're being interviewed in the studio heroically trying to keep their eyes above her neckline.

Regardless of the reason viewers tune in for sex-charged information, they certainly do tune in. That fact is not lost on a station closer to home, the CBS affiliate in Cleveland, Ohio: WOIO. In a segment heavily and provocatively advertised by the station beforehand, their news anchor Sharon Reed

stripped on air before dashing off to join a throng of temporary nudists participating in an installation by photographer Spencer Tunick, who's gained international fame by convincing multitudes of men and women to voluntarily pose naked for his fleshy panorama shots.

The reviews of Reed's participative report were mixed. Don Shelby, an anchor at the CBS affiliate in St. Paul and Minneapolis said, "This threatens to turn us [news broadcasters] into something of a cartoon, if we weren't already." [1]Going further, the chairman of the Radio-Television News Directors Association in Washington, DC, complained, "I think the general reaction in the industry has been one of surprise and disgust. I don't see how this can engender confidence in the quality of news we think we are doing, and it manages to justify the harsh criticism that we often face in our industry." [2]

On the other side, neither WOIO nor Sharon Reed backed down. Station executives insisted that the core story—Tunick's photography event—was legitimate local news, and the anchor's participation was analogous to conveying the reality of a flash flood by reporting underneath an umbrella from beside a rushing stream. As for Reed personally, she made no apologies for using her assets to increase ratings for her station and, simultaneously, her own profile in her profession's arena. "I'm in it to win," she said. "When did that become a crime?"

That last quote came from the *New York Times*. The newspaper took advantage of the situation to run its own nude picture of Reed. [3]

Product Sincerity, Prurience, and Objectification

Ethical issues visible in the Sharon Reed broadcast include product sincerity, prurience, and objectification. Product sincerity measures openness and transparency about what's being sold. In the case of Reed's report, there are two front-running possibilities, two clearly distinct products being offered for viewers' consumption:

1. A news story about a flamboyant picture taker's visit to Cleveland
2. A video of a woman stripping

Here's one way to sharpen the question about what's really going on: Had federal broadcasting rules *not* allowed the unclothed images, would WOIO still have covered the event, would the station have broadcast a story more or less like the one it did but with the reporter clothed? For its part, the station insists it would have. Further, its basic argument for broadcasting the nude version is clearly reasonable. Both WOIO and Reed remind critics that participating in an event is an excellent way to understand and convey it. That's why sports reporters pick up bats and try to hit pitched baseballs, and fashion reporters dress in the season's hot shoes and exhibit them on camera, and war reporters visit the front lines. The fact, consequently, that Reed got involved with her story fits perfectly with the claim that she's doing the best and most professional job possible of portraying what happened. Still, it's also probably true that she could've uncovered herself without beaming the images across the airwaves. More, the *way* she took everything off wasn't exactly discreet. In a moment reminding some viewers of the artistic and historical significance of the disrobed body, and others of a bar with poles, Reed stared intently at the camera as she slowly unsnapped her bra and slipped out of her final clothing layer.

Does it matter? Whether the station was trying to win over viewers with a news story that happened to include nudity, or with nudity that happened to include some news, is there a *responsibility* for the people at WOIO to be sincere about their strategy? There are solid reasons for affirming that the responsibility is limited.

- Viewers aren't morons; they know how to change channels. If they see something they don't like on WOIO, they're free to try another offering. As long as that's true, as long as viewers can see for themselves what's being offered and therefore make their own fully informed decisions, what the broadcaster is *claiming* diminishes in importance.

- The fact that a product being offered for consumption isn't what it claims to be is a perfectly understood part of our economic and business world. It goes on all the time and everywhere. Teenagers buying whipped cream chargers (whippets) don't come to the grocery store because they expect to have pie that night at dinner. The cashier knows why they're buying the canister, the store owner does too and the manufacturer. Everyone knows, which means there's no attempt to deceive. It's true that the canister packaging insists that the product is for use with whipped cream, but that's not really a lie, just a formality.

Product sincerity, in conclusion, is relative. When people can see for themselves what's being offered, or everyone knows what's going on, a lie isn't really a lie. Or at least the case can be made that it's not.

Going back to Reed's story, this much is clear: exactly how her report would be presented was well publicized. Through a massive promotional campaign leading up to the event, the station made sure everyone knew beforehand what was coming. Even accepting the informed consent of the viewers, however, a business ethics that sticks with firm duties—one that orients right and wrong with basic rules about always telling the whole truth—may disapprove of what happened on WOIO. This is the position anchorman Don Shelby took when asked about the infamous report. As Shelby put it, "This threatens to turn us into something of a cartoon." He meant that Reed's news broadcast was simply and factually insincere: it claimed to convey important events about the real world, but really offered viewers a piece of ratings-grubbing, skin-flashing entertainment.

In the end, the two guiding questions about product sincerity as they relate to Sharon Reed remain open: Was she telling the truth when asserting that hers was a legitimate news story that rightfully included sex (as opposed to a chance to use sex to boost ratings with the help of a dubious news event)? And does it matter whether she was telling the truth?

Prurience is an immoderate and unwholesome interest or desire, especially related to sex. On this front, the ethical question is simple: is there anything wrong with sitting in front of your TV and watching someone take their clothes off? Anyone who's watched the Olympics has noticed that beach volleyball gets a little more coverage than the purely athletic competition seems to merit, and some viewers seem more interested in watching the male swimmers stretch on their blocks and prepare to fire into the water than they do in following the actual swimming. People like to look at nice bodies, but where does checking someone out cross into the objectionably unwholesome?

This question is especially well adapted to a community or a cultural ethics, which is a sense of right and wrong that's not determined by preset rules or viewers' free choices so much as community standards. What's right or wrong, from this perspective, is set by a society's customs and expectations. Swinging this viewpoint around to Sharon Reed's report, one important aspect is that it was carefully set to air after 10 p.m. when, presumably, children would be tucked away in bed. The station didn't have any choice in the matter (at least not if it wanted to keep its broadcasting license) because nudity simply isn't allowed before that time. In the United States, these standards are usually set by the Federal

Communications Commission (FCC), which is the national government's regulatory commission for what can and can't be shown on open airways. The members of that agency are chosen, ultimately, by elected officials, and those officials, presumably, are in touch with what the public feels is appropriate. The argument can be made here that because a democratically elected government drew the line between the acceptable and the unwholesome at 10 p.m., the line is there. Period.

Refining the point, certain depictions of nudity, degrees of it, and things that happen to go on while people aren't wearing clothes are limited in similar ways by the FCC, and in all these areas, lines are getting drawn between healthy and immoderate viewer interest. The definition of what counts as prurience, finally, may find an ethical foundation on a community's verdict about whether it's happening.

Objectification is dehumanization; it drains away the person inside a body. If you set the reporter Sharon Reed next to a blow-up doll of Sharon Reed, objectification is what happens when you go from the first to the second. The charge or accusation of objectification is that by volunteering to take her clothes off on TV, Reed is violating a moral duty to herself, the duty to protect her own dignity and humanity. As an experienced TV reporter, the professional skills Reed had developed involve the sophisticated ability to investigate, understand, and report on current affairs. There's nobility in those cultivated talents, and Reed has a responsibility to herself to promote them. When she takes her clothes off, though, everyone loses sight of what truly makes her an accomplished person. In the same way, those that participate in the nude spectacle—the TV station, the viewers—are violating a duty to her: by sending Reed out there to be ogled, or by doing the ogling, they're violating their responsibility to see her as an accomplished reporter, and not an empty piece of eye candy. If that's right, finally, then Reed shouldn't have taken her clothes off, and viewers shouldn't have watched if she did.

One strong argument against this duty-based reasoning is that respect for others can be condescending and patronizing. Who are we to tell Reed when she is and isn't an object? It's far better to let everyone make their own decisions and respect them for doing so. The case could even be made that Reed's highest dignity as a human lies precisely in her ability to use and display her body as she chooses. If stripping moves Reed toward accomplishments that will make her happy—if it helps her achieve the success as in her profession—then she shouldn't be obstructed. From this perspective, telling Reed to keep her clothes on isn't a respectable ethical recommendation; it's an insulting attack on her right to go out into the world and find what she wants. Listening to her, it sounds like she may have had this argument in mind when she asserted, "I'm in it to win. When did that become a crime?"

There's at least one further route to follow in defense of Reed's disrobing. In the twenty-nine-second advertising segments promoting her presentation, art is heavily featured. It's steamy art, true, but nonetheless the kind of thing we're used to seeing in museums. The first shot is a bronze sculpture of three female nudes knotted in a passionate embrace. Next comes a painting on the same subject. Both these shots apparently come from museums. Reed appears in the following scene; it's a head shot balanced by a partially visible statue of a male nude just to her right. The statue's visible section is its waist area. Similar juxtapositions lead to a climactic (and blurry) tease of men and women gathering without their clothes to pose for Spencer Tunick's artistic photos.

Art, the message is, includes bodies. Far from presenting a cheap thrill, Reed is participating in the illustrious history of high and noble aesthetic representation. Everyone will have to decide for themselves whether Spencer Tunick's panorama shots of naked herds deserve to be called art. But the fact that they could be opens the way to claiming that those stripping down for him aren't being reduced to pinups; they're being elevated to one of the higher human callings, which is the thoughtful and provocative depiction of what it means to be human in all its dimensions.

Conclusion. Sex certainly sells. It's also certain that sexual selling raises ethical questions: is it insincere, unwholesome, or exploitive of the person doing the selling?

Getting on Top to Get Ahead

Some people who are in it to win consider going further than taking their clothes off. "Based on the questions I receive from readers," writes *Huffington Post* columnist Joy Chen, "there seems to be a substantial segment of charming, ambitious female blog readers among you who wonder: 'Should I have sex with my boss to get ahead in my career?' Perhaps there is an equally large number of good-looking male readers among you who are in the same predicament, but too shy to ask." [4] No, she answers, and runs through a list of practical reasons why the strategy is flawed.

Regardless of whether sleeping with the boss will help you up the career ladder, the ethics of the strategy divide along a number of lines. The arguments against even trying to convert sex into a promotion start with appeals to honesty and fairness. Granting special favors to a superior—no matter what they may be—almost inevitably requires lying if they're to be repaid with a promotion or pay raise or some other professional compensation since most organizations require that some kind of internal evaluation justify the selection of one employee instead of others for a move up. The practical reality is that people involved in this kind of relationship are probably going to end up misleading others about what's really going on. And even if no one asks, the equally fundamental value of fairness gets breached when promotions that supposedly are based on specific job-performance skills end up being distributed in accordance with different motives.

Another, though related, argument against what Chen calls the "sleep-up strategy" emerges from utilitarian theory. Starting with the premise that ethical good is just whatever heightens a society's general welfare and happiness, it seems as though a world in which *everyone* is uniformly getting ahead by working hard will be less rancorous and angry than a world where some people are getting ahead through hard work, while others are flying under the radar, suddenly appearing in higher-level posts for reasons that others don't understand or that don't conform with expectations. Resentment can grow quickly, as well as charges of capriciousness and unfairness. If the boss happens to be a heterosexual woman, for example, with a taste for sinewy, dark men, and if promotions are doled out as part of pillow talk, then large numbers of workers aren't even going to have the opportunity to ask just how far they'll go to get that salary raise. It's true, of course, that some individuals *will* benefit when sleeping up occurs. But for the *general* welfare to be favored, their pleasures are going to need to outweigh quite a bit of workplace frustration.

The third strong ethical argument against sleeping with the boss to get ahead relates to the earlier consideration of disrobing for the camera. If you can make an argument that a news reporter shouldn't take off clothes to win more viewers because it's dehumanizing and objectifying, the same reasoning may be transferred with even greater force to taking off the clothes and not stopping there. In both cases, individuals are drained of their professionalism. Within the business world, they sacrifice the judgment and skills that make them what they are as qualified supervisors and laboring employees. When the particular dignity that belongs to those who develop real skills in the economic world is stripped away, what's left is nothing more than selfish individuals placating immediate and base desires.

One response to this last argument is to deny the premise, which means to dispute the basic assumptions. In this case, denying the premise could mean asserting that skills in the business world *aren't* limited to the kinds of things that show up on paper: the number of tasks you're able to complete each hour, the scores you receive in customer satisfaction surveys, and so on. Business is much broader than that. Like money, it's everywhere, as broad as life itself. If this is the starting point, it follows that the notion of business skills must be taken to include all that.

Next, if that's what business skills are, if they're everything you can bring to bear on the economic world, then sex is going to factor into the mix. It's going to be something employable just like any other ability. Some people are born with great mathematical minds, and they use the quality to get ahead by finding good engineering jobs guaranteeing high pay. Others are born with tremendous athletic skill. They may use that ability to win a college scholarship and so receive an education that the next person—who's the same in every other way—won't be able to access. There are people who have a natural talent for selling and leverage that; others put a sharp visual sense of balance and harmony to use in an interior design company. Sculptors and carpenters turn capable hands into money. If, finally, there's someone out there with great sex appeal and the ability to use it, why shouldn't they? Theirs is a talent just like everyone else's.

Filling this out by reference to ethical theory, there are two kinds of foundations that may be laid underneath the assertion that using bedroom skills to get ahead isn't any different from dressing for success or staying late at the office. The first is obvious: fairness. If one person can use their skills, then others should be able to use theirs. One response to this argument is that any talent may be used *as long as* it's directly relevant to professional responsibilities. Letting people use their erotic skills is only fair, the argument goes, if you happen to be in Amsterdam, a few counties in Nevada, or some other place where prostitution is legal.

The second theoretical foundation for an ethics of sleeping up is the privileging of individual rights and human freedom as the highest values in the workplace. If freedom guides ethics, then constraining the talents that may be used to succeed becomes immoral because it's a constraint on individual liberty. Freedom, the argument continues, is one of those things you can't limit: either you let people make their own decisions about getting ahead or you don't.

The Ethics of Individual Freedom and the Wide-Open Market Economy

The employment of an ethics of freedom to justify the bedroom strategy for career advancement illustrates one reason why proponents of freedom maximization in the economic world frequently set their view of individual rights in tandem with the ideal of an unobstructed market economy. An unobstructed marketplace is sometimes called a laissez-faire economy (laissez-faire is French for "leave to do"), and it's one where individuals and organizations compete against each other with minimal regulation, oversight, and limitation. The purchase of trash bags is a decent example. If you buy Glad bags and find they rip when you're taking the trash out and so leave your kitchen floor stained with coffee grounds, it doesn't take much effort to go to the store and buy a different brand. On the other hand, trash *collection* is much less competitive. Especially in those cities where the local government runs the trash trucks, you're going to find it difficult to change companies if you don't like the service you're getting. Now, with respect to the trash bag company, if all the design specialists got their jobs by getting it on with the CEO, no one will be surprised to discover that they don't know too much about making good bags. This kind of company, therefore, one where professional excellence isn't rewarded, is probably also one that'll produce leaking bags and soon go out of business. The marketplace, consequently, does some of the work to professionalize the office that a freedom-based ethics can't do. Of course, if the marketplace is obstructed—if consumers can't easily switch from one provider to another, as in the trash collection case—then it's less likely that experts in sleeping up will be weeded out.

A stronger point can be made. Practices many consider inappropriate, undignified, or reprehensible—like sleeping with the boss to get ahead—may surrender to economic reality more quickly and completely than they do to purely ethical arguments. It's possible that the best way (the most efficient, practical, and certain) to cure behaviors many label egregious—everything from under-the-table bribes to racial discrimination—is to simply let market forces of competition do their job.

KEY TAKEAWAYS

- Using sexual images and suggestions for economic reasons raises ethical issues of sincerity, prurience, and objectification.
- Sleeping with the boss for career advancement opens issues concerning the intrinsic nobility of the individual in a business setting and the limits of acceptable strategies for advancement.

- The possibility of sleeping with the boss to advance professionally illustrates one reason rights theorists in the economic world tend to favor market-driven economies.

REVIEW QUESTIONS

1. What—if anything—is wrong with taking off your clothes to earn some money?
2. Is there an ethical difference between stripping for *Playboy* or *Playgirl* magazine and Reed's disrobing? If so, what is it? If not, why are they ethically the same? Use the concepts of *prurience* and *objectification* to answer.
3. Your boss wants to sleep with you, and it's clear that visiting a hotel will help your career. What are two arguments against? What's an argument in favor?
4. Some ethical theorists believe individual freedom and the pursuit of happiness are the highest ethical values. Why might this kind of theorist also favor wide-open market economies with competition among companies?

[1] David Carr, "When a TV Talking Head Becomes a Talking Body," *New York Times*, November 25, 2004, accessed June 1, 2011, http://www.nytimes.com/2004/11/25/arts/television/25tube.html?_r=1.

[2] David Carr, "When a TV Talking Head Becomes a Talking Body," *New York Times*, November 25, 2004, accessed June 1, 2011, http://www.nytimes.com/2004/11/25/arts/television/25tube.html?_r=1.

[3] David Carr, "When a TV Talking Head Becomes a Talking Body," *New York Times*, November 25, 2004, accessed June 1, 2011, http://www.nytimes.com/2004/11/25/arts/television/25tube.html?_r=1.

[4] Joy Chen, "Should You Have Sex With Your Boss to Get Ahead?," *Huffington Post*, May 18, 2010, accessed June 1, 2011, http://www.huffingtonpost.com/joy-chen/should-you-have-sex-with_b_580512.html.

11.2 Bad Sex: Harassment

LEARNING OBJECTIVE

1. Discuss sexual harassment in its principal contexts.

The Boss Wants to Sleep with You

The flip side of you deciding to sleep with the boss to get ahead is the boss deciding to sleep with you. In ethical terms, however, and in legal ones also, this situation isn't just a reversed copy of the previous. When the sleep-up strategy begins with some guy or gal having a few drinks and deciding to make a run through the promotion shortcut, the boss can decline. There'll be some awkward talk and red faces, but a week later the whole thing will probably have evaporated. What happens, though, when the person initiating the deal isn't so much an opportunist as a predator, and when it's not so much about making a quick and steamy bargain as it is a continuously leveled demand?

Sexual harassment with respect to the law is defined this way by the US Equal Employment Opportunity Commission (EEOC): "Unwelcome sexual advances, requests for sexual favors, and other verbal or physical conduct of a sexual nature constitutes sexual harassment when submission to or rejection of this conduct explicitly or implicitly affects an individual's employment, unreasonably interferes with an individual's work performance, or creates an intimidating, hostile or offensive work environment." [1]

The clichéd image of sexual harassment—which may have gotten to be the cliché by being the most accurate and common—is of a middle-age man hiring and hitting on the nubile account executive. She gets the message pretty quickly about exactly why she was selected for the job, and what she's going to need to do to keep it or advance upward. Whether that's the most typical scenario or not, both legal and ethical considerations of the issue account for varied exploitation scenarios: harassment can work against diverse people in multiple ways. According to the EEOC statement,

- The victim as well as the harasser may be a woman or a man. The victim does not have to be of the opposite sex.
- The harasser can be the victim's supervisor, an agent of the employer, a supervisor in another area, a coworker, or a nonemployee.
- The victim does not have to be the person harassed but could be anyone affected by the offensive conduct.
- Unlawful sexual harassment may occur without economic injury to the victim.
- The harasser's conduct must be unwelcome. [2]

A number of ambiguities knot attempts to deal with harassment in the courts. Starting with the term *sexual advances*, everyone knows from their own experience that someone standing fifty yards off and staring can be tremendously disconcerting, while someone else rushing up, draping themselves over us, and sighing, "You're hot!" can be a funny joke. It's hard to set down in words exactly what an *advance* is. Similar uncertainties plague attempts to define just what constitutes the *unwelcome* part of unwelcome advances because, again, different individuals have very distinct ways of feeling and expressing displeasure.

On the other end, even if the advance is clear, and even if it's clearly unwelcome, when do accumulated come-ons add up to a hostile work environment? In some situations, people will feel pressured months after a single polite invitation to dinner has been firmly refused, while in other places the boss's daily proposal to "Get blind drunk together and see what happens" will seem more absurd than threatening. None of this changes the fact that the law's intention is clear.

People aren't allowed to make sex an employment requirement or contaminate the workplace by acting like it's a singles' bar. Anyone who breaks those rules may be subject to prosecution, especially if the behavior is persistent and continues even after discomfort has been explicitly reported. How is the gap between a clear legal intention and a messy real world bridged? Courts have sought to alleviate the problem of different people seeing things in different ways with a reasonable person model. The basic questions at the core of harassment cases—"Is it an unwanted sexual advance?" and "Is it a hostile work environment?"—are answered, as far as the law is concerned, by the response a reasonable person would give if informed of the situation. Of course, reasonable people once believed the earth was flat, so it's not clear that the reasonable person definition will entirely withstand the tremendous variety of situations in which people come together. Still, the model certainly advances the discussion. The fact that any accusation of harassment, or any defense in the face of an accusation, must pass through the test does wring out extreme cases. The accuser who complains that the boss once winked, or the boss who claims not to have realized that advances were unwelcome even after receiving a glass of ice water in the lap, probably won't get much sympathy in the eyes of a judge.

Sex, Harassment, and Ethics

Sexual harassment is difficult to justify, and easy to condemn, with nearly all mainstream ethical theories.

- The general welfare, most agree, is well served by a workplace where everyone can work, where labor can be done without the impediments of annoying and molesting come-ons. There are other spots and times that are designated for romantic socializing, and in general, we all get along most harmoniously when we keep our various activities in the places they're expected to be. Exceptions exist, but looking at the situation broadly, utilitarianism—which sets the general welfare as the highest good—comes down against overly aggressive advances at work.
- More individualistic and liberty-oriented ethics that privilege freedom and each person's unique expression and aspirations as the guiding ideal for action will likely agree that a workplace plagued by harassment is one where individuals' freedom to pursue their own hopes and careers is being significantly impeded. The harasser, of course, can always insist that he or she is free to toss out as many blunt invitations as he or she may choose, but it must be remembered that all freedom-based theories restrict us to actions that don't limit the freedom of others.

- Basic duty theory, which orients ethics in the workplace around the specific imperative to honesty, also rejects harassment because no sane boss is going to admit to it. Harassment, in other words, will likely lead to lying. Along the same lines, the duty to fidelity (keeping our promises) also prohibits harassment assuming the original working agreement was about work and not romance. Finally, the duty to respect others as dignified human beings—worthy of being treated as ends and not means—leaves little room for hostile workplaces.

An ethical review of workplace sexual harassment shows that the practice is difficult to justify. Similar confidence can be attached to a related subject: victimization. Victimhood, in its extreme form, is falsely claiming to suffer harassment as a way of injuring another, very likely a supervisor. Since the accusation is a lie, it will, in most cases, fail an ethical review. Also in terms of the utilitarian principle of the greatest good, it's probable that society won't be benefited by people flinging false accusations of sex harassment. In general, the ethical difficulties surrounding victimhood are practical. They surround this question: how can individuals be protected against retributive and false claims of harassment without making the accusation impossible to level?

Probably the most interesting—and conflictive—ground for the subject of sexual advances in the office is the intercultural workplace: situations where employees from distinct nations with divergent customs and habits are asked to work together.

Academic studies have carefully shown how cultural differences affect attitudes about sex, sexual advances, and hostility at work. In one study, American, Australian, and German collegians were offered written scenarios of sexual overtures in offices. Responses from all three nationalities were similar, but as a group, they were far more likely to brand the episodes with terms like *harassment* than were their peers from Brazil. Faced with the same scenarios, the Brazilians tended to see only innocuous pokes at romance and sex that didn't constitute abuse of power or create a hostile environment. A similar experiment showed a comparable split between typical adults living in the United States (more prone to see harassment) and Ecuador (more likely to see scenarios as flirtatious or harmless sexual jousting). [3]

Researchers speculate that the distinct responses to the situations don't indicate superficial differences of opinion, or divergences in local laws, but go much deeper into sweeping ways people understand sex and socializing and men and women together. South American culture is generally more eroticized, more tolerant of displays of nudity, and more accepting of raw gestures toward sex. Of course you can't miss how much more comfortable men and women are with their displayed bodies if you visit Carnival in Brazil, but it goes beyond that. Something simple—a comment asserting that the workday passes more agreeably when the woman a few cubicles down wears one of her shorter skirts—comes off very differently in South America (where few would object) than the United States (where just citing the example will make some people wince). The expectations, acceptance, and enjoyment surrounding sex and suggestion at work, the conclusion is, aren't any different from the rules governing which side of the street you drive on, or how much can be revealed at the beach; they're different at different places. [4]

Cultural differences don't make much difference as long as cultural places remain fixed. But in a world of multinational corporations and falling trade barriers, large organizations (and small ones too) are going to explore international markets. Mixed nationalities in the office are going to follow. Then what? What happens if an American TV station, impressed by the rating-busting success of Russian Sergei Moskvin—the producer behind the topless news program, *Naked Truth*—invites him to come to America? No one should be too surprised if Moskvin spends the first day in the office bouncing around asking female reporters to give him a waist-up look. And no one should be too surprised if one, a few, or all of the reporters (including the men) protest and maybe file a lawsuit. In ethical terms, there are a number of strategies for resolving these clashes of expectations and customs. In general, they divide into two groups:

1. Those working from a culturalist ethical perspective
2. Those planted in one of the traditional approaches

Office Sex from a Culturalist Perspective

A culturalist ethics defines right and wrong as simply aligning with a society's accepted rules and norms for behavior. For example, in the States we consider ownership of land that we've legally purchased to be legitimately ours; part of what we morally owe each other is respect for possessions. According to the customs and traditions practiced by indigenous peoples in southern Mexico, however, the very idea of private land is immoral. All land, in the ethical sense, belongs to everyone, which explains why the plots used for farming are divided and re-divided each year in accord with the dictates of the village chief or consul. So which society is right? Should possession of a plot be determined by a deed or by the chief's voice? According to a culturalist ethics, either one. It just depends on where you happen to be when the decision gets made. Wherever you are, if you decide in accordance with local customs and traditions, you're right.

Moving this over to the issue of harassment, the answer to the question "What's an unwelcome sexual advance?" isn't answered by recourse to specific dos and don'ts; it's simply the common practice and expectations of those making up the larger culture where the business is located. If repeatedly making suggestive comments about how much better the day feels when the woman down the row is short-skirted counts as a hostile work environment in the United States, then it *is* a hostile one. If the same tone and words are accepted as perfectly normal and appropriate in Brazil, then they are appropriate. No further ethical discussion is required.

Departing from this origin, there are two main resolutions to sex problems coming up in international offices:

1. The "When in Rome..." solution (or local deference ethical strategy) accepts the basic culturalist argument that right and wrong is nothing more than the customs and habits of those forming a society. People joining that society (like Sergei Moskvin coming to America) can expect a kind of grace period while they figure things out, but they must ultimately come into line with local practices. Moskvin will be excused, in other words, for asking women to take off their shirts, but only for the first few days. Expecting others to adapt to local customs is a reasonable way to manage intercultural ethical conflicts, and it works well for those receiving workers from other places. The catch is that the same logic works the other way. If an American multinational media company expands into the Russian market, then the local partners are going to be standing on solid ground when they begin asking for a level of exposure—female, male, both, or whatever—that doesn't sit well in the United States. In this kind of situation, employees sent abroad will naturally be uneasy about expectations. Probably some will embrace the change with a sense of adventure while others will recoil, but regardless of the attitude, everyone will probably find themselves in at least a few uncomfortable situations. As for the larger organization trying to hold a business together while spanning various nations and cultures, this is an incurable difficulty with simply accepting local ethics. The resulting ethical schizophrenia—rules within an organization switching as fast as employees are assigned to one or another country—makes setting a specific and coherent corporate culture in the area of sex almost impossible.

2. The multicultural respect ethical strategy also accepts the basic culturalist argument that right and wrong are defined mainly by the customs and habits of those forming a society. In this case, however, people moving to other places aren't expected to adapt. Those others are expected to accept. When, for example, people from other places come to America, basic respect for the autonomous value and dignity of their customs and habits demands that their behavior be tolerated, even if it gives offense to many locals. In the case of Sergei Moskvin, people in the office will just have to deal with the fact that for him there's not a big difference between exposing one's face to the camera and one's chest.

This respectful response to intercultural ethical conflict is reasonable, even laudable for its tolerance of diversity. The problem, however, underlying the "When in Rome..." strategy continues within a context of multicultural respect: it leaves organizations in an impossible situation when it comes to formalizing policies and procedures governing all those working in all the international offices.

Office Sex from a Traditional Perspective

Most traditional ethical theories approach the multicultural workplace more objectively. They insist that the moral rules of right and wrong transcend cultural diversity, and so open the way to claiming that certain behaviors are acceptable, and others unacceptable, no matter where the workplace happens to be or what countries the employees call home. The Russian news producer Sergei Moskvin plays by the same rules as the Ohio anchorwoman Sharon Reed, and that goes whether they're in Russia, Ohio, or anywhere else.

The traditional approaches—especially duty theory and rights-based thought—work together fairly well in the areas of sexual innuendo, advances, and harassment: the actions they recommend can be construed to more or less fall in line with standard practices in America and Europe (which, not surprisingly, are also centers of the theories' historical development and interpretation). That clears the way to affirming that those who come to the United States to work will need to adapt their behavior dealing with sex in the office to something resembling the codes of conduct normally in place here. More, organizations opening offices overseas will also implement those codes because the codes' justification rests on arguments that function independently of local habits.

One clear advantage to this solution to questions about sexual advances in the office is that it allows more or less uniform regulations for conduct, no matter who happens to be working, or where they happen to be. The main problem, however, with this solution is that it breeds accusations of insensitivity to other cultures and customs. More broadly,

American attitudes about sex in the workplace—when they're forced on those who work for American multinationals in other countries—lead to charges of cultural imperialism.

In the economic world, cultural imperialism, which fits besides terms like the *ugly American* and *globalization*, is the charge that US companies are imposing attitudes on local populations, imposing on people with different histories and customs who value and want to preserve their different ways of being—and getting—together.

KEY TAKEAWAYS

- Sexual harassment occurs when unwelcome sexual advances or conduct creates a hostile work environment.
- Because sexual language is frequently suggestive more than explicit, and because diverse individuals relate to their own sexuality in distinct ways, it's very difficult to form explicit rules defining sexual harassment.
- Sexual behavior is culturally diverse, leading to problems in workplaces with international participants.

REVIEW QUESTIONS

1. In your own words, what is sexual harassment?
2. Sketch two ethical arguments against sex harassment in the workplace.
3. Why might cultural diversity create sexual conflicts in an office?
4. What is the *multicultural respect* response to sexual tensions in an international office?
5. Why might a multinational corporation's policy dealing with sexual issues seem sensible in the United States but be viewed with hatred by employees in overseas offices?

[1] "Facts about Sexual Harassment," U.S. Equal Employment Opportunity Commission, last modified June 27, 2002, accessed July 1, 2011, http://www.eeoc.gov/facts/fs-sex.html.
[2] "Facts about Sexual Harassment," U.S. Equal Employment Opportunity Commission, last modified June 27, 2002, accessed July 1, 2011, http://www.eeoc.gov/facts/fs-sex.html.
[3] Jennifer Zimbroff, "Cultural Differences in Perceptions of and Responses to Sexual Harassment," *Duke Journal of Gender Law and Policy* (2007): 1311, accessed June 1, 2011,http://www.law.duke.edu/shell/cite.pl?14+Duke+J.+Gender+L.+& + Pol%27y+1311; E. R DeSouza and C. S. Hutz, "Reactions to Refusals of Sexual Advances among U.S. and Brazilian Men and Women," *Sex Roles* 34, nos. 7–8 (1996): 549–65.
[4] Eros R. DeSouza, "Gender Differences in the Interpretation of Social-Sexual Behavior: A Cross-Cultural Perspective on Sexual Harassment," *Journal of Cross-Cultural Psychology*, September 1, 1997.

11.3 Drugged
LEARNING OBJECTIVES

1. Define workplace drugs.
2. Review recent history of social attitudes toward drugs.
3. Consider problems caused by drugs at work and the reasons for their use.
4. Discuss the ethics of drug testing.

Rehab

Amy Winehouse's chart-topping, Grammy-winning song "Rehab" is an old-fashioned piece of rock-and-roll defiance:

> *They tried to make me go to rehab*
> *I said no, no, no*
> *I ain't got the time*
> *I won't go, go, go* [1]

It's also a statement about drugs in the workplace, and a very impacting one when the workplace is a concert hall and the worker standing up in front singing is collapsing under the weight of abuse, falling out of her clothes, tripping across the stage, forgetting the lyrics. Winehouse's picture is all over the Internet with cocaine dabbing her nose. She's been filmed inhaling crack. When people notice that her arms are laced with cuts, she explains that she knives herself during withdrawals as a distraction from the aching need for another drink or shot or whatever. Still, she sings that she's not going to "go, go, go," and everyone out in the crowd sings it right along with her.

Where's the line? Does it get crossed when she finally gets to the point where she can't walk out on stage? Or will the line get drawn when people stop paying money to watch her sing and the profits dry up? Or maybe there is no line, maybe she means what she sings and there won't be any stopping. And no matter where the line is, who decides? Is it her equally distraught, on-and-off husband? Her manager, her record label, her fans? No one at all except Amy Winehouse?

Sooner or later her story is going to end badly, but the questions will keep getting asked because drugs lace so deeply through professional lives. In most offices the boost comes from coffee, Red Bull, anti-depression pills, or the prescription amphetamine Ritalin (which, to complete the ladder, is used to cut cocaine). Then there are the relaxers, the cigarettes, the gin tonic, the Valium. In between, there's a broad and colorful spectrum of chemicals that help people go to work, do their work, and get away from work. Some athletes—or just guys wanting to fill out a suit—are using steroids. Others respond to the stress of the workday with high blood pressure or similar, and there are drugs for that too.

The ethics of drugs at work starts with a straightforward question, and then divides into two areas of debate. The question is "What counts as a drug?" The two areas of debate are the following:

1. What should happen when a worker wants to use drugs or alcohol, and that goes against an employer's policy and wishes?
2. What should happen when the organization doesn't intervene in a worker's drug use, or actually encourages it because the organization benefits from the use?

What Is a Drug?

The technical definition of a drug is a substance affecting the structure or function of the body or of one's consciousness. When discussed in business ethics, only a slice of the broad category is applicable. The subject here isn't diabetes medications and similar doctor-prescribed substances; the dosing under consideration is recreational drugs and those substances taken to improve performance temporarily, but that don't seem medically necessary and that may not be medically desirable, especially because they cause negative effects further down the line. Steroids are an easy example.

In the area of business ethics and drugs, it can be stated that, loosely, a drug means a substance providing a temporary and artificially desirable state, one followed by a comedown or a reversal to a level below the original condition. Under this definition, the reason a Red Bull is a drug and, say, taking a nap isn't is that while both provide some good working hours, Red Bull eventually leaves you even more tired than when you started. It comes with a letdown not affecting those who choose a nap. Something similar, but over a longer term, happens to those who use cigarettes to tighten their concentration. For many, nicotine works; it helps get work done. Later, however, when you try to kick the habit, it'll be hard to concentrate on anything at all for months. What, finally, makes a drug a drug is that in essence it's something that lets you borrow against the future.

A Brief History of Drugs (with Lessons That Could Be Applied to Sex)

One warning should be inserted before any ethical consideration of drugs, sex, and similar themes in the workplace: both the legal rules as well as social attitudes are subject to change over time. The fact that rules *can* change doesn't mean they will or should, but simple prudence demands that anyone trying to form a justifiable position in any particular ethical situation should be aware of how significantly society's broad view of the subject can transform in relatively short periods.

The way we think about almost everything evolves, but the case of attitudes toward alcohol, marijuana, and similar substances go beyond gradual developing: they can turn so abruptly that they fall into the category of social paradigm shifts. The word paradigm (from the Greek word *paradeigma*) could be translated as "pattern." Think of it as a pattern of thought or a pattern of processing things. More than an attitude, a paradigm is a worldview, an almost instinctual way of seeing and understanding experience. A paradigm shift is a change in the way we perceive things as we try to understand them.

As an abstract example, you've seen three-dimensional boxes drawn on paper with just a set of twelve lines. You look, and one face seems to be in front and the other behind. But when you blink, the box seems to have shifted and reversed: now the front is the back and the back is front. Called a *Necker Cube*, this experience of certain things in the world that make perfect sense even when seen in opposed ways is analogous to a social paradigm shift. In both cases, something is out there, and all of a sudden we see it in an entirely different but equally true way. Another, more human example, of a paradigmatic shift has been lived by all of us when as boys and girls we passed through puberty. Suddenly, and almost inexplicably, the way most of us saw members of the opposite sex was different. As it happens, this adolescent shift is based on biological transformations, but the cause can be anything. What's important is that fundamental views modify very quickly, and over the course of the 1980s in America, fundamental views about drugs in the workplace modified significantly and fast.

In 1981, an American military jet crashed while trying to land on the USS Nimitz, an aircraft carrier. Numerous crew members were killed. Subsequent tests showed some were high on marijuana. That worrisome result—along with the suspicion that drugs may have contributed to the accident—provoked testing of soldiers across the armed services. Positive results were startlingly high. Quickly, zero-tolerance policies were imposed within the military. Soon, the restrictions spread to the civilian side of the federal government. By 1988, the Drug-Free Workplace Act had been promulgated; it required that most companies doing business with the government certify that they maintained a drug-free workplace. More, federal contractors were asked to publish a policy explicitly prohibiting the use and distribution of unlawful drugs at work, and also institute a drug awareness program emphasizing the potential dangers of substance abuse. Soon, even businesses not engaged with the government were customarily advertising themselves as drug-free workplaces.

None of this seems remarkable now, but it would have seemed so in 1976 when then-presidential candidate Jimmy Carter campaigned in favor of decriminalizing marijuana use and his leading expert on illicit drugs believed that cocaine wasn't a serious public health threat. At the time, Dr. Robert DuPont was head of the National Institute of Drug Abuse, and he too supported marijuana decriminalization (though he later changed his mind after learning that thirteen-year-olds in suburban neighborhoods like his own were passing around joints at their birthday parties). While tolerance dominated political attitudes toward drugs, the media was busy glamorizing them, especially cocaine. A widely read article informed Americans that "among hostesses in the smart sets of Los Angeles and New York, a little cocaine, like Dom Perignon and Beluga caviar, is now *de rigueur* at dinners. Some party givers pass it around along with the canapés on silver trays…the user experiences a feeling of potency, of confidence, of energy." [2]

It seems like that must have been a long time ago. It's not, though—only a few decades. And there's no reason to believe we won't see similar shifting in the coming years; we just don't know what will change and which way it'll go. Regardless, the lesson for business ethics is simple and applies whether the subject is drugs or sexual advances or whatever in the workplace. It's that the broadly accepted rules and social attitudes should be handled—and relied on—with care.

What's Wrong with Drugs at Work?

The most commonly discussed issue in the area of drugs and work involves the organization's interest in promoting and enforcing a drug-free workplace. Of course space is made for coffee. It's true that the drink can leave people irritable and aggressive, but the effects are mild and since almost everyone uses it, there's not much to do by way of dissuasion anyway. And pushing into the slightly stronger stuff, most organizations accept the occasional wine and beer shindig in the office corridors on Friday afternoons to loosen the atmosphere a bit. For the most part, however, companies want their workers straight for two reasons: productivity and safety.

A study published in the *Journal of the American Medical Association* (*JAMA*) asserted that postal workers testing positive for illegal drugs (typically marijuana and similar) were significantly more likely to be fired, injured, disciplined, or

absent than their non-using peers. [3] If that study accurately represents reality, then companies stand on firm ground when arguing that because they have a right to expect a full day's good work for a full day's pay, they can demand that employees be drug free. If they're not, the argument goes, the statistics indicate that they're less productive. And if they're absent, then their coworkers who count on them being there may end up being less productive also. Drug use, finally, becomes an ethical breach of the duty to fidelity. It violates the responsibility employees have to honor their commitments to employers.

Moving in a slightly different direction, all public companies hold responsibilities to their shareholders. They include, in most cases, the obligation to make a profit—and to make as large a profit as possible within the parameters of normal business practice. That obligation may well go unfulfilled, however, if a workplace is not drug free. Because companies frequently pay health insurance premiums for their employees, workplace injuries climbing in number and severity resulting from drug use ultimately add to the firm's operating costs. And these subtract from the annual profit.

The stakes rise as occupations become more prone to accidents affecting those *outside* the company or organization. While a walking mailman probably can't do too much damage to others no matter how many swigs he takes from his hip flask, a crane operator, a school bus driver, an airplane pilot, a technician at a nuclear power plant, all these kinds of posts demand that employers take aggressive steps to ensure workers are well suited to carry out their duties. If they're impaired and make mistakes, there's no telling who or how many may suffer. What's certain is that lawyers will chase to the scene of any accident fitting those characteristics. As the punitive lawsuits pile up, the catastrophic accident caused by drug use will probably turn out to be a financial disaster for the company. It will also be an ethical nightmare. Assuming the drug use causing the accident was preventable—a more scrupulous and sternly applied policy would've cleaned out the workplace and so avoided the accident—all the major ethical theories produce condemnation:

- The duty to avoid harming others is broken.
- The utilitarian imperative to serve the general welfare is breached.
- The right to individual freedom of the accident's victims gets jeopardized or destroyed.

Summarizing, the following concerns lead to policies within most organizations—as well as concrete actions—aiming to control how employees treat their mind and bodies:

- Drugged employees can be less productive.

- Employees using drugs can cause *others* to be less productive.
- Medical insurance and other costs elevate as drug use rises.
- Risks to third parties increase with drug use.

Against these powerful arguments in favor of limiting or eliminating drugs in the workplace, individuals naturally chafe at demands made by their employer that go beyond specific job tasks. Many of them figure that they're paid to do a job, and as long as they're doing it, the boss ought to leave them alone. While it's clear that the Amy Winehouse situation is an extreme one, it's also quite typical in terms of its basic structure. On one side, the people writing her paycheck want her getting to the workplace on time and then performing well. They want her remembering the lyrics and they'd prefer that she not fall off the stage. She, on the other hand, wants to enjoy her leisure time as she pleases, and she'd prefer that others just leave her to do her work in the way she sees fit.

Drug Tests: Actions by the Organization to Stop Drug Use

From the management's side, a number of actions may be taken to diminish drug use in the workplace. Most are noncontroversial. Just like cigarette boxes come with dire warnings, so too company policy handbooks and employee bulletin boards are used to underline the potentially negative effects of use and abuse. More positively, drug-free lifestyles may be encouraged through an organizational culture stressing healthy choices. Special bonuses may be given to those who quit smoking (or certain privileges may be denied to those who don't). Possibly, a gym membership will be included with a standard contract. Biking to work may be encouraged (the advertising agency Crispin Porter Bogusky has a bike repair shop right in its offices). More incentives could be added but, in general, steps organizations take to encourage physically healthy lives receive little resistance and do, at least indirectly, discourage substance abuse.

With increasing frequency, intrusive steps are also being taken to separate drugs from work. Drugs tests are the most notable. Over the course of the last decade, scientific advances have made these probes easier to administer and less expensive to apply. That, combined with hardening attitudes about drugs in society and at work, has led to increasingly frequent testing. The checks are applied to filter new employees and also (though less frequently) to guarantee the condition of those already on the payroll.

This testing is a controversial practice both legally and ethically. There *is* agreement on one point: no one can be forced to take a drug test. At least with respect to work-related activities (as opposed to police-related events including drunk driving), any employee is always free to say no, to quit, and leave. Within the business world, all drug testing must be consensual. Informed consent is an employee agreeing to undergo a drug test (or a series of them, or at least be open to possible testing) only after fully understanding the reason the organization is asking for the test, what is being tested for, and knowing—fully—the extent to which he or she may refuse. Beyond simply having information, informed consent also implies deliberation. In a complicated situation, few are able to make good decisions instantly; typically, sleeping on a question or something similar is necessary for an individual to feel as though he or she may consent to a test in a confident and informed way. Finally, consent must be voluntary in the sense that those agreeing to it understand what pressures are operating to encourage one or another decision. Naturally, people are going to feel a variety of tugs and pulls (from peers, from a union or civil rights organization, from management) to make a certain decision. For the decisions to be voluntary, those pressures must be understood and accounted for. Basically, informed consent means those subjected to the test can't be railroaded.

In some fields, refusal to submit may lead to termination (commercial airline pilot). In others where an employer has no health-connected reason to seek a test, and no reason to suspect that drug use or abuse is occurring, the employee should know that refusal can be an option, both legally and ethically.

Legality and Types of Drug Tests

Legally, the question about the employee's right to say no to test is a moving target. Currently, the federal government and most states allow drug screening as part of the hiring process and generally allow tests on existing employees as a condition for continued employment *if* there's reasonable ground for suspicion of use. Grounds for suspicion include slurring words, acting disoriented, seeming unfocused, and similar. Most college students have a pretty good idea. Some states, including Minnesota, allow tests to be performed on random employees even without cause for suspicion. In this case, advance notice is required of the random test process.

As for the kinds of tests that are applied, urine is common. Obviously, bosses sniffing alcohol on the breath is a functioning, though unscientific, check. Saliva can be analyzed. Because traces of drugs remain detectable in hair for much longer than urine (about three months versus three days) and because it's easy to clip a few strands, this type of drug test is not uncommon.

Ethics of Drug Tests

Ethically, justifications for drug tests rest on the legitimate reasons organizations have for wanting to weed out users from the workforce: drugged employees can be less productive, and cause others to be less productive, and use may raise operating costs as well as pose risks to third parties. The linchpin argument is that these concerns give organizations a right—and also a responsibility—to do all they can to create drug-free workplaces. Tests serve that obligation. Because they're a reasonable way to keep worker performance up, operating costs down, and everyone as safe as possible, employers have a responsibility to apply them.

Critics of drug testing also muster strong arguments. Most rest on convictions relating to individual dignity and rights. Putting their argument into the largest perspective, it's simply a fact that if, as a society, we decided to rid ourselves of all cocaine use, we could do that in a week. We'd only need to legislate that every single citizen would visit a government office every single morning and pee in a cup. Positive results would trigger an automatic jail sentence. Cocaine—along with its accompanying problems—would disappear in little more time than it takes to broadcast a just-say-no TV ad.

No one advocates this truly zero-tolerance enforcement strategy, however. The central reason no one proposes total testing is that basic convictions concerning human rights provide two direct forms of protection. First, our intrinsic dignity as individuals guarantees some measure of privacy. Privacy is the right to be left alone by others, to conceal ourselves from their prying eyes. What we do inside our own homes and with our own time is our—and no one else's—business.

This right to a dignified space for me stands on its own, but also extends as the right to define my own unique identity for myself. If everything we think and do is seen by others (imagine your life filmed and broadcast on TV twenty-four hours a day), then we no longer have a self. All our energy and time would get devoted to presenting an image and appearance for others. Privacy is the space each of us needs to create ourselves as who we are. Drug testing finally, insofar as it intrudes on our private reality, also intrudes on the right each of us has to be ourselves.

The right to privacy can be construed slightly differently in terms of *humiliation* and *exposure*. Being forced to pee in a cup is embarrassing; it's being treated like a farm animal. On this front, the right to privacy is the guarantee that certain private things like that won't intersect with anyone else unless we make that decision ourselves. The other articulation,

exposure, is especially pertinent today. In an electronic world, personal information about ourselves, once it's tapped into a computer, can end up anywhere at any time. In the end, who knows who's going to get their hands on our lab results? Or when? Because it could be anyone into the indefinite future, there's an element of invasive exposure in many drug-testing procedures.

The same fundamental rights that protect privacy also guarantee freedom—the right to pursue our own happiness in the ways we as individuals determine. Of course this right gets suspended the second our drug use ruins *someone else's* freedom by injuring them in a car wreck, but until then, drug tests are going to appear as a violation of fundamental liberty. According to this argument, the *reason* we're out in the economic world to begin with, the reason we're going to work and earning money, is precisely to allow us to pursue our happiness in the ways we choose (by providing shelter, some drinks on Friday night, the occasional gift for the ones we love, opportunities for our children, and similar). If, finally, the reason we go to work is to *have and express our freedom*, and the first thing we do when we get to work is accept the imposition of a drug test designed to find out exactly what we were smoking Friday night, then the entire point of going to work in the first place is undermined.

Besides the privacy and freedom arguments against drug testing, there's also a slippery slope concern. A slippery slope is the idea that once you start doing something, it'll be difficult to stop doing more and more of it. Start with the proposal that random drug testing will be performed in a workplace once a month on one employee, and the sample will be tested only for some hard drug, say, heroin. For most people in most offices, that doesn't sound very threatening, and even though it may be a violation of basic rights, some will be tempted to simply accept the measure because, really, it's not that big a deal, not worth a fight. So the program is implemented. A few months later, the proposal comes down to test not one, but *two* employees every month. Again, not a big deal and no one objects. Then the test gets expanded to check for cocaine. You see where this is going. The process repeats and, in the end, everyone's getting tested all the time for everything. The slippery slope argument against drug testing in the workplace is that individual liberties are so important that they must be entirely protected from the very beginning. Stated slightly differently, rights can't be done halfway. You either have or protect them, or you don't. If that's persuasive, then *everyone* should band together against drug testing, even those who've never had a drink or smoke in their lives.

A fourth argument against drug testing is about half ethical, half technical. It concerns drug test reliability. Even top-notch manufacturers concede that their products produce false positives in some very infrequent cases. A 1 percent error rate seems, on the face of it, acceptable, but if you personally happen to be that 1 percent, your perspective may change. Of course, to a certain extent this objection can be answered by technical advances: if a 1 percent error rate is too high, the product can be improved and now it's 0.1 percent or 0.01 percent. Probably, however, there'll always be *some* possibility of error, and as long as there is, the argument remains that the ethical cost of misidentifying a clean worker as a user outweighs the benefits accrued from correctly identifying those who really are using.

Finally, in the face of the organization's justifiable desire to impose drug tests, the arguments against accepting testing are:

- The right to privacy
- The right to freedom
- Slippery slope concerns
- Imperfect testing

KEY TAKEAWAYS

- In the workplace, the term drugs may be used to denote a substance affecting the mind or body in a temporary and artificially positive way.
- Social attitudes toward drugs in the workplace have altered very rapidly over the previous decades and may (or may not) continue to change.
- Drug use at work can enhance performance.
- Drug use at work can lead to less productive employees, higher costs of doing business, and risks to third parties.
- Drug testing at work pits the employer's legitimate interest in maximizing worker performance against individual rights to privacy and freedom.

REVIEW QUESTIONS

1. What is a social paradigm shift?
2. What are some legal substances that count as a drug at work? What are some illegal ones?
3. What are some reasons an employee may want to use drugs at work?
4. Justify in ethical terms the application of drug tests to employees of the aircraft maker Boeing.
5. Describe two distinct reasons why someone who has never used a drug in his or her life might refuse a test at

work. Convert those reasons into well-founded ethical arguments.

[1] Amy Winehouse, "Rehab," *Back to Black* (Island Records, 2010), audio CD.
[2] "Thirty Years of America's Drug War: A Chronology," PBS, Frontline, accessed June 1,
2011, http://www.pbs.org/wgbh/pages/frontline/shows/drugs/cron/.
[3] Craig Zwerling, James Ryan, and Endel John Orav, "The Efficacy of Pre-employment Drug Screening for Marijuana and Cocaine in Predicting Employment Outcome," *Journal of the American Medical Association* 264, no. 20 (1990): 2639–643, doi:10.1001/jama.1990.03450200047029. Study quoted in William Shaw, *Moral Issues in Business*, 10th ed. (Belmont: Thomson Higher Education, 2007), 335.

11.4 The Organization Wants You to Use Drugs?
LEARNING OBJECTIVE

1. Examine the ethics of organizations facilitating drug use by employees.

When Drugs and the Workplace Mix

The conflict between organizations demanding drug-free workplaces (and testing to be sure they get them) and individual rights to privacy and freedom center most discussions of drugs at work. There's another area of debate, however. What happens when your employer *wants* you to use drugs?

Take the case of Amy Winehouse. Everyone interested in music—and many who aren't—know all about her. Every time she gets photographed inhaling something that looks illegal or gets videoed tripping out of a party with her dress slipping down her chest, the images, the sound, and the story race across TV channels and the social web and she's back in circulation. People talk, remember her songs, ask if she's got anything new coming out, and wonder when she'll bring her notorious road show to their town. Anyone who didn't know better would be tempted to suspect that the whole thing was fake, a giant scam dreamed up by a genius publicist to get Winehouse all the free attention today's connected world can generate.

Pop stars tend to have short shelf lives and long lists of people making money off their fame. Those on the periphery of Winehouse's success—her managers and promoters and publicists and lawyers and accountants—all know that she probably won't be providing their income for long, and it's in their financial interest to maximize what she can give while she still can. Will her body and life suffer from her cocaine use? Yes, but most of that damage probably won't register until after the flow of money she's producing has slowed to a trickle. Given that reality, her corporate sponsors have little professional reason to want to intervene in her life to help her slow down the intake. Just the opposite, actually.

Something similar occurs in the world of professional sports. Anyone who's watched professional football or soccer players has witnessed this scene: the athlete down and writhing on the field, clutching frantically at a knee or ankle. Teammates slink away, concerned about their companion but also thanking God it wasn't them. Trainers hurry onto the field. Commercials interrupt the drama. TV returns and the game goes on. Then, five minutes later, he's back like nothing happened. Commentators approvingly acknowledge the guy's toughness. Advertisers are relieved because viewers stay fixed to the screen. The team owners in their box are happy to be getting their money's worth from their employees. For every one of them, drugs and the workplace are an excellent mix.

The Ethics of Drugging Employees

There are two broad categories of organizationally sanctioned employee drug abuse. The first is the employee doing it, and managers don't get in their way. The second category belongs to those organizations actively encouraging drug use. It goes without saying that the next higher degree of involvement: sneaking drugs into an employee's drink or diet is both illegal (a form of assault) and an unethical breach of individual privacy and freedom rights.

Complicit organizations know employees are using drugs and don't intervene—they may suspend drug testing or refuse to initiate it—because the use suits the organization's interest. This could be the football coach who just doesn't want to know how his lineman suddenly exploded with muscle over the summer. Or the complicity could be for the young lawyer in the firm who works to all hours and always seems peppy and alert. One day someone may notice a pill case dropping out of her purse, but no one's going to ask any questions as long as she keeps cranking out those billable hours.

Should questions be asked? One answer is simply "No." The football player and lawyer are free individuals pursuing their own welfare as they see fit and as they're free to do. They're not hurting anyone else along the way and should be left alone. This argument, based on the values of individual rights and freedom, is very strong.

Things become more complicated, however, in a case like Amy Winehouse's, one where she's clearly being damaged by her abuse. The root question is straightforward: when should I go out of my way—or perhaps even harm my own interests—to help out someone else? If I'm Winehouse's manager, and I'm making money off her publicity-grabbing drug episodes, at what point do I need to say the money isn't worth it, and my human responsibility for the well-being of those around me requires that I try to do something (like send her to rehab)? This scenario involves Samaritanism, which itself makes up an entire area of ethical study.

Samaritanism—taken from the biblical parable of the Good Samaritan—is the ethical responsibility to step in and help others. Most duty theorists contend that we have an unavoidable responsibility to help others in need as long as the cost to ourselves is not disproportionately burdensome and as long as there's some possibility of actually aiding. Taking a simple example, a person who can't swim has no responsibility to jump in after a drowning man, but Michael Phelps would have an obligation to get in the water unless the flow was so violent and fast that even he would be powerless to help. As for the manager faced with a self-destructing client, it's hard to see—from this ethical perspective—what could erase his obligation to help Winehouse clean up since the only thing he has to lose is money.

The Ethics of Drugging Employees: Enabling Organizations

Enabling organizations actively encourage or at least facilitate drug use by employees because it serves their interest. Of course almost *all* organizations engage in this facilitating to some small extent. The New Year's office party where drinks are free and free-flowing is, at bottom, a drug event where alcohol hopefully washes away some of the resentments and angers accumulated over the preceding twelve months.

More aggressively, many occupations (especially those directly involving selling) require employees to be cool—and *look* cool—under pressure. This can be difficult. A story from the *Atlantic* magazine discusses beta-blockers, which are essentially blood-pressure medications that coincidentally reduce the outward appearance of nervousness: they help you avoid the sweat beading on the forehead, trembling hands, and dry mouth. [1] As the story notes, beta-blockers aren't nearly as potent or dangerous as the doping of North Korean Olympic athletes, but they're not a harmless over-the-counter medication either.

Beta-blockers carry real risks. Even granting the risk, though, it's not hard to imagine that more than one supervisor has found a way to get the *Atlantic* magazine story into the e-mail of an employee who's had a history of tightening up at key moments. In fact, the business consultant Keith Ferrazzi once made the recommendation on his web page, but then withdrew it after receiving complaints: "I originally included a reader's recommendation of the beta blocker Propranolol in this list of public speaking tips, but have removed it after taking to heart the concern of many KF.com readers." [2]

Somewhat more ominously, there's the infamous case of the Studio 54 busboys at the height of the club's popularity. Blonde (frequently) and naked (usually) except for tight spandex shorts, they were plied with drugs to increase their energy level and commitment to customer service in all imaginary ways. The busboys, it must be noted, were more than willing participants, but the fact that everyone agreed doesn't necessarily make the scene ethical. One useful tool for evaluating this exuberant but also troubling situation is the already developed notion of informed consent. In order for the case to be made that drugging willing employees is acceptable, it will help to fulfill the following requirements:

- Employees must fully understand *what* they're being given, as well as the risks and benefits.

- Employees must fully understand *why* the drugs are being provided.

- Employees must be given a clear indication of what acceptance or rejection means for their career.

- Employees must be allowed a *deliberative* decision—the option should be offered for consideration, not thrown at them for a sudden yes-no answer.

The fact that an employee makes an informed decision to use performance-enhancing drugs at work doesn't rinse an enabling employer of all ethical responsibility. Business is just like any other aspect of life in the sense that employers, like everyone else, have a duty of Samaritanism or beneficence— that is, a responsibility to look out for the long-term welfare of others so long as their own welfare isn't significantly affected. Further, the responsibility to respect the humanity of others and not use them as a simple tool in our schemes (to see them as ends and not means) translates as a demand that organizations advocating internal drug use clarify what their own motives are. Finally, if the drugs are illegal, the possibility that people will end up in jail needs to be factored into consideration.

Going beyond the ethical discussion involving only employer and employee, there are a number of broader and difficult questions that could be pressed, especially by proponents of utilitarian theory. If right and wrong is ultimately defined by the general public welfare, it may be difficult to justify drugs in the workplace even if employer and employee wholeheartedly agree to use them. What happens, for example, at *other* workplaces? In the highly competitive field of professional sports, it's clear that when one team starts using some substance, others will have to join in or get beaten on the playing field. In other occupations the need to imitate

to succeed may not be so immediate, but there still may be an undertow. If Amy Winehouse is eating up all the free publicity in the music business with her drug-fueled exploits, aren't other musicians going to feel pressured to follow along? If a sales team at Smith's Tires is using beta-blockers and winning deals, aren't the sellers at Jones' Tires going to start feeling the need to swallow some pills? If the effects, finally, of drug use in the workplace go beyond that particular spot, then the effects on those outsiders need to be accounted for in order for a final decision to be well justified.

KEY TAKEAWAYS

- In some cases employee drug use may serve the organization's interests.

- Organizations may be complicit with or enabling of employee drug use.

REVIEW QUESTIONS

1. Can you provide your own example from the business world of an organization that is complicit with respect to employee drug use?
2. Can you provide your own example from the business world of an organization that is enabling with respect to employee drug use?
3. Why might Samaritanism diminish workplace pressure on employees to use drugs?
4. What are the requirements for informed consent when it comes to employees accepting the organization's invitation to use drugs?

[1] Carl Elliott, "In Defense of the Beta Blocker," *Atlantic*, August 2008, accessed June 1, 2011, http://www.theatlantic.com/magazine/archive/2008/08/in-defense-of- the-beta-blocker/6961/.
[2] Keith Ferrazzi, "10 Tips to Banish Your Public Speaking Fear for Good," *Keith Ferrazzi: Business is Human. Relationships Power Growth* (blog), August 26, 2009, accessed June 1, 2011, http://www.keithferrazzi.com/personal-branding/10-tips-to-banish-your-public-speaking-fear-for-good/.

11.5 Case Studies

Holly Madison for PETA

PETA (People for the Ethical Treatment of Animals) is an animal rights organization. According to their website, "PETA focuses its attention on the four areas in which the largest numbers of animals suffer the most intensely for the longest periods of time: on factory farms, in the clothing trade, in laboratories, and in the entertainment industry." [1] Both an organization and a cause, PETA depends on public attention and donations. Attention is necessary because raising consciousness about animal suffering is more or less a prerequisite to fighting against it. Nearly all companies causing animal suffering as part of their daily business struggle mightily to hide it from their consumers: what's not seen, the reasoning goes, isn't a problem. PETA wants cruel animal treatment to be seen.

Donations are also necessary because PETA is a nonprofit. Many people give cash, but some give their time and themselves. Celebrities can be especially helpful given their ability to generate interest and grab attention in a noisy world. One celebrity participant is the Hollywood actress Alicia Silverstone. In August of 2010, she was featured in a video on PETA's home page. Here's the accompanying text: "Sexy Hollywood star Alicia Silverstone bares all in PETA's first ever naked veggie testimonial, shot by acclaimed director Dave Meyers." [2]

Much of the video is shot in slow motion. Silverstone pulls herself out of a swimming pool, leans into the camera, holds it with her smoky eyes, and talks about the advantages of being a vegetarian. No clothes are visible. [3]

QUESTIONS

1. Alicia Silverstone praises the virtues of vegetarianism nude. Do you believe this is an example of product sincerity—that is, of openness and honesty about what's being sold?
○ What is the product here?
○ What elements of its presentation might seem insincere?
○ What elements of its presentation might seem sincere?
○ On balance, why do you believe the short video is sincere or insincere?

2. Almost certainly some people watched this video because they wanted to see a nude woman.
○ What is a prurient interest?
○ Make the case that this video promotes a prurient interest.
○ Assuming the video promotes a prurient interest, who should feel ethically ashamed of their action: Silverstone, PETA, the viewers, and some combination, someone else?

3. Silverstone could have filmed her monologue with her clothes on. Make the case that she should have because her decision to strip down to get attention results in her objectification.
○ In terms of the ethics of objectification, is there any difference between letting people see you in a video and on a nude beach? Why or why not?
○ PETA is a respected nonprofit organization (which isn't to say everyone agrees with their methods and cause,

only that most respect their dedication and altruism). Does that give them a license to objectify Silverstone? Why or why not?
○ Should this book's web page include a link to watch the video? Justify your answer in ethical terms.

Milan?

The question posted by Chourok C on the *Yahoo! Answers* web page begins this way:

> I just started this job 2 weeks ago as the CEO's personal assistant. He is married 3x and is a very charismatic man, the CEO of a self-built multi-million empire.
> After a few days, he suddenly asked me if he could take me out to diner in London, if I book my flights and hotel he will afterwards reimburse me. [4]

It was then, she relates, that she knew he wanted to sleep with her. In her words, she's "totally not interested, but wants to preserve the job by not rejecting him." So she made an excuse to get out of it and her post continues: "He then bothered me for hours about giving him good reasons why I couldn't go. Then he said OK, next week we will go to Milan! He is a very powerful man, and I just get nervous of him. But I really do not want to lose my job. What should I do?" [5]

QUESTIONS

1. What should she do? Justify in ethical terms.
2. Here's an answer posted by aznelepahnt5: "If he's good-looking, and there's a guarantee that you'll get better pay/promoted, then yes, you should do it." [6] Make the case that she's ethically free to follow the advice, to say yes to advance her career.
3. Make the case that Chourok C is *not* ethically free to go to Milan with him in order to advance her career, regardless of whether she's attracted to him or not.
4. The poster called Srta. Argentina answers, "He can't fire you because you rejected his sexual advances. You can sue him if he does. And you can file a sexual harassment claim against him." [7]
○ What is sexual harassment?
○ Sketch the harassment case against the CEO.
○ At what point in the chronology does the CEO's behavior cross from the ethically acceptable to the unacceptable? Why?
○ If the CEO hired you to form an ethical defense of his behavior, what would the case look like?
5. The poster called Skater Boi proposes an aggressive solution: "Get a voice recorder and record what he says. blackmail if he tries to fire you." [8] It sounds like the blackmail Skater Boi is proposing would entail

threatening a sex harassment lawsuit unless the boss gives her favorable treatment. Ethically, is there any difference between the boss threatening to fire her unless he gets what he wants and her threatening to turn him in unless she gets what she wants? If so, what is it? If not, why not?

International Affair

A newspaper account gives an idea of how different the world can be on the other side of national and cultural borders. The report tells of an unnamed executive, a twenty-two-year-old woman from St. Petersburg who found herself locked out of her office after resisting her boss's lewd advances. She took her case to court, "hoping to become only the third woman in Russia's history to bring a successful sexual harassment action against a male employer." [9]

She didn't make it.

According to the judge who ruled against her, everything had just been part of normal courtship and romance. He went so far as to affirm, "If we had no sexual harassment we'd have no children."

Sexual harassment—as the concept is defined and understood in America—is a customary part of life in the Russian workplace. In Russia, 40 percent of female professionals have had sex with their boss at least once, according to the story. Yes, that's 40 percent. Rounding out the picture, "Eighty per cent of those who participated in the survey said they did not believe it possible to win promotion without engaging in sexual relations with their male superiors. Women also report that it is common to be browbeaten into sex during job interviews." [10]

QUESTIONS

1. What is a culturalist ethics?

2. American multinationals are sometimes accused of being ugly and imperialist because they force members of other cultures to accept a system of values and rules that conflict with local practices, beliefs, and customs.
   o How could that accusation be described when an American company installs itself and its American policies for employee behavior in Russia? What basic values support the accusation?
   o An American laboring in a multinational corporation is assigned to open and manage an office in Russia, one that will be staffed by locals. How could a cultural ethics be transformed into an obligation that all those in the office more or less

adapt to the customary expectations of sex in the workplace brought from the States?

3. Back in America, direct and explicit demands of sex for work are uncommon. Sex *at* work, however, or at least sexiness and attractiveness, does seem to connect with job offers according to what economists Markus Mobius and Tanya Rosenblat found when they got together and performed a series of experiments discussed in their paper "Why Beauty Matters." Their conclusions about the power of attractiveness in the typical US workplace can be partially summarized by recounting one test. *Employers were divided into two groups and asked to hire a few job applicants. Some employers got a stack of CVs. Others got the CVs with a photo attached. The two groups then sorted out the applicants that they would like to hire. Comparing the results revealed a beauty premium. The fact that someone—whether it was a man or a woman—was physically attractive converted in the mind of employers into a job qualifier. That is, those men and women who were good looking were also judged as the most likely good workers, the kind you want to hire because they're capable and will do a good job. [11]* Is there a single ethical argument that could be set against the Russian custom of demanding sex to get a job, and the American custom of (to some extent) demanding sexiness to get a job?

Drugs and Drug Testing at Coke

John Pemberton came up with the original Coca-Cola recipe in 1886 and sold it out of Jacob's Pharmacy in Atlanta, Georgia. Advertised as a medicine, the drink was supposed to cure headaches and impotence.

Coke certainly delivered a rush. Brewed to contain a massive dose of cocaine, the drink was virtually guaranteed to succeed. Not surprisingly, many over-the-counter medicines started boosting their appeal by including the coca leaf extract. By the end of the century, however, public attitudes began turning. Rather than a cure, cocaine came to be seen as a ruinous addiction. Coke responded by radically cutting the cocaine in the drink, and by 1903 there was none, though the product still contained (and to this day contains) flavoring from the same coca leaf that earlier provided the drug. Finally, in 1914, the Harrison Act effectively outlawed the sale and distribution of cocaine both on its own and as an ingredient.

The other side of the original Coca-Cola jolt came from the kola nut, which added a slightly bitter taste to the drink, and lots of caffeine. ("Coca" corresponds with the coca leaf and cocaine, "Cola" with the kola nut and caffeine.) That additive also fell out of the public's favor, though not to the extent or depth of cocaine. In 1911, the US government sued to get the substance removed on the grounds of its pernicious effects, but failed (*United States v. Forty Barrels and Twenty Kegs of Coca-Cola*). The next year the Food and Drug Act defined caffeine as "habit forming" and "deleterious," and required that the substance be listed on Coke's label.

QUESTIONS

1. An accounting office manager stumbles on a warehouse full of the original, cocaine Coca-Cola.
   o Make the case that he has a responsibility to provide the bottles to his workers and encourage them to drink the liquid down. What benefits could the manager hope to receive? Why does the manager hold a professional responsibility to achieve those benefits?
   o Make the case that the manager has a responsibility to provide bottles of both the original (now illegal) formula and today's formula to staff members, and allow them to choose to drink either one, both, or neither.
   o Make the case that he has a responsibility to provide bottles of only today's formula to staff members, and allow them to drink it or not.
   o Make the case that, ethically, he should tolerate no Coca-Cola of any kind in the workplace.

2. In a web posting, mmafan, from Dayton, Ohio, writes about his experience working for the Coca-Cola Company: "We even had someone witness a merchandiser, on the clock, in uniform, and in a company vehicle, smoking a joint in a store parking lot. Not only did the union prevent Coke from terminating or disciplining him, they protected him from submitting to a drug test. So Coke had to just let it go. All the union did was protecting the lazy, the incompetent, and the screw-ups if you ask me." [12] In response, the union could mount a number of arguments to defend their decision to not let Coke administer a drug test. The most frequently cited ethical reasons to refuse drug tests are the following:
   o To protect the right to privacy
   o To protect the right to freedom
   o Because of slippery slope concerns
   o Because of imperfect testing

   Which of these kinds of arguments would best support the union's decision to protect the employee from a drug test? What would the argument look like?

3. Mmafan believes the union did nothing more than "protect the lazy, the incompetent, and the screw-ups." This complaint is actually the root of a powerful and thoughtful ethical argument in favor of drug testing

because drug-free workplaces maximize employee performance. Fill out the argument:
   o Whose obligations are served by drug tests?
   o What are those obligations?
   o Name an ethical theory that forcefully supports the use of drug testing in the workplace. What's the reasoning?

4. The Coca-Cola Company's history is laced with cocaine.
   o Given the fact that cocaine was a key ingredient in getting the Coca-Cola Company off the ground; does that organizations have any right to preclude the use of drugs in the workplace or anywhere else? Why or why not?
   o When Coke included coke, the substance was legal, and a respected medicine. Should that fact affect your answer to the previous question? Why or why not?

Acid Rock

Ultimate-Guitar.com is a guitar and rock site. One of its articles begins this way: "Of the many articles in Ultimate Guitar which deal with the history of musicians in this day of modern music, there is one participant who seems missing. The history of this participant is responsible for influencing a huge range of artists, possibly second to none." [13]

The participant is LSD. Without that, the column affirms, there'd be no Grateful Dead, Carlos Santana, Jimi Hendrix, Doors, Beatles, or Pink Floyd. At least not as we now know them. The article covers a lot of ground, but the basic point is that taking the illegal drug LSD helped these guys become great musicians. In the comments section, *many* people responded.

QUESTIONS

1. ATL_420 writes, "I don't know about y'all, but I have recorded music while tripping on acid. I was the most talented I have ever been on guitar during those hours." Assume you are the manager of ATL_420's band. Convince yourself that you have an ethical duty to make sure he's got all the LSD he needs when he's in the recording studio. Make the case, in other words, that you should be an enabler.

2. Strat_Monkey says, "I'm going to go with what I've heard from several drug-using musicians which is basically: Yes, Drugs CAN open your mind and allow you to make better music, BUT if you take too many you will f*ck yourself up good and proper. Moderation is the key here." How would someone who subscribes to a utilitarian ethics (the greatest good for the greatest

number should be sought) define the term *moderation*? What kinds of fears would this ethicist have about allowing Strat_Monkey to use LSD?

3. Ramco addresses this to the article's author:

If this article causes even one person to try LSD then you are a monster.

LSD is a fungus that degenerates the brain stem, and continues to remain in the brain for years, causing "acid flashbacks" at unexpected and inopportune times. With the exception of heroin, LSD has the worst long-term effects of any drug.

Also, LSD has given us some of the WORST music ever. There are plenty of drug-inspired songs that only appeal to those on drugs.

I am disappointed in UG for approving this article which is nothing but an advertisement for LSD, which is not only dangerous but also illegal.

Use two distinct ethical theories to develop two independent arguments that the article's author is a monster.

4. Assume that both sides of this argument have some hold on the truth. In some cases LSD really did help musicians produce excellent music, but the effects of LSD use are also extremely harmful. How do you decide where to draw the line? How much social harm are you willing to tolerate for some good music? Justify.

5. One way for music company executives to manage the fact that some of their acts use a lot of drugs is with complicity—that is, adopting a kind of "don't ask, don't tell" policy. Even though drug use wouldn't be encouraged, it wouldn't be tested for either. What are some of the ethical advantages to this approach? What are some of the disadvantages?

6. In the comments section of the Ultimate-Guitar.com article, kosarsosar adds this about a hallucinogenic drug: "It didn't do much for me, however it did make my girlfriend run around the house flapping her arms like a bird." Ethically, is there anything wrong with taking a drug that does that to you? If so, what? If not, why not?

[1] "Our Mission Statement," PETA (People for the Ethical Treatment of Animals), About, accessed June 1, 2011, http://www.peta.org/about/index.asp.

[2] PETA (People for the Ethical Treatment of Animals) home page, accessed June 1, 2011,http://www.peta.org. Screenshot of PETA homepage featuring Alicia Silverstone from Business Ethics Workshop, http://businessethicsworkshop.com/Chapter_11/peta.html.

[3] "I am an Actor and I am a Vegetarian: Now Featuring Alicia Silverstone," PETA (People for the Ethical Treatment of Animals), Vegetarian Testimonials, accessed June 1,

2011,http://veggietestimonial.peta.org/psa.aspx?CID=8ce2420c-021c-49bc-91c5-b02a8775e2a2.

[4] Chourok C, "My boss wants to sleep with me?," *Yahoo! Answers,* accessed June 1, 2011,http://answers.yahoo.com/question/index?qid=20090419030102AAbYEDf.

[5] Chourok C, "My boss wants to sleep with me?," *Yahoo! Answers,* accessed June 1, 2011,http://answers.yahoo.com/question/index?qid=20090419030102AAbYEDf.

[6] aznelephant5, comment on Chourok C, "My boss wants to sleep with me?," *Yahoo! Answers,* accessed June 1, 2011, http://answers.yahoo.com/question/index?qid=20090419030102AAbYEDf.

[7] Srta. Argentina, comment on Chourok C, "My boss wants to sleep with me?," *Yahoo! Answers,* accessed June 1, 2011, http://answers.yahoo.com/question/index?qid=20090419030102AAbYEDf.

[8] Skater Boi, comment on Chourok C, "My boss wants to sleep with me?," *Yahoo! Answers,* accessed June 1, 2011, http://answers.yahoo.com/question/index?qid=20090419030102AAbYEDf.

[9] Adrian Blomfield, "Sexual Harassment Okay as It Ensures Humans Breed, Russian Judge Rules," *Telegraph,* July 29, 2008, accessed June 1, 2011,http://www.telegraph.co.uk/news/worldnews/europe/russia/2470310/Sexual-harrassment-okay-as-it-ensures-humans-breed-Russian-judge-rules.html.

[10] Adrian Blomfield, "Sexual Harassment Okay as It Ensures Humans Breed, Russian Judge Rules," *Telegraph,* July 29, 2008, accessed June 1, 2011,http://www.telegraph.co.uk/news/worldnews/europe/russia/2470310/Sexual-harrassment-okay-as-it-ensures-humans-breed-Russian-judge-rules.html.

[11] Markus Mobius and Tanya Rosenblat, "Why Beauty Matters," June 24, 2005, accessed June 1, 2011, http://citeseerx.ist.psu.edu/viewdoc/download?doi=10.1.1.118.3553&rep=rep1&type=pdf.

[12] mmafan, comment on Isgchas, "It sounds like working for Coke is bad all over the country. Does anybody work for a union shop? Is that any better?," Indeed, accessed June 1, 2011, http://www.indeed.com/forum/cmp/Coca--Cola/get-job-at-Coca-Cola/t10481/p2.

[13] Kalakala, "LSD and 60's Music: What We Owe to It. Part 1," Ultimate-Guitar.com, August 12, 2006, accessed June 1, 2011, http://www.ultimate-guitar.com/columns/junkyard/lsd_and_60s_music_what_we_owe_to_it_part_1.html.

NOTES:

Chapter 12:
Advertising and Consumer Protection

Chapter Overview

This chapter considers the ethics of selling by examining advertising, and the ethics of buying by examining conceptions of the consumer.

12.1 Two Kinds of Advertising
LEARNING OBJECTIVES

1. Define and characterize informational advertising.
2. Define and characterize branding advertising.

Old Spice

One reason guys like to have the controller when couples are watching TV is so they can flip the channel fast when ads like this come on:

> *Viewed from the waist up, you see a perfectly bodied man wrapped in a low-slung towel. With gleaming eyes locked on the camera he intones, "Hello, ladies, look at your man, now back to me, now back at your man, now back to me." While guys at home cringe, he comes to an indisputable conclusion, "Sadly, he isn't me." After letting the reality sink in, he soothes his female viewers with the information that "He could at least smell like me if he switched to Old Spice body wash." Next, he asks us to "Look down," and while everyone's eyes drop to his towel, some green screen magic allows him to seamlessly appear on a romantic sailboat in the Caribbean. His hand overflows with diamonds, then a bottle of Old Spice arises along with them, and we learn that, "Anything is possible when your man smells like Old Spice."*

Advertising is about enticing consumers. It comes in many forms, but the two central strategies are (1) informational and (2) branding.

Ads: Information and Branding

There are more and less sophisticated ways of enticing consumers. At the lowest level, there are product-touting ads and comparisons giving straight information. When Old Spice set aside some money to sell their body wash, they could have gone that route, they could've dabbed some product on a shirt and asked random women to stop, take a sniff, and report on the scent. Then magazine spreads could be produced announcing that "three out of four women like the Old Spice scent!" A bit more aggressively, women could

be given a blind sniff test featuring Old Spice and Axe products, or Old Spice and some "leading brand," one probably chosen because it fares particularly poorly in the comparison test. In any of its forms, this is informational advertising. It presents facts and hopes that reasonable consumers buying body wash will choose Old Spice.

Other kinds of informational advertising include price comparisons (Old Spice costs less than Axe) and quality comparisons (the Old Spice scent lingers eight hours after showering, and Axe is gone after only six). Naturally, different kinds of products will lend themselves to different kinds of factual and informational claims. Sometimes, finally, this kind of advertising is called transactional because it's directly about the exchange of money for a good or service.

Moving toward more sophisticated—or at least less rational and direct—advertising, there's branding, which is the attempt to convert a product into a brand. In the advertising and marketing world, the word *brand* has a very specific meaning. It's not the name of the company making the product, not the words Old Spice or Kleenex. Instead, a brand is a product or company's *reputation*; it's what you think of when you hear the name and it's the feelings (good or bad) accompanying the name. Technically, a brand is what a product or company is left with when you take everything away. Exemplifying this in the case of Old Spice, imagine that tomorrow all their production factories burn down, their warehouses flood, and their merchandise sells out at every store. Basically, the company has nothing left, no factories to make product, no stock to ship out, and no items left to sell on any shelf. Now, if you were a wealthy investor, would you *buy* this company that has nothing? You might.

You might because it still has its brand, it still has a reputation in people's minds, and that can be worth quite a bit. Frequently, when we visit a store and stand in front of shelves packed with different versions of a single kind of item, we don't have time or the patience to carefully go through and compare price per ounce or to Tweet questions to friends about what they recommend. We choose one body wash—or one style of underwear or Eveready batteries instead of Duracell—because of an idea about that product planted in our mind. Maybe we don't know exactly where the idea came from, or exactly what it is, but it's there and guides us to one choice instead of another. It makes a product seem like it's *our* kind of product (if it's the one we end up buying) or not our kind of product.

The Old Spice commercial is an exercise in branding. It's funny, sexy, embarrassing, and extremely sophisticated. Looking at the commercial, the first question to ask is "in the most literal terms, what's the message?" Is it that Old Spice is a good value? No, there's no talk about price. Is it that Old Spice smells good? No, the only claim is that it can make you smell like an attractive actor. Is it that the actor (and former pro football player) Isaiah Mustafa uses Old Spice? No, he says he does, but that's not the message. If anything, *his* message to potential consumers is that, if he wanted to, he could steal their girlfriends. This is not the kind of information that wins market share.

Fortunately for Old Spice, branding isn't about facts or truths; it's about producing an attitude and connecting with a specific sense of humor and outlook on life. Like a style of clothes or a preference for a certain kind of music, Old Spice is conveying a personality that you appreciate and like or, just as easily, dislike. That's why the whole commercial comes off as a kind of joke about a certain vision of attraction and romance and sex. Do you enjoy the joke? If you don't, then Old Spice is going to have to find a different way to get into your (or your boyfriend's) wallet. If you *do* like it, if the whole thing seems zany and funny and you wouldn't mind pulling it up on YouTube to watch again, then you've been branded. Old Spice has found a way to get past all the defenses we usually set up when we see advertising, all the skepticism and cynicism, and gotten us to feel like we're part of something that includes that company's products.

In broad strokes, finally, there are two kinds of advertising, two strategies for influencing consumption choices. One works by appealing to facts and provides information; the other appeals to emotions and creates a lifestyle. Both kinds of advertising raise ethical questions.

1. Informational ads provoke questions about truth and lies.
2. Branding efforts provoke questions about the relation between our products and who we are as individuals and a culture.

KEY TAKEAWAYS

- Informational advertising employs facts to persuade consumers.
- Branding advertising attempts to attach a personality and reputation to a product.

REVIEW QUESTIONS

1. Can you think of an example of an informational ad? What information is provided, and how does it persuade consumers?
2. Can you think of an example of a branding ad? What personality and attitude are attached to the product? How might those characteristics persuade consumers?

12.2 Do Ads Need to Tell the Truth?
LEARNING OBJECTIVES

1. Delineate different types and degrees of deceitful advertising.
2. Discuss legal and regulatory responses to deceitful advertising.
3. Map the ethical issues surrounding deceptive ads.

Types of Deceitful Advertising

An initial way to distinguish informational advertising from branding is by asking whether consumers are supposed to ask whether the claims are true. In the case of the Old Spice body wash TV spot, there's no question. The actor asserts that "anything is possible with Old Spice" as diamonds flow magically from his hands. But no one would buy the product expecting to receive diamonds. They wouldn't because branding ads are neither true nor false. Like movies, you enjoy them (or you don't) without worrying about whether it could really happen. Informational ads, on the other hand, derive their power from selling consumers hard facts. When the ad claims the product costs less than similar offerings from rivals, the first question is "really?" When the answer is "no," the advertising is deceitful.

There are four ways that informational advertising can be deceitful:

1. False claims directly misrepresent the facts. For example, an Old Spice body wash ad could announce that it costs less per ounce than Axe. When you go to the store, however, the opposite is true. It may be that the manufacturer's suggested retail price is less, or Axe is on a special sale, but if the ad says Old Spice is cheaper and it's not, that's a false claim.
2. Claims that conceal facts are more common than directly false ones because they're not flatly untrue and so can't be easily disproven. A body wash, for example, may conveniently leave out the fact that chemical scents frequently react differently with different skin types and body temperatures, meaning a product may smell great on one man but come off as nauseating when used by most others. Another set of examples surround the infamous *fine print* on contracts. Every day, someone somewhere receives an offer for a free issue of a

magazine and sends the business reply card in. It's not until a few months later; however, that they realize that getting the free one also committed them to buying a year's worth. Another example of a concealed fact is a juice made from "natural ingredients," and it turns out the natural ingredient is sugar, which is natural, but not the fruit juice from real oranges you were expecting.

3. Ambiguous claims resemble concealed facts in not being directly untrue. Where claims that conceal facts manipulate consumers by leaving something out, ambiguous claims mislead by putting too much in. For example, a body wash may announce that it "kills the smelly bacteria that women hate most," and that may be true, but the implication that *only* Old Spice does that is misleading because *all* soaps and washes wipe out some bacteria. Just water washes a good bit away. Similarly, Viagra announces that before using the product, men should check with their doctor to "ensure that you are healthy enough to engage in sexual activity." The misleading idea is that the rock and rolling will be so intense it could be life threatening. The truth is that the drug itself may be dangerous for the unhealthy. Finally, cigarette companies use a similar strategy when they advertise light cigarettes as (truly) containing less cancer-causing tar, but they leave out the fact that the lower nicotine levels cause many smokers to light up more often and so take in as much, or even more, than they otherwise would have. In every case, the ad's claim is technically true, but it leads consumers toward possibly false assumptions that just happen to make the product more attractive.

4. Puffery is a technical term in the advertising world. It signifies expressed views that are clearly subjective exaggerations or product slogans, and not meant to be taken literally. In the Old Spice ad, the actor's claim that "anything is possible with Old Spice" is actually an ironic joke about puffery: the ad is poking fun at those other personal care products that in essence claim the women (or men) will come running. Here are two standard examples of puffery: Budweiser is "The King of Beers" and Coke is "The Real Thing." More generally, any product labeled "The Finest," and all services that announce them "Can't be beat!" are engaging in the practice. Of course these kinds of slogans can be harmless with respect to their violation of strict truth telling, but they do place a burden on consumers to be wary.

Deceitful advertising, finally, is not the same as false advertising. All false ads are also deceitful, but there are many ways of being deceitful that don't require directly false claims.

Legal Responses to Deceptive Advertising

Created in the early 1900s, the Federal Trade Commission (FTC) was originally tasked with enforcing antitrust laws. With time, its responsibilities have expanded to include consumer protection in the area of marketing and advertising. Today, many legal conflicts over truth and sales run through its offices.

The act authorizing the FTC to begin regulating advertising declares that "unfair and deceptive practices" are illegal, and the agency is charged with the responsibility to investigate and prevent them. [1] In judging what counts as deceptive, two models are frequently used. The reasonable consumer standard is the looser of the two. It presumes that protections should only be extended to cover advertising that would significantly mislead a thoughtful, moderately experienced consumer. One advantage of this stance is that it allows the FTC to focus on the truly egregious cases of misleading advertising, and also on those products that most seriously affect individual welfare. Very close attention is paid to advertising about things we eat and drink, while fewer resources are dedicated to chasing down garden-variety rip-offs that most consumers see through and avoid. One borderline case is the *FTC v. Cyberspace.com*. In that case, and according to their press release, the FTC charged that the defendants

> engaged in an illegal scheme to deceive consumers by mailing $3.50 "rebate" checks to millions of small businesses and consumers. The check came with an attached form that looked like an invoice and used terms like "reference number," and "discount taken," making it look like there was a previous business relationship. By cashing the checks, the FTC alleged that many small businesses and consumers unknowingly agreed to allow the defendants to become their Internet Service Provider. After the checks were cashed, the defendants started placing monthly charges of $19.95 to $29.95 on the consumers' telephone bills. According to the FTC, the defendants then made it very difficult to cancel future monthly charges and receive refunds. [2]

The judge sided with the FTC.

Whether or not these businesspeople should have seen through the free-money scam and thrown the "check" in the trash, it's certain that the FTC should have stepped in under the ignorant consumer standard. Within this framework—which is much stricter than the reasonable consumer version—consumers are protected even from those scams and offers that most people recognize as misleading. One point to make is that the "ignorant consumer" isn't synonymous with dumb. Though the category does catch some people who probably should've tried a bit harder in school, other ignorant consumers may include immigrants who have little experience with American advertising practices and customs. The elderly too may fall into this category, as might people in situations of extreme or desperate need. One example would be late-night TV commercials appealing to people in deep debt. Some ads promise that loan consolidation will lower their overall debt. Others imply that filing for bankruptcy will virtually magically allow a start-over from scratch. Both claims are false, but when creditors are calling and threatening to take your home and your car, even the most reasonable people may find themselves vulnerable to believing things they shouldn't because they *want* to believe so desperately.

The federal government, finally, through the FTC has the power to step in and protect these consumers. Strictly from a practical point of view, however, their resources are limited. The task of chasing down every ad that might confuse or take advantage of someone is infinite. That factor, along with good faith disagreements about the extent to which companies should be able to shine a positive light on their goods and services, means (1) the ignorant consumer standard will be applied only sparingly by government regulators, and (2) borderline cases of advertising deceit will be with us for the foreseeable future.

The Ethics of Deceitful Advertising

One way to enter the ethical debate about dubious product claims is by framing the subject as a conflict of rights. On one side, producers have a right to talk sunnily about what they're selling: they're free to accentuate the positives and persuade consumers to reach for their credit card. On the other side, consumers have a right to know what it is that they're buying. In some fields, these rights can coexist to some significant extent. For example, with respect to food and drink, labeling standards imposed on producers can allow consumers to literally see what's in their prospective purchase. Given the transparency requirement, companies can make a strong argument that they should be allowed to advocate their products with only minimal control because consumers are free to check exactly what it is they're buying.

Even these clear cases can become blurry, however, since some companies try to stretch labeling requirements to the breaking point to suit their purposes. One example comes from breakfast cereal boxes. On the side, producers are required to list their product's ingredients from high to low. At the top you expect to see ingredients including flour or similar, as quite a bit of it goes into most dry cereals. At the

bottom, there may be some minor items added to provide a bit of flare to the taste.

One specific ingredient many parents worry about is sugar: they don't want to send their little ones off to school on a massive sugar high. So what do manufacturers do? They comply with the letter of the regulation, but break the spirit by counting sugar under diverse names and so break up its real weight in the product. Here are the first few lines of the ingredients list from Trix cereal:

> *Corn (Whole Grain Corn, Flour, Meal), Sugar, Corn Syrup, Modified Corn Starch, Canola and/or Rice Bran Oil, Corn Starch, Salt, Gum Arabic, Calcium Carbonate, High Fructose Corn Syrup, Trisodium Phosphate, Red 40, Yellow 6, Blue 1.*

Sugar is sugar, corn syrup has a lot of sugar, high fructose corn syrup has even more sugar. We'd have to get a chemist to tote up the final results, but it's clear that a reasonable consumer should figure this is a sugar bomb. Is it fair, though, to assume that an immigrant mother—or *any* mother not well versed in sugar's various forms—is going to stop and do (or be able to do) a comprehensive ingredient investigation? The question goes double after remembering that the first image consumers see is the product's advertising on the box featuring a child-friendly bunny.

More generally, in terms of a pure rights-based argument, it's difficult to know where the line should get drawn between the right of manufacturers to sell, and the right of consumers to know what they're buying. The arguments for pushing the line toward the consumer and thereby allowing manufacturers wide latitude to make their claims include the following:

1. Free speech. The right for people to say whatever they want doesn't get suspended because someone is trying to sell a product. Further, on their side, consumers are completely free to buy whatever they want, they're free to listen to pitches from competing merchants, and they can consult the Consumer Reports web page and talk to friends. Ours is, after all, a *free* market, and advertisers participate in it. The right to make whatever advertising claims one wishes is justified on principle, on the ideal of a liberal (in the sense of free) economic world.

2. Marketers have a moral responsibility to do everything they possibly can to sell because they're obligated to serve their employers' interest, which is to make money, presumably. In this case, deceitful advertising may be morally objectionable but less so than failing to turn the highest profit possible.

3. Within the context of an open market economy, one way to help it function efficiently, one way to get products and services sent where they're supposed to go in a way that benefits everyone, is by maximizing the amount of information consumers have before they purchase. And one way to maximize information, it could be argued, is by letting competing sellers advertise freely against each other. They can say whatever they like about themselves and point out exaggerations and untruths in the claims of competitors. This is similar to what happens in courtrooms where plaintiffs are allowed to say more or less whatever they want and defendants can do that too. Both sides cross-examine each other, and in the end, the jury weighs through it all and decides guilt or innocence. Returning to the economic realm, the argument is that the best way to get the most information possible out to consumers is by allowing a vibrant advertising world to flourish without restriction.

On the other side, distinct arguments are frequently proposed to defend the position that sellers should operate within tight restrictions when advertising the virtues of their goods and services. The consumer should be vigorously shielded; the reasoning goes, from claims that could be deceptive. Arguments include the following:

1. Consumers have a fundamental ethical right to know what they're buying, and even mildly ambiguous marketing techniques interfere with that right. If a box of breakfast cereal is marketed with a harmless and helpful bunny, then the ingredients of Trix cereal better be harmless and helpful (and not sugar bombs). Everyone agrees, finally, that advertisers have a right to free speech, but that right stops when it conflicts with consumers' freedom to purchase what they really want.

2. Advertisers are just like everyone else insofar as they're bound by an ethical duty to tell the truth. That duty trumps their obligation to sell products and help companies make profits.

3. *Both* advertisers *and* the manufacturing companies are duty bound to treat everyone including consumers as ends and not as means. The basic ethical principle here is that no one should be treated as an instrument, as a way to get something else. There's no problem with advertising a product and allowing consumers to decide whether they want it, but when the advertising becomes deceptive, consumers are no longer being respected as dignified human beings; they're being treated as simply means to ends, as *ways* the company makes money. Consumers become, in a sense, indistinguishable from the machines in the factory, nothing more than cogs in the process of making owners wealthy.

4. Purchasing a product is also the signing of an implicit contract between producer and consumer. The consumer gives good money and expects a good product, one in line with the expectations raised by advertising. Just as companies are right to apply drug tests to workers because those companies have a right to a full day's good labor for a full day's pay, so too when the consumer pays full price for a product it should fully meet expectations.

5. Though the *idea* of allowing marketers to say whatever they want may sound good because it allows consumers to maximize information about the products that are out there, the theory only works if consumers have massive amounts of time to study the messages from every producer before making every purchase. In reality, no one has that much time and, as a result, advertisers must be limited to making claims that are clearly true.

There's a lot of space between truths and lies in advertising; there are many ways to not quite tell the whole truth. Both legally and ethically, the limits of the acceptable can be blurry.

KEY TAKEAWAYS

- Deceitful advertising occurs along a range from exaggerations to direct falsehoods.
- Legal responses to deceitful advertising may be organized through the FTC.
- The degree of consumer legal protection depends on premises about the marketplace sophistication of the consumer.
- Ethical debates concerning deceitful advertising pit the rights of marketers to sell against the rights of consumers to know what they are purchasing.

REVIEW QUESTIONS

1. What's the difference between deceitful advertising and direct falsehoods?
2. Define the *reasonable consumer standard* for consumer protection. How is it different from the *ignorant consumer standard*?
3. What are two arguments in favor of granting marketers wide latitude to promote their products?
4. What are two arguments in favor of forcing marketers to stay very close to the pure truth when promoting their products?

[1] Section 5, Federal Trade Commission Act.
[2] "Bogus 'Rebate' Offers Violate Federal Law," Federal Trade Commission, August 5, 2002, accessed June 2, 2011, http://www.ftc.gov/opa/2002/08/cyberspace.shtm.

12.3 We Buy, Therefore We Are: Consumerism and Advertising

LEARNING OBJECTIVES

1. Define consumerism.
2. Discuss the power and problems surrounding advertising that creates desires.
3. Consider special issues surrounding advertising and children.
4. Investigate the penetration of advertising in life.

What Is Consumerism?

The word *consumerism* is associated with a wide range of ideas and thinkers, ranging from American economist John Kenneth Galbraith and his book *The Affluent Society* to the French postmodern philosopher Jean Baudrillard. While definitions of the word and responses to it vary, consumerism in this text is defined in two parts:

1. We identify ourselves with the products we buy. Consumerism goes beyond the idea that our brands (whether we wear Nike shoes or TOM's shoes, whether we drive a Dodge Charger or a Toyota Prius) are *symbols* of who we are. Consumerism means our products aren't just things we wear to make statements. They *are* us; they incarnate the way we think and act.
2. If we are what we buy, then we need to buy in order to be. Purchasing consumer items, in other words, isn't something we do to dispatch with necessities so that we can get on with the real concerns of our lives—things like falling in love; starting a family; and finding a satisfying job, good friends, and fulfilling pastimes. Instead, buying becomes the way we do all those things. The consumption of goods doesn't just dominate our lives; it's what we do to live.

The subject of consumerism goes beyond business ethics to include every aspect of economic life and then further to cultural studies, political science, and philosophy. Staying within business ethics, however, and specifically with advertising, the subject of consumerism provokes the following questions:

- Does advertising create desires (and is there anything wrong with that)?
- Do advertisers have a responsibility to restrain their power?
- Should there be different rules for advertising aimed at children?
- Is advertising too intrusive in our lives?

Does Advertising Create Desires (and Is There Anything Wrong with That)?

Our society is affluent. With the exception of marginal cases, all Americans today eat better, enjoy more effective shelter from winter cold and summer heat, are healthier, and live longer than, say, the king of France in 1750. In fact, necessity in the sense of basic life needs hardly exists. We struggle heroically to afford a better car than our neighbor, to have a bigger home than our high-school classmates, to be thin and pay the doctor for a perfectly shaped nose, and so on, but no one worries about famine. Our economic struggles aren't about putting food on the table; they're about eating in the most desirable restaurant.

How do we decide, however, what we want—and even what we want desperately—when we don't truly *need* anything anymore? One answer is that we create needs for ourselves. All of us have had this experience. For our entire lives we lived without iPhones (or even without cell phones), but now, somehow, getting halfway to work or campus and discovering we left our phone at home causes a nervous breakdown.

Advertising plays a role in this need creation. Take the Old Spice body wash ad. Body wash as a personal grooming product was virtually unheard of in the United States until only a few years ago. More, as a product with specific characteristics, it's hard to see how it marks an advance over old-fashioned soap. This absence of obvious, practical worth at least partially explains why the Old Spice ad provides very little information about the product and nothing by way of comparison with other, similar options (like soap). Still, the Old Spice body wash is a hit. The exact techniques the ad uses are a matter for psychologists, but as the sales numbers show, the thirty-second reel first shown during the Super Bowl has herded a lot of guys into the idea that they need to have it. [1]

Is there anything wrong with that? One objection starts by pointing out that corporations producing these goods and selling them with slick ad campaigns aren't satisfying consumer needs; *they're trying to change who consumers are* by making them need new things. Instead of fabricating products consumers want, corporations now fabricate consumers to want their products, and that possibly violates the demand that we respect the dignity and autonomy of others. The principle, for example, that we treat others as ends and not means is clearly transgressed by any advertising that creates needs. First, guys out in the world *aren't* being respected as "ends," as individuals worthy of respect when corporations stop producing their required products better or more cheaply. Second, guys out in the word *are* being treated as means—as simple instruments of the corporations' projects—when their desires are manipulated and used to satisfy the *corporations'* desire to make money.

Another argument against this kind of desire-creating advertising starts from a rights approach. According to the theory that freedom is the highest good, we're all licensed to do whatever we want *as long as* our acts don't curtail the freedom of others. The argument could be made that using sophisticated advertising campaigns to manipulate what people want is, in effect, curtailing their freedom at the most fundamental level. Old Spice's advertising strategy is enslaving people to desires that they didn't freely choose.

A final argument against need creation with advertising is the broad utilitarian worry that consumers are being converted into chronically, even permanently unhappy people because they have no way to actually satisfy their desires. If you work to attain something you've been told you're supposed to want, and the second you get it some new company enters with the news that now there's something else you need, the emotional condition of not being satisfied threatens to become permanent. Like mice trapped on a running wheel, consumers are caught chasing after a durable satisfaction they can't ever reach.

On the other side of the argument, defenders and advocates of desire-creating advertisements like the one Old Spice presented claim (correctly) that their announcements *aren't* violating the most traditional and fundamental marketing duty, which is to tell the truth. The Old Spice ad, in fact, doesn't really say anything that's either true or false. Given that, given that there's no attempt to mislead, the company is perfectly within its rights to provide visions of new kinds of lives for consumers to consider, accept or reject, buy or pass over.

Stronger, advocates claim that consumers are adults and attempts to shield them from ads like those Old Spice produced *don't* protect their identity and dignity; instead, they deny consumers options. Consequently, ethical claims that ads aiming to generate new desires should be constrained actually *violate* consumer dignity by treating them like children. We should all be free, the argument concludes, to redefine and remake ourselves and our desires in as many ways as possible. By offering options, advertising is expanding our freedom to create and live new, unforeseen lives.

Do Advertisers Have a Responsibility to Restrain Their Power?

The Old Spice ad didn't end after its thirty seconds of fame on the Super Bowl broadcast. The actor Isaiah Mustafa went on to became a Twitter sensation. By promising to respond to questions tweeted his way, he effectively launched a second phase of the marketing effort, one designed to stretch out the idea that body wash is big and important: it's what people are talking about, and if you *don't* know about it and what's going on, you're out of the loop, not relevant. The tone of the invitation to Twitter users to get involved stayed true to the original commercial. Mustafa asked people to "look for my incredibly manly and witty and amazing responses" to their questions. [2]

On YouTube, Mustafa's status went to instant legend: not only has his commercial been viewed about *20 million* times (by people who actually *want* to watch and pay attention and at zero cost to Old Spice), there's also a long list of copycat videos, derivative videos, spoof videos, and on and on. The depth of the advertising campaign is now virtually infinite. You could pass years watching and listening and reading the social media generated and inspired by the original commercial.

All that is advertising. It's not paid, it's not exactly planned, but it is part of the general idea. When Old Spice spent big money to get a Super Bowl slot for their ad, they weren't only trying to reach a large audience; they were also hoping to do exactly what they did: set off a firestorm of attention and social media buzz.

Called viral advertising, this consumer-involved marketing strategy drives even further from traditional, informational advertising than the activity of branding. Where branding attempts to attach an attitude and reputation to a product or company independent of specific, factual characteristics, viral ads attempt to involve consumers and exploit *them* to do the company's promotional work. When viral advertising is working, the activity of branding is being carried out for free by the very people the advertising is meant to affect. In a certain sense, consumers are advertising to themselves. Of course, consumers aren't rushing to donate their energy and time to a giant corporation; they need to be enticed and teased. The Super Bowl ad with its irresistible humor and sex-driven come-on does that—it provokes consumers to get involved.

Viral ads—and the techniques of public enticement making them spread contagiously—come in many forms. One ethical discussion, however, surrounding nearly all viral advertising can be framed as a discussion about knowledge and resource exploitation. Two critical factors enabled Old Spice, along with its advertising agency Wieden+Kennedy, to generate so much volunteer help in their endeavor to get the body wash buzz going:

1. Knowledge of consumer behavior
2. Tremendous resources—especially money and creative advertising talent—that allowed them to act on their knowledge

Compared with the typical person watching a TV commercial, the raw power of Old Spice is nearly immeasurable. When they aim their piles of money and sharp advertising experts toward specific consumers, consumers are overwhelmed. Without the time required to learn all the skills and strategies employed by today's advertisers, they literally don't even know what's hitting them. From that fact, this ethical question arises: Don't today's sophisticated marketers have a responsibility to *inform* consumers of what they're up to so that potential purchasers can at least begin to defend themselves?

Making the last point stronger, isn't the economic asymmetry—the huge imbalance in monetary power and commercial knowledge favoring today's professional advertisers—actually *an obligation* to restraint, a responsibility to *not* employ their strongest efforts given how comparatively weak and defenseless individual consumers are? The "yes" answer rests on the duty of fairness—that is, that we treat equals equally and un-equals unequally. In this case, the duty applies to companies just as it does to people. Frequently people say to large, muscle-bound characters caught up in a conflict with someone smaller, "Go pick on someone your own size." It's simply unfair to challenge another who really has no chance. This duty comes forward very graphically on a video snippet from MTV's *Jersey Shore* when a thin girl attacks the physically impressive Ronnie. He just shoves her aside. When her boyfriend, however, who's about Ronnie's size and age, shows up and starts swinging, he ends up getting a good thumping. Leaving aside the ethics of fistfights, it doesn't take profound thought to see that Ronnie understands his superior physical power is also a responsibility when harassed by a comparative weakling to hold himself in check. [3]

While the case of Old Spice and Wieden+Kennedy isn't quite as transparent as Ronnie on the street, it does obey the same logic: all their power and marketing expertise is both a power over consumers and an equally forceful responsibility not to exercise it. Compare that situation with the famous "I'm a Mac, I'm a PC" advertising campaign. No one objects to

powerhouse Apple taking some figurative swings at powerhouse Microsoft since that company clearly has the means to defend itself. When a corporation manipulates innocent and relatively powerless individual consumers at home on the sofa, however, it's difficult to avoid seeing something unfair happening.

The argument on the other side is that consumers *aren't* powerless. There's no real imbalance of might here because consumers today, armed with their Twitter accounts and Facebook pages, are perfectly capable of standing up to even the mightiest corporations. Viral messaging, in other words, goes both ways. Old Spice may use it to manipulate men, but individual men are perfectly free and capable of setting up a Facebook group dedicated to recounting how rancid Old Spice products actually are. Beneath this response, there's the fundamental claim that individuals in the modern world are free and responsible for their own behavior, and if they end up voluntarily advertising for Old Spice and don't like it, they shouldn't complain: they should just stop tweeting messages to Isaiah Mustafa.

Further, the proposition that consumers need to be *protected* from Old Spice is an infringement on the dignity of those who are out in the world buying. Because today's consumers connected to social media are alert and plugged in, because even a solitary guy in pajamas in his basement running his own YouTube channel or Facebook group can be as influential as any corporation, attempts to shield him are nothing less than disrespectful confinements of his power. Protection, in this case, is just another word for condescension.

Should There Be Different Rules for Children?
The discussion of knowledge and resource exploitation leads naturally to the question about whether children should be subjected to advertising because the knowledge imbalance is so tremendous in this particular case.

According to a letter written by a number of respected psychologists to their own professional association, children should receive significant shielding from advertising messaging. The first reason is a form of the general concern that advertising is creating desires as opposed to helping consumers makes good decisions about satisfying the desires they have: "The whole enterprise of advertising is about creating insecure people who believe they need to buy things to be happy." [4]

The problem with advertising that creates insecurity is especially pronounced in the case of society's youngest members because once that attitude of constant need and consequent unhappiness is bred into these consumers, it's difficult to see how it will be removed. Since they've known nothing else, since they've been taught from the very start that the natural condition of existence is to not have the toys and things that are needed, they have no way of escaping into a different (non-consumerist) way of understanding their reality. Finally, if this entire situation is set inside a utilitarian framework, it's clear that the ethical verdict will fall somewhere near reprehensible. If, as that ethical theory affirms, moral good is just any action contributing to social welfare and happiness, then advertisements consigning children to lifetime dissatisfaction must be prohibited.

The second part of the psychologists' argument elaborates on the condition of children as highly vulnerable to commercial message techniques. Children aged three to seven, for example, gravitate toward the kind of toys that transform themselves (for example, Transformers). Eight- to twelve-year-olds love to collect things. Armed with these and similar insights about young minds, marketers can exploit children to want just about anything. The virtual defenselessness of children, the point is, cannot be denied.

Still, there is a case for child-directed advertising. It's that where children are defenseless, parents have a responsibility to step in. First, they can turn off the TV. Second, no young child can buy anything. Children depend on money from mom and dad, and to the extent that parents enable children to live their advertising wants, its parents who are at fault for any feelings of insecurity and dissatisfaction affecting their kids.

Whether advertising aimed at children is right or wrong, the stakes are certainly high. Children under twelve are spending around $30 billion a year, and teenagers are hitting $100 billion in sales. [5]

Are Ads Too Intrusive in Our Lives?

Another sentence from that letter written by concerned psychologists indicates a distinct area of ethical concern about advertising: "The sheer volume of advertising is growing rapidly and invading new areas of childhood, like our schools." [6]

It's not just children in their schools. We all go to concerts at the American Airlines Center, our shirts and shoes are decorated with the Nike swoosh, public parks are sponsored by corporations, the city bus is a moving billboard, the college football championship will be determined at the FedEx Orange Bowl. Every day it's harder to get away from ads, and

each year the promotions and announcements push closer to those parts of our lives that are supposed to be free of economic influence. Maybe someday we'll attend Mass at the Diet Coke Cathedral, weigh guilt and innocence in the Armor All courthouse, elect senators to vote in the Pennzoil chamber.

And maybe that's OK. The push of advertising into everything is a proxy for a larger question about the difference between business life and life. It could be that, at bottom, there is no difference. We are Homo economics'. The anti-romanticists were right all along: love can be bought with money, fulfillment is about consuming, and that bumper sticker "He who dies with the most toys wins" is true.

Since serious thought about what really matters in life began in Greece 2,500 years ago, people have promoted the idea that there are more important things than money and consumption. Those usually ill-defined but nonetheless more important things have always explained why most poets, artists, priests, and philosophy professors haven't had much in the way of bank accounts. Possibly, though, it's the other way. Maybe it's not that there are more important things in life that lead some people away from wealth and consumption; maybe it's that some people who don't have much money and can't buy as much as their neighbors explain away their situation by imagining that there are more important things.

Who's right? The ones, who say money and economic life should be limited because the really important things are elsewhere, or the ones who say there are no other things and those who imagine something else are mainly losers? It's an open question. Whatever the answer, it will go a long way toward determining the extent to which we should allow advertising into our lives. If there's only money and consumption, then it's difficult to see why the reach of the branding factories and viral marketers should be significantly limited. If, on the other hand, there's life outside the store, then individuals and societies wanting to preserve that part of them may want to constrain advertising or require that it contribute to noneconomic existence.

KEY TAKEAWAYS

- Consumerism places our entire life within the context of consumer goods and services.
- Advertising can create desires.
- Advertising creating desires raises questions about whether ads violate consumers' dignity and rights.

- The knowledge and financial power of companies (and their ad agencies) may also be an obligation for restraint.
- Children are especially vulnerable to sophisticated advertising and may require special protections.
- Discussion of the advertising that creates needs is a proxy for a larger discussion about the role of money and consumption in our lives.

REVIEW QUESTIONS

1. Put into your own words the definition of consumerism.
2. How can an ad create a desire?
3. Why might an advertiser seek to create a desire?
4. Make the case that ads that create desires violate a consumer's basic rights.
5. Why might a consumer want advertisers to create desires?
6. What is a viral ad?
7. With reference to the concept of economic asymmetry, why is advertising aimed at children the subject of special concern?
8. Why might an advertising company feel obligated to limit the places in which its work appears in the name of protecting the noneconomic parts of our lives?
9. Why might someone want advertising to be everywhere?

[1] Noreen O'Leary and Todd Wasserman, "Old Spice Campaign Smells Like a Sales Success, Too," July 25, 2010, *Adweek*, accessed June 2, 2011,http://www.adweek.com/news/advertising-branding/old-spice-campaign-smells-sales-success-too-107588.

[2] Meena Hartenstein, "Old Spice Guy Takes Web By Storm in Viral Ad Campaign, Creating Personalized Videos for Fans, Celebs," *New York Daily News*, July 14, 2010, accessed June 2, 2011, http://www.nydailynews.com/entertainment/tv/2010/07/14/2010-07-14_old_spice_guy_takes_web_by_storm_in_viral_ad_campaign_creating_personalized_vide.html.

[3] Nicholas Graham, "Jersey Shore Fight: Ronnie Gets Into Vicious Fight," *Huffington Post*, August 1, 2010, accessed June 2, 2011,http://www.huffingtonpost.com/2010/01/08/jersey-shore-fight-ronnie_n_416259.html.

[4] Rebecca Clay, "Advertising to Children: Is it Ethical? *Monitor On Psychology* 31, no. 8 (September 2000), 52, accessed June 2, 2011,http://www.apa.org/monitor/sep00/advertising.aspx.

[5] Rebecca Clay, "Advertising to Children: Is it Ethical? *Monitor On Psychology* 31, no. 8 (September 2000), 52, accessed June 2, 2011,http://www.apa.org/monitor/sep00/advertising.aspx.

[6] Rebecca Clay, "Advertising to Children: Is it Ethical? *Monitor On Psychology* 31, no. 8 (September 2000), 52, accessed June 2, 2011,http://www.apa.org/monitor/sep00/advertising.aspx.

12.4 Consumers and Their Protections
LEARNING OBJECTIVES

1. Delineate the issue of consumer protection from defective goods and services.

2. Outline five conceptions of the consumer.
3. Consider the ethics of consumer protection surrounding each conception of the consumer.

Google Search: Make Money on the Stock Market

One of the top results of a Google search for "make money on the stock market" links you to a page called 2stocktrading.com. It claims, "If you just follow my technique, then I guarantee you will be able to turn $2000 into $1.7 Million in just 1.9 years!"

People turn small amounts into large amounts fast on Wall Street. It happens every day. Many of those people, however, have spent years in school studying economics and business and then decades more studying data and preparing for a speculative opportunity. That studious patience may be a good way to find success, but it isn't the 2stocktrading.com recommendation. According to them, "You don't need to spend hours reading charts, doing technical analysis and stuff like that."

So what *do* you do to prepare for sudden riches? You've got to buy a special book that they sell on the website. Then,

> *you follow 5 simple steps explained in the book. Within 10 minutes, you have found a stock trade that is bound to make you money in any market condition…Go make coffee. Have a little breakfast. And wait for the market to open…Call your broker to place an order.*
> *That's it…Your job is done for today.*
> *Trust me.*

Of every one hundred people who read the pitch from 2stocktading.com in this business ethics textbook, how many do you think will take a second to check out the site? And of that group, what percentage will actually spend some time reading through the whole page? And of that group, which percentage will end up sending in money?

Everybody would like to know the answer to that last question for this reason: everyone has been ripped off, and afterward, everyone has looked at themselves and asked, "Well, was it *my* fault?" Sometimes the answer is disagreeable, and it's comforting to know that at least *some* people out there—like the ones sending in money to 2stocktrading—are even more gullible.

The business ethics surrounding the consumer mainly concerns gullibility, mistreatment of the consumer, and responses to the mistreatment. The questions are about how much freedom consumers should have to spend their money and how much responsibility suppliers should take for their goods and services. One way of organizing the answers is by considering five conceptions of the consumer, five ways of arranging the rights and responsibilities surrounding the act of spending money:

1. The wary consumer
2. The contracting consumer
3. The protected consumer
4. The renegade consumer
5. The capable consumer

The Wary Consumer

Caveat emptor is Latin; it translates as "Let the buyer beware." As a doctrine, caveat emptor means the consumer alone is responsible for the quality of the product purchased. If, in other words, you send your money to 2stocktrading.com and you end up losing not only that but also the cash invested in disastrous stock choices, that's your problem. You don't have any claim against this particular get-rich-quick scheme. And if you don't like the results, that only means you should have been a more careful consumer.

The doctrine of caveat emptor entered the American legal lexicon in 1817 (*Laidlaw v. Organ*). Since then, the legal tide has flowed in the other direction: toward consumer protection and the idea that offering a good or service for sale is also, implicitly, the offer of some kind of guarantee. If a product doesn't do what a reasonable person expects, then there may be room for a legal claim against the seller.

On the ethical front, caveat emptor sits at one extreme of the buyer-seller relation. It's what you have when you buy a used car marked *As Is*. Even if it's a lemon, you're stuck with it. As far as justifying this view of the consumer and mounting an argument that our economic life ought to be organized by the idea that when buyers hand over their money, they get their item and nothing else, there are several routes that may be followed:

- Caveat emptor maximizes respect for the consumer. By placing *all* responsibility in the consumer's hands, a high level of dignity and freedom is invested in those who buy. It's true that when there's a rip-off, there's no recourse, but it's also true that the consumer is allowed to make decisions based on any criteria he or she sees fit. The case of 2stocktrading.com is a good example. Reading about the scheme, it's normal to be tempted to say, really, these guys shouldn't be allowed to advertise their service. What they're claiming is clearly untrue (if their stock-picking system really worked so well, they'd spend their time picking stocks, not trying to sell other people ideas about how to pick stocks). And it's true that

were consumers banned from sending money in, more than a few would be better off. But do we really want a society like that, one where we don't get to make our own choices, even if they're bad ones? A critical component of showing respect for others is allowing them to mess up. Its worth, the argument closes, allowing those mess ups if what we get back for them is consumers endowed with the dignity of making their own decisions.

- Another argument justifying caveat emptor is that it maximizes a certain kind of economic efficiency. When deals are done, they're done and everyone moves on. This allows two kinds of savings. First, there are no expensive lawsuits where everyone pays and mainly lawyers walk away with the cash. Second, though it's impossible to put a number on the cost, it's certain that a huge amount of resources are devoted in our economy today to warnings and similar that are meant to protect companies against consumer claims of fraud and abuse and lawsuits. Take, for example, the TV ads we see for prescription drugs. Sometimes it seems like half the airtime is devoted to reciting warnings and complications associated with the medication. In a world of pure caveat emptor, those kinds of efforts could be minimized because sellers wouldn't have to worry so much about getting sued. With respect to ethics, finally, it may be possible to argue here that maximizing economic efficiency is also the best way to maximize a society's happiness, and if it is, then the doctrine of caveat emptor is sanctioned by utilitarian theory.

On the other side, there are also solid ethical arguments against envisioning consumers as protected only by their own wariness.

- An ethics of care sets the maintenance of a community—of its relationships and unity—as the highest value. If that's the final definition of good, if what we seek in the business world is smooth and continuing cooperation everywhere along the line from the production to the sale and finally to the use of products, then it's difficult to see how sellers could wash their hands after a transaction, or why buyers would be restrained from complaining when things don't work out the way they were supposed to.

- In our society, an ethics based on virtue also stands against the caveat emptor model of consumption. Proponents of virtue ethics typically cite senses of fairness and civility as key components of a good ethical life. If they are, it seems clear that customers who don't receive what they honestly thought they were getting should be listened to and compensated, not ignored and spurned.

In conclusion, caveat emptor envisions consumers as free and empowers them to do as they wish. However, by freeing sellers to be as unscrupulous as they like, it may create an economic society that seems more savage than civil.

The Contracting Consumer

The contractual view of the consumer sees transactions as more than a simple passing of money one way and a good or services the other. The transaction is also the creation of an implicit contract. It's true that nothing may be written on a piece of paper or signed, but the contract's terms may nonetheless be deduced from the transaction itself. In order to begin deducing, the nature of a contractual relationship should first be summarized in general form. Entering into a contract implies the following three requirements:

1. *Freedom*. Neither party may be forced into the agreement. One of the memorable scenes from the *Godfather* movies involves the mafia's attempt to win a movie role for young Frank Sinatra. The Hollywood executive resists the casting, until he wakes up one morning with the severed head of his favorite horse in his bed. A contract is quickly sent out. That's not a true story, but it's an example of entering a contract under duress. A more subtle violation of contractual freedom occurs on the 2stocktrading web page. If you scroll to the bottom you find the price of the product is about $200, *but* if you buy immediately you're eligible for a half-price discount. The aim here is to limit the consumer's freedom to think things through before entering into a purchasing contract by forcing a yes-no decision right now.

2. *Information*. Both buyers and sellers must have reasonably complete knowledge of the agreement they together enter. The issues here range from simple to complicate. If the price, for example, is set in dollars, does that mean US dollars or the Canadian version? More thorny would be the question as to what exactly you receive when you send in your money to 2stocktrading.com. They claim you'll get the stock-picking secrets, but what exactly does that mean? Is it a textbook in economics, a subscription to the *Wall Street Journal*, a crystal ball? If you go through the company's web page carefully, you get the idea that a set of books will be mailed your way, but again, exactly how these books convey secret knowledge is harder to see.

3. *Honesty*. Both sides have to tell the truth. Consumers who send in checks must have money in their accounts. Sellers who promise stock tips that will make you rich must, in fact, send you good stock tips.

The vision of the consumer as entering a contractual relationship essentially moves ethical questions into the legal realm. What's *morally* right or wrong becomes a matter of contract law, and decisions made on the ethical front loosely parallel those that would be taken in the courts.

The ethical work that needs to be done here occurs in the deduction of exactly what terms and clauses make up the implicit contract as it's implied by the circumstances of the agreement. In the field of law, of course, we know what the contract's terms are because they're actually spelled out on a piece of paper. In the case of the contractual view of the consumer, it will be necessary to start with a specific ethical theory, and move from there to the conceiving of an agreement entered into by both sides.

An ethical theory of traditional duties, which values honesty highly, may move all the claims made on the 2stocktrade.com web page directly over to the implicit contract. If, it follows, the people selling the stock-picking service say you'll get rich in two years by following their recommendations and you follow them and you don't get rich, the sellers have not fulfilled their contract. Both economically and ethically, they haven't held up their end of the bargain. At this point, the concept of an implied warranty activates. An implied warranty, just like an implicit contract, elaborates what consumers may claim from sellers if the good or service fails to meet expectations. In this case, one where the implicit contract guaranteed wealth, it seems obvious that consumers who don't make any money should get their original purchase price back. They may also be able to claim that any money lost on the stock market should be refunded because it was invested underneath the assumption that it would produce a gain. At the outside extreme, they might be able to demand the wealth they were supposed to receive for their investments.

Looking at this situation differently—which means using a different ethical theory to produce the terms of an implicit contract between 2stocktrading.com and a consumer—a culturalist ethics may not be quite so stringent. A culturalist ethics accords right and wrong with the habits and customs of a society. And in America today, there's a common understanding that in a free market, sellers are sometimes going to get a little overenthusiastic about their products. Of course consumers have a right to expect some truth from advertisements, but there's also an agreement that exaggerations occur. In this case, the implicit contract would require that stock-picking tips actually be delivered, but it might not require that the people who use them actually get rich or make any money at all. If, in other words, reasonable people in our society who read the web page don't come away believing they'll really rake in the cash by using the stock-picking techniques, then the implicit contract arising between seller and buyer doesn't include that guarantee.

Regardless of how the implicit contract—and consequent implied warranty—are construed, there's a significant disadvantage to this approach: ambiguity. Law firms earn their entire income by disputing what *written* contracts actually mean in the real world. If even perfectly explicit and signed agreements between buyers and sellers don't yield easy determinations about the obligations imposed on the two sides, then answering those questions for implicit contracts, ones where nothing is written, is going to be tremendously difficult. The theory of the consumer as entering a contractual relationship with the seller certainly makes sense, but in practice, it may not help resolve problems.

The Protected Consumer

Most economic transactions don't threaten grave losses even when they go wrong. You buy a half gallon of milk at the grocery store, bring it home, and find the package was slightly punctured so the milk is curdled. You buy a pen and no ink flows. You pay for a nice haircut and get butchered. These kinds of economic hiccups occur all the time and the defects normally don't matter too much. The defect definitely *does* matter, however, when you buy a car and a design error causes the gas pedal to get stuck, leading to wild, unbreakable speeding and entire families are dying in flaming wrecks. While it's unclear how many people have been victims of Toyota's gas pedal manufacturing error, it has become stuck at full acceleration on multiple occasions and has caused real human suffering completely incomparable with the kinds of petty losses typical consumers absorb every day. [1]

Another important aspect of buying a Toyota, or any car, is that it's a complex transaction. That means there's a large distance between the individual who actually takes your money, and the people in faraway plants who physically made the car. In the case of 2stocktrading.com, it may well be that the people who invented the stock-picking system get the money directly when you hit the Internet "Buy" button. A car, however, is typically purchased in a dealership from a salesman who may not even know where the car he's selling is made. Even if he does know, he certainly can't tell you where all the components came from. In today's interconnected world, more and more products are like cars—they're composed of parts that come from all over the place and then they're shipped halfway across the country (or

the world) for sale by people who have nothing to do with any design or manufacturing flaws.

These two factors—the possibility of severe injury coupled with the difficulty in locating who, exactly, is to blame—support the proposal that in some cases ethics may not be enough to protect consumers. Legal protections with sharp teeth could work better. These protections generally move along two lines: manufacturer liability and government safety regulation.

Manufacturer liability is the consumer right to sue manufacturers—and not just the local dealership with which a sales contract is signed—for injuries caused by a defective product. As for specific types of defects incurring liability suits, there are three:

1. Design defects are errors in the product's blueprint. The physical manufacturing, in other words, may be perfect, but because the design isn't, consumers may be harmed.
2. Manufacturing defects are part of the production process. In this case, a product may be generally safe but dangerous in a specific instance when it comes off the assembly line missing a bolt.
3. Instructional defects involve poor or incomplete instructions for a product's safe use. The product may be designed and built well, but if the instructions tell you it's OK to use the blow-dryer in the shower, there could be problems.

The legal origin of manufacturer liability is *MacPherson v. Buick Motor Company*. In that 1916 case, Donald MacPherson was injured when his Buick veered out of control. A defective wheel caused the accident, one that Buick purchased from another company. Buick argued that they weren't liable for MacPherson's injury for two reasons: a quasi-independent dealership, not Buick itself, sold the car, and Buick didn't even make the wheel that failed. The court ruled against both arguments. The result was a concept of legal liability extending beyond explicit contracts and direct manufacturing: the concept of due care recognizes that manufacturers are in a privileged position to understand the potential dangers of their products and have, therefore, an obligation to take precautions to ensure quality. Those obligations remain in effect regardless of who ultimately sells the product and no matter whether a subcontractor or the larger corporation itself made the defective part.

Over the last century, the notion of due care has strengthened into the legal doctrine of strict product liability. This holds that care taken by a manufacturer or supplier—no matter how great—to avoid defects is immaterial to court considerations of liability. If a product is defective and causes harm, liability claims may be filed no matter how careful the manufacturer had been in trying to avoid problems.

Proponents of these legal protections argue that social welfare is improved when companies exist under the threat of serious lawsuits if their products cause damage. Critics fear that liability suits can be unfair: companies may act in good faith to produce safe products, but nonetheless fail, and be forced to pay massive amounts even though they took all precautions they honestly believed necessary.

Government safety regulation is the second main legal route toward a protected consumer. As is the case with liability protection, government regulation has expanded over the last century. Key moments include the establishment of the National Highway Traffic Safety Administration in 1970 and the Consumer Product Safety Commission in 1972. These federal agencies are charged with advocating for consumers by imposing regulations, and then enforcing them through the agencies' legal arms. In actual practice, the agencies frequently act in cooperation with manufacturers to ensure public safety. For example, when news broke that Toyota gas pedals were sticking, causing runaway vehicles, the NHTSA pressured Toyota to redesign the gas pedal and then recall the malfunctioning vehicles to have their pedals replaced.[2]

Regulatory action resembles the extension of liability protection in that proponents believe the measures serve the social welfare. People live better when governmental forces work to ensure protection from defective products. Almost inevitably, the argument in the background is a version of utilitarianism; it's that the ethical good equals whatever actions serve the public welfare and happiness. If society as a whole lives better with strict regulations in effect, then imposing them is good.

Critics fear that the cost of these regulations may become burdensome. In straight economic terms, an argument could be mounted that the dollars and cents spent by corporations in their attempts to comply with regulations are actually superior to the social cost of letting some defective goods out into the marketplace. There's a possibility, here, to meet advocates of regulation on their own ground by claiming that at least in monetary terms, society is better off with less regulation, not more. It's much easier, however, to put a price tag on the cost of complying with safety rules than it is to measure in terms of dollars the cost of injuries and suffering that could have been avoided if more stringent safeguards had been in place. (Of course, if you happen to be one of those few people who gets a seriously defective item—like a

car that speeds out of control—then for you it's pretty clear that the regulations are recommendable no matter the cost.) Another argument cautioning against regulatory action is that bureaucratic overreach threatens legal paternalism. Legal paternalism is the doctrine that, just as parents must restrict the freedom of their children in the name of their long-term welfare, so too regulators in Washington, DC (or elsewhere) must restrict the freedom of citizens because they aren't fully able to act in their own self-interest. One simple example is the seatbelt. In the late 1960s, federal action required the installation of seatbelts in cars. Subsequently, most states have implemented laws requiring their use, at least by drivers. Society as a whole is served by these regulations insofar as injuries from traffic accidents tend to be reduced. That doesn't change the fact, however, that people who are alone in their cars and presumably responsible for their own welfare are being forced to act in a way they may find objectionable. Parallel discussions could be followed on the subject of motorcycle helmets, bicycle helmets, and similar.

Conclusion. Liability lawsuits against manufacturers, together with government regulations, protect consumers from dangerous goods and services. The protections cost money, however, and regulations may seem intrusive or condescending to some buyers.

The Renegade Consumer

The best defense can be a good offense. That's probably the idea the owner of a chronically breaking-down Range Rover had when he parked his car on a public street in front of the dealership where he bought it and pasted bold letters on the side announcing that the car is a lemon. Probably, the display put a dent in the dealership's business. [3]

It was work and sacrifice for the car owner, though. Whoever it was had to hatch the plan and then go out and buys stick-on lettering to spell the message on the Range Rover's side. Then it was necessary to give up use of the car for the duration of the protest. (It also might have been necessary to constantly plug a parking meter with coins.) Regardless of the cost, the renegade consume seeks justice against product defects by going outside the system. Instead of making ethical claims against producers based on the idea of an implicit contract, and instead of seeking refuge underneath governmental protection agencies, this kind of buyer enters a no-holds-barred battle against (perceived) dirty sellers.

Parking a car marked lemon in front of the dealership that sold it is an old—and potentially effective—maneuver. Today's social media, however, allows newer strategies with possibly higher impacts and less inconvenience. One example is Rip-off Report, a website allowing consumers to post complaints for all to see. Browsing the page, it takes only a moment to grasp that the site compiles more or less unedited consumer rebellions. There are stories of being gypped by department stores, robbed by banks, defrauded by plumbers, and nearly everything imaginable. People can add their own comments, and a convenient search box allows anyone to get a quick check on any company they may be considering doing business with. The website's tagline, finally, is very appropriate. It reads, "Don't let them get away with it. Let the truth be known!"[4]

These two sentences correspond well with the two ethical categories into which the renegade consumer naturally falls:

- The imperative "don't let them get away with it" fits the conception of the renegade consumer as acting in the name of retributive justice.
- The imperative "let the truth be known!" fits the conception of the renegade consumer as a consumer advocate.

Retributive justice proposes that it's ethically recommendable to seek revenge against those who have wronged you. "You cost me time, money, and trouble," the logic runs, "and now I'll return the favor." The notion is probably as old as humanity, and it appears in many of history's oldest texts. (The Bible's Matthew 5:38 contains the proverbial "An eye for an eye and a tooth for a tooth.")

Two aspects of retributive justice are significant. First, there's a strong sense of *proportionality* in the idea. The code isn't "A life for an eye" because the goal of retributive justice is to make things even again; it's to restore a balance that was there before the problematic transaction. Retributive justice is a theory of proportional revenge. In the case of the lemon Range Rover, it seems about right that a dealership that refuses to fix (or replace or refund) a client's defective car should in turn see losses to its business that approximately equal the money they save by mistreating consumers. The second point to make about the notion of retributive justice is that it fits within and is a subset of the duty to fairness. What drives retributive justice is a notion that the two sides of an economic exchange should be treated in the same way, equally.

These two characterizations of retributive justice are important because they separate the calculated act of vengeance from being nothing more than a blind and angry outburst. It's normal when we've been wronged to want to simply strike out at the one who's mistreated us. Probably, there's a good bit of that anger behind the Range Rover owner and many of the rip-off reports. What makes those acts also ethically respectable, however, is their containment within the rules of proportionality and the duty to fairness.

The renegade consumer can also find an ethical slot in the category of consumer advocate. When the Rip-off Report asks contributors to let the truth be known, reports are enlisted not as individuals seeking revenge but as wronged consumers performing a public service. Here, the rule of fairness is not in effect; instead, it's the utilitarian idea of the general good. If what ought to be done is just that which brings the greatest happiness to the greatest number, then the public calling out of car dealerships that don't stand behind their product becomes a public utility or good. Renegade consumers become consumer advocates when they help others avoid their fate.

Renegade consumers are the mirror image of caveat emptor consumers. Both place extremely high levels of responsibility in the hands of the buyer. The difference is that the caveat emptor vision places that entire responsibility in the consumers' buying judgment and so disarms them: it places an ethical restriction against consumer complaints because the entire transaction process is wrapped in the idea that before anything else the consumer should be wary about what's being purchased. Renegade consumers also take full responsibility, but their obligations come at the end of the process, not the beginning: they rebalance the scales after a seller tries to get away with taking money for a defective product. Instead of swallowing their loss, renegade consumers act to make sure that the seller who cheated them pays a price.

The Capable Consumer

The capable consumer is a free market ideal. The combined economic-ethical notion underneath it is that business functions most smoothly—and thus produces quality of life at a maximum pace—when consumers play their marketplace role efficiently. Their marketplace role is to use purchasing decisions to reward good companies, ones that produce better goods at a lower cost, while penalizing those companies producing inferior goods. As successful companies grow, and as poor performers fall away, the general welfare improves: products do their jobs more satisfyingly, and people gain more disposable income for pleasure spending (because necessities will be less expensive). If, finally, right and wrong in the economic world is about bringing the greatest good and happiness to the most people, then the marketplace economy supports this moral demand:

a society should do everything possible to perfect the consumer. The perfected consumer is

- able,
- informed,
- free,
- rational.

The able buyer is sufficiently experienced to manage marketplace choices. Just about everyone has been taken in at one point or another by unrealistic promises like those made on the 2stocktrading.com web page. The difference between the incapable and the capable is the ability to learn; it's a kind of acquired instinct that sets off warning signals when an offer sounds *too* good: it might be too good to be true. Specifically on the stock-picking deal, able consumers don't need to carefully study the whole spiel before realizing that, probably, the best thing to do is close the web page.

The informed buyer is sufficiently knowledgeable about a specific product category to make a good purchasing choice from within the various options. Different types of items, of course, require different levels of expertise. Making a good decision about a garage door opener is much easier than making a good decision about a car because the latter is so much more complicated and filled with highly specialized components. For example, Dodge spends a lot of time lauding their cars and trucks as including a hemi, but not many people understand what the actual benefits of that feature are. In fact, many people don't even know what a hemi is. It's always possible, of course, to learn about the intricacies of car engines, but in the real world of limited time, qualifying as an informed buyer requires only one of these two skills: either you know a lot about what you're buying, or you learn which sources of information can be trusted. The search for a trustworthy source may lead to *Consumer Reports* magazine or Rip-off Report or something else, but the result should be a purchasing decision guided by real understanding.

The free buyer has choices. No amount of education about car quality will help anyone who only has one product to select. Most consumer items, however, do provide choices—abundantly. Standing in front of the shelves in any supermarket shows that the ideal of the consumer as free is, to a large extent, satisfied in our society. Still, there are exceptions. Cable TV and phone services can be limited in certain areas, as can electricity providers and sanitation services.

Rational buyers use their experience and information to make good choices. For the qualities of the ideal consumer to cash out, they must be orchestrated by careful thought. Of course this hardly seems worth mentioning in the abstract. All buyers are perfectly rational when they're reading a textbook section about buying. It's easy to be cold and analytical sitting on a sofa. The problem comes when the actual buying is *happening*. Dealers use all kinds of tricks and techniques to get consumers to, at least momentarily, suspend their good judgment and leap. One of the most common is the disappearing deal, which can be found on the 2stocktrading.com site and almost inevitably appears in the car buying experience. The salesman always has some special opportunity that you can get *now*, but if you wait until tomorrow, well…Sometimes the claim is that there's a sale on, but it's ending tonight. Or there's only one left in stock and another customer has been asking about it. The salesman shakes his pen at you and pushes the contract across the desk and the car right behind him is gleaming and new and in those moments the capable consumer is the one who takes a deep breath.

Conclusion

Most ethical questions surrounding consumers are about how much freedom they should have to spend their money. In the case of the wary consumer—the *caveat emptor* buyer—freedom is maximized, but the dealer takes no responsibility for what's sold. In the cases of the contracting, protected, and renegade consumer, buyers sacrifice some of their freedom in return for the guarantee that if a good is defective, they'll have some recourse against the dealer. In many cases, the freedom that consumers lose is minimal or even positive (most people are happy to not be free to buy a lemon car).

It's inescapably true, however, that when you force dealers to stand behind what they sell, there are goods and services that they won't bring to market. This newspaper story, for example, relates how it came to pass that holiday season cookie makers in California had to make do one December without those little silver ball sprinkles that frequently decorate the season's cookies. A crusading lawyer had decided the balls might be harmful, and the threat of a lawsuit caused the item to be removed from store shelves. [5] Probably, most people were able to enjoy their holiday celebrations just fine without the sprinkles, but the stakes go up when drug manufacturers are forced to consider pulling effective diabetes drugs like Avandia off the market because of a discovery that it may increase the risk of heart attacks. [6]

KEY TAKEAWAYS

- Wary consumers are safeguarded from defective goods and services only by their own caution. They enjoy maximum freedom in the marketplace and suffer minimal protection.

- The contracting consumer is protected from defective goods and services by the affirmation that their purchase is also an implicit contract with the seller guarantying quality similar to expectations.
- The protected consumer is safeguarded from defective goods and services by liability lawsuits and governmental regulatory action.
- The renegade consumer takes individual action to penalize sellers whose products fail to meet expectations.
- The capable consumer minimizes the need for buyer protection while maximizing a market economy's efficient functioning.

REVIEW QUESTIONS

1. What does *caveat emptor* mean?
2. What are some purchases that are typically made within a consumer ethics of caveat emptor?
3. What is an implicit contract? How is it created from a particular transaction?
4. What are the two main ways that consumers are backed up by legal protections?
5. How do renegade consumers create protections against defective products?
6. What characteristics make up a capable consumer?

[1] "Toyota to Replace 4 Million Gas Pedals After Crashes," *Fox News*, November 25, 2009 accessed June 2, 2011, http://www.foxnews.com/us/2009/11/25/toyota-replace-million-gas-pedals-crashes.

[2] "Toyota Announces Fix for Gas Pedal Sticking Problem," *US Recall News*, November 26, 2009, accessed June 2, 2011, http://www.usrecallnews.com/2009/11/toyota-announces-fix-for-gas-pedal-sticking-problem.html.

[3] "Range Rover Owner Advertises Faults On Lemon Parked Outside Dealer," Jalopnik, June 3, 2009, accessed June 2, 2011, http://jalopnik.com/5277286/range-rover-owner-advertises-faults-on-lemon-parked-outside-dealer.

[4] Rip-off Report home page, http://www.ripoffreport.com.

[5] Carol Ness, "Bay Area Faces Holidays Without Little Silver Balls on Baked Goods," *San Francisco Chronicle*, December 23, 2003, accessed June 2, 2011,http://articles.sfgate.com/2003-12-23/news/17524040_1_dragees-holiday- cookies-silver-balls.

[6] Andrew Clark, "Relief for GlaxoSmithKline as US Regulators Reject Ban on Avandia, "*Guardian*, July 15, 2010, accessed June 2, 2011,http://www.guardian.co.uk/business/2010/jul/15/glaxosmithkline-avandia-fda-expert-committee.

12.5 Case Studies

We Can Lie Too

Tappening is run by a couple of guys who don't like bottled water. The liquid is fine, but they worry about those small transparent bottles. First, the air gets polluted when they're fabricated and then, after they've been emptied and tossed in the trash, the plastic doesn't quickly break down and reenter the ecosystem.

The Tappening people also notice that bottled-water advertising can be deceitful. The labels and ad campaigns are known to feature mountain streams in forest paradises, breeding the idea that the water is pumped from pristine natural sources when the truth is a lot of it comes from the tap, usually with some filtering applied.

Faced with the distasteful situation—polluting water bottles and deceitful advertising—the Tappening crew could've put together some of their own ads revealing the true source of common bottled waters and the destiny of the containers, but they chose to mount a more aggressive campaign. One effort is a print ad with a crying polar bear drawn at the center, sitting on a melting arctic glacier. Under the title "Bottled Water," the text says, "98% melted ice caps, 2% polar bear tears." At the bottom, in small print, a message reads, "If bottled water companies can lie, we can too." [1]

QUESTIONS

1. In broad strokes, there are four types of deceitful advertising: those that make false claims, conceal facts, make ambiguous claims, and engage in puffery.
   - The Tappening ad makes two apparently false claims. What are they, and what makes them seem false?
   - What are the producers trying to communicate with their claims?
   - Does the fact that the ad admits at the bottom that it's a lie diminish (or entirely eliminate) the fact that false claims are made? Why or why not?
   - The people at Tappening believe that bottled water ads featuring flowing natural streams can be deceitful because frequently the water comes (essentially) from a faucet. What specific kind of deceitful advertising is that? Explain.
   - Is there any puffery in the Tappening print ad? If so, where?
2. Here's one thing the Tappening polar bear ad neglects to inform people: Tappening isn't just trying to get us to stop drinking bottled water; they're also trying to sell something. Water bottles. They cost $14.95 (plus $3

shipping and handling). For the money you get a Tappening plastic bottle made for reuse and emblazoned with the company's slogan: "Think Global. Drink Local." You can also buy a message shoulder bag from the company. It announces that it's "Made with 100% post-consumer recycled materials: yesterday's discarded bottles and yogurt containers." That costs $49.95, plus the shipping and handling. [2] Make the case that Tappening is engaging in deceitful advertising by concealing facts in its polar bear ad. More broadly, what is the ethical case against Tappening?

3. No one doubts that reusable water bottles can be better for the environment than disposable ones. Does the fact that Tappening's purpose is noble diminish the moral objection to the company's deceitful advertising? Explain.

4. For consumers, water bottles are not high stakes. If some guy reads the Tappening ad, gets caught up in the message that bottled water is environmentally disastrous ("98% melted ice caps, 2% polar bear tears"), visits the web page and, in the passion of the moment, buys ten reusable water bottles and the shoulder bag, he'll be out about $250. It's doubtful that his life will be significantly worsened by that kind of monetary loss. Later on, however, he may feel conned when he realizes that the air was polluted to make his presumably environmentally friendly water bottles, and most of the time when he needs bottled water, it's not foreseen, and so he ends up just buying the disposable bottles anyway. The reusable containers with their enviro-friendly slogans get left at home and forgotten and the only thing that really changes is the guys at Tappening made some money.

   o As considered against this background, do you believe the FTC should get involved to rein in Tappening's deceitful advertising? In ethical terms, why or why not?

   o The FTC can use one of two standards for deciding whether action is required to combat deceitful advertising: the ignorant consumer standard and the reasonable consumer standard. Could both standards lead to action against Tappening or only the ignorant standard? Explain.

5. Make the case that, in ethical terms, bottled water companies should be allowed to freely label their bottles with flowing, natural streams even though the water is taken from a city supply and filtered.

Consumerism

Two curious news stories. The first comes from the BBC and tells of a shopaholic, a woman who purchased so much she could hardly fit it all in her apartment. When she passed away from pneumonia, it took more than a day to find her body underneath all the purchases. A friend commented, "It gave her pleasure to buy things, she only bought things she really liked." [3]

The second story relates that in India, according to a UN report, there are about 560 million cell phone users, but only 360 million people have access to toilets. [4]

QUESTIONS

1. Consumerism replaces the model of the consumer as someone who buys necessities in order to get on with their lives, with the model of the consumer as someone who buys in order to live. Can you put that definition in your own words?

2. How could the story of a woman buried and dead underneath her endless purchases be construed as an example of consumerism?

3. How could the story of India having more cell phones than toilets be construed as an example of consumerism?

4. One way of characterizing much of the work of advertising agencies is as nurturing consumerism. Can you make the ethical case that advertising agencies should be banned from society?

5. In ethical terms, make the case that consumerism is good.

She's Gotta Have It…or Maybe Not

Statistics aren't available, but the amount of time guys spend spilling seduction lines—and the amount of time women spend dealing with them—is very high. Most women can deal with it coming from most guys, but what happens when the lines come from a powerful corporation?

The giant pharmaceutical company Boehringer Ingelheim has stumbled onto a drug (Flibanserin) that makes women want sex. That's not going to earn them any money, though. To get sales, they've got to convince women that they *want* to want to have sex. The problem is interesting. The drug company has discovered the cure to a disease that, by definition, no one has. If a woman—or a man—doesn't feel like having sex, then she doesn't feel like she's missing something by not doing it. The opposite is the case. She doesn't want to do it, so the fact that she doesn't feel like doing it isn't a problem at all. It's perfect, actually. What the company needs to do, therefore, is create a desire. It has to make women want (or even need) something they didn't know they wanted.

According to the *New York Times*, "Boehringer has been trying to lay the consumer groundwork with a promotional campaign about women's low libido, including a Web site, a Twitter feed and a publicity tour by Lisa Rinna, a soap opera star and former *Playboy* model who describes herself as someone who has suffered from a disorder that Boehringer refers to as a form of 'female sexual dysfunction.'" [5]

That advertising campaign is geared to create a desire for a form of women's Viagra by convincing women that they're supposed to want sex, and there's something wrong with them if they don't. The effort has its critics. Here's one argument: "Boehringer's market campaign could create anxiety among women, making them think they have a condition that requires medical treatment. 'This is really a classic case of disease branding,' said Dr. Adriane Fugh-Berman, an associate professor at Georgetown University. 'The messages are aimed at medicalizing normal conditions, and also preying on the insecurity of the patient.'" [6]

QUESTIONS

1. Dr. Fugh-Berman says that Boehringer's marketing campaign is "aimed at medicalizing normal conditions."
   o What does "medicalizing normal conditions" mean?
   o How does "medicalizing a normal condition" serve Boehringer's purpose?

2. The goal of Boehringer's marketing is to create a desire for a product. There are a number of ethical objections to this kind of campaign.
   o What does it mean to say that trying to convince low-libido women (or men) that they need a drug to want more sex is to treat them as a means and not an end?
   o How could the attempt to sell the idea that women (or men) need to need sex be construed as a violation of their basic right to freedom?

3. Boehringer created a web page dedicated to its sex drug—http://www.sexbrainbody.com—which has since been taken down. On it, a successful actress and *Playboy* model left a testimonial. It concluded with her encouraging readers to learn about sexual health and to feel comfortable talking about it. "Both," she asserted, "play an important role in overall health and well-being. It's time to focus on you!" [7]
   o What are some of the ways this message—and the messenger—create the need for consumers to have

sexual health the way the Boehringer pharmaceutical company defines the term?
   o Justify, from an ethical perspective Boehringer's use of these techniques.
   o Boehringer has decided to take the page down. What ethical argument may have convinced them to do that?

4. A *New York Times* article relates that prestigious medical journals have published research affirming that low libido really is a problem, and one suffered by a large number of women. The article also notes that "such studies have been financed by drug companies." [8]
   o What is knowledge and resource exploitation by advertisers?
   o Make the case that the knowledge and resources at the disposal of Boehringer and its advertising company are also an ethical obligation to *not* use that power to sell products.

5. Assume the critics are right. Assume that women (or men) with low libidos aren't suffering any kind of medical problem; they're just not that into sex, and there's no reason why that condition should be "cured." Make the case that even so, Boehringer is ethically justified in trying to create the need for their desire-enhancing pill.

6. A pharmaceutical company stumbles upon a drug that kills the sex drive for men and for women. The company devotes millions of dollars to a seductive advertising campaign designed to convince consumers that they really want to not want sex, and therefore they need this new medication. Make the case that this is not only ethically acceptable but laudable.

Hot Coffee

In a world of get-rich-quick schemes, few are mentioned more frequently than lawsuits. One of the reasons is the infamous McDonald's coffee case (*Liebeck v. McDonald's Restaurants*). This is what happened in 1992 in Albuquerque, New Mexico. Stella Liebeck, seventy-nine, was riding in a car driven by her grandson. They stopped at a McDonald's drive-through, where she purchased a Styrofoam cup of coffee. Wanting to add cream and sugar, she squeezed the cup between her knees and pulled off the plastic lid. The entire thing spilled back into her lap. The searing liquid left her with extensive third-degree burns. Eight days of hospitalization—which included skin grafts—were required.

Initially, she sought $20,000 from McDonald's, which was more or less the cost of her medical bills. McDonald's refused. They went to court. There it came to light that about seven hundred claims had been made by consumers between

1982 and 1992 for similar incidents. This seems to indicate that McDonald's knew—or at least should have known—that the hot coffee was a problem.

Most of the rest of the case turned around temperature questions. McDonald's admitted that they served their coffee at 185 degrees, which will burn the mouth and throat and is about 50 degrees higher than typical homemade coffee. More importantly, coffee served at temperatures up to 155 degrees won't cause burns, but the danger rises abruptly with each degree above that limit. So why did McDonald's serve it so hot? Most customers, the company claimed, bought on the way to work or home and would drink it on arrival. The high temperature would keep it fresh until then. Unfortunately, internal documents showed that McDonald's knew their customers intended to drink the coffee in the car immediately after purchase. Next, McDonald's asserted that their customers wanted their coffee hot. The restaurant conceded, however, that customers were unaware of the serious burn danger and that no adequate warning of the threat's severity was provided.

Finally, the jury awarded Liebeck $160,000 in compensatory damages and $2.7 million in punitive damages (about two days' worth of McDonalds' coffee sales). The judge, however, reduced the $2.7 million to $480,000. McDonald's threatened to appeal, and the two sides eventually came to a private settlement agreement. [9]

QUESTIONS

1. What does *caveat emptor* mean?
   o According to this doctrine, who is responsible for Stella Liebeck's burns? Explain.
   o Does the fact that she's seventy-nine years old make it more difficult to justify a caveat emptor attitude in this case?
   o One aspect of the caveat emptor doctrine is that it maximizes respect for the consumer as an independent and autonomous decider. Could that be a reason for affirming that a seventy-nine-year-old is a *better* candidate than most for a caveat emptor ethics of consumption?
2. In general terms, what does it mean to claim that an implicit contract arises around a transaction? How does that contract protect the consumer?

3. From the information provided, and from your own experience, what are the main terms of the implicit contract surrounding the purchase of coffee at a fast-food drive-through?
   o What does the restaurant owe the consumer?
   o What does the consumer owe the restaurant?
4. In order for an implicit contract to arise, the following three conditions must be met:
   o Both sides must enter the contract freely.
   o Both sides must be reasonably informed of the agreement's terms.
   o Both sides must be honest.

   Were these three conditions met in the McDonald's coffee case? Explain.
5. Make the case that the original offer by Liebeck—$20,000 from McDonald's to cover the medical bills—is ethically recommendable within the structure of an implicit contract. Use the concept of an *implied warranty*.

6. The concept of manufacturer liability gives consumers the right to sue manufacturers for defective goods. There are three kinds of product defect:
   o Design defects (errors in the product's design)
   o Manufacturing defects (errors in the production of one specific case of a generally safe product)
   o Instructional defects (poor or incomplete instructions for a product's safe use)

   Which (if any) of these defects are applicable in the McDonald's coffee case? Explain.
7. What is the concept of *strict product liability*, and how could it be applicable in this case?
8. In ethical terms, justify the original jury award to Liebeck: $160,000 in compensatory damages and $2.7 million in punitive damages (about two days of McDonalds' coffee sales).
9. Of these three ethical structures for conceiving of the coffee-buying consumer and her protections—caveat emptor, the implicit contract, and manufacturer liability—which do you believe is best? Why?

Cancel the Account

This is a condensed version of a dialogue between Vincent Ferrari and AOL, an Internet services provider known especially for its e-mail.

AOL Rep:	Hi, this is John at AOL. How may I help you today?
Vincent:	I wanted to cancel my account.
AOL Rep:	OK. You've had this account for a long time.
Vincent:	Yep!

AOL Rep:	You've used this quite a bit. What was the cause for turning this off today?
Vincent:	I just don't use it anymore.
AOL Rep:	Do you have a high-speed connection like DSL or cable?
Vincent:	Yep.
AOL Rep:	OK.
AOL Rep:	How long have you had that, the high speed?
Vincent:	Years.
AOL Rep:	Well, actually, I'm showing a lot of usage on this account.
Vincent:	Yeah a long time ago, not recently.
AOL Rep:	I'm looking at this account…
Vincent:	Either way, whatever you're seeing…
AOL Rep:	Well, what's the cause for turning this off today?
Vincent:	I don't use it.
AOL Rep:	Well, OK. Is there a problem with the software itself?
Vincent:	No. It's just I don't use it. I don't need it. I don't want it. I don't need it anymore.
AOL Rep:	So when you use it, the computer, is it for business or for school?
Vincent:	Dude, what difference does it make? I don't want the AOL account anymore. Can you please cancel it?
AOL Rep:	Well, on June second this account was signed on. It's been on for seventy-two hours.
Vincent:	I don't know how to make it any clearer.
AOL Rep:	Last year was five hundred fou—last month was 545 hours of usage.
Vincent:	I don't know how to say this any clearer, so I am just going to say this one last time. Cancel the account please.

AOL Rep:	Well explain to me what's—wha—why?
Vincent:	I am not explaining anything to you. Cancel the account.
AOL Rep:	Wha—what's the matter man? We're just—I'm just trying to help.
Vincent:	You're not helping me. You're not helping me.
AOL Rep:	I am trying to, OK.
Vincent:	Listen, I called to cancel the account. Helping me would be canceling the account. Please help me and cancel my account.
AOL Rep:	No it wouldn't actually.
Vincent:	Cancel my account!
AOL Rep:	Turning off your account would be the worst—
Vincent:	Cancel the account! Cancel the account!
AOL Rep:	Is your dad there?
Vincent:	I'm the primary payer. I'm the primary person on the account, not my dad. Cancel the account!
AOL Rep:	OK, 'cause I'm just trying to figure out—
Vincent:	Cancel the account! I don't know how to make this any clearer for you. Cancel the account. The card is mine, in my name. The account is mine and in my name. When I say, "cancel the account," I don't mean help me figure out how to keep it. Cancel the account.

This went on for almost five minutes. Part of the audio can be heard here:

Cancel AOL

Back in the days before Internet, exchanges like this would've been entirely positive for AOL. The worst that could've happened is that the company would lose the client, who they were going to lose anyway. By dragging the cancellation out, they may have convinced him to stay on, so that's what they did.

Today, with Internet, things are different. Ferrari (who, apparently, suspected that AOL would try some shenanigans) taped the conversation and posted it. The Slashdot effect—a website overwhelmed by a huge spike in traffic—followed immediately. It wasn't long before Ferrari and his conversation were appearing on shows like *Today*. The damage to the AOL brand was catastrophic. Revenue plummeted, and with no hope for recovery, the company that owned and controlled AOL at the time, Time Warner, sold off the shriveled remains.

Certainly, the Ferrari tape didn't alone bring down AOL, not even close, but it's difficult for any company to be profitable when recordings like Ferrari's are going out over national TV and available for anyone to hear, twenty-four hours a day, seven days a week, forever, online.

QUESTIONS

1. After listening to the Ferrari tape, what would consumers associate with the AOL brand? How is that brand different from a pure economic understanding of the value of AOL as a company?

2. In broad strokes, what is retributive justice? How did it work in this case? How is *this* case study in *this* textbook involved?

3. As an ethical theory, most conceptions of retributive justice highlight a notion of proportionality.
   o   What does proportionality mean?
   o   Just in general terms, and from the provided information, did Ferrari's response to AOL satisfy the proportionality requirement? Why or why not?

4. Ferrari couldn't have foreseen the how fast and how much his AOL-bashing would grow. Part of the reason is that much of the negative publicity wasn't provided directly by him. NBC rebroadcast his tape through millions of TV sets. Countless blogs and websites excerpted sections and linked to the original. (Eventually, the transcript even turned up in a business ethics textbook.) Should Ferrari take responsibility for how far things went? Justify.

5. Two ethical values support consumer revenge in the marketplace: fairness and public welfare. Fairness is the idea that the company hurt the consumer, so the consumer ought to hurt the company. Public welfare is the idea that by publicly attacking companies, consumers actually do *other* consumers a favor by warning them away from poor service providers. Sketch an ethical

justification for Ferrari's action based on the idea that he's serving the public welfare.

6. In *ethical* terms, what are some advantages of consumer revenge when compared with these other forms of consumer protection: the concept of the implied contract, the legal right to sue?

[1] "New Tappening Ads Tell Lies—Honest," *Adweek*, July 23, 2009, accessed June 2, 2011,http://www.adweek.com/aw/content_display/creative/news/e3i04a c5aa7296d367cc7c7c9623bc3df48.

[2] Tappening, order page, accessed June 2, 2011,http://www.tappening.com/Order_Tappening_Bottle.

[3] "Shopaholic Died under Purchases," *BBC*, July 28, 2009, accessed June 2, 2011,http://news.bbc.co.uk/2/hi/uk_news/england/manchester/8173271 .stm.

[4] "India Has More Mobile Phones Than Toilets: UN report," *Telegraph*, April 15, 2010, accessed June 2, 2011,http://www.telegraph.co.uk/news/worldnews/asia/india/7593567/I ndia-has-more-mobile-phones-than-toilets-UN-report.html.

[5] Duff Wilson, "Push to Market Pill Stirs Debate on Sexual Desire," *New York Times*, June 16, 2010, accessed June 2, 2011,http://www.nytimes.com/2010/06/17/business/17sexpill.html?src= me&ref=business.

[6] Duff Wilson, "Push to Market Pill Stirs Debate on Sexual Desire," *New York Times*, June 16, 2010, accessed June 2, 2011,http://www.nytimes.com/2010/06/17/business/17sexpill.html?src= me&ref=business

[7] Melissa Castellanos, "Lisa Rinna on 'Sex, Brain, Body' Connection," CBS News, May 18, 2010, accessed June 2, 2011,http://www.cbsnews.com/stories/2010/05/18/entertainment/main 6496015.shtml?tag=mncol;lst;2.

[8] Duff Wilson, "Push to Market Pill Stirs Debate on Sexual Desire," *New York Times*, June 16, 2010, accessed June 2, 2011,http://www.nytimes.com/2010/06/17/business/17sexpill.html?src= me&ref=business.

[9] Consumer Attorneys of California, "The Actual Facts About the McDonalds' Coffee Case," The 'Lectric Law Library, 1995, accessed June 2, 2011,http://www.lectlaw.com/files/cur78.htm.

NOTES:

Chapter 13:
Corporations and Social Responsibility

Chapter Overview

This chapter defines different legal structures for businesses and explores ways that individual companies may be understood not only as pursuing economic goals but also as possessing broad ethical responsibilities in society.

13.1 What Kind of Business Organizations Are There?
LEARNING OBJECTIVES

1. Distinguish and define the principal ways of organizing a business.
2. Consider liability and ethical responsibility as they relate to different forms of businesses.
3. Sketch the organizational structure of a corporation.

Paramount Pictures

Movies from Paramount Pictures begin with an image of a mountain flashed onto the screen. That mountain, reputedly, was quick-sketched on a notepad by the company's founder W. W. Hodkinson. Hodkinson got started in the movie business in the early 1900s when he opened a theater in Ogden, Utah. He shuffled films faster than his competitors (the town's two other movie houses), and so came to dominate the local market. Soon he expanded to the big city of Salt Lake, then Los Angeles, and onward.

Looking to keep his enterprise growing, Hodkinson founded a company called Paramount to provide up-front money to cash-strapped movie producers. In exchange, he got exclusive rights to screen their work in theaters. Grateful for the help, for the trust, and above all for the cash, struggling moviemakers including Adolph Zukor, Samuel Goldfish (later Goldwyn), and Cecil B. DeMille signed on to the project in five-year deals. By 1915, they were all wealthier.

Now that they no longer needed his up-front money, Zukor and the rest started trying to squirm out of their deal. Having initially taken the risk to launch their careers, Hodkinson refused to let them go. So Zukor and friends hatched a plan. Pretending to have been faced down by Hodkinson, they not only embraced the deal they'd already inked, but they also extended it for twenty-five more years in exchange for a lump sum. They took that money, opened a line of credit, and began secretly buying Paramount stock. When they accumulated enough, they took it over, and in what would be

a good premise for a revenge movie, they kicked Hodkinson out of his own company.

Types of Businesses

One lesson of Hodkinson's story is that the way a business is organized is critically important. He left Paramount open to a financial sneak attack by not keeping the whole company in his name as a sole proprietorship. When he let shares go out—when he allowed others to buy part ownership in his enterprise—he was setting himself up for what happened. Of course it's also true that he probably wouldn't have had the money needed to get the enterprise going in the first place had he not gotten a capital injection from selling off pieces of ownership.

Every form of business organization comes with advantages and disadvantages, and the specific *kinds* of organization that may be formed are numerous and change from state to state. There are, however, a number of basic types:

*   Sole proprietorship
*   Partnership
*   Limited liability company
*   S corporation
*   Nonprofit organization
*   Corporation

A sole proprietorship is the easiest kind of business to start. All you need to do is go down to the county courthouse and fill out a DBA, which is a form officially registering that you're opening a business with the name you choose. DBA means *doing business as*, so Jan Jones can go register her company as JJ's Midnight Movie House, and she doesn't need to do anything more: her tax ID number for the business is just her Social Security number, and when she's filling out her IRS forms, she counts her profits as income, just like a paycheck. Benefits of a sole proprietorship include the speed and ease of getting it going. Further, sole proprietors can take advantage of tax accounting fitted to business reality. If you're Jan Jones and you sign contracts to pay $2,500 to rent a vacant warehouse along with the rights to show Paramount's *Mommie Dearest*, and you receive $3,000 from ticket buyers, you don't pay income tax on the whole $3,000, only on the $500 profit. Finally, sole proprietorships have the advantage of belonging to their owner: she can do whatever she wants with her company without fear of being taken over by someone else.

The main disadvantage of a sole proprietorship is that the company really is an extension of you, and you're on the hook for whatever it does. So if you screen your movie and no one shows up, you can't just call the whole thing a bad idea, declare bankruptcy, and walk away. Your lenders can sue you personally for the $2,500 you agreed to pay as JJ's Midnight Movie House. Worse, if people *do* show up, but someone smokes in the theater, which starts a fire and causes injuries, those injured people can sue you personally, and maybe take everything you own. The fact that Jan Jones has to take full responsibility for what her company does is called unlimited liability. That liability, finally, is legal, but it's also clear that there's an ethical dimension to the responsibility. While few assert that it's morally wrong to fail in business, there is a reasonable objection to be made when those who fail try to avoid paying the cost.

A partnership resembles a sole proprietorship. The main difference, obviously, is that there's more than one owner: maybe there are two partners with 50 percent each or one with 50 percent and then a group of smaller shareholders each owning 10 percent of the enterprise. The bookkeeping is pretty straightforward since profits are allotted in accordance with how great a share each partner owns. All partnerships must have, finally, at least one general partner who faces unlimited liability for the company's actions. On the ethical front, responsibility starts getting murky as you move to multiple owners. If the theater burns down, and one individual partner had been assigned (and failed) the task of making sure there were a few fire extinguishers around, does that one partner bear the entire ethical burden of the injuries? Is it doled out in accordance with the percentage owned? What if one of the owners just kicked some money in as a favor to a friend, and wasn't involved in the actual operation, does *she* bear any responsibility for what happened?

Limited liability companies (LLC) and S corporations are very similar. They're both hybrids of partnerships and corporations. From the partnership side they take the tax structure. Called pass-through taxation, profits are divided among the partners or shareholders. Then those individuals pay taxes on the money like its income, a normal paycheck. What these two take from the corporate side—and the main reason people form an LLC or an S corporation—is that the enterprise's legal status provides *some* protection against liability lawsuits. If you, Jan Jones, and a few others form an LLC and the theater burns and people get injured, you may get out without losing all you have. Creditors and lawyers for the injured will be able to sue the company and probably take any money left in the till, but they'll have a harder time trying to take your personal car or the house you live in. Specific

rules, it's important to note, vary depending on the business and the location, but both options are typically limited to a certain number of participants.

On the responsibility front, this is the pressing ethical question: If the theater burns down for an LLC, the owners will likely enjoy some legal protection. Does that protection, however, extend to the ethics? Is there any difference in terms of *moral responsibility* between a partnership operating a burning theater and an LLC?

Nonprofit corporations exist in a class by themselves. Usually formed to serve a charitable or civic cause, they don't have to pay taxes since they don't make profits: they spend all their income promoting the cause they're set up to serve. The operators of nonprofits often enjoy complete protection from liability claims. What about the ethics? If a nonprofit screens *Mommie Dearest* to raise money for the cause of orphans, and the theater burns, does the fact that the entire endeavor was arranged for the public good provide moral protection from guilt when people get hurt?

Technically, what most of us mean when we use the term corporation is a C corporation (as opposed to an S corporation). One financial difference between the two is that a C corporation is taxed twice. First, the government takes a chunk of the corporation's profits before they're distributed to the company's owners, who are all those individuals holding shares. Then when the shareholders get their part, each must pay taxes on it again. Another difference is that C corporations are not limited in terms of number of shareholders. Finally, most of the corporations that people are familiar with are public, meaning that the company's shares are available for purchase by anyone with the money to spend. There are, it should be noted, private corporations (and the similar "closely held" corporations) where share allocation is limited to a group or single person, but again, most of the commonly referenced incorporated companies are listed for public sale in places including the New York Stock Exchange, and you or I may become partial owners. In fact, and as the story of W. W. Hodkinson teaches, if we get enough money, we can buy the shares to take over the business.

Corporations step away from easier-to-form partnerships by providing protection to owners against liability claims. In the case of C corporations, that protection is significant. In many cases, the protection is *total*: completely insulated from liability, shareholders can lose their investment if the company does something it shouldn't and gets sued, but their personal possessions are completely safe. This is the case, for example, with the mega movie chain Regal Cinemas. The price of one share of that company today was $13.77. If you buy that, then no matter what the company does tomorrow, the most you could possibly lose is a little under $15. No one likes to lose $15, but still, there's a very large freedom from responsibility here. If Regal tries to save some money (and therefore boost its share price and your profit) by intentionally not charging their fire extinguishers, and on the day a blockbuster gets released ten theaters in various states burn with accompanying human suffering and a major number of deaths, the company may go bankrupt under a flood of lawsuits and justifiable public outrage. But you, one of the owners, would be out three $5 bills.

Corporations play a very large role in business ethics for two reasons. First, their independence from their specific owners opens questions about who—if anyone—should take moral responsibility for what the corporation does. Second, because corporations today have grown so large and powerful, because they touch all our lives in so many ways so often, the ethical questions they raise become hard to avoid. Both these dimensions of the modern corporation, the ethical ambiguity and the potentially huge size, relate to the history of the institution.

A Very Brief History and Description of the Corporation
Exxon Mobil's market value is around $450 billion. Just to compare, the GDP of Portugal—the total value of all goods and services produced in the country each year—is about $250 billion (when converted to US dollars). Wal-Mart's revenues are climbing above $375 billion, which is a full third of the total revenues (in the form of taxes) collected by the US federal government from individuals. If Wal-Mart were a sovereign nation, it would be China's fourth largest export market. Less abstractly, the size and penetration of the Ford Motor Company can be felt just by going out on the street and watching their products pass by. And if you go to a movie from Paramount, or laugh for a while with the Comedy Channel, or check out music videos on MTV, you're patronizing the behemoth called Viacom.

All these businesses, along with the rest of the corporations on the *Fortune* 500 list and then the many that didn't make the top tier, change our lives most every day. If you outfitted your dorm room or apartment at Wal-Mart, it was a decision made by an executive buyer that determined the choices you'd have. If you're thinking about voting this year, Jon Stewart at Comedy Central is doing all he can to guide the way you decide which lever to pull. If you go to see a concert next weekend, an MTV executive may have been the one who originally pulled that group out of obscurity. Publicly held

corporations, all this means, aren't just places where we go to work, or manufacturers that supply our necessities: they set the parameters and directions of our lives.

The first corporations extended directly from governments. In 1600, the English monarchy designated the British East India Company to manage international trade between the homeland and the Indian subcontinent. Shareholders did extremely well. By the 1800s, private enterprise was breaking away from tight governmental association; the corporation as we know it today began taking shape when individuals started claiming a right to freely associate for their economic benefit without direct governmental oversight and license.

Modern corporations are formed by a group of people who fill out the papers and register the name. Once it's created, however, the business exists as a *legally distinct entity*. In the eyes of the law, it is

- perpetual—it can survive even after its founders have passed away;
- responsible—just like a person—in the narrow sense in that it holds specific legal obligations and rights.

In 1819, the US Supreme Court defined a corporation as "an artificial being, invisible, intangible and existing only in the contemplation of the law." [1] This legal independence clears the way for owners (shareholders) to escape liability claims made against the corporation. Because the business stands on its own, because it is a "being," all claims must be made against it, not the shareholders standing behind.

Corporations are structured in diverse ways, but the basic governing form starts with the shareholders electing a board of directors. Wal-Mart, for example, is governed by a fifteen-member board, which is elected each year. The board holds two main responsibilities. One is oversight; it keeps track of what's going on and reports back to shareholders. The other responsibility is operational. The board selects individuals who'll run the company on a day-to-day basis. Frequently, a chief executive officer (CEO) leads this team and is ultimately responsible for making sure Wal-Mart is buying from suppliers at the lowest possible price, getting goods into the stores before stock runs out, and convincing customers to return and do more buying.

If the CEO and management team is good, there's a decent chance the company will be successful and grow. Good leadership, however, can't alone explain the mega-dimensions of today's larger corporations. One critical element of the corporate structure that contributes to the size is the owner-as-shareholder model. The model allows businesses to collect large amounts of cash quickly. Simply by printing up and selling more shares, a corporation raises potentially huge sums. That capital can be reinvested in the business—maybe to build new Wal-Mart stores in growing suburbs—and the corporation's value goes up. It's true that the original shareholders now own less of the company on a percentage basis (because there are more owners), but their shares are worth more because the company is worth more, so they're unlikely to complain. As long as that virtuous cycle continues, well-run corporations can grow very quickly.

While all that growth is going on, the actual owners—shareholders—can be at home sitting in front of the TV. Many shareholders, actually, have almost no idea of what's happening inside the company they partially own. With respect to business ethics, this adds another level of complexity to the question about whom, if anyone, should be held *morally* responsible for what the corporation does. If you just go out in the street and ask a passerby, "Who do you think bears moral responsibility for what a company does?" the answer you'll probably get is the owners. But in the case of corporations, they're protected *legally* by a liability firewall, and now they're also protected *structurally* by the fact that they—along with the multitude of other owners scattered all over the country and even the globe—aren't necessarily involved in making the company's operational decisions. These two factors combined have thrust this question to the forefront of questions about ethics in the economic world: can these artificial beings called corporations themselves have moral responsibilities to go along with their legal responsibility to operate within the law?

KEY TAKEAWAYS

- Businesses can be organized in various ways.
- The way a business is organized affects economic questions about profits, legal questions about liability, and ethical questions about responsibility.
- In sole proprietorships and partnerships, owners take economic, legal, and moral responsibility for what the company does.
- In public corporations, owners are shielded from legal responsibility for the enterprise's actions; the question about moral responsibility remains open.
- The structure of corporations—the ability to sell shares publicly—is instrumental in their ability to grow economically.

REVIEW QUESTIONS

1. What are the main ways of organizing a business?
2. What kind of business organization might be suitable for a plumber? Explain.
3. Why might someone choose to organize as an LLC instead of a sole proprietorship?
4. In legal terms, what is the relation between a corporation and those individuals who found the corporation?
5. In what ways does the structure of a corporation protect its owners from absorbing ethical responsibility for the company's actions?
6. How can corporations raise money?

[1] Trustees of Dartmouth College v. Woodward, 17 U.S. (4 Wheat.) 518 (1819).

13.2 Three Theories of Corporate Social Responsibility
LEARNING OBJECTIVE

1. Define and discuss the three main theories of corporate social responsibility.

Corporations as Responsible

A Civil Action was originally a novel, but more people have seen the movie, which was distributed by W. W. Hodkinson's old company, Paramount. One of the memorable scenes is John Travolta playing a hotshot lawyer speeding up a rural highway to Woburn, Massachusetts. He gets pulled over and ticketed. Then he continues on his way to investigate whether there's any money to be made launching a lawsuit against a company that allowed toxic industrial waste to escape into the town's aquifer. The polluted water, Travolta suspects, eventually surfaced as birth defects. After checking things out, he races his Porsche back to Boston at the same speed. Same result. [1]

One of the movie's messages is that many corporations are like greedy lawyers—they have little sense of right and wrong, and their behavior can only be modified by money. The lesson is that you can't make Travolta slow down and drive safely by appealing to the right of others to use the road without being threatened by speeding Porsches, or by pleading with him to respect general social well-being that is served when everyone travels at about the same speed. If you want him to slow down, there's only one effective strategy: raise the traffic ticket fine. Make the money hurt. Analogously for companies, if you want them to stop polluting, hit them with harder penalties when they're caught.

What if that's not the only way for corporations to exist in the world, though? What if people who directed businesses began understanding their enterprise not only in financial terms (as profits and losses) but also in ethical ones? What if companies became, in a certain moral sense, like people, members of society bound by the same kinds of duties and responsibilities that you and I wrestle with every day? When companies *are* seen that way, a conception of *corporate social responsibility* comes forward.

Three Approaches to Corporate Responsibility

According to the traditional view of the corporation, it exists primarily to make profits. From this money-centered perspective, insofar as business ethics are important, they apply to moral dilemmas arising as the struggle for profit proceeds. These dilemmas include: "What obligations do organizations have to ensure that individuals seeking employment or promotion are treated fairly?" "How should conflicts of interest be handled?" and "What kind of advertising strategy should be pursued?" Most of this textbook has been dedicated to these and similar questions.

While these dilemmas continue to be important throughout the economic world, when businesses are conceived as holding a wide range of economic *and* civic responsibilities as part of their daily operation, the field of business ethics expands correspondingly. Now there are large sets of issues that need to be confronted and managed outside of, and independent of the struggle for money. Broadly, there are three theoretical approaches to these new responsibilities:
1. Corporate social responsibility (CSR)
2. The triple bottom line
3. Stakeholder theory

Corporate Social Responsibility (CSR)

The title corporate social responsibility has two meanings. First, it's a general name for any theory of the corporation that emphasizes both the responsibility to make money and the responsibility to interact ethically with the surrounding community. Second, corporate social responsibility is also a specific conception of that responsibility to profit while playing a role in broader questions of community welfare.

As a specific theory of the way corporations interact with the surrounding community and larger world, corporate social responsibility (CSR) is composed of four obligations:
1. The **economic responsibility** to make money. Required by simple economics, this obligation is the business version of the human survival instinct. Companies that don't make profits are—in a modern market economy—doomed to perish. Of course there are special cases. Nonprofit organizations make money (from their own activities as well as through donations

and grants), but pour it back into their work. Also, public/private hybrids can operate without turning a profit. In some cities, trash collection is handled by this kind of organization, one that keeps the streets clean without (at least theoretically) making anyone rich. For the vast majority of operations, however, there have to be profits. Without them, there's no business and no business ethics.

2. The **legal responsibility** to adhere to rules and regulations. Like the previous, this responsibility is not controversial. What proponents of CSR argue, however, is that this obligation must be understood as a proactive duty. That is, laws aren't boundaries that enterprises skirt and cross over if the penalty is low; instead, responsible organizations accept the rules as a social good and make good faith efforts to obey not just the letter but also the spirit of the limits. In concrete terms, this is the difference between the driver who stays under the speed limit because he can't afford a traffic ticket, and one who obeys because society as a whole is served when we all agree to respect the signs and stoplights and limits. Going back to John Travolta racing his Porsche up and down the rural highway, he sensed none of this respect. The same goes for the toxic company W. R. Grace Incorporated as it's portrayed in the movie: neither one obeys regulations and laws until the fines get so high they've got no choice. As against that model of behavior, a CSR vision of business affirms that society's limits will be scrupulously obeyed, even if the fine is only one dollar.

3. The **ethical responsibility** to do what's right even when not required by the letter or spirit of the law. This is the theory's keystone obligation, and it depends on a coherent corporate culture that views the business itself as a citizen in society, with the kind of obligations that citizenship normally entails. When someone is racing their Porsche along a country road on a freezing winter's night and encounters another driver stopped on the roadside with a flat, there's a social obligation to do something, though not a legal one. The same logic can work in the corporate world. Many industrial plants produce, as an unavoidable part of their fabricating process, poisonous waste. In Woburn, Massachusetts, W. R. Grace did that, as well as Beatrice Foods. The law governing toxic waste disposal was ambiguous, but even if the companies weren't legally required to enclose their poisons in double-encased, leak-proof barrels, isn't that the right thing to do so as to ensure that the contamination will be safely contained? True, it might not be the right thing to do in terms of pure profits, but

from a perspective that values *everyone's* welfare as being valuable, the measure could be recommendable.

4. The **philanthropic responsibility** to contribute to society's projects even when they're independent of the particular business. A lawyer driving home from work may spot the local children gathered around a makeshift lemonade stand and sense an obligation to buy a drink to contribute to the neighborhood project. Similarly, a law firm may volunteer access to their offices for an afternoon every year so some local schoolchildren may take a field trip to discover what lawyers do all day. An industrial chemical company may take the lead in rehabilitating an empty lot into a park. None of these acts arise as obligations extending from the day-to-day operations of the business involved. They're not like the responsibility a chemical firm has for safe disposal of its waste. Instead, these public acts of generosity represent a view that businesses, like everyone in the world, have some obligation to support the general welfare in ways determined by the needs of the surrounding community.

Taken in order from top to bottom, these four obligations are *decreasingly* pressing within the theory of corporate social responsibility. After satisfying the top responsibility, attention turns to the second and so on. At the extremes, the logic behind this ranking works easily. A law firm on the verge of going broke probably doesn't have the responsibility to open up for school visits, at least not if the tours interfere with the accumulation of billable hours and revenue. Obviously, if the firm *does* go broke and out of business, there won't be any school visits in any case, so faced with financial hardship, lawyers are clearly obligated to fulfill their economic obligations before philanthropic ones.

More difficult questions arise when the economic responsibility conflicts with the legal one. For example, to remain profitable, an industrial plant may need to dispose of waste and toxins in barrels that barely meet legally required strengths. Assuming those legal limits are insufficiently strict to guarantee the barrels' seal, the spirit of the law may seem violated. The positive economic aspect of the decision to cut corners is the ability to stay in business. That means local workers won't lose their jobs, the familial stresses of unemployment will be avoided, suppliers will maintain their contracts, and consumers will still be served. The negative, however, is the possibility—and the reality at Woburn—that those toxins will escape their containers and leave a generation of workers' children poisoned.

Knowing what we do now about those Woburn children, there's no real conflict; anything would have been better than

letting the toxins escape. If necessary, the company should have accepted bankruptcy before causing the social damage it did. At the time of the decision, however, there may have been less certainty about exactly what the risks and benefits were. Even among individuals promoting a strong sense of corporate responsibility for the surrounding community, there may have been no clear answer to the question about the proper course of action. Regardless, corporate social responsibility means every business holds four kinds of obligations and should respond to them in order: first the economic, then the legal, next the ethical, and finally the philanthropic.

The Triple Bottom Line

The triple bottom line is a form of corporate social responsibility dictating that corporate leaders tabulate bottom-line results not only in economic terms (costs versus revenue) but also in terms of company effects in the social realm, and with respect to the environment. There are two keys to this idea. First, the three columns of responsibility must be kept separate, with results reported independently for each. Second, in all three of these areas, the company should obtain sustainable results.

The notion of sustainability is very specific. At the intersection of ethics and economics, **sustainability** means the long-term maintenance of balance. As elaborated by theorists including John Elkington, here's how the balance is defined and achieved economically, socially, and environmentally:

- **Economic sustainability** values long-term financial solidity over more volatile, short-term profits, no matter how high. According to the triple-bottom-line model, large corporations have a responsibility to create business plans allowing stable and prolonged action. That bias in favor of duration should make companies hesitant about investing in things like dot-coms. While it's true that speculative ventures may lead to windfalls, they may also lead to collapse. Silicon Valley, California, for example, is full of small, start-up companies. A few will convert into the next Google, Apple, and Microsoft. What gets left out, however, of the newspaper reports hailing the accomplishments of a Steve Jobs or a Bill Gates are all those other people who never made it—all those who invested family savings in a project that ended up bankrupt. Sustainability as a virtue means valuing business plans that may not lead to quick riches but that also avoid calamitous losses.

Moving this reasoning over to the case of W. R. Grace dumping toxins into the ground soil, there's a possible economic-sustainability argument against that kind of action. Corporations trying to get away with polluting the environment or other kinds of objectionable actions may, it's true, increase their bottom line in the short term. Money is saved on disposal costs. Looking further out, however, there's a risk that a later discovery of the action could lead to catastrophic *economic* consequences (like personal injury lawyers filing huge lawsuits). This possibility leads immediately to the conclusion that concern for corporate sustainability in financial terms argues against the dumping.

- **Social sustainability** values balance in people's lives and the way we live. A world in which a few *Fortune* 500 executives are hauling down millions a year, while millions of people elsewhere in the world are living on pennies a day can't go on forever. As the imbalances grow, as the rich get richer and the poor get both poorer and more numerous, the chances that society itself will collapse in anger and revolution increase. The threat of governmental overthrow from below sounds remote—almost absurd—to Americans who are accustomed to a solid middle class and minimal resentment of the wealthy. In world history, however, such revolutions are quite common. That doesn't mean revolution is coming to our time's developed nations. It may indicate, however, that for a business to be stable over the long term, opportunities and subsequently wealth need to be spread out to cover as many people as possible.

The fair trade movement fits this ethical imperative to shared opportunity and wealth. Developed and refined as an idea in Europe in the 1960s, organizations promoting fair trade ask businesses—especially large producers in the richest countries—to guarantee that suppliers in impoverished nations receive reasonable payment for their goods and services even when the raw economic laws of supply and demand don't require it. An array of ethical arguments may be arranged to support fair trade, but on the front of sustainability, the lead argument is that peace and order in the world depend on the world's resources being divided up in ways that limit envy, resentment, and anger.

Social sustainability doesn't end with dollars; it also requires *human respect*. All work, the logic of stability dictates, contains dignity, and no workers deserve to be treated like machines or as expendable tools on a production line. In today's capitalism, many see—and the perception is especially strong in Europe—a world in which dignity has been stripped away from a large number of trades and professions. They see minimum wage workers who'll be fired as soon as the next economic downturn arrives. They see bosses hiring from temporary agencies, turning them over fast, not even bothering to learn their names. It's certainly possible that these kinds of attitudes, this contempt visible in so many workplaces where the McJob reigns, can't continue. Just as people won't stand for pennies in wages while their bosses get millions, so too they ultimately will refuse to accept being treated as less dignified than the boss.

Finally, social sustainability requires that corporations as citizens in a specific community of people maintain a healthy relationship with those people. Fitting this obligation into the case of W. R. Grace in Woburn, it's immediately clear that any corporation spilling toxins that later appear as birth defects in area children isn't going to be able to sustain anything with those living nearby. Any hope for cooperation in the name of mutual benefit will be drowned by justified hatred.

- **Environmental sustainability** begins from the affirmation that natural resources—especially the oil fueling our engines, the clean air we breathe, and the water we drink—are limited. If those things deteriorate significantly, our children won't be able to enjoy the same quality of life most of us experience. Conservation of resources, therefore, becomes tremendously important, as does the development of new sources of energy that may substitute those we're currently using.

Further, the case of an industrial chemical company pouring toxins into the ground that erupt years later with horrific consequences evidences this: not only are resources finite, but our earth is limited in its ability to naturally regenerate clean air and water from the smokestacks and runoff of our industries. There are, clearly, good faith debates that thoughtful people can have about *where* those limits are. For example, have we released greenhouse gases into the air so heavily that the earth's temperature is rising? No one knows for sure, but it's certain that *somewhere* there's a limit; at some point carbon-burning pollution will do to the planet what toxic runoff did in Woburn: make the place unlivable. Sustainability, finally, on this environmental front means actions must be taken to facilitate our natural world's renewal. Recycling or cleaning up contamination that already exists is important here, as is limiting the pollution emitted from factories, cars, and consumer products in the first place. All these are actions that corporations must support, not because they're legally required to do so, but because the preservation of a livable planet is a direct obligation within the triple-bottom-line model of business responsibility.

Together, these three notions of sustainability—economic, social, and environmental—guide businesses toward actions fitted to the conception of the corporation as a participating citizen in the community and not just as a money machine.

One deep difference between corporate social responsibility and the triple bottom line is cultural. The first is more American, the second European. Americans, accustomed to economic progress, tend to be more comfortable with, and optimistic about, change. Collectively, Americans want business to transform the world, and ethical thinking is there (hopefully) to help the transformations maximize improvement across society. Europeans, accustomed to general economic decline with respect to the United States, view change much less favorably. Their inclination is to slow development down, and to keep things the same as far as possible. This outlook is naturally suited to sustainability as a guiding value.

It's important to note that while sustainability as a business goal puts the breaks on the economic world, and is very conservative in the (nonpolitical) sense that it favors the current situation over a changed one, that doesn't mean recommending a pure freeze. Sustainability isn't the same as Ludditism, which is a flat resistance to all technological change.

The Luddites were a band of textile workers in Britain in the 1800s that saw (correctly) that mechanized looms would soon rob them not only of their livelihood but also of their way of life. To stop the change, they invaded a few factories and broke everything in sight. Their brute strategy succeeded very briefly and then failed totally. Today, Ludditism is the general opposition to new technologies in any industry on the grounds that they tear the existing social fabric: they force people to change in the workplace and then everyplace, whether they like it or not. There's an element of (perhaps justifiable) fear of the future in both Ludditism and the business ethics of sustainability, but there are differences between the two also. For example, sustainability concerns don't always stand against technological advances. Actually, innovation is favored *as long as* advances are made in the name of maintaining the status quo. For example, advances in wind power generation may allow our society to continue using energy as we do, even as oil reserves dwindle, and with the further benefit of limiting air pollution.

Stakeholder Theory

Stakeholder theory, which has been described by Edward Freeman and others, is the mirror image of corporate social responsibility. Instead of starting with a business and looking out into the world to see what ethical obligations are there, stakeholder theory starts in the world. It lists and describes those individuals and groups who will be affected by (or affect) the company's actions and asks, "What are their legitimate claims on the business?" "What rights do they have with respect to the company's actions?" and "What kind of responsibilities and obligations can they justifiably impose on a particular business?" In a single sentence, stakeholder theory affirms that *those whose lives are touched by a corporation hold a right and obligation to participate in directing it.*

As a simple example, when a factory produces industrial waste, a CSR perspective attaches a responsibility directly to factory owners to dispose of the waste safely. By contrast, a stakeholder theorist begins with those living in the surrounding community who may find their environment poisoned, and begins to talk about business ethics by insisting that they have a right to clean air and water. Therefore, they're stakeholders in the company and their voices must contribute to corporate decisions. It's true that they may own no stock, but they have a moral claim to participate in the decision-making process. This is a very important point. At least in theoretical form, those affected by a company's actions actually become something like shareholders and owners. Because they're touched by a company's actions, they have a right to participate in managing it.

Who are the stakeholders surrounding companies? The answer depends on the particular business, but the list can be quite extensive. If the enterprise produces chemicals for industrial use and is located in a small Massachusetts town, the stakeholders include:

- Company owners, whether a private individual or shareholders
- Company workers
- Customers and potential customers of the company
- Suppliers and potential suppliers to the company
- Everyone living in the town who may be affected by contamination from workplace operations
- Creditors whose money or loaned goods are mixed into the company's actions
- Government entities involved in regulation and taxation
- Local businesses that cater to company employees (restaurants where workers have lunch, grocery stores where employee families shop, and similar)
- Other companies in the same line of work competing for market share
- Other companies that may find themselves subjected to new and potentially burdensome regulations because of contamination at that one Massachusetts plant

The first five on the list—shareholders, workers, customers, suppliers, and community—may be cited as the five cardinal stakeholders.

The outer limits of stake holding are blurry. In an abstract sense, it's probably true that everyone in the world counts as a stakeholder of any serious factory insofar as we all breathe the same air and because the global economy is so tightly linked that decisions taken in a boardroom in a small town on the East Coast can end up costing someone in India her job and the effects keep rippling out from there.

In practical terms, however, a strict stakeholder theory—one insistently bestowing the power to make ethical claims on *anyone* affected by a company's action—would be inoperable. There'd be no end to simply figuring out whose rights needed to be accounted for. Realistically, the stakeholders surrounding a business should be defined as those tangibly affected by the company's action. There ought to be an unbroken line that you can follow from a corporate decision to an individual's life.

Once a discrete set of stakeholders surrounding an enterprise has been located, stakeholder ethics may begin. The purpose of the firm, underneath this theory, is to maximize profit on a collective bottom line, with profit defined not as money but as human welfare. The collective bottom line is the summed effect of a company's actions on *all* stakeholders. Company managers, that means, are primarily charged not with representing the interests of shareholders (the owners of the company) but with the more social task of coordinating the interests of *all* stakeholders, balancing them in the case of conflict and maximizing the sum of benefits over the medium and long term. Corporate directors, in other words, spend part of the day just as directors always have: explaining to board members and shareholders how it is that the current plans will boost profits. They spend other parts of the day, however, talking with other stakeholders about *their* interests: they ask for input from local environmentalists about how pollution could be limited, they seek advice from consumers about how product safety could be improved and so on. At every turn, stakeholders are treated (to some extent) like shareholders, as people whose interests need to be served and whose voices carry real force.

In many cases transparency is an important value for those promoting stakeholder ethics. The reasoning is simple: if you're going to let every stakeholder actively participate in a corporation's decision making, then those stakeholders need to have a good idea about what's going on. In the case of W. R. Grace, for example, it's important to see that a stakeholder theory would not necessarily and immediately have acted to prohibit the dumping of toxins into the soil. Instead, the theory demands that all those who may be affected know what's being dumped, what the risks are to people and the environment, and what the costs are of taking the steps necessary to dispose of the chemical runoff more permanently and safely.

As already noted, we know now what W. R. Grace should have done under most every ethical theory. At the time, however, stakeholders fully informed of the situation may have been less sure because it wasn't so clear that the runoff would cause so many problems (or any problems at all). Given that, owners may have favored dumping because that increases profits. Next, what about workers in town? It's important to keep in mind that the safe removal of the waste may have lowered company profits and potentially caused some layoffs or delayed wage hikes. As stakeholders, they may have been willing to agree to the dumping too. The same goes for community politicians who perhaps would see increased tax revenue as a positive effect of high corporate profits.

What's certain is that stakeholder theory obligates corporate directors to appeal to all sides and balance everyone's interests and welfare in the name of maximizing benefits across the spectrum of those whose lives are touched by the business.

Conclusion on the Three Forms of Corporate Social Responsibility

Traditionally, the directors of companies have had an extremely difficult but very narrowly defined responsibility: guide the enterprise toward money. The best companies have been those generating the highest sales, gaining the most customers, and clearing the largest profits. As for ethical questions, they've been arranged around the basic obligation to represent the owners' central interest, which presumably is to profit from their investment. Consequently, the field of business ethics has mainly concerned conflicts and dilemmas erupting inside the company as people try to work together to win in the very competitive economic world. The idea of corporate social responsibility—along with the related ideas of the triple bottom line and stakeholder theory—opens a different kind of business ethics. Morality in the economic world is now about corporate directors sensing and responding to a broad range of obligations, ones extending through the town where the business is located and then out into surrounding communities and through society generally. In Woburn, Massachusetts, in the early 1980s, this conflict between two ways of running a business played out in the

Hollywood depiction of the lawyer played by John Travolta. At the movie's beginning, right and wrong for a business got decided in dollars and without broader sensibility. Travolta's law firm existed to make money and operated by accepting only cases that promised big payouts. That's what brought Travolta to Woburn, the chance to sue deep-pocketed W. R. Grace for poisoning the land with toxic runoff and for destroying the lives of families living near the pools of contamination. Over the course of the movie, however, Travolta becomes attached to Woburn's cause and the social good of fighting for a clean environment. By the end, he's risking his firm's high profits—and, according to his law-firm partners, all common sense—to make sure that harmed people living in town get their good lives back, and to ensure that a Woburn-like toxic disaster won't happen again.

In terms of business ethics, it's not difficult to interpret Travolta's transformation from a businessman taking care of the bottom line, to one engaged by a broader vision of social responsibility. Each of the three discussed theories— corporate social responsibility, the triple bottom line, stakeholder theory—can be fit into the movie *A Civil Action*. In terms of corporate social responsibility, Travolta came to believe that his job as the law firm's leader obligated him to satisfy his economic responsibility to make money for the firm by suing for financial damages while also acting legally. Further, his firm needed to satisfy the ethical responsibility to help others in Woburn gets their good lives back. Here, there is a basic duty to help others in need when you have the capability. Finally, there was an element of philanthropy in Travolta's endeavor because his law firm pursued a case that served the greater good even though more profitable work opportunities were available.

In terms of the triple bottom line of economics, society, and the environment, Travolta came to believe that his job as the law firm's leader obligated him to take account of and do well in all three areas. It was no longer enough to win money; his business had a moral responsibility to win for society and to win for the environment also. The long-term goal was to ensure the economic sustainability of his firm, the sustainability of healthy family life in Woburn, and the sustainability of clean earth and air in that part of Massachusetts.

In terms of stakeholder ethics, Travolta came to believe that his job as the law firm's leader obligated him not only to work for the firm's owners (including himself) but also to take direction from those who would be affected by the firm's actions. That meant considering—trying to balance and to

add up—the interests of his partners and all those who lived in Woburn.

Finally, because Travolta's story was also a Hollywood story, his transformation on the big screen was presented as the change from an aloof bad guy to a caring good guy. It's not clear, however, in the real world whether a corporate ethics based on social responsibility, the triple bottom line, or all stakeholders is actually recommendable. The debate between the two ways of thinking about business—the traditional, profit-centered view and the broader, socially responsible view—is hard-fought and intensified by good arguments on both sides.

KEY TAKEAWAYS

- Corporations may have obligations that go beyond generating profits and include the larger society.
- Corporate social responsibility as a specific theory affirms that corporations are entities with economic, legal, ethical, and philanthropic obligations.
- Corporations responsible for a triple bottom line seek sustainability in the economic, social, and environmental realms.
- Corporate ethics built on stakeholder theory seek to involve all those affected by the organization in its decision-making process.

REVIEW QUESTIONS

1. For corporate advocates of the specific CSR theory, what are the responsibilities the corporation holds, and how are conflicts between those responsibilities managed?
2. Create a hypothetical situation in which philanthropy would not be required of a corporation by CSR theory.
3. What does *sustainability* mean within each of the three columns of the theory of the triple bottom line?
4. How does the fair trade movement fit together with the triple-bottom-line theory of corporate responsibility?
5. Who are the stakeholders in stakeholder ethics?
6. What does it mean for a corporate director to "balance stakeholder interests"?
7. What basic elements do CSR, the triple bottom line, and stakeholder theory have in common?

[1] *A Civil Action*, directed by Steven Zaillian (New York: Scott Rudin, 1998), film.

13.3 Should Corporations Have Social Responsibilities? The Arguments in Favor

LEARNING OBJECTIVE

1. Define and elaborate the major arguments in favor of corporations having social and environmental responsibilities.

Why Should Corporations Have Social Responsibilities?

Broadly, there are three kinds of arguments in favor of placing corporations, at least large and fully developed ones, within an ethical context of expansive social and environmental responsibilities:

1. Corporations are morally required to accept those responsibilities.
2. The existence of externalities attaches companies, in operational and economic terms, to those responsibilities.
3. Enlightened self-interest leads to voluntarily embracing those responsibilities.

The Moral Requirement Argument

The moral requirement that business goals go beyond the bottom line to include the people and world we all share is built on the following arguments:

- Corporations are already involved in the broad social world and the ethical dilemmas defining it. For example, factories producing toxic waste are making a statement about the safety and well-being of those living nearby every time they dispose of the toxins. If they follow the cheapest—and least safe—route in order to maximize profits, they *aren't* avoiding the entire question of social responsibility; they're saying with their actions that the well-being of townspeople doesn't matter too much. That's an ethical stance. It may be good or bad, it may be justifiable or not, but it's definitely ethics. Choosing, in other words, not to be involved in surrounding ethical issues *is* an ethical choice. Finally, because companies are inescapably linked to the ethical issues surrounding them, they're involved with some form of corporate social responsibility whether they like it or not.

- Corporations, at least well-established, successful, and powerful ones, can be involved in the effective resolution of broad social problems, and that ability implies an obligation. Whether we're talking about a person or a business, the possession of wealth and power is also a duty to balance that privilege by helping those with fewer resources. Many accept the argument that individuals who are extraordinarily rich have an obligation to give some back by, say, creating an educational foundation or something similar. That's why people say, "To whom much is given, much is

expected." Here, what's being argued is that the same obligation applies to companies.

- Corporations rely on much more than their owners and shareholders. They need suppliers who provide materials, employees who labor, a town where the workplace may be located, consumers who buy, air to breathe, water to drink, and almost everything. Because a business relies on all that, the argument goes, it's automatically responsible—to some extent—for the welfare and protection of those things.

- Because businesses cause problems in the larger world, they're obligated to participate in the problems' resolution. What kinds of problems are caused? Taking the example of an industrial chemical factory, toxic waste *is* produced. Even though it may be disposed of carefully, that doesn't erase the fact that barrels of poison are buried somewhere and a threat remains, no matter how small. Similarly, companies that fire workers create social tensions. The dismissal may have been necessary or fully justified, but that doesn't change the fact that problems are produced, and with them comes a responsibility to participate in alleviating the negative effects.

Taken together, these arguments justify the vision of any particular enterprise as much more than an economic wellspring of money. Businesses become partners in a wide world of interconnected problems and shared obligations to deal with them.

The Externality Argument

The second type of argument favoring corporate social responsibility revolves around *externalities*. These attach corporations to social responsibilities not morally but operationally. An externality in the economic world is a cost of a good or service that isn't accounted for in the price (when that price is established through basic laws of supply and demand). For example, if a corporation's factory emits significant air pollution, and that results in a high incidence of upper respiratory infections in the nearby town, then a disproportionately high number of teachers and police officers (among others) are going to call into work sick throughout the year. Substitute teachers and replacement officers will need to be hired, and that cost will be borne by everyone in town when they receive a higher tax bill. The corporation owning the pollution-belching factory, that means, gets the full amount of money from the sale of its products but doesn't pay the full cost of producing them since the broader public is shouldering part of the pollution bill. This strikes many as unfair.

Another example might be a company underfunding its pension accounts. The business may eventually shut its doors, deliver final profits to shareholders, and leave retired workers without the monthly checks they'd been counting on. Then the government may have to step in with food stamps, welfare payments, and similar to make up for the shortfall, and in the final tabulation, the general public ends up paying labor costs that should have been borne by shareholders.

Externalities, it should be noted, aren't always negative. For example, the iPhone does a pretty good job of displaying traffic congestion in real time on its map. That ability costs money to develop, which Apple invested, and then they get cash back when an iPhone sells. Apple doesn't receive, however, anything from those drivers who don't purchase an iPhone but still benefit from it: those who get to where they're going a bit faster because everyone who *does* have an iPhone is navigating an alternate route. More, *everyone* benefits from cleaner air when traffic jams are diminished, but again, that part of the benefit, which should channel back to Apple to offset its research and production costs, ends up uncompensated.

Whether an externality is negative or positive—whether a company's bottom line rises or falls with it—a strong argument remains for broad corporate responsibility wherever an externality exists. Because these parts of corporate interaction with the world aren't accounted for in dollars and cents, a broad ethical discussion must be introduced to determine what, if any, obligations or benefits arise.

The Enlightened Self-interest Argument
The third kind of argument in favor of corporations as seats of social responsibility grows from the notion of enlightened self-interest. Enlightened self-interest means businesses take on broad responsibilities because, on careful analysis, that public generosity also benefits the company. The benefits run along a number of lines:

- Corporations perceived as socially engaged may be rewarded with more and more satisfied customers. TOM's shoes is an excellent example. For every pair of shoes they sell, they give a pair away to needy children. No one doubts that this is a noble action—one displaying corporate vision as going beyond the bottom line—but it's also quite lucrative. Many people buy from TOMS *because* of the antipoverty donations, and those customers feel good about their footwear knowing that a child somewhere is better off.

- Organizations positively engaged with society or the environment may find it easier to hire top-notch employees. All workers seek job satisfaction, and given that you spend eight hours a day on the job, the ingredients of satisfaction go beyond salary level. Consequently, workers who select from multiple job offers may find themselves attracted to an enterprise that does some good in the world. This point can also be repeated negatively. Some organizations with more checkered reputations may find it difficult to hire good people even at a high salary because workers simply don't want to have their name associated with the operation. A curious example to fit in here is the Central Intelligence Agency. Some people will accept a job there at a salary lower than they'd make in the private realm because it's the CIA, and others won't work there even if it's their best offer in terms of money because it's the CIA.

- Organizations taking the initiative in regulating themselves in the name of social betterment may hold off more stringent requirements that might otherwise be imposed by governmental authorities. For example, a lab fabricating industrial chemicals may wrap their toxic waste in not only the legally required single, leak-proof barrel but a second as well, to positively ensure public safety. That proactive step is not only good for the environment, but it may help the bottom line if it effectively closes off a regulatory commission's discussion about requiring *triple* barrel protections.

Enlightened self-interest starts with the belief that there are many opportunities for corporations to do well (make money) in the world by doing good (being ethically responsible). From there, it's reasonable to assert that *because* those opportunities exist, corporations have no excuse for not seeking them out, and then profiting from them, while helping everyone else along the way.

One basic question about enlightened self-interest is, "Are corporations making money because they're doing good deeds, or are they doing good deeds because it makes them money?" In terms of pure consequences, this distinction may not be significant. However, if the reality is that social good is being done *only* because it makes money, then some will object that corporate social responsibility is twisting into a clever trick employed to maximize profits by deceiving consumers about a business's intention. CSR becomes an example of cause egoism—that is, giving the false appearance of being concerned with the welfare of others in order to advance one's own interests.

- There are three broad arguments in favor of corporate social responsibility: it is morally required, it's required by externalities, it serves the interest of the corporation.

REVIEW QUESTIONS

1. In your own words, what are a few reasons a corporation may feel directly required to respond to broad social obligations?
2. What is an example of an externality? How could the existence of that externality be transformed into an argument in favor of corporate social responsibility?
3. List three ways a corporate bottom line may be improved by serving the public welfare.

13.4 Should Corporations Have Social Responsibilities? The Arguments Against

LEARNING OBJECTIVES

1. Define and elaborate the major arguments in favor of the corporate purpose as limited to increasing profits.
2. Define and elaborate major arguments against corporations accepting broad social and environmental responsibilities.

The Only Corporate Responsibility Is to Increase Profits

In 1970, just as the idea of corporate social responsibility was gaining traction and influential advocates in the United States, the economist Milton Friedman published a short essay titled "The Social Responsibility of Business is to Increase its Profits." Possibly the most provocative single contribution to the history of business ethics, Friedman set out to show that large, publicly owned corporations ought to be about making money, and the ethical obligations imposed by advocates of CSR should be dismissed. His arguments convinced some and not others, but the eloquent and accessible way he made them, combined with the fact that his ideas were published in a mainstream publication—the *New York Times Magazine*—ensured their impact. [1]

Businesses, as discussed at the chapter's beginning, come in all shapes and sizes. When the topic is social responsibility, however, attention frequently fixes on very large corporations because they're so big (and therefore able to do the most good) and powerful (the philosophies driving them tend to set the tone for business life in general). Friedman's essay concerns these large, publicly held corporations. Here are his arguments.

The Argument That Businesses *Can't* Have Social Responsibilities

A business can't have moral responsibilities any more than a wrench can. Only humans have moral responsibilities because only we have consciousness and intentions: we're the only things in the world that can control our actions, that can distinguish between what we want to do and what's right to do. Therefore, only we can have responsibilities in the ethical sense. What, then, is a business? Nothing more than a tool, something we make to further our ends. It may work well or poorly, but no matter what, it doesn't do what *it* wishes, so we can't blame or credit the business, only those individuals who use it for one purpose or another.

In Woburn, Massachusetts, according to this argument, it makes no sense to say that W. R. Grace has some kind of corporate responsibility to keep the environment clean. A company doesn't have any responsibilities. It's like a wrench, a thing out in the world that people use, and that's all. Would you accuse a wrench of being irresponsible if someone uses it to loosen the bolts on some truckers' tires and so causes an accident and disastrous spill of toxins? You'd probably accuse the person who *used* the wrench of acting irresponsibly, but blaming the wrench for something would be madness.

The Argument That Corporate Executives Are Responsible Only to Shareholders

Corporate executives are employees of the owners of the enterprise. They're contracted and obligated to conduct the business as the owners' desire, not in accord with the wishes of some other people out in the world advocating broad social concerns. Executives in this sense are no different from McDonald's burger flippers: they're hired and agree to do a certain thing a certain way. If they don't like it, they're free to quit, but what they can't do is take the job and then flip the hamburgers into the trash because their friends are all texting them about how unhealthy McDonald's food is.

What do corporate owners desire? According to Friedman, the typical answer is the highest return possible on their investment. When you buy shares of the industrial chemical maker W. R. Grace, you check once in a while what the stock price is because price (and the hope that it's going up) is the reason you bought in the first place. It follows, therefore, that executives—who in the end work for you, the owner—are duty bound to help you get that higher share price, and the quickest route to the goal is large profits.

What about the executive who decides to dedicate time and a corporation's resources to social welfare projects (to things like reducing runoff pollution even further than the law requires or hiring released felons as a way of easing their passage back into society)? Friedman is particularly cutting on this point. It's despicable selfishness. There's nothing easier than generosity with other people's money. And that's what, Friedman hints, CSR is *really* about. It's about corporate executives, who like the idea of receiving accolades for their generous contributions to society, and they like it even more because the cash doesn't come out of their paycheck; it's subtracted from shareholder returns. There's the seed of an argument here, finally, that not only is corporate social responsibility not recommendable, it's reproachable: in ethical terms, corporate leaders are duty bound to refuse to participate in social responsibility initiatives.

The Argument That Society Won't Be Served by Corporate Social Responsibility

One serious practical problem with the vision of corporate executives resolving social problems is *it's hard to be sure that their solutions will do well.* Presumably, corporate executives got to be executives by managing businesses profitably. That's certainly a difficult skill, but the fact that it has been mastered doesn't automatically imply other talents. More, given the fact that corporate executives frequently have no special training in social and environmental issues, it's perfectly reasonable to worry that they'll do as much harm as good.

One example of the reversed result comes from *Newsweek*. Executives at the magazine probably thought they were serving the public interest when they dedicated space in their April 28, 1975, issue to the threatening and impending environmental disaster posed by global…cooling. Not a very enticing subject, they probably could've done more for their circulation numbers by running a story (with lots of pictures) about the coming summer's bathing suit styles, but they did the science to stoke broad discussion of our environmental well-being. As for the stoking, they certainly succeeded. Today, many scientists believe that global warming is the real threat and requires corporations to join governments in reducing carbon emissions. They have a hard time getting their message out cleanly, though, when there's someone around bringing up that old *Newsweek* article to discredit the whole discussion.

The Right Institution for Managing Social Problems Is Government

Social problems shouldn't be resolved by corporations because we already have a large institution set up for that: government. If members of a society really are worried about carbon emissions or the disposal of toxic waste at chemical plants, then they should express those concerns to elected representatives who will, in turn, perform their function, which is to elaborate laws and regulations guiding the way all of us—inside and outside of business—live together. Government, the point is, should do its job, which is to regulate effectively, and those in the business world should do their job, which is to comply with regulations while operating profitably.

Underneath this division of labor, there's a crucial distinction. Friedman believes that human freedom is based to some significant degree in economic life. Our fundamental rights to our property and to pursue our happiness are inviolable and are expressed in our working activities. The situation is complicated, however, because it's also true that for us to live together in a society, *some* restrictions must be placed on individual action. No community can flourish if everyone is just doing what they want. There's room for quite a bit of discussion here, but in general, Friedman asserts that while government (and other outside institutions) have to be involved in regulation and the imposing of limits, they shouldn't start trying to mold and dictate basic values in the economic realm, which must be understood in principle as a bastion of individual liberty and free choices.

At this juncture, Friedman's essay reaches its sharpest point. The notion of corporate social responsibility, Friedman asserts, is not only misguided; it's dangerous because it threatens to violate individual liberty. Stronger, the violation may ultimately lead to socialism, the end of free market allocation of resources because rampant political forces take control in the boardroom.

The movement to socialism that Friedman fears comes in two steps:

1. Environmental activists, social cause leaders, and crusading lawyers will convince at least a handful of preening business executives that working life isn't about individuals expressing their freedom in a wide-open world; it's about serving the general welfare. The notion of corporate social responsibility becomes a mainstream concern and wins wide public support.

2. With the way forced open by activists, the risk is that government will follow: the institution originally set up to regulate business life while guaranteeing the freedom of individuals will fall into the custom of imposing liberty-wrecking rules. Under the weight of these intrusive laws, working men and women will be forced to give up on their own projects and march to the cadence of government-dictated social welfare projects. Hiring decisions, for example, will no longer be about companies finding the best people for their endeavors; instead, they'll be about satisfying social goals defined by politicians and bureaucrats. Friedman cites as an

example the hiring of felons. Obviously, it's difficult for people coming out of jail to find good jobs. Just as obviously, it's socially beneficial for jobs to be available to them. The problem comes when governments decide that the social purpose of reinserting convicts is more important than protecting the freedom of companies to hire anyone they choose. When that happens, hiring quotas will be imposed—corporations will be forced to employ certain individuals. This intrusive workplace rule will be followed by others. All of them will need to be enforced by investigating agents and disciplining regulators. As their numbers grow and their powers expand, freedom will be squeezed. Ultimately, freedom may be crushed by, as Friedman puts it, "the iron fist of Government bureaucrats." [2]

It's difficult to miss the fact that Friedman's worries were colored by the Cold War, by a historical moment that now feels remote in which the world really did hang in the balance between two views of working life: the American view setting individual freedom as the highest value and the Soviet view raising collectivism and the general welfare above all personal economic concerns and liberties.

Still, and even though today's historical reality is quite different from the 1970s, the essence of Friedman's objection to CSR hasn't changed. It's that you and I get to be who we are by going out into the world and making something of ourselves. When our ability to do that gets smothered beneath social responsibility requirements, we may help others (or possibly not), but no matter what, we sacrifice ourselves because we've lost the freedom to go and do what we choose. This loss isn't just an inconvenience or a frustration: it's the hollowing out of our dignity; it's the collapse of our ability to make ourselves and therefore the end of the opportunity to be someone instead of just anyone.

The Best Way for Corporations to Be Socially Responsible Is to Increase Profits

The final major argument against corporate social responsibility in its various forms is that the best way for most corporations to *be* socially responsible is to contribute to the community by doing what they do best: excelling in economic terms. When corporations are making profits, the money isn't just disappearing or piling up in the pockets of the greedy super rich (though some does go there); most of it gets sent back into the economy and everyone benefits. Jobs are created, and those that already exist get some added security. With employment options opening, workers find more chances to change and move up: more successful corporations mean more freedom for workers.

Further, corporations don't get to be successful through luck, but by delivering goods and services to consumers at attractive prices. Corporate success, that means, should indicate that consumers are doing well. Their quality of life improves as their consumer products improve, and those products improve best and fastest when corporations are competing against each other as freely as possible.

What about the public welfare in the most general sense, the construction of parks, schools, and similar? Here, too, corporations do the best for everyone by concentrating on their own bottom line. More hiring, sales, and profits all also mean more tax revenue flowing to the government. And since elected governmental entities are those organizations best equipped to do public good, the most a corporation can hope for with respect to general social welfare is to succeed, and thereby generate revenues for experts (or, at least democratically elected officials) to divide up wisely.

The term marketplace responsibility, finally, names the economic and social (and political) view emerging from Friedman's arguments. The title doesn't mean ethical responsibility in the marketplace so much as it does the specific conception of ethical responsibility that the open marketplace produces. It has two aspects: first, the notion of corporate social responsibility is misguided and dangerous, and second, the corporate purpose of profit maximization serves the social welfare while cohering with the value of human freedom that should be paramount in business ethics.

Conclusion: Corporate Social Responsibility versus Marketplace Responsibility

Advocates of corporate social responsibility believe corporations are obligated to share the burden of resolving society's problems. They maintain that the responsibility stands on pure moral grounds. More, there are operational reasons for the responsibilities: if businesses are going to contaminate the environment or cause distress in people's lives, they should also be actively working to resolve the problems. Finally, there's the strong argument that even if the corporate purpose should be to make profits, social responsibility is an excellent way to achieve the goal.

Advocates of marketplace responsibility—and adversaries of the corporate social responsibility model—argue that by definition corporations can't have moral responsibilities. Further, to the extent ethical obligations control corporate directors, the obligations are to shareholders. More, corporate directors aren't experts at solving social problems, and we already have an institution that presumably does have expertise: government. Finally, there's a strong argument that even if the corporate purpose should include broad social responsibilities, free individuals and corporations in the world making profits is an excellent way to achieve the goal.

KEY TAKEAWAYS

- The first argument against theories of corporate social responsibility is corporations can't have ethical responsibilities.
- The second argument is corporate executives are duty bound to pursue profits.
- The third argument is corporations are ill-equipped to directly serve the public good.
- The fourth argument is social issues should be managed by government, not corporations.
- The fifth argument is marketplace ethics reinforce human freedom and corporate social responsibility threatens society with socialism.
- The sixth argument against theories of corporate social responsibility is the best way for corporations to serve the public welfare is by pursuing profits.

REVIEW QUESTIONS

1. What does it mean to say that, in ethical terms, a corporation is no different from a wrench?
2. What primary responsibility do corporate directors have to shareholders? Why do they have it?
3. Why should social issues be managed by government and not corporations?
4. What is the connection between corporate social responsibility and the threat to freedom posed by socialism? How does socialism limit freedom?
5. What is an example of a company doing good by doing well—that is, making profits—and for that reason improving the general welfare? How can the example be converted into an argument against the theory of the corporation as having social responsibilities?

[1] Milton Friedman, "The Social Responsibility of Business Is to Increase Its Profits," *New York Times Magazine*, September 13, 1970, accessed June 7, 2011,http://www.colorado.edu/studentgroups/libertarians/issues/friedman-soc-resp-business.html.
[2] Milton Friedman, "The Social Responsibility of Business Is to Increase Its Profits," *New York Times Magazine*, September 13, 1970, accessed June 7, 2011,http://www.colorado.edu/studentgroups/libertarians/issues/friedman-soc-resp-business.html.

13.5 Case Studies

Casinos and Crime

Earl Grinols and David Mustard are economists and, like a lot of people, intrigued by both casinos and crime. In their case, they were especially curious about whether the first causes the second. It does, according to their study. Eight percent of crime occurring in counties that have casinos results from the legalized gambling. In strictly financial terms—which are the ones they're comfortable with as economists—the cost of casino-caused crime is about $65 per adult per year in those counties. [1]

When casinos come to town, the following specific crimes increase:

- Robbery (in all three major categories: of individuals, of their homes, of their cars)
- Aggravated assault
- Rape

The crimes also increased to some extent in neighboring counties.

Situation: A casino regular runs out of money after a string of bad cards. She coasts out to the street and drops her purse in front of an out-of-towner. When the chivalrous guy bends over to pick it up for her, she picks his back pocket. With the $100 stolen from the wallet, she heads back into the casino, spends $40 on hard liquor, loses the rest at the roulette table, and goes home. She wakes up alone, though some underwear she finds on her floor makes her think she probably didn't start the night that way. She can't remember.

QUESTIONS

1. Sole proprietorship
   - What is a sole proprietorship?
   - What are the basic legal steps to take on the way to making a sole proprietorship?
   - How are taxes paid in this kind of organization?
   - In most casino states and counties, laws protect owners from liability claims arising from problems caused by gambling. In ethical terms, however, if you're the sole proprietor of the casino, do you feel any responsibility for this episode? Why or why not? If you feel responsibility, to whom would it be? What could you do to set things right?

2. Partnership
   - In business, what is a partnership?
   - You own only 5 percent of a partner-owned casino, and don't pay too much attention to what goes on

inside. In fact, you don't like gambling and only invested in the enterprise as a favor to a friend. Do you feel any ethical responsibility for this episode? Why or why not?

3. Nonprofit organization
   o What is a nonprofit organization?
   o You're an equal partner in a nonprofit organization that runs the casino to support the cause of building schools for children in impoverished sections of Peru. You spend a few months every year down there building schools and giving free English-language classes. In ethical terms (and regardless of what the law allows), do you believe anyone involved in this episode should be able to sue you personally for their suffering? Why or why not?

4. Large, public corporation
   o Large public corporations protect their owners from the ethical implications of what the corporation does through the business's organizational structure. What is that structure, and how does it protect shareholders?
   o Say that the casino under discussion in this set of questions is the MGM Grand Hotel and Casino in Las Vegas, which is owned by a large, public corporation. You have five shares of stock inherited a few years ago when a relative died. You are legally protected from liability claims. In ethical terms, however, do you believe that anyone involved in this episode should be able to sue you personally—or just plain blame you—for their suffering? Why or why not?

5. The woman in the story is your eighteen-year-old daughter. Does that change any of your answers?

6. What is an externality? What externalities probably belong to casinos? Are there any *positive* externalities that probably belong to casinos?

7. Pigouvian taxes (named after economist Arthur Pigou, a pioneer in the theory of externalities) attempts to correct externalities—and so formalize a corporate social responsibility—by levying a tax equal to the costs of the externality to society. The casino, in other words, that causes crime and other problems costing society, say, $1 million should pay a $1 million tax.
   o In terms of casinos, would such a tax more or less satisfy any ethical claim that could be made against them for the social problems they cause? Why or why not?
   o The way these social scientists measured the cost of each crime was, more or less, by totaling the *quantifiable* costs—that is, those things that

could receive a price tag fairly readily. If, for example, your car gets stolen and sold for parts by a desperate gambler, you can put a price on the crime's cost by checking the car's Kelly Blue Book value. Added to that there are administrative costs—at the police station, the insurance company—and those too may be figured in terms of time and wages. Still, quite a bit of the cost of crime escapes (as the authors readily admit) their measure. Their calculations don't include lost productivity, social service, and welfare costs. They also don't include emotional costs, the tears, and distress of the victim. Is there any way for those cost—especially the emotional suffering—to be put into dollars and cents? If so, how? If not, is there some other kind of requirement that could be strapped onto casinos to help make them socially responsible for their activities?

Grace

The W. R. Grace Company was founded by, yes, a man named W. R. Grace. He was Irish and it was a shipping enterprise he brought to New York in 1865. Energetic and ambitious, while his company grew on one side, he was getting civically involved on the other. Fifteen years after arriving, he was elected Mayor of New York City. Five years after that, he personally accepted a gift from a delegation representing the people of France. It was the Statue of Liberty.

Grace was a legendary philanthropist. He provided massive food donations to his native Ireland to relieve famine. At home, his attention focused on his nonprofit Grace Institute, a tuition-free school for poor immigrant women. The classes offered there taught basic skills—stenography, typewriting, bookkeeping—that helped students enter the workforce. More than one hundred thousand young women have passed through the school, which survives to this day.

In 1945, grandson J. Peter Grace took control of the now worldwide shipping company. A decade later, it became a publicly traded corporation on the New York Stock Exchange. The business began shifting from shipping to chemical production.

By the 1980s, W. R. Grace had become a chemical and materials company, and it had come to light that one of its plants had been pouring toxins into the soil and water underneath the small town of Woburn, Massachusetts. The poisons worked their way into the town's water supply and then into the townspeople. It caused leukemia in newborns.

Lawsuits in civil court, and later investigations by the Environmental Protection Agency, cost the corporation millions.

J. Peter Grace retired as CEO in 1992. After forty-eight years on the job, he'd become the longest-reigning CEO in the history of public companies. During that time, he also served as president of the Grace Institute.

The nonfiction novel *A Civil Action* came out in 1996. The best-selling, award-winning chronicle of the Woburn disaster soon became a Hollywood movie. The movie, starring John Travolta, continues to appear on television with some regularity.

To honor the Grace Institute, October 28 was designated "Grace Day" by New York City in 2009. On that day, the institute defined its mission this way: "In the tradition of its founding family, Grace Institute is dedicated to the development of the personal and business skills necessary for self-sufficiency, employability, and an improved quality of life." [2]

QUESTIONS

1. The specific theory of corporate social responsibility encompasses four kinds of obligations: economic, legal, ethical, and philanthropic.
   o How are business leaders meant to organize these four responsibilities? Which ones take precedence over the others and why?
   o Judging the man named W. R. Grace through the lens of CSR, how well did he respond to his obligations? Explain.
   o Judging the company's more recent activities in the 1980s through the lens of CSR, how well did it respond to its obligations? Explain.

2. The triple-bottom-line theory of corporate responsibility promotes three kinds of sustainability: economic, social, and environmental.
   o What does the term *sustainability* mean within this theory and within each of the three categories?
   o The W. R. Grace Company has a long history. From the information provided, what are some of the steps the company has taken to become economically sustainable? Explain.
   o What are some of the steps the W. R. Grace Company has taken to promote social sustainability? Explain.
   o What is environmental sustainability? How can the dumping of toxic waste in Woburn be categorized

as unethical within the area of environmental sustainability concerns? Explain.

3. Stakeholder theory affirms that for companies to perform ethically, management decisions must take account of and respond to stakeholder concerns.
   o What is a *stakeholder*?
   o Looking back at the early company in New York in the 1800s, who would have been some of the stakeholders surrounding the Grace shipping company?
   o Looking to more recent history, to the corporation as a producer of industrial chemicals in Woburn, Massachusetts, who were some of the major stakeholders surrounding Grace?
   o Explain why the Grace Institute, which receives generous support from the W. R. Grace industrial chemical corporation—and the women receiving training there—are stakeholders in the W. R. Grace Corporation.
   o The Grace Institute—the people employed there and the women receiving free training—depend to some extent on the chemical company being profitable. Could you construct an argument in favor of the chemical company being environmentally irresponsible if that allows profits and therefore necessary support for the Institute?

4. As this question is being written, the share price of W. R. Grace is $26.17, and there are a total of 72,780,100 shares out there in the world. You've saved some money from a summer job and invested in Grace, 100 shares to be exact. That costs you $2,617, and means you own a not-overwhelming 0.000137 percent of the company. Next, you e-mail this to the CEO: "I worked hard for my $2,617, I bought stock to see that amount rise, and I want you to pour a little bit more of the profits into research and development of new products, and a little less into the Grace Institute." Assuming the CEO is a proponent of stakeholder ethics, what do you suppose the response would be?

5. There are a number of arguments supporting the proposal that corporations are autonomous entities (apart from owners and directors and employees) with ethical obligations in the world. The *moral requirement argument* contains four elements:
   o Corporations are already involved in the broad social world and the ethical dilemmas defining it, and therefore they are obligated to participate and help solve problems.
   o Well-established, successful, and powerful corporations *can* be involved in the effective

resolution of broad social problems, and that ability implies an obligation to do so.

o Corporations rely on much more than their owners and shareholders. They need suppliers, employees, a town in which to locate, consumers, air to breathe, and water to drink. That reliance implies an obligation to care for the welfare and protection of those things.

o Because businesses cause problems in the larger world, they're obligated to participate in the problems' resolution.

How can each of these general arguments be specified in the case of W. R. Grace?

6. Summarize the externality argument in favor of corporations having ethical obligations in the world. How can it be specified in the case of W. R. Grace?

The Body Shop

The Body Shop is a cosmetics firm out of England, founded by Anita Roddick. "If business," she writes on the company's web page, "comes with no moral sympathy or honorable code of behaviors, then God help us all."[3]

Moral sympathy and an honorable code of behaviors has certainly helped The Body Shop. Constantly promoted as an essential aspect of the company and a reason to buy its products, the concept of corporate social responsibility has been a significant factor in the conversion of a single small store in England to a multinational conglomerate.

Maybe it has been *too* significant a factor. That's certainly the suspicion of many corporate watchers. The suspicion isn't that the actual social responsibility has been too significant but that the actions of corporate responsibility have been much less energetic than their promotion. The social responsibility has been, more than anything else, a marketing strategy. Called *green washing*, the accusation is that only minimally responsible actions have been taken by The Body Shop, just enough to get some good video and mount a loud advertising campaign touting the efforts. Here's the accusation from a website called thegoodhuman.com:

> *The Body Shop buys the palm oil for their products from an organization that pushed for the eviction of peasant families to develop a new plantation. So much for their concern about creating "sustainable trading relationships with disadvantaged communities around the world."* [4]

QUESTIONS

1. What is the enlightened self-interest argument in favor of corporate social responsibility? How does the case of The Body Shop illustrate and make that argument?

2. From the perspective of the enlightened self-interest argument in favor of corporate social responsibility, what can be made of the accusation that The Body Shop is a green washer? Explain.

3. With reference to Milton Friedman's marketplace ethics—essentially the idea that corporations have only one ethical responsibility, to make money—what can be made of the green washing accusation? Is it possible that it's not so much an accusation as a compliment?

4. If a corporation acts in a way that does good in the world, does motive matter, does it matter *why* the corporation does what it does? Justify your answer.

Greed Is Good

It's probably the most repeated business ethics line in recent history. Michael Douglas—playing Wall Street corporate raider Gordon Gekko—stands in front of a group of shareholders at Teldar Paper and announces, "Greed is good."

Teldar has been losing money, but the company, Douglas believes, is fundamentally strong. The problem's the management; it's the CEO and chief operations officer and all their various vice presidents. Because they don't actually own the company, they only run it, they're tempted to use the giant corporation to make their lives comfortable instead of winning profits for the actual owners, the shareholders. As one of those shareholders, Douglas is proposing a revolt: get rid of the lazy executives and put in some new directors (like Douglas's friends) who actually want to make money. Here's the pitch. Douglas points at the CEO and the rest of the management team up at their table:

> *All together, these men sitting up here own less than 3 percent of the company. And where does the CEO put his million-dollar salary? Not in Teldar stock; he owns less than 1 percent.*

Dramatic pause. Douglas earnestly faces his fellow shareholders.

> *You own the company. That's right—you, the stockholder. And you're all being royally screwed over by these bureaucrats with their steak lunches, their hunting and fishing trips, their corporate jets and golden parachutes. Teldar Paper has 33 different vice presidents, each earning over 200 thousand dollars a year. Now, I have spent the last two months*

analyzing what all these guys do, and I still can't figure it out. One thing I do know is that our paper company lost 110 million dollars last year. The new law of evolution in corporate America seems to be survival of the un-fittest. Well, in my book you either do it right or you get eliminated.

He adds,

In the last seven deals that I've been involved with, there were 2.5 million stockholders who have made a pretax profit of 12 billion dollars. [5]

QUESTIONS

1. Douglas says, "In my book you either do it right or you get eliminated."
   o   In economic terms, what does "do it right" mean?
   o   In *ethical* terms, and with reference to a marketplace morality resembling the one Milton Friedman proposes, what does "do it right" mean?
2. The structure of most large, publicly held corporations separates owners from actual managers who are hired to run the company. They're employed agents of the owners. What does that mean as far as their ethical obligations go with respect to the *purpose* of the company they are leading?
3. In the real world, the paper company Weyerhaeuser promotes itself as socially and environmentally responsible. On their web page, they note that they log the wood for their paper from certified forests at a percentage well above that required by law. [6] Carefully defining a "certified forest" would require pages, but basically the publicly held corporation is saying that they don't just buy land, clear-cut everything, and then move on. Instead, and at a cost to themselves, they leave some trees uncut and plant others to ensure that the forest they're cutting retains its character.
   o   How could Douglas's speech at Teldar be rewritten as a criticism of the management at Weyerhaeuser?
   o   What specific criticism would Douglas launch at Weyerhaeuser managers who spend corporate money planting trees?
   o   If it turned out that the sustainable forest initiative cost Weyerhaeuser some money up front, but ultimately won them positive publicity and consequently more consumers, would Douglas approve of the practice? Explain.
4. One broad argument against the various ideas of corporate social and environmental responsibility is that corporations can't have moral responsibilities at all. How could that argument be specified in the case of Weyerhaeuser?

5. According to the Weyerhaeuser web page, the US government sets certain rules for sustainability with respect to forests. Weyerhaeuser complies and then goes well beyond those requirements. According to Milton Friedman and the ideals of marketplace responsibility, broad questions about social and environmental corporate responsibilities should be answered by democratically elected governments because that's the institution we've developed to manage our ethical life. Governments should try to succeed in the ethical realm by making good laws; companies should try to succeed in the economic realm by making good profits.
   o   Weyerhaeuser notes on its web page that in China and Uruguay it obeys local regulations with respect to logging. Apparently, however, the company isn't doing quite as much in those places to avoid the environmental problem of deforestation. Land is very inexpensive in vast, poor nations like these two, and it looks like Weyerhaeuser more or less does what's required and that's it. Maybe the company simply buys acres, cuts them, and moves on. Make the case that *in ethical terms*, the corporate actions in Uruguay and China are more respectable than the actions here in the States.
6. The first part of Douglas's speech concerned problems with the corporate organization's structure, and with out-of-control managers: people employed to run a company who promptly forget who their bosses are. The speech's second part is about what drives life in the business world:

The point is, ladies and gentleman, that greed—for lack of a better word—is good.

Greed is right.

Greed works.

Greed clarifies, cuts through, and captures the essence of the evolutionary spirit.

Greed, in all of its forms—greed for life, for money, for love, knowledge—has marked the upward surge of mankind.

   Greed, Douglas says, is an imperfect word for what he's describing. What words might have been better? What words might advocates of marketplace ethics propose?
7. One word that might have worked better than greed is ambition. Whether the word is greed or ambition, it has, according to the Douglas character, marked the upward surge of mankind. Assume that's true. Can you speculate about how the upward surge would play out in a developing nation like Uruguay when a multinational comes to town, brings money, creates jobs, and wrecks the forests?

[1] Earl Grinols and David Mustard, "Measuring Industry Externalities: The Curious Case of Casinos and Crime," accessed June 7, 2011, http://casinofacts.org/casinodocs/Grinols-Mustard-Casinos_And_Crime.pdf.

[2] "Our Mission," Grace Institute, accessed June 1, 2011,http://www.graceinstitute.org/mission.asp.

[3] "Our Values," The Body Shop, accessed June 7, 2011,http://www.thebodyshop.com/_en/_ww/services/aboutus_values.aspx.

[4] "Green wash of the Week: The Body Shop Business Ethics," *The Good Human*, September 30, 2009, accessed June 7, 2011, http://www.thegoodhuman.com/2009/09/30/greenwash-of-the-week-the-body-shop-business-ethics.

[5] *Wall Street*, directed by Oliver Stone (Los Angeles: Twentieth Century Fox, 1987), film.

[6] "Forest Certification," Weyerhaeuser, accessed June 7, 2011,http://www.weyerhaeuser.com/Sustainability/Footprint/Certification.

NOTES:

NOTES:

Chapter 14:
Economics and the Environment

Chapter Overview

Chapter 14 explores the multiple relations linking business, the environment, and environmental protection. The question of animal rights is also considered.

14.1 The Environment
LEARNING OBJECTIVES

1. Consider damage done to the environment in a business context.
2. Delineate major legal responses to concerns about the environment.

Cancun

Cancun, Mexico, is paradise: warm climate, Caribbean water, white sand beaches, stunning landscapes, coral reefs, and a unique lagoon. You can sunbathe, snorkel, parasail, shoot around on jet skis, and drink Corona without getting carded. Hordes of vacationers fill the narrow, hotel-lined peninsula—so many that the cars on the one main street snarl in traffic jams running the length of the tourist kilometers. It's a jarring contrast: on one side the placid beaches (until the jet skis get geared up), and on the other there's the single road about a hundred yards inland. Horns scream, oil-burning cars and trucks belch pollution, tourists fume. Cancun's problem is that it can't handle its own success. There's not enough room for roads behind the hotels just like there's not enough beach in front to keep the noisy jet skiers segregated from those who want to take in the sun and sea quietly.

The environment hasn't been able to bear the success either. According to a report,

> *The tourist industry extensively damaged the lagoon, obliterated sand dunes, led to the extinction of varying species of animals and fish, and destroyed the rainforest which surrounds Cancun. The construction of 120 hotels in 20 years has also endangered breeding areas for marine turtles, as well as causing large numbers of fish and shellfish to be depleted or disappear just offshore.* [1]

For all its natural beauty, environmentally, Cancun is an ugly place. Those parts of the natural world that most tourists don't see (the lagoon, the nearby forest, the fish life near shore) have been sacrificed so a few executives in suits can make money.

From its inception, Cancun was a business. The Mexican government built an airport to fly people in, set up rules to draw investors, and made it (relatively) easy to build hotels on land that only a few coconut harvesters from the local plantation even knew about. From a business sense, it was a beautiful proposition: bring people to a place where they can be happy, provide new and more lucrative jobs for the locals, and build a mountain of profit (mainly for government insiders and friends) along the way.

Everything went according to plan. Those who visit Cancun have a wonderful time (once they finally get down the road to their hotel). College students live it up during spring break, young couples take their children to play on the beach, and older couples go down and remember that they do, in fact, love each other. So fish die, and people get jobs. Forests disappear, and people's love is kindled. The important questions about business ethics and the environment are mostly located right at this balance and on these questions: how many trees may be sacrificed for human jobs? How many animal species can be traded for people to fall in love?

What Is the Environment?

Harm to the natural world is generally discussed under two terms: the environment and the ecosystem. The words' meanings overlap, but one critical aspect of the term ecosystem is the idea of interrelation. An ecosystem is composed of living and nonliving elements that find a balance allowing for their continuation. The destruction of the rain forest around Cancun didn't just put an end to some trees; it also jeopardized a broader web of life: birds that needed limbs for their nests disappeared when the trees did. Then, with the sturdy forest gone, Hurricane Gilbert swept through and wiped out much of the lower-level vegetation. Meanwhile, out in the sea, the disappearance of some small fish meant their predators had nothing to feed on and they too evaporated. What makes an ecosystem a system is the fact that the various parts all depend on each other, and damaging one element may also damage and destroy another or many others.

In the sense that it's a combination of interdependent elements, the tourist world in Cancun is no different from the surrounding natural world. As the traffic jams along the peninsula have grown, making it difficult for people to leave and get back to their hotels, the tourists have started migrating away, looking elsewhere for their vacation reservations. Of course Cancun isn't going to disappear, but if you took that one road completely away, most everything else would go with it. So economic realities can resemble environmental ones: once a single part of a functioning system disappears, it's hard to stop the effects from falling further down the line.

What Kinds of Damage Can Be Done to the Environment?

Nature is one of nature's great adversaries. Hurricanes sweeping up through the Caribbean and along the Eastern Seaboard of the United States wipe out entire ecosystems. Moving inland, warm winters in northern states like Minnesota can allow some species including deer to reproduce at very high rates, meaning that the next winter, when conditions return to normal, all available food is eaten rapidly at winter's onset and subsequent losses to starvation are massive and extend up the food chain to wolves and bears. Lengthening the timeline, age-long periods of warming and cooling cause desertification and ice ages that put ends to giant swaths of habitats and multitudes of species.

While it's true that damaging the natural world's ecosystems is one of nature's great specialties, evidence also indicates that the human contribution to environmental change has been growing quickly. It's impossible to measure everything that has been done, or compare the world today with what would have been had humans never evolved (or never created an industrialized economy), but one way to get a sense of the kind of transformations human activity may be imposing on the environment comes from extinction rates: the speed at which species are disappearing because they no longer find a habitable place to flourish. According to some studies, the current rate of extinction is around *a thousand* times higher than the one derived from examinations of the fossil record, which is to say, before the time parts of the natural world were being severely trashed by developments like those lining the coast of Cancun, Mexico. [2]

In an economics and business context, the kinds of damage our industrialized lifestyles most extensively wreak include:

- Air pollution
- Water pollution
- Soil pollution
- Contamination associated with highly toxic materials
- Resource depletion

Air pollution is the emission of harmful chemicals and particulate matter into the air. Photochemical smog—better known simply as *smog*—is a cocktail of gases and particles reacting with sunlight to make visible and poisonous clouds. Car exhaust is a major contributor to this kind of pollution, so smog can concentrate in urban centers where traffic jams are constant. In Mexico City on bad days, the smog is so thick it can be hard to see more than ten blocks down a straight street. Because the urban core is nestled in a mountain valley that blocks out the wind, pollutants don't blow away as they do in many places; they get entirely trapped. During the winter, a brown top forms above the skyline, blocking the view of the surrounding mountain peaks; the cloud is clearly visible from above to those arriving by plane. After landing, immediately upon exiting the airport into the streets, many visitors note their eyes tearing up and their throats drying out. In terms of direct bodily harm, Louisiana State University environmental chemist Barry Dellinger estimates that breathing the air in Mexico's capital for a day is about the equivalent of smoking two packs of cigarettes. [3] This explains why, on the worst days, birds drop out of the air dead, and one longer-term human effect is increased risk of lung cancer.

Greenhouse gasses, especially carbon dioxide released when oil and coal are burned, absorb and hold heat from the sun, preventing it from dissipating into space, and thereby creating a greenhouse effect, a general warming of the environment. Heat is, of course, necessary for life to exist on earth, but fears exist that the last century of industrialization has raised the levels measurably, and continuing industrial expansion will speed the process even more. Effects associated with the warming are significant and include:

- Shifts in vegetation, in what grows where
- Rising temperatures in lakes, rivers, and oceans, leading to changes in wildlife distribution
- Flooding of coastal areas, where many of our cities are located (Cancun could be entirely flooded by only a small rise in the ocean's water level.)

Another group of chemicals, chlorofluorocarbons (CFCs), threaten to break down the ozone layer in the earth's stratosphere. Currently, that layer blocks harmful ultraviolet radiation from getting through to the earth's surface where it could cause skin cancer and disrupt ocean life. Effective international treaties have limited (though not eliminated) CFC emissions.

Coal-burning plants—many of which produce electricity—release sulfur compounds into the air, which later mix into water vapor and rain down as sulfuric acid, commonly known as acid rain. Lakes see their pH level changed with subsequent effects on vegetation and fish. Soil may also be poisoned.

Air pollution is the most immediate form of environmental poison for most of us, but not the only significant one. In China, more than 25 percent of surface water is too polluted for swimming or fishing. [4]

Some of those lakes may have been ruined in the same way as Onondaga Lake near Syracuse, New York. Over a century ago, resorts were built and a fish hatchery flourished on one side of the long lake. The other side received waste flushed by the surrounding cities and factories. Problems began around 1900 when the fish hatchery could no longer reproduce fish. Soon after, it was necessary to ban ice harvesting from the lake. In 1940, swimming was banned because of dangerous bacteria, and in 1970, fishing had to be stopped because of mercury and PCB contamination. The lake was effectively dead. To cite one example, a single chemical company dumped eighty tons of mercury into the water during its run on the coast. Recently, the New York state health department loosened restrictions slightly, and people are advised that they may once again eat fish caught in the lake. Just as long as it's not more than one per month. Those who do eat more risk breakdown of their nervous system, collapse of their liver, and teeth falling out. [5]

Like liquid poisons, solid waste can be dangerous. Paper bags degrade fairly rapidly and cleanly, but plastic containers remain where they're left into the indefinite future. The metal of a battery tossed into a landfill will break down eventually, but not before dropping out poisons including cadmium. Cadmium weakens the bones in low doses and, if exposure is high, causes death.

At the industrial waste extreme, there are toxins so poisonous they require special packaging to prevent even minimal exposure more or less forever. The waste from nuclear power plants qualifies. So noxious are the spent fuel rods that it's a matter of national debate in America and elsewhere as to where they should be stored. When the Chernobyl nuclear plant broke open in 1986, it emitted a radioactive cloud that killed hundreds and forced the permanent evacuation of the closest town, Pripyat. Area wildlife destruction would require an entire book to document, but as a single example, the surrounding pine forest turned red and died after absorbing the radiation storm.

Finally, all the environmental damage listed so far has resulted from ruinous substance *additions* to natural ecosystems, but environmental damage also runs in the other

direction as depletion. Our cars and factories are sapping the earth of its petroleum reserves. Minerals, including copper, are being mined toward the point where it will become too expensive to continue digging the small amount that remains from the ground. The United Nations estimates that fifty thousand square miles of forest are disappearing each year, lost to logging, conversion to agriculture, fuel wood collection by rural poor, and forest fires.[6] Of course, most of those tree losses can be replanted. On the other hand, species that are driven out of existence can't be brought back. As already noted, current rates of extinction are running far above "background extinction" rates, which are an approximation of how many species, would disappear each year were the rules of nature left unperturbed.

Conclusion. Technically, there's no such thing as preserving the environment because left to its own devices the natural world does an excellent job of wreaking havoc on itself. Disruptions including floods, combined with wildlife battling for territory and food sources, all that continually sweeps away parts of nature and makes room for new species and ecosystems. Still, changes wrought by the natural world tend to be gradual and balanced, and the worry is that our industrialized lifestyle has become so powerful that nature, at least in certain areas, will no longer be able to compensate and restore any kind of balance. That concerns has led to both legal efforts, and ethical arguments, in favor of protecting the environment.

The Law

Legal efforts to protect the environment in the United States intensified between 1960 and 1970. The Environmental Protection Agency (EPA) was established in 1970 to monitor and report on the state of the environment while establishing and enforcing specific regulations. Well known to most car buyers as the providers of the mile-per-gallon estimates displayed on the window sticker, the EPA is a large agency and employs a workforce compatible with its mission, including scientists, legal staffers, and communications experts.

Other important legal milestones in the field of environmental protection include:

- The Clean Air Act of 1963 and its many amendments regulate emissions from industrial plants and monitor air quality. One measure extends to citizens the right to sue companies for damages if they aren't complying with existing regulations: it effectively citizenries' law enforcement in this area of environmental protection.
- The Clean Water Act, along with other, related legislation, regulates the quality of water in the

geographic world (lakes and rivers), as well as the water we drink and use for industrial purposes. Chemical composition is important, and temperature also. Thermal pollution occurs when factories pour heated water back into natural waterways at a rate sufficient to affect the ecosystem.

- The Wilderness Act, along with other legislation, establishes areas of land as protected from development. Some zones, including the Boundary Waters Canoe Area in northern Minnesota, are reserved for minimal human interaction (no motors are allowed); other areas are more accessible. All wilderness and national park areas are regulated to protect natural ecosystems.

- The Endangered Species Act and related measures take steps to ensure the survival of species pressed to near extinction, especially by human intrusion. One example is the bald eagle. Subjected to hunting, loss of habitat, and poisoning by the pesticide DDT (which caused eagle eggs to crack prematurely), a once common species was reduced to only a few hundred pairs in the lower forty-eight states. Placed on the endangered species list in 1967, penalties for hunting were increased significantly. Also, DDT was banned, and subsequently the eagle made a strong comeback. It is no longer listed as endangered.

- The National Environmental Policy Act of 1969 requires that an environmental impact statement be prepared for many major projects. The word environment in this case means not only the natural world but also the human one. When a new building is erected in a busy downtown, the environmental impact statement reports on the effect the building will have on both the natural world (how much new air pollution will be released from increased traffic, how much water will be necessary for the building's plumbing, how much electricity will be used to keep the place cool in the summer) and also the civilized one (whether there's enough parking in the area for all the cars that will arrive, whether nearby highways can handle the traffic and similar). Staying with the natural factors, the statement should consider impacts—positive and negative—on the local ecosystem as well as strategies for minimizing those impacts and some consideration of alternatives to the project. The writing and evaluation of these statements can become sites of conflict between developers on one side and environmental protection organizations on the other.

Two major additional points about legal approaches to the natural world should be added. First, they can be expensive; nearly all environmental protection laws impose costs on business and, consequently, make life for everyone more costly. When developers of downtown buildings have to create a budget for their environmental impact statements, the expenses get passed on to the people who buy condos in the building. There's no doubt that banning the pesticide DDT was good for the eagle, but it made farming—and therefore the food we eat—more expensive. Further, clean water and air stipulations don't only affect consumers by making products more expensive; the environmental responsibility also costs Americans jobs every time a factory gets moved to China or some other relatively low-regulation country. Of course, it's also true that, as noted earlier, around 25 percent of China's surface water is poisonous, but for laid-off workers in the States, it may be hard to worry so much about that.

Second, these American laws, regulations, and agencies don't make a bit of difference in Cancun, Mexico. Even though Cancun and America wash back and forth over each other (Cancun's hotels were constructed, chiefly, to host American visitors), the rights and responsibilities of legal dominion over the environment stop and start at places where people need to show their passports. This is representative of a larger reality: more than most issues in business ethics, arguments pitting economic and human interests against the natural world are international in nature. The greenhouse gases emitted by cars caught in Cancun traffic are no different, as far as the earth is concerned, from those gases produced along clogged Los Angeles freeways.

KEY TAKEAWAYS

- Ecosystems are natural webs of life in which the parts depend on each other for their continued survival.
- In a business context, the major types of pollution include air, water, soil, and contamination associated with highly toxic materials.
- Resource depletion is a type of environmental damage.
- Numerous laws regulate the condition and use of the environment in the United States.

REVIEW QUESTIONS

1. What is an example of an ecosystem?
2. Explain one way that an ecosystem can resemble an economic system.
3. What are some effects of smog?
4. What's an *environmental impact statement*?
5. Why are the business ethics of the environment more international in nature than many other subjects?

[1] "Cancun Tourism," TED, Trade & Environment Database, case no. 86, accessed June 8, 2011, http://www1.american.edu/TED/cancun.htm.

[2] Kent Holsinger, "Patterns of Biological Extinction," lecture notes, University of Connecticut, August 31, 2009, accessed June 8, 2011,http://darwin.eeb.uconn.edu/eeb310/lecture-notes/extinctions/node1.html.

[3] "Is Air Pollution Killing You?" *Ivanhoe Newswire*, May 2009, accessed June 8, 2011,http://www.ivanhoe.com/science/story/2009/05/572a.html.

[4] "More than 25% of China's Surface Water Contaminated," *China Daily*, July 26, 2010, accessed June 8, 2011, http://www.chinadaily.com.cn/china/2010-07/26/content_11051350.htm.

[5] The Upstate Freshwater Institute Onondaga Lake page, October 22, 2010, accessed June 8, 2011, http://www.upstatefreshwater.org/html/onondaga_lake.html; "2010–2011 Health Advisories: Chemicals in Sportfish and Game," New York State Department of Health, 2011, accessed June 8, 2011, http://static.ongov.net/WEP/wepdf/2009_AMP-FINAL/Library/11_SupportingDocs/L11.10.11_HealthAdvisory2010-2011.pdf.

[6] Rhett A. Butler, "World Deforestation Rates and Forest Cover Statistics, 2000–2005,"*Mongabay.com*, November 16, 2005, accessed June 8, 2011,http://news.mongabay.com/2005/1115-forests.html.

14.2 Ethical Approaches to Environmental Protection
LEARNING OBJECTIVES

1. Outline five attitudes toward environmental protection.
2. Consider who should pay for environmental protection and cleanup.

The Range of Approaches to Cancun

Cancun is an environmental sacrifice made in exchange for tourist dollars. The unique lagoon, for example, dividing the hotel strip from the mainland was devastated by the project. To construct the roadwork leading around the hotels, the original developers raised the earth level, which blocked the ocean's high tide from washing over into the lagoon and refreshing its waters. Quickly, the living water pool supporting a complex and unique ecosystem clogged with algae and became a stinky bog. No one cared too much since that was the street side, and visitors had come for the ocean. Still, one hotel developer decided to get involved. Ricardo Legorreta who designed the Camino Real Hotel (today named Dreams Resort) said this about his early 1970s project: "Cancun is more water than land. The Hotel Camino Real site was originally 70 percent water. It had been filled during the urbanization process. I wanted to return the site to its original status, so we built the guest room block on solid rock and the public areas on piles, and then excavated what was originally the lagoon. The difference in tide levels provides the necessary water circulation to keep the new lagoon clean." [1]

Specific numbers aren't available, but plainly it costs more to dig out the ground and then build on piles than it does to just build on the ground. To save the lagoon, the owners of the Camino Real spent some money.

Was it worth it? The answer depends initially on the ethical attitude taken toward the environment generally; it depends on how much, and how, value is assigned to the natural world. Reasonable ethical cases can be made for the full range of environmental protection, from none (total exploitation of the natural world to satisfy immediate human desires) to complete protection (reserving wildlife areas for freedom from any human interference). The main positions are the following and will be elaborated individually:

- The environment shouldn't be protected.
- The environment should be protected in the name of serving human welfare.
- The environment should be protected in the name of serving future generations' welfare.
- The environment should be protected in the name of serving animal welfare.
- The environment should be protected for its own sake.

The Environment Shouldn't Be Protected

Should individuals and businesses use the natural world for our own purposes and without concern for its welfare or continuation? The "yes" answer traces back to an attitude called free use, which pictures the natural world as entirely dedicated to serving immediate human needs and desires. The air and water and all natural resources are understood as belonging to everyone in the sense that all individuals have full ownership of, and may use, all resources belonging to them as they see fit. The air blowing above your land and any water rolling through it are yours, and you may breathe them or drink them or dump into them as you like. This attitude, finally, has both historical and ethical components.

The history of free use starts with the fact that the very idea of the natural world as needing protection at all is very recent. For almost all human history, putting the words environment and protection together meant finding ways that *we* could be protected from *it* instead of protecting it from us. This is very easy to see along Europe's Mediterranean coast. As opposed to Cancun where all the buildings are pushed right up to the Caribbean and open to the water, the stone constructions of Europe's old coastal towns are huddled together and open away from the sea. Modern and recently built hotels obscure this to some extent, but anyone walking from the coast back toward the city centers sees how all the old buildings turn away from the water as though the builders feared nature, which, in fact, they did.

They were afraid because the wind and storms blowing off the sea actually threatened their existences; it capsized their boats and sent water pouring through roofs and food supplies. Going further, not only is it the case that until very recently nature threatened us much more than we threatened it, but in those cases where humans *did* succeed in doing some damage, nature bounced right back. After a tremendously successful fishing year, for example, the supply of food swimming off the coastlines of the Mediterranean was somewhat depleted, but the next season things would return to normal. It's only today, with giant motorized boats pulling huge nets behind, that we've been able to truly fish out some parts of the sea. The larger historical point is that until, say, the nineteenth century, even if every human on the planet had united in a project to ruin nature irrevocably, not much would've happened. In that kind of reality, the idea of free use of our natural resources makes sense.

Today, at a time when our power over nature is significant, there are two basic arguments in favor of free use:
1.   The domination and progress argument
2.   The geological time argument

The domination and progress argument begins by refusing to place any necessary and intrinsic value in the natural world: there's no autonomous worth in the water, plants, and animals surrounding us. Because they have no independent value, those who abuse and ruin nature can't be automatically accused of an ethical violation: nothing intrinsically valuable has been damaged. Just as few people object when a dandelion is pulled from a front yard, so too there's no necessary objection to the air being ruined by our cars.

Connected with this disavowal of intrinsic value in nature's elements, there's high confidence in our ability to generate technological advances that will enable human civilization to flourish on the earth no matter how contaminated and depleted. When we've drilled the last drop of the petroleum we need to heat our homes and produce electricity to power our computers, we can trust our scientists to find new energy sources to keep everything going. Possibly solar energy technologies will leap forward, or the long-sought key to nuclear fission will be found in a research lab. As for worries about the loss of wildlife and greenery, that can be rectified with genetic engineering, or by simply doing without them. Even without human interference, species are disappearing every day; going without a few more may not ultimately be important.

Further, it should be remembered that there are many natural entities we're happy to do without. No one bemoans the extinction of the virus called variola, which caused smallpox. That disease was responsible for the death of hundreds of millions of humans, and for much of history has been one of the world's most terrifying scourges. In the 1970s, the virus was certified extinct by the World Health Organization. No one misses it; not even the most devoted advocate of natural ecosystems stood up against the human abuse and final eradication of the virus. Finally, if we can destroy one part of the natural world without remorse, can't that attitude be extended? No one is promoting reckless or wanton destruction, but as far as those parts of nature required to live well, can't we just take what we need until it runs out and then move on to something else?

To a certain extent, this approach is visible in Cancun, Mexico. The tourist strip has reached saturation and the natural world in the area—at least those parts tourists won't pay to see—has been decimated. So what are developers doing? Moving down the coast. The new hotspot is called Playa del Carmen. Extending south from Cancun along the shoreline, developers are gobbling up land and laying out luxury hotels at a nonstop rate and with environmental effects frequently (not in every case) similar to those defining Cancun. What happens when the entire area from Cancun to Chetumal is cemented over? There's more shoreline to be found in Belize, and on Mexico's Pacific coast, and then down in Guatemala.

What happens when *all* shoreline runs out? There's a lot of it around the world, but when the end comes, it'll also probably be true that we won't need a real natural world to have a natural world, at least those parts of it that we enjoy. Already today at Typhoon Lagoon in Disney World, six-foot waves roll down for surfers. And visitors to the Grand Canyon face a curious choice: they can take the trouble to actually walk out and visit the Grand Canyon, or, more comfortably, they may opt to see it in an impressive IMAX theater presentation. There's no reason still more aspects of the natural world, like the warm breezes and evening perfection of Cancun, couldn't be reproduced in a warehouse. Of course there are people who insist that they want the real thing when it comes to nature, but there were also once people who insisted that they couldn't enjoy a newspaper or book if it wasn't printed on real paper.

Next, moving on to the other of the two arguments in favor of free use, there's the idea that we might as well use everything without anxiety because, in the end, we really can't seriously affect the natural world anyway. This sounds silly at first; it seems clear that we can and do wreak havoc: species disappear and natural ecosystems are reduced to dead zones.

However, it must be noted that our human view of the world is myopic. That's not our fault, just an effect of the way we experience time. For us, a hundred years is, in fact, a long time. In terms of geological time, however, the entire experience of *all* humanity on this earth is just the wink of an eye. Geological time understands time's passing not relative to human lives but in terms of the physical history of the earth. According to that measure, the existence of the human species has been brief, and the kinds of changes we're experiencing in the natural world pale beside the swings the earth is capable of producing. We worry, for example, about global warming, meaning the earth's temperature jumping a few degrees, and while this change may be seismically important for us, it's nothing new to the earth. As Robert Laughlin, winner of the Nobel Prize in physics, points out in an article set under the provocative announcement "The Earth Doesn't Care if You Drive a Hybrid," six million years ago the Mediterranean Sea went bone dry. Eighty-five million years before that there were alligators in the Arctic, and two-hundred million years before that Europe was a desert. Comparatively, human industrialization has changed nothing. [2]

This geological view of time cashes out as an ethical justification for free use of the natural world for a reason nearly the opposite of the first. The argument for free use supported by convictions about domination and progress borders on arrogance: it's that the natural world is unimportant, and any problems caused by our abusing it will be resolved by intelligence and technological advance. Alternatively, and within the argument based on geological time, our lives, deeds, and abilities are so trivial that it's absurd to imagine that we could seriously change the flow of nature's development even if we tried. We could melt nuclear reactors left and right, and a hundred million years from now it wouldn't make a bit of difference. That means, finally, that the idea of preserving the environment isn't nobility: it's vanity.

The Environment Should Be Protected in the Name of Serving Human Welfare

The free-use argument in favor of total environmental exploitation posits no value in the natural world. In and of itself, it's worthless. Even if this premise is accepted, however, there may still be reason to take steps in favor of preservation and protection. It could be that the ecosystems around us should be safeguarded not for them, but for *us*. The reasoning here is that we as a society will live better and happier when lakes are suitable for swimming, when air cleans our lungs instead of gumming them up, when a drive on the freeway with the car window down doesn't leave your face feeling greasy. Human happiness, ultimately, hinges to some extent on our own natural and animal nature. We too, we must remember, are part of the ecosystem. Many of the things we do each day—walk, breathe, find shelter from the elements—are no different from the activities of creatures in the natural world. When that world is clean and functioning well, consequently, we fit into it well.

Wrapping this perspective into an ethical theory, utilitarianism—the affirmation that the ethically good is those acts increasing human happiness—functions effectively. For visitors to Cancun, it seems difficult to deny that their trip will be more enjoyable if the air they breathe is fresh and briny instead of stinky and gaseous as it was in some places when the lagoon had decayed into a pestilent swamp. Understood in this way, we could congratulate Architect Legorreta for his expensive decision to carve out a space for the tides to reenter and refresh the inland lake. It's not, the argument goes, that he should be thanked for rescuing an ecosystem, but that by rescuing the ecosystem he made human life more agreeable.

Another way to justify environmental protection in the name of human and civilized life runs through a rights-based argument. Starting from the principle of the right to pursue happiness, a case could be built that without a flourishing natural world, the pursuit will fail. If it's true that we need a livable environment, one where our health—our breathing, drinking, and eating—is guaranteed, then industrialists and resort developers who don't ensure that their waste and contamination are controlled aren't just polluting; they're violating the fundamental rights of everyone sharing the planet.

Bringing this rights-based argument to Cancun and Legorreta's dredging of the lagoon, it's possible to conclude that he absorbed a pressing responsibility to do what he did: in the name of protecting the right of others to live healthy lives, it was necessary to renew the dead water. Again, it must be emphasized that the responsibility isn't to the water or the animals thriving in its ecosystem. They're irrelevant, and there's no obligation to protect them. What matters is human existence; the obligation is to human rights and our dependence on the natural world to exercise those rights.

The Environment Should Be Protected in the Name of Serving Future Generations' Welfare

The idea that the environment should be protected so that future generations may live in it and have the choices we do today is based on a notion of social fairness. Typically in ethics, we think of fairness in terms of individuals. When applying for a job at a Cancun hotel, fairness is the imperative that all those applying get equal consideration, are subjected to similar criteria for selection, and the selection is based on ability to perform job-related duties. When, on the other hand, the principle of fairness extends to the broad social level, what's meant is that groups taken as a whole are treated equitably.

One hypothetical way to present this notion of intergenerational fairness with respect to the environment and its protection is through the previously discussed notion of the veil of ignorance—that is, the idea that you imagine yourself as removed from today's world and then reinserted at some future point, one randomly assigned. You may come back tomorrow, next year, next decade, or a hundred years down the line. If, the reasoning goes, that's your situation, and then very possibly you're going to urge contemporary societies to protect the environment so that it'll be there for you when your time comes around, whenever that might be. Stated slightly differently, it's a lot easier to wreck the environment when you don't have to think about others. Fairness, however, *obligates* us to think of others, including future others, and the veil of ignorance provides one way of considering their rights on a par with the ones we enjoy now. What does this mean in terms of Cancun? We should enjoy paradise there, no doubt, but we should also ensure that it'll be as beautiful for our children (or any randomly selected future generation) as it is for us. In this case, the re dredging of the lagoon serves that purpose. By helping maintain the status quo in terms of the natural ecosystems surrounding the hotels, it also helps to maintain the possibility of enjoying that section of the Caribbean into the indefinite future.

There's also a utilitarian argument that fits underneath and justifies the position that our environment should be protected in the name of future generations. This theory grades acts ethically in terms of their consequences for social happiness, and with those consequences *projected forward in time*. To the extent possible, the utilitarian mind-set demands that we account for the welfare of future generations when we act today. Of course the future is an unknown, and that tends to weigh decisions toward their effects on the present since those are more easily foreseen. Still, it's not difficult to persuade most people that future members of our world will be happier and their lives fuller and more rewarding if they're born onto an at least partially green earth.

The Environment Should Be Protected in the Name of Serving Animal Welfare

One of the more frequently voiced lines of reasoning in favor of ecosystem preservation starts with a fundamental shift from the previous arguments. Those arguments place all intrinsic value in *human* existence: to the extent we decide to preserve the natural world, we do so because it's good for us. Preservation satisfies our ethical duties to ourselves or to those human generations yet to come. What now changes is that the natural world's creatures get endowed with a value independent of humans, and that value endures whether or not we enjoy or need to fit into a web of healthy, clean ecosystems. Animals matter, in other words, regardless of whether they matter for us.

Ethically, the endowment of nonhuman animals with intrinsic worth is to treat them, to some extent, or in some significant way, *as* human. This treatment is a subject of tremendous controversy, one orbiting around the following two questions:

- *Are* nonhuman animals worthy of moral consideration? What do they do, what qualities do they possess that lead us to believe they should have rights and impose obligations on you and me?

- Granting that nonhuman animals do hold value in themselves and impose obligations on humans by their very existence, how far do the obligations go? If we're given a choice on a speeding highway between running over a squirrel and hitting a person, do we have a moral obligation to avoid the person (and run down the squirrel)? If we do, then it seems that the intrinsic worth of an animal is less than that of a human being, but how much less?

Questions about whether animals have rights and impose obligations are among the most important in the field of environmental ethics. They will be explored in their own section of discussion that follows. In this section, it will simply be accepted that nonhuman animals do, in fact, have autonomous moral standing. It immediately follows that their protection is, to some extent, a responsibility.

In terms of an ethics of duties, the obligation to protect animal life could be conceived as a form of the duty to beneficence, a duty to help those who we are able to aid, assuming the cost to ourselves is not disproportionately high. Protecting animals is something we do for the same reason we protect people in need. Alternatively, in terms of the utilitarian principle that we act to decrease suffering in the world (which is a way of increasing happiness), the argument could be mounted that animals are, in fact, capable of suffering, and therefore we should act to minimize that sensation just as we do in the human realm. Finally, rights theory—the notion that we're free and should not impinge on the freedom of others—translates into a demand that we treat the natural world with respect and with an eye to its preservation in order to guarantee that nonhuman animals may continue to pursue their own ends just as we demand that we humans be allowed to pursue ours.

With the obligation for the protection of—or at least noninterference with—nonhuman animals established, the way opens to extend the conservation to the natural world generally. Because animals depend on their habitat to express their existence, because their instincts and needs suggest that they may be free only within their natural environment, the first responsibility derived from the human obligation to animals is one to protect their wild and natural surroundings. As an important note here, that habitat—the air all animals breathe, the water where fish swim, the earth housing burrowing animals—is not protected for its own sake, only as an effect of recognizing the creatures of the natural realm as dignified and worthy of our deference.

What does this dignity conferred on animal life mean for Cancun? The dredging and revivifying of the lagoon by Legorreta fulfills an obligation under this conception of the human relation to the natural world. It's a different obligation from those developed in the previous cases, however. Before, the lagoon was cleansed in the name of improving the Cancun experience for vacationers; here, it's cleansed so that it may once again support the land and aquatic life that once called the place home. As for whether that improves the vacation experience, there's no reason to ask; it's only necessary to know that saving animals probably requires saving their home.

The Entire Environmental Web Should Be Protected for Its Own Sake

The environment as a whole, the total ecosystem including all animal and plant life on Earth—along with the air, water, and soil supporting existence—should be protected according to a number of ethical arguments:

- The least difficult to persuasively make is the case that the obligation flows from human welfare: we're happier when our planet is healthy.
- It's more difficult, but still very possible, to make a reasonable case that the obligation to protection attaches to the autonomous value and rights of nonhuman animals. In order to protect all of them, the reasoning goes, we should preserve all elements of the natural world to the extent possible because we can't be sure which ones may, in fact, play an important role in the existence of one or another kind of creature.
- Finally, the most difficult case to make is that humans are obligated to protect the total environment—all water

and air, every tree and animal—because all of it and every single part holds autonomous value. This Earth-wide value translates into an Earth-wide obligation: the planet—understood as the network of life happening above and under its surface—becomes something like a single living organism we humans must protect.

What distinguishes the third argument from the previous two is that we don't save the greater natural ecosystem in the name of something else (human welfare or habitat preservation for nonhuman animals) but for itself.

It's easy to trivialize the view that every element of the natural world demands respect and therefore some degree of protection. Do we really want to say that a child experimenting out in the driveway with worms, or pulling up plants to see the roots is failing a moral obligation to the living world? What about the coconut trees felled to make room for Cancun's hotels? Perhaps if they were unique trees, or if a certain species of bird depended on precisely those limbs and no others for its survival, but do we want to go further and say that the standard trees—a few hundred out of millions in the world—should give developers pause before the cement trucks come wheeling in? For many, it will be easier to conclude that if a good project is planned—if there's money to be earned and progress to be made—then we can cut down a few anonymous trees that happen to be standing in the way and get on with our human living.

On the other hand, sitting on the sand in Cancun, it's difficult to avoid sensing a happening majesty: not a reason to pull out your camera and snap, but a living experience that can only be had by a natural being participating, breathing air as the wind blows across the beach, or swimming in the crisp water. There may be a kind of aesthetic imperative here, a coherent demand for respect that we feel with our own natural bodies. The argument isn't that the entire natural ecosystem should be preserved because it feels good for us to jump in the ocean water—it feels good to jump in the shower too—the idea is that through our bodies we experience a substance and value of nature that requires our deference. Called the aesthetic argument in favor of nature's dignity, and consequently in favor of the moral obligation to protect it, there may be no proper explanation or reasoning, it may only be something that you know if you're in the right place at the right time, like Cancun in the morning.

The response to the aesthetic argument is that we can't base ethics on a feeling.

If We Decide to Protect the Environment, Who Pays?

Much of the stress applied to, and the destruction wrought on the environment around Cancun could be reversed. That costs money, though. Determining exactly how much is a task for biologists and economists to work out. The question for ethical consideration is, who should pay? These are three basic answers:

1. Those who contaminated the natural world
2. Those who enjoy the natural world
3. Those who are most able

The answer that the costs should be borne by those who damaged nature in the first place means sending the bill to developers and resort owners, to all those whose ambition to make money on tourism got roads paved, forests cleared, and foundations laid. Intuitively, placing the obligation for environmental cleanup on developers may make the most sense, and in terms of ethical theory, it fits in well with the basic duty to reparation, the responsibility to compensate others when we harm them. In this case, the harm has been done to those others who enjoy and depend on the natural world, and one immediate way to compensate them is to repair the damage. A good model for this could be Legorreta's work, the expense taken to raise a portion of a hotel and so once again allow tide water to freshen the lagoon. Similar steps could be taken to restore parts of the ruined coral reef and to replant the forest behind the hotel area.

The plan makes sense, but there's a glaring problem: times change. Back when Cancun was originally being laid out in the 1960s, ecological concerns were not as visible and widely recognized as they are today. That doesn't erase the fact that most hotel companies in Cancun laid waste to whatever stood in the way of their building, but it does allow them to note that they are being asked to pay today for actions that most everyone thought were just fine back when they were done. It's not clear, finally, how fair it is to ask developers to pay for a cleanup that no one envisioned would be necessary back when the construction initiated.

The proposal that those who enjoy and depend on the natural world should bear primary responsibility for protecting and renewing it also makes good sense. This reasoning is to some extent implemented in America's natural parks where fees are charged for entry. Those revenues go to support the work of the forestry service that's required to ensure that visitors to those parks—and the infrastructure they need to enjoy their time there—don't do harm to the ecosystems they're coming to see, and also to ensure that harm done by others (air pollution, for example, emitted by nearby factories) is cleansed by nature's organic processes.

On a much larger scale, a global one, this logic is also displayed in some international attempts to limit the emission of greenhouse gasses. The specific economics and policy are complicated and involve financial devices including carbon credits and similar, but at bottom what's happening is that governments are getting together and deciding that we all benefit from (or even need) reduced emissions of waste into the air. From there, attempts are made to negotiate contributions various countries can make to the reduction effort. As for the cost, most economists agree that the expense of pollution control measures will, for the most part, be passed along as hikes in the cost of consumer goods. Everyone, in other words, will pay, which matches up with the affirmation that everyone benefits.

Finally, the response that those most able to pay should bear the brunt of the cost for protecting the natural world is a political as much as an environmental posture. One possibility would be a surtax levied on wealthy members of society, with the money channeled toward environmental efforts. This strategy may find a solid footing on utilitarian grounds where acts benefitting the overall welfare remain good even if they're burdensome or unfair to specific individuals. What would be necessary is to demonstrate that the sum total of human (and, potentially, nonhuman animal) happiness would be increased by more than the accumulated displeasure of those suffering the tax increase.

KEY TAKEAWAYS

- The attitude that the environment shouldn't be protected has both historical and ethical roots.
- Confidence in the human ability to control the environment diminishes concerns about protecting its current state.
- The power of nature viewed over the very long term diminishes concerns about protecting its current state.
- Environmental protection in the name of serving human welfare values the natural world because it's valuable for us.
- Environmental protection in the name of serving future generations' welfare derives from a notion of social fairness.
- Environmental protection in the name of serving animal welfare connects with a notion of moral autonomy in nonhuman animals.
- Environmental protection for its own sake values the entire set of the world's ecosystems.

- If the environment is protected, the costs may be made the responsibility of various parties.

REVIEW QUESTIONS

1. Briefly, what is the history of the free-use attitude toward the natural world?

2. How can technology make environmental protection a wasted effort?

3. How can the idea of geological time become an argument against taking expensive steps to protect the natural world?

4. What are some reasons why our ethical obligations to ourselves may lead us to protect the natural world?

5. What is the difference between protecting the natural world because we humans are valuable, and because animals are valuable?

6. What kind of experiences with nature may result in the sensation that, as an interdependent whole, the natural world holds value?

7. If the decision is made to protect nature, who are some individuals or groups that might be asked to pay the cost?

[1] Ricardo Legorreta, Wayne Attoe, Sydney Brisker, and Hal Box, *The Architecture of Ricardo Legorreta* (Austin: University of Texas Press, 1990), 108.
[2] George Will, "The Earth Doesn't Care: About What Is Done to or for It," *Newsweek*, September 12, 2010, accessed June 8, 2011,http://www.newsweek.com/2010/09/12/george-will-earth-doesn-t-care-what-is-done-to-it.html?from=rss.

14.3 Three Models of Environmental Protection for Businesses

LEARNING OBJECTIVE

1. Outline three business responses to environmental responsibility.

The Role of Businesses in Environmental Protection

Protecting the environment is itself a business, and many organizations, especially nonprofits, take that as their guiding purpose. The World Wildlife Fund, the Audubon Society, and National Geographic exemplify this. Their direct influence over the natural world, however, is slight when compared against all the globe's for-profit companies chugging away in the name of earning money. Whether the place is Cancun, or China, or the United States, the condition of the natural world depends significantly on what profit-making companies are doing, the way they're working, the kinds of goods they're producing, and the attitude they're taking toward the natural world. Three common attitudes are
1. accelerate and innovate,

2. monetize and count,
3. express corporate responsibility.

Business and Environmental Protection: Accelerate and Innovate

There's a subtle difference between environmental conservation and protection. Conservation means leaving things as they are. Protection opens the possibility of changing the natural world in the name of defending it. One way for a business to embrace the protection of nature is through technological advance. New discoveries, the hope is, can simultaneously allow people to live better, and live better with the natural world. Looking at a stained paradise like Cancun, the attitude isn't so much worry that we're ruining the world and won't be able to restore a healthy balance, it's more industrially optimistic: by pushing the accelerator, by innovating faster we'll resolve the very environmental problems we've created.

Examples of the progressive approach to environmental protection—as opposed to the conservative one—include solar and wind power generation. Both are available to us only because of the explosion of technology and knowledge the industrialized, contaminating world allows. Because of them, we can today imagine a world using energy at current rates without doing current levels of environmental damage. Here's a statement of that aim from a wind power company's web page: "Our goal has always been to produce a utility-scale wind turbine that does not need subsidies in order to compete in electricity markets." [1]

The idea, in other words, is that electricity produced by this company's windmills will be as cheap (or cheaper) than that produced from fossil fuels, including coal. To reach that point, the development of very strong yet lightweight materials has been necessary, along with other technological advances. If they continue, it may be that American energy consumption can remain high, while pollution emitted from coal-burning electricity plants diminishes. One point, finally, that the wind turbine company web page doesn't underline quite so darkly is that they'll make a lot of money along the way if everything goes according to plan. This incentive is also typical of an accelerate-and-innovate approach: not only should industrialization go forward faster in the name of saving the environment, so too should entrepreneurialism and profit.

In broad terms, the business attitude toward employing innovation to protect the environment acknowledges that human activity on earth has done environmental damage, and that matters. The damage is undesirable and should be reversed. The way to reverse, however, isn't to go backward by doing things like reducing our energy use to previous levels. Instead, we keep doing what we're doing, just faster. The same industrialization that caused the problem will pull us out.

Business and Environmental Protections: Monetize and Count

A cost-benefit analysis is, theoretically, a straightforward way of determining whether an action should be undertaken. The effort and expense of doing something is toted on one side, and the benefits received are summed on the other. If the benefits are greater than the costs, we go ahead; if not, we don't. Everyone performs cost-benefit analyses all the time. At dinner, children decide whether a dessert brownie is worth the cost of swallowing thirty peas. Adults decide whether the fun of a few beers tonight is worth a hangover tomorrow or, more significantly, whether getting to live in one of the larger homes farther out of town is worth an extra half-hour in the car driving to work every morning.

Setting a cost-benefit analysis between a business and the environment means adding the costs of eliminating pollution on one side and weighing it against the benefits of a cleaner world. The ethical theory underneath this balancing approach to business and nature is utilitarianism. The right act is the one most increasing society's overall happiness (or most decreasing unhappiness), with happiness measured in this case in terms of the net benefits a society receives after the costs of an action have been deducted.

The most nettlesome problem for businesses adopting a cost-benefit approach to managing environmental protection is implementation. It's hard to know exactly what all the costs are on the business side, and what all the benefits are on nature's side. Then, even if all the costs and benefits are confidently listed, it's equally (or more) difficult to weigh them against each other. According to a report promulgated by the nonprofit Environmental Defense Fund, North Carolina's coal-fired electricity plants could install smokestack scrubbers to significantly reduce contaminating emissions. The cost would be $450 million. The benefits received as a result of the cleaner air would total $3.5 billion. [2]This seems like a no-brainer. The problem is that when you dig a bit into the report's details, it's not entirely clear that the benefits derived from cleaner air add up to $3.5 billion. More troubling, it looks like it's hard to put any price tag at all on them. Here are a few examples:

- According to the report, "It is estimated that pollution from power plants triggers more than 200,000 asthma attacks across the state each year and more than 1,800

premature deaths." The word *estimated* is important. Further, how do you put a dollar total on an asthma attack or a death?

- According to the report, "One should be able to see out 93 miles on an average day in the Smoky Mountains, but now air pollution has reduced this to an average of 22 miles." How do you put a dollar total on a view?

- According to the report, "Air pollution contributes to significant declines in populations of dogwood, spruce, fir, beech, and other tree species." What is "significant?" What's the dollar value of a dogwood? [3]

The list of items goes on, but the point is clear. A cost-benefit analysis makes excellent sense in theory, but it's as difficult to execute as it is to assign numbers to human experiences. If the attempt is nonetheless made, the technical term for the assigning is monetization.

A final set of hurtles to clear on the way to implementing a cost-benefit approach to business and the environment involves formalizing mechanisms for paying the costs. Two common mechanisms are regulation and incentives.

Regulations are imposed by federal or local governments and come in various forms. Most directly, and staying with electrical plants in Carolina, the plants could be required to install smokestack scrubbers. Costs of the installation would, to some significant extent, be passed on to consumers as rate hikes, and the benefits of cleaner air would be enjoyed by all. It's worth noting here that the contamination producers in question—coal-burning electricity plants—are pretty much stuck where they are in geographic terms. You can't produce electricity in China and sell it in the States. Other kinds of businesses, however, may be able to avoid regulations by packing up and heading elsewhere. This, of course, complicates the already knotted attempt to tote up the benefits and costs of environmental protection.

A more flexible manner of regulating air and other types of pollution involves the sale of permits. There are multiple ways of mounting a permit trade, but as a general sketch, the government sets an upper limit to the amount of air pollution produced by all industry, and sells (or gives) permits to specific operating businesses. In their turn, these permits may be bought and sold. So an electric company may find that it makes economic sense to install scrubbers (limiting its pollution output) and then sell the remaining pollution amount on its license to another company that finds the cost of limiting its emissions to be very high. One advantage of this approach is that, while it does limit total contamination, it allows for the fact that it's easier for some polluters than others to cut back.

As opposed to regulations that essentially force businesses to meet social pollution goals, incentives seek the same results cooperatively. For example, tax incentives could be offered for environmental protection efforts; money paid for the scrubbers a company places in their smokestacks may be deducted from taxes at a very high rate. Similarly, matching funds may be offered by government agencies: for every dollar the company spends, the government—which in this case means you and I and everyone who pays taxes—chips in one also.

Alternatively, government agencies including the Environmental Protection Agency may provide public recognition to anti-contamination efforts undertaken by a business, and in the hands of a strong marketing department those awards may be converted into positive public relations, new consumers, and extra profits that offset the original pollution control costs.

Specific awards tied to government agencies may not even be necessary; the incentive can be drawn from a broad range of sources. A good example comes from the *Washington Post*. A long and generally quite positive news story recounts Wal-Mart's efforts to encourage suppliers in China to increase energy efficiency while decreasing their pollution output. Basically, Wal-Mart told suppliers that they need to clean up or they'll get replaced. According to the account, not only is the effort bearing fruit, but it's working better than government regulations designed to achieve similar ends: "In many cases, Wal-Mart is first trying to bring firms up to government standards. Suppliers may not care about government fines, but they care about orders from the buyers." [4]

As for Wal-Mart, their cause is served by the free publicity of the story when it's distributed to almost a million newspaper readers in the Washington, DC, area and then projected broadly on the Internet. Further down the line, the good publicity ended up getting cited here. Going back to the specific newspaper story, it finishes with a clear acknowledgment of the public relations dynamic. These are the article's last lines: "Wal-Mart sees this not just as good practice but also good marketing. 'We hope to get more customers,' said Barry Friedman, vice president for corporate affairs in Beijing. 'We're not doing it solely out of the goodness of our hearts.'" [5]

One notable problem with the incentive approach is identical to its strength: since participation is voluntary, some heavy polluters may choose not to get involved.

As a final point about incentives, many industrial plants already receive incentives to *not* protect the environment. To the extent they're allowed to simply jet sulfur and other contamination into the air, they are, in effect, forcing society generally to pay part of their cost of production. Every time someone in Carolina falls ill with an asthma attack, the consequences are suffered by that individual while the profits from electricity sales go to the electric company. As previously discussed, these externalities—these costs of production borne by third parties—actually encourage businesses to follow any route possible to make outsiders pay the costs of their operations. One route that's frequently possible, especially for heavy industry, involves letting others deal with their runoff and waste.

Business and Environmental Protections: Corporate Social Responsibility

The third posture an organization may adopt toward environmental protection falls under the heading of corporate social responsibility. The attitude here is that companies, especially large, public corporations, should humanize their existences: an attempt should be made to see the corporation, in a certain sense, as an individual person. Instead of being a mindless machine built to stamp out profits, the business is re-envisioned as a seat of economic *and* moral responsibility. Responding to ethical worries isn't someone else's concern (say, the government's, which acts by imposing regulations), instead, large companies including Wal-Mart take a leading role in addressing ethical issues.

The *Washington Post*'s flattering presentation of Wal-Mart in China fits well here. The story actually presents Wal-Mart as transitioning from a vision of itself as a pure profit enterprise to one exercising corporate citizenship. Originally,

> *Wal-Mart only cared about price and quality, so that encouraged suppliers to race to the bottom on environmental standards. They could lose contracts because competition was so fierce on price.*

Now, however,

> *Wal-Mart held a conference in Beijing for suppliers to urge them to pay attention not only to price but also to "sustainability," which has become a touchstone.* [6]

Sustainability means acting to protect the environment and the people surrounding an operation so that they may continue to contribute to the profit-making enterprise. As a quick example, a logging operation that clear-cuts forests isn't sustainable: when all the trees are gone, there's no way for the company to make any more money. Similarly in human terms, companies depending on manual labor need their employees to be healthy. If a factory's air pollution makes everyone sick, no one will be able to come in to work.

For Wal-Mart in China, one step toward sustainability involved energy efficiency. A supplier installed modern shrink-wrapping machines to replace work previously done by people wielding over-the-counter hair dryers. In theoretical terms at least, the use of less energy will help the supplier continue to produce even as worldwide petroleum supplies dwindle and energy costs increase. Steps were also taken, as the newspaper story notes, to limit water pollution: "Lutex says it treats four tons of wastewater that it used to dump into the municipal sewage line. That water was supposed to be treated by the city, but like three-quarters or more of China's wastewater, it almost certainly wasn't." [7]

More examples of Wal-Mart suppliers making environmentally conscious decisions dot the newspaper story, and in every case these actions may be understood as serving the long-term viability of the supplier's operations. Stakeholder theory is another way of presenting corporate social responsibility. The idea here is that corporate leaders must make decisions representing the interests not only of shareholders (the corporation's owners) but also of all those who have a stake in what the enterprise is doing: the company exists for *their* benefit too. Along these lines, Wal-Mart encouraged farmers in China to abandon the use of toxic pesticides. The corporation contracted with farmers under the condition that they use only organic means to kill pests and then allowed their products to be sold with a label noting their Wal-Mart-confirmed clean production. The real lives of locals who eat that food and live on the now less-contaminated land are markedly improved. As another farming-related example of dedication to the well-being of the Chinese making up their manufacturing base, Wal-Mart sought "to help hundreds of small farmers build rudimentary greenhouses, made of wood and plastic sheeting, in which they grow oranges in midwinter to sell to Wal-Mart's direct farm program. Zhang Fengquan is one of those farmers; he gathers more than three tons of nectarines from more than 400 trees in his greenhouse. Asked what he did during the winter before the greenhouse was built, he said he worked as a seasonal laborer. Or played the popular Chinese board game mah-jongg." [8]

In both cases, Wal-Mart is not simply abandoning its workers (or its suppliers' workers) once they punch out. As stakeholders in the company, Wal-Mart executives feel a responsibility to defend employees' well-being just as they feel a responsibility to bring good products to market in the name of profit.

The fact that Wal-Mart's recent actions in China can be presented as examples of a corporation expressing a sense of responsibility for the people and their natural world that goes beyond immediate profit doesn't mean that profit disappears from the equation. Shareholders are stakeholders too. And while corporate attitudes of social responsibility may well result in an increasingly protected environment, and while that protection may actually help the bottom line in some cases, there's no guarantee that the basic economic tension between making money and environmental welfare will be resolved.

Conclusion. Businesses can react to a world of environmental concern by trusting in technological innovation, by trusting in governmental regulation, and by trusting in a concept of corporate responsibility. It is currently uncertain which, if any, of these postures will most effectively respond to society's environmental preoccupations.

KEY TAKEAWAYS

- One business response to concerns about the environment is to participate in the process of technological innovation to produce cleaner, more efficient ways of living.

- One business response to concerns about the environment is to participate in, and act on cost-benefit studies of environmental protection.

- One business response to concerns about the environment is to express corporate responsibility: to make the business a seat of economic *and* ethical decisions.

REVIEW QUESTIONS

1. What's the difference between environmental protection and environmental conservation?
2. How has industrialization caused environmental problems? How can it resolve those problems?
3. What is a *cost-benefit analysis*?
4. With respect to the environment, how can a cost-benefit analysis be used to answer questions about business and environmental protection?

5. What is practical problem with the execution of a cost-benefit analysis strategy for responding to environmental problems?

6. What's the difference between a corporation guided by profit and one guided by a sense of social responsibility?

7. Why might a stakeholder theory of corporate decision making be good for the environment?

[1] The Wind Turbine Company home page, accessed June 8, 2011,http://www.windturbinecompany.com.

[2] "The North Carolina Clean Smokestacks Plan," *Environmental Defense Fund*, March 2001, accessed June 8, 2011, http://apps.edf.org/documents/700_NCsmokestacks.PDF.

[3] "The North Carolina Clean Smokestacks Plan," *Environmental Defense Fund*, March 2001, accessed June 8, 2011, http://apps.edf.org/documents/700_NCsmokestacks.PDF.

[4] Steve Mufson, "Wal-Mart Presses Vendors in China to Meet Higher Standards," *Washington Post*, February 26, 2010, accessed June 8, 2011,http://www.washingtonpost.com/wp-dyn/content/article/2010/02/26/AR2010022603339_pf.html.

[5] Steve Mufson, "Wal-Mart Presses Vendors in China to Meet Higher Standards," *Washington Post*, February 26, 2010, accessed June 8, 2011,http://www.washingtonpost.com/wp-dyn/content/article/2010/02/26/AR2010022603339_pf.html.

[6] Steve Mufson, "Wal-Mart Presses Vendors in China to Meet Higher Standards," *Washington Post*, February 26, 2010, accessed June 8, 2011,http://www.washingtonpost.com/wp-dyn/content/article/2010/02/26/AR2010022603339_pf.html.

[7] Steve Mufson, "Wal-Mart Presses Vendors in China to Meet Higher Standards," *Washington Post*, February 26, 2010, accessed June 8, 2011,http://www.washingtonpost.com/wp-dyn/content/article/2010/02/26/AR2010022603339_pf.html.

[8] Steve Mufson, "Wal-Mart Presses Vendors in China to Meet Higher Standards," *Washington Post*, February 26, 2010, accessed June 8, 2011,http://www.washingtonpost.com/wp-dyn/content/article/2010/02/26/AR2010022603339_pf.html.

14.4 Animal Rights
LEARNING OBJECTIVES

1. Elaborate arguments in favor of and against the proposition that animals have ethical rights.

2. Distinguish questions about animal rights from ones about animal suffering.

Do Animals Have Rights?

Were these a textbook in environmental ethics, two further questions would be added to this subsection's title: which rights, which animals? It's clear that chimps and dolphins are different from worms and, even lower, single-cell organisms. The former give coherent evidence of having some level of conscious understanding of their worlds; the latter seem to be little more than reactionary vessels: they get a stimulus, they react, and that's it. Questions about where the line should be drawn between these two extremes, and by what criteria, fit within a more specialized study of the environment. In business ethics, attention fixes on the larger question of whether animals can be understood as possessing ethical rights as we customarily understand the term.

There are two principal arguments in favor of understanding at least higher-order nonhuman animals as endowed with rights:

1. The cognitive awareness and interest argument

2. The suffering argument

And there are three arguments against:

1. The lack of expression argument

2. The absence of duties argument

3. The anthropomorphism suspicion argument

The **cognitive awareness and interest argument** in favor of concluding that animals do have ethical rights begins by accumulating evidence that nonhuman animals are aware of what's going on around them and do in fact have an interest in how things go. As for showing that animals are aware and interested, in higher species evidence comes from what animals do. Most dogs learn in some sense the rules of the house; they squeal when kicked and (after a few occurrences) tend to avoid doing whatever it was that got them the boot. Analogously, anyone who's visited Sea World has seen dolphins respond to orders, and seemingly understand that responding well is in their interest because they get a fish to eat afterward.

If these deductions of animal awareness and interest are on target, the way opens to granting the animals an autonomous moral value and standing. Maybe their ethical value should be inferior to humans who demonstrate sophisticated understanding of their environment, themselves, and their interests, but any understanding at all does bring animals into the realm of ethics because determinations about whose interests should be served in any particular situation are what ethical discussions concern. The reason we have ethics is to help those who have specific interests have them satisfied in ways that don't interfere with others and their attempts to satisfy their distinct interests. So if we're going to have ethical principles at all, then they should apply to dogs and dolphins because they're involved in the messy conflicts about who gets what in the world.

Putting the same argument slightly differently, when the owner of a company decides how much of the year-end profits should go to employees as bonuses, that's ethics because the interests of the owner and the employees are being weighed. So too when decisions are made at Sea World about how often and how intensely animals should be put to work in entertainment programs: the interests of profits (and human welfare) are being weighed against the interests of individual dolphins. As soon as that happens, the dolphins are granted an ethical standing.

The **suffering argument** in favor of concluding that animals do have ethical rights fits neatly inside utilitarian theory. Within this ethical universe, the reason we have ethical rules is to maximize happiness and minimize suffering. So the first step to take here is to determine whether dogs and similar animals do, in fact, suffer. Of course no dog complains with words, but no baby does either, and no one doubts that babies suffer when, for example, they're hungry (and whining). When dogs would be expected to suffer, when they get slapped in the snout, they too exhibit clear signs of distress. Further, biological studies have shown that pain-associated elements of some animal nervous systems resemble the human version. Of course dogs may not suffer on the *emotional* level (if you separate a male and female pair, there may not be any heartbreak), and it's true that absolute proof remains elusive, but for many observers there's good evidence that some animals do, in fact, feel pain. If, then, it's accepted that animals suffer, they ought to be included in our utilitarian considerations by definition because the theory directs us to act in ways that maximize happiness and minimize suffering. It should be noted that the theory can be adjusted to include only human happiness and suffering, but there's no necessary reason for that, and as long as there's not, the establishment of animal suffering is enough to make a reasonable case that they are entities within the ethical world, and ones that require respect.

On the other side, the arguments *against* granting animals a moral standing in the world begin with the **lack of expression** argument. Animals, the reasoning goes, may display behaviors indicating an awareness of the world and the ability to suffer, but that's not enough to merit autonomous moral standing. To truly have rights, they must be *claimed*. An explicit and demonstrated awareness must exist of what ethics are, and why rules for action are attached to them. Without that, what separates animals from a sunflower? Like dogs, sunflowers react to their environment; they bend and twist to face the sun. Further, like dogs, sunflowers betray signs of suffering: when they don't get enough water they shrivel. Granting, finally, animals rights based on their displaying some reactions to their world isn't enough to earn a moral identity. Or if it is, then we end up in a silly situation where we have to grant sunflowers moral autonomy. Finally, because animals can't truly explain morality and demand rights, they have none.

Another way to deny animal rights runs through the **absence of duties argument**. Since animals don't have duties, they *can't* have rights. All ethics, the argument goes, is a two-way street. To have rights you must also have responsibilities; to claim protection against injury from others, you must also display consideration before injuring others. The first question to ask, consequently, in trying to determine whether animals should have rights is whether they have or could have responsibilities. For the most part, the answer seems to lean toward no. Were a bear to escape its enclosure in the zoo and attack a harmless child, few would blame the bear in any moral sense; almost no one would believe the animal was guilty of anything other than following its instincts. People don't expect wild animals to distinguish between their own interest and instinct on one side, and doing what's right on the other. We don't even expect that they *can* do that, and if they can't, then they can't participate in an ethical world any more than trees and other natural creatures that go through every day pursuing their own survival and little more.

The last argument against granting moral autonomy or value to animals is a **suspicion of anthropomorphism**. Anthropomorphism is the attribution of human qualities to nonhuman things. When we look at dogs and cats at home, or chimpanzees on TV, it's difficult to miss the human resemblance, the blinking, alert eyes, and the legs stretching after a nap, the howls when you accidentally step on a tail, the hunger for food, the thirst and need to drink. In all these ways, common animals are very similar to humans. Given these indisputable similarities, it's easy to imagine that others must exist also. If animals look like we do (eyes, mouth, and nose), and if they eat and drink as we do, it's natural to assume they feel as we do: they suffer sadness and boredom; they need affection and are happy being cuddled. And from there it's natural to imagine that they think as we do, too. Not on the same level of sophistication, but, yes, they feel loyalty and experience similar inclinations. All this is false reasoning, however. Just because something *looks* human on the outside doesn't mean it experiences some kind of human sentiments on the inside. Dolls, for example, look human but feel nothing.

Transferring this possibility of drawing false conclusions from superficial resemblances over to the question about animal rights, the suspicion is that people are getting fooled. Animals may react in ways that look like pain to us but aren't pain to them. Animals may appear to need affection and construct relationships tinted with loyalty and some rudimentary morality, but all that may be just us imposing our reality where it doesn't actually exist. If that's what's happening, then animals shouldn't have rights because all the qualities those rights are based on—having interests, feeling pain and affection—are invented for them by us.

Corresponding with this argument, it's hard not to notice how quickly we rush to the defense of animals that look cute and vaguely human, but few seem very enthusiastic about helping moles and catfish.

Dividing Questions about Animal Rights from Ones about Animal Suffering

The debate about whether animals should be understood as possessing rights within the ethical universe is distinct from the one about whether they should be subjected to suffering. *If* animals do have rights, then it quickly follows that their suffering should be objectionable. Even if animals aren't granted any kind of autonomous ethical existence, however, there remains a debate about the extent to which their suffering should be considered acceptable.

Assuming some nonhuman animals do, in fact, suffer, there are two major business-related areas where the suffering is especially notable:

- Research
- Consumer goods

The case of research—especially medical and drug development—provides some obvious justification for making animals suffer. One example involves a jaw implant brought to market by the firm Vitek. After implantation in human patients, the device fragmented, causing extensive and painful problems. Later studies indicated that had the implant been tested in animals first, the defect would've been discovered and the human costs and pain avoided. [1] From here, it's easy to form an argument that if significant human suffering can be avoided by imposing on animals, then the route should be followed. Certainly many would be persuaded if it could be proven that the net animal suffering would be inferior to that caused in humans. (As an amplifying note, some make the case that testing on humans can be justified using the same reasoning: if imposing significant suffering on a few subjects will later help many cure a serious disease, then the action should be taken.)

The case of animal testing in the name of perfecting consumer goods is less easily defended. A *New York Times* story chronicles a dispute between the Perdue chicken company and a group of animal rights activists. The activists got enough money together to purchase a newspaper ad decrying poultry farm conditions. It portrayed chickens as crowded together so tightly that they end up fiercely attacking and eating each other. Even when not fighting, they wallow

in disease and convulse in mass hysteria. [2] Though Perdue denied the ad's claims, many believe that animals of all kinds are subjected to extreme pain in the name of producing everything from cosmetics, to dinner, to Spanish bullfights. When animals are made to suffer for human comfort or pleasure—whether the result is nice makeup, or a tasty veal dish, or an enthralling bullfight—two arguments quickly arise against subjecting animals to the painful treatment. The utilitarian principle that pain in the world should be minimized may be applied. Also, a duty to refrain from cruelty may be cited and found persuasive.

KEY TAKEAWAYS

- Cognitive awareness and directed interest by animals may be sufficient to grant them autonomous ethical rights.
- Accepting that animals suffer may be sufficient to grant them autonomous ethical rights.
- The fact that animals do not explicitly claim ethical rights may be sufficient to deny them those rights.
- The fact that animals don't have duties may be sufficient to deny them ethical rights.
- Anthropomorphism may lead to erroneously seeing animals as possessing autonomous ethical value.
- The question about whether animal treatment causing suffering is ethically acceptable may be managed independently of the question about whether animals possess rights.

REVIEW QUESTIONS

1. What are the basic steps of the cognitive awareness and interest argument?
2. What are the basic steps of the suffering argument?
3. What are the basic steps of the lack of expression argument?
4. What are the basic steps of the absence of duties argument?
5. What are the basic steps of the anthropomorphism suspicion argument?
6. In ethical terms, how is animal suffering for research reasons distinct from the suffering of a Spanish bullfight?

[1] Lauren Myers, "Animal Testing Necessary in Medical Research," *Daily Wildcat*, November 6, 2007, accessed June 8, 2011, http://wildcat.arizona.edu/2.2255/animal-testing-necessary-in-medical-research-1.169288.
[2] Barnaby Feder, "Pressuring Perdue," *New York Times*, November 26, 1989, accessed June 8,

2011, http://www.nytimes.com/1989/11/26/magazine/pressuring-perdue.html.

14.5 Case Studies

Yahoo! Answers: Why Should We Save the Planet?

Some people argue that there's no ethical requirement to protect the environment because the natural world has no intrinsic value. Against that ethical posture, here are four broad justifications for environmental protection. Each begins with a distinct and fundamental evaluation:

1. The environment should be protected in the name of serving human welfare, which is intrinsically valuable.
2. The environment should be protected in the name of serving future generations because they're valuable and merit intergenerational fairness.
3. The environment should be protected to serve animal welfare because there's an independent value in the existence and lives of animals.
4. The entire environmental web should be protected for its own sake because the planet's collection of ecosystems is intrinsically valuable.

On a Yahoo! forum page, a student named redbeard_90 posts the question "why should we save the planet?" and partially explains this way: "With the entire constant talk of 'saving the planet' and stopping global warming, should we actually try to stop it? Perhaps in a way, this is humans transforming the planet to better suit us?" [1]

QUESTIONS

1. It sounds like redbeard_90 might think that humans doing damage to the environment is OK because it's just a symptom of "humans transforming the planet to better suit us."
   o Where is redbeard_90 placing value?
   o What might redbeard_90's attitude be toward the *free use* conception of the human relation with the environment?
   o What is the *domination and progress argument* against worrying about saving the planet? How could that argument fit together with what redbeard_90 wrote?

2. The response by a woman named Super Nova includes this reasoning: "We should try to save the planet because there would be less people with health problems. Did you know that there are more people with respiratory problems because of all the air pollution contributing to it? Also, we should think about future generations on Earth and how it would affect our future. Also, global warming is affecting our essential natural resources like food and lakes are drying up and it is causing more droughts in the world."

The overall tone of her answer is strong with conviction.
   o It sounds like Super Nova wants to save the planet. What values sit underneath her desire? Why does she think environmental protection is important?
   o Does it sound like she believes nature in itself has value? Why or why not?

3. The poster named Luke writes an animated response, including these sentences:

The first thing we need to do is help make some changes in our national mind set from one that lets us believe that our earth can recover from anything, to one that lets us believe that our earth could use a little help.

Developing cleaner ways to produce electricity is not going to hurt a thing; if it does nothing but make the air we breathe cleaner it works for me.

Developing alternative fuels to power our transportation needs, again won't hurt a thing, reduce the demand for oil you reduce the price we pay for it, I think everyone can say "that works for me" to this.

I'm a global warming advocate but, not because of some unfounded fear of Doomsday but (as you may have guessed by now) because it won't hurt a thing to help our earth recover from years of industrial plunder.

   o Some people are worried about human welfare, some people care a lot about the welfare of the planet, some people mix a little of both. Where would you say Luke comes down? Justify by specific reference to his words.
   o Some people who are concerned about the earth's welfare are most interested in helping nonhuman animals; others are more interested in the natural world in its totality. Where would you say Luke comes down here? Why?
   o Environmental *conservation* efforts can be conservative in the sense that they try to undo damage to the earth by limiting industrialization. The idea of environmental protection leaves open the possibility of using industrial advances—the same forces that have been contaminating the earth—to help resolve the problem. Does Luke sound more like a conservationist or a protector? Explain.

4. The poster named scottsdalehigh64 is the most intense. He's also fairly experienced: assuming his username is true and he graduated high school in 1964, he's about retirement age now. He writes, "There is an alternate question: Why do we think we have a right to be so destructive to other life forms on the planet? Perhaps the

best answer is that we want to leave a good place to live for the species that are left when we go extinct."

Unlike most of the other posters, he doesn't include any personal note or "best wishes" type line in his response. He's focused and intense.

- o How much value does scottsdalehigh64 place in human existence?
- o Where does he place value? What does scottsdalehigh64 think is worth aiding and protecting?
- o Just from his words, how do you imagine scottsdalehigh64 would define "a good place to live?"

5. Scottsdalehigh64 doesn't seem to like those who are "destructive to other life forms on the planet."
- o Could an argument be built that, in preparing for our own eventual extinction, we should make sure that we eliminate *all* life-forms that are destructive to other life forms? What would that elimination mean? What would need to be done? How could it be justified?
- o In a newspaper column, the philosopher Jeff McMahan appears to tentatively endorse scottsdalehigh64's vision. He proposes that we "arrange the gradual extinction of carnivorous species, replacing them with new herbivorous ones." [2] If, in fact, we decided to wipe out meat-eating animals and leave the world to plants and plant eaters, would we be valuing most highly ourselves? Nonhuman animals? The entire natural world? Something else? Explain your response.

6. An excited poster, KiRa01, announces, "Just live like there's no tomorrow!!!!" With respect to the environment, justify his attitude in ethical terms.

Going Green

Fifty years ago airports were designed to reward fliers with architecture as striking as the new experience of flight was rare and exciting. From those early days, only a few airports remain unspoiled by renovation and expansion. The Long Beach Airport south of Los Angeles is a survivor. The low lines of midcentury modern architecture captivate today's visitors just as they did the first ones. The restaurant overlooking the tarmac remains as elegant and perfectly simple as always. Walking the concourse, it's easy to imagine men in ties and women and children in their Sunday clothes waiting for a plane while uniformed porters manage their suitcases.

Flying is different today—no longer exciting and rare, it's just frustrating and crowded. Recognizing that reality, when the large European nations combined to form an airplane manufacturer, they didn't choose a distinguished and elevated name for their enterprise, they just called it Airbus: a company that makes buses that happen to go up and down. Airplanes are tremendously polluting. In the United States, large passenger flights account for about 3 percent of released greenhouse gasses. That doesn't sound like much, but when you compare the number of flights with car trips, it's clear that each airplane is billowing massive carbon dioxide. And the problem is only getting worse, at least on the tourism front. Over the course of the next decade, global tourism will double to about 1.6 billion people annually.

Tourists aren't the only fliers. Planes are also taken by people heading to other cities to talk about tourism. One of them, Achim Steiner, is the executive director of the United Nations Environment Program. At a recent conference in Spain, he said, "Tourism is an extraordinary growth industry, it's the responsibility of operators—from hoteliers to travel companies—as well as governments to ensure that sites are sustainable." [3]

Sustainability has at least two sides. On one side, there's the economic reality: revenue provided by visitors pays for needed services. An example comes from the Masai Mara park reserve in Kenya. In villages surrounding the park, schools were forced to close when political unrest scared away the tourists and their money. On the other side, sustainability also means environmental protection. According to Steiner, there's the possibility that "Masai Mara could be overused to the point where it loses its value."

QUESTIONS

1. According to Steiner, "Hoteliers, travel companies, and governments are responsible" for ensuring the sustainability of sites including Masai Mara. In most discussions about *paying* the costs of a clean environment, three groups are signaled:
- o Those who contaminate the natural world
- o Those who enjoy the natural world
- o Those who are most able to pay

How do each of these three fit into Steiner's vision?

2. Airplane exhaust contributes significantly to the damage currently being done to the environment. Steiner rode an airplane to a city to talk about that damage.
- o What is a cost-benefit analysis?

o How could a cost-benefit analysis be used to show that his boarding the plane and going was actually an environmentally respectable act?

3. Fifty years ago, airplanes contributed almost no pollution to the environment because so few could afford to fly. One way to limit the amount of pollution into the air is through incentives. In the airplane case, a large tax could be attached to an airline ticket, thus providing an incentive to tourists to stay home or use alternate sources of transportation. Of course, for the very wealthy, the tax will be more absorbable and, presumably, airplane travel would tend toward its origins: flying would be something the rich do. How could a utilitarian analysis be used to justify the action of, in essence, reserving plane flying for the rich in the name of helping the environment?

4. The airport at Long Beach is a low-ranking historical treasure. Tourists will never flock to see it, but it does incarnate and vivify a time in the recent past. The airport at Long Beach is also a business. That may lead its directors to initiate remodeling and expansion plans that will destroy the airport's original essence.

   o Is preserving the natural world like the preservation of a historical architectural treasure? If so, why? If not, why not?

   o Using standard arguments against the business responsibility to preserve the natural world (free use, domination and progress, geological time), make the case that progress should be allowed to destroy the Long Beach Airport's historical authenticity if that course of action is profitable.

   o Using standard arguments in favor of the business responsibility to preserve the natural world (preservation for human welfare, for future generations, for the sake of the thing itself), make the case that the Long Beach Airport should be preserved.

   o If the airport is preserved, who should pay? Why?

5. In ethical terms, make the case that it's more important to preserve the Masai Mara park reserve in Kenya than the Long Beach Airport.

IBM and IBM

Bernadette Patrick moved away from her home in Endicott, New York, saying this about the town: "It was very neighborly and well kept, with lots of kids and families. Then all of a sudden it seemed like they put a skull and crossbones on all the doors. It was like a scene from a science fiction movie." [4]

The science fiction part is the large, white metal boxes attached to Endicott homes. With tubes burrowing down in the earth and shooting up high into the air, they're wired to pump air from below and jet it above. The idea is to disperse toxic vapors rising up through the ground. The vapor's source is industrial solvents poured down drains and dripped out of leaky pipes at the local IBM factory over the course of its seventy-five-year history.

Those seventy-five years have otherwise been good ones. IBM money and jobs drove the small town forward. As Wanda Hudak put it, "The IBM plant paid for a lot of college educations and cottages at Perch Pond." [5] The good feelings ended when a company IBM hired started showing up at people's homes to test the air and offer to install the mechanical ventilation systems.

QUESTIONS

1. IBM is paying millions for cleanup efforts. They're installing air cleaners on homes and pumping contaminated groundwater to the surface for safe disposal. An IBM spokesman said this about the toxic pollution, "None of it was done intentionally, but we still are sticking around to take care of it. We feel obligated legally, ethically. We are not going anywhere." [6]

   o Make the ethical case that those who contaminated the environment—IBM—should pay all the cleanup costs.

   o Make the case that those who benefit from a clean environment—the locals who work at the company and those who don't—should pay for the cleanup.

2. When the extent of the environmental pollution became clear, it was also evident that the cleanup would be tremendously expensive. In general terms, how could a cost-benefit analysis be mounted to decide between going forward with the environmental cleanup or closing the factory, shuttering the town, and moving on?

3. One critical element of the notion of corporate social responsibility is the idea of sustainability.

   o In both environmental and economic senses, what is sustainability?

   o What would be sustained by a cleanup in this case? How?

4. One critical element of the notion of corporate social responsibility is the idea of stakeholder theory.

   o Who are the obvious stakeholders in this case?

   o Thinking about the situation from the directorship of IBM, what are the company's responsibilities to each of the stakeholders?

5. The IBM of Endicott, New York, is an IBM of the past, one focused on factories and making business machines like typewriters and photocopiers. The IBM of today leaves most hard manufacturing to foreign firms in low-cost countries. What IBM now wants to do now, according to their advertising, is "build a smarter planet." That means solving problems like this one reported by CNN: *Stockholm bogs down in rush-hour traffic. A series of bridges connecting Sweden's capital creates bottlenecks that cause gridlock and air pollution, waste millions of gallons of fuel, hamper public transportation, and endanger pedestrians.* [7] The solution? Swede governmental officers decided on a congestion fee, on charging vehicles money for entering the city at peak traffic times. The aim was to seriously reduce the number of cars downtown at rush hours. That's easier said than done, however. Stopping people at toll booths would just make the problem worse: it would add yet another air-polluting stop to the traffic through town. So IBM was hired to produce camera technology allowing license plate numbers to be recorded and recognized automatically. Then monthly bills were generated and mailed out to the car owners. As CNN reported, these were the results: *Traffic fell 35 percent almost immediately and stayed down 22 percent—and not just at peak times or solely downtown. Emissions also dropped by 14 percent. The streets became more pedestrian friendly, and the buses began finishing their routes so quickly that the city had to rewrite the schedules. The fee schedule makes it obvious when traffic will be the worst, so drivers who trek in during peak hours know they'll pay more for what will probably be a maddening experience. As a result, people seem to be cutting out unnecessary trips: bundling afterschool pickups, say, with visits to the grocery store. In short, Swedes are driving smarter.* [8] When IBM protects the environment by cleaning up Endicott, they're losing money; when IBM protects the environment by selling smart systems to the Swedes, they're profiting.

    o   Make the case that, ethically, IBM's actions in Endicott are nobler than the actions in Sweden.

    o   Make the case that, ethically, IBM's actions in Sweden are nobler than the actions in Endicott.

6. In the world of business ethics and the environment, one of the more spirited debates is this: should we slow down technology and industrialization to use less and pollute less, or speed up industrialization and technology in the hope that we'll discover solutions to the environmental problems caused by industrialization and technology?

    o   How does the case of IBM incarnate that debate?

    o   Does the decision about where you come down depend on where you place value (human welfare versus environmental welfare)? Explain.

7. With respect to the environment and money, there are two formulas for thinking about IBM's project in Sweden:

    a. The aim was to clean up the environment, and money happened to be made along the way.

    b. The aim was to make money, and cleaning up the environment happened to be a good strategy for profit.

    In terms of basic values and ethics, outline the difference between these two visions. Thinking about ethics and IBM in Endicott and in Sweden, what's more important: the intentions of a company when it acts, or the consequences of the actions? Explain.

Windmills and Condors

The wind farms of Northern California produce clean electricity. Every light bulb illuminated by the giant turbines represents less destruction of the earth by mining and drilling operations and less contamination of the air by coal- and oil-fired power plants. It also represents fewer California Condors.

The spinning blades of the windmills erected in spots including the Altamont Pass are proving deadly for the rare birds, which are a kind of vulture. Here's a reaction by the environmental writer and activist Jim Wiegand: "For all the 'green energy' believers out there, this is a video you have to see. Each year across America thousands of eagles, hawks, owls, falcons, vultures and condors perish at green energy wind farms. This video will open your eyes and your mind when you see how easily a soaring vulture is smashed by the innocent looking blades of a prop wind turbine."[9]

Fatal Accident with Vulture on a Windmill
The video shows a large and calm vulture cycling slowly around a modern wind turbine and then getting struck by one of the spinning blades. The bird drops out of the air. Left on the ground beside the towering contraption, it drags and struggles to flap its broken wing.

QUESTIONS

1. Unlike single-cell creatures, vultures seem to have awareness and interest in their environment. They notice distressed animals, circle patiently, and in the end descend to eat the carcass.

    o   How can this behavior be translated into an argument that animals have ethical rights?

    o   How can the claim that aware and interested vultures have independent ethical rights be mustered into an argument against installing wind turbines in areas that threaten vultures, no matter how much clean electrical energy they may generate?

2. If you have a chance to see the video and watch the fallen bird struggling and dying on the ground, do the images change your feelings about the importance of protecting this creature?

   o Assume the bird writhing on the ground is, in fact, suffering in a way not completely unlike human suffering. How can this behavior be translated into an argument that animals have ethical rights?

   o Make the case that the video doesn't allow the conclusion that birds suffer.

3. Assume that, for whatever reason, you're convinced that those condors being cut down by California wind turbines have ethical rights comparable with the ones we deposit in human animals. Can you nonetheless outline an argument in favor of continued windmill use because of the clean energy it provides?

   o Make your case by appeal to a utilitarian argument.

   o Make your case by appeal to a cost-benefit analysis.

   o Make your case by appealing to the idea that the environment should be protected in its entirety because, as an interlocked set of ecosystems, it holds autonomous value.

4. If you can make the case that some nonhuman animals that have autonomous ethical rights should be allowed to meet their end in the name of clean energy, could you make the same argument for human animals? Imagine, for example, that actually constructing these wind turbines leads to high worker fatalities, say, 10 times higher than any other kind of work. Could those deaths be justified ethically in the name of clean energy? Why or why not?

The PETA Homepage

People for the Ethical Treatment of Animals are possibly the most active animal-rights organization in the United States. On the day this case study was written, the organization's home page featured pictures of a sad-eyed Dalmatian, a noble elephant, and a cuddly rabbit. There was also a tease to a story set underneath a picture of smiling, former President Clinton. It read, "What's the secret behind this former president's newly trim waistline, enhanced energy, and improved cardiovascular health? A vegan diet! Read more." [10]

QUESTIONS

1. A vegan diet excludes all products derived from animals and promotes plant-based eating. In this PETA ad, what values probably underlie the strategy (is the appeal to

protect animals made in the name of human welfare, animal welfare, or general environmental welfare)? Justify.

2. What is anthropomorphism? How could the phenomenon of anthropomorphism lead someone to posit autonomous ethical dignity, and rights, in nonhuman animals that really shouldn't be considered worth protecting any more than trees?

3. From the description provided of the PETA home page, how could it be described as inviting anthropomorphism?

4. Were you in charge at PETA, an organization fighting for animal an right that depends on donations, would you use the phenomenon of anthropomorphism to boost your organization's revenue?

   o What is an argument in favor of the strategy?

   o What is an argument against the strategy?

[1] "Why Should We Save the Planet?," *Yahoo! Answers*, accessed June 8, 2011,http://answers.yahoo.com/question/index?qid=20080610193018AA7IQt2.

[2] Jeff McMahan, "The Meat Eaters," *New York Times*, September 19, 2010, accessed June 8, 2011, http://opinionator.blogs.nytimes.com/2010/09/19/the-meat-eaters.

[3] James Kanter, "How Do You Measure Green Tourism?," *New York Times*, October 6, 2008, accessed June 8, 2011, http://green.blogs.nytimes.com/2008/10/06/is-there-any-such-thing-as-green-tourism.

[4] Janet Gramza, "Life in the Plume: IBM's Pollution Haunts a Village," *Post-Standard*, January 11, 2009, accessed June 8, 2011,http://www.syracuse.com/specialreports/index.ssf/2009/01/life_in_the_plume_ibms_polluti.html.

[5] Janet Gramza, "Life in the Plume: IBM's Pollution Haunts a Village," *Post-Standard*, January 11, 2009, accessed June 8, 2011,http://www.syracuse.com/specialreports/index.ssf/2009/01/life_in_the_plume_ibms_polluti.html.

[6] Janet Gramza, "Life in the Plume: IBM's Pollution Haunts a Village," *Post-Standard*, January 11, 2009, accessed June 8, 2011,http://www.syracuse.com/specialreports/index.ssf/2009/01/life_in_the_plume_ibms_polluti.html.

[7] Jeffrey M. O'Brien, "IBM's Grand Plan to Save the Planet," *CNN Money*, April 21, 2009, accessed June 8, 2011,http://money.cnn.com/2009/04/20/technology/obrien_ibm.fortune/index.htm.

[8] Jeffrey M. O'Brien, "IBM's Grand Plan to Save the Planet," *CNN Money*, April 21, 2009, accessed June 8, 2011,http://money.cnn.com/2009/04/20/technology/obrien_ibm.fortune/index.htm

[9] C. Taibibi, "California Condors, Wind Farms on Collision Course," *Examiner.com*, August 30, 2009, accessed June 8, 2011, http://www.examiner.com/wildlife-conservation-in-national/california-condors-wind-farms-on-collision-course.

[10] Peta.org, "Try Bill Clinton's New Diet!," accessed June 8, 2011,https://secure.peta.org/site/Advocacy?cmd=display&page=UserAction&id=3315.

NOTES:

Chapter 15:

The Star System and Labor Unions

Chapter Overview

This chapter investigates ethical issues raised by extreme disparities in income and wealth. Issues surrounding labor unions are also considered.

15.1 What Is the Star System?
LEARNING OBJECTIVE

1. Define and characterize the star system in contemporary business life.

Cash Break Zero

Hard times, according to the *Los Angeles Times*, have come to Hollywood: "Today, actors who used to make $15 million are making $10 million. The filmmakers who used to make $10 million are making $6 million. As one prominent agent put it, 'Everyone is in free fall. It's just brutal out there.'" [1]

The news isn't all bleak, however, for Hollywood's top actors, directors, and producers. Though they're being forced to settle for these embarrassingly small up-front paychecks, they're getting a higher percentage on the back end. The key concept is *cash break zero*—the point where the money a studio spent making, promoting, and distributing a film is balanced by the income from ticket sales in theaters, cable rights, home rentals, and similar. Once that break-even number has been hit, actors and film-makers that are being forced to cut their up-front salary are getting a large chunk of the profits. This arrangement can lead to huge rewards, but the talent only rakes it in if they're willing to bet on themselves making a movie that generates more money than it cost.

According to the *Times*, one exemplary winner is director Michael Bay, who pocketed $80 million for his successful—but not earth-shatteringly popular—movie *Transformers*. In the new Hollywood arrangement, just modest box-office success can translate into a giant payday. For those who make stinkers, however, they're walking away with their reduced up-front salary and nothing more. One major result, finally, of tying compensation to profits is that the distance between the big winners and everyone else in Hollywood increases dramatically. Just like a few movies every year break through the clutter of entertainment options to become must-see shows, so too some paychecks rocket above the rest.

The question about whether stars should get less at the beginning but potentially much more later on is a hot topic in Hollywood, but it doesn't connect with too many people's actual lives. In the words of one successful producer, "The studio pays for the lead actor or actress, but after that, well, the talent is just getting grinded. Everyone else is lucky to be working." [2]

Young people stepping off the bus in Hollywood and getting grinded is a long tradition. Even the biggest names tell stories about working the restaurant night shift six times a week so they're free to audition all day long, and then getting nothing but bit-parts for years. Once in a while someone catches a real break, but most of the time what breaks is the actor. After absorbing endless rejections, there's no direction left but the one leading back to the bus station, and then a long ride back home. The Hollywood blogger T. R. Locke provides a list of the reasons why:

- There are 120,000 SAG (Screen Actors Guild) actors in Hollywood.
- At any given time 85 percent of them are out of work.
- The average salary of a SAG actor is less than $10,000 a year.
- Most of them are just trying to earn the required $7,500 a year to keep their health benefits.
- Less than 1 percent is the ones you read about and know: the real stars, the actors who make million-dollar salaries. [3]

The reality is sobering. In Hollywood the real paycheck difference—the salary separation dividing top talent from just the average—is $10,000 versus $80 million. When Michael Bay cashed his *Transformer*'s check, he got enough to pay the yearly salary of *eight thousand* actors. That $79,990,000 gap separating Bay from each one of those aspiring stars explains Locke's good advice for Hollywood newcomers: "The best way to achieve your dreams is to wake up." [4]

Hollywood actors aren't the only ones staring across giant wealth gaps. If a typical employee at Microsoft who has, like many Americans, a net worth of about $100,000, spends $150 at the bars on a big Friday night, it would be about proportional to what Microsoft chairman Bill Gates would do to his net worth ($57 billion) were he to blow through...$85 million. In fact, just one Bill Gates party night could pay a weekend-long bender for every single adult in Wyoming. And if Gates wanted to hire actors in Hollywood, he could get a year of services from six million of them. If every single man, woman, and child living in Rhode Island, Montana, Delaware, South Dakota, Alaska, North Dakota, Vermont, and Wyoming were actors, he could hire them all for a year.

Bill Gates is not the richest man in the world. The Mexican Carlos Slim is. Rounding the numbers off, and using the average Mexican per-capita earning, he could hire ten million people to work a year for him. In US terms, he could hire a personal assistant for every adult in Florida.

Wall Street executive Stephan Schwarzman earned $702,440,573 in 2009: about enough to hire twelve thousand teachers for New York City's public schools. Oracle CEO Larry Ellison earned $560 million: enough to pay ten thousand junior-level software engineers. Occidental Petroleum CEO Ray Irani got $223 million: enough to pay five thousand gas station attendants. The list goes on. Reality imitates Hollywood: nearly every field of work has its stars. [5]

What Is the Star System?
The star system in the economic world is a winner-take-almost-all structure for distributing wealth: those who are successful in any particular field take home a vastly disproportionate share of the revenue. This is easy to see in the movies and some other places (big-time professional sports, for example), but what makes the star system a pressing issue in business ethics is that it seems to be expanding through our economic lives. To begin getting a sense of the expansion—exactly what it is and means—two distinctions may be drawn:
1. Individual worth versus salary (or income)
2. Vertical versus horizontal expansion of the star system

Individuals can separate from the larger population mass in terms of individual worth, and in terms of salary. Loosely, the first is how much money someone would have if they sold everything they owned and concentrated the dollars in a single bank account; the second is the amount an individual gets paid each year to *do* something. These two measures may be very distinct—someone may be a star in one category and ordinary in the other. Indra Tamang is a Nepalese immigrant who served a wealthy New Yorker as butler for many years. In terms of salary, he could not be called a star. When his matron passed away, however, she left him just under $10 million (and cut her own children out in the process). That rocketed Tamang into the upper end of the net-worth scale, even while his always-modest salary went to zero. [6]

At the other extreme, but still in New York, basketball player Eddy Curry received $10 million to play a single year's worth of basketball for the New York Knicks, clearly establishing him in the top echelon of earners. Still, he's not worth much. In fact, he's worth around zero: his house is in foreclosure, and creditors are suing for his cars. It's not clear where all the money went, but a pretty good clue comes from the fact that one of his creditors is charging a jaw-dropping 85 percent interest rate, and that's only legal in Nevada. [7] Finally, it's clear that the Nepalese butler and the high-rolling basketball player are extreme cases. More typically, individual worth and salary dovetail: those who make a lot end up having a lot. Still, the difference between them remains as two dimensions of a star system.

The second distinction to draw through an examination of gaping wealth differences is horizontal versus vertical. Vertical wealth imbalances measure the distance between top earners and typical ones. It's the distance between the hyper rich, a Bill Gates in Seattle or a Carlos Slim in Mexico City, and the guy pouring cement at a Seattle construction site or the waitress serving tamales in a Mexico City restaurant.

According to Internal Revenue Service's tax returns, in the fifteen years from 1992 to 2007, the four hundred wealthiest Americans have seen their average yearly income jump from about $50 million a year, to $350 million. That's about $300 million of extra space between the big earners and everyone else.[8] As a parallel statistic, according to a Hofstra political science professor, "The ratio of executive salary to the average paycheck during the mid-twentieth century was about thirty to one. In the last decade it has ranged from three hundred to over five hundred to one." [9]

Though there are many ways to measure the star system, there's a common conclusion: in terms of pure dollars, the rich are getting richer relative to everyone else.

As against the star system's vertical measure, horizontal expansion refers to the number of fields of activity where large wealth imbalances are prevalent. Some occupations fairly naturally lead to all or near-nothing incomes: wildcat oil drilling, hedge-fund managing, movie acting. Other fields seem naturally inclined to resist divergences. There aren't many farmers on lists of the hyper wealthy. Plumbers frequently earn a solid income, but rarely climb above that. The idea of the star system's horizontal expansion is that more and more careers resemble the first set of occupations, while fewer and fewer resemble the second set. It's difficult to find raw statistics to prove this expansion, but it's not hard to locate reasons for suspecting it.

One important reason the star system may be spreading is technological advancement. Justin Bieber, for example, is a cute adolescent boy from Canada with a nice singing voice and good instincts for catchy pop licks. Had he appeared forty years ago, he may have become known around his hometown of London, Ontario. With a lot of long drives and late nights, he may have become a star in his Canadian province and earned a nice concert income for a while. Thanks to YouTube, however, he was able to jump straight from singing a few songs a few times in remote Canadian towns to international superstardom. Similarly, lawyers that may once have become successful in a single courthouse can now buy cheap, late-night advertising on a cable network and set up branch offices around an entire state or even the nation. Anyone sitting at home with a laptop can use the camera to film themselves pitching some product or service and then display the commercial around the world using Google Ads for only a few pennies. What's happening is that people who have a good product or service or pitch are today able to scale up their success very rapidly and inexpensively. No one is saying that it's easy to become an overnight international sensation in any profession, but the *opportunities* to do that are expanding as our world becomes more interconnected.

One further point. Twenty years ago, if Justin Bieber had become successful in Ontario, he would've taken attention and economic opportunity away from some other aspiring singers in a Canadian province. Today, his success crowds out other potential preteen heartthrobs all around the world. Something similar has happened in corporate boardrooms as companies that used to operate in a state or a region have become international behemoths. It used to be that big-time CEOs managed hundreds of employees. The CEO of Wal-Mart today is responsible for millions. For young and ambitious employees entering the Wal-Mart company, that means, there's a lot more competition than there used to be for that one slot on top of the pyramid.

Conclusion. The star system isn't measured or defined by one specific statistic; it's a constellation of ideas involving the increasing concentration of wealth within a profession—and within the economy generally—in the hands of a few individuals.

KEY TAKEAWAYS

- The star system in the economic world is a winner-take-almost-all structure of wealth distribution.

- In the contemporary economic world, wealth imbalances are growing vertically and horizontally.

REVIEW QUESTIONS

1. Name a field of economic activity characterized by the star system. Explain.
2. Name a field of economic activity that resists the star system. Why does it resist?
3. With an example, explain the difference between vertical and horizontal wealth imbalances in a society.

[1] Patrick Goldstein and James Rainey, "Hollywood Gets Tough on Talent: $20-million Movie Salaries Go Down the Tubes," *Los Angeles Times*, August 3, 2009, accessed June 9, 2011, http://latimesblogs.latimes.com/the_big_picture/2009/08/want-to-make-10-million-a-movie-forget-about-it-hollywood-gets-tough-on-talent.html.

[2] Patrick Goldstein and James Rainey, "Hollywood Gets Tough on Talent: $20-Million Movie Salaries Go Down the Tubes," *Los Angeles Times*, August 3, 2009, accessed June 9, 2011, http://latimesblogs.latimes.com/the_big_picture/2009/08/want-to-make-10-million-a-movie-forget-about-it-hollywood-gets-tough-on-talent.html.

[3] T. R. Locke, "I'm an ACTOR… Should I Move to New York or Hollywood?," T. R. Locke, October 16, 2009, accessed June 9, 2011, http://www.trlocke.com/2009/10/i'm-an-actor…-should-i-move-to-new-york-or-hollywood.

[4] T. R. Locke, "I'm an ACTOR… Should I Move to New York or Hollywood?," T. R. Locke, October 16, 2009, accessed June 9, 2011, http://www.trlocke.com/2009/10/i'm-an-actor…-should-i-move-to-new-york-or-hollywood.

[5] David, "12 Highest Paid People of 2009," *Business Pundit*, December 28, 2009, accessed June 9, 2011, http://www.businesspundit.com/12-highest-paid-people-of-2009.

[6] Coryn Brown, "New York Butler's $8.4 Million Inheritance Includes 2 Dakota Apartments," *AOL Real Estate*, *aol.com*, May 18, 2010, accessed June 9, 2011,http://www.housingwatch.com/2010/05/18/new-york-butler-inherits-8-4-million-and-dakota-condo.

[7] Trey Kerby, "Eddy Curry Makes a Lot, Spends a Lot and Owes a Lot of Money," *Yahoo! Sports*, May 25, 2010, accessed June 9, 2011,http://sports.yahoo.com/nba/blog/ball_dont_lie/post/Eddy-Curry-makes-a-lot-spends-a-lot-and-owes-a-?urn=nba-243600.

[8] Sam Gustin, "Super Rich Made $345 Million Each in 2007 as Their Tax Rates Plummeted," *AOL DailyFinance*, accessed June 9, 2011,http://www.dailyfinance.com/story/super-rich-made-344-million-each-in-2007-as-their-tax-rates-plu/19362705.

[9] David Michael Green, "America's Race to the Bottom," *David Michael Greens* (blog), *The Smirking Chimp*, December 12, 2009, accessed June 9, 2011.

15.2 Questions Provoked by the Star System

LEARNING OBJECTIVES

1. Discuss different formulas for distributing wages and wealth in society.
2. Consider different ways individuals are compensated for their labor.
3. Define cronyism and distinguish it from a star system.

4. Discuss theoretical notions of envy.

How Should Wages Be Distributed?

From a business ethics perspective, a modern society striated by extreme income or wealth imbalances provokes questions:

- How should wages be distributed?
- What counts as compensation?
- What's the difference between a star system and crony capitalism?
- Why do we want to be stars?

Beginning with the question about wage distribution, in today's economy a multitude of architectures may determine compensation levels for individuals at work. The appeal to market forces is the most straightforward. When the question is "How much should Bill Gates get?" the direct answer is whatever he can find a way to earn. This rationale has nothing to do with how hard Gates works. He may well struggle mightily, but it could also be that he sat down for a few mornings, jammed the lines of code composing the Windows operating system into his computer, and he hasn't done a thing since. He'd still be fully justified in claiming his billions because people are willing to pay his company to get the product.

Expanding the logic that people should receive whatever they can get someone to pay them, no one thinks twice about applying that way of thinking to paintings. The worth of a Picasso that goes on sale tomorrow is no more or less than what the highest bidder offers. So too, the argument goes, should wages be determined.

This subject will be returned to later, but provisionally it may be stated that this method of apportioning money fits well with the contemporary star system. It fits because if some few people find ways of accumulating huge sums in the open marketplace, that's not a problem or an injustice. If anything, it's an indication that the market economy, which privileges individual initiative and freedom, is working as it should.

Another way of thinking about how wages and wealth should be distributed is value generated for society. Under this formula, few would deny that Bill Gates—whose software contributes mightily to making our lives easier—deserves healthy compensation. However, does he deserve more than the top-notch elementary school teacher who every year sends thirty children forward, ready to contribute to society? What about a paramedic? It's true that Gates has touched most all our lives, but he hasn't *saved* any.

With respect to ethically justifying this form of wealth distribution, it fits together well with the utilitarian ideal of acting in the name of the common welfare. When economic incentives are put in place to highly reward those performing tasks that provide for happiness when measured across an entire community, even those who don't care about anyone but themselves will find their efforts channeled toward the general welfare.

On the question, finally, about gaping imbalances in income and wealth distribution, deciding to apportion money in terms of value added for society may not shrink the disparities. It's true that Wall Street speculators may have a harder time justifying million-dollar bonuses, but others may claim their place on the spectrum's upper end (Scientists? Teachers?). And with respect to someone like Gates, he'd stand on solid ground demanding huge riches based on his role in software development.

A third structure for dividing wealth is effort, measured by, say, number of hours toiling or amount of measurable work done. American Apparel employs this formula when dividing up wages among sewers at its Los Angeles factory. The sewers are grouped, and each member receives a respectable hourly base wage, and then a bonus depending on how many garments their team produces. Some groups produce faster than others and so make more money, but no individual rises above the pack as drastically as financier Stephan Schwarzman did on Wall Street when he earned $702,440,573 in one year. To underline the difference, if Schwarzman worked twenty-four hours every day of the year, he'd be getting $80,000 an hour. No sewer at American Apparel gets anything close to that.

Ethically justifying a structure for wealth distribution based on pure effort may lead toward the duty to fairness. If there's broad agreement that all individuals should have an equal opportunity to pull down a big paycheck, then aligning the paycheck with effort makes sense. It works especially well by eliminating advantages some people have over others as a result of luck. Someone born with a knack for math may do better on Wall Street than another born without, but both have it in their power to work equally hard. If, consequently, we want to ensure that all society's members have the same shot at becoming wealthy, setting paycheck decisions to accord with effort may function well.

With respect to a star system, finally, it's immediately clear that this method of dividing wages drastically suppresses income differences. It may be that Wall Street maven Stephan Schwarzman works harder and longer than any sewer at

American Apparel (or he may not), but there's no way he works $80,000 an hour harder.

A still flatter system of wealth distribution is precisely flat wealth distribution—that is, everyone gets the same check at the end of the month. Retirees collecting Social Security approximate this reality. Though it's true that Social Security payments vary depending on factors including how much individuals contributed during their working lives and how early they began accepting benefits, there's no room whatsoever for a star system. Near-blind equality across the board, in fact, is one of the main principles guiding the Social Security system.

Of course, one reason people are willing and, for the most part, happy to participate in Social Security's relatively flat payment system is that they *aren't* working. When people are working, when they receive a check for labors accomplished during preceding weeks, it becomes difficult to justify giving everyone the same amount regardless of how many hours they may have put in or effort exerted. In a certain sense, it actually becomes impossible because such a distribution breaks the link between work and payment (even someone who sucked their thumb all day would receive the same wage as the dedicated nurse) and so the entire discussion about dividing up salary levels evaporates. Dispersing money to the population becomes a political task more than an economic one. It is, it must be underlined, quite possible to ethically justify a flat wealth distribution system; it's just that the justification would rest on social and political grounds, not economic and business ones.

The last structure for wealth division is in terms of need. Everyone gets the funding necessary to maintain a quality of life comparable with that of everyone else. A gesture in this direction is made in the United States by government welfare programs, a notable example being food stamps (about 40 million Americans, or 12 percent of the population, receive them). The idea behind the benefits is that those unable to afford the grocery store should receive a supplemental income to guarantee a sufficiently stocked kitchen cabinet. There are many and heated debates about the extent to which government institutions should be redistributing wealth by channeling tax revenue. It is clear, however, that giving to all members of society in accordance with their need will eliminate the star system. It may be true that some will *receive* vastly more than others (for example, those with serious physical disabilities), but there wouldn't be any outsized accumulation of wealth; there wouldn't be any Bill Gates out there with $50 billion in the checking account.

Conclusion. The star system in American business life is not necessary; other systems of wealth distribution are possible and justifiable. However, the star system does fit together well with the proportioning of wealth through open market forces.

What Counts as Compensation?
The president of the United States receives "only" $400,000 annually. Then again, he also gets a brass band striking up a tune in his honor every time he goes out the front door. Michael Bloomberg spent 108 million of his own dollars to be elected mayor of New York City in 2010. Since the job's salary is $225,000, he'd need to work 480 years just to break even. On the other hand, with a police escort he has a lot less trouble with the cross-town traffic frustrating so many New Yorkers, no matter how wealthy they may be. On Wall Street, *quants* are quantitative analysts: people who use mathematical algorithms (among other tools) to buy and sell stock. Their compensation can reach astronomical heights, which explains why some people who have the talent to be math professors at universities give up campus life for the world of finance. Others, however, decide against finance and in favor of the campus and a paycheck that struggles to reach six figures. In 1993, basketball superstar Michael Jordan left the game and signed up to play minor league baseball with the Birmingham Barons. Not everyone, reality teaches, wants to be a star, at least not in purely financial terms.

It's also true, however, that most people who could be financial stars forgo that possibility only because they get what *they perceive* to be a better offer. The better offer may not appear so wonderful to many—it takes a certain kind of person to choose minor league baseball over the NBA, or campus life instead of glittering Wall Street—but the decision nonetheless makes sense for the deciders (and to enough outside observers for the choice to avoid being labeled insane). The point is that compensation, what you want to get back for doing your job, comes in many flavors, and it's hard to put a universal price tag on them. Many would thoroughly enjoy the perks of being president, but probably few see why living a life of the mind at a remote university is preferable to being rich in New York City. Regardless, one of the difficulties in gauging and fully delineating the star system as it exists in professional life is accounting for the kinds of benefits that don't appear on paychecks.

What's the Difference between the Star System and Crony Capitalism?
Cronyism is partiality to others because they're friends and allies. Normally, cronyism also includes some expectation of reciprocity: favors are exchanged. Crony capitalism is an

insiders' game in business, one where decisions are made on the basis of personal relationships and loyalties more than unbiased judgments and professional considerations.

About cronyism, everyone engages in it to some extent. When children come around in December selling gift wrap to raise money for their school, one girl may knock on the door and give a tremendous presentation along with some discount options, but you still buy more from the boy who mumbles and forgets most of the samples because he's your sister's son and also because you hope that when your children get older, your sister will do the same favor for you. In the neighborhood and on a small scale, it's difficult to object to outbreaks of personal allegiance at the cost of economic purity. In fact, an ethics of care—one that sets the preservation of social and family bonds as the highest moral good—actually endorses this kind of cronyism. The problem comes further up the scale when personal relations guide decisions about *other people's* money, either directly or indirectly. One example is the bailout of Boston's One United Bank. It was located in the district of a powerful congressman and led at one point by the husband of a powerful congresswoman. When the bank collapsed under the weight of bad loans, it should've been put out of business. In fact, the Federal Deposit Insurance Corporation, a regulating arm of the US government, ordered the bank to stop making loans. Still, after a string of telephone calls stretching from the bank to the congresswoman and then on to the congressman in charge of doling out government bailout funds, a $12 million check got written. The incompetent bankers at One United got to keep working, and US taxpayers got a seven-figure bill. [1]

The purely economic description of this kind of bailout is "privatizing the profits and publicizing the losses," meaning that when a company does well, the private sector people— the managers and shareholders—keep the profits, and when money is lost, the bill is charged to the public sector, to taxpayers. This kind of practice may well encourage wealth accumulation among a few people with powerful friends in government since their insider connections grant them a tremendous advantage on the economic playing field: they can bet everything knowing that if they lose, they'll just get their stake back to try again.

Ethically, a number of arguments may be quickly mounted against cronyism:

- In terms of basic duties, including the duty to fairness, cronyism fails because economic players aren't getting the same opportunity to succeed. In the banking example, the duty to fairness doesn't mean all bankers necessarily succeed equally, but it does require that the difference between winning and losing gets determined in terms of the skills of banking (attracting depositors, correctly determining which loans are good and which should be avoided and similar). Cronyism replaces banking expertise with social and political maneuverings at the core of success, which is unfair by definition, just as it would be to screen applicants for a bartending job by asking them all to participate in a running race.

- Another duty-based argument against cronyism is that it can be construed as a form of stealing. When political friends provide taxpayer dollars to a business, there's no one person who can claim to have been robbed, but as a collective, taxpayers find someone has taken their money.

- A utilitarian argument against crony capitalism would succeed by showing that an economic system distorted by political favoritism is less efficient, and therefore, less supportive of the general welfare than one where only those who are best at one or another activity gain rewards.

Conversely, and in support of crony capitalism, an ethics of egoism could be mustered. Viewed from the perspective that whatever is best for me personally is also ethically recommendable, it's hard to find fault with individuals in the world seeking to use *all* their resources—including friendships and discreet deals with government bigwigs—to succeed. An argument could even be made that if everyone simply accepted that we should all use every resource at our disposal, there might be a balance in the distribution of favors and underhanded advantages.

Regardless of the ethical defensibility of crony capitalism, there are important differences between it and a star system, at least a star system conceived in its purest form. The central contrasts:

- The concentration of income in the hands of a few within a working star system generally traces back to their professional talents, as opposed to their personal connections.

- The income concentration frequently results from an economic system allowing for successes to be transparently replicated on a tremendous scale, as opposed to sneaky, back-room deals.

An illustrative example of the difference comes from the top of the *Forbes* 400 list. The world's two wealthiest individuals, according to the ranking, are Carlos Slim and Bill Gates. While everyone knows Gates, few people outside of Mexico have heard the name Carlos Slim, which isn't remarkable given that he's never invented anything, participated in the providing of an improved service, or even found a way to get typical goods and services to market more efficiently than anyone else. What Slim *has* done very well is pay off politicians.

In the early 1990s, Mexico, like many developing nations, was selling off inefficient state assets. One of them was *Telefonos de Mexico* (Telmex), the sole provider of telephone services for the country. Slim, together with a group of investors, bought the company in a shady deal (it's not clear how much, if any, money the Mexican people received in exchange for the company their taxes built) and then got national legislators to grant them an effective monopoly. With no competition, the new directors of Telmex were free to charge whatever they wished for phone service, and they didn't hesitate. They also didn't bother investing in system improvements, so, until recently, multiline technology was not even introduced in the country. People and businesses who wanted to have more than one line had to have a second (or third, or fourth) line physically wired to their location. As the telecommunications industry around the world exploded—the demand for services including Internet shooting through the roof—people in Mexico had to wait for a crew to come out and run a wire. The wait was months or more. The people at Telmex were in no rush since their friends in the national legislature were busy assuring that no competitor could sweep in and take the client. The result, twenty years later, is that Slim is one of the world's wealthiest individuals, and Mexicans pay among the world's highest phone bills for abysmally poor service.

Except for the accrued wealth part, Slim's story is completely different from Bill Gates'. Though defenders of Apple enjoy pointing out that Microsoft's Windows operating system came after, and looked suspiciously like the early Apple operating systems (almost as though it was a copy with just enough changes to claim originality), few deny that Windows, along with MS Office, have responded nimbly to consumer demands, and responded more skillfully than comparable offerings from competitors. And in a world where software can be mass-stamped as a small plastic disc or downloaded rapidly over the Internet, the Microsoft success has galloped across the economy: the Windows operating system along with MS Office almost immediately went to the extreme of creating a monopoly in America and elsewhere. No payoffs to politicians or other cronyism-stoking was necessary. The lesson is that in at least some parts of the interconnected world, quality differences (even small ones) between competing products can translate quickly into huge business success because consumers across the spectrum almost all make the same buying decision.

Something similar could be written about Wal-Mart, as well as other companies. Though it's true that the price difference between a Wal-Mart cart of items and one from a competitor isn't too great, the fact that there's even an incremental difference quickly leads to a slaughtering of huge chunks of competition because there's no difference between winning by a little and winning by a lot. In an interconnected world, most people hear very quickly that Wal-Mart is cheaper, and overwhelmingly respond by going there. What's important is that whether the company is Microsoft, Wal-Mart, or a similar enterprise, market domination—along with the associated enrichment of a few individuals—has followed from genuine quality as determined by consumer decisions flocking together in an open market.

Both crony capitalists and the leaders in an economic star system build mountainous wealth, but the former do so at the cost of others by denying consumers choices or by short-circuiting the market's natural functioning, while the latter do so by satisfying consumer demands and taking full advantage of a smooth-running market economy.

Do We Want to Want to Be Like the Stars? The Psychology of Envy

Though questions about envy—"What is it?" "What causes it?" "Is it OK to feel it?"—generally belong to studies in psychology, they're inescapable in the economic world when a few participants have money flowing in so fast that it's not worth the five seconds of their time required to bend down and pick up a twenty-dollar bill they dropped.

In sweeping terms, there are two broad emotional—as opposed to ethical—reactions to the hyper rich and the question about whether the rest of us want to be like them. The first response is, "Yes, obviously." This makes sense. Most of us have lists of consumer goods we'd like to buy—an iPad, a new dress, a vacation trip—and it'd be nice to swipe the credit card without worrying about the balance. This reaction, it should be noted, isn't just a pleasant thought: it may also contain traces of envy or, stronger, of resentment and even anger. Anyone who internalizes what it would mean (and how great it could be) to receive a wage that exceeds by thousands of dollars per hour the one we currently get, is going to be vulnerable to disliking or even hating those who have so much more.

The other way to make sense of the star system's vast wealth disparities comes from a proposition on the subject found in Aristotle's *Rhetoric*, book 2, chapter 10. There, Aristotle proposes that envy of others decreases as their distance increases. These distances may include years: few of us envy the medieval kings and queens of Europe. We know they had servants waiting on their every desire, but that doesn't make us want to be them or get angry at their privileged lives. No one's mad at Henry VIII; he's just someone we see portrayed on the History Channel. Alternatively, the distance separating us from others who have more than we do could be measured in space and culture. We feel less envious of those people we hear about who may be tremendously wealthy but who live in some far-off place we've never visited and speak a language we'll never understand. We may read about their exotic lives in a magazine, but it doesn't affect us emotionally. Finally, the distance can also be economic: Aristotle's proposition is that the hyper wealthy—Bill Gates, Warren Buffett—are *so* far away from us that we don't feel stung and angry when confronted with statistics about their wealth. Their lives are just too different to relate with.

We only sense envy, Aristotle affirms, for those who come from similar backgrounds, for those who desire and chase similar things, and for those whose economic and social status isn't too far above our own. We need, in other words, to already be like others in some ways in order to want to be like them in others. For this reason, it can drive you crazy when your next door neighbor gets a sparkling Mercedes, but when a Saudi prince buys his seventh Rolls Royce, you don't bat an eye.

Why is envy distance limited? According to Aristotle, when those who are like us end up getting more than we do, it's a reproach to us: *it's our fault* that we didn't get the promotion or the better-paying job at the start-up company. If we're like our neighbors in most every way except for the fact that they're bringing in more money, that means we somehow blew the chance to get that much ourselves.

Finally, these two very different reactions to astronomically wealthy members of our society have important consequences for the ethical verdict reached about the star system. One of the criticisms launched at modern economies characterized by extreme wealth disparities is that the disparities poison society with rancor and envy. No matter, the argument goes how positive the inventions of a Bill Gates may be, the social welfare his work generates is cancelled by the sourness and resentment his personal wealth creates. If that's true, then maybe we should impose limits on the economic success of individuals.

On the other hand, if Aristotle is right and we don't rage when we find ourselves dwarfed by giant wealth, the star system becomes much easier to justify on the grounds that the prospect of endless money incentivizes people to invent goods and services that make all our lives better.

- Wages and wealth may be assigned in accordance with multiple formulas.
- The assignment of wages and wealth may be justified by reference to multiple theories.
- Money is only one of several ways people are rewarded for their work.
- Cronyism, which works through personal favors, may result in wealth disparities, but it is not synonymous with or necessary for a star system.
- A decision about how envy works affects ethical evaluations of an economic star system.

REVIEW QUESTIONS

1. Name a field of work where market forces typically determine wages. Does the star system naturally take root there? Why or why not?
2. What's the difference between wages based on "value generated for society" and "effort exerted"? Can you cite examples to indicate that one resists a star system more than another?
3. What's a job where the main compensation isn't money? Why do people want that job?
4. What are two ethical arguments against crony capitalism?
5. Why might someone be more envious of a neighbor whose house is slightly larger than their own than of a Saudi prince with eight luxury homes scattered around the world?

[1] John Stossel, "Crony Capitalism," *John Stossel's Take* (blog), *Fox Business News*, December 23, 2009, accessed June 9, 2011, http://www.foxbusiness.com/on-air/stossel/blog/2009/12/23/crony-capitalism.

15.3 Ethics: Justifying and Criticizing the Star System
LEARNING OBJECTIVES

1. Define and consider the main ethical arguments supporting a star system.
2. Define and consider the main ethical arguments reproaching a star system.

Justifying the Star System: Rights

In evaluating the ethics of the star system, three arguments are commonly mounted in favor of respecting vast wealth disparities:

1. The rights argument
2. The social welfare argument
3. The fairness argument

The rights argument defends the respectability of wealth concentrations by affirming that *not* allowing those accumulations is a violation of human freedom. From this perspective, all ethics centers on individual opportunity: right and wrong is about guaranteeing that free individuals can pursue whatever goals and as much money as they like on the way to finding their own happiness. Concerns about society's overall welfare become secondary and derivative.

Ethics that make freedom the highest value can be used in a thought experiment inspired by the philosopher Robert Nozick to produce a substantial defense of an economic star system. It goes this way:

1. Imagine that everyone in our society has the same income, everything goes forward as perfect equality, and no one complains.
2. Next, imagine that NBA superstar Kobe Bryant proposes a new contract with his team. It stipulates that the ticket price for every home game will go up five dollars, and that extra five bucks goes directly to him.
3. The team owners say, "No."
4. Kobe says, "I'm going to quit, and go get a job as a gym teacher at the school near my house."
5. The owners change their mind.
6. Some season ticket holders, angry at the new price, cancel their purchase, but most say, "Yeah, it's worth an extra five dollars to see Kobe."
7. A total of 17,500 people fit into the Forum, the Los Angeles basketball arena where Kobe Bryant plays, and he plays forty-one games there each year.
8. Kobe pockets an extra $3,590,000. Annually.

Does anyone have a problem with this? Is there someone who didn't agree to the arrangement, to this new society where one guy—Kobe Bryant—is suddenly a lot richer than everyone else? Is there someone who's being forced to do something they don't want to do? Is anyone else being denied the chance to renegotiate their own contract or search for a different job? Are there *any* legitimate grounds someone can stand on to launch a complaint?

Further, if someone *does* complain, if they say Kobe shouldn't have proposed the new contract, the owners shouldn't have agreed to it, or the spectators shouldn't have ponied up the extra money, then isn't the complaint itself unethical? Isn't anyone launching those criticisms really just trying to limit the freedom of someone else?

The rights-based argument affirming the star system's respectability is powerful and hard to stop once it gets going. If you buy the premise—if you accept that business ethics is fundamentally about ensuring the right to individual freedom—it's nearly impossible to break the chain of arguments against those who'd try to limit the choices Kobe Bryant and his adoring fans can make, no matter how much wealth piles up for the one player.

Moving the argument over to a broader consideration of the American star system, something like the Kobe Bryant thought experiment actually happens with respect to Hollywood celebrities, especially within the cash-break-zero reality currently gripping the movie capital. Big-name actors are essentially saying that they want a dollar (or whatever the relevant number is) from everyone who pays to see their movie. In this case, as in the Kobe example, the owners of the enterprise are perfectly free to find different actors if they don't like the terms of the deal they're being offered. And on the consumer side, moviegoers entering a theater are free to look up at the listings and choose another show if they don't like the idea of padding the pockets of a particular Hollywood celebrity. Moviegoers are also perfectly free to walk out of the theater and redirect their entertainment dollars at museums, vacation travel, web browsing, or a novel. The list is interminable, and as long as it is, it becomes difficult to deny ethical acceptance to the movie attraction that's making one star incredibly rich.

The Logic of Rights: License or Responsibility?

The Kobe Bryant thought experiment illustrates how a rights-based ethics licenses individuals to accumulate wealth without accumulating moral guilt. In the hands of its most dedicated defenders, however, the logic of rights goes further. It's not just a license to accumulate; it's something nearer to a responsibility. Taking the case of Bill Gates, when he piles up astronomical wealth, he isn't only expressing his freedom; he's inciting others to pursue *their* freedom: he's providing them an example, he's offering them products they may freely choose to purchase or reject, and he's offering them tools they can use to pursue their own goals. With respect to those tools, many small businesses have gotten off the ground with the help of—and been *able* to get off the ground because of—the spreadsheet, publishing, and word-processing software found in MS Office. The fact, therefore, that Gates (and his fellow stars) are so rich in an open market economy shows that their ethical aptitude and performance is just as stellar as their economic one. They aren't obnoxiously greedy; they're the most dedicated servers of pure ethics because they're living free and helping others be that way too.

Those who criticize Gates' wealth in the name of spreading the money around to more needful members of society may sound noble, but they're not. They should be reprimanded for distorting expressions of human freedom. Stronger, broad demands for wealth's redistribution—which may occur, for example, through increased taxes levied on the wealthy or through pressure to donate to charitable causes—are *not* virtuous calls to social responsibility: they're deplorable violations of basic human rights.

Justifying the Star System: General Welfare

The utilitarian argument defending the star system as ethically acceptable affirms that the general welfare can be served by wealth imbalances. If moral good and bad only reflect whether the general welfare is served, the argument builds this way:

1. Breakthrough developments of consumer goods are encouraged by a star system because it allows inventors to reap a significant portion of the economic reward.
2. Breakthrough developments can positively impact social welfare incrementally (Apple's iPad), and sometimes be revolutionary (the invention of the assembly line).
3. The broad social happiness provided by these breakthroughs outweighs unhappiness attributed to giant wealth imbalances. (This is especially true if the imbalances are sufficiently great to preclude envy in the terms Aristotle proposed.)

This argument may be formulated slightly differently as a hypothetical question. Imagine you could have one of these two lives:

1. A typical middle-class European or American today. You're far from rich but you can always afford decent food and a night out here and there. You've got a car that doesn't break down too much. There's a microwave to make popcorn in the kitchen, a TV in the main room, and some clothes you like in the closet. On the other hand, you need to go to work in the morning and clean grime out of the shower occasionally.
2. King of England. In 1600. You never have to clean the shower, but then again, the shower hasn't been invented. There are no flush toilets either. You get whatever clothes you want, but they better be warm since there's no heat for your castle except the fireplace. You don't have a microwave, and even if you did, there's no electricity to run it. You get from place to place fairly well on the country's best horse.

This is a hard choice: live better in objective terms in the present or better in subjective terms in the past. It's a way of asking, "What's more important: how well you live, or, how well you live relative to everyone else?"

There's no right or wrong response here. This is a question that's as much about psychology and economics as it is about morality. However, if you go for the first, you're leaning toward the utilitarian argument justifying wealth imbalances. As long as those imbalances are functioning to encourage life-improving innovations, then the stark economic inequalities they leave in their wake become acceptable.

Justifying the Star System: Fairness

The fairness argument justifying the star system is increasingly persuasive as technological advances allow communication and operational organization to cover the globe instantly. That has opened the way for single individuals to amass tremendous responsibilities in vast organizations and then claim that it's only fair that their reward be equally massive.

Only fifty years ago the largest department and grocery stores in the United States were mostly local concerns; crossing one or two state lines was a big deal. Of course expansive companies including the telegraph transmitter Western Union (which now specializes in international money transfers) and the Ford Motor Company have been around for more than a century, but neither compares in size, reach, or number of employees to today's Wal-Mart. With more than two million workers spread across the globe, CEO Michael Duke holds management responsibilities dwarfing the ones known by corporate heads in the past. To the extent that's right, if it's true that Duke's responsibilities are astronomically high, then shouldn't he receive a wage commensurate with the difference?

The fairness argument favoring the star system—at least in those cases where high salary reflects high responsibility—is that it would be arbitrary and unequal to simply put a lid on managers' compensation if there's no corresponding lid on the size of management responsibility. Concretely in Wal-Mart's case, a store manager overseeing the work of, say, a hundred employees makes about $100,000. By that logic (the business pays $1,000 of salary for every employee managed), Michael Duke, who oversees the work of two million people, should make about $2 *billion*. That's a hundred times what he actually makes.

When Wal-Mart wanted to open a store in Chicago recently, a local alderman complained about the CEO's salary this way: "How can you go to bed at night and sleep knowing you make this kind of money?" [1]

One response allowed by an argument appealing to fairness is that it's difficult for CEO Duke to sleep because he's making so little. His wage is massively unfair in its paltriness.

Criticizing the Star System: Social Welfare

In evaluating the ethics of the star system, these arguments are commonly mounted against respecting vast wealth disparities:

- The social welfare argument
- The duty to beneficence argument
- The virtue argument

The social welfare argument against the star system is the most obvious and commonly cited, it's that, essentially, Aristotle is wrong and wealth differences—especially extreme disparities—are ethically reproachable because of the emotional turmoil they cause within a community. While it may be true that allowing vast wealth accumulation motivates innovators and managers to perform exceptionally well, and while their work may benefit society significantly, the upside fails to outweigh the human cost of the resentment. The social rancor of inequality isn't worth the benefits provided by highly paid innovators.

Criticizing the Star System: Duty to Beneficence

The beneficence argument against the star system operates from the duty to help others when doing so requires no unreasonable sacrifice of our own interests. Most discussions of beneficence revolve around acts. For example, if a man is drowning in a lake and you don't know how to swim, you have no responsibility to jump in. But if you're Michael Phelps in exactly the same situation, then the duty to save the flailing man applies.

Transposing the discussion into monetary terms, one basic question is, "At what point does my accumulated money translate into a responsibility to charity?" If a woman works a few overtime hours to buy a new pair of boots for the upcoming winter, there's no clear duty to share the cash with a neighbor in similar circumstances. By contrast, when Alice Walton (daughter of Wal-Mart founder Sam Walton) who's worth $18 billion walks down a street near her home outside of Fort Worth, Texas, she'd have a hard time convincing those passing by that she couldn't establish, say, a generous college scholarship program for society's neediest members without suffering any tangible loss. Probably, most people at the very top of the wealth pyramid could dedicate large chunks of cash to charitable causes without severely denting their quality of life. In these circumstances, the duty to beneficence becomes pressing.

With respect to the star system, it's important to note that beneficence doesn't form an argument against high incomes or even astronomical wealth accumulation; it does, however, argue against the *maintenance* of large disparities. A society oriented by the duty to beneficence would, in other words, tolerate a star system, but only a fleeting one, a reality where people could make tremendous amounts, but not without feeling a charitable responsibility (or something similar) that would significantly diminish the economic gap separating them from the general population.

Criticizing the Star System: Virtue

Virtue ethics eschews reliance on social outcomes (the utilitarian model) as well as strict rules for action (the duty model). Instead, decisions are left in the hands of those who've been taught to think and be virtuous, with the key to virtue frequently being located as those actions that take a middle road between extremes.

A virtue argument against wealth concentration begins by locating extreme situations. At one pole, the star system grows exponentially. Market rules function without reserve, and traditional wealth-redistribution measures are scuttled. The progressive income tax, for example, is replaced by a flat charge for all citizens. (The justification: everyone uses roads and other services more or less equally, so they should all pay the same tax dollars). Further, social attitudes could be adjusted. The idea of earning huge amounts and accumulating even more usually elicits both respect and also suspicion of greed. That could be changed: schools and other institutions could be adjusted to teach that getting extremely rich is an unmixed good, and suspicions by others of greed is nothing more than cloaked envy.

Toward the other extreme, there's the vision of a broadly equitable society. Redistributive taxation is heightened. In Denmark, for example, the highest earners pay an eye-popping 68 percent of their salary. On top of that, estate taxes paid on an individual's death could be hiked to ensure that money doesn't build up over successive generations. Then, on the social level, attitudes could be bred in our schools, churches, and similar institutions that any significant wealth difference above the mean is worrisome and their possessors aren't admirable so much as ugly hoarders. These combined economic and social actions would almost certainly reduce wealth differences across the social spectrum.

Next, and building above this foundation of extremes, the virtue ethicist would navigate a moderate course. Redistributive measures undertaken by the government may not reach the 68 percent taxation rate, but they wouldn't allow the wealthy to use accounting tricks and similar measures to drop their total payments to levels comparable with what middle class individuals pay. Then, with respect to social attitudes, a balanced sense of pride and shame would need to be instilled in the community, one that granted successful entrepreneurs like Bill Gates respect for their accomplishments, but one that also taints his (or anyone's existence) when that wealth reaches a point where it's enough to hire six million struggling Hollywood actors for a year.

KEY TAKEAWAYS

- Arguments ethically justifying the star system may be based on rights and freedom, the general welfare, and appeals to fairness.
- Arguments criticizing the star system may be based on the general welfare, the duty of beneficence, and virtue.

REVIEW QUESTIONS

1. Can you take the Nozick-inspired thought experiment concerning Kobe Bryant and re-create it in your own words and with a different example?
2. What is an example of the star system serving the general welfare by promoting innovation?
3. Why might the contemporary star system be considered fair?
4. Why does the star system harm the general welfare?
5. How might the duty to beneficence be applied to Bill Gates? Why would the duty tend to preclude an economic star system?

[1] Alice Gomstyn, "Wal-Mart CEO Pay: More in an Hour Than Workers Get All Year?," *ABC News*, July 2, 2010, accessed June 9, 2011, http://abcnews.go.com/Business/walmart-ceo-pay-hour-workers-year/story?id=11067470.

15.4 Unions
LEARNING OBJECTIVES

1. Define a labor union.
2. Discuss the ethics of union membership.

Hollywood Writers

Movie theater lobbies are inevitably lined with advertising posters for upcoming attractions. A standard poster carries a recognizable celebrity face (or, if you don't recognize it, the expression is so beaming and confident that you immediately assume you missed the news of a huge new star's arrival). The movie's title is there, and the lead actors' names too. Sometimes the director gets big billing. The producer, the studio, they're easy to locate. You need to go a long way down the poster, though, and into the fine print, to find the writer's name.

Inside the industry's day-to-day working life, writers don't get much respect. Longtime agent Nancy Nigrosh writes that frequently they're not invited to the screening or any other film-opening festivity. She paints the situation bleakly: "Unless you hire your own hardworking publicist you'll be sitting at the kiddy table and arguing politely with security at the star's tent at the premier because here's the other thing: nobody cares." [1]

The heart of the reason no one cares is the way films are composed. It's not like a novel or a poem or even journalism where one person more or less shepherds a work from beginning to end. Instead, scripts are written and then rewritten by someone else. Then another author is called in for some further adjustments and it's all reworked while the filming actually happens, and by the time the movie's done, it's almost impossible to figure out who deserves credit for which words. In that kind of situation, writers find themselves in a bad spot when it comes to bargaining for money. It's true that the studios need writers, and that provides some leverage, but they don't usually need any *particular* writer. There are exceptions, but since movie scripting is usually an assembly-line process, substituting one with another probably won't affect the final product too much in most cases.

One response to this reality is that workers organize and sell their labor collectively. Conceptually, the idea is simple. When employers threaten to replace individual workers with others who'll perform the same services for even less credit and at a lower price, the other employees—seeing that they could be next in line to face replacement—stand together in support of their colleague.

Whether the workers are Hollywood writers, Detroit autoworkers assembling cars, or hotel maids cleaning the rooms and making up the beds, the strategy of forming an alliance to defend common interests can work by reversing the star system. The star system promotes the general welfare by freeing individuals to pursue their own interests. In labor unions, individuals promote their own interests by defending the general welfare or, at least, the collective welfare of their fellow laborers.

Unions: Definition and Quick History

A labor union is an organization of wage earners formed to promote job-related interests, especially with respect to wages and working conditions. A union can be as informal as a band of salespeople telling the boss they're not going to come in the next morning unless the coffeemaker is fixed. Most discussion, however, surrounds larger and more formalized unions: members pay dues, hold elections to choose leaders, and in the largest instances, hire a professional management team to advocate for the laborers' common interests.

Two inflection points mark the history of labor unions in the United States. The Wagner Act (more formally, the National Labor Relations Act) was approved in Washington, DC, in 1935. It blocked employers from mistreating or firing workers attempting unionize a shop's workforce. The act also prohibited the summary firing of workers who've gone out on strike. The freedom to organize, along with the power to strike effectively, quickly translated into more unions, more walkouts, and two large organizations guiding the efforts of many smaller trade unions: the American Federation of Labor (AFL) and the Congress of Industrial Organizations (CIO). While it's true that in the years after World War II business-damaging strikes grew more frequent, wages also rose and nourished a broad American middle class. Organized labor came to play a central role in business life. The maturation of organized labor in the United States harmonized with world events. Political parties dedicated to workers—especially the hard labor sectors—swept the globe, frequently leading to socialist and communist societies. Those movements eventually reached US shores. In 1947, communists eager to maximize their influence took control of sectors of the United Auto Workers Union, the Detroit collective making nearly all the cars Americans drove. Pictures from the time—auto workers waving signs announcing they're for "Tommie the Commie" seem far out of sync with today's reality but serve to remind how quickly the world's orienting values and ideologies can change. [2]

In that same heated year, 1947, congress responded to sweeping unionization and complaints that the workers' organizations had become too powerful with the Taft-Hartley Act. It prohibited the so-called closed shop, which is a workplace where being hired carries with it the requirement to already be a union member. It allowed, however, a union shop, a workplace where all employees are required to join or at least pay the dues associated with joining. Later, the US Supreme Court ruled that even though striking workers couldn't be fired for walking off (in accordance with the Wagner Act), they could be permanently replaced. Over time, this significantly diminished union strength since those going on strike were now risking their jobs.

As decades rolled forward, the counter union tide on the legal front eventually replicated as important changes in American industry. Many of the skilled and heavy laboring jobs involving cars, steel, and similar industries that had responded well to organizational efforts began drying up for at least two reasons. Increased international trade allowed companies to shift many labor-intensive tasks to other countries with lower wages. Also, jobs that remained Stateside faced the threat of machines taking over many functions. Detroit assembly lines formerly composed of blue-collar workers are now dominated by sophisticated robots. Politically, organized labor also dimmed over the second half of the twentieth century. In the 1980s, the nation's air traffic controllers went on strike. President Reagan fired them all and hired new ones. Reagan also challenged the world's communist nations; the collapse of countries explicitly guided by the collective welfare of laborers was rapid and nearly complete.

Today, organized labor unions play roles in most sectors of American economic life, but their influence is limited, except in a few areas. Government workers continue to be very highly unionized: more than half of all union laborers in the United States today have government jobs. Unions also remain in small fields that resist marketplace forces. The National Football League players, for example, are unionized: you can't just send their jobs overseas. Also, workers in the health-care field have a fairly high unionization rate: you can't replace a nurse with a machine (at least, not yet). In political terms, and though diminished, unions continue to be a notable force. The single largest outside spender in the 2010 election campaign was the American Federation of State, County and Municipal Employees. AFSCME spent a whopping $90 million (much coming from workers' dues) to support candidates around the country. Still, with only 1.6 million members, the group is no larger than the United Auto Workers union back in 1970 when US population was only two-thirds of today's number. Currently, the UAW has about 400,000 active members.

Three questions asked about unions in the field of business ethics are:
1. Who should be a union member?
2. What kinds of demands should unions make?
3. What kinds of actions can unions justifiably undertake?

Membership
In principle, a unionized workplace incorporates all employees: the idea of a union is a united workers front presented to management when wages and conditions are discussed. In practice, however, the ideal often falls short.

For example, the Writers Guild of America (WGA) represents Hollywood's writers: they're the people penning scripts for everything from TV sitcoms to big-budget movies to the annual Oscar Awards. With around twelve thousand members, the union members produce around one hundred scripts and rewrite a week through the major studios. Without their work, quite a bit of the show time industry halts. It doesn't all halt, though. According to the *New York Times*, in the 1980s, nearly all Hollywood's writing came from Guild members, but the percentage has now dropped to about half. Union writers are being displaced by freelancers. [3]

While the scriptwriting evolution from the 1980s to today is essentially the move away from—though not a complete departure from—unionization in Hollywood, there are three strong arguments in favor of reversing the trend and refortifying the writers' collective. They're based on

- fairness,
- solidarity,
- respect.

On the other side, there's one main argument frequently set up against the proposal that the model workplace become something close to a union shop:

- the right to free agency, along with a derived duty to individuality

The first argument supporting broad union membership rests on fairness. Gains in wages and improvements in working conditions don't come for free. Take, for example, the WGA demand that residuals go to writers. The union is saying that those receiving credit for the program script should receive money not only at filming but also later on if the show is a hit and ends up getting repeatedly shown into the indefinite future. On almost any night somewhere in the United States, one of the *Die Hard* movies is broadcast, and licensing rights are subsequently divvied up among those who made the film. The actors, the directors, the producers, everyone wants as much as they can get, and for writers to take a share, they need professional negotiators who can bargain hard, as well as lawyers and other experts who understand the complicated laws and dynamics of residual payments. The money to pay for these services comes from union dues, and if writers who aren't in the union nonetheless receive these hard-bargained benefits, they're free riders. They get the advantages of unionization without paying the cost. If, the argument concludes, freelance writers want to receive long-term benefits, then they should pay their fair share to the operation making them possible.

The second argument in favor of drawing workers into unions rests on a notion of solidarity. Solidarity, in this sense, is the moral obligation to share in the struggles of others facing challenges similar to those we face. For example, when William Russell Grace immigrated to New York in 1865 and set up a successful business (now called simply Grace Incorporated), one of the steps he took as an expression of solidarity with immigrants coming after him was to set up a free school where new arrivals could learn basic skills helping them find employment in their new country. Called the Grace Institute, there's an ethical solidarity incarnated in the school, one uniting immigrants around their shared experiences and common hardships. Broad social movements also provide abundant examples of the ethics of solidarity. A case could be made, for instance, that women and African Americans have a special obligation to unite with homosexuals seeking workplace equality because women and African Americans too know, and have shared the suffering of discrimination.

It's true that the case of Hollywood film writers isn't so dramatic as immigration or broad job discrimination, but the ethics are the same. Because all scriptwriters share a common vocation, similar challenges, and common hardships, they have a duty to stand together. Unionization is an expression of that solidarity. People don't sense the obligation to join up as a way of getting higher wages; instead, the union becomes a site of empathy, of mutual experience and support.

The third argument in favor of obligating new workers to join the union is based on a duty of respect. When a group of individuals have labored to form a cooperative in the name of their mutual benefit, those joining the occupation have a duty to honor those efforts by not undercutting them. The crucial point here is that, in many cases, there's no middle ground. It'd be one situation if Hollywood writers could work on their own without affecting the efforts of unionized script producers, but that's not usually the case. Workers who refuse to join and participate in the WGA and who forge their own contracts and reimbursements are also undermining union efforts because, presumably, the reason producers go outside the union to hire is that freelancers are cheaper. If that's right, and if new writers coming to town don't respect the existing union structure, then market forces are eventually going to put the union out of business: instigated by the need to maximize profits, owners and managers will hire nonunion workers to replace the more expensive, organized ones as fast as possible.

This is, in essence, what has started happening in Hollywood. To the extent the studios are funding independent projects pitched by freelancers, they're replacing higher-cost union talent with writers who are willing to work for very little in exchange for the chance to get a break, be famous, and be a star (in the relatively dim world of script writing). There's a problem here, obviously: if writers are allowed to work for something near slave wages to get a break, then as soon as they're established in the industry, some younger dreamers are going to come along and undercut them just as they earlier undercut the WGA workers. That's economics, though. The moral imperative is that respect for others' unionization efforts is also an obligation to not undermine them.

Set up against these three arguments in favor of union shops, there's the powerful rights-based argument. If ethical discussion starts from the premise that each of us owns ourselves, and we're free to use and sell our abilities as we like, then no one can pressure us to sign up for a union without violating our intrinsic liberty. In terms of Hollywood scriptwriting, this is the right to free agency.

Derived from the right to free agency there is a right to self-definition: each of us is uniquely qualified to define who we are and which desires guide our working life. This derivative argument resists the entire concept of unionized activity because collective bargaining eliminates individuality. What allows labor unions to work, what gives them strength at the negotiating table, is precisely that they compact an entire workforce into a single model of interests and demands; it's that focus and the united voice of the workers behind it that allow union leaders the strength they need to bargain effectively. This strategy can, no doubt, work, but only by forcing all scriptwriters to renounce their singularity and uniqueness in the business world: they all demand to be paid in accordance with the same pay structure, to be covered by the same set of benefits, to labor in the same working conditions, and so on.

The lynchpin, finally, to this argument is that because unions function by erasing the individuality of specific workers, we're all morally prohibited from joining. Doing so is a violation of the fundamental obligation we all have to ourselves to express our freedom by being who we are. We are duty-bound to resist any nameless, faceless mass, whether that mass happens to be a labor union or any other collective.

The Card Check
One hot spot of union membership debate is the proposed Employee Free Choice Act or so-called card check legislation. If enacted, this law would make an important change to the process of forming a workplace union. As currently regulated, the process typically goes like this. It's necessary to get at least 30 percent of the workforce to sign

cards stating their preference to be represented in collective bargaining. Once the number has been reached, the list is forwarded to the National Labor Relations Board and to the employer. The list is checked. If the numbers are verified, a secret-ballot election follows: workers are asked to vote on whether they want to be represented by a labor union. The majority rules. What card check legislation changes is the secret ballot component. No longer necessary, if organizers can simply accumulate a list of 50 percent of the workers requesting unionization, then the structure will be applied.

The main objection to the secret ballot's elimination is that workers may be intimidated into putting their names on the list. The reason for a secret vote in the current system is to allow those preferring not to be unionized a chance to express that without fear of retribution from their peers. Not surprisingly, the US Chamber of Commerce and other business groups lobby against the legislation. For their part, the major unions see card check as an opportunity to expand their membership and lobby in favor.

Regardless of the legislative value, the ethical debate underneath the card check parallels the one about a union shop. For those valuing solidarity, unionization—even with pressure—may seem recommendable. More, because a union draws its strength from forcibly uniting the divergent workers into a set of single demands, the greater good that's served by the united front simply outweighs protests that may be expressed by individuals. So while it's true that workplace pressures following the approval of card check legislation may make some employees uncomfortable, they should be more strongly guided by a sense of fairness (if they want to benefit, they've got an obligation to join), by a sense of solidarity ("we're all workers"), and by a sense of respect (some workers are dedicating their energy to lead a cause serving everyone).

On the other side, for those whose ethical orientation begins from the idea of individual rights, self-ownership and the duty to self-definition, any organizational structure that presents the risk of violating individual freedom will, on principle, be rejected. The kinds of pressures on individuals that may be applied by peers in the attempt to get them to sign the union card are so fundamentally in violation of our deepest rights that the legislation must be voted down, even at the potential cost of power for workers at the bargaining table.

Union Demands: The Workplace and Public Policy
The two stalwart demands made by organized labor unions on behalf of employees are wage hikes and working

conditions. The balance between these two concerns shifts depending on the kind of work being done. When a Hollywood writer arrives on a soundstage to straighten out final kinks in a script, the kinds of working-condition issues being faced may be trivial (Is the coffee hot? Are there some nonfattening snacks around somewhere?). When a coal miner takes the elevator down into the earth, the questions are more serious. What kind of emergency safeguards protect against a collapsed shaft? How careful are foremen to ensure that tired workers nearing the end of their shift aren't assigned to work on the more dangerous of the heavy machines or set off dynamite charges? A coal miners' union, clearly, is going to expend a greater effort bargaining for safe conditions than the WGA.

On the compensation side, one challenge union's face is melding the distinct interests of diverse members into a single bargaining strategy. If you check the WGA website, you'll find union involvement on issues ranging from direct pay for work to health-care benefits and pensions. A twenty-five-year-old just breaking in is going to be more concerned, possibly, about getting as much cash now as possible for work done, while an older writer will begin asking about paying medical bills and living decently in retirement. In translating these diverse situations into a collective set of negotiating points, simple market forces will play a role (a union active in a field heavily stocked with younger workers will have to take account of that, or people will stop participating), but other structures may be erected to resolve problems also. A utilitarian structure, for example, may provide a way for union leaders to justify decisions making some members unhappy.

Finally, unions don't only represent workers before employers; they can also carry labor issues into the political arena. As noted, AFSCME spent $90 million supporting (and opposing) candidates around the country during the 2010 midterms. Unions can also—and frequently do—provide voting guides advising members on which candidates will better respond to their immediate interests. With respect to specific issues, and besides the already mentioned card check legislation, unions lobby elected representatives and government agencies in areas including workplace safety, the minimum wage, and health care.

KEY TAKEAWAYS

- Labor unions allow workers to organize and bargain collectively for improvements in wage and working conditions.

- Ethical arguments in favor of workers joining unions may be built upon notions of fairness, solidarity, and respect.
- The right to free agency, along with a derived duty to individuality, forms the basis for an ethical stand against joining unions.
- Unions take sides in workplace issues, and broader political debates.

REVIEW QUESTIONS

1. Why might the notion of fairness convince a worker to join a labor union?
2. In your own words, and with respect to labor unions, what does *solidarity* mean?
3. How does joining a union harm one's sense of individuality? Why might that harm be an ethical argument against union membership?
4. What is card check legislation, and how might it advance the interests of labor unions?
5. How can a union represent the interests of members beyond negotiating with a specific employer?

[1] Anne Thompson, "Screenwriting in Hollywood: A Modest Proposal," *Variety*, October 2, 2008, accessed June 9, 2011,http://blogs.indiewire.com/thompsononhollywood/screenwriting_in_hollywood_a_modest_proposal#.
[2] June 9, 2011, *Life Magazine* 22, no. 12 (March 24, 1947), 31, accessed June 9, 2011,http://books.google.com/books?id=AUoEAAAAMBAJ&pg=PA31&dq=
uaw+membership+local+600+ford&hl=en&ei=5KbBTKbcNML98Ab01LGdBg&sa=
X&oi=book_result&ct=result&resnum=6&ved=0CEoQ6AEwBQ#v=
onepage&q=uaw%20membership%20local%20600%20ford&f=false.
[3] Michael Cieply and Brookes Barnes, "Writers Say Strike to Start Monday," *New York Times*, November 2, 2007, accessed June 9, 2011,http://www.nytimes.com/2007/11/02/business/media/02cnd-hollywood.html?pagewanted=all.

15.5 Union Strikes
LEARNING OBJECTIVES

1. Define a labor strike.
2. Consider ethical justifications for striking.
3. Weigh responsibilities set against striking.
4. Consider the rights of employers and strikebreakers.

The Hollywood Writers' Strike
The most contentious area, both economically and ethically, of union action involves strikes: workers collectively walking off the jobsite in an attempt to pressure employers to accede to their demands. The Writers Guild of America (WGA) led one of the most publicized recent walkouts when Hollywood script writers put down their pencils and closed their

laptops—at least officially—in November of 2007. By the time they returned in early 2008, the economic damage wrought in the Los Angeles basin was massive, $3.5 billion according to some estimates, but the resolution ultimately satisfied most members of the moviemaking community. During the strike, two constellations of ethical issues came to the fore. First, questions involved

- the right for workers to not work,
- the right of employers to find someone who will work,
- the rights of third parties to go on with their lives and work.

The second set of questions involved responses to the strike:

- Who in Hollywood, if anyone, is obligated to support the writers?
- Is it OK to take a striker's job?

Justifying Not Working

Some Hollywood writers are contracted by faceless studios to churn out rewrites for movies; others generate TV dramas and soap operas. There's work to be done inventing jokes for sitcoms like *The Office*, and opening monologues for Jay Leno's *Tonight* show need to be written a few days every week. As the writers' strike extended, the walkout's effects beamed into living rooms. Almost immediately, Leno went into reruns. *The Office*, which had a few episodes in the can, lasted several weeks. The moviemakers—many of whom live underneath piles of scripts submitted unsolicited by writers—kept going.

Out on the picket lines, Leno zipped around in his vintage sports car to support the stoppage, and occasionally stopped to chat with the strikers and crack good-humored jokes. Of course Leno, who makes millions a year, probably didn't really need his paychecks. Others in Hollywood, however, live from day to day and without much room for unemployment. Set designers, prop companies, on-site catering services, all the people surrounding the now-halted industry saw their income wither. In the face of the injurious consequences, three arguments nonetheless favor and justify the writers' walkout.

1. The *rights argument* in favor of the workers' strike is direct and convincing for many: all individuals have a right to *not* go to work in the morning. Whether we're talking about a union action or just someone who wakes up with a hangover, any ethical theory that takes its bearings from individual rights is generally going to turn in a verdict in favor of the worker's right to stay home.

2. The *last resort argument* affirms that workers are justified in striking when three conditions are met: First, there must be a just cause. The driving issue cannot be petty

angers or interpersonal conflicts of some kind; instead, the motive must be wages or working conditions that are out of step with industry norms or reasonable expectations. In the writers' case, this condition may have been met because they represented one of the few talent sectors not benefitting from payments for programming broadcast over new media, especially the Internet. Second, there must be proper authorization, which means the workers themselves must support the action, and have reached a well-deliberated decision. In the writer's case, most did support the action, which had been planned for months. Third, the strike must be a last resort, meaning attempts to find solutions must've been fully explored. Here too writers met the condition as long negotiations had explored most possible solutions.

3. The *marketplace argument* is the rawest of the justifications for striking, and it answers the ethical question with economic facts. If workers can get away with striking, the reasoning goes, and then they're justified. The argument is less flippant than it sounds. If workers *really are* being underpaid for their labors, then when an employer seeks others to replace those who've walked out, none will emerge, at least none capable of doing the work well. On the other hand, if market conditions determine that the striking workers are demanding more than they legitimately should within the current economic context, then when an employer tries to replace strikers with fresh hires, the cost of doing so will be less than the wage increase the strikers are demanding.

On the other side, the kinds of arguments normally set up to obligate striking workers to return to their stations involve responsibilities to the larger community:

1. The *public safety* argument applies only in selected situations. The famous air-traffic controllers' strike in the 1980s involved the safety of fliers. Similarly, police officers, firefighters, and similar may find it difficult to justify a full-fledged strike given the serious suffering that may result. There are many borderline cases, however. For example, in Tennessee some fire departments collect fees directly from those they protect. In one case, a man who hadn't paid found that his house was on fire and called the department; they responded, but only to protect nearby homes from the fire's spread. They watched the flaming home burn to the foundation without intervening because the bill hadn't been paid. Of course, the situation would've been different had a person been trapped inside. In this case, however, the loss and dispute was entirely about money. [1]

2. The *public welfare argument* against workers going on strike weighs in when strikes affect third parties, people outside the initial dispute. The scriptwriters' walkout, for example, left a large chunk of Hollywood unemployed. The most rudimentary way to elaborate the argument is simply to note that the suffering caused across the entire industry by the five-month writers' strike almost surely outweighed the benefits the writers finally obtained. It should also be remembered, however, that if some workers somewhere don't draw the line against owners and employers, those employers will have no incentive to not push *everyone's* wages down, ultimately affecting the welfare of most all the industry's participants.

3. The *immediate welfare argument* against the writers' strike finds support in an ethics of care. An ethics of care values most highly an individual's immediate social web; concern for those people who are nearest outweighs abstract rules or generalized social concerns. In the case of the Hollywood writers' strike, the suffering incurred by families and friends related to particular strikers may be taken to outweigh any benefits the broad union collective won from the action.

Finally, it's important to note that strikes don't need to be long-term walkouts. The dynamic and ethics surrounding the refusal to work change when, for example, a union decides to go on strike for only a single day as a way of pressuring management.

Standing in Line and Crossing It: The Ethics of Supporting Strikes and Breaking Them

The Hollywood writers' strike featured some big-name backing. Jay Leno cruised around in his Bugatti; Steve Carell, star of *The Office*, refused to cross the picket lines; and Sally Field mingled with writers in the Disney Studios lot. These shows of support scored public relations points and provoked this question: what obligation do workers in related fields hold to support strikers?

The range of responses corresponds well with those already outlined to justify the unionization of workers in a particular shop.

- One way to oblige workers in related fields to support strikers is the argument from fairness. When workers in a certain industry strike and win concessions, those gains may be cited by other workers as justifying their own demands. In fact, in Hollywood the writers themselves had used this strategy in the past: instead of going on strike, they'd waited for the directors union (Directors Guild of America) to negotiate demands with the major studios and then used those results to make their own

case for concessions. The argument for supporting striking workers based on fairness is that *all* workers for a particular company or across an industry may well benefit when one group makes gains, and if that's so, then those other groups also have a responsibility to support the strikers when they're sacrificing.

- A second argument is based on solidarity, on the idea that an alliance between workers in an industry is ethically natural: there's an obligation to share in a struggle when facing similar challenges. Because other members of the Hollywood community are uniquely positioned to understand the realities and hardships of screenwriting life, they have a duty to act on that empathy.

As events transpired, the WGA did, in fact, receive wide support from across Hollywood, but the solidarity was far from complete. As this outburst from a writer's blog shows, some network studios tried to keep their soap operas in production by hiring strikebreakers, or scabs, as they're known to picketers:

> *The scab writer's work under fake names, work from home and use different email addresses so only the executive producer knows the real identities of the scabs. These tend to be experienced soap writers who aren't currently on a show. They are then promised employment after the strike is over. While they're scabbing, they get paid less than union writers.* [2]

This under-the-table scripting captures a conflict inherent in the union's attempt to use economic force against employers. On one side, by cutting off their labor, strikers are trying to win concessions through economic force. But their success depends on the suspension of basic economic rules: as this blogger is admitting, there *are* scriptwriters out there willing to work at current wages for the studios. It sounds like they may even be willing to work for less.

For these secretive scriptwriters, what ethical justifications can be mounted for what is, in essence, picket-line crossing? The blog post decrying scab workers actually rallied some to post arguments in the strikebreakers' defense. One comes from a poster named Jake: "Maybe he [the blogger writing the original post complaining about strikebreakers] has unlimited funds somewhere and can stay out of work forever, but some need to support themselves now." [3]

The argument here is that we all have fundamental duties to ourselves that must be served before deferring to others. It's not, in other words, that scriptwriters should feel no obligation to their colleagues, but all of us have a deeper responsibility to our own welfare (and possibly to that of our family members who may depend on us), and that responsibility takes precedence when the situation becomes extreme, when going without work represents more than just an inconvenience.

Another argument wraps through the following exchange between two blog readers. The first, who registers his comment anonymously, writes, "I'm a little amazed by some of these comments…Do you guys [who support strikebreakers] not know about unions? Do you not understand what it *means* to cross a picket line?…People need to work for just (as in fair) pay." [4]

This response comes from a poster named Tim: "Anonymous said, 'Do you not understand what it means to cross a picket line?' Yes, it means you are trying to work for someone who wants to pay you. In moral terms, it's just a voluntary mutually beneficial exchange that for the most part is no one else's business. Members of a union do and should have the right to refuse to provide a service, but they don't have a right to prevent others from providing the service." [5] Tim's argument is based on the principle of free agency and the ethics of freedom. According to him, what are morally right is any action particular scriptwriters and studio owners agree to undertake. The only ethical obligation individuals have is to *not* violate the freedom of others and, according to Tim; everyone involved in this strikebreaking is acting freely without stopping others from doing the same. The strikers, like the strikebreakers, may go to work—or not go—whenever they like. To the extent that's right, ethical objections shouldn't be raised against either choice.

The key phrase in Tim's response is that the strikebreaking writers' actions are "no one else's business." Those defending the union could choose to intervene here and assert that the claim is fundamentally wrong. Ethics depends on compassionately taking account of others' interests, and factoring them into your own decisions: what writers decide to do must serve not only their own but also the general welfare. Possibly, Tim could respond to this by asserting that in a market economy the best way to serve the general welfare is for individuals to pursue their own success. There are responses to this argument too, and the discussion continues.

KEY TAKEAWAYS

- A rights argument and a marketplace argument may lend ethical support to workers' decision to strike.

- Ethical arguments against striking may derive from broad social concerns, or justifiably privileging one's own interests.
- Arguments in favor of supporting strikers from outside the union may stand on conceptions of fairness or solidarity.
- Both strikebreakers and employers may claim the right to bypass union demands based on economic realities, or their rights as free agents.

REVIEW QUESTIONS

1. Explain the marketplace argument in favor of the right for workers to strike.
2. How could a union worker ethically justify not joining companions on the picket lines?
3. Outline an argument from fairness that could be made against strikebreakers.
4. Sketch two arguments that could be made in favor of independent writers swooping in and taking union jobs when the SGA goes out on strike.

[1] Jason Hibbs, "Firefighters Watch as Home Burns to the Ground," *WPSD*, September 29, 2010, accessed June 9, 2011, http://www.wpsdlocal6.com/news/local/Firefighters-watch-as-home-burns-to-the-ground-104052668.html.
[2] John Aboud, "Scabbing Doesn't Pay (For Long)," *United Hollywood* (blog), November 8, 2007, accessed June 9, 2011, http://unitedhollywood.blogspot.com/2007/11/scabbing-doesn-pay-for-long.html.
[3] Jake, November 8, 2007 (6:44 a.m.), comment on John Aboud, "Scabbing Doesn't Pay (For Long)," *United Hollywood Blog*, November 8, 2007,http://unitedhollywood.blogspot.com/2007/11/scabbing-doesn-pay-for-long.html.
[4] Anonymous, November 8, 2007 (8:15 a.m.), comment on John Aboud, "Scabbing Doesn't Pay (For Long)," *United Hollywood Blog*, November 8, 2007,http://unitedhollywood.blogspot.com/2007/11/scabbing-doesn-pay-for-long.html.
[5] Tim, November 8, 2007 (8:32 a.m.), comment on Anonymous, "Scabbing Doesn't Pay (For Long)," *United Hollywood Blog*, November 8, 2007,http://unitedhollywood.blogspot.com/2007/11/scabbing-doesn-pay-for-long.html.

15.6 Case Studies

Jim Webb's Speech

At the height of the American economic boom running from 2000 to 2008, a freshly elected senator from Virginia gave a sobering speech. He said,

> When one looks at the health of our economy, it's almost as if we are living in two different countries. The stock market is at an all-time high, and so are corporate profits. But these benefits are not being fairly shared. When I graduated from college, the average corporate CEO made 20 times what the

average worker did; today, it's nearly 400 times. In other words, it takes the average worker more than a year to make the money that his or her boss makes in one day. In short, the middle class of this country, our historic backbone and our best hope for a strong society in the future, is losing its place at the table. Our workers know this, through painful experience. [1]

QUESTIONS

1. What is the star system?

2. According to Senator Webb (and doing the math), when he was in college around 1966, a corporate CEO had to labor eighteen days to make the money the average worker earned in about a year. Now, CEOs only need a day to reach a worker's yearly total.
   - What is vertical wealth imbalance?
   - In terms of the days a CEO must labor to net the average worker's yearly pay, where does the star system line get drawn? Webb seems to think it's somewhere between eighteen days and one day, but where would you draw the distinction? How would you justify your decision?

3. Webb says the "middle class of this country" is disappearing. How does this claim relate to the idea of horizontal wealth imbalances?

4. When Webb asserts that the benefits of a healthy economy aren't being "fairly shared," he's making an ethical claim, saying the wealth concentration is wrong. He was speaking on national TV and so didn't have time to flesh things out, but how could an argument be formulated to support his claim?

5. Jim Webb is a United States senator. When the United States was founded, there was about one senator for every twenty-five thousand people. Today, it's one in three million. The salary of a US senator is $175,000; the salary of the average American worker is about $40,000.
   - Besides money, what kinds of compensation do you imagine Webb gets for his job?
   - Do you believe Webb's compensation (salary plus other nonmonetary benefits) qualifies him as a star? Why or why not?
   - Does the fact that Webb represents more constituents than the original senators convert into a case that Webb's salary should be higher relative to his constituents than the salary granted to senators two hundred years ago? Explain.
   - Make the case that Webb has an ethical responsibility to donate a significant part of his salary to public service causes.

6. Part of the reason Webb's talk lacked specifics was that, as a US senator, he doesn't want to offend any particular person or large company. (He probably wants their money for his reelection campaign, or at least he doesn't want them funding his opponent.) Others, however, who share his opinion about wage imbalances aren't similarly constrained. One notable example comes from the web page *Daily Kos*, a politically oriented site with a huge readership and located on the left fringe of American politics, somewhere between rowdy and rabid. On that page, the following point was added to Webb's speech: *As an example of this inequality, look no further than Ford Motor Company. Just this week, Ford announced a staggering $12.7 billion loss, the highest in company history. This came after a year in which the company announced that it was cutting more than 40,000 jobs (30,000 of them union jobs). So what to do in a company that's failed to deliver innovative products to the market, completely misjudged consumer trends, and managed itself into a fiscal bind? You award bonuses to the top management.* [2] The web page went on to explain that Ford CEO Alan Mulally would be giving performance bonuses to his top executives because, according to Mulally, "You have to keep the talented people you really need."
   - Just from the provided facts, why might someone be suspicious that CEO Mulally participates in crony capitalism? How might he respond to the charge?
   - Justify the *Daily Kos* attack on Mulally's bonuses in terms of general social welfare, and in terms of the duty to beneficence.
   - Make the case that the bonuses are justified in ethical terms with the language of rights.
   - Through the language of rights, argue that those who criticize the bonuses—like writers at *Daily Kos*—are ethically despicable.

7. Consider these four jobs: US senator, political commentator on a widely read web page (regardless of whether it happens to tilt left or right), CEO of Ford, and union worker on a car assembly line.
   - Who do you expect would earn most and least were wages divided only by market forces? Loosely, how would wages be apportioned? Would the differences reach star system proportions?
   - How would you rank their wage order in terms of value generated for society? Loosely, how would wages be apportioned? Would the differences reach star system proportions?
   - How would you rank their wage order in terms of effort? Loosely, how would wages be apportioned?

Would the differences reach star system proportions?

First You Get the Money…

The film *Scarface* cost $25 million to make and has earned back about $200 million so far. The story follows Tony Montana as he enters the cocaine dealing business. His mentor tells him that to survive over the long term you've got to fly under the radar and stay small. Comfortably wealthy, yes, but wildly rich, no. Montana isn't so sure. Later he decides the advice is directly bad, kills the mentor who gave it to him, and expands his business as far and as fast as he can. As moviegoers learn at the film's end, the mentor was probably right.

QUESTIONS

1. Though the initial reviews were mixed, time has proven the film's popular appeal. More than twenty years after its release, *Scarface* continues to be a rental favorite, a standard campus feature, and a late-night TV standard.
    o   How can the notion of the general welfare be used to justify giving big bucks to the stars making the film: actor Al Pacino, director Brian De Palma, and writer Oliver Stone?
    o   Can you form an argument against the concentration of money in the hands of a very few people that would work equally well against Al Pacino's (presumed) wealth and Tony Montana's?
2. Given the way Montana got wealthy, can the duty to beneficence argument against the star system still be applied to him? Why or why not?
3. Possibly the movie's most repeated line is Al Pacino as Tony Montana explaining that to be successful in America, "First you get the money, then you get the power, then you get the women."
    o   What is Aristotle's theory of envy?
    o   Does the story the movie tells about Montana's life—coming to America with nothing as an immigrant and getting ahead by killing and drug dealing—make you more or less envious of his success (at least the money and power parts), or does it not make any difference?
    o   How does envy factor into ethical considerations of the star system?
4. Amado Carrillo Fuentes—better known as *Lord of the Skies*—was a serious innovator before he died in a Mexico City Hospital during a plastic surgery procedure to transform his appearance. While everyone else in his profession was flying small Cessna-like aircraft around Latin America and over the border into the States, he

broke every limit by buying full-size Boeing passenger planes, hollowing them out, filling them with cocaine, and flying multimillion-dollar shipments. Though he never made the *Forbes* list of the world's most powerful and wealthy (unlike other traffickers from the same Mexican state of Sinaloa, including Joaquín Guzmán), there's no doubt that Carrillo Fuentes got extraordinarily wealthy by bringing innovation to the cocaine business. Bill Gates got extraordinarily wealthy by bringing innovation to the software business. One argument frequently presented in favor of outsized rewards in the business world is that it can stimulate innovative ideas. Does the fact that creativity in the business world can do social good *and* social harm weaken this argument in favor of the star system? Explain.

The Delta Vote

When Delta Airlines absorbed Northwest Airlines in 2008, the expanded Delta employed about twenty thousand flight attendants or *FAs* as they're called in the industry. The thirteen thousand Delta FAs weren't unionized; the seven thousand that came over from Northwest were.

The nation's largest flight attendant union, the Association of Flight Attendants (AFA) saw the opportunity to build membership numbers and lobbied the united workforce to unionize. The question went to a vote and the results were excruciatingly close: votes in favor fell 328 short out of 18,760 cast. Subsequently, the *USA Today* published a roundup of media reports and readers reactions. [3]

QUESTIONS

1. One argument in favor of joining labor unions works from fairness, the idea that if workers are *benefitting* from the work done by a collective, they should sign up and contribute their share of the dues required to pay for the lawyers and the negotiators a major union needs to operate.
    o   How does the following reaction to the "no" vote intersect with the fairness argument? Flight attendant Cindy Hanks said, "I'm ecstatic. There is no reason for a union at Delta. I get paid more than my co-workers [who worked for Northwest before the merger]. I have an open-door policy with my management. Whenever I have a complaint, I am listened to, and there is always a resolution. I'm not left in the dark." [4]
2. One person added this comment below the story about the culture around Delta: "Nobody cares about workers' rights, including the workers." [5] One argument in favor of joining labor unions works from a notion of

solidarity. With respect to labor unions, what's the solidarity argument for joining the FA union at Delta?

3. Delta spokeswoman Betsy Talton reacted this way to the "no" vote, "We have said all along that we believe our direct relationship works well for our people and our company,"
   o One argument against joining a labor union is the duty to individuality derived from the right to free agency. What is the right to free agency? What is the derived duty to individuality?
   o How can Talton's reaction be buttressed in ethical terms by reference to the right and derived duty?

4. The vote at Delta was a secret ballot. What is *card check* legislation, and what does it do? How might that law have changed the results at Delta?

5. Some of the responses to the Delta vote didn't concern the specific FA union but the question of unions generally. For example, one commenter believes a stigma attaches to union membership, a bad one. As he puts it, "I have read pro union people are lazy and want protection." Another commentator adds that unions have, "basically destroyed the auto industry and the steel industry." [6] How can this criticism of unions and union workers be converted into an ethical argument in favor of an economic star system?

6. A person identified as dinstinctM wrote, "Labor unions BUILT the American middle class. The middle class that is shrinking as unions have been decimated." [7] This is an economic claim. Assume it's true. How can it be converted into an ethical claim in favor of the FA union?

Responding to a Transit Strike

The web page titled "How to Commute By Bicycle, All of a Sudden" begins this way: "There is a transit workers' strike in NYC today. If you need to get somewhere, consider riding your bike. Even though it's 22 degrees right now (8:33 EST), this is not a crazy suggestion." [8]

When you need to preface a suggestion with the assurance that it's not crazy, you can be pretty sure that the situation is bad.

The New York City transit strike began on December 20, 2005, and ran three days. Representing the subway operators, bus drivers, and some related personnel, there was the Transport Workers Union, Local 100 (TWU). On the other side, representing the city—and the traveling, tax-paying public—there was the Metropolitan Transit Authority (MTA). Wages and retirement age were the main issues. The MTA argued (correctly) that the transit workers' wages were much higher than the national norm, and their retirement age

extremely low. The workers argued (correctly) that the job of driving in New York City was more stressful than in most other places. When negotiations failed, public transportation stopped a few days before Christmas, leaving millions of daily commuters stranded.

For some commuters, the bike became an option. In the abstract—sitting in a warm room reading about it—the possibility doesn't sound so bad, get some good exercise and brisk fresh air on the way to work and back. There are real problems, though. The air can be dangerously cold and streets in winter are icy. It also needs to be remembered that the sun goes down early in December, so people biking home at night along the roadside are pedaling in the dark. Falls are common. Falls in front of oncoming cars are especially bad.

QUESTIONS

1. The transit workers strike was actually illegal. After a similar walkout years before, the Taylor Law had been enacted; it barred transportation workers from leaving their posts and implemented arbitration methods for settling disputes. When the workers ignored the law, a judge hit them with fines and sentenced their leaders to short jail terms.
   o In the face of the strike's illegality, how can a rights argument be mounted to ethically justify the walkout?
   o Is the rights argument affected by the fact that many commuters suffered?

2. The "last resort argument" justifying a workers strike is activated when three conditions are met: (1) There must be a just cause; (2) there must be proper authorization; and (3) the strike must be a last resort—that is, attempts to find solutions must've been fully explored. In this case, the transport workers national union actually ordered the local to go back to work. The national union, in other words, didn't authorize the strike, but the actual workers on the scene did. Does this count as *proper authorization?* In a union organization, which, ultimately, gets to decide whether a strike is appropriate, the organizing management selected to speak for the collective, or the individual workers on the ground? Explain.

3. What is the public safety argument against a union going out on strike? From the information provided, how could it be implemented in this case?
   o How would the public safety argument against the strike differ from the public welfare argument?
   o In general terms, is there public welfare argument that could be sketched in *favor* of the strike?

Air and Bus Traffic: Stars and Collectives

The early 1980s were seismic years in American business. Newly elected President Reagan promoted waves of deregulation legislation, and the openness loosed a breed of entrepreneurs bringing innovative goods and services to the marketplace so rapidly that entire segments of business life erupted in disorder. One especially affected area was transportation, and one very affected transporter was the venerable Greyhound bus lines. This report from San Jose State University summarizes:

> *Deregulation of the transportation industry made the competition for passengers stiff. New entrepreneurs who paid low wages entered the business and offered fare prices much lower than the more established inter-city lines. The newly deregulated airline industry made things even worse for Greyhound. Low-cost passenger airline carriers sprang up. People Express, for example, charged only $23 for a flight between New York City and Buffalo. Greyhound charged $41 for the trip. A flight by Southwest Airlines from San Francisco to Phoenix was only $60, compared to a Greyhound's bus ticket to the same location costing $79.* [9]

When a higher-quality service (a fast plane ride) actually costs *less* than a lower-quality service (a slow bus trip), the simple rules of economics are, sooner or later, going to put the bus company out of its misery.

To survive, Greyhound had to cut its prices, which meant cutting costs. The prices of buses and gasoline and similar were fairly fixed, leaving wages to be targeted. Greyhound went to the workers collective, the local Amalgamated Transit Union, and proposed a 9.5 percent wage cut.

The answer was no. Greyhound insisted. A strike ensued.

Greyhound was prepared. They'd already recruited more than a thousand new hires in anticipation of the walkout, and agreed to pay them the salary the union had refused. A tremendous segment of business was lost while the company struggled to bring still more drivers aboard but, eventually, it became clear that the union would have to break, which it did.

In the aftermath, a stinging article was written: "Leave the Slave-Driving to Us." That's a play on the Greyhound advertising line "Leave the Driving to Us," and it pretty clearly displays where the author comes down on the ethics of labor walkouts broken by replacement workers. [10]

QUESTIONS

1. From the "Leave the Slave-Driving to Us" article: "After the strike got underway the Bus Lines tried to run scab buses. In response, the striking Greyhound workers carried out militant actions that were effective as far as they went. For example, pickets from Local 1225 in San Francisco, together with some supporters, tried to block the departure of buses from the 7th Street depot in downtown San Francisco. There was then a cop attack on the picket line and a melee ensued. Only one bus left the station. It soon experienced a collision with another vehicle (the driver of the other vehicle just happened to be a striking Greyhound driver) and it was forced to retreat to the S.F. depot."

   o   When the striking Greyhound driver drove his car or pickup into the bus, he probably damaged his own vehicle. Who should pay for the repairs? Justify.

   o   Is it possible to argue that, ethically, Greyhound should pay? Explain.

   o   Who should pay to repair the damaged Greyhound bus? Why?

   o   The "cop attack" was, presumably, police officers clearing strikers from the public road. The police are frequently unionized. Do they have, as union workers, any responsibility to leave the strikers alone?

2. From the "Leave the Slave-Driving to Us" article: "During any strike material pressures (rent or house payments, utility bills, RV financing, etc.) may influence strikers' decisions. Since Greyhound is not merely a bus line, but a conglomerate with revenues from many lines of business, its capacity to bear losses from a strike is much greater than that of individual strikers to bear the loss of wages. Even those who have substantial savings may run short during a long strike. To succeed, they had to convince other transport workers and their unions to strike in sympathy with them. But of course, that's illegal under existing contracts and laws. But that only means that the ranks needed to take matters into their own hands from the very beginning. The rank and file did not have to respect the law."

   o   What is Greyhound's structural economic advantage over the workers?

   o   Does the Greyhound economic advantage provide an ethical justification for the workers to illegally (in terms of contractual commitments) try to get others in related fields to strike in support of the Greyhound workers? Explain.

3. The marketplace test showed the strike was, in purely economic terms of supply and demand, not justified. The company was able to find workers at the wages it wanted to offer.
    o Ethically, does the economic reality justify the strikebreakers' actions in crossing the picket lines? Explain.
    o The "Leave the Slave-Driving to Us" author considers these strikebreakers to be slaves. What is the ethical argument behind this insult?

4. From the "Leave the Slave-Driving to Us" article: "'Greyhound Lines Chair Frank Nagotte pulled down a hefty $447,000 in salary and benefits' in 1983 [that's 1,004,000 in today's dollars]. In general, Greyhound management was slated to receive a 7–10% salary/benefit increase. Despite the competition from lower air fares cited by Greyhound management, the Bus Lines division alone earned a profit that has been estimated at $5 million in the first nine months of 1983."
    o The chairman's salary and benefits was about one million in today's dollars. In terms of basic rights, how could he justify taking that mountain of money home after firing the drivers?
    o In terms of the value his work generated for society, how could chairman Nagotte justify taking the mountain of money home after firing the drivers?
    o In terms of his responsibilities as chairman, how could Nagotte justify taking the mountain of money home after firing the drivers?
    o What ethical argument could the drivers use to justify demanding that the chairman take a salary and benefit cut in line with the one he was asking from the drivers?

5. The fundamental cause of the Greyhound problem was competition from new transportation companies providing better service at lower cost, including Southwest Airlines, founded by Rollin King and Herb Kelleher. They're both bright stars in the American economic star system.
    o Make the case that King and Kelleher have an ethical obligation to support the Greyhound drivers who lost their jobs. What is the case? What kind of support do they owe?
    o Convert the Greyhound experience into an ethical argument that no employee at Southwest should seek to unionize.

[1] Jim Webb, "Democratic Response of Senator Jim Webb to the President's State of the Union Address," *New York Times*, January 23, 2007, accessed June 9, 2011, http://www.nytimes.com/2007/01/23/washington/23webb-transcript.html?_r=1&oref=slogin.
[2] Mark Sumner, "Jim Webb and Economic Reform," *Daily Kos*, January 26, 2007, accessed June 9, 2011, http://www.dailykos.com/storyonly/2007/1/26/295137/-Jim-Webb-and-Economic-Reform.
[3] Ben Mutzabaugh, "Delta Attendants Vote Against Union," *USA Today*, November 4, 2010, accessed June 9, 2011, http://travel.usatoday.com/flights/post/2010/11/delta-attendants-vote/129933/1.
[4] Ben Mutzabaugh, "Delta Attendants Vote Against Union," *USA Today*, November 4, 2010, accessed June 9, 2011, http://travel.usatoday.com/flights/post/2010/11/delta-attendants-vote/129933/1.
[5] distinctM, November 4, 2010 (11:02 a.m.), comment on Ben Mutzabaugh, "Delta Attendants Vote Against Union," *USA Today*, November 4, 2010, accessed June 9, 2011, http://travel.usatoday.com/flights/post/2010/11/delta-attendants-vote/129933/1.
[6] Timatl2002, November 4, 2010 (10:08 p.m.), comment on Ben Mutzabaugh, "Delta Attendants Vote Against Union," *USA Today*, November 4, 2010, accessed June 9, 2011, http://travel.usatoday.com/flights/post/2010/11/delta-attendants-vote/129933/1.
[7] distinctM, November 5, 2010 (3:17 p.m.), comment on Ben Mutzabaugh, "Delta Attendants Vote Against Union," *USA Today*, November 4, 2010, accessed June 9, 2011, http://travel.usatoday.com/flights/post/2010/11/delta-attendants-vote/129933/1.
[8] "How to Commute By Bicycle, All of a Sudden," *Days of Leisure* (blog), accessed June 9, 2011, http://www.daysofleisure.com/writing/How_to_commute_by_bicycle,_all_of_a_sudden.html.
[9] Herbert Oestreich, "The Great Greyhound Strikes," Mineta Transportation Institute College of Business, San Jose State University, September 2001, 2001, accessed June 9, 2011, http://www.angelfire.com/al/silverball/strikes.html.
[10] Daniel, "1983: Leave the Slave-Driving to Us—Chris Fillmer," *Libcom.org*, June 17, 2007, accessed June 9, 2011, http://libcom.org/library/1983-leave-slave-driving-us-chris-fillmer.

NOTES: